Islamic Leaders:
Their
Biographies
&
Accomplishments
(From Muhammad to the present)

SAUL SILAS FATHI

Islamic leaders: Their biographies and accomplishments

Copyright 2012 by Saul Silas Fathi

Library of Congress Number: 2012915407

ISBN#:   978-0-9777117-6-5   Hardcover

ISBN#:   978-0-9777117-5-8   Tradepaper

Book Design: Elaine Lanmon

Cover design: Daniel Middleton

Art / Photo: iStockPhoto

All rights reserved. No part of this book may be reproduced or transmitted in any form or any means, electronic or mechanical, including photocopying, recording, or by any information storage and retrieval system, without permission in writing from the copyright owner.

This book was printed in the United States of America

Other books by Saul Silas Fathi:

A)   Full Circle: Escape from Baghdad and the return
          ISBN# 978-0-9777117-8-9 (Trade paper)
B)   History of the Jews and Israel
          ISBN# 978-0-9777117-3-4 (Trade paper)

(INGRAM: LIGHTNINGSOURCE)

***

ACKNOWLEDGEMENT

I owe deep gratitude to Elaine Lanmon and Nellie Corean for their assistance in typing, editing and researching this manuscript; for their patience, their valuable advice and dedication to this massive project.

***

Author/Lecturer: Saul Silas Fathi

Saul Silas Fathi was born to a prominent Jewish family in Baghdad, Iraq. At age 10, he was smuggled out of Baghdad through Iran and eventually reached the state of Israel. He began writing a diary at age 11 and had several stories published in Israeli youth magazines. In 1958, he worked his way to Brazil where he nearly starved. In 1960, he came to the U.S. on a student exchange visa. After Basic Training in Fort Benning, Georgia, he was sent to helicopter school at Fort Bragg, North Carolina, and there enrolled at the University of Virginia. Within a few months, Saul was shipped to South Korea where he served with the 1st Cavalry Division, 15th Aviation Company, the famed helicopter division in the Vietnam War. Saul retired in 2003 and began writing his memoirs, Full Circle: Escape from Baghdad and the return. Today, he lives in Long Island, New York, with his wife Rachelle. He is also a certified linguist, fluent in English, Hebrew, Arabic, and Portuguese.

Mr. Fathi has lectured at 160+ organizations since 2006, and authored 2 books: "Full Circle: Escape from Baghdad and the return" (ISBN#978-0-977117-8-9) and "History of the Jews and Israel" (ISBN# 978-0-9777117-3-4). Mr. Fathi will be publishing a major book on Islam shortly.

www.saulsilasfathi.com / fathi@optonline.net

***

T.O.C. ISLAMIC BIOGRAPHIES

Introduction:	16
Abbas ibn Firnas (810–887):	21
Abbas I (Abbas the Great), (1557-1629):	21
Abbas II (Abbas Hilmi) (1874-1944):	21
Abbas, Mahmud (1935-):	21
Abd Al-Azir ibn Saud (1880-1953):	22
Abd al-Majid or Abdulmecit (1823-1861):	24
Abd al-Malik ibn Marwan (646-705):	24
Abd al-Qadir al-Jilani (1077-1166):	27
Abd al-Rahman I, (731-788):	28
Abd al-Rahman III (890-961):	36
Abdul Aziz ibn Abdul Rahman al Saud (1879-1953):	38
Abdul Ghani, Abdul Aziz (1939-):	38
Abdul Hamid II (1842-1918):	38
Abdul ilah ibn Ali (1912-1958):	39
Abdul Maguid, Esmat (1924-):	39
Abdul Rahman, Omar (1938-):	39
Abdullah I ibn Hussein al Hashem (1882-1951):	40
Abdullah al-Ma'mun (786-833):	40
Abdullah ibn Abdul Aziz al Saud (1923-):	41
Abdullah, Sheikh Muhammad (1905-1982):	42
Abraham (1948 BCE-):	42
Abu Al-Abbas Al-Suffah (750-754):	42
Abu al Qasim Muhammad (....-....):	43
Abu Bakr al-Razi (841-925):	43
Abu Bakr al-Siddiq (573-634):	44
Abu Dhabi city:	46
Abu Hamid al-Ghazali (1058-1111):	46
Abu Hanifah (700-767):	47
Abu Hurairah (601- 679):	49
Abu 'l-Afia (-):	49
Abu Musa Island:	50
Abu Muslim (728-755):	50
Abu Nakr (-):	50
Abu Sufyan (728-755):	50
Abu-Simbel:	51
Abul A'la Mawdudi (1903-1979):	51
Abul Hasan al-Ash'ari (873-941):	53

Abul Hasan al-Mas'udi (895-957): 54
Abul Hasan al-Shadhili (1197-1258): 55
Abul Qasim al-Zahrawi (936-1013): 57
Abyssinian Campaigns (1935-1941): 58
Aflaq, Michel (1910-1989): 58
Aga Khan (1800–1881): 59
Ahmad ibn Hanbal (778-855): 59
Ahmad ibn Yahya (1895-1962): 62
Ahmad Khan, Sir Sayyid (1817-1898): 61
Aishah bint Abu Bakr (also Ayisha 610-677): 62
Akbar the Great (1542–1605): 63
Al-Ahmar, Abdullah ibn Hussein (1933-2007): 66
Al-Assad, Hafez (1930-2000): 66
Al-Assad, Rifaat (1937-   ): 67
Al Badr, Muhammad (1926 -1996): 67
Al Banna, Sabri (1937-2002): 67
Al-Battani (850–922): 67
Al Baz, Abdul Aziz ibn Abdullah (1911-1999): 68
Al Beidh, Ali Salim (1939-   ): 68
Al-Biruni, Abu al-Rayḥān Muhammad ibn Aḥmad (973-1048): 68
Al-Bukhari (809-870): 72
Al-Farabi (Al-Pharabius 870–950): 73
Al-Hafiz, Amin (1921-2009): 81
Al Hakim, Tawfiq (1898-1987): 81
Al-Hallaj (858-922): 81
Al-Hamid I (-   ): 83
Al Husseini, Faisal (1940-2001): 84
Al-Husseini, Hajj Muhammad Amin (1897-1974): 84
Al-Idrisi (1100–1166): 85
Al Iryani, Abdul Rahman (1908-1998): 85
Al-Jazari, Badi'al-Zaman Abu al-'Izz Ismā'īl ibn al-Razāz (1136–1206): 86
Al-Khursani, Abu Muslim Abd Rahman ibn Muslim (700-755): 92
Al-Khwarizmi (780-847): 94
Al-Kindi (801-873): 96
Al-Mahdi, Muhammad ibn Al-Hasan (869-941): 98
Al Maktum, Rashid ibn Said (1914-1990): 104
Al-Ma'mun (786-833): 106
Al-Mansur (914-1002): 104
Al-Mansur (754-775): 104
Al-Mansur, Abu Ja'far Abdallah Ibn Muhammad (714-775): 105
Al-Mutanabbi (915-968): 107

Al-Mu'tasim, Abu Ishaq Abbas (794-842): 108
Al-Mutawakkil, Ala Allah Ja'far ibn (821-861): 111
Al-Nimeiri, Gaafar Muhammad (1930-2009): 114
Al Quwatli, Shukri (1891-1967): 114
Al Sabah, Abdullah III ibn Salim I (1895-1965): 114
Al Sabah, Ahmad I Ivn Jabar II (1885-1950): 115
Al Sabah, Jaber III ibn Ahmad I (1926-2006): 115
Al Sabah, Sabah III ibn Salim I (1913-1977): 116
Al Sadr, Musa (1928-1978): 117
Al Said, Nuri (1888-1958): 117
Al Saud, Saud ibn Abdul Azi (1902-1969): 117
Al Shaabi, Qahtan Muhammad (1920-1981): 116
Al Shafi'i (767-820): 117
Al Sistani, Ali Husseini (1930-   ): 119
Al-Tabari (839-923): 119
Al-Tahtawi, Rifah (1801-1873): 121
Al Thani, Ali ibn Abdullah (1894-1976): 121
Al Thani, Hamad ibn Khalifa (1932-   ): 121
Al Utaiba, Juheiman ibn Saif (1939-1980): 121
Al-Zarqali (1028–1087): 122
Al-Zawahiri, Ayman (1950-   ): 122
Ali Ibn Abi Talib (599-661): 123
Ali Khamanei, Hussein (1939-   ): 137
Ali Pasha (1744-1822): 138
Ali, Salim Rubai (1935-1978): 138
Amin Dada, Idi (1925 -   ): 138
Amr ibn al-As (573-664): 139
Antonius, George (1892-1942): 139
Aoun, Michel (1935-   ): 139
Arabi Pasha (1839-1911): 140
Arafat, Yasir (1929-   ): 140
Arif, Abdul Rahman (1916-   ): 141
Arif, Abdul Salam (1929-1966): 141
Asbar, Ali Ahmad Said (1930-   ): 141
Askia Muhammad I, the Great (1443-1538): 141
Assad Rifaat (1937-   ): 142
Atef, Muhammad (1944-2001): 142
Attasi, Nur al Din (1929-1992): 142
Awrangzeb Alamgir (1618-1707): 142
Ayatullah Khomeini (1902-1989): 144
Ayub Kahn, Muhammad (1907-1974): 147
Azikiwe, (Benjamin) Nnamdi (1904-1996): 147
Aziz, Tariq (1936-   ): 147

Azzam, Abdullah (1941-1989): ... 148
Babur (1483-1530): ... 148
Bakdash, Khalid (1912-1995): ... 148
Bakhtiar, Shahpur (1914-1991): ... 148
Bakr, Ahmad Hassan (1912-1982): ... 149
Bani Sadr, Abol Hassan (1933-): ... 149
Banu Musa brothers: ... 149
Barakah: ... 149
Barbarossa (Turkish, Khayr ad-Din Pasha .1483-1546): ... 150
Barzani, Masud (1946-): ... 150
Barzani, Mustafa (1904-1979): ... 150
Barzargan, Mahdi (1905-1995): ... 150
Bayezid I (1347-1403): ... 151
Bayezid II (1447-1512): ... 151
Bello, Alhaji Sir Ahmadu (1906-1966): ... 151
Ben Bella, Ahmed (1916-2012): ... 151
Berri, Nabih (1938-): ... 152
Beyazid (1347-1403): ... 152
Bhutto, Benazir (1953-): ... 152
Bhutto, Zulfikar Ali (1928-1979): ... 153
Bilal ibn Rabah (579-641): ... 153
Bin Laden, Osama (or Usama, 1957-2011): ... 155
Bishara, Azmi (1956-): ... 156
Bitar, Salah al Din (1912-1980): ... 156
Boumedienne, Houari (1925-1978): ... 156
Bourguiba, Habib Ali (1903-): ... 156
Boutros-Ghali, Boutros (1922-): ... 157
Chalabi, Ahmad (1944-): ... 157
Chehab, Fuad (1902-1973): ... 157
Darwish, Mahmud (1941-): ... 158
Dost Muhammad (1798-1863): ... 158
Dowlatabadi, Mahmud (1940 -): ... 158
El Cid (1040-1099) ... 158
El Saadawi, Nawal (1931-): ... 158
Emin Pasha (Mehmed Eduard Schnitzer) (1840-1992): ... 159
Enver Pasha (1881-1922): ... 159
Fahd ibn Abdul Aziz al Saud (1921-): ... 159
Faisal I ibn Hussein al Hashem (1885-1933): ... 160
Faisal I (or Feisal) (1885-1933) ... 160
Faisal ibn Abd al-Aziz ibn Saud (1905-1975): ... 160
Faisal II ibn Ghazi al Hashem (1935-1958): ... 160
Fakhr al-Din al-Razi (1149-1209): ... 161
Farouk (1920-65) King of Egypt (1936-1952). ... 162

Farrakhan, Louis (1933-): 162
Fatimah bint Muhammad (605-633): 163
Franjieh, Suleiman (1910-93): 168
Gabriel: 169
Gailani, Rashid Ali (1892-1965): 169
Gemayel, Bashir (1947-1982): 170
Gemayel, Pierre (1905-1984): 170
Genghis Khan (or Jenghiz Khan) (1167-1227): 170
Ghashmi, Ahmad Hussein (1938-1978): 171
Ghazi ibn Faisal I al Hashem (1912-1939): 171
Glubb (Pasha), Sir John Bagot (1897-1986): 171
Golpaygani, Muhammad Reza Musavi (1899-1993): 172
Habash, George (1926-2008): 172
Habibi, Emile Shukri (1921-96): 172
Hafiz, Amin (1921-): 173
Hafsah (609-665): 173
Hagar (-): 173
Hamad ibn Isa (1950-): 173
Hamdi, Ibrahim (1943-1977): 173
Hariri, Rafiq (1944-2005): 174
Harun al-Rashid (766-809): 174
Hasan Al-Banna (1906-1949): 177
Hasan al-Basri (642-728): 179
Hasan Ibn Ali (625-669BCE): 181
Hasan Muhammad Abdille Sayyid (1864-1920): 181
Hashim (-): 181
Hawatmeh, Nayif (1934-): 181
Heikal, Muhammad Hassanein (1923-): 181
Helou, Charles (1912-2001): 182
Himayun (1508-1556): 182
Hoss, Salim (1929-….): 182
Hoveida, Amir Abbas (1919-1979) 183
Hrawi, Elias (1925-2006): 183
Hulagu Khan (1217-1265): 183
Hunayn ibn Ishaq (809-871): 184
Husain ibn Ali (-): 184
Husayn ibn Ali (1856-1931): 184
Husayn ibn Mansur al-Halaj (858-922): 185
Husayn (-): 185
Hussain ibn Ali (625-680): 185
Hussein ibn Talal al Hashem (1935-1999): 187
Hussein, Qusay Saddam (1966-2003): 188
Hussein, Saddam (1937-2005): 188

Hyder Ali (1722-1982): 189
Ibn Abd al-Wahhab, Muhammad (1703-1792): 189
Ibn al Arabi (d. 1240): 193
Ibn Al-Haytham, Alhazen (965-1040):..193
Ibn Al-Nafis (1213-1288): 204
Ibn Arabi (1165-1240): 204
Ibn Batuttah (1332-1406):...206
Ibn Hanbal, Ahmad (780-855): 208
Ibn Harith, Muthana (-):...208
Ibn Hazm al-Andalusi (994-1064):..208
Ibn Ishaq (704-767): 210
Ibn Jubayr (1145-1217): 211
Ibn Khaldun (1332-1406): 211
Ibn Rushd (Averroes 1126-1198): 213
Ibn Sinna, Abu Ali Husayn (Avicenna) (980-1037):.........................215
Ibn Taymiyyah (1263-1328):..226
Ibn Tufayl (1101-1185): 228
Ibn Tulun, Ahmad (835-884):...229
Ibrahim Pasha (1789-1848): 231
Idris, Yusuf (1927-1991): 232
Inn, Ismet (1884-1973): 232
Iqbal, Muhammad (1876-1938):...232
Isa II ibn Salman (1933-1999): 233
Ismail (-): 233
Ismail, Abdul Fattah (1936-1986 233
Ismail I Safavi (d. 1524): 233
Ismail ibn Ja'far (-):...233
Ismail Pasha (1830-1895): 234
Jadid, Salah (1926-1993): 234
Ja'far (-): 235
Ja'far al-Sadiq (700-765): 235
Jabir ibn Hayyan (738-813): 236
Jalal ad-Din Rumi, Muhammad Balkhi (1207-1273): 238
Jamal al-Din al-Afghani (1838-1897):..247
Jibran, Khalil (1883-1931): 248
Jibril, Ahmad (1938-): 249
Jumblat, Kamal (1917-1977): 249
Jumblat, Walid (1949-): 249
Junaid of Baghdad (d. 910): 250
Ka'b bin Al Ashraf (-): 250
Kabir (1440-1518): 250
Karami, Rashid (1921-1987): 250
Kashani, Abol Qasim (1884-1962): 251

Kassem, Abdul Karim (1914-1963): 251
Khaddam, Abdul Halim (1932-   ): 251
Khadijah bint Khuwailid (555-619): 252
Khalaf, Salah (1932-1991): 253
Khalifa, Abdallah Muhammad (1846-1899): 254
Khalid ibn al-Walid (584-642): 254
Khatami, Muhammad (1943-   ): 256
Khatib, Ahmad (1940-   ): 256
Khoei, Abol Qasim (1899-1992): 257
Khosrau I (d. 579): 257
Khosrau II (d. 628): 257
Khosrow I (531-579): 257
Khouri, Bishara (1890-1964): 258
Khwajah Naqshband (1317-1389): 258
Kublai Kahn (1214-1294): 259
Lahoud, Emile (1936-   ): 260
Lawrence of Arabia (Thomas Edward 1888-1935): 260
Liaqat Ali Khan, Nawabzada (1895-1951): 261
Mahdi, the (-   ): 261
Mahdi of Sudan, the (1844-1885): 262
Mahfouz, Naguib (1911-   ): 264
Mahmud II (1784-1839): 264
Mahmud of Ghazna (967-1030): 265
Malaika, Nazik (1923-2001): 267
Malcolm X (1925-1965): 268
Malik ibn Anas (711-795): 270
Mansa Musa (ruled 1307-1337): 272
Mansur, Husain al (also known as al Hallaj, the Wool Carder) (-   ): 272
Mariyah or Marya or Meriem (-   ): 272
Marwan II (684-750): 272
Masudi, Abd al-Hasan Ali ibn al-Hussyn, (d. 956): 272
Mehmed II (Muhammad II, the Conqueror (1430-1481): 273
Mehemet Ali (1769–1849): 273
Midhat Pasha 1822-1883): 273
Mimar Sinan (1489-1588): 274
Montazeri, Hussein Ali (1922-2009): 276
Moussa, Amr (1936-   ): 276
Muawiya ibn Abi Sufyan (605-680): 276
Muawiya II, ibn Yazid (661-684): 279
Mubarak, Muhammad Hosni (1928-   ): 282
Mughira ibn Shuba (-   ): 283
Muhammad Abduh (1849-1905): 283
Muhammad Ali (1769-1849): 285

Muhammad Ali Cassius Marcellus Clay (1942-): 285
Muhammad, Ali (1952-): 287
Muhammad Ali Jinnah (1876-1948): 288
Muhammad, Ali Masser (1939-): 289
Muhammad Ali Pasha (-): 290
Muhammad of Ghor (d. 1206): 290
Muhammad I (-): 290
Muhammad Ibn Abdallah ibn al-Muttalib (Prophet of Islam 570-632): 290
Muhammad's wives and children: 310
Muhammad ibn al-Qasim (694-715): 316
Muhammad Ilyas (1885-1944): 318
Muhammad Iqbal, Sir (1877-1938): 319
Muhammad, Khalid Shaikh (1965-): 321
Muhammad, Khwarazmshah (1200-1220): 321
Muhammad Musadeq (-): 321
Muhammad Reza Pahlavi (1944-1979): 321
Muhammad Riza Shah (-): 322
Muhammad V (or Mehmet V, 1844-1918): 322
Muhammad Yunus (1940-): 322
Muhyi al Din, Khalid (1922-): 324
Muhyiddin ibn Arabi (1165-1240): 325
Mu'in al-Din Chishti (1142-1236): 325
Mujibar Rahman, Sheikh (1920-1975): 326
Mullah Sadra (1571-1641): 327
Murad I (1326?-1389) 328
Murad II (1403-1451): 329
Murtadd (-): 329
Musa ibn Nusayr (639-716): 330
Musavi, Mir Hussein (1941-): 332
Muslim ibn al-Hajjaj (817-875): 332
Mussadiq, Muhammad (1881-1967): 333
Mustafa IV (1778-1808): 333
Mustafa Kemal Ataturk (1881-1938): 334
Nabulsi, Suleiman (1908-1976): 352
Nadir Shah (1688-1747): 352
Nahas (Pasha), Mustafa (1879-1965): 353
Nasir al-Din al-Tusi (1201-1274): 354
Nasser, Gamal Abdul (1918-1970): 356
Neguib, Muhammad (1901-1984): 357
Nizam al-Mulk (1020-1092): 357
Nizar (-): 359
Nur Al-Din Zangi (1117-1174): 359
Oqba ibn Nafi (-): 362

Orkhan (1288-1362): 362
Osman I (1258-1326): 362
Pahlavi, Muhammad Reza Shah (1919-1980): 363
Pahlavi, Reza Shah (1878-1944): 364
Qaboos ibn Said (1940-   ): 364
Qaddafi, Muammar al- (1942- 2011): 364
Qasim, Abdul Karim (1914-1963): 365
Qassam, Izz al Din (1881-1935): 366
Rabi'a al-Adawiyyah (717-801):.. 366
Rafsanjani, Ali Akbar Hashemi (1934-   ): 367
Rajagopalachariar, Chakravarti (1878-1972): 368
Rajai, Muhammad Ali (1933-81): 368
Rajavi, Massoud (1948-   ):... 369
Ranjit Singh (1780-1839):.. 369
Rashid Ali al-Ghailani (1892-1965):.. 369
Reza Shah Pahlavi (Reza Kahn) (1878-1944): 370
Saad ibn Abu Waqqas (-   ): 370
Saada, Antun (1902-1949): 370
Sabri, Ali (1920-1991): 371
Sadi (or Saadi, Bin Shiraz, 1184-1291): 371
Sa'id Nursi (1877-1960): 371
Sadat, Muhammad Anwar (1918-1981):.. 373
Saladin, Jalal Ad-Din Ayyubi (1138-1193): 374
Salam, Saeb (1905-2005):.. 388
Salih, Ali Abdullah (1942-   ):... 388
Sallal, Abdullah (1917-2001):.. 389
Salman II ibn Hamad (1895-1961): 389
Sarkis, Elias (1924-1985): 389
Saud:... 390
Sawdah (-   ): 390
Sayyab, Badr Shakir: (1926-1964):.. 390
Sayyid Qutb (1906-1966):.. 391
Seku Ahmadu Lobbo (1775-1845): 393
Selim I (1470-1520): 393
Selim III (1761-1808): 393
Shah Jahan (1592-1666):.. 394
Shah Waliullah (1703-1762): 396
Shamil (1798-1871): 398
Shamyl of Daghestan (1796-1871): 398
Shapur I (or Sapor I (241-272):.. 399
Shariati, Ali (1933-1977): 400
Shariatmadari, Muhammad Kazem (1903-1986):.................................. 400
Shaykh Ahmad Sirhindi (1564-1624): 400

Shaykh Sa'di of Shiraz (1174-1290): 402
Shihab al-Din Suhrawardi (1154-1191): 404
Shishkali, Adib (1901-1964): 405
Shuqairi, Ahmad (1908-1980): 406
Solh, Riyad (1894-1951): 406
Suharto (1921-2008): 406
Sukarno, Achmad (1901-1970): 407
Sulaiman the Magnificent (1494-1566): 407
Sultan Husayn (1694-1729): 408
Sultan Muhammad II (1429-1481): 410
Tahman, Tungku (Prince) Abdul (1903-1990): 412
Taimur ibn Faisal (1885-1956): 412
Talabani, Jalal (1933-   ): 412
Talal ibn Abdullah al Hashem (1909-1972): 413
Taleqani, Mahmud (1910-1979): 413
Tariq ibn Zaid (700-712): 413
Tariq ibn Ziyad (650-728): 414
Tewfik Pasha (Muhammad Tewfik 1852-1892): 415
Timur the Conqueror (1336-1405): 416
Tipu Sultan (1753-1799): 419
Touma, Emile (1918-1985): 419
Toure (Ahmed) Sekou (1922-1984): 419
Ubaydallah ibn Jahsh (-   ): 419
Umar, al-Hajj (1797-1864): 420
Umar Al-Khayyam (1048–1131): 420
Umar ibn Abd al-Aziz (682-719): 426
Umar ibn al-Khattab, Al-Farooq (586-644): 428
Umar ibn Said Tal (or al-Hajj Umar or Umar Tal) (1797-1864): 439
Umar II (717-720): 439
Umm Salamah (-   ): 439
Usama bin Zayd (-   ): 440
Uthman Dan Fodio (1754-1817): 440
Uthman ibn Affan (579-656): 441
Velayati, Ali Akbar (1945-   ): 456
Waraqah ibn Mawfal (-   ): 456
Wazir, Khalil (1935-1988): 456
Yahya al-Nawawi (1233-1277): 456
Yamani, Ahmad Zaki (1930-   ): 458
Yassin, Ahmad (1937-   ): 458
Yazid II, bin Abd al-Malik (687-724): 459
Zaghlul Pasha, Saad (1850-1927): 460
Zahedi, Fazullah (180-1963): 460
Zaid ibn Sultan, Al Nahyan (1915-2004): 460

Islamic Leaders

Zaim, Hosni (1890-1949: 460
Zayd ibn Ali (695-740): 461
Zayd ibn Harithah (-): 461
Zaynab bin Jaysh (-): 461
Zayyad (-): 461
Zubayr ibn al Awwam (-): 462

***

Introduction
Islam: Its leaders and their accomplishments

Dear reader: In this book you will be introduced to hundreds of Islamic leaders, their biographies and accomplishments, since the days of the Prophet Muhammad to the present. They are presented in alphabetical order, not in order of importance nor chronologically.

In less than a century after Muhammad's death Islam swept through Asia, Africa and Europe, dominating an area larger than that of the Roman Empire at its peak. Today, one in 5 people on the face of this earth is a Muslim. A total of 1.6 billion people; the second largest religion in the world and the fastest-growing.

For a period of 400 years, from the Eighth to the Twelfth Century, the achievements of this synthesized culture were unsurpassed. In fact, much of the science and literature of the European Renaissance was inspired by Islamic models. I Urge everyone to learn about it.

Islam (=Submission): Is the monotheistic religion articulated by the Qur'an, a text considered by its adherents to be the verbatim word of God (Arabic: *Allāh*), and by the teachings and normative example (called the *Sunnah* and composed of *Hadith*) of Muhammad, considered by them to be the last prophet of God. An adherent of Islam is called a *Muslim*.

God (Allah): Muslims believe that God is one and incomparable and the purpose of existence is to worship God. Muslims also believe that Islam is the complete and universal version of a primordial faith that was revealed at many times and places before, including through Abraham, Moses and Jesus, whom they consider prophets. They maintain that previous messages and revelations have been partially changed or corrupted over time, but consider the Qur'an to be both the unaltered and the final revelation of God.

Islam's most fundamental concept is a rigorous monotheism, called Tawhid. God is described in chapter 112 of the Qur'an as: "Say: He is God, the One and Only; God, the Eternal, Absolute; He begetteth not, not is He begotten; and there is none like unto Him." **(Qur'an 112:1-4)** Muslims repudiate the Christian doctrine of the Trinity and divinity of Jesus, comparing it to polytheism, but accept Jesus as a prophet. In Islam, God is beyond all comprehension and Muslims are not expected to visualize God.

Muslims believe that creation of everything in the universe is brought into by God's sheer command "'Be' and so it is." and that the purpose of existence is to worship God. He is viewed as a personal God who responds whenever a person in need or distress calls Him. There are no intermediaries, such as clergy, to contact God who states "We are nearer to him than (his) jugular vein" *Allāh* is the term with no plural or gender used by Muslims and Arabic-speaking Christians and Jews meaning the one God.

Holy Qur'an: It is divided into 114 suras, or chapters, which combined contain 6,236 *āyāt*, or verses. Muslim jurists consult the H*adith*, or the written record of Prophet Muhammad's life, to both supplement the Qur'an and assist with its interpretation. The science of Qur'anic commentary and exegesis is known as T*afsir*. To Muslims, the Qur'an is perfect only as revealed in the original Arabic; translations are necessarily deficient because of language difference, the fallibility of translators, and the impossibility of preserving the original's inspired style.

Predestination: In accordance with the Islamic belief in predestination, or divine preordainment (*al-qadā wa'l-qadar*), God has full knowledge and control over all that occurs. For Muslims, everything in the world that occurs, good or evil, has been preordained and nothing can happen unless permitted by God. According to Muslim theologians, although events are pre-ordained, man possesses FREE WILL in that he has the faculty to choose between right and wrong, and is thus responsible for his actions.

Five Pillars of Islam
The Pillars of Islam (A*rkan al-Islam*; also *Arkan ad-din*, "pillars of religion") are five basic acts in Islam, considered obligatory of all believers. The Quran presents them as a framework for worship and a sign of commitment to the faith. They are (1) Shahadah (Creed), (2) daily prayers (Salat), (3) Almsgiving (Zakah), (4) Fasting during Ramadan (Sawm), and (5) Pilgrimage to Mecca (Hajj) at least once in a lifetime. The Shi'a and Sunni sects both agree on the essential details for the performance of these acts.

1. **Testimony** (*Shahadah*)
   The Shahadah, which is the basic creed of Islam that must be recited under oath with the specific statement: " '*ashadu 'al-lā ilah illā-llāhu wa 'ashadu 'anna Muhammadan rasūlu-llāh*", or "I testify there are no deities other than God alone and I testify that Muhammad is the Messenger of God." Muslims must repeat the *Shahadah* in prayer, and non-Muslims wishing to convert to Islam are required to recite the creed.

2. **Prayer** (*Salah*)

Ritual prayers, called Ṣalāh or Ṣalāt, must be performed five times a day. Salah is intended to focus the mind on God, and is seen as a personal communication with Him that expresses gratitude and worship. Salah is compulsory but flexibility in the specifics is allowed depending on circumstances. The prayers are recited in the Arabic language, and consist of verses from the Qur'an.

- **Mosque (Masjid)**
  A mosque is in place of worship is a place of worship for Muslims, who often refer to it by its Arabic name, M*asjid*. The word M*osque* in English refers to all types of buildings dedicated to Islamic worship. Although the primary purpose of the mosque is to serve as a place of prayer, it is also important to the Muslim community as a place to meet and study. Shi'a Islam permits combining prayers in succession.

3. **Fasting** (*Sawm of Ramadan*)
Fasting, from food, drink and sex must be performed from dawn to dusk during the month of Ramadhan. The fast is to encourage a feeling of nearness to God, and during it Muslims should express their gratitude for and dependence on Him, atone for their past sins, and think of the needy. But missed fasts usually must be made up quickly. The fasting ends daily at sun-down and continues for 30 days.

4. **Alms-giving** (*Zakat and Sadaqah*)
"Zakat" is giving a fixed portion of accumulated wealth by those who can afford it to help the poor or needy, and also to assist the spread of Islam. It is considered a religious obligation (as opposed to voluntary charity) that the well-off owe to the needy because their wealth is seen as a "trust from God's bounty". The Qur'an and the Hadith also suggest a Muslim give even more as an act of voluntary alms-giving (S*adaqah*).

5. **Pilgrimage** (*Hajj*)
The pilgrimage, called the H*ajj* during the Islamic month of *Dhu al-Hijjah* in the city of Mecca. Every able-bodied Muslim who can afford it must make the pilgrimage to Mecca at least once in his or her lifetime. Rituals of the Hajj include walking seven times around the Kaaba, touching the black stone if possible, walking or running seven times between Mount Safa and Mount Marwah, and symbolically stoning the Devil in Mina.

Jihad and the Military: Jihad means "to strive or struggle" (in the way of God) and is considered the "Sixth Pillar of Islam" by a minority of Sunni Muslim authorities. Jihad, in its broadest sense, is classically defined as "exerting one's utmost power, efforts, endeavors, or ability in contending with an object of disapprobation. Jihad, when used without any qualifier, is understood in its military aspect. Jihad also refers to one's striving to attain religious and moral perfection. Some Muslim authorities, especially among the Shi'a and Sufis, distinguish between the "greater jihad", which pertains to spiritual self-perfection, and the "lesser jihad", defined as warfare.

Within Islamic jurisprudence, jihad is usually taken to mean military exertion against non-Muslim combatants in the defense or expansion of the Ummah. Others have argued that the goal of Jihad is global conquest. Jihad is the only form of warfare permissible in Islamic law and may be declared against terrorists, criminal groups, rebels, apostates, and leaders or states that oppress Muslims or hamper proselytizing efforts.

Under most circumstances and for most Muslims, jihad is a collective duty (*Fard Kifaya*): Its performance by some individuals exempts the others. For most Shi'as, offensive jihad can only be declared by a divinely appointed leader of the Muslim community, and as such is suspended since Muhammad al-Mahdi's occultation in 868 AD.

Muhammad (610-632): Muhammad (570–June 8, 632) was a trader later becoming a religious, political, and military leader. However, Muslims do not view Muhammad as the creator of Islam, but instead regard him as the last messenger of God, through which the Qur'an was revealed. Muslims view Muhammad as the restorer of the original, uncorrupted monotheistic faith of Adam, Abraham, Moses, Jesus, and other prophets.

For the last 22 years of his life, beginning at age 40 in 610 CE, Muhammad started receiving revelations that he believed to be from God. The content of these revelations, known as the Qur'an, was memorized and recorded by his companions. During this time, Muhammad preached to the people of Mecca, imploring them to abandon polytheism. After 12 years of preaching, Muhammad and the Muslims performed the Hijah ("emigration") to the city of Medina (formerly known as *Yathrib*) and the Meccan migrants (*Muhajirun*), Muhammad established his political and religious authority. By 630 Muhammad was victorious in the nearly bloodless Conquest of Mecca, and by the time of his death in 632 (at the age of 63) he untied the tribes of Arabia into a single religious polity.

Rise of the caliphate and civil war (632–750):
With Muhammad's death in 632, disagreement broke out over who would succeed him as leader of the Muslim community. Umar ibn al-Khattab, a prominent companion of Muhammad, nominated Abu Bakr, who was

Muhammad's companion and close friend. Others added their support and Abu Bakr was made the First Caliph.

- **The Rashidun (Rightly-Guided Caliphs):**
  Abu Bakr's death in 634 resulted in the succession of Umar ibn al-Khattab as the caliph, followed by Uthman ibn al-Affan, Ali ibn Abi Talib and Hasan ibn Ali. The first 4 caliphs are known as *al-khulafa' ar-rāshidūn* ("Rightly Guided Caliphs"). Under them, the territory under Muslim rule expanded deeply into Persian and Byzantine territories. When Umar was assassinated in 644, the election of Uthman as successor was met with increasing opposition. In 656, Uthman was also killed, and Ali assumed the position of caliph. After fighting off opposition in the first civil war (the "First Fitna"), Ali was assassinated by Kharijites in 661. Following this, Mu'awiyah seized power and began the Umayyad dynasty, with its capital in Damascus.

Islamic Accomplishments:
Islamic civilization flourished in what is sometimes referred to as the "Islamic Golden Age". Public hospitals established during this time, are considered "the first hospitals" in the modern sense of the word, and issued the first medical diplomas to license doctors of medicine. The Guinness World Records recognizes the University of Al Karaouine, founded in 859, as the world's older degree-granting university. An important pioneer in this, Ibn al-Haytham is regarded as the father of the modern scientific method and often referred to as the "world's first true scientist." Discoveries include gathering the data used by Copernicus for his heliocentric conclusions and Al-Jahiz's proposal of the theory of natural selection. Rumi wrote some of the finest Persian poetry and is still one of the best selling poets in America. Legal institutions introduced include the trust and charitable trust (Waqf).

***

ISLAMIC BIOGRAPHIES IN ALPHABETICAL ORDER:

Abbas ibn Firnas (810–887): An Andalusian scientist, musician and inventor. He developed a clear glass used in drinking vessels, and lenses used for magnification and the improvement of vision. He had a room in his house where the sky was simulated, including the motion of planets, stars and weather complete with clouds, thunder and lightning. He is most well known for reportedly surviving an attempt at controlled flight.

***

Abbas I (Abbas the Great 1557-1629): Shah of Persia (1587-1628), of the Safavid dynasty. In 1597 he ended the raids of the Uzbeks, and subsequently (1603-23) he conquered extensive territories from the Turks. He maintained diplomatic contacts with Europe, and with English aid he took (1622) Hormoz from the Portuguese and founded what is now the port of Bandar Abbas. At his capital at Esfahan, he erected many palaces, mosques, and gardens and did much to improve public works in Persia.

***

Abbas II (Abbas Hilmi, 1874-1944): Last khedive of Egypt (1892-1914): son and successor of Tewfik Pasha. Nominally, he ruled in subordination to the Ottoman Empire, but in fact Egypt was controlled by the British resident-at first Lord Cromer, and later Lord Kitchener. Although he resisted complete British rule, Abbas met with little success; in 1899 he was forced to admit the British claim to rule jointly with Egypt over Sudan. When Turkey joined the Central Powers in World War I, Britain declared Egypt a British protectorate and deposed Abbas. He lived thereafter in Switzerland, where he died. He wrote *The Anglo-Egyptian Settlement* (1930).

***

Abbas, Mahmud (1935-   ): Palestinian politician; prime minister of Palestinian Authority, 2003 — born of middle class parents in Safad, Palestine, he and his family fled to Syria during the 1948-49 Arab Israeli war. Abbas graduated in law at Damascus University and then earned a doctorate in history at the Oriental College, Moscow. On 1965 he was one of the founder members of Fatah. Three years later, he was elected a member of the Palestine National Council.

***

Abd Al-Azir ibn Saud (1880-1953): Muhammad ibn Saud, the charismatic founder of the Saudi dynasty (also known as the House of Saud), was born around 1703. After succeeding his father as the ruler of the oasis principality of Diriyyah at the age of forty, he formed an alliance with Muhammad ibn Abd al-Wahhab, the renowned Islamic scholar and reformer of Arabia, in 1744 and thereby laid the foundations of the modern Saudi State. The two Muhammads thus joined together to create a formidable politico-religious alliance in Arabia. To further strengthen their relationship, Muhammad ibn Saud married Ibn Abd al-Wahhab's daughter in 1744. The first Saudi State was established around 1744 and it endured until it was destroyed in 1818 by the forces of Muhammad Ali Pasha, the powerful Ottoman viceroy of Egypt. Modeled on the first Saudi State, another politico-religious order then emerged in Arabia in 1824, but incessant internal strife and political rivalry led to its disintegration in 1891. However, the credit for laying the foundations of the Kingdom of Saudi Arabia, the modern Saudi State, must go to Abd al-Aziz ibn Saud, who was undoubtedly one of the most charismatic and influential Arab leaders of modern times.

Abd al-Aziz ibn Abd al-Rahman ibn Faisal al-Saud, known as Ibn Saud for short, was born in Riyadh, the capital of modern Saudi Arabia, but he spent his early years in Kuwait. Exasperated by his battles with his brothers, Abd al-Rahman ibn Faisal was eventually forced to leave Arabia in 1891 after Riyadh was captured by Muhammad ibn Rashid, the ruler of Najd and a political rival of the al-Sauf family. During his exile in Kuwait, however, he maintained close contact with his supporters back home, hoping one day to return to his native Riyadh in triumph. Ibn Saud received training in all aspects of desert warfare and soon became an expert in launching military raids. His years of training in military strategy and desert warfare equipped him with much-needed skills and experience to organize and launch the military expeditions to reclaim his ancestral homeland from his rivals.

Even after Kuwait became a British protectorate in 1899, they struggled to protect their political and economic interests in the region from German and French encroachment. Following the death of the charismatic Rashidi ruler Muhammad ibn Abdullah in 1897, Riyadh was rocked by both political upheaval and social uprisings. The situation deteriorated further as his successor, Abd al-Aziz ibn Mitaab, ruthlessly suppressed the uprising. Despite the volatile situation at home, the new Rashidi ruler – supported by the Ottomans – launched an unprovoked attack on Kuwait, which was still then a British protectorate, in 1900. But thanks to the British, the Rashidi ruler's attempt to annex Kuwait failed miserably. Indeed, Ibn Mitaab's attack on Kuwait backfired in a spectacular fashion, as Shaykh al-Mubarak al-Saba, the ruler of Kuwait, and Abd al-Rahman ibn Faisal, the father of Ibn Saud, now united to fight and drive out the Rashidis from Arabia. Leading a ten thousand strong force, the two men attacked the Rashidi forces with great success. During this period the twenty-two year old Ibn Saud spearheaded the attack on Riyadh, his native city.

In the ensuing battle, the city's governor was slain by Abdullah ibn Jelawi, Ibn Said's cousin, and they inflicted a crushing defeat on their enemy. The fall of Riyadh marked the beginning of the end for the Rashidis, as the House of Saud swiftly reasserted its authority across the country under the able stewardship of Ibn Saud and his father. Thereafter, Ibn Saud urged the local clerics and the people of Riyadh to pledge allegiance to his father, Abd al-Rahman ibn Faisal, as their new sovereign; the people responded to his call and pledged their allegiance to him. Later, Ibn Saud's popularity and standing with the masses prompted his father to abdicate in favor of his son, who accordingly became the King.

With Riyadh now firmly in his grip, Ibn Saud was eager to extend his rule across the rest of Arabia, but he knew that would not be an easy task given that the Rashidis were in full control in Najd. Thus, over the next five decades, he married more than a dozen times, fathering around forty sons and fifty daughters. He knew that forming alliances through multiple marriages not only helped to extend his family ties, it also strengthened his political powerbase. In 1912, he established a special fighting force which came to be known as the *Ikhwan* (the 'Brotherhood'). The members of this force were loyal supporters of the House of Saud and strict adherents of Islam as interpreted by Muhammad ibn Abd al-Wahhab.

With the support of the *Ikhwan* troops, Ibn Saud first conquered the wealthy region of Hasa (situated on the coast of the Persian Gulf) and then went on to smash the Rashidis of Najd in 1921. Five years later, he ousted the Hashimites from the Hijaz, thus extending his rule and authority over the holy cities of Mecca and Medina which brought him much-needed revenue for his fledgling administration from the visiting pilgrims. Not keen on pursuing endless military conquests, Ibn Saud swiftly disbanded the *Ikhwan* and focused his full attention on improving the economic fortunes of his new kingdom. He established a Council of Ministers to oversee the affairs of the State, and appointed close members of his family to key positions within the Government. Thus his two eldest sons, Saud and Faisal, were offered high-ranking Government posts in the province of Najd and Hijaz. During this period he also enforce the *Shari'ah* (Islamic law) across the State and in due course this became the supreme law of the land.

Then, in 1930, Ibn Saud established a Ministry of Foreign

Affairs and appointed his second son, Faisal, as Foreign Minister and he played a key role in establishing diplomatic relations with some of the world's leading powers, including the United States of America. Two years later, the formation of the Kingdom of Saudi Arabia was officially announced. This was followed, in the mid-1930s, by the discovery of the world's largest oil reserves beneath the barren deserts of Arabia. By the 1940s, Saudi Arabia's diplomatic relations with the powerful industrial Western nations (especially the United States) was formalized. The special US-Saudi relationship was formalized by Ibn Saud and President Roosevelt during their meeting onboard the US naval ship USS Quincy in 1945. Thanks to the new petrodollars, the once backward and poverty-stricken desert kingdom suddenly became one of the world's most prosperous countries.

Ibn Saud, the founder of the Kingdom of Saudi Arabia, eventually died at the age of seventy-three and was buried in his native Riyadh. He was succeeded by his eldest son, Saud, who ruled the kingdom for eleven years before abdicating in favor of his younger brother, Faisal. Like his father, Faisal was a wise and able ruler, but he was assassinated in 1975. Khalid, Ibn Saud's fourth son, then ascended the Saudi throne and ruled for seven years until his death in 1982. He was succeeded by Fahd who ruled the kingdom until his death in 2005. Abdullah, his half-brother, then succeeded him as King.

**

Abd al-Majid or Abdulmecit (1823-1861): Ottoman sultan (1839-1861), son and successor Mahmud II to the throne of the Ottoman Empire. The rebellion of Muhammad Ali was checked by the intervention (1840-41) of England, Russia, and Austria. Abd al-Majid was influenced by the British ambassador, Viscount Stratford de Redcliffe, who helped persuade the sultan to introduce Western reforms. Two decrees (1839, 1856) led to many changes but did not have permanent effect. Confident in British and French support, Abd al-Majid resisted (1853) the Russian claim to act as protector of the Orthodox Christians in the Ottoman Empire. This was a primary cause of the Crimean War. Turkey received no concrete gains at the Congress of Paris (1856; see Paris, Congress of). The sultan was succeeded by his brother, Abd al-Aziz. Ottoman sultan; modernizer of the army through "Tanzimat".

**

Abd al-Malik ibn Marwan (646-705): After Muawiyah's death in 680, his son, Yazid, ascended the Umayyad throne, but he failed to live up to his father's expectations. His heavy-handed tactics backfired in a spectacular fashion after the grisly murder of Hussain at the plain of Karbala. After three years of political chaos and mismanagement, Yazid was succeeded by his twenty-one year old son, Muawiyah ibn Yazid, who, unlike his father, was a sickly but peace-loving young man who abdicated within months of his accession. This led to more political chaos and uncertainty, as there was no obvious candidate to succeed him. After much political infighting and wrangling, the veteran politician Marwan ibn Hakam, who served as governor of Medina for a long period, was sworn in as the fourth Caliph of the Umayyad dynasty.

Thus Abdullah ibn Zubair, the son of the renowned Zubair ibn Awwam, assumed control of the entire Hijaz, while Mu'sab ibn Zubair proclaimed himself the administrator of Iraq on behalf of his brother. By contrast, Marwan ibn Hakam, the newly appointed Umayyad Caliph, found himself in charge of only southern Syria. He then proceeded to Egypt and brought this important country under Umayyad control. However, he was succeeded in 685 by his son, Abd al-Malik, who went on to become one of the Umayyad dynasty's most successful rulers, along with Muawiyah ibn Abi Sufyan.

Abd al-Malik ibn Marwan ibn Hakam was born in Medina during the early years of Caliph Uthman's reign. His father, Marwan ibn Hakam, was an influential member of the Umayyah clan. When Caliph Uthman was brutally murdered by a group of insurgents in 656, Abd al-Malik was still in his early teens. When the supporters of Abdullah ibn Zubair drove out the Umayyads from Mecca and Medina, Abd al-Malik, who was in his mid-thirties at the time, moved with his entire family to Syria where he became his father's chief political advisor after the latter's ascension to the Umayyad throne in 684. A year later, he succeeded his father as the Umayyad Caliph in 685; he was in his early forties at the time.

The Byzantines threatened to invade the Umayyad territories at the same time. In short, Abd al-Malik could not have ascended the Umayyad throne at a more dangerous and challenging time. After signing a peace treaty with the Byzantines and agreeing to pay them an annual tribute, he reorganized and expanded his armed forces in order to crush all political and military opposition against his rule in the Hijaz, Iraq and the neighboring territories. His failure to reassert his authority in Iraq prompted Abd al-Malik to change his political and military strategy, and he decided to consolidate his position in Syria and Egypt, and patiently wait to deal with his opponents at the right moment. For the next five years, he took no action against the rebels in Iraq.

Now there were only two main contenders for the Caliphate, namely Abdullah in Mecca and Abd al-Malik in Damascus. Like

Hussain ibn Ali, Abdullah rebelled against the Umayyads soon after the death of Muawiyah in 680, having flatly refused to acknowledge Yazid as Caliph. Although Hussain was brutally murdered by Yazid's forces at Karbala, Abdullah continued his opposition against Yazid and his successors, and in so doing established his authority across Hijaz and parts of Iraq.

Sensing Abdullah's vulnerability, Abd al-Malik personally led a military expedition to Iraq and in the ensuing war, he not only defeated his opponents but also reasserted Umayyad authority across that country. He then dispatched a large army to Mecca under the command of the notorious Hajjaj ibn Yusuf in order to bring Abdullah to heel. Following Abdullah's defeat at the hands of the Umayyad forces in 692, Abd al-Malik reunited the Muslim world under his leadership and restored peace and security throughout his dominion. It is true that two of the most notorious military generals, Ubaydullah ibn Ziyad and Hajjaj ibn Yusuf, thrived during his reign.

After restoring the political unity of the Muslim world, Abd al-Malik authorized fresh military campaigns in different parts of the world. He dispatched a large army under the command of Hassan ibn al-Nu'man which, despite an initial setback, went on to capture Carthage from the Byzantines and establish Islamic rule across North Africa. In addition to this, he instigated a series of campaigns against the Hindu rulers of Kabul.

Abd al-Malik's influence extended far beyond the political and military spheres. He became a champion of the Arabic language and actively promoted it throughout his dominion. This forced all his foreign officials and civil servants to learn Arabic. Then, between 696 and 698, he abolished and phased out regional coinage, thereby removing the distinction between the Sasanian dirham (silver) and Syriac, Egyptian and Palestinian dinars (gold) and replacing them with a standard Arabic coinage for the first time.

Abd al-Malik planned and constructed the magnificent *Qubbat al-Sakhra* (or the 'Dome of the Rock'). Constructed in 692 on the site of the rock (*Sakhra*) from which the Prophet Muhammad ascended to heaven (*Miraj*), this breathtaking Islamic edifice is today considered to be one of the world's most famous mosques along with the *Masjid al-Haram* (the Sacred Mosque) in Mecca and the *Masjid al-Nabi* (the Prophet's Mosque) in Medina. The Dome of the Rock is one of the Muslim world's most spectacular and breathtaking works of architecture.

Caliph Abd al-Malik's highly productive reign of two decades came to an end at the age of fifty-nine; he was buried in Damascus. He must be considered one of the Muslim world's most successful rulers.

Historians often refer to him as the 'father of Kings' because he was succeeded by his four sons, al-Walid, Sulaiman, Yazid II and Hisham.

Abd al-Malik, c.646-705, 5th Umayyad caliph (685-705); son of Marwan I. At his accession, Islam was torn by dissension and threatened by the Byzantine Empire. With the help of his able general al-Hajjaj, Abd al-Malik overthrew the rival caliphs and united Islam. His battles with Byzantine forces were without final result. A caliph; came to power in 685 ACE and ruled for 20 years (Iraq). Promoted the Arabic language; caused great expansion of the Islamic Empire. Umayyad caliph (685-705) who restored Umayyad power after a period of civil war; the Dome of the Rock was completed under his auspices in 691.

***

Abd al-Qadir al-Jilani (1077-1166): The great spiritual leaders were eager to understand the true nature of reality, which would enable them to move closer to Divine proximity – the origin of all that exists. One of the Muslim world's most influential, and arguably the most revered, Sufi (or spiritual teacher and guide) was Abd al-Qadir al-Jilani.

Sayyid Muhyi al-Din Abu Muhammad Abd al-Qadir Hasani al-Jilani was born in Nif, a district town of Jilan in the province of Tabaristan, located on the coast of the Caspian Sea. His family traced their lineage back to Hasan, the eldest son of Caliph Ali and a grandson of the Prophet. Abd al-Qadir received his early education in Arabic, committed the whole Qur'an to memory and studied aspects of *Hadith* (Prophetic traditions) at home under the supervision of his mother and maternal grandfather.

In 1095, Abd al-Qadir left his native Jilan and journeyed to Baghdad, which was the capital of the Muslim world at the time. After a long and eventful journey, he finally reached Baghdad. At the time Baghdad was a thriving center of Islamic learning and commercial activity.

Under Shaykh al-Dabbas's instruction, Abd al-Qadir not only learned the theories and methods of Sufism, but also became exposed to a new universe of meaning, purpose and spiritual fulfillment. Being a Sufi himself, the *Hanbali* jurist Abu Sa'id also played a decisive role in Abd al-Qadir's early quest for spirituality and fulfillment.

Abd al-Qadir's remarkable and unique ability to combine Islamic traditionalism with Islamic spirituality made him a hugely popular figure during his lifetime. Thanks to his intellectual brilliance and unique style of delivery, hundreds of non-Muslims (including Jews and Christians) embraced Islam and thousands of ordinary Muslims began to take their faith seriously. He became one of the first Sufi scholars in the annals of Islam to acquire such a mass following. More than seventy thousand people used to attend his lectures at any one time and around four hundred scribes used to write down his talks for the benefit of posterity. He was one of the most meticulous followers of the Prophetic *sunnah*.

Thanks to his band of dedicated scribes, Abd al-Qadir's lectures were preserved in the form of books and manuscripts for the benefit of posterity. In total, more than twenty-four books and manuscripts have been attributed to him. Abd al-Qadir argued that man was a creature of God Who created him only to serve Him. Abd al-Qadir did not consider God to be a theological construct or a logical abstract; rather, he believed, He is One Who resides in our hearts and continues to influence us in every sphere of our lives. Named after him, the *Qadiriyyah* Sufi Order is today followed by millions of people throughout the Muslim world.

Abd al-Qadir himself once remarked, 'My foot is on the head of every saint.' He died at the venerable age of around eighty-nine and was buried in Abbasid Baghdad.

***

Abd al-Rahman I (731-788): Or, his full name by patronymic record, Abd al-Rahman ibn Mu'awiya ibn Hisham ibn Abd al-Malik ibn Marwan (731-788) was the founder of the Umayyad Emirate of Córdoba (755), a Muslim dynasty that ruled the greater part of Iberia for nearly three centuries (including the succeeding Caliphate of Córdoba). The Muslims called the regions of Iberia under their dominion al-Andalus. Abd al-Rahman's establishment of a government in al-Andalus represented a branching from the rest of the Islamic Empire, which had been brought under the Abbasid following the overthrow of the Umayyads from Damascus in 750.

He was also known by appellations *al-Dakhil* ("the Immigrant"), *Saqr Quraish* ("the Falcon of the Quraysh") and the "Falcon of Andalus". Variations of the spelling of his name include **Abd ar-Rahman I**, **Abdul Rahman I** and **Abderraman I**.

Flight from Damascus:

Born near Damascus in Syria, Abd al-Rahman, grandson of Hisham ibn Abd al-Malik, was the son of the Umayyad prince Mu'awiyah ibn Hisham and a Berber concubine. He was twenty when his family, the ruling Umayyads, were overthrown by a popular revolt known as the Abbasid Revolution, occurring in the year 750. Abd al-Rahman and a small selection of his family fled Damascus, where the center of Umayyad power had been; people moving with him include his brother Yahiya, his four-year old son Sulayman, and some of his sisters, as well as his former Greek slave (a freedman), Bedr. The family fled from Damascus to the River Euphrates. All along the way the path was filled with danger, as the Abbasids had dispatched horsemen across the region to try to find the Umayyad prince and kill him. The Abbasids were merciless with all Umayyads that they found. Abbasid agents closed in on Abd al-Rahman and his family while they were hiding in a small village. He left his young son with his sisters and fled with Yahiya.

Abd al-Rahman, Yahiya and Bedr quit the village narrowly escaping the Abbasid assassins. Later, on the way south, Abbasid horsemen again caught up with the trio: Abd al-Rahman and his companions then threw themselves into the River Euphrates. While trying to swim across the dangerous Euphrates, Abd al-Rahman is said to have become separated from his brother Yahiya, who began swimming back towards the horsemen, possibly from fear of drowning. The horsemen beseeched the escapees to return, and that no harm would come to them. Yahiya returned to the near shore, and was quickly dispatched by the horsemen. They cut the head off their prize, leaving Yahiya's body to rot. Al-Maqqari quotes prior Muslim historians as having recorded that Abd al-Rahman said he was so overcome with fear at that moment, that once he made the far shore he ran until exhaustion overcame him. Only he and Bedr were left to face the unknown.

Exile years:

After barely escaping with their lives, Abd al-Rahman and Bedr continued south through Palestine, the Sinai, and then into Egypt. Abd al-Rahman had to keep a low profile as he traveled. It may be assumed that he intended to go at least as far as northwestern Africa (Maghreb), the land of his mother, which had been partly conquered by his Umayyad predecessors. The journey across Egypt would prove perilous. At the time, Abd al-Rahman ibn Habib al-Fihri was the semiautonomous governor of Ifriqiya (roughly, modern Tunisia) and a former Umayyad client. The ambitious Ibn Habib, a member of the illustrious Fihrid family, had long sought to carve out Ifriqiya as a private dominion for himself. Ibn Habib broke openly with the Abbasids and invited the remnants of the Umayyad dynasty to take refuge in his dominions. Abd al-Rahman was only one of several surviving Umayyad family members to make their way to Ifriqiya at this time.

But Ibn Habib soon changed his mind. He feared the presence of prominent Umayyad exiles in Ifriqiya, a family more illustrious than his own, might become a focal point for intrigue among local nobles against his own usurped powers. Around 755, believing he had discovered plots involving some of the more prominent Umayyad exiles in Kairouan, Ibn Habib turned against them. At the time, Abd al-Rahman and Bedr were keeping a low profile, staying in Kabylia, at the camp of a Nafza Berber chieftain friendly to their plight. Ibn Habib dispatched spies to look for the wayward Umayyad prince. When Ibn Habib's soldiers entered the camp, the Berber chieftain's wife Tekfah hid Abd al-Rahman under her personal belongings to help him go unnoticed. Once they were gone, Abd a-Rahman and Bedr immediately set off westwards.

In 755, Abd al-Rahman and Bedr reached modern day Morocco near Ceuta. Their next step would be to cross the sea to al-Andalus, where Abd al-Rahman could not have been sure whether or not he would be welcomed. Following the Berber Revolt of the 740s, the province was in a state of confusion, with the Muslim community torn by tribal dissensions among the Arabs and racial tensions between the Arabs and Berbers. At that moment, the nominal ruler of al-Andalus, emir Yusuf ibn 'Abd al-Rahman al-Fihri (another member of the Fihrid family, and a favorite of the old Arab settlers (Baladiyun), mostly of south Arabian or 'Yemenite' tribal stock) was locked in a contest with his vizier (and son-in-law) al-Sumayl ibn Hatim al-Qilabi, the head of the new settlers (Shamiyum, the Syrian Junds or military regiments, mostly of north Arabian Qaysid tribes, which had arrived only in 742).

Among the Syrian Junds were contingents of old Umayyad clients, numbering perhaps 500, and Abd al-Rahman believed he might tug on old loyalties and get them to receive him. Bedr was dispatched across the straits to make contact. Bedr managed to line up three Syrian commanders – Obeid Allah ibn Uthman and Abd Allah ibn Khalid, both originally of Damascus, and Yusuf ibn Bukht of Qinnasrin The trio approached the Syrian arch-commander al-Sumayl (then in Zaragoza) to get his consent, but al-Sumayl refused, fearing Abd al-Rahman would try to make himself emir. As a result, Bedr and the Umayyad clients sent out feelers to their rivals, the Yemenite commanders. Although the Yemenites were not natural allies (the Umayyads are a Qaysid tribe), their interest was piqued.

The emir Yusuf al-Fihri, had proven himself unable to keep the powerful al-Sumayl in check and several Yemenite chieftains felt their future prospects were poor, whether in a Fihrid or Syrian-dominated Spain, that they had a better chance of advancement if they hitched themselves to the glitter of the Umayyad name. Although the Umayyads did not have a historical presence in the region (no member of the Umayyad family was known to have ever set foot in al-Andalus before) and there were grave concerns about young Abd al-Rahman's inexperience, several of the lower-ranking Yemenite commanders felt they had little to lose and much to gain, and agreed to support the prince. Bedr returned to Africa to tell Abd al-Rahman of the invitation of the Umayyad clients in al-Andulus. Abd al-Rahman landed at Almunecar in al-Andalus, to the east of Malaga in September 755; however, his landing site was unconfirmed.

Fight for power:

Upon landing in al-Andalus, Abd al-Rahman was greeted by clients Abu Uthman and Ibn Khalid and an escort of 300 cavalry. During his brief time in Málaga, he was able to amass local support quickly. Waves of people made their way to Málaga to pay respect to the prince they thought was dead, including many of the aforementioned Syrians. One famous story which persisted through history related to a gift Abd al-Rahman was given while in Málaga. The gift was a beautiful young slave girl, but Abd al-Rahman humbly returned her to her previous master.

News of the prince's arrival spread like wildfire throughout the peninsula. During this time, emir al-Fihri and the Syrian commander al-Sumayl, pondered what to do about the new threat to their shaky hold on power. They decided to try to marry Abd al-Rahman into their family. If that did not work, then Abd al-Rahman would have to be killed. Abd al-Rahman was apparently sagacious enough to expect such a plot. In order to help speed his ascension to power, he was prepared to take advantage of the feuds and dissensions. However, before anything could be done, trouble broke out in northern al-Andalus. Zaragoza, an important trade city on the Upper March of al-Andalus, made a bid for autonomy.

Al-Fihri and al-Sumayl rode north to squash the rebellion. This might have been fortunate timing for Abd al-Rahman, since he was still getting a solid foothold in al-Andalus. By March 756, Abd al-Rahman and his growing following of Umayyad clients and Yemenite Junds, were able to take Sevilla without violence. After settling his bloody business in Zaragoza, al-Fihri turned his army back south to face the "pretender". The fight for the right to rule al-Andalus was about to begin. The two contingents met on opposite sides of the River Guadalquivir, just outside the capital of Córdoba on the plains of Musarah.

The river was, for the first time in years, overflowing its banks, heralding the end of a long drought. Nevertheless, food was still scarce, and Abd al-Rahman's army suffered from hunger. In an attempt to demoralize Abd al-Rahman's troops, al-Fihri ensured that his troops not only were well fed, but also ate gluttonous amounts of food in full view of the Umayyad lines. An attempt at negotiations soon followed in which it is likely that Abd al-Rahman was offered the hand of al-Fihri's daughter in marriage and great wealth. Abd ar-Rahman, however, would settle for nothing less than control of the emirate, and an impasse was reached. Even before the fight began, dissension spread through some of Abd al-Rahman's lines. Specifically, the Yemeni Arabs were unhappy that the prince was mounted on a fine Spanish steed. And the prince's mettle was untried in battle, after all! The Yemenis observed significantly that such a fine horse would provide an excellent mount to escape from battle.

Being the ever-wary politician, Abd al-Rahman acted quickly to regain Yemeni support, and rode to a Yemeni chief who was mounted on a mule named "Lightning". Abd al-Rahman averred that his horse proved difficult to ride and was wont to buck him out of the saddle. He offered to exchange his horse for the mule, a deal to which the surprised chief readily agreed. The swap quelled the simmering Yemeni rebellion. Soon both armies were in their lines on the same bank of the Guadalquivir. Abd al-Rahman had no banner, and so one was improvised by unwinding a green turban and binding it round the head of a spear. Subsequently the turban and the spear became the banner and symbol of the Andalusian Umayyads. Abd al-Rahman led the charge toward al-Fihri's army. Al-Sumayl in turn advanced his cavalry out to meet the Umayyad threat. After a long and difficult fight "Abd ar-Rahman obtained a most complete victory, and the field was strewn with the bodies of the enemy". Both al-Fihri and al-Sumayl managed to escape the field (probably) with parts of the army too.

Abd al-Rahman triumphantly marched into the capital, Córdoba. Danger was not far behind, as al-Fihri planned a counterattack. He reorganized his forces and set out for the capital Abd al-Rahman had usurped from him. Again Abd al-Rahman met al-Fihri with his army; this time negotiations were successful, although the terms were somewhat changed. In exchange for al-Fihri's life and wealth, he would be a prisoner and not allowed to leave the city limits of Córdoba. Al-Fihri would have to report once a day to Abd al-Rahman, as well as turn over some of his sons and daughters as hostages. For a while al-Fihri met the obligations of the one-sided truce, but he still had many people loyal to him; people who would have liked to see him back in power.

Al-Fihri eventually did make another bid for power. He quit Córdoba and quickly started gathering supporters. While at large, al-Fihri managed to gather an army allegedly numbering to 20,000. It is doubtful, however, that his troops were "regular" soldiers, but rather a hodge-podge of men from various parts of al-Andalus. Abd ar-Rahman's appointed governor in Sevilla took up the chase, and after a series of small fights, managed to defeat al-Fihri's army. Al-Fihri himself managed to escape to the former Visigoth capital of Toledo in central al-Andalus; once there, he was promptly killed. Al-Fihri's head was sent to Córdoba, where Abd al-Rahman had it nailed to a bridge. With this act, Abd ar-Rahman proclaimed himself the emir of al-Andalus. One final act had to be performed, however: al-Fihri's general, al-Sumayl, had to be dealt with, and he was garroted in Córdoba's jail.

Rule:

Indeed, Abd al-Rahman only proclaimed himself as emir, and not as caliph. This was likely because al-Andalus was a land besieged by many different loyalties, and the proclamation of caliph would have likely caused much unrest. Abd al-Rahman's progeny would, however, take up the title of caliph. In the meantime, a call went out through the Muslim world that al-Andalus was a safe haven for friends of the house of Umayyah, if not for Abd al-Rahman's scattered family that managed to evade the Abbasids. Abd al-Rahman probably was quite happy to see his call answered by waves of Umayyad faithful and family. He was finally reacquainted with his son Sulayman, whom he last saw weeping on the banks of the Euphrates with his sisters. Abd ar-Rahman's sisters were unable to make the long voyage to al-Andalus. Abd al-Rahman placed his family members in high offices across the land, as he felt he could trust them more than non-family. The Umayyad family would again grow large and prosperous over successive generations. However, by 763 Abd ar-Rahman had to get back to the business of war. Al-Andalus had been invaded by an Abbasid army.

Far away in Baghdad, the current Abbasid caliph, al-Mansur, had long been planning to depose the Umayyad who dared to call himself emir of al-Andalus. Al-Mansur installed al-Ala ibn-Mugith (also known as al-Ala) as governor of Africa (whose title gave him dominion over the province of al-Andalus). It was al-Ala who headed the Abbasid army that landed in al-Andalus, possibly near Beja (in modern day Portugal). Much of the surrounding area of Beja capitulated to al-Ala, and in fact rallied under the Abbasid banners against Abd al-Rahman. Abd al-Rahman had to act quickly. The Abbasid contingent was vastly superior in size, said to have numbered 7,000 men. The emir quickly made for the redoubt of Carmona with his army. The Abbasid army was fast on his heels, and laid siege to Carmona for approximately two months. Abd al-Rahman must have sensed that time was against him as food and water became scarce, and his troops morale likely came into question. Finally Abd al-Rahman gathered his men as he was "resolved on an audacious sally". Abd al-Rahman hand-picked 700 fighters from his army and led them to Carmona's main gate.

There, he started a great fire and threw his scabbard into the flames. Abd al-Rahman told his men that time had come to go down fighting than die of hunger. The gate lifted and Abd al-Rahman's men fell upon the unsuspecting Abbasids, thoroughly routing them. Most of the Abbasid army was killed. The heads of the main Abbasid leaders were cut off. Their heads were preserved in salt, and identifying tags pinned to their ears. The heads were bundled together in a gruesome package and sent to the Abbasid caliph who was on pilgrimage at Mecca. Upon receiving the evidence of al-Ala's defeat in al-Andalus, al-Mansur is said to have gasped, "God be praised for placing a sea between us"! Al-Mansur hated, and yet apparently respected Abd al-Rahman to such a degree that he dubbed him the "Hawk of Quraysh" (The Umayyads were from a branch of the Quraysh tribe).

Despite such a tremendous victory, Abd al-Rahman had to continuously put down rebellions in al-Andalus. Various Arab and Berber tribes fought each other for varying degrees of power, some cities tried to break away and form their own state, and even members of Abd al-Rahman's family tried to wrest power from him. During a large revolt, dissidents marched on Córdoba itself; However, Abd al-Rahman always managed to stay one step ahead, and crushed all opposition; as he always dealt severely with dissidence in al-Andalus. Despite all this turmoil in al-Andalus, Abd al-Rahman wanted to take the fight back east to Baghdad. Revenge for the massacre of his family at the hands of the Abbasids must surely have been the driving factor in Abd al-Rahman's war plans. However his war against Baghdad was put on hold by more internal problems. The seditious city of Zaragoza on the Upper March revolted in a bid for autonomy. Little could Abd al-Rahman have known that as he set off to settle matters in that northern city, his hopes of warring against Baghdad would be indefinitely put on hold.

Problems in the Upper March:

Zaragoza proved to be a most difficult city to reign over for not only Abd ar-Rahman, but his predecessors as well. In the year 777–778, several notable men including Sulayman ibn Yokdan al-Arabi al-Kelbi, the self-appointed governor of Zaragoza, met with delegates of the leader of the Franks, Charlemagne. "(Charlemagne's) army was enlisted to help the Muslim governors of Barcelona and Zaragoza against the Umayyad (emir) in Cordoba..." Essentially Charlemagne was being hired as a mercenary, even though he likely had other plans of acquiring the area for his own empire. After Charlemagne's columns arrived at the gates of Zaragoza, Sulayman got cold feet and refused to let the Franks into the city. It is possible that he realized that Charlemagne would want to usurp power from him. Charlemagne's force eventually headed back to France via a narrow pass in the Pyrenees, where his rearguard was wiped out by Basque and Gascon rebels (this disaster inspired the epic Chanson de Roland).

Now Abd al-Rahman could deal with Sulayman and the city of Zaragoza without having to fight a massive Christian army. In 779 Abd ar-Rahman offered the job of Zaragoza's governorship to one of Sulayman's allies, a man named al-Husayn ibn Yahiya. The temptation was too much for al-Husayn, who murdered his colleague Sulayman. As promised, al-Husayn was awarded Zaragoza with the expectation that he would always be a subordinate of Córdoba. Within two years, however, al-Husayn broke off relations with Abd al-Rahman and announced that Zaragoza would be an independent city-state.

Once again Abd al-Rahman had to be concerned with developments in the Upper March. He was intent on keeping his important northern border city within the Umayyad fold. By 783 Abd al-Rahman's army advanced on Zaragoza. It appeared as though Abd al-Rahman wanted to make clear to this troublesome city that independence was out of the question. Included in the arsenal of Abd al-Rahman's army were thirty-six siege engines. Zaragoza's famous white granite defensive walls were breached under a torrent of ordnance from the Umayyad lines. Abd al-Rahman's warriors spilled into the city's streets, quickly thwarting al-Husayn's desires for independence.

Military and social reforms and constructions works:

After the aforementioned period of conflict, Abd al-Rahman continued in his improvement of al-Andalus' infrastructure. He ensured roadways were begun, aqueducts were constructed or improved, and that a new mosque was well funded in his capital at Córdoba. Construction on what would in time become the world famous Great Mosque of Córdoba was started circa the year 786. Abd al-Rahman knew that one of his sons would one day inherit the rule of al-Andalus, but that it was a land torn by strife. In order to successfully rule in such a situation, Abd al-Rahman needed to create a reliable civil service and organize a standing army. He felt that he could not always rely on the local populace in providing a loyal army; and therefore bought a massive standing army consisting mainly of Berbers from North Africa as well as slaves from other areas.

The total number of army-men under his command were nearly 40,000. As was common during the years of Islamic expansion from Arabia, religious tolerance was practiced. Abd al-Rahman continued to allow Jews and Christians and other monotheistic religions to retain and practice their faiths. They did, however, have to pay a tribute tax for this privilege. Abd al-Rahman's policy of taxing non-Muslims, which was often carried out by later rulers, changed the religious dynamic of al-Andalus. Possibly because of excessive tribute taxes "the bulk of the country's population must have become Muslim". However, other scholars have argued that though 80% of al-Andalus converted to Islam, it did not truly occur until near the 10th century.

Christians more often converted to Islam than Jews although there were converted Jews among the new followers of Islam. There was a great deal of freedom of interaction between the groups: for example, Sarah, the granddaughter of the Visigoth king Wittiza, married a Muslim man and bore two sons who were later counted among the ranks of the highest Arab nobility.

Conclusion:

The date of Abd al-Rahman's death is disputed, but is generally accepted to be sometime around 785 through 788. Abd al-Rahman died in his adopted city of Cordoba and was supposedly buried under the site of the Mezquita. Abd al-Rahman's alleged favorite son was his choice for successor and would later be known as Hisham I. Abd ar-Rahman's progeny would continue to rule al-Andalus in the name of the house of Umayyah for several generations, with the zenith of their power coming during the reign of Abd al-Rahman III.

Legends:

In his lifetime, Abd al-Rahman was known as *al Dakhil* ("the immigrant"). But he was also known as *Saqr Quraish* ("The Falcon of the Quraish"), bestowed on him by one of his great enemies, the Abbasid caliph al-Mansur.

***

Abd al-Rahman III (890-961): The Umayyads ruled the Muslim world from 661 to 750, but when the Abbasids came to power they put most of the Umayyad princes to the sword. Only a handful of the Umayyad princes escaped the ensuing massacre. Abd al-Rahman, the grandson of Umayyad ruler Hisham ibn Abd al-Malik, was one of them. He fled Damascus and travelled on foot and by ship for many years before he finally reached North Africa, where he received a warm welcome from the Berber tribe of Banu Nafisa (in present-day Morocco). In 756, he led an army into battle and defeated the governor's forces before proceeding to Cordova, the capital of *al-Andalus*, and in so doing inaugurated Umayyad rule in Spain. Abd al-Rahman and his descendants went on to rule Muslim Spain for nearly three centuries. During this period Muslim

Spain produced a number of influential rulers, but the most outstanding of them all was Caliph Abd al-Rahman III.

Abd al-Rahman ibn Muhammad, better known as Abd al-Rahman III, was born in Cordova during the reign of his grandfather, Amir Abdullah. Young Abd al-Rahman grew up under the care of his Frankish mother, Muzna, and his grandfather, Amir Abdullah. His mother, Muzna, and grandmother, Iniga, were of European origin. Young Abd al-Rahman was aware of the difficult challenges which confronted his country and contributed as much as he could to alleviating the problems until Amir Abdullah died in 912.

Abd al-Rahman succeeded his grandfather at the age of twenty-two and became the new ruler of Islamic Spain. Immediately after becoming Caliph, his main priority was to restore political stability and civil order across *al-Andalus*. The Abbasid Caliph in Baghdad, he reminded his people, would not come to their aid should the neighboring Christian powers decide to attack *al-Andalus*. His message to his people was very loud and clear: unite or you will be consigned to the dustbin of history.

After establishing political and civil order across Cordova and its immediate surroundings, Abd al-Rahman turned his attention to other major cities like Seville and Toledo. But when these self-appointed rulers rejected his conciliatory measures, he launched military actions against them. Since Ordono II, the Christian ruler of Leon, was the chief instigator of these raids, Abd al-Rahman sent an expedition and inflicted a crushing defeat on his forces in 923. After successfully subduing these cities, Abd al-Rahman finally restored peace, order and security across much of *al-Andalus*. In 929, at the age of thirty-nine, he became the undisputed master of Islamic Spain and adopted the title of *al-Khalifah al-Nasir li-din Allah* ('the Caliph, the Defender of the Religion of God').

Indeed, under Abd al-Rahman's stewardship, Spain became a beacon of light for the rest of Europe. When there was hardly a college or library worth its name in Europe, *al-Andalus* boasted some of the finest, and also largest, libraries and educational institutions in the Western world. He transformed the Academy in Cordova into one of the world's most dazzling centers of higher education and research. The thriving and tolerant civil society, known as the *convivencia,* fostered by Caliph Abd al-Rahman enabled everyone including Muslims, Jews and Christians to live and work together in peace and tranquility. Renowned Jewish thinkers such as Ibn Gabirol and Judah Halevi also lived and thrived in Islamic Spain.

Then, in 936, Caliph Abd al-Rahman ordered the construction of a new palace city which became known as *Madinat al-Zahra* (or 'the dazzling city'). This mammoth project took more than forty years to complete. It was in fact Caliph al-Hakam, his son and successor, who finally achieved this in 976.

For nearly eight centuries, under her Mohammedan rulers, Spain set to all Europe a shining example of a civilized and enlightened State. Mathematics, astronomy and botany, history, philosophy and jurisprudence were to be mastered in Spain, and Spain alone.

His reign of forty-nine years was therefore a truly remarkable period in the history of Islamic Spain and Europe as a whole. Caliph Abd al-Rahman III died in Cordova at the age of seventy-one. *Al-Andalus* began to decline after his death and the Umayyads of Spain were eventually ousted from power in 1031.

***

Abdul Aziz ibn Abdul Rahman al Saud (1879-1953): founder and king of Saudi Arabia. Born in Diraiya, central Arabia, Abdul grew up in Kuwait, where his ruling al Saud family was exiled following its defeat in 1891. In 1902 he regained Diraiya and neighboring Riyadh from the rival Rashid clan, which was allied with the Ottoman empire. Yet it was not until October 1953, a month before his death, that Abdul issued a decree appointing a council of ministers as an advisory body. At age 21 he departed Kuwait to subdue the two holy places: Mecca and Medina.

***

Abdul Ghani, Abdul Aziz (1939-   ): Yemeni political; North Yemeni prime minister, 1975-80, 1983-90, 1994-97 Born into a Shafii Sunni family in the Hujariya region of North Yemen, Abdul went to a teacher training college in Aden, South Yemen. He supported Salih in the civil war that erupted in May 1994 and was appointed premier after it ended in July. Following the 1997 parliamentary poll, Abdul was replaced as the prime minister by Faraj Said Ghanim.

***

Abdul Hamid II (1842-1918): Ottoman sultan (1876-1909). He succeeded his brother Murad V and ruled until his deposition following the 1908 Young Turk revolution. His war with Russia (1877-78) was resolved by the Treaty of San Stefano (1878), subsequently modified by the congress of Berlin (1878).

***

Islamic Leaders

Abdul ilah ibn Ali (1912-1958): Iraqi regent, 1939-53; crown prince, 1953-58 Son of Sharif Ali ibn Hussein, King of Hijaz, Abdul moved to Baghdad along with the family when Hijaz fell to Abdul Aziz ibn Abdul Rahman al Saud in 1925. Following the death in 1939 of his cousin and brother in law, King Ghazi of Iraq, he became regent on behalf of four year old King Faisal II. After the seizure of power by anti British officers, led by Rashid Ali Gailani in April 1941, the pro British Abdul and the rest of the royal family fled. But two months later they returned to Baghdad following Gailani's defeat by the British. When Faisal II came of age in 1953 and ascended the throne, he named Abdul crown prince. By then Abdul was widely regarded in Iraq as an agent of British imperialism. He was assassinated during the antimonarchist coup of 14 July 1958.

***

Abdul Majuid, Esmat (1924-   ): Egyptian diplomat and politician; secretary general of the Arab league. 1991-2001 Born into a middle class family in Alexandria, Abdul trained as a lawyer at universities in his native city and Paris. He joined the Foreign Service when he was twenty seven. In May 1991, following the expulsion of Iraq from occupied Kuwait, in which Egypt played an important role, Abdul was unanimously elected secretary general of the Arab league, the event signifying the restoration of Egypt as leader of the Arab world after twelve years of ostracization following its unilateral peace treaty with Israel in 1979. In 2001 he was succeeded by Amr Moussa.

***

Abdul Rahman, Omar (1938-   ): Egyptian Islamist leader Born into a poor peasant family in Gamaliya village, Daqaliya district, in the Nile delta, Abdul went blind in infancy as a result of diabetes. He was educated in local religious schools before joining al Azhar University in 1955. After securing a doctorate in literature in 1965 he became a lecturer in Islamic studies at the al Azhar's branch at Fatyum in the Nile delta. Following the bombing of the World Trade Center in New York in February 1993 and the aborting of a plan to bomb the United Nations and other targets some weeks later, Abdul was arrested as a suspect, found guilty in October 1995, and sentenced to life imprisonment for seditious conspiracy for a bombing plot. In early 1999, from his high security jail in the US, he endorsed the unilateral cease-fire declared by al Gamaat al Islamiya.

***

Abdullah I ibn Hussein al Hashem (1882-1951): Emir of Tran Jordan, 1921-46, King of Jordan 1946-51 Son of Sharif Hussein ibn Ali al Hashem of Hijaz, Abdullah was educated in Istanbul, where his father was kept under surveillance from 1891 until the coup by the Young Turks in 1908. From 1912 to 1914 Abdullah represented Mecca in the Ottoman parliament. He participated in the Arab revolt against the Ottomans that, led by his father, erupted in June 1916. When Sharif Hussein declared himself King of Hijaz in 1917, Abdullah became his foreign minister. Most of them considered Abdullah a traitor, a lackey of the British, who had made underhanded deals with the Zionists at the expense of Arab interests. In July 1951, Shurki Ashu, a young Palestinian, assassinated Abdullah as he entered al Aqsa Mosque in East Jerusalem for Friday prayers. King of Jordan; assassinated in 1951.

***

Abdullah al-Ma'mun (786-833): The question of political succession has often been a major stumbling block in Islamic political history. Keen to avoid a similar conflict after his death, the celebrated Abbasid Caliph Harun al-Rashid took the unusual step of nominating his successor during his own lifetime. According to the agreement formulated by Harun, he was to be succeeded by his son, Muhammad, who became known as Caliph al-Amin. It also stated that al-Amin, in turn, was to be succeeded by his brother, Abdullah, who later became known as Caliph al-Ma'mun. Al-Ma'mun denounced his brother as a traitor and this set the two brothers against each other, leading to considerable political infighting and loss of life. Al-Ma'mun not only went on to become one of the Muslim world's most prominent rulers, but also carved out an important place for himself in the intellectual history of Islam.

Abdullah al-Ma'mun ibn Harun al-Rashid was born in Baghdad after his father's accession to the Abbasid throne at the age of twenty-two. The Caliph invited the leading scholars to come and teach al-Ma'mun. He thus received a thorough education in Arabic language, literature and aspects of Islamic sciences. Young al-Ma'mun acquired considerable knowledge of Islamic sciences and became thoroughly familiar with the Qur'an.

In 809, Caliph Harun al-Rashid died at the age of forty-three. During his reign of twenty-two years he completely transformed the fortunes of the Abbasid Empire. He restored peace, order and security throughout his vast empire. Under Harun's patronage, Baghdad became one of the Muslim world's most famous educational, cultural and architectural centers.

Al-Ma'mun was keen to reward his staff handsomely so as to prevent corruption, bribery and malpractice from rearing their ugly heads within his Government, and in this respect he was very successful. Like his father, al-Ma'mun transformed Baghdad into a thriving city. Under his stewardship, it became the world's most dazzling capital city, being renowned for its schools, colleges, hospitals, markets, bookshops and libraries. As a generous patron of learning and education, he transformed the *bait al-Hikmah* ('the House of Wisdom'), which was originally founded by his father Caliph Harun al-Rashid, into one of the Muslim world's most famous libraries and research centers. He not only expanded its activities and renamed it as *dar al-Hikmah* ('the Abode of Wisdom'), he also went out of his way to recruit some of the Muslim world's brightest minds.

Al-Ma'mun chose to champion the views of the Mu'tazilites with the result that, during his reign, Mu'tazilism became the official creed of the State. Unlike the Islamic traditionalists, who argued that the Qur'an was the uncreated Word of God, al-Ma'mun – like the Mu'tazilites – considered it to be a created Word of God.

Caliph al-Ma'mun's reign of two and a half decades came to an end when he was forty-seven. He died in the village of Budandun (in present-day Pozanti) during a military expedition he led against the Byzantines. His body was transferred to Tarsus where he was laid to rest following a simple funeral. His half-brother Abu Ishaq Muhammad Mu'tasim Billah succeeded him as Caliph.

***

Abdullah ibn Abdul Aziz al Saud (1923-   ): Saudi Arabian crown Prince, 1982, son of Abdul Aziz al Saud and Asi al Shuraim of the Rashid clan, which was defeated by Abdul Aziz in 1921, Abdullah was born and educated in Riyadh. He started his career as governor of Mecca and became deputy defense minister and commander of the national Guard in 1963. When Khalid ibn Abdul Aziz acceded the throne in 1975 he appointed Abdullah as second deputy premier. Washington's relations with Riyadh soured when it emerged that fifteen of the nineteen hijackers of 9/11 were Saudi nationals. Abdullah I (Abdullah ibn Husayn), 1882-1951, king of Jordan (1946-51), b. Mecca; son of Husayn ibn Ali of the Hashemite family.

During World War I, Abdullah, with British support, led Arab revolts against Turkish rule. After the war, the unsuccessfully fought against Ibn Saud for control of the Hejaz. In 1921, Great Britain made Abdullah the emir of Transjordan as well as placed Abdullah's brother Faisal as king of Iraq. In World War II, Abdullah strongly opposed the

Axis powers. Following the partition of Palestine (May, 1948) he led the troops of his British-trained force, the Arab Legion, against the newly declared state of Israel. Abdullah annexed the portions of Palestine now known as the West Bank. His foreign policy was directed toward creation of an Arab federation, preferably under Hashemite rule. In 1951 he was assassinated in Jerusalem.

***

Abdullah, Sheikh Muhammad (1905-1982): Kashmiri Muslim leader. He began his career as an activist in the Kashmir Muslim Conference in the 1930s, agitating against the arbitrary rule of the Hindu Dogra Maharaja of Kashmir. Later, as the leader of the Muslim National Conference, he established close links with the Indian National Congress and Jawaharlal Nehru.

***

Abraham: First of the patriarchs of Israel, from whom the Israelites traced their descent. He is revered by Jews, Christians and Muslims. The biblical stories of Abraham are of varying date and origin, and it is uncertain how much historical fact they contain. According to the book of Genesis (the first book of the Old Testament), Abraham lived in the middle of the 2nd millennium BC at Haran in northern Mesopotamia. He was divinely called to leave his home and family and go to a new land, Canaan. It is recorded that God made a covenant (or agreement) with him, promising him a multitude of descendants to whom he would give Canaan forever, provided that he and all his male descendants were circumcised. Accordingly, Abraham's wife Sarah, although aged over 90, gave birth to a son, Isaac. God subsequently tested Abraham's faith by asking him to sacrifice Isaac to him. When Abraham showed his readiness to do this, a ram was substituted for the sacrifice and God confirmed his covenant. Through Ishmael, his son by Hagar, the maidservant of Sarah, he is considered by Muslims an ancestor of the Arabs, and is frequently mentioned (as Ibrahim) in the Koran.

***

Abu Al-Abbas Al-Suffah (750-754): Abu al-Abbas as-Saffah, d. 754, 1st Abbasid caliph (749-54). **Abu al Qasim Muhammad:** also known as the Hidden Imam. He was the Twelfth Imam of the Shiah, who was said to have gone into hiding in 874 to save his life; in 934 his "Occultation" was declared God it was said had miraculously concealed the Imam and he could make no further direct contact with Shi'as. Shortly before the

Last Judgment, he would return as the Mahdi to inaugurate a golden age of justice and peace, having destroyed the enemies of God.

***

Abu al Qasim Muhammad: Also known as the Hidden Imam. He was the Twelfth Imam of the Shiah, who was said to have gone into hiding in 874 to save his life; in 934 his "Occultation" was declared God it was said had miraculously concealed the Imam and he could make no further direct contact with Shi'as. Shortly before the Last Judgment, he would return as the Mahdi to inaugurate a golden age of justice and peace, having destroyed the enemies of God.

***

Abu Bakr al-Razi (841-925): 'The greatest clinician of Islam and of the whole Middle Ages. He was the most celebrated and probably the most original of the Arabic writers.' Some historians have compared him with Hippocrates, the famous Greek physician, while according to others he was one of history's most pioneering medical practitioners. This remarkable Muslim physician and philosopher was none other than Abu Bakr al-Razi.

Abu Bakr Muhammad ibn Zakariyya ibn Yahya al-Razi, known in the West as Rhazes, was born in the Persian city of Rayy (located close to modern Tehran), at the time a thriving center of educational and commercial activity. He became fascinated by music and musical theory, and during this period learned to play the flute with considerable proficiency. Inspired by the works of Jabir ibn Hayyan, the father of Islamic alchemy and chemistry, al-Razi became a widely respected authority on experimental alchemy.

Despite this, his eyesight continued to deteriorate, eventually forcing him to turn his back on alchemy and chemistry for good, and instead he began to study medicine under Abul Hasan Ali ibn Sahl al-Rabbani's guidance. Al-Razi soon became a respected intellectual and skilled medical practitioner. This prompted al-Mansur ibn Ishaq, the city's governor, to appoint him director of the local hospital.

In addition to mastering alchemy, medicine and philosophy, al-Razi acquired considerable proficiency in logic, cosmology, theology and aspects of mathematics. Unlike al-Ash'ari and al-Kindi, he espoused a championed a purely rationalistic philosophy. Thus, reason and revelation, he argued, were incompatible and any attempts to reconcile the two were bound to fail.

Al-Razi became a champion of Platonic philosophy. Not surprisingly, his philosophical worldview revolved around the five eternal principles of Creator, Universal Soul, Primeval Matter, Time and Space. Human reason, in his opinion, was far superior to revelation and, as such, he was one of the most rationalistic of all Muslim philosophers. His philosophical thought never took off in the Muslim world.

Although accused of heresy, al-Razi's unflinching faith in God prevented his most vociferous critics from branding him an unbeliever or atheist. He read extensively and wrote copiously; on one occasion he wrote more than twenty thousand pages in a single year. In old age, when he could no longer read or write due to failing eyesight, he paid people to read books to him so that he could continue to learn.

Along with Ibn Sina and al-Zahrawi, al-Razi must be considered one of the most influential Muslim physicians of all time. He managed two of the leading hospitals of his day; one was based in Rayy and the other was located in Baghdad. His *Kitab al-Hawi* was arguably the most comprehensive medical work ever produced in Arabic and consisted of twenty-five hefty volumes. The Latin translation of this book was begun in 1280 and completed in 1542. Considered to be one of the masterpieces of medical writing, it was used as a standard textbook on smallpox and measles until the modern period. Al-Razi authored one hundred and eighty-four books and treatises on all branches of learning, including eighty books on philosophical and theological topics alone. But, according to other historians, he wrote more than two hundred and forty books, most of which have, unfortunately, perished.

Hailed as the 'Arab Galen' across medieval Europe, al-Razi became blind toward the end of his life, due to excessive reading and writing. He died at the age of about eighty-four and was buried in his native Rayy.

***

Abu Bakr al-Siddiq (573-634): If piety, righteousness and love for Islam were the only criteria for selection, then after the Prophet Muhammad, Abu Bakr would certainly have led the way.

Abdullah ibn Abi Quhafah, better known by his patronymic Abu Bakr, was born into the clan of Taym of the noble Quraysh tribe; he was only two years younger than the Prophet himself.

The situation in Mecca had become so degenerate that the Arabs buried their baby girls alive because they were considered to be an economic burden on their families.

After Muhammad received his first revelation (*Wahy*) from God, through the angel Gabriel, in the year 610 (while he was busy meditating on the Mount of Light (*Jabal al-Nur*)), he shared the good news with his immediate family before approaching his best friend, Abu Bakr. As soon as the Prophet informed him about his Prophetic mission, Abu Bakr accepted it without any hesitation whatsoever.

For the next twenty-three years, Abu Bakr provided unflinching help and support to the Prophet. In the tenth year of Muhammad's Prophethood, a momentous event took place. *Al-Isra wa'l Miraj* (or the Prophet's miraculous night journey from Mecca to Jerusalem, and ascension to heaven) occurred, and it was on this occasion that the five daily prayers were prescribed. Abu Bakr became known as *al-Siddiq* or 'the truthful' one.

After the Prophet's migration to Medina in 622, Abu Bakr purchased a plot of land where the foundations of *Masjid al-Nabi* (or the 'Prophet's mosque') were laid in 623; he also led the first *hajj* (pilgrimage) to Mecca on behalf of the Prophet. Although the Prophet did not directly nominate a successor before he died, by nominating Abu Bakr to lead the daily prayers he had implicitly pointed the way forward, but the Prophet was keen to give the people a say in the election or selection of their rulers.

After the Prophet passed away in 632, the news of his death spread across Arabia like wildfire; they thought that Islam would fizzle out after the Prophet's death. After considerable discussion and debate, it was unanimously agreed by the companions of the Prophet to elect Abu Bakr *khalifat Rasoul Allah* ('successor to the Messenger of God'). After being elected the first Caliph of Islam, Abu Bakr went straight to the Prophet's mosque where he delivered his first address to the people. He declared:

'O people! I have been selected as your trustee although I am no better than anyone of you. If I am right, obey me. If I happen to be wrong, set me right, God willing. I ask you to obey me as long as I obey God and His messenger. If I disobey God and His messenger, you are free to disobey me.'

Caliph Abu Bakr did not decide anything unilaterally. He formed an advisory council consisting of the leading companions of the Prophet and he regularly consulted them before authorizing or undertaking any issues of importance.

In the year 633, Abu Bakr authorized Khalid ibn al-Walid, the great Muslim military commander, to take action against the subversive activities of the Persians. The Muslim army defeated the Persians and brought peace and order to that area. In the following year, elements of the Byzantine army began to instigate military raids and other provocative actions against the Muslim territories. After consulting his advisory council, the Caliph took decisive action against the Byzantines.

In just over two years, Caliph Abu Bakr helped transform the fortunes of Islam. More importantly, encouraged and supported by Umar, he brought together all the parchments (*Suhuf*) on which the Qur'an was written during the Prophet's lifetime and compiled them in the form of one book (*Mushaf*).

Only the love and pleasure of God, the Absolute Reality, mattered to Abu Bakr. This great servant of Islam breathed his last at the age of sixty-one and was buried in Medina next to the Prophet, his mentor and guide. Such was the greatness of Caliph Abu Bakr that the Prophet once stated, 'Abu Bakr's name shall be called out from all the gates of Paradise, and he will be the first person of my community to enter it.'

***

Abu Dhabi city: capital of United Arab Emirates and Abu Dhabi emirate Pop 520,000. Located on the offshore island of the same name, Abu Dhabi was founded by members of the Aal bu Falah clan of the Bani Yas Tribe in 1761. A quarter of a century later they transferred their base from the al Jiwa oasis to Abu Dhabi. With the formation of a confederation of seven emirates, called the United Arab Emirates in 1971, Abu Dhabi was selected as its interim capital, later confirmed as the capital city.

***

Abu Hamid al-Ghazali (1058-1111): Under Abul Hasan al-Ash'ari's guidance, speculative theology (*Ilm al-kalam*) became a powerful force within the Islamic intellectual firmament. Prior to that, under Hasan al-Basri's tutelage, Sufism (or Islamic mysticism) had become a potent force in the Muslim world. These rationalistic, philosophical, theological and mystical trends continued to compete for the hearts and minds of Muslims until the indomitable personality of al-Ghazali emerged in the eleventh century to champion and reassert traditional Islamic thought and practices as never before.

Abu Hamid Muhammad ibn Muhammad ibn Muhammad al-Tusi al-Ghazali, known in the Latin West as Algazel, was born in the historic town of Tus in Khurasan (in present-day Mashhad in Iran). Al-Ghazali attended the class of a local Sufi tutor and attained proficiency in Arabic language, grammar, Qur'an, *Hadith*, jurisprudence (*Fiqh*) and aspects of Sufi thought and poetry before he was fifteen.

Al-Ghazali was barely twenty years old when he traveled to Nishapur to pursue advanced instruction in Islamic sciences. It was during this period that he composed his *al-Mankhul min Ilm al-Usul* (A

Summary of the Science of Fundamentals), wherein he elucidated the fundamental principles of Islamic law and legal methodology.

In 1085 al-Juwayni died and al-Ghazali was asked to become professor of Islamic thought at the Nizamiyyah College in Baghdad by none other than Nizam al-Mulk himself, the great Seljuk Prime Minister and founder of the Nizamiyyah College. At the age of thirty-four, he became the youngest professor at Nizamiyyah. This was an extraordinary honor for young al-Ghazali since the Nizamiyyah College of Baghdad was the Oxford or Harvard of its time.

Al-Ghazali was profoundly disturbed by the apparent conflict between the views of the rationalists, who argued that human reason (*Aql*) was superior to revelation (*Wahy*), and the traditionalists who considered Divine revelation to be infallible and, therefore, more authoritative in comparison with fallible human reason. The more al-Ghazali questioned the more he doubted the very foundation of knowledge. Thus, for a period, he became a fully-fledged sceptic, living in a state of doubt and depression.

Al-Ghazali began studying and analyzing the works of the philosophers and theologians. He found no common ground on which all theologians could agree. He argued, therefore, that scholastic theology would be of no value to anyone unless they believed in the indispensability of human reason. Astonishingly, al-Ghazali was only thirty-six when he authored his hugely influential *Tahafut*.

After this, al-Ghazali immersed himself in the ocean of Sufi thought and practices. Following a thorough study of the works of prominent Sufis like Abu Talib Amr al-Makki, Harith al-Muhasibi, Abul Qasim al-Junayd al-Baghdadi, Abu Bakr al-Shibli and Abu Yazid al-Bistami, al-Ghazali realized that 'empirical' – as opposed to 'theoretical' – knowledge was the foundation of Sufism. He devoted all his time and energy to seeking experiential knowledge in order to move closer to Divine proximity like the Sufis. He found peace of mind and intellectual reassurance in the message of Sufism.

Al-Ghazali's philosophical and theological views also exerted considerable influence on renowned Jewish and Christian thinkers like St Thomas Aquinas, Ramon Lull, Blaise Pascal and Musa bin Maimon (Moses Maimonides) among others. Al-Ghazali eventually returned to his native Tus in 1110 and, a year later, he died at the age of fifty-three. He was buried in the cemetery close to Sanabad.

***

Abu Hanifah (700-767): The principles of *Shari'ah* (Islamic law) are derived from the Qur'an and the normative practice (*sunnah*) of the Prophet

Muhammad. After the death of the Prophet, his leading companions, such as Abu Bakr al-Siddiq, Umar ibn al-Khattab, Uthman ibn Affan and Ali ibn Abi Talib, assumed the leadership of the Muslim community. The *Shari'ah* was not codified in a systematic way at the time. At such a critical time in Islamic history, Abu Hanifah emerged to develop one of Islamic history's most influential legal syntheses.

Numan ibn Thabit ibn Zuta ibn Mah, better known by his patronymic Abu Hanifah, was born in Kufah (in modern Iraq) during the reign of the great Umayyad Caliph Abd al-Malik ibn Marwan. Of Persian origin, Abu Hanifah was brought up in a relatively wealthy Muslim family. He was very fortunate to have met a number of prominent companions, including Anas ibn Malik, Sahl ibn Sa'd, Abu al-Tufayl Amir ibn Watihilah and Jabir ibn Abdullah.

Caliph Sulaiman, al-Walid's successor, was a relatively benevolent ruler who promoted learning and scholarship. By all accounts, Abu Hanifah was a late starter and most of his peers were way ahead of him when he began his studies, but after he started he was determined to reach the very summit of Islamic learning and scholarship. Abu Hanifah went on to become one of the Muslim world's greatest intellectuals and jurists.

Abu Hanifah went to Mecca to perform the sacred *hajj* (pilgrimage) and enrolled at the school of Ata ibn Abu Rabah, who was considered to be one of the giants of Islamic learning and wisdom at the time.

In the year 720, when Abu Hanifah was twenty-one, he left Mecca for Medina where he learned *Hadith* from Sulaiman and Salim ibn Abdullah. Sulaiman was an aide of *ummul Mu'minin* (the 'mother of the believers') Maymuna, the wife of the Prophet, and Salim was a grandson of Umar, the second Caliph of Islam. Abu Hanifah became a great repository of Islamic knowledge.

The vast corpus of juristic pronouncements (*fatawa*) developed by Abu Hanifah and his trusted disciples became so large that, over time, a school of Islamic legal thought emerged named after him. Known as the *Hanafi Madh'hab*, this school of legal thought is most prevalent in India, Pakistan, Bangladesh, Afghanistan, Turkey, Syria, Iraq and Egypt. Towards the end of his life, Abu Hanifah was imprisoned by the Abbasid Caliph Abu Ja'far al-Mansur for refusing to take of the post of *Qadi* (Judge) of the Abbasid Empire. Abu Hanifah died in prison at the age of around sixty-seven and was buried in Baghdad.

***

Abu Hurairah (601- 679): Amongst the companions of the Prophet, one man more than any other, stands out like a shining star for his utter devotion and dedication to preserving the *ahadith* (or sayings of the Prophet); he was Abu Hurairah.

His pre-Islamic name was Abd ash-Shams but after embracing Islam he changed it to Abd al-Rahman ibn Sakhr, although he became well known by his nickname, 'Abu Hurairah' (meaning the 'father of the kitten'), received due to his love and affection for his pet kitten. Born into the Daws tribe of southern Arabia, Abu Hurairah was about twelve when Muhammad became a Prophet and started preaching Islam in Mecca. Abu Hurairah was still in his teens when the Prophet began to preach the message of Islam to his kith and kin. This was followed by an open call to all the people of Mecca.

After preaching in Mecca for more than a decade, the Prophet left his native city and moved to the nearby oasis of Madinah, where he received a warm welcome. At the time Abu Hurairah was in his early twenties. It was not until seven years after the Prophet's migration (H*ijrah*) to Madinah that Abu Hurairah came to hear about the Prophet and his mission. Immediately he set out for Madinah in order to meet the Prophet. He set out for Khaybar – which is located around one hundred and sixty kilometers from Madinah – and after a long and exhausting journey, he formally became a Muslim at the hands of the Prophet. He was about thirty at the time. As a perceptive individual who was blessed with a highly retentive memory, he became one of the most learned among the companions of the Prophet.

Abu Hurairah is a legend in Islamic history for not only narrating a vast quantity of Prophetic traditions, but also for his unique memory power. According to the historian and traditionist Abd al-Rahman ibn Ali ibn al-Jawzi, Abu Hurairah narrated five thousand three hundred and seventy-four *Hadith* in total, more than any other companion of the Prophet, including the Prophet's wife, Aishah. Abu Hurairah breathed his last at the age of seventy-eight and was buried in Madinah, the city of the Prophet.

***

Abu 'l-Afia: Tudrus ha-Levi Ben Uyssuf Ben Tudrus: Head of the Jewish community of Castile, who exercised great influence over Alfonso X. He wrote Biblical and Talmudic commentaries with cabbalist tendencies: his Talmudic commentary *Osar ha-kabod* (Treasury of Glory) contained references to the mystical Zohar (Splendor). He exchanged verses with his contemporary Abraham Bedersi. He is not to be confused with his namesake Tudrus Ben Yuhuda Abu'l-Afia.

***

Abu Musa Island: An offshore island on the Gulf on the eve of the independence of the Trucial emirate of Sharjah in 1971, Muhammad Reza Shah Pahlavi of Iran pressed his claim to three islands at the mouth of the Gulf, including Abi Musa. After Iranian troops had landed there, Britain, the erstwhile imperial power in the region, meditated. In 1994 the Gulf Cooperation Council took up the matter and urged Iran to agree to refer the issue of its occupation of Abu Musa and Greater and Lesser Tumb Islands to the International Court of Justice, but to avail. A decade later the matter remained unresolved.

***

Abu Muslim (728-755): Persian leader of the Abbasid revolution. By political and religious agitation he raised (747) the black banners of the Abbasids against the ruling Umayyad family. In 749 he established Abu al-Abbas as-Saffah, the head of the Abbasid family, as caliph of Islam. Abu Muslim became governor of Khorasan, but the caliph al-Mansur feared his power and treacherously murdered him.

***

Abu Nakr: Father of Aisha, acclaimed first Caliph after the Prophet's death. Arguably the first adult male convert to Islam, and a close colleague and devout disciple of the Prophet Muhammad. The only man to accompany Muhammad when he escaped from Mecca. He was chosen to head the prayers by the Prophet in the last week of his life, which gave him a critical edge to become his acknowledged successor.

***

Abu Sufyan: A Meccan tribal leader who raised an army and attacked Medina. nobleman of Mecca who for ten years commanded the pagan opposition to early Islam after Muhammad's migration to Medina. After his acceptance of Islam, prepared for by the marriage of his daughter Umm Habiba to Muhammad, he would become a loyal ally of the Prophet. He would serve as a provincial governor in the Yemen for the first two Caliphs and is traditionally considered to have fought at Yarmuk. Legitimate father of Yazid and Muawiya and possibly to others such as Amr and Zayyad. Meccan leader who opposed Muhammad; fought in battles. A Quraysh leader who surrendered Mecca to Muhammad in 629.

***

Abu-Simbel: Abu-Simbel or Ipsambul, village, S Egypt, on the Nile River. Its two temples were hewn (1250 BC) our of rock cliffs during the reign of Ramses II. To avoid the rising waters caused by the construction of the Aswan High Dam in the 1960s, the colossal statues of Ramses II and the temples were cut into 950 blocks and reassembled farther inland. The project, sponsored by UNESCO and funded by more than 50 nations, was completed in 1966.

***

Abul A'la Mawdudi (1903-1979): If the nineteenth century was the age of European domination of the Muslim world, then the twentieth century must be considered the period when the Muslims finally woke from sleep and began to liberate their lands from foreign occupation. But following the departure of the British, French, Italians and the other European colonial powers from the Muslim world, a powerful and pertinent debate took place in all the Muslim countries concerning their political and constitutional futures. One Islamic scholar and activist contributed more to this debate than probably any other Muslim thinker or reformer of his generation; he was Abul A'la Mawdudi of Pakistan.

Sayyid Abul A'la Mawdudi, better known as Mawlana Mawdudi, was born in the town of Aurangabad in the Indian state of Hyderabad (located in present-day Andhra Pradesh). Born and brought up in a family where learning, personal piety and devotion to Sufism was valued and respected, young Mawdudi received his early education at home from his father. His further education was interrupted at the age of seventeen when his father suddenly died in 1920. Mawdudi was forced to abandon his studies and work to earn a living.

Mawdudi then became editor of the prominent *al-Jam'iyat*, the official publication of Jam'iat-i Ulama-i Hind, a national Islamic umbrella organization which represented the Indian Muslims at the time.

Following his resignation as editor of *al-Jam'iyat* in 1928, Mawdudi left Delhi and moved to Hyderabad. As a journalist and editor of *al-Jam'iyat*, he was clean-shaven and wore Western clothes, but now he grew a beard and adopted a revivalist approach to Islam. He took charge of *Tarjuman al-Qur'an* (Interpretation of the Qur'an) in 1932. This was a monthly Islamic journal which was originally founded and published by an independent Muslim scholar in Hyderabad. This convinced Mawdudi that his intellectual efforts were having the desired effect and thus he continued to champion the cause of the Indian Muslims and write prolifically.

Mawdudi continued to publish the *Tarjuman* from Hyderabad until 1937, when Sir Muhammad Iqbal invited him to move to Pathankot (located in East Punjab, India) and help him to establish an Islamic research center there. After his move to Pathankot in 1938, he continued to edit and publish the *Tarjuman* and also began work on the proposed research center. With the active support of a number of leading Indian Islamic scholars, in 1941 he formally launched the *Jama'at-i-Islami* (The Islamic Organization), an Islamic political party, in order to reform Indian politics, culture and society in the light of Islam. This situation changed radically following the formation of Pakistan as an independent country in 1947. Along with his close friends and supporters, Mawdudi left India in favor of Pakistan and tried to establish an Islamic political, economic and cultural order there.

It was the formation of *Jama'at-i-Islami* in 1941 – and his subsequent migration to Pakistan in 1947 – which provided the ideal opportunity for Mawdudi to engage in politics on a full-time basis for the first time. He actively campaigned for an Islamic constitution, as well as the need to implement the *Shari'ah* (Islamic law) in that country. Mawdudi did not believe in the pursuit of intellectual activity minus socio-political activism. And although his political activism landed him in prison on more than one occasion, he remained as firm and steadfast as ever. He believed there was no room for the depoliticisation of Islam. Accordingly, Mawdudi and his *Jama'at-i-Islami* fully embraced socio-political activism.

As an Islamic ideologue and author, Mawdudi wrote more than one hundred books and treatises on all aspects of Islam. However, it is his *Tafhim al-Qur'an* (Towards Understanding the Qur'an), a voluminous Urdu translation and commentary on the Qur'an, which is today considered to be his most influential work. His critics have argued that his books read more like manuals for socio-political action, rather than works of Islamic wisdom and spirituality, but the *Jama'at-i-Islami* party which he founded and led for more than three decades continues to operate in Pakistan, India, Bangladesh and Sri Lanka to this day.

Mawdudi is today considered to be one of the most widely-read Muslim authors of modern times. He died in a hospital in Buffalo (New York) at the age of seventy-five and was buried in front of his house in Lahore. Prior to his death, Mawdudi received the prestigious King Faisal International Award for his services to Islam.

***

Abul Hasan al-Ash'ari (873-941): After the death of Caliph Uthman, huge controversy ensued within the Islamic State regarding the question of leadership and political legitimacy. During this period, a number of political factions emerged including the *Shi'at Ali, khawarij,* M*urji'ah* and the *Mu'tazilah*. Of these factions, the most politically neutral were the *Mu'tazilah* who later acquired a largely philosophical and theological contour under the influence of Wasil ibn Ata. Famous Abbasid rulers like Harun al-Rashid and his son al-Ma'mun became ardent champions of Mu'tazilism. Abul Hasan al-Ash'ari, one of the Muslim world's most influential theologians (M*utakallimun*), emerged to turn the tables on Mu'tazilism.

Abul Hasan Ali ibn Ismail al-Ash'ari was born in Basrah (in modern Iraq) into a distinguished Muslim family which traced its lineage back to Abu Musa al-Ash'ari, who was a prominent companion of the Prophet. Al-Ash'ari mastered Arabic grammar, literature, Islamic sciences and the philosophical and theological doctrines of Mu'tazilism from an early age.

Al-Ash'ari was considered to be far superior to all of them on account of his mastery of the finer points of Mu'tazilite philosophy and theology. According to al-Ash'ari, the Prophet Muhammad appeared to him in a dream and instructed him to champion the cause of Islamic orthodoxy, rather than that of Mu'tazilism. Suddenly, it was as if al-Ash'ari woke up from a deep sleep, only to discover that he had already spent four decades of his life studying and championing the cause of an un-Islamic creed. He went straight to the central mosque in Basrah, which at the time was packed to its maximum capacity. He stepped onto the *minbar* (pulpit) and delivered a historic announcement. This announcement was to mark the beginning of the end for philosophical rationalism and the resurgence of Islamic traditionalism. 'Lo! I repent that I have been a Mu'tazilite.' The Mu'tazilite rationalists lost one of their most formidable champions. Al-Ash'ari now became the Mu'tazilites most formidable intellectual adversary.

Al-Ash'ari's repudiation of Mu'tazilism was both comprehensive and monumentally effective. He composed more than ninety books and treatises on all aspects of Islamic beliefs (*Aqidah*) and theology (*kalam*), in refutation of the Mu'tazilite creed, and aspects of Islamic epistemology and philosophy.

Led by eminent Islamic scholars like Ahmad ibn Hanbal, the traditionalists vehemently opposed the philosophical interpretation of Islamic theological matters. Al-Ash'ari stated that the Qur'an was the uncreated (*Ghair Makhluq*), eternal Word of God, and that only the ink, paper and individual letters were created. The Mu'tazilite creed was eventually rooted out from the intellectual and cultural lives of Muslims.

Al-Ash'ari was not only an outstanding Islamic intellectual; he was also one of the greatest religious thinkers of all time. He died and was buried in a place close to *Bab Al-Basrah* (or 'the Gate of Basrah'); he was sixty-eight at the time. Ash'arism became the most dominant religious theology in the Muslim world.

***

Abul Hasan al-Mas'udi (895-957): After the emergence of Islam in seventh century Arabia, the once illiterate and uncivilized Bedouins of the desert burst onto the global stage under the banner of their new faith and transformed the course of human history. The Arabs crushed the mighty Roman and Persian Empires and carved out for themselves one of the greatest empires in history. Muslims prepared the way for the emergence of modern science, culture and civilization. The tenth century was one of the most intellectually productive periods in the history of Islam, for it was during this period that great Muslim thinkers like Ibn Sina, al-Farabi, al-Razi, al-Biruni and Ibn al-Haytham lived and thrived. Al-Mas'udi, the famous Muslim scholar and polymath, also lived during this period and contributed immensely to the development of science, philosophy, Islamic history, geology, geography and natural history.

Abul Hasan Ali ibn Hussain ibn Ali al-Mas'udi was born in Baghdad during the reign of the Abbasid Caliph Mu'tadid. Al-Mas'udi grew up at a time when the influence of Mu'tazilism was still very strong within the intellectual and cultural circles of Baghdad, which at the time was one of the Muslim world's foremost centers of philosophical and scientific learning. After completing his formal education, he left his native Baghdad and travelled extensively in pursuit of knowledge. Like Ibn Sina, al-Razi and al-Biruni (who were his contemporaries), the incessant pursuit of knowledge and wisdom became his main preoccupation in life.

Everywhere he went al-Mas'udi carefully observed both the geographical and demographical make-up of the place, and took copious notes about the locals, their culture, traditions and social habits. Three centuries before Marco Polo and Ibn Batuttah were born, al-Mas'udi travelled across a significant part of the then-known world on his own. From his native Baghdad, he journeyed across Persia and reached India while he was still in his twenties. From India, he retreated to Kirman in Persia, where he stayed for a period of time before returning again to India. After a short stay in Madagascar, he set out for what is now the Gulf State of Oman, via Basrah. Al-Mas'udi then travelled across the Middle East and Asia in pursuit of knowledge, and in the process he became a pioneering cultural explorer as well as a great geographer.

Prior to al-Mas'udi's time, some of the Muslim world's great thinkers and scientists (like al-Khwarizmi, al-Kindi and al-Sarakhsi) had researched and written extensively on these subjects. Indeed, al-Khwarizmi's celebrated book *Kitab Surat al-Ard* (Book on the Shape of Earth) was a pioneering work in the field of geography which later inspired other Muslim scientists and geographers to pursue advanced research in this subject.

It was during his stay in Basrah that al-Mas'udi recorded his ideas and thoughts on a wide range of subjects (including history, geology and geography) in the form of a book. He paved the way for other Muslim thinkers, such as Ibn Khaldun, to pursue their sociological analysis of culture and society. The accounts of his journeys were accurate, vivid and comprehensive. Considered to be one of the most comprehensive works ever written on the subject of history, geology and geography, al-Mas'udi completed the first draft of his book in 947. He later revised it in 956 and a French translation was published in Paris between 1861 and 1877 in nine bulky volumes.

In addition to being a pioneering explorer, a gifted geologist and an outstanding geographer, al-Mas'udi was also a historian of the highest caliber. Along with al-Baladhuri, al-Tabari, al-Isfahani, Ibn al-Athir and Ibn Khaldun, he is today considered to be one of the Muslim world's greatest historians.

Hailed as a masterpiece, al-Mas'udi's work has recently been published in English in thirty-eight volumes. He did not collect a large quantity of information and compile it in chronological order; instead he adopted a critical approach to writing and interpreting history.

Toward the end of his life, al-Mas'udi left Basrah and moved to Syria for a period. He then went to Cairo where he composed another voluminous work on history. Entitled *Akhbar al-Zaman* (An Account of Times), this work on history and culture consisted of around thirty volumes.

Al-Mas'udi became known as the 'Herodotus and Pliny of the Arabs'. He died at the age of sixty-two and was buried in al-Fustat, Egypt.

***

Abul Hasan al-Shadhili (1197-1258): According to a famous Prophetic tradition (*Hadith*), at the turn of every century there will emerge a *Mujaddid* (or religious regenerator) who will call the Muslims back to the original, pristine message of Islam. Eminent Sufi sages like Hasan al-Basri, Abd al-Qadir al-Jilani, Jalal al-Din Rumi, Khwajah Naqshband, Shihab al-Din Umar Suhrawardi, Mu'in al-Din Chishti and Najm al-Din Kubra (who contributed immensely to the preservation and dissemination of Islam as a religion and a way of life) were not considered to be *Mujaddid*. Of the numerous Sufi Orders (*Tariqah*) which emerged in the Muslim world over the last fourteen centuries, the *Qadiriyyah*, *Naqshbandiyyah* and the *Chishtiyyah* are considered to be the most popular and prominent. However, the Sufi Order founded by Abul Hasan al-Shadhili, the great North African Sufi scholar and sage, also played a pivotal role in the preservation of Islamic thought and practices in North Africa, as well as the dissemination of Islam across Europe and America.

Abul Hasan Ali ibn Abdullah al-Shadhili, known as Imam Shadhili for short, was born in the district of Ghumara, located close to modern Ceuta in Morocco. Living during this relatively peaceful rule of the al-Mohads (this dynasty was founded in the middle of the twelfth century by Abu Abdullah Muhammad ibn Abdullah ibn Tumart, a prominent North African Islamic reformer of the time), Shadhili became a devout student of Islam from an early age.

His time with Shaykh Mashish represented a major turning point in Shadhili's life, for it was during this period that he mastered the rigorous methods of Sufism and began to experience Islamic spirituality in its highest form. After completing his training with Shaykh Mashish, Shadhili left his native Morocco and moved to a town called Shadhila in Tunisia; henceforth he became known as Imam Shadhili. The movement started by him later became known as *Tariqah al-Shadhiliyyah* (or the *Shadhiliyyah* Sufi Order). Islamic spirituality – as championed by Shadhili – thus spread across Tunisia, Morocco and many other parts of North Africa during his own lifetime.

In 1244, at the age of forty-seven, Shadhili claimed to have been blessed with another vision wherein he was instructed to leave Tunisia and go to Egypt to propagate Islam there. Accompanied by his family, friends and disciples, he left North Africa and moved to Alexandria where he established a *Shadhiliyyah Zawiyyah*.

To prove there was no contradiction between the Prophetic way (M*inhaj al-sunnah*) and the ways of *Tasawwuf*, Shadhili took part in the Battle of al-Mansura, where the Muslims fought against the Crusaders led by St. Louis of France. He insisted on taking part in the battle, despite being blind, and thereby proved that one does not have to become a hermit to be a Sufi.

The age of Shadhili was indeed one of the most significant periods in the annals of Sufism. These influential Sufis inspired the Muslim masses to reject the forces of materialism and self-indulgence which threatened to overwhelm Islamic societies both in the East and the West. At the same time, the Muslim world faced a serious political and military threat from the Mongol hordes. As it transpired, the

Mongols soon overran the fragile defense put up by the Muslims and marched into Baghdad, the capital of the Abbasid Caliphate, in 1258 and reduced the great city to rubble.

Unlike, for example, Jalal al-Din Rumi or Ibn al-Arabi, Shadhili did not write any books or treatises. The main focus of his teachings was the attainment of inner purification and spiritual illumination through the incessant practice of *dhikr*, or invocation of Divine Names and Attributes (*al-asma wa'l Sifat*). After Shadhili's death at the age of sixty-one, collections of his invocations, or litanies (A*dkhar*), were published by his prominent disciples (such as Abul Abbas al-Mursi) and later became the bedrock of *Shadhiliyyah* teachings.

Buried in the village of Humaithra on the coast of the Red Sea, Imam Shadhili's enduring message of Islamic morality, ethics, spirituality and gnosis continues to influence millions of Muslims across North Africa, Egypt, Sudan, Turkey, Iran, parts of East Africa and the Balkans to this day.

***

Abul Qasim al-Zahrawi (936-1013): After the Umayyads were ousted from power by the Abbasids in 750, Prince Abd al-Rahman ibn Muawiyah fled Damascus and arrived in North Africa. From there he reached Cordova, the capital of *al-Andalus* (Muslim Spain) in 756, and swiftly assumed control of that country. By unifying Spain under his able leadership, he also inaugurated one of the most memorable periods in European history. Under the guidance of his descendants such as Abd al-Rahman II and Muhammad I, Spain became one of the most advanced European nations of the time. Caliph Abd al-Rahman III and his successors turned Cordova into a thriving center of intellectual, cultural and literary activities. Al-Zahrawi was one such outstanding scholar and scientist whose contribution and achievement in the field of medicine and surgery was unique and unprecedented.

Abul Qasim Khalaf ibn Abbas al-Zahrawi, known in medieval Europe as Abulcasis, was born in the royal suburb of al-Zahra in Cordova during the glorious reign of Caliph Abd al-Rahman III. After completing his early education in Arabic and aspects of Islamic and physical sciences, al-Zahrawi developed a keen interest in the medical sciences. He went on to serve the Caliph in the capacity of personal physician until the latter died in 961 at the age of seventy-one, having ruled Islamic Spain for no less than half a century. Al-Zahrawi was barely twenty-five when al-Hakam ascended the throne in Cordova and asked him to serve as hi personal physician.

The libraries of Cordova were packed with books and manuscripts on all the sciences of the day. Such was al-Hakam's enthusiasm for learning and scholarship that the historians have compared him with the Abbasid Caliph Abdullah al-Ma'mun who was also a formidable champion of higher education and learning.

As a pioneer of surgical anatomy, al-Zahrawi performed a large number of operations, ranging from simple Caesarean sections, to more complex and delicate eye operations. He not only invented a large number of surgical tools, but also performed numerous operations using the same tools and equipment. He also trained midwives to carry out emergency Caesarean operations and other clinical procedures on women. As an accomplished dentist, he was thoroughly familiar with all aspects of oral hygiene and dentistry.

After a lifetime devoted to medical research and surgery, al-Zahwari eventually decided to write a book on the subject. Consisting of thirty chapters, this book was in fact a massive encyclopedia on medicine and surgery and soon after its publication it became one of the most sought-after surgical textbooks of its time. This book was rated so highly by the Europeans that it was prescribed to all medical students at Europe's leading universities until as late as the eighteenth century.

Al-Zahrawi became famous in the West as the 'father of surgery'. He died at the age of seventy-seven and was buried in his native Cordova.

***

Abyssinian Campaigns (1935-1941): Conflicts between Italy, Abyssinia (Ethiopia), and later Britain. War broke out from Italy's unfulfilled ambition of 1894-96 to link Eritrea with Somalia, and from Mussolini's aim to provide colonies to absorb Italy's surplus unemployed population. In 1934 and 1935 incident5s, possibly contrived, took place at Walwal and elsewhere. On 3 October 1935 an Italian army attacked the Ethiopian forces from the north and east. Eventually the Ethiopians mustered 40,000 men, but there were helpless against the highly trained troops and modern weapons of the Italians.

***

Aflaq, Michel (1910-1989): Syrian political thinker and politician. Born into a Greek Orthodox family in Damascus Aflaq received his higher education at the University of Sorbonne, Paris, where he came under leftist influence. Back in Damascus in 1934, he taught history at a prestigious secondary school. Together with Salah al Din Bitar a fellow teacher in 1940, he established a study circle called the Movement of Arab Renaissance. They published pamphlets in which they expanded revolutionary, socialist Arab nationalism, committed to achieving Arab unity as the first step. In 1942 Aflaq devoted himself full time to politics. During the Iran-Iraq war Aflaq was the butt of many attacks by Iran, anxious to depict Iraq, guided by a Christian, as a state that had deviated from Islam. Significantly, after his death in 1989 the Iraqi media disclosed that Aflaq had converted to Islam before his demise.

***

Aga Khan (Turkish, aga, 'master', khan, 'ruler'). Title borne by leaders of the Nizari or eastern branch of the Ismaili sect of Shiite Islam. The first Aga Khan, Hassan Ali Shah of Kirman (d. 1881), fled to Afghanistan and Sind after leading an unsuccessful revolt in Iran in 1838. Winning British favor he settled in Bombay, where in 1866 the Arnold judgment gave him control of the affairs of the Indian Khoja community. His grandson, Sultan Muhammad Shah (1877-1957), played an active part in Indian politics, attempting to secure Muslim support for British rule, particularly as President of the All-India Muslim League (1913). He was leader of the Muslim delegation to the Round Table Conference in 1930-32. He was succeeded by his grandson, Prince Karim. A title used by the Ismaili Imams of the Nizari line.

***

Ahmad ibn Hanbal (778-855): Islamic history is replete with scholars who distinguished themselves by the breadth of their learning and courage. They also endured considerable personal and financial hardship, and were often made to suffer for their faith and conviction, but they never bowed before a King or Queen. To them, the life of this world was like an illusion; without a reality of its own. Ahmad ibn Hanbal was one such towering scholar and reformer who emerged to defend traditional Islam at a critical time in Islamic history, and thereby left his indelible mark in the annals of Islam.

Abu Abdullah Ahmad ibn Muhammad ibn Hanbal al-Shaybani was born into the noble Arab tribe of al-Shayban. Ahmad's grandfather, Hanbal ibn Hilal, occupied a prominent position as governor of the province of Sarakhs under the Umayyads, while his father, Muhammad, was a valiant warrior who participated in a *jihad* (military expedition) led by the Umayyads and died on the battlefield while he was in his thirties. Ahmad was about two years old when his father died. He attended his local schools and successfully committed the entire Qur'an to memory before he was ten. He thus combined his education in *Fiqh* (Islamic jurisprudence) and *Hadith* under the guidance of Abu Yusuf Yaqub ibn Ibrahim with his extra-curricula activities.

Ahmad then studied *Hadith* and *Fiqh* for another four years under the guidance of Haytham ibn Bishr, who was one of the foremost scholars of *Hadith* in Baghdad. After completing his studies under the renowned scholars of Baghdad, he travelled to other major centers of Islamic learning (including Basrah, Kufah, Makkah, Madinah, Yemen and Syria) in pursuit of *Hadith*. Ahmad became widely recognized as an eminent scholar of *Hadith*, having mastered all the nuances and intricacies of this subject under the tutelage of the Yemeni scholar Abd al-Razzaq ibn Hammam, the author of the highly rated *Musannaf*.

Since Ahmad's main preoccupation in life was the pursuit of knowledge, he happily travelled long distances in search of Islamic knowledge and wisdom. His critical examination of *Hadith* literature enabled him to ascertain their relevance to Islamic law and legal theory. He started teaching *Hadith* and *Fiqh* at the age of forty, and soon gathered around him a large following. Unflustered by the mass attention he now received, Ahmad continued to lead a simple and ascetic lifestyle, far removed from the wealth and luxuries of this world.

If any of his well-wishers sent him any money or gifts, Ahmad gave them away to the poor and needy. When he ran out of money, which he did regularly, he used to skip meals. His sincerity, simplicity and profound insight into Islamic teachings made him very popular with the masses in Baghdad.

The Mu'tazilites believed that the Qur'an was created (contrary to the traditional Islamic view, which stated that the Qur'an was the uncreated Word of God). When the Caliph eventually ordered all the defiant scholars to be brought to his palace in chains, they all relented save one. That indomitable scholar was Ahmad ibn Hanbal. Ahmad remained as firm as ever, refusing to bow before the scourge of rationalism, which at the time was threatening to undermine the very foundation of Islam. He continued his struggle against the Mu'tazilites until, in 846, Mutawakkil ala Allah ascended the Abbasid throne and reversed his predecessor's harsh policies. The new Caliph also freed Ahmad from captivity so he could resume his normal activities. During this period he wrote numerous books on *Hadith* and *Fiqh* including his famous *al-Musnad*, which contains more than thirty thousand *ahadith*.

Ahmad ibn Hanbal died and was buried in Baghdad at the age of around seventy-seven. After his death, a new school of Islamic legal thought emerged named after him. The *Hanbali Madh'hab* is today followed mainly in Palestine and Saudi Arabia.

***

Ahmad Khan, Sir Sayyid (1817-1898): The Asian subcontinent has produced some of the Muslim world's most influential rulers, thinkers and reformers. Thus, famous Mughal rulers like Akbar the Great, Shah Jahan and Awrangzeb feature in this book on account of their enduring political and cultural contributions. These remarkable and gifted individuals were pioneers in their chosen fields of endeavor. Sir Sayyid Ahmad Khan, an illustrious Indian Muslim educationalist and reformer, also belongs to this select group of inspirational subcontinental Muslims.

Sayyid Ahmad Khan, also known simply as Sir Sayyid, was born in Delhi, the capital of India, during the reign of the Mughal Emperor Akbar Shah II. His ancestors originally hailed from Arabia and settled in Heart before moving to Delhi during the sixteenth century. While Ahmad Khan was a child his devout father, Sayyid Muhammad Muttaqi Khan, embraced Sufism (Islamic mysticism); thus he retreated from worldly affairs and became an ascetic (*Zahid*). During his early years, Ahmad became very fond of Persian poetry. After the successive deaths of his older brother and father, his whole outlook on life changed. He grew a beard and became a practicing Muslim.

Following the horrific events of 1857 known as the Indian Mutiny, which led to the mass slaughter of Muslims at the hands of the British army as well as the expulsion of the last Mughal ruler, Bahadur Shah Zafar II, from India, more than three centuries of Mughal rule came to an abrupt end. A year later, Queen Victoria was proclaimed Empress of India. Dismayed by the political upheavals of the time, Ahmad initially decided to leave India and settle in Egypt, but soon he changed his mind and instead decided to work with his fellow Muslims to improve their social, political, economic and cultural conditions. He felt opposing the British would be both futile and suicidal for the future of Indian Muslims; thus he decided to cooperate with the British authorities. He therefore declared his loyalty to the Crown and this, of course, endeared him to the ruling British elites.

Many of Ahmad's recommendations for change were accepted and implemented by the ruling elite, in order to facilitate better communication between the rulers and the ruled. Ahmad became a powerful voice for educational and cultural reform across the country. He argued that there was no contradiction between modern science and Islamic teachings. The Indian Muslims, he felt, had nothing to fear from modern Western science and educational philosophy. In 1864, the British authorities helped him to establish a scientific society in Ghazipur in order to translate high quality, modern Western philosophical and scientific literature into Urdu, so as to make the treasures of modern scientific knowledge and scholarship accessible to the Indian Muslims.

During his stay in England, Ahmad became profoundly impressed by the scientific and technological achievements of the Western world and he hoped that his college would inspire the Indian Muslims to revive the Islamic intellectual and cultural heritage. After his return from England, he enlisted the help of several prominent British officials, including Lord Northbrook and Lord Lytton, and together they laid the foundations of the Muhammadan Anglo-Oriental College (MAO) in 1877. Now known as Aligarh Muslim University, this famous institution of higher education has produced generations of renowned Indian Muslim scholars, thinkers and leaders, including Mawlvi Abdul Haq, Ziauddin Ahmad, Muhammad Ali Jauhar, Liaquat Ali Khan and Zakir Hussain among others.

Heavily influenced by nineteenth century European philosophical and scientific thought, Ahmad attempted to reconcile religion and science, as if Islam and scientific thought were somehow incompatible. Given his ultra-rationalistic approach to the Qur'an, it is not surprising that the *ulama* severely criticized him for his neo-Mu'tazilite approach to the Islamic scriptural sources.

In recognition of his outstanding services to his people, Ahmad was knighted by the British Government in 1888. He died at the age of eighty-one and was buried in Aligarh.

***

Ahmad ibn Yahya (1895-1962): ruler of North Yemen, 1948-62, Eldest son of Imam Yahya of the Hamid al Din branch of the Rassi dynasty, which for centuries has governed the northern and eastern highlands of Yemen, inhabited by Zaidi tribes and later under the suzerainty of the Ottoman Turks, which ended in 1918. Suffering from ill health, Ahmad passed on much of his authority to his eldest son, Muhammad al Badr before his death in September 1962, which triggered a military coup and ended the 1,064 year rule of the Rassi dynasty.

***

Aishah bint Abu Bakr (also Ayisha; 610-677): Women have played a critical role in Islamic history. Of all the illustrious Muslim women who had played an instrumental role in the emergence and development of Islam as a religion, culture and civilization, one stands out over all others. That outstanding woman was Aishah bint Abu Bakr. Her achievements were so varied and startling that no other woman in Islamic history can be compared to her. She is, therefore, the most influential single Muslim woman in history.

Aishah bint Abi Bakr ibn Abi Quhafah was born into the Banu Taym clan of the Quraysh tribe of Makkah. Her father, Abu Bakr al-Siddiq, and her mother, Umm Ruman, became Muslims very early on. She not only possessed a photographic memory; she was also a gentle and cultured lady.

Aishah was married to the Prophet when she was very young, although at the time she had matured both intellectually and physically way beyond her age. After her marriage, Aishah became the youngest wife of the Prophet; she was also much wiser than, and intellectually far superior to, the others. She was the only wife of the Prophet who was a maiden.

When Aishah went to live with the Prophet in the small apartment attached to his mosque in Madinah, she was perhaps around thirteen years old. The Prophet had no possessions other than a straw mat, a thin mattress, a pillow made of dry tree barks and leaves, a leather water container, a small plate and a cup for drinking water. The Prophet not only occupied himself in prayers and meditation, but also reminded his wives, children and followers not to become lured by the wealth, glitter and riches of this world.

Since the Prophet used to visit Abu Bakr frequently, Aishah knew the Prophet very well even before their marriage. No other person claimed to know the Prophet as well as Aishah. Aishah's enquiring mind and willingness to learn and disseminate knowledge endeared her to the Prophet. That is why Caliphs Abu Bakr al-Siddiq, Umar ibn al-Khattab and Uthman ibn Affan, who were three of the most prominent companions of the Prophet and outstanding jurists in their own right, regularly consulted her before deciding on complex and intractable legal issues during their reigns.

Aishah memorized and related more than two thousand *ahadith* of the Prophet, and was brave enough to lead an army into the battlefield and wage war. Known reverentially as *ummul Mu'minin* (the 'mother of the believers'), Aishah passed away at the age of sixty-seven.

***

Akbar the Great (1542–1605): After the death of Amir Timur in 1405, the vast empire he had created began to rapidly disintegrate, thanks to his immediate descendants who fought each other for overall political supremacy: in the process they only succeeded in diving the Timurid Empire into several principalities. From Kabul, Babar launched raids into India and routed his opponents with great skill and determinations before establishing Mughal supremacy in 1526. Babar, the founder of the Mughal Empire, died soon afterward without fully consolidating his new kingdom. Humayun, his son and successor, was too romantic, fun-loving and indecisive to make much of an impact. He also died in his forties without securing Mughal rule. It was left to the genius of Akbar, the greatest of Mughal Emperors and one of the most influential rulers of Muslim India, to fully consolidate Mughal rule throughout the subcontinent.

Abul Fath Jalal al-Din Muhammad was born in Umarkot in the northern Indian province of Sind (in present-day Pakistan). Akbar was born at a time when his father had lost much of his power to his opponents – including his own brothers – before he took military action in order to regain his lost territories. Since he had few supporters in Sind, he proceeded to Persia to ask the reigning Safavid monarch, Shah Tahmasp, for his political and military support. Backed by the Safavids, Humayun spearheaded military action against his rebellious brothers Kamran, Askari and Hindal. During this period of military campaigns, Humayun and his family were forced to move from one place to another, which deprived young Akbar of much in the way of formal education and training. For this reason, he failed to gain proficiency in literacy.

Blessed with a prodigious memory and sharp intellect, Akbar learned and mastered a wide range of subjects including history, philosophy, religion, art and poetry with ease. He was only thirteen when his father suddenly died in 1556 and, as expected, he succeeded him as the ruler of the Mughal Empire. His accession to power was to mark the beginning of a glorious era in the history of Muslim India.

After ascending the Mughal throne, Akbar instigated military action in order to regain the lost territories, and thereby restore political stability, social peace and security across the Mughal dominion. However, as Akbar began to tighten his grip on India, the aged Bairam Khan increasingly became a liability.

Akbar was only eighteen when he became a fully-fledged Mughal ruler and military commander. Keen to expand Mughal rule further, he then took the fight to the rulers of the neighboring territories. Thus, from 1568 to 1569, he conducted military expeditions against the Rajputs of Rajasthan as they began to threaten Mughal interests. He took the capital of Gujarat without encountering much resistance and thus connected his empire to the Arabian Sea, thereby opening up a naval route to the rest of the world. Following this astonishing series of conquests, Akbar managed to establish Mughal power and authority throughout northern India. According to his son Salim (who later became Emperor Jahangir), 'Although he was illiterate, so much became clear to him through constant intercourse with the learned and the wise in his conversations with them...'

As an intelligent ruler, Akbar knew that brute force only breaks; it does not mend and fix. Since all the previous Indian Muslim dynasties had disintegrated within a few decades of their inception, Akbar was determined not to allow the same to happen to the Mughals. He decided to win the hearts and minds of his people – that is, particularly the Muslims and Hindus. He appointed provincial governors who were responsible for overseeing the affairs of their own provinces and regularly reported directly to him.

As a fiercely monotheistic religion, Islam preaches the absolute Oneness of God (*Tawhid*), thus negating all forms of associationism (*shirk*). By contrast, the Hindus believe in multiple gods and goddesses, and also worship statues, idols and various animals. As such, these two religions are more diametrically opposed to each other than probably any of the other major world faiths. Akbar's approach to inter-faith dialogue proved both inept and foolish. Far from uniting the two rival religious factions, this only served to make matters worse, because both orthodox Muslims and Hindus considered Akbar's religious eclecticism very offensive.

As a religious freethinker, Akbar was fascinated by religion and philosophy and regularly engaged in religious discussion and debate with the leading Muslim, Hindu and Christian scholars of his time, for he was very keen to discover the truth about religion. He accepted the authority of the Qur'an, but also believed in the spiritual unity of religions (that is to say, he believed that all religions were true and authentic in their essence, only their forms differed). This became the basis of his new religious synthesis, namely *din-i-Ilahi* (or 'the Divine Religion').

Akbar's long reign of forty-nine years represented one of the most glorious periods in the history of Mughal India. He also built some of India's most magnificent buildings including the breathtaking Fatehpur Sikri, which is today considered to be one of the most beautiful sites in India along with the immortal Taj Mahal. As a ruler, Akbar was determined and ruthless, but also benevolent; his most famous motto was 'Servant of all and master of none.' He died at the age of sixty-three and was buried inside the mausoleum he had prepared for himself at Sikandra, located about five miles west of Agra, India.

The third and greatest of the Moguls, who ruled India from 1555 to 1605. At 13 he inherited a fragile empire, but military conquests brought Rajasthan, Gujarat, Bengal, Kashmir, and the north Deccan under his sway. He introduced a system of civil and military service which ensured loyalty and centralized control, and made modifications to the land revenue system which reduced pressure on peasant cultivators. Akbar created the basis for Mogul control over India until the early 18th century, and also left a distinctive mark on Muslim-Hindu relations in India. Son of Humayun, who retook Kandahar and Heart in Afghanistan; Akbar claimed the throne at age 13; he moved the capital from Delhi to Agra; died in 1555 after entering Delhi, India.

***

Al-Ahmar, Abdullah ibn Hussein (1933-2007): Yemeni political. Son of Shaikh Hussein ibn Nasser al Ahmar, head of the Hashid tribal confederation, who was executed in 1959 for his part in a failed coup against Imam Ahmad ibn Yahya al Ahmar succeeded his father. When civil war erupted in September 1962, soon after Imam Ahmad's death, al Ahmar sided with the republicans. In the 1994 Yemeni Civil War he actively sided with the government. Following the 1997 general election, in which the Isah secured fifty three seats, he was reelected parliamentary speaker. With the tenure of the parliament extended to six years, al Ahmar's status remained unchanged until 2003.

***

Al-Assad, Hafez (1930-2000): Syrian politician, secretary general of the Ba'athist party and president of Syria from 1971-2000. Assad is one of the longest-serving and most influential leaders of the Middle East; after positions as an air force general and defense minister, he became prime minister after a bloodless coup in 1970, and was elected president the following year. In the effectively one-party state that Assad created, he was re-elected president in 1978, 1985, and 1991. He lost the Golan Heights in the Yom Kippur War against Israel in 1973, but won increasing influence in Lebanon after committing some 50,000 troops to the civil war there (1975 – 1990). president 1971-2000 Born Hafiz Wahhash in the family of a notable in Qurdaha, an Alawi village near Latakia, Assad enrolled at the Homs military academy in 1951 and graduated as an air force pilot four years later. During the last days of his rule was marked by his consistency and tenacity. A distant and authoritarian personality, he combined realism with a cool calculating disposition. He was strongly anti-Zionist and a major supporter of Palestinian guerrilla organizations.

***

Islamic Leaders

Al-Assad, Rifaat (1937-   ): Syrian politician Born in the family of a rural notable in Qurdaha, an Alawi village near Latakia. Assad joined the Baath party in 1952. He did his military service during the period when Syria was part of the United Arab Republic (1958-61). After the Ba'athist coup of March 1963, Assad was put through a crash course at the Homs military academy. In late 1999 the government closed down a port in Latakia that had been built illegally by Assad, and warned him that he faced prosecution if he returned home. Following Hafiz Assad's death in 2000, Assad described the accession of Bashar Assad as unconstitutional.

***

Al Badr, Muhammad (1926-1996): ruler of North Yemen, 1962 As the eldest son of Imam Ahmad ibn Yahya al Badr assisted his father in administering North Yemen and fulfilling specific assignments. In 1955 when Imam Ahmad faced an armed revolt by two of his brothers, al Badr mobilized the Bakil and Hashid tribal confederations and saved his father's throne. Al Badr was named crown prince. The resulting civil war lasted until 1970. As the rapprochement between the royalist and republican sides, brokered by Saudi Arabia, was based on acceptance of a republic in North Yemen, al Badr went into self exile in Britain.

***

Al Banna, Sabri (1937-2002): Palestinian leader Born into a prosperous, plantation owning family in Jaffa al Banna and his family fled to the al Bureij refugee camp in the Gaza strip after the established of Israel in May 1948. They then moved to the West Bank city of Nablus. In August 2002, the Iraqi government claimed that al Banna had entered the country illegally and that when confronted by a security unit in his Baghdad apartment, he committed suicide. Other reports suggested that al Banna had been killed by the Iraqi security unit in a shoot out.

***

Al-Battani (850–922): An astronomer who accurately determined the length of the solar year. He contributed to numeric tables, such as the Tables of Toledo, used by astronomers to predict the movements of the sun, moon and planets across the sky. Some of Battani's astronomic tables were later used by Copernicus. Battani also developed numeric tables which could be used to find the direction of Mecca from different locations.

Knowing the direction of Mecca is important for Muslims, as this is the direction faced during prayer.

***

Al Baz, Abdul Aziz ibn Abdullah (1911-1999): Saudi Arabian religious leader Born into a religious family in Riyadh al Baz studied the Quran and Sharia. After going blind at sixteen he became a student of Shaikh Muhammad ibn Abdul Wahhab, the grand lufti, to train as an Islamic judge. The next year he was appointed grand mufti of Saudi Arabia, a job that had been left vacant since 1969, and president of the Supreme Religious Council. Among his several books is Inquiry and clarification of Many Hajj and Umra Issues.

***

Al-Beidh, Ali Salim (1939-   ): South Yemeni and Temeni political Born into a religious family in the Hadramaut region, al Beidh participated in the armed nationalist struggle of the South Yemen conducted by the National Liberation Front against Britain. In 1996 as leader of the National Opposition Front, al Beidh demanded a referendum in the south to secure better terms for the region. Two years later he was sentenced to death in absentia for his role in the 1994 civil war.

***

Al-Biruni, Abu al-Rayḥān Muhammad ibn Aḥmad (973-1048): (born 5 September 973 in Kath, Khwarezm, died in the year 13 December 1048 in Ghazni), known as **Alberonius** in Latin and **Al-Biruni** in English, was a Persian-Chorasmian Muslim scholar and polymath of the 11th century and from an early age, he became interested in mathematics and the physical sciences.

Al-Biruni is regarded as one of the greatest scholars of the medieval Islamic era and was well versed in physics, mathematics, astronomy and natural sciences. He also distinguished himself as a historian, chronologist and linguist. He was conversant in Chorasmian, Persian, Arabic, Sanskrit and Turkic, and also knew Greek, Hebrew and Syriac. He spent a large part of his life in Ghazni in modern-day Afghanistan, capital of the Ghaznavid dynasty which ruled eastern Iranian lands and the northwestern Indian subcontinent.

In 1017 he traveled to the Indian subcontinent and became the most important interpreter of Indian science to the Islamic world. He is given titles such as the "founder of Indology" and the "first anthropologist". He was an impartial writer on custom and creeds of various nations and was given the title al-Ustdadh ("The Master") for his remarkable description of early 11th century India. He also made contributions to Earth sciences and is regarded as the "father of geodesy" for his important contributions to that field, along with his significant contributions to geography.

Life:

He was born in the outer district of Kath, the capital of the Afrighid dynasty of Chorasmia. The word Biruni means "outer-district" in Persian and so this became his nisba: "al-Bīrūnī" = "the Birunian". His first twenty-five years were spent in Chorasmia where he studied Fiqh, theology, grammar, mathematics, astronomy, medics and other sciences.

He was sympathetic to the Afrighids, who were overthrown by the rival dynasty of Ma'munids in 995. Leaving his homeland, he left for Bukhara, then under the Samanid ruler Mansur II the son of Nuh. There he also corresponded with Avicenna.

In 998, he went to the court of the Ziyarid Amir of Tabaristan, Shams al-Mo'ali Abul-Hasan Ghaboos ibn Wushmgir. There he wrote his first important work, *al-Athar al-Baqqiya 'an al-Qorun al-Khaliyya* (literally: "The remaining traces of past centuries" and translated as "Chronology of ancient nations" or "Vestiges of the Past") on historical and scientific chronology, probably around 1000 A.D., though he later made some amendments to the book. Accepting the definite demise of the Afrighids at the hands of the Ma'munids, he made peace with the latter who then ruled Chorasmia. Their court at Gorganj (also in Chorasmia) was gaining fame for its gathering of brilliant scientists.

In 1012, al-Biruni returned to his native Khwarizm where he resumed his studies. In 1017, Mahmud of Ghazni took Rey. Most scholars, including al-Biruni, were taken to Ghazna, the capital of the Ghaznavid dynasty. Biruni was made court astrologer and accompanied Mahmud on his invasions into India, living there for a few years. Biruni became acquainted with all things related to India. He may even have learned some Sanskrit. During this time he wrote the *Kitab Ta'rikh al-Hind*, finishing it around 1030.

Mathematics and Astronomy:

Ninety-five of 146 books known to have been written by Bīrūnī, about 65 percent, were devoted to astronomy, mathematics and related subjects like mathematical geography. Biruni's major work on astrology is primarily an astronomical and mathematical text, only the last chapter concerns astrological prognostication. His endorsement of astrology is limited, in so far as he condemns horary astrology as 'sorcery'.

Biruni wrote an extensive commentary on Indian astronomy in the *Kitab Ta'rikh al-Hind*, in which he claims to have resolved the matter of Earth's rotation in a work on astronomy that is no longer extant, his *Miftah-ilm-alhai'a (Key to Astronomy)*:

> "The rotation of the earth does in no way impair the value of astronomy, as all appearances of an astronomic character can quite as well be explained according to this theory as to the other. There are, however, other reasons which make it impossible."

Physics:

Al-Biruni contributed to the introduction of the experimental scientific method of mechanics, unified statics and dynamics into the science of mechanics and combined the fields of hydrostatics with dynamics to create hydrodynamics.

Geography:

Bīrunī also devised his own method of determining the radius of the earth by means of the observation of the height of a mountain and carried it out at Nandana in India.

Pharmacology and Mineralogy:

Due to an apparatus he constructed himself, he succeeded in determining the specific gravity of a certain number of metals and minerals with remarkable precision.

History and Chronology:

Biruni's main essay on political history, Kitab al-Musāmara fī akbār Kᵛārazm (Book of conversation concerning the affairs of Kᵛārazm) is now known only from quotations in Bayhaqī's Tarikh-e mas'ūdī. In addition to this, various discussions of historical events and methodology are found in connection with the lists of kings in his al-Āthār al-Baqqiya and in the Qanun, as well as elsewhere in the Āthār in India and scattered throughout his other works

History of Religions:

Bīrūnī is one of the most important Muslim authorities on the history of religion. Al-Biruni was a pioneer in the study of comparative religion. He studied Zoroastrianism, Judaism, Hinduism, Christianity, Buddhism, Islam and other religions. He treated religions objectively, striving to understand them on their own terms rather than trying to prove them wrong. His underlying concept was that all cultures are at least distant relatives of all other cultures because they are all human constructs.

Al-Biruni divides Hindus into an educated and an uneducated class. He describes the educated as monotheistic, believing that God is one, eternal and omnipotent, eschewing all forms of idol worship. He recognizes that uneducated Hindus worshipped a multiplicity of idols yet points out that even some Muslims (such as the Jabiriyya) have adopted anthropomorphic concepts of God. (Ataman, 2005)

Indology:

Biruni's fame as an Indologist rests primarily on two texts. Al-Biruni wrote an encyclopedic work on India called "Tarikh Al-Hind" (History of India, also known as "Indica," or simply "India") in which he explored nearly every aspect of Indian life, including religion, history, geography, geology, science and mathematics. He explores religion within a rich cultural context. As an example of Al-Biruni's analysis, is his summary of why many Hindus hate Muslims. He explains that Hinduism and Islam are totally different from each other. Moreover, Hindus in 11th century India considered all foreigners, not just Muslims, impure and refused to have any connection with them. Furthermore, when the Muslims entered India, the land had already been devastated by two previous invasions by the Sakas and the Hunas. Al-Biruni collected books and studied with Hindu scholars to become fluent in Sanskrit. He translated books both from Sanskrit to Arabic and vice versa.

Works:

Most of the works of Al-Biruni are in Arabic, although he wrote one of his masterpieces, the *Kitab al-Tafhim,* apparently in both Persian and Arabic, showing his mastery over both languages. Biruni's catalogue of his own literary production up to his 65th lunar/63rd solar year (the end of 427/1036) lists 103 titles divided into 12 categories: astronomy, mathematical geography, mathematics, astrological aspects and transits, astronomical instruments, chronology, comets, an untitled category, astrology, anecdotes, religion and books of which he no longer possesses copies.

Persian work:

Although he preferred Arabic to Persian in scientific writing, his Persian version of the Al-Tafhim is one of the most important of the early works of science in the Persian language and is a rich source for

Persian prose and lexicography. The book covers the Quadrivium in a detailed and skilled fashion.

In 1031, when he was around fifty-eight, al-Biruni left India and returned to Ghazna. He spent the rest of his life in Ghazna and passed away at the age of seventy-eight. In the intellectual history of Islam, the period from 973 to 1051 is known as the 'Age of al-Biruni'.

***

Al-Bukhari (809-870): The life and teachings of the Prophet Muhammad are an important source of inspiration, guidance and instruction for more than a billion Muslims across the globe today. The Arabic word *Hadith* refers to a 'saying' or 'utterance' of the Prophet. Muslims scrupulously emulate his deeds and actions (*sunnah*) in every sphere of their lives. In Islamic history, one man stands over and above all others when it comes to collecting, editing, analyzing and verifying the sayings and utterances of the Prophet. He is none other than Imam al-Bukhari.

Abu Abdullah Muhammad ibn Ismail ibn Ibrahim ibn Mughirah ibn Bardizbah al-Bukhari was born in Bukhara, in Muslim Central Asia. Of Persian origin, al-Bukhari's ancestors were farmers who were taken captive during the Muslim conquest of that region in the early days of Islam. Muhammad was the younger of two sons, and became well-known as al-Bukhari.

Al-Bukhari was evidently a gifted student who possessed a photographic memory and great analytical skills. After successfully completing his initial education at the age of twelve, al-Bukhari pursued advanced training in Islamic sciences and specialized in *Hadith* literature. In fact, he was barely twenty when he came to be recognized as one of the foremost scholars of *Hadith* in his locality.

After completing his higher education in Bukhara, al-Bukhari left his native city and went to Makkah, along with his mother and brother, to perform the sacred *hajj* (pilgrimage). From Makkah he travelled to other great centers of Islamic learning in Egypt, Syria and Iraq before settling in Basrah where he conducted advanced research in *Hadith*. During his sojourns he came into contact with some of the foremost *Hadith* scholars of his time, including Ahmad ibn Hanbal, Abu Bakr ibn Abu Shaiba, Ishaq ibn Rahawaih, Ali ibn al-Madini and Yahya ibn Ma'in.

After rigorous and systematic investigation of the *ahadith*, the M*uhaddithun* (or 'scholars of *Hadith*') classified them into different categories such as sound (*Sahih*), good (*hasan*), recurrent (M*utawatir*), solitary (*ahad*), weak (*daeef*), fabricated (*maudu*) and so on and so forth. Al-Bukhari not only mastered the science of *Hadith*, but also committed around half a million *Hadith* to memory. He ate most frugally, and led a very simple and austere lifestyle. After collecting more than half a million *Hadith*, he systematically investigated and examined them in order to ascertain their veracity.

Al-Bukhari composed his first book on *Hadith* during his stay in Madinah, when he was only eighteen. He contributed more to Islamic thought and scholarship than any other scholar of his generation. Of all his works, his most seminal contribution was *Jami al-Sahih*, better known as *Sahih al-Bukhari*. This anthology is today widely considered to be the most authentic book of Islamic teachings after the Holy Qur'an. Al-Bukhari sifted through more than half a million *ahadith* and chose only the most authentic ones for inclusion in his *Jami al-Sahih*, which consisted of a total of seven thousand, two hundred and twenty-two Prophetic narrations.

Al-Bukhari settled in a small town adjacent to his native Bukhara and passed away at the age of approximately sixty-one.

***

Al-Farabi (Al-Pharabius 870–950): was a rationalist philosopher, scientist, cosmologist, logician, musician and mathematician of the Islamic world, who attempted to describe, geometrically, the repeating patterns popular in Islamic decorative motifs. His book on the subject is titled *Spiritual Crafts and Natural Secrets in the Details of Geometrical Figures*.

Biography:

The sources for his life are scant which makes the reconstruction of his biography beyond a mere outline nearly impossible. The earliest and more reliable sources, i.e., those composed before the 6th/12th century. The sources prior to the 6th/12th century consist of: (1) an autobiographical passage by Farabi, preserved by Ibn Abī Uṣaibiʻa. In this passage, Farabi traces the transmission of the instruction of logic and philosophy from antiquity to his days. (2) Reports by Al-Masudi, Ibn al-Nadim and Ibn Hawqal, as well as by Said Al-Andalusi (d. 1070), who devoted a biography to him.

When major Arabic biographers decided to write comprehensive entries on Farabi in the 6th-7th/12th-13th centuries, there was very little specific information on hand; this allowed for their acceptance of invented stories about his life which range from benign extrapolation on the basis of some known details to tendentious reconstructions and legends. The sources from the 6th/12th century and later consist essentially of three biographical entries, all other extant reports on Farabi being either dependent on them or even later fabrications: 1) the

Syrian tradition represented by Ibn Abī Uṣaibiʻa. 2) The Wafayāt al-aʻyān wa-anbāʼ abnāʼ az-zamān ("Deaths of Eminent Men and History of the Sons of the Epoch"; trans. by Baron de Slane, Ibn Khallikan's Biographical Dictionary, 1842–74) compiled by Ibn Khallikan. 3) the scanty and legendary Eastern tradition, represented by Ẓahīr-al-Din Bayhaqī.

From incidental accounts it is known that he spent significant time in Baghdad with Christian scholars including the cleric Yuhanna ibn Haylan, Yahya ibn Adi, and Abu Ishaq Ibrahim al-Baghdadi. He later spent time in Damascus, Syria and Egypt before returning to Damascus where he died in 950-1.

Name:

His name was Abu Nasr Muhammad b. Muhammad Farabi, as all sources and especially the earliest and most reliable, Al-Masudi, agree. In modern Turkish scholarship and some other sources, the pronunciation is given as Uzluḡ rather than Awzalaḡ, without any explanation.

Birthplace:

Abu Nasr Muhammad ibn Muhammad ibn Tarkhan ibn Uzalagh al-Farabi, better known in the Latin West as Alpharabius, was born in Wasij, a small village located close to Farab in the province of Transoxiana in Turkistan. Of Turkish origin, his father initially served as an army captain, and later he became a prominent member of the Persian military service.

Blessed with an unrivalled linguistic ability, al-Farabi continued to develop this ability throughout his life and probably knew more languages and dialects than any other Muslim thinker of his generation. Arabic and Persian aside, he mastered Turkish, Greek, Syriac and Hebrew, not to mention many other local languages and dialects. He went on to receive advanced training in linguistics and Islamic sciences. He became so proficient in *Fiqh* (Islamic jurisprudence) that he was appointed Q*adi* (judge) while he was still in his twenties.

Origin:

There exists a difference of opinion on the ethnic background of Farabi. According to the Oxford Encyclopedia of African Thought "*[...] because the origins of al-Farabi were not recorded during his lifetime or soon after his death in 950 C.E. by anyone with concrete information, accounts of his pedigree and place of birth have been based on hearsay...*

Iranian origin theory:

Medieval Arab historian Ibn Abī Uṣaibi'a (died in 1269) - al-Farabi's oldest biographer - mentions in his 'Oyūn that al-Farabi's father was of Persian descent. Sogdian have been mentioned as his native language and the language of the inhabitants of Farab. Muhammad Javad Mashkoor argues for an Iranian-speaking Central Asian origin.

Turkish origin theory:

The oldest known reference to a possible Turkish origin is given by the medieval historian Ibn Khallikan (died in 1282), who in his work Wafayāt (completed in 669/1271) states that Farabi was born in the small village of Wasij near Farab (in what is today Otrar, Kazakhstan) of Turkish parents. Oxford professor C.E. Bosworth notes that "great figures [such] as al-Farabi, al-Biruni, and ibn Sina have been attached by over enthusiastic Turkish scholars to their race".

Life and Education:

Al-Farabi spent almost his entire life in Baghdad, capital of Abbasids that ruled the Islamic world. In the auto-biographical passage about the appearance of philosophy preserved by Ibn Abī Uṣaibi'a, Farabi has stated that he had studied logic with Yūḥannā b. Ḥaylān up to and including Aristotle's Posterior Analytics. His studies of Aristotelian logic with Yūḥannā in all probability took place in Baghdad, where Al-Masudi tells us Yūḥannā died during the caliphate of al-Moqtader (295-320/908-32). He also lived and taught for some time in Aleppo. Later on Farabi visited Egypt; and complete six sections summarizing the book Mabāde' in Egypt in 337/July 948-June 949. He returned from Egypt to Syria. In Syria, he was supported and glorified by Saif ad-Daula, the Hamdanid ruler of Syria.

Contributions:

Farabi made contributions to the fields of logic, mathematics, music, philosophy, psychology, and education.

Alchemy:

Al-Farabi wrote: *The Necessity of the Art of the Elixir*.

Logic:

Though he was mainly an Aristotelian logician, he included a number of non-Aristotelian elements in his works. He is also credited for categorizing logic into two separate groups, the first being "idea" and the second being "proof".

Music:

Farabi wrote a book on music titled Kitab al-Musiqa (*The Book of Music*). He presents philosophical principles about music, its cosmic qualities and its influences. Al-Farabi's treatise *Meanings of the Intellect* dealt with music therapy, where he discussed the therapeutic effects of music on the soul.

Philosophy:

As a philosopher, Al-Farabi was a founder of his own school of early Islamic philosophy known as "Farabism" or "Alfarabism", though it was later overshadowed by Avicennism. Al-Farabi's school of philosophy "breaks with the philosophy of Plato and Aristotle [... and ...] moves from metaphysics to methodology, a move that anticipates modernity". In his attempt to think through the nature of a First Cause, Alfarabi discovers the limits of human knowledge".

Al-Farabi had great influence on science and philosophy for several centuries, and was widely regarded to be second only to Aristotle in knowledge (alluded to by his title of "the Second Teacher" in his time. His work, aimed at synthesis of philosophy and Sufism, paved the way for the work of Ibn Sina (Avicenna).

Al-Farabi also wrote a commentary on Aristotle's work, and one of his most notable works is *Al-Madina al-Fadila* where he theorized an ideal state as in Plato's *The Republic*. Al-Farabi departed from the Platonic view in that he regarded the ideal state to be ruled by the prophet-imam, instead of the philosopher-king envisaged by Plato. Al-Farabi argued that the ideal state was the city-state of Medina when it was governed by the prophet Muhammad as its head of state, as he was in direct communion with Allah whose law was revealed to him.

Physics:

Al-Farabi thought about the nature of the existence of void. He may have carried out the first experiments concerning the existence of vacuum, in which he investigated handheld plungers in water. He concluded that air's volume can expand to fill available space, and he suggested that the concept of perfect vacuum was incoherent.

Psychology:

In psychology, al-Farabi's *Social Psychology* and *Model City* were the first treatises to deal with social psychology. He stated that "an isolated individual could not achieve all the perfections by himself, without the aid of other individuals." He wrote that it is the "innate disposition of every man to join another human being or other men in the labor he ought to perform." He concluded that in order to "achieve what he can of that perfection, every man needs to stay in the neighborhood of others and associate with them."

His *On the Cause of Dreams*, which appeared as chapter 24 of his *Book of Opinions of the people of the Ideal City*, was a treatise on dreams, in which he distinguished between dream interpretation and the nature and causes of dreams.

Philosophical thought:

The main influence on al-Farabi's philosophy was the neo-Aristotelian tradition of Alexandria. A prolific writer, he is credited with over one hundred works. Some other significant influences on his work were the planetary model of Ptolemy and elements of Neo-Platonism, particularly metaphysics and practical (or political) philosophy (which bears more resemblance to Plato's *Republic* than Aristotle's *Politics*).

He tried to gather the ideas of Plato and Aristotle in his book "The gathering of the ideas of the two philosophers". His success should be measured by the honorific title of "the second master" of philosophy (Aristotle being the first), by which he was known.

Metaphysics and cosmology:

In contrast to al-Kindi, who considered the subject of metaphysics to be God, al-Farabi believed that it was concerned primarily with being *qua* being (that is, being in of itself), and this is related to God only to the extent that God is a principle of absolute being.

Al-Farabi's cosmology is essentially based upon three pillars: Aristotelian metaphysics of causation, highly developed Plutonian emanational cosmology and the Ptolemaic astronomy. In his model, the universe is viewed as a number of concentric circles; the outermost sphere or "first heaven", the sphere of fixed stars, Saturn, Jupiter, Mars, the Sun, Venus, Mercury and finally, the Moon. At the centre of these concentric circles is the sub-lunar realm which contains the material world. Each of these circles represent the domain of the secondary intelligences (symbolized by the celestial bodies themselves), which act as causal intermediaries between the First Cause (in this case, God) and the material world. Furthermore these are said to have emanated from God, who is both their formal and efficient cause. This departs radically from the view of Aristotle, who considered God to be solely a formal cause for the movement of the spheres, but by doing so it renders the model more compatible with the ideas of the theologians.

The process of emanation begins (metaphysically, not temporally) with the First Cause, whose principal activity is self-contemplation. And it is this intellectual activity that underlies its role in the creation of the universe. The First Cause, by thinking of itself, "overflows" and the incorporeal entity of the second intellect "emanates" from it. Like its predecessor, the second intellect also thinks about itself, and thereby brings its celestial sphere (in this case, the sphere of fixed stars) into being, but in addition to this it must also contemplate upon the First Cause, and this causes the "emanation" of the next intellect. The cascade of emanation continues until it reaches the tenth intellect, beneath which is the material world. It should be noted that this process is based upon necessity as opposed to will. In other words, God does not have a choice whether or not to create the universe, but by virtue of His own existence, He causes it to be. This view also suggests that the universe is eternal, and both of these points were criticized by al-Ghazali in his attack on the philosophers.

In his discussion of the First Cause (or God), al-Farabi relies heavily on negative theology. He says that it cannot be known by intellectual means, such as dialectical division or definition, because the terms used in these processes to define a thing constitute its substance. This would suggest that the more philosophically simple a thing is, the more perfect it is. Each succeeding level in this structure has as its principal qualities multiplicity and deficiency, and it is this ever-increasing complexity that typifies the material world.

Epistemology and eschatology:

Human beings are unique in al-Farabi's vision of the universe because they stand between two worlds: the "higher", immaterial world of the celestial intellects and universal intelligibles and the "lower", material world of generation and decay; they inhabit a physical body, and so belong to the "lower" world, but they also have a rational capacity, which connects them to the "higher" realm. Each level of existence in al-Farabi's cosmology is characterized by its movement towards perfection, which is to become like the First Cause; a perfect intellect. Human perfection (or "happiness"), then, is equated with constant intellection and contemplation.

Al-Farabi divides intellect into four categories: potential, actual, acquired and the Agent. The first three are the different states of the human intellect and the fourth is the Tenth Intellect (the moon) in his emanational cosmology. By thinking, al-Farabi means abstracting universal intelligibles from the sensory forms of objects which have been apprehended and retained in the individual's imagination.

This motion from potentiality to actuality requires the Agent Intellect to act upon the retained sensory forms; just as the Sun illuminates the physical world to allow us to see, the Agent Intellect illuminates the world of intelligibles to allow us to think. This illumination removes all accident (such as time, place, and quality) and physicality from them, converting them into primary intelligibles, which are logical principles such as "the whole is greater than the part". Because the Agent Intellect knows all of the intelligibles, this means that when the human intellect knows all of them, it becomes associated with the Agent Intellect's perfection and is known as the acquired Intellect.

And it is by choosing what is ethical and contemplating about what constitutes the nature of ethics that the actual intellect can become "like" the active intellect, thereby attaining perfection. It is only by this process that a human soul may survive death, and live on in the afterlife.

According to al-Farabi, the afterlife is not the personal experience commonly conceived of by religious traditions such as Islam and Christianity. Any individual or distinguishing features of the soul are annihilated after the death of the body; only the rational faculty survives (and then, only if it has attained perfection), which becomes one with all other rational souls within the agent intellect and enters a realm of pure intelligence.

Psychology, the soul and prophetic knowledge:

In his treatment of the human soul, al-Farabi draws on a basic Aristotelian outline, which is informed by the commentaries of later Greek thinkers. He says it is composed of four faculties: The *appetitive* (the desire for, or aversion to an object of sense), the *sensitive* (the perception by the senses of corporeal substances), the *imaginative* (the faculty which retains images of sensible objects after they have been perceived, and then separates and combines them for a number of ends), and the *rational*, which is the faculty of intellection. It is the last of these which is unique to human beings and distinguishes them from plants and animals. It is also the only part of the soul to survive the death of the body.

Special attention must be given to al-Farabi's treatment of the soul's *imaginative* faculty, which is essential to his interpretation of prophet hood and prophetic knowledge. Therefore what makes prophetic knowledge unique is not its content, which is also accessible to philosophers through demonstration and intellection, but rather the form that it is given by the prophet's imagination.

Practical philosophy (ethics and politics):

The practical application of philosophy is a major concern expressed by al-Farabi in many of his works, and while the majority of his philosophical output has been influenced by Aristotelian thought, his practical philosophy is unmistakably based on that of Plato. In a similar manner to Plato's *Republic*, al-Farabi emphasizes that philosophy is both a theoretical and practical discipline; labeling those philosophers who do not apply their erudition to practical pursuits as "futile philosophers". Al-Farabi compares the philosopher's role in relation to society with a physician in relation to the body; the body's health is affected by the "balance of its humors" just as the city is determined by the moral habits of its people. The philosopher's duty, he says, is to establish a "virtuous" society by healing the souls of the people, establishing justice and guiding them towards "true happiness".

Of course, al-Farabi realizes that such a society is rare and will require a very specific set of historical circumstances in order to be realized, which means very few societies will ever be able to attain this goal. *Ignorant* societies have, for whatever reason, failed to comprehend the purpose of human existence, and have supplanted the pursuit of happiness for another (inferior) goal, whether this be wealth, sensual gratification or power. Al-Farabi also makes mention of "weeds" in the virtuous society; those people who try to undermine its progress towards the true human end.

Al-Farabi rightly earned the coveted title of *al-Mu'allim al-Thani* (The Second Teacher) with Aristotle being *al-Mu'allim al-awwal* (The First Teacher). The great Jewish philosopher and theologian Musa bin Maimon (better known as Maimonides) once told one of his friends that al-Farabi's works on logic were 'finer than flour' and urged him not to bother consulting the works of other logicians.

Unlike al-Ghazali and many other prominent Islamic thinkers, al-Farabi considered philosophy to be entirely unified. He argued that both Plato and Aristotle expounded the same truth. As a devout Muslim and also a practicing Sufi, al-Farabi focused more on the spiritual, than on the practical, dimension of things.

Al-Farabi was in his early seventies when political instability began to spread across Baghdad, and this prompted him to move to Damascus in 942. Here he worked as a gardener for a period before moving to Egypt, only to return to Damascus again in 949. A year later, he died at the age of eighty and was buried in Damascus following a simple funeral led by Sayf al-Dawlah himself. Al-Farabi's works influenced prominent Jewish and Christian thinkers like St Thomas Aquinas, John Duns Scotus, Musa bin Maimon (Maimonides) and Leo Strauss among others.

***

Al-Hafiz, Amin (1921-2009): Syrian politician, president 1963-1966. The son of a Sunni policeman in Aleppo. Hafiz became a noncommissioned officer in the French Syrian Social Forces during the Second World War. After his release from jail in June 1967 he went into exile in Lebanon. When the Afaw led faction of the Baath party seized power in Iraq about a year later, he moved to Baghdad. Hafiz continued his anti Assad activities, later heading the National Alliance of the Liberation of Syria, an umbrella body of various anti Assad factions.

***

Al Hakim, Tawfiq (1898-1987): Egyptian writer Born of a Turkish father and an Egyptian mother in Alexandria al Hakim secured a law degree from Cairo University. In 1925 he went to Paris to obtain a doctorate in law. Instead of concentrating on his studies, he soaked himself in the cultural, artistic and theatrical life of the city. By then his literary career was well established. Having attempted light entertainment in Ali Baba, al Hakim opted for authoring intellectual plays fill of ideas and philosophic reflections. At the time of the 1952 revolution, al Hakim was director of the National Library in Cairo He supported the new regime. After Nasser's death in 1970 al Hakim criticized him in his booklet. The return of consciousness (1975).

***

Al-Hallaj (858-922): The origin of Sufism (or the mystical dimension of Islam) is often traced back to the Qur'an and the normative practice (*sunnah*) of the Prophet by its adherents. Thus, far from being an alien intrusion into the Muslim world, Sufism embodies the very heart and soul of Islam as a religion and way of life. Like the Prophet and his close companions, the early Sufis, like Hasan al-Basri, Ja'far al-Sadiq and Rabi'a al-Adawiyyah renounced worldly pleasures and engaged in devotional activities and did so without wearing the label of Sufi. Scores of outstanding Sufi personalities like Dawud al-Ta's, Shaqiq al-Balkhi, Habib al-Ajami, Ibrahim ibn Adham, Maruf al-Karkhi, Hasan al-Basri and Rabi'a al-Adawiyyah emerged to warn both the rulers and the people of the dangers of excessive materialism. Al-Hallaj was probably one of the most prominent exponents of this strand of Sufism.

Abul Mughith Hussain ibn Mansur ibn Muhammad al-Hallaj was born at Tur near al-Bayda in the Persian province of Fars. According to one account, his ancestors were originally Zoroastrians (followers of Zoroaster, the ancient Persian prophet and sage). His father, Mansur, was a devout Muslim who earned his living as a wool-carder; hence the title 'al-Hallaj'. Encouraged by his father, young al-

Hallaj committed the entire Qur'an to memory as a child and then pursued further education in Arabic and traditional Islamic sciences. Thereafter, he travelled to the Iraqi city of Wasit where he completed his higher education under the tutelage of its leading scholars. Founded in 702 by Hajjaj ibn Yusuf, the governor of the Umayyad ruler Abd al-Malik ibn Marwan, Wasit became a prominent center of Islamic learning and scholarship in Iraq.

After completing his higher education, al-Hallaj left Wasit and moved to Basrah, which was also the home of Hasan al-Basri and Rabi'a al-Adawiyyah, and there he married the daughter of a local Sufi. From Basrah, he went to Makkah where he became renowned for his devotional and ascetic practices. After completing the sacred *hajj* (pilgrimage), he went to Baghdad which at the time was one of the Muslim world's foremost centers of Islamic learning and spirituality. Here he became a student of Abul Qasim al-Junayd al-Baghdadi (also known as al-Junayd al-Baghdadi), who was a Sufi scholar of considerable influence.

Al-Hallaj left Baghdad and became a wandering Sufi. During his travels in and around Khurasan he gathered around him a sizeable following and eventually went to Makkah to perform his second pilgrimage. From Makkah he went to Turkistan and from there he reportedly travelled to India and as far as the borders of China. He became familiar with the Hindu mystical concepts of 'self-annihilation' and 'extinction' which, in turn, influenced his own mystical views. He returned to Baghdad when he was about fifty and a large following gathered around him. He became such an outspoken exponent of Sufism that even the Mu'tazilites considered him to be an opportunist and charlatan. This prompted the ruling Abbasid elites to expel him from Baghdad, after which he again returned to Makkah and performed yet another pilgrimage. After completing this third pilgrimage, he returned to Baghdad completely transformed.

Al-Hallaj ignored the advice of his fellow Sufis and began to advocate the need for spiritual and moral reformation in Baghdad. He was eventually apprehended by the Abbasid authorities and imprisoned for nine years. The Abbasid elites promptly put him on trial charged with blasphemy and treason. The trial was no more than a show; thus everyone expected him to be found guilty. Mocked, vilified and branded a heretic by the orthodox religious scholars, and also shunned and excommunicated by his fellow Sufis, al-Hallaj was sentenced to death by hanging.

As one of the Muslim world's most radical and controversial mystical thinkers, al-Hallaj's life and thoughts are riddled with contradictions, paradoxes, and unusual insights into Islamic spirituality and gnosis. Following in the footsteps of Abu Yazid al-Bistami (who was one of the first Sufi thinkers to argue that 'self-annihilation and extinction' represented the peak of mystical experience), al-Hallaj became one of the most eloquent and bravest revealers of mystical secrets and truths. Central to al-Hallaj's mystical philosophy was the concept of love (*mahabbah*). Like Rabi'a al-Adawiyyah, he advocated the pursuit of disinterested love, that is to seek the Beloved only for His sake, rather than out of fear of eternal damnation or promise of reward. Al-Hallaj's expression of spontaneous, disinterested love proved hugely controversial because he claimed to have experienced the 'essence of union' (*Ayn al-jam*), where the lover and the Beloved became one (*ittihad*); thus he blurred the crucial distinction between the Creator and His creation.

Al-Hallaj expressed his mystical ideas and experiences in beautiful, unforced and refreshing poetic couplets. He composed around forty-six books and treatises on different aspects of Islamic mysticism.

'I do not cease swimming in the seas of love, rising with the wave, then descending; now the wave sustains me, and then I sink beneath it; love bears me away where there is no longer any shore.' (Diwan al-Hallaj). (Kitab al-Tawasin): 'I have seen my Lord with the eye of my heart, and I said: 'Who are you?' He said: 'You.'

Taken literally, these mystical utterances and outburst are indeed heretical and blasphemous. Al-Hallaj argued that he was neither a heretic nor a blasphemer; rather he was an exponent of mystical experience in its highest form.

He was sentenced to death at the age of sixty-four for preaching 'heretical' ideas. His persecutors severely tortured and flogged him, before amputating his limbs one by one. His body was then cremated and his ashes scattered in the Tigris.

Other equally renowned Islamic scholars and Sufis, like Abu Bakr al-Shibli, Abd al-Qadir al-Jilani, Abu Hamid al-Ghazali, Fakhr Rumi and Sir Muhammad Iqbal, have exonerated him of the charge of self-deification and belief in monism. True to form, nearly eleven centuries after his death, al-Hallaj continues to polarize the Sufis, Islamic philosophers and theologians to this day.

***

Al-Hamid I: to the throne of the Ottoman Empire (Turkey). He suffered severe defeats in the second of the Russo-Turkish Wars with Catherine II, but suffered no major territorial losses when peace was made at Jassy in 1792. An ardent reformer, Selim set out to rebuild the Turkish navy on European lines, to reform the army, and to curb the Janissaries. In 1798

Selim joined the second coalition against France in the French Revolutionary Wars. Turkish forces lost Jaffa to Napoleon Bonaparte, who had invaded (1799) Syria after taking Egypt, but they held out at Acre and forced Napoleon to retreat. In 1801 the French left Egypt, which was restored to the sultan. In 1804 the Serbs under Karageorge revolted.

In 1806 war with Russia broke out again. A revolt of the Janissaries and conservatives who opposed his reforms led to Selim's deposition and imprisonment in 1807. Mustafa IV was placed on the throne. A loyal army marched on Constantinople to restore Selim. It entered the city in 1808, just after Selim had been strangled on Mustafa's orders. Mustafa was executed and another of Selim's cousins, Mahmud II, was put on the throne. During Selim's reign Egypt became virtually independent under Muhammad Ali, as did Albania under Ali Pasha. Selim's well-intentioned and efficient reforms came too late to arrest the decay of the Ottoman empire

***

Al Husseini, Faisal (1940-2001): Born in Baghdad to Abdul Qadir, the field commander during the 1936-39 Arab Revolt in Palestine during the time his family took refuge there al Hussein grew up in Cairo where he obtained a university degree. In 1979 he opened the Arab Studies Center in East Jerusalem which the Israeli authorities regarded as a front for coordinating PLO activities in the Occupied Territories. In the preliminary talks that led to the Middle East Peace Conference in Madrid in October 1991 he acted as a bridge between US secretary of State James Baker and Arafat. During his trip to Kuwait to repair the damaged relations between the emirate and the PLO al Hussein died of a heart attack.

***

Al-Husseini, Hajj Muhammad Amin (1897-1974): Palestinian religious and political leader. Born into a prominent religious family in Jerusalem al Hussein received his secondary education in the city, studied for a year at al Azhar University in Cairo and then enrolled at the Ottoman school of administration in Istanbul. As the leader of an Arab nationalist group in Jerusalem, the Arab Club he considered Palestine to be part of Greater Syria and opposed Jewish immigration into Palestine. In December sir Herbert ordered the establishment of a five member Supreme Muslim Council charged with running religious endowments and courts and mosques to be elected indirectly. He insisted demand that restrictions on Jewish immigration should be coupled with the establishment of an Arab national government made him the most significant political leader of Arab Palestinians.

In April 1936, as his behest, various Arab groups united to form the Arab Higher Committee under his leadership. Al Husseini took refuge in the Muslim shrines of Jerusalem and then managed to flee, first to Lebanon and then Syria From there he continued to direct the Arab revolt, which ended in March 1939 with a death toll of 3,232 Arabs 329 Jews and 135 Britons. soon after the outbreak of the Second World War in September 1939 al Husseini arrived in Baghdad as a political refugee and began rallying anti Zionist and anti British sentiments in Iraq. At the end of the war al Husseini was arrested by the French forces but soon managed to escape to Cairo. After the Palestine War his attempts to form a government of all Palestine in the Egyptian occupied Gaza Strip were cold shouldered by Cairo. He moved to Beirut in 1959.

***

Al-Idrisi (1100–1166): Moroccan traveler, cartographer and geographer, educated in Cordoba, Spain, famous for an important geographical work on the Seven Climes (1154) for Roger II of Sicily. It contains one map for each clime (i.e. climatic zone); the maps of later manuscripts suggest that those in the autograph were colored. Also, he produced the first map of the world for Roger, the Norman King of Sicily. al-Idrisi also wrote the Book of Roger, a geographic study of the peoples, climates, resources and industries of all the world known at that time. In it, he incidentally relates the tale of a Moroccan ship blown west in the Atlantic and returning with tales of faraway lands.

***

Al Iryani, Abdul Rahman (1908-1998): Yemeni politician; president of North Yemen, 1967-74, Born into a notable Zaidi family in Saada, Iryani received religious education and trained as an Islamic judge. Having failed to strike a deal with the royalists, Nasser freed Sallal in September 1966. On his return home Sallal purged his rivals, including Iryani, who now found himself under house arrest in Cairo. He was overthrown in a bloodless coup by Col. Ibrahim Hamdi in June 1974. He went into Exile to Lebanon and then to Syria. He was allowed to return home in October 1981.

***

Al-Jazari, Badi'al-Zaman Abu al-'Izz Isma'il ibn al-Razāz (1136–1206): was an Arab or a Kurdish Muslim polymath: a scholar, inventor, mechanical engineer, craftsman, artist, and mathematician from Jazirat ibn Umar (current Cizre), who lived during the Islamic Golden Age (Middle Ages). He is best known for writing the *Book of Knowledge of Ingenious Mechanical Devices* in 1206, where he described fifty mechanical devices along with instructions on how to construct them.

Biography:
Little is known about al-Jazari and most of that comes from the introduction to his *Book of Knowledge of Ingenious Mechanical Devices*. He was named after the area in which he was born (the city of Jazirat ibn Umar). Like his father before him, he served as chief engineer at the Artuklu Palace, the residence of the Mardin branch of the Turkish Artuqid dynasty which ruled across eastern Anatolia as vassals of the Zangid rulers of Mosul and later Ayyubid general Saladin. He was born in the Kurdish city of Tor, now located in the district of Cizre in south-Eastern Turkey.

His *Book of Knowledge of Ingenious Mechanical Devices* appears to have been quite popular as it appears in a large number of manuscript copies, and as he explains repeatedly, he only describes devices he has built himself. According to Mayr, the book's style resembles that of a modern "do-it-yourself" book.

Some of his devices were inspired by earlier devices, such as one of his monumental water clocks, which were based on that of a Pseudo-Archimedes. He also cites the influence of the Banu Musa brothers for his fountains, al-Asturlabi for the design of a candle clock, and Hibat Allah ibn al-Husayn (d. 1139) for musical automata. Al-Jazari goes on to describe the improvements he made to the work of his predecessors, and describes a number of devices, techniques and components that are original innovations which do not appear in the works by his predecessors.

Mechanisms and methods:
While many of al-Jazari's inventions may now appear to be trivial, the most significant aspect of al-Jazari's machines are the mechanisms, components, ideas, methods, and design features which they employ.

Camshaft:
The camshaft, a shaft to which cams are attached, was first introduced in 1206 by al-Jazari, who employed them in his automata, water clocks (such as the candle clock) and water-raising machines. The

Crankshaft and crank-slider mechanism:

The eccentrically mounted handle of the rotary hand mill in 5th century BC Spain that spread across the Roman Empire constitutes a crank. The earliest evidence of a crank and connecting rod mechanism dates to the 3rd century AD Hierapolis sawmill in the Roman Empire. The crank also appears in the mid-9th century in several of the hydraulic devices described by the Banū Mūsā brothers in their *Book of Ingenious Devices*.

In 1206, al-Jazari invented an early crankshaft, which he incorporated with a crank-connecting rod mechanism in his twin-cylinder pump. Like the modern crankshaft, Al-Jazari's mechanism consisted of a wheel setting several crank pins into motion, with the wheel's motion being circular and the pins moving back-and-forth in a straight line. The crankshaft described by al-Jazari transforms continuous rotary motion into a linear reciprocating motion, and is central to modern machinery such as the steam engine, internal combustion engine and automatic controls.

He used the crankshaft with a connecting rod in two of his water-raising machines: the crank-driven Baqqiya chain pump and the double-action reciprocating piston suction pump. His water pump also employed the first known crank-slider mechanism,

Escapement mechanism in a rotating wheel:

Al-Jazari invented a method for controlling the speed of rotation of a wheel using an escapement mechanism.

Mechanical controls:

According to Donald Routledge Hill, al-Jazari described several early mechanical controls, including "a large metal door, a combination lock and a lock with four bolts."

Segmental gear:

A segmental gear is "a piece for receiving or communicating reciprocating motion from or to a cogwheel, consisting of a sector of a circular gear, or ring, having cogs on the periphery, or face." Professor Lynn Townsend White, Jr. wrote:

> Segmental gears first clearly appear in al-Jazari, in the West they emerge in Giovanni de Dondi's astronomical clock finished in 1364, and only with the great Sienese engineer Francesco di

Giorgio (1501) did they enter the general vocabulary of European machine design.

Water-raising machines:
Al-Jazari invented five machines for raising water, as well as watermills and water wheels with cams on their axle used to operate automata, in the 12th and 13th centuries, and described them in 1206. It was in these water-raising machines that he introduced his most important ideas and components.

Saqiya chain pumps:
The first known use of a crankshaft in a chain pump was in one of al-Jazari's Baqqiya machines. The concept of minimizing intermittent working is also first implied in one of al-Jazari's *Baqqiya* chain pumps, which was for the purpose of maximizing the efficiency of the Baqqiya chain pump. Al-Jazari also constructed a water-raising Baqqiya chain pump which was run by hydropower rather than manual labor, though the Chinese were also using hydropower for chain pumps prior to him. Saqiya machines like the ones he described have been supplying water in Damascus since the 13th century up until modern times, and were in everyday use throughout the medieval Islamic world.

Double-action suction pump with valves and reciprocating piston motion:
Citing the Byzantine siphon used for discharging Greek fire as an inspiration, al-Jazari went on to describe the first suction pipes, suction pump, double-action pump, and made early uses of valves and a crankshaft-connecting rod mechanism, when he invented a twin-cylinder reciprocating piston suction pump. This pump is driven by a water wheel, which drives, through a system of gears, an oscillating slot-rod to which the rods of two pistons are attached. The pistons work in horizontally opposed cylinders, each provided with valve-operated suction and delivery pipes. The delivery pipes are joined above the centre of the machine to form a single outlet into the irrigation system. This water-raising machine had a direct significance for the development of modern engineering. This pump is remarkable for three reasons:

- The first known use of a true suction pipe (which sucks fluids into a partial vacuum) in a pump.
- The first application of the double-acting principle.
  The conversion of rotary to reciprocating motion, via the crank-connecting rod mechanism, al-Jazari's suction piston pump

could lift 13.6 meters of water, with the help of delivery pipes. This was more advanced than the suction pumps that appeared in 15th-century Europe, which lacked delivery pipes. It was not, however, any more efficient than a noria commonly used by the Muslim world at the time.

Water supply system:

Al-Jazari developed the earliest water supply system to be driven by gears and hydropower, which was built in 13th century Damascus to supply water to its mosques and Bipartisan hospitals. The system had water from a lake turn a scoop-wheel and a system of gears which transported jars of water up to a water channel that led to mosques and hospitals in the city.

Automata:

Al-Jazari built automated moving peacocks driven by hydropower. He also invented the earliest known automatic gates, which were driven by hydropower. He also created automatic doors as part of one of his elaborate water clocks, He also invented water wheels with cams on their axle used to operate automata. According to *Encyclopedia Britannica*, the Italian Renaissance inventor Leonardo da Vinci may have been influenced by the classic automata of al-Jazari.

Mark E. Rosheim summarizes the advances in robotics made by Arab engineers, especially Al-Jazari, as follows:

> Unlike the Greek designs, these Arab examples reveal an interest, not only in dramatic illusion, but in manipulating the environment for human comfort. Thus, the greatest contribution the Arabs made, besides preserving, disseminating and building on the work of the Greeks, was the concept of practical application. This was the key element that was missing in Greek robotic science.
>
> The Arabs, on the other hand, displayed an interest in creating human-like machines for practical purposes but lacked, like other preindustrial societies, any real impetus to pursue their robotic science.

Drink-serving waitress:

One of al-Jazari's humanoid automata was a waitress that could serve water, tea or drinks. The drink was stored in a tank with a reservoir from where the drink drips into a bucket and, after seven minutes, into a cup, after which the waitress appears out of an automatic door serving the drink.

Hand-washing automaton with flush mechanism:

al-Jazari invented a hand washing automaton incorporating a flush mechanism now used in modern flush toilets. It features a female humanoid automaton standing by a basin filled with water. When the user pulls the lever, the water drains and the female automaton refills the basin.

Peacock fountain with automated servants:

Al-Jazari's "peacock fountain" was a more sophisticated hand washing device featuring humanoid automata as servants which offer soap and towels. Mark E. Rosheim describes it as follows:

> Pulling a plug on the peacock's tail releases water out of the beak; as the dirty water from the basin fills the hollow base a float rises and actuates a linkage which makes a servant figure appear from behind a door under the peacock and offer soap. When more water is used, a second float at a higher level trips and causes the appearance of a second servant figure — with a towel!

Musical robot band:

Al-Jazari's work described fountains and musical automata, in which the flow of water alternated from one large tank to another at hourly or half-hourly intervals. This operation was achieved through his innovative use of hydraulic switching.

Al-Jazari created a musical automaton, which was a boat with four automatic musicians that floated on a lake to entertain guests at royal drinking parties. The drummer could be made to play different rhythms and different drum patterns if the pegs were moved around.

Clocks:

Al-Jazari constructed a variety of water clocks and candle clocks. These included a portable water-powered scribe clock, which were a meter high and half a meter wide, reconstructed successfully at the Science Museum (London) in 1976. Al-Jazari also invented monumental water-powered astronomical clocks which displayed moving models of the Sun, Moon, and stars.

Candle clocks:

According to Donald Routledge Hill, al-Jazari described the most sophisticated candle clocks known to date. Hill described one of al-Jazari's candle clocks as follows:

> The candle, whose rate of burning was known, bore against the underside of the cap, and its wick passed through the hole. Wax collected in the indentation and could be removed periodically so that it did not interfere with steady burning. The bottom of the candle rested in a shallow dish that had a ring on its side connected through pulleys to a counterweight. As the candle burned away, the weight pushed it upward at a constant speed. The automata were operated from the dish at the bottom of the candle. No other candle clocks of this sophistication are known.

Al-Jazari's candle clock also included a dial to display the time and, for the first time, employed a bayonet fitting, a fastening mechanism still used in modern times.

Elephant clock:

The elephant clock was described by al-Jazari in 1206 is notable for several innovations. It was the first clock in which an automaton reacted after certain intervals of time (in this case, a humanoid robot striking the cymbal and a mechanical robotic bird chirping) and the first water clock to accurately record the passage of the temporal hours to match the uneven length of days throughout the year.

Castle clock:

Al-Jazari's largest astronomical clock was the "castle clock", which was a complex device that was about 11 feet (3.4 m) high, and had multiple functions besides timekeeping. It included a display of the zodiac and the solar and lunar orbits, and an innovative feature of the device was a pointer in the shape of the crescent moon which travelled across the top of a gateway, moved by a hidden cart, and caused automatic doors to open, each revealing a mannequin, every hour. Another innovative feature was the ability to re-program the length of day and night in order to account for their changes throughout the year. Another feature of the device was five automaton musicians who automatically play music when moved by levers operated by a hidden camshaft attached to a water wheel. Other components of the castle clock included a main reservoir with a float, a float chamber and flow regulator, plate and valve trough, two pulleys, crescent disc displaying the zodiac, and two falcon automata dropping balls into vases.

Weight-driven water clocks:

Al-Jazari invented water clocks that were driven by both water and weights. These included geared clocks and a portable water-powered scribe clock, which were a meter high and half a meter wide. The scribe with his pen was synonymous to the hour hand of a modern clock. al-Jazari's famous water-powered scribe clock was reconstructed successfully at the Science Museum (London) in 1976.

Miniature paintings:

Alongside his accomplishments as an inventor and engineer, al-Jazari was also an accomplished artist. In *The Book of Knowledge of Ingenious Mechanical Devices*, he gave instructions of his inventions and illustrated them using miniature paintings, a medieval style of Islamic art.

***

Al-Khursani, Abu Muslim Abd Rahman ibn Muslim (700-755): Or al-Khurasani AKA Behzādān pour Vandād Hormozd was an Abbasid general of Persian origin, who led the first major and organized liberal movement against the Umayyad dynasty.

Life and Origin:

His original name was Behzadan, prior to his father Vandad Hurmoz's conversion to Islam, who adopted the name of 'Moslem' for himself. His birthplace remains obscure, though the oldest historical reference, the 11th century *Al-Mahasin al-Isfahan* written by Mafzal Ibn-Sa'd Maforukhi Esfahani, claims he was born in the town of Fereidan in the central Iranian province of Isfahan. It is also claimed he was born in the village of Sanjerd or Makhowan near the city of Merv in what is now Turkmenistan.

Crushing a Shiite rebellion in Bukhara:

There was an Arab by the name Sharik ibn Shaikh al-Mahri in Bukhara, who wanted to spread Shi'a Islam firmly and oppose anyone against him. Soon, he got the support of several local rulers and many local people.

When this news reached Abu Muslim (Khurasani), he along Ziyad ibn Salih came there to find out what the details, and soon they got involved in a fight. Abu Muslim fought Sharik ibn Shaikh al-Mahri and his Shiite supporters for thirty-seven days with no victory, everyday Abu Muslim's side was losing soldiers and several taken as prisoners. After that, all of a sudden Sharikh ibn Shaikh (Shiite leader) died, and his supporters started to crumble & fear, but they were still hostile. The rebellion was eventually crushed and most of the Shi'a supporters were hanged.

Rise and revolution:

Abu Muslim was a major supporter of the Abbasid cause, having met with their Imam Ibrahim ibn Muhammad in Mecca, and was later a personal friend of Abu al-'Abbas Al-Saffah, the future Caliph. He observed the revolt in Kufa in 736 tacitly. With the death of the Umayyad Caliph Hisham ibn Abd al-Malik in 743, the Islamic world was launched into civil war. Abu Muslim was sent to Khorasan by the Abbasids initially as a propagandist and then to revolt on their behalf. He took Merv in December 747 (or January 748), defeating the Umayyad governor Nasr ibn Sayyar, as well as Shayban al-Khariji, a Kharijite aspirant to the caliphate. He became the de facto Abbasid governor of Khorasan, and gained fame as a general in the late 740s in defeating the peasant rebellion of Bihafarid, the leader of a syncretic Persian sect that were Mazdaism. Abu Muslim received support in suppressing the rebellion both from purist Muslims and Zoroastrians. In 750, Abu Muslim became leader of the Abbasid army and defeated the Umayyads at Battle of the Zab. Abu Muslim stormed Damascus, the capital of the Umayyad caliphate, later that year.

His heroic role in the revolution and military skill, along with his conciliatory politics toward Shi'a, Sunnis, Zoroastrians, Jews, and Christians, made him extremely popular among the people. Although it appears that Abu al-'Abbas trusted him in general, he was wary of his power, limiting his entourage to 500 men upon his arrival to Iraq on his way to Hajj in 754. Abu al-'Abbas' brother, al-Mansur (r. 754-775), advised al-Saffah on more than one occasion to have Abu Muslim killed, fearing his rising influence and popularity. It seems that this dislike was mutual, with Abu Muslim aspiring to more power and looking down in disdain on al-Mansur, feeling al-Mansur owed Abu Muslim for his position. When the new caliph's uncle, Abdullah ibn Ali rebelled, Abu Muslim was requested by al-Mansur to crush this rebellion, which he did, and Abdullah was given to his nephew as a prisoner. Abdullah was ultimately executed.

Relations deteriorated quickly when al-Mansur sent an agent to inventory the spoils of war, and then appointed Abu Muslim governor of Syria and Egypt, outside his powerbase. After an increasingly acrimonious correspondence between Abu Muslim and al-Mansur, Abu Muslim feared he was going to be killed if he appeared in the presence of the Caliph. He later changed his mind and decided to appear in his presence due to a combination of perceived disobedience, al-Mansur's promise to keep him as governor of Khorasan, and the assurances of some of his close aides, some of whom were bribed by al-Mansur. He went to Iraq to meet with al-Mansur in Madain in 755. Al-Mansur proceeded to enumerate his grievances against Abu Muslim, who kept reminding the Caliph of his efforts to enthrone him. Against al-Muslim were also charges of being a Zendic or heretic. Al-Mansur then signaled five of his guards behind a portico to kill him. Abu Muslim's mutilated body was thrown in the river Tigris, and his commanders were bribed to acquiesce to the murder.

***

Al-Khwarizmi (780-847): The origin of all the physical sciences can, one way or another, be traced back to mathematics. According to the historians, archaeological excavations carried out in the Nile Valley and Mesopotamia have shown that counting was familiar to both ancient Egyptians and the Babylonians. The Chinese and Indians also devised their own distinctive ways of counting, just as the Arabs used the positions of their fingers to help them count during the time of the Prophet Muhammad.

Though the zero-based number system was known to the ancient Indians, it was the Muslims who invented the word 'zero'. Derived from the Arabic *sifr*, meaning 'nothing' or 'nil'. When the Muslim mathematicians were busy conducting complex and sophisticated mathematical equations in their research laboratories in Baghdad, Damascus, Cairo and Merv, the Europeans were struggling to perform simple mathematical calculations using Roman numerals. By contrast, the introduction of Arabic numerals represented nothing short of a major revolution in mathematical study and research. No other mathematician played a more pivotal role in the development of algebra and Arabic numerals that al-Khwarizmi. That is why he is today considered to be one of the greatest mathematical geniuses of all time.

Abu Abdullah Muhammad ibn Musa al-Khwarizmi was born in Khwarizm, in the Central Asian province of Khurasan. Al-Khwarizmi's family migrated to the district of Qurtrubulli, located on the outskirts of Baghdad, when he was still a child. The students who were considered to be most capable and gifted by their tutors were then encouraged to pursue research in medicine, astronomy, alchemy and mathematics, thereby widening their intellectual horizons.

When al-Khwarizmi's reputation as an accomplished religious scholar, scientist and mathematician reached the corridors of power in Baghdad, the reigning Abbasid Caliph, Abdullah al-Ma'mun, invited him to join his celebrated *bait al-Hikmah* (The House of Wisdom) in

Baghdad around 820; he was around forty at the time. Originally founded by Harun during his reign as Caliph, the *bait al-Hikmah* became one of the Muslim world's most famous and influential libraries and centers of research under Caliph al-Ma'mun's patronage. As expected, al-Khwarizmi occupied a prominent position in *bait al-Hikmah*, where he studied and conducted research in a host of disciplines including astronomy, geography, history, music and mathematics, which was his favorite subject. He authored an influential book on history entitled *Kitab al-Tarikh* (The Book of History), which later inspired celebrated Muslim historians like Abul Hasan al-Mas'udi and al-Tabari to produce their own works on the subject.

The Muslim scientists and mathematicians not only translated and preserved ancient Greek intellectual heritage (such as Euclid's *Elements*, Ptolemy's *Almagest* and the vast corpus of Aristotelian logic for the benefit of posterity), they also explored and analyzed the intellectual and cultural contribution of other ancient civilizations, including those of Persia, India and China. According to some historians, al-Khwarizmi's quest for knowledge took him all the way to India, where he mastered traditional Indian science and mathematics. It was also during his stay in India that he became familiar with the zero-based decimal system for the first time. During this period al-Khwarizmi discovered that the ancient Indians used a blank space to denote 'nothing' or 'nil' (S*unya*), which inspired him to coin the Arabic word *sifr* meaning 'nothing', just as its Latin equivalent, *ciphrium*, later came to denote 'zero'. His discovery of the concept of 'zero' enabled him to lay the foundations of a new decimal system, which is today widely known as Arabic numerals, and in so doing he revolutionized the study of mathematics forever.

Al-Khwarizmi's complete mastery of Greek, Indian and Babylonian mathematics enabled him to critically evaluate the contribution of the ancients before he went on to develop his own fresh ideas and thoughts on the subject. The originality of his mathematical contribution is most evident from the fact that the word 'algebra' was derived directly from the title of his famous book on the subject, entitled *Kitab al-Mukhtasar fi Hisab al-Jabr wa'l Muqabalah* (The Summarized Treatise on the Process of Calculation for Transposition and Cancellation). He used around eight hundred different demonstrative equations to show how calculations of integration and equation could be performed.

Al-Khwarizmi's book on arithmetic entitled *Kitab al-Jam' wa'l Tafriq bi'l Hisab al-Hindi* (The Book of Aggregation and Division in Indian Mathematics) was not only a pioneering mathematical contribution, it also became a hugely influential book. After Bon

Compagni translated it into Latin in 1157, it became a popular textbook on arithmetic throughout medieval Europe. Al-Khwarizmi's scholarship had such a pervasive influence on Western science and technology that he became known as 'Algorithm' across Europe, and throughout the centuries his Latinized name became synonymous with the word 'arithmetic' in the West. Without al-Khwarizmi's seminal contributions in arithmetic, algebra, trigonometry and other branches of mathematics, it would not have been possible for Copernicus, Kepler, Galileo, Newton and others to achieve as much as they did in the fields of astronomy, physics, mathematics and chemistry.

Al-Khwarizmi was also a brilliant astronomer and geographer. He not only accurately measured and determined the sphericity of the earth, he also suggested ways in which the process could be made easier in the future, by improving the device he had invented. Towards the end of his life he authored a book on geography entitled *Kitab Surat al-Ard* (The Book on the Shape of the Earth). In this book, he went to great lengths to correct Ptolemy's misconceptions about different aspects of geography, geology and other related sciences.

In total, al-Khwarizmi authored more than a dozen books on all the sciences of his time. He died at the age of sixty-seven and was laid to rest in Baghdad.

***

Al-Kindi (801-873): Rescued from being a footnote in history by the Prophet Muhammad, the Arabs embraced learning, culture and civilization like never before. It was al-Kindi, that hugely influential Islamic philosopher – known in the West as the 'philosopher of the Arabs' (*faylasuf al-Arab*) – who played a central role in the development of philosophical thought in the Muslim world.

Abu Yusuf Yaqub ibn Ishaw al-Kindi, known in the Latin West as Alkindus, was born in the Iraqi city of Kufah. Along with Basrah, Baghdad, Damascus, Makkah and Madinah, Kufah was one of the foremost centers of Islamic learning at the time.

After completing his formal education in Kufah, al-Kindi moved to Baghdad, the political capital of the Islamic world, to pursue advanced training in the religious and philosophical sciences. After the death of Harun al-Rashid in 809, his son al-Ma'mun – having defeated al-Amin – became the Caliph and vigorously promoted the study of the rational sciences, including Greek philosophy and science, across the Muslim world. In Baghdad, al-Kindi enjoyed the patronage of Caliph al-Ma'mun who encouraged him to pursue his studies at the *bait al-Hikmah* (House of Wisdom), the celebrated library and research center originally founded by Harun al-Rashid. At the *bait al-Hikmah*, al-Kindi devoted all his time and energy to the study of mathematics, astronomy, chemistry, musical theory and philosophy.

Along with other luminaries of the time, including al-Khwarizmi the great mathematician and scientist, and al-Farghani the renowned astronomer, al-Kindi became a prominent member of *bait al-Hikmah*. Given al-Kindi's intellectual brilliance and great linguistic abilities, Caliph al-Ma'mun became very fond of him and asked him to spearhead the pioneering task of translating Greek, Persian and Indian philosophical, mathematical and scientific works into Arabic for the benefit of the Muslim scholars and researchers. Thanks to al-Kindi and his colleagues, the study of comparative thought became one of the foremost intellectual preoccupations of the early Muslim philosophers and scientists.

Al-Kindi was appointed chief astrologer at the Caliphal court in Baghdad when he was only thirty-two years old. However, it was in the fields of optics, music and philosophy that he made some of his most original contributions. For the first time in the history of optics, al-Kindi fully explained the principle of rectilinear progress of light emerging from a luminous object. Using a lit candle, hence becoming known as the 'candle experiment', al-Kindi was able to demonstrate that light progressed in a straight line. His contribution in the field of musical theory was equally remarkable. Since musical songs formed an important part of Arab culture, he was keen to develop a theoretical understanding of music – a branch of learning which the Muslims later exported to the West.

Though al-Kindi's contributions in optics and musical theory were nothing short of remarkable, today he is most famous for his philosophical originality and writings. The author of twenty-two books on philosophy, he became a towering figure in this subject both in the Muslim world and in the West, where he became widely known as the 'philosopher of the Arabs'. To al-Kindi, philosophy consisted of three parts, ranked in order of importance: theology, mathematics and physics.

Al-Kindi remained a devout Muslim all his life. He considered religion and philosophy to be compatible in the same way that reason and revelation are harmonious. According to him, philosophy relates to the nature of God, Divine Attributes, creation and time. Unlike many other great Muslim philosophers, such as Ibn Sina, he believed that creation was not eternal; rather he considered time, space and the chain of causality to be finite. Only God was infinite, he argued, because He was the first cause which was not an effect. Al-Kindi was quick to point out that perfect order and harmony in creation was a further indication of the existence of God, although al-Ghazali later thoroughly discredited the teleological argument for the existence of God.

Al-Kindi authored exactly two hundred and forty-two books and treatises on all the sciences of his day. The vast majority of all his books are no longer extant. Influential European thinkers like Roger Bacon considered him to be one of the world's greatest minds. In the Muslim world he became known as the 'father of Islamic philosophy'. Al-Kindi died at the age of seventy-two.

***

Al-Mahdi, Muhammad ibn Al-Hasan (869-941): Muḥammad ibn al-Ḥasan al-Mahdi (born c. July 29, 869 (15 Sha'aban 255 AH), *in Occultation* since 941) is believed by Twelver Shi'a Muslims to be the Mahdi, an ultimate savior of humankind and the final Imam of the Twelve Imams. Twelver Shi'a believe that al-Mahdi was born in 869 and did not die but rather was hidden by God in 941 (this is referred to as *the Occultation*) and will later emerge with Isa (Jesus Christ) in order to fulfill their mission of bringing peace and justice to the world. He assumed the Imamate at 5 years of age. Some Shi'ite schools do not consider ibn-al-Hasan to be the Mahdi, although the mainstream sect Twelvers do.

Sunnis believe that the Mahdi has not yet been born, and therefore his exact identity is only known to Allah. Aside from the Mahdi's precise genealogy, Sunnis accept many of the same Hadiths Shi'as accept about the predictions regarding the Mahdi's emergence, his acts and his universal Khilafat. Sunnis also have a few more Mahdi Hadiths which are **not** present in Shi'a collections.

Birth and early life according to Twelver Shi'a:

In Shi'a sources even in historical works of Ibn Babuya the birth of Imam was miraculous which must be considered as hagiography. Aside from Shi'as works almost nothing is known about the life of this Imam. According to Yaan Richard some even cast doubt on his actual existence.

Even though, most scholars say Al Mahdi was born in 869 AD. His mother is Narjis. There are a couple of narrations regarding the origin of his mother. One is that his mother, Narjis was a Byzantine slave. Another narration says she was a black slave from Africa. Other narration says that she was a Byzantine Princess who pretended to be a slave so that she might travel from her kingdom to Arabia. Mohammad Ali Amir-Moezzi, in Encyclopedia of Iranica, suggests that the last version is "undoubtedly legendary and hagiographic".

To support Imam Mahdi's claim, Twelver Shi'as along with some other Muslim sects quote the following Hadith: "I and `Ali are the fathers of this nation; whoever knows us very well also knows Allah, and whoever denies us also denies Allah, the Unique, the Mighty. And from `Ali's descendants are my grandsons al-Hasan and al-Husayn, who is the masters of the youths of Paradise, and from al-Husayn's descendants, shall be nine: whoever obeys them obeys me, and whoever disobeys them also disobeys me; the ninth among them is their Qa'im and Mahdi."

The eleventh Imam of the Twelve Imams Hasan al-Askari died on 1 January 874 AD (8th Rabi' al-awwal, 260 AH) and since that day, his son Mahdi is believed by Shi'as to be the Imam, appointed by Allah, to lead the believers of the era. The most popular account of al-Mahdi in Shi'a literature is taken from his father's funeral. It is reported that as the funeral prayer was about to begin, al-Mahdi's uncle, Ja'far ibn Ali approached to lead the prayers. However, al-Mahdi approached and commanded, *"Move aside, uncle; only an Imam can lead the funeral prayer of an Imam."* Ja'far moved aside, and the five-year-old child led the funeral prayer for his father. It is reported that it was at this very moment that al-Mahdi disappeared and went into *Ghaybat*, or occultation

In a Hadith widely regarded as authentic, Muhammad said,

> *"Even if the entire duration of the world's existence has already been exhausted and only one day is left before the Day of Judgment, Allah will expand that day to such a length of time, as to accommodate the kingdom of a person out of Ahl al-Bayt who will be called by my name and my father's name. He will then fill the Earth with peace and justice as it will have been filled with injustice and tyranny before then"*

The Occultation:

Twelver Shi'as believes that for various reasons, Allah concealed the twelfth and current Imam of the Twelve Imams, al-Mahdi, from mankind.

Period:

The period of occultation (*Ghaybat*) is divided into two parts:

- *Ghaybat al-Sughra* or Minor Occultation (874–941), consists of the first few decades after the Imam's disappearance when

communication with him was maintained through deputies of the Imam.
- *Ghaybat al-Kubra* or Major Occultation began 941 and is believed to continue until a time decided by Allah, when the Mahdi will reappear to bring absolute justice to the world.

Minor Occultation:
During the Minor Occultation (*Ghaybat al-Sughra*), it is believed that al-Mahdi maintained contact with his followers via deputies (Arab. *an-nuwāb al-arba'a* literal: the four leaders).

Also, during the oppressive rule of the later Abbasid caliphs, the Shi'a Imams were heavily persecuted and held prisoners, thus their followers were forced to consult their Imams via messengers or secretly.

Shi'a Tradition holds that four deputies acted in succession to one another:

1. Uthman ibn Sa'id al-Asadi
2. Abu Ja'far Muhammad ibn Uthman
3. Abul Qasim Husayn ibn Ruh al-Nawbakhti
4. Abul Hasan Ali ibn Muhammad al-Samarri

In 941 (329 AH), the fourth deputy announced an order by al-Mahdi, that the deputy would soon die and that the deputyship would end and the period of the Major Occultation would begin.

The fourth deputy died six days later and the Shi'a Muslims continue to await the reappearance of the Mahdi. In the same year, many notable Shi'a scholars such as Ali ibn Babwayh Qummi and Muhammad ibn Yaqub Kulayni, the learned compiler of al-Kafi also died.

Major Occultation:
According to the last letter of al-Mahdi to Ali ibn Muhammad al-Samarri "from the day of your death [the last deputy] the period of my major occultation (al ghaybatul kubra) will begin. Hence forth, no one will see me, unless and until Allah makes me appear."[1] Another view is that the Hidden Imam is on earth "among the body of the Shi'a" but "incognito." "Numerous stories" exist of the Hidden Imam "manifesting himself to prominent members of the ulama."

Reappearance:
Twelver Shi'as cite various references from the Qur'an and reports, or Hadith, from Imam Mahdi and the Twelve Imams with

regard to the reappearance of al-Mahdi who would, in accordance with Allah's command, bring justice and peace to the world by establishing Islam throughout the world.

> At this time, Imam al-Mahdi will come wielding Allah's Sword, the Blade of Evil's Bane, Zulfiqar, the Double-Bladed Sword. He will also come and reveal the texts in his possession, such as al-Jafr and al-Jamia.

> Shi'as believes that Jesus will also come (after Imam Mahdi's re-appearance) and follow the Imam Mahdi to destroy tyranny and falsehood and to bring justice and peace to the world.

Titles:
The 12th Imam is known by many titles in Shi'a Islam, including:

- Al-Mahdi (the Guided one)
- Al-Muntathar (the Awaited one)
- Al-Qa'im (the Rising one)
- Sahab az-Zaman (the Master of the Age)
- Imam az-Zaman (the Leader of the Age)
- Wali al-'Asr (the Guardian of the Era or alternatively, the Guardian in the Twilight [of man])
- Al-Hujjah (the Proof [of Allah's justice])

Sunni view:
The majority of Sunni Muslims do not consider the son of Hasan al-Askari to be the Mahdi nor to be in occultation. However, they do believe that the Mahdi will come from Muhammad's family, more specifically from Al-Hasan's descendants. Sunnis believe that the Mahdi has not yet been born, and therefore his exact identity is only known to Allah.
Abu Sa'id al-Khudri narrated that Muhammad said:

Our Mahdi will have a broad forehead and a pointed (prominent) nose. He will fill the earth with justice as it is filled with injustice and tyranny. He will rule for seven years
—Abu Sa'id al-Khudri

Umm Salamah said:

> I heard the Messenger of Allah say: "The Mahdi is of my lineage and family"
> —Umm Salamah,

He would protect the Muslims from destruction and would restore the religion to its original position.

Sunnis also believe that Jesus will return alongside the Mahdi, with the only difference being that they disagree with the Shi'a regarding exactly who the Mahdi is.

Scholarly observations:
Some scholars, including Bernard Lewis also point out, that the idea of an Imam in occultation was not new in 873 but that it was a recurring factor in Shi'a history.

Consequence of occultation of Twelfth Imam:
The occultation of 12th Imam left a considerable gap in leadership of Shi'as. According to Shi'as beliefs the Imam was both the spiritual and political head of the community. After the greater occultation, the role of Imam as the head of community left vacant, which did not theoretically matter at the beginning of Occultation because Shi'as had no political power at that time. This problem has caused continuing tension between government and religion throughout the Shi'as history.

Muhammad Al-Mahdi
Imam of Twelver Shi'a Islam

Rank	12th Twelver Imam
Birthplace	Samarra, Iraq
Buried	n/a – in Occultation
Life Duration	Before Imamate: 5 years
	(255 – 260 AH)
	Imamate: Occultation
	(260 AH – present)
	-Minor Occultation: 70 years
	(260 – 329 AH)
	-Major Occultation: ???
	(329 AH – present)

Titles
- Al-Mahdi (Arabic for Guided One)
- Al-Qa'im (Arabic for One who Rises)
- Al-Hujjah (Arabic for The Proof)
- Sahib az-Zaman (Arabic for Master of the Era)
- al-Muntadhar (Arabic for the Awaited One)
- Hujjatullah (Arabic for Proof of Allah)
- al-Gha'ib (Arabic for The Unseen One)
- Sahib al-Amr (Arabic for Master of Command)
- Imam al-'Asr (Arabic for Imam of the Age)
- Onikinci Ali (Turkish for Twelfth Ali)

Father	Hasan al-'Askari
Mother	Narjis

Ali – Hasan – Husayn
al-Sajjad – al-Baqir – al-Sadiq
al-Kadhim – al-Rida – al-Taqi
al-Hadi – al-Askari – al-Mahdi

***

Al Maktum, Rashid ibn Said (1914-1990): ruler of Dubai emirate in the United Arab Emirates, 1990; vice president of the UAE 1990, prime minister of the UAE, 1971-79, 1990 Born in Dubai al Maktum was educated there and in Britain. After the death of Shaikh Rashid in October 1990, al Maktum took over his father's positions; vice president and premier of the UAE, and the ruler of the Dubai emirate. Under his leadership, Dubai has been developed successfully as a tourist resort for Europeans. ruler of the Dubai emirate in the United Arab Emirates, 1958-90, vice president of the UAE 1971-90, prime minister of the UAE 1979-90 Born in Dubai al Maktum belonged to the Aal bu Falasa section of the Bani Yas tribe. Following the founding of the United Arab Emirates in July 1971, a Supreme Council of seven rulers was established, with Shaikh Zaid al Nahyan of Abu Dhabi as its president and al Maktum its vice president. At the behest of Shaikh Zaid the Supreme Council called on al Maktum to become the UAE's prime minister in July 1979.

***

Al-Mansur (914-1002): (Muhammad ibn Abi-Amir al-Mansur Billah), Moorish regent of Cordoba, known in Spanish as Almanzor. He became steward to Princess Subh, wife of the caliph Hakim II, and under her patronage and by clever manipulation he rose to become (978) royal chamberlain for Hakim's successor, the young Hisham II. Al-Mansur kept Hisham in seclusion at his court and assumed complete control over the caliphate. A great warrior, he reorganized the army and undertook many campaigns against the Christian states of N Spain; he sacked Barcelona (985), razed the city of Leon (988), and destroyed the church and shrine of St. James at Santiago de Compostela (998). Before he died he appointed one of his sons as his successor.

***

Al-Mansur (754-775): [Arab., the victorious], 2nd Abbasid caliph and founder of the city of Baghdad. His name was in full Abu Ja'far Abd-Allah al-Mansur. He was brother and successor of consolidated his empire even though it was threatened by internal strife and foreign wars. He could not prevent the secession of Muslim Spain, however, under the Umayyad prince Abd ar-Rahman I. Mansur lived at first, as his brother had, near Kufa, but in 762 he began to build a new city, Baghdad. Abbasid caliph (754-75). Strongly suppressed Shii dissidents and moved the capital of the empire to the new city of Baghdad.

***

Al-Mansur, Abu Ja'far Abdallah Ibn Muhammad (714-775): Al-Mansur or Abu Ja'far Abdallah ibn Muhammad al-Mansur (95 AH – 158 AH (714 AD – 775 AD);[1] was the second Abbasid Caliph from 136 AH to 158 AH (754 AD – 775 AD).

Biography:
Al-Mansur was born at the home of the 'Abbasid family after their emigration from the Hejaz in 95 AH (714 AD). "His father, Muhammad, was reputedly a great-grandson of Abbas ibn Abd al-Muttalib, the youngest uncle of Mohammad; his mother, as described by 14th century Moorish historian Ali Ibn-Abd Allah's Roudh el Kartas was a "Berber woman given to his father." He reigned from Dhu al-Hijjah 136 AH until Dhu al-Hijjah 158 AH (754 AD – 775 AD). In 762 he founded as new imperial residence and palace city Madinat as-Salam (the city of peace), which became the core of the Imperial capital Baghdad.

Al-Mansur was concerned with the solidity of his regime after the death of his brother, Abu'l 'Abbas, who later become known as-Saffah (the blood spreader = bloody). In 755 he arranged the assassination of Abu Muslim. Abu Muslim was a loyal freed man from the eastern Iranian province of Khorasan who had led the Abbasid forces to victory over the Umayyads during the Third Islamic Civil War in 749-750. At the time of al-Mansur he was the subordinate, but undisputed ruler of Iran and Transoxiana. The assassination seems to have been made to preclude a power struggle in the empire.

During his reign, literature and scholarly work in the Islamic world began to emerge in full force, supported by new Abbasid tolerances for Persians and other groups suppressed by the Umayyads. Although the Umayyad caliph Hisham ibn Abd al-Malik had adopted Persian court practices, it was not until al-Mansur's reign that Persian literature and scholarship were truly appreciated in the Islamic world. *Shu'ubiya* was a literary movement among Persians expressing their belief that Persian art and culture was superior to that of the Arabs; the movement served to catalyze the emergence of Arab-Persian dialogues in the eighth century.

Perhaps more importantly than the emergence of Persian scholarship was the conversion of many non-Arabs to Islam. The Umayyads actively tried to discourage conversion in order to continue the collection of the jizya, or the tax on non-Muslims. The inclusiveness of the Abbasid regime, and that of al-Mansur, saw the expansion of Islam among its territory; in 750, roughly 8% of residents in the Caliphate were Muslims. This would double to 15% by the end of al-Mansur's reign.

In 756, Al-Mansur sent over 4,000 Arab mercenaries to assist the Chinese in the An Shi Rebellion against An Lushan. After the war, they remained in China. Al-Mansur was referred to as "A-p'u-ch'a-fo" in the Chinese T'ang Annals.

Al-Mansur died in 775 on his way to Mecca to make hajj. He was buried somewhere along the way in one of the hundreds of graves that had been dug in order to hide his body from the Umayyads. He was succeeded by his son, al-Mahdi.

According to a number of sources, the Imam Abu Hanifah an-Nu'man was imprisoned by al-Mansur. Imam Malik ibn Anas, the founder of another school of law, was also flogged during his rule, but al-Mansur himself did not condone this - in fact, it was his cousin, who was the governor of Madinah at the time, who did so. Al-Mansur, in turn, punished his cousin, and reattributed Imam Malik.

Character:

Al-Masudi in *Meadows of Gold* recounts a number of anecdotes that present aspects of this caliph's character.

A very impressive aspect of this caliph's character is that when he died he left in the treasury six hundred thousand Dirhams and fourteen million dinars.

Al-Mansur : **Abbasid**

Sunni Islam titles

Preceded by **Caliph of Islam** Succeeded by
As-Saffah 754 – 775 **Al-Mahdi**

***

Al-Ma'mun (786-833): (Abu al-Abbas Abd Allah al- Ma'mun), Abbasid caliph (813-33); son of Harun al-Rashid. He succeeded he brother al-Amin after a bitter civil war, but was unable to enter Baghdad until 819. He was himself one of the Mu'tazilites, holding that the Qur'an was created in time, i.e., that it was not an uncreated eternal existent. He persecuted the orthodox bitterly, Al-Ma'mun's reign was one of great cultural achievement, and he was especially interested in the work of scientists, particularly of those who knew Greek. He established (830) in Baghdad the *House of Wisdom,* an institution that translated Greek works into Arabic.

***

Al-Mutanabbi (915-968): Like Aramaic and Hebrew, Arabic is a Semitic language. However, unlike the other Semitic languages, Arabic is today a global language. As the *lingua franca* of the Arab world, Arabic is the official language of almost all the Middle Eastern and North African countries. Although the Abbasid era is generally considered to be the Golden Ago of Islamic science, philosophy and literature, it was during the reign of Harun al-Rashi and his son, al-Ma'mun, that Baghdad became the world's foremost center of philosophical, scientific and literary activities. The Arabs soon became the messengers of knowledge, wisdom and literature. Widely considered to be the greatest of all Arabic poets, al-Mutanabbi lived and thrived during this Golden Age of Arabic literature and poetry.

Abul Tayyib Ahmad ibn Hussain al-Jufi, better known as al-Mutanabbi (the 'would-be prophet'), was born in the southern Iraqi city of Kufah. He experienced considerable social and economic hardship as a child. His family was forced to leave their home and stay away for about two years on the outskirts of Samawa due to the Qarmatian insurrection.

When al-Mutanabbi was about twelve, his family returned to Kufah where he began to compose poetry. He was a voracious reader of Arabic poetry and became thoroughly familiar with the works of his illustrious predecessors like Hasan ibn Hani (better known as Abu Nuwas), Habib ibn Aws (also known as Abu Tammam), and Walid ibn Ubayd al-Buhturi. These celebrated Arabic poets lived and thrived in and around Baghdad during the early Abbasid period.

Al-Mutanabbi began his poetic career in Kufah where he became popular after composing his early poems. After leaving Kufah, he moved to Baghdad in 928. Lack of response from the locals forced him to leave Baghdad and go to Syria, where he stayed for about two years. Here he earned his livelihood working as a freelance singer and entertainer, but his failure to attain instant success had a profoundly negative psychological impact on him.

Al-Mutanabbi began to sympathize with the plight of this religious sect. Like the latter, he was a passionate activist and a pessimistic thinker whose philosophy of life was gloomier than even the Qarmatians. He eventually became a fully-fledged member of this group.

Later, when the Syrian authorities arrested a group of Qarmatians and threw them into prison, al-Mutanabbi happened to be one of them. It was Badr al-Kashani, the incumbent governor of Damascus, who recognized al-Mutanabbi's poetic talent and recruited him into his court. Soon his fame reached the Hamdanid ruler Sayf al-Dawlah, who recruited him to his famous court in Aleppo.

The Hamdanid dynasty was established during the early part of the tenth century by Abu al-Haji Abdullah and their rule extended all the way from northern Iraq and Syria, to Armenia in the north. Al-Mutanabbi stayed with the Hamdanid ruler for nearly a decade and during this period he regularly accompanied him on his military campaigns.

As a master of the Arabic language, al-Mutanabbi composed poetry for all occasions and to suit all tastes. His way with words, emotional spontaneity and, especially, his ability to capture the mood of the moment has remained unrivalled in the history of Arabic poetry. And although it is true that outstanding classical Arabic poets like Zuhayl ibn Abi Sulma, Tirimmah ibn Hakim, Bashshar ibn Burd, Abu Nuwas and Abu Tammam laid the foundations of early Arabic poetry, it was in the works of al-Mutanabbi that Arabic poetry reached its peak and greatest glory. As a Muslim and proud Arab, he was very fond of the history and symbolism of pre-Islamic Arabia, its culture and heritage. His poetry reflected nationalistic, philosophical, mystical, romantic as well as cultural themes.

After a decade at Sayf al-Dawlah's court in Aleppo, al-Mutanabbi moved to Egypt for a period, before returning to his native Kufah. From Kufah he went to Baghdad and eventually settled in the Persian city of Shiraz, where he graced the court of the Buwayhid (or Buyid) ruler Adud al-Dawlah for a long time. Ambushed by a group of desert bandits, al-Mutanabbi died at the age of fifty-three while he was on his way to Baghdad.

***

Al-Mu'tasim, Abu Ishaq Abbas (794-842): Abu Ishaq 'Abbas al-Mu'tasim ibn Harun (Arabic: 'Ishāq al-Mu'tasim ibn Harun) (794 – January 5, 842) was an Abbasid caliph (833-842). He succeeded his half-brother al-Ma'mun. In Arabian communities, al-Mu'tasim is an example of the magnanimity because of the famous incident "Wa Mu'tasimah".

Early life:

Abu Ishaq was born to a Turkic slave mother. His father was then caliph Harun al-Rashid, Abu Ishaq led the pilgrimage in A.H. 200 (815-816) and in 201. Abu Ishaq defeated these Kharijites

In A.H. 214 (829-830) Abu Ishaq subdued Egypt and executed some leading rebels. He returned in 215 to join al-Ma'mun in a campaign against the Byzantines. Abu Ishaq commanded forces that captured thirty Byzantine strongholds.

Caliphate:

Al-Tabari records that al-Mu'tasim was hailed caliph on August 9, 833. He promptly ordered the dismantling of al-Ma'mun's military base at Tyana. He sent Ishaq ibn Ibrahim ibn Mu'sab against a Khurramite revolt centered near Hamadhan. Ishaq soundly defeated the rebels. Their survivors, under Nasr, fled to the Byzantines.

One of the most difficult problems facing this Caliph, as faced his predecessor, was the uprising of Babak Khorramdin. Babak first rebelled in A.H. 201 (816-817) and overcame a number of caliphate forces sent against him. Finally, al-Mu'tasim provided clear instructions to his general al-Afshin Khaydhar ibn Kawus. Following these al-Afshin patiently overcame the rebel, securing a significant victory of this reign. Babak was brought to Samarra in A.H. 223 (837-838). He entered the city spectacularly riding on a splendid elephant. He was executed by his own executioner and his head sent to Khurasan. His brother was executed in Baghdad.

In that same year of Babak's death, the Byzantine emperor Theophilus launched an attack against a number of Abbasid fortresses, Al-Mu'tasim launched a well planned response. Al-Afshin met and defeated Theophilus on July 21, 838, known as Battle of Anzen. Ankara fell to the Muslim army of 50,000 men (with 50,000 camels and 20,000 mules) and from there they advanced on the stronghold of Amorium. A captive escaped and informed the caliph that one section of Amorium's wall was only a frontal façade. By concentrating bombardment here, al-Mu'tasim captured the city.

On his return home, he became aware of a serious conspiracy centered on al-Abbas ibn al-Ma'mun. A number of senior military commanders were involved. Al-Abbas was executed, as were, among others, al-Shah ibn Sahl, Amr al-Farghana, 'Ujayf ibn 'Anbasa and Akhmad ibn al-Khalil.

The ghilman (sing, Ghulam) were introduced to the Caliphate during al-Mu'tasim's reign. The ghilman were slave-soldiers taken as prisoners of war from conquered regions, in anticipation of the Mamluk system and made into caliphal guard. The *ghilman*, personally responsible only to the Caliph, were to revolt several times during the 860's, killed 4 caliphs and be replaced by the Mamluk system, based on captured Turkish children, trained and molded within the Islamic lands.

The *ghilman*, along with the S*hakiriya* which had been introduced in the reign of al-Ma'mun, had irritated the Arab regular soldiers of the Caliph's army. The Turkic and Armenian *ghilman* agitated the citizens of Baghdad, provoking riots in 836. The capital was moved to the new city of Samarra later that year, where it would remain until 892 when it was returned to Baghdad by al-Mu'tamid.

The Tahirid dynasty, which had come to prominence during al-Ma'mun's reign after the military province of Khurasan was granted to Tahir bin Husain, continued to grow in power. They received the governorships of Samarqand, Farghana and Herat. Unlike most provinces in the Abbasid Caliphate, which were closely governed by Baghdad and Samarra, the provinces under the control of the Tahirids were exempted from many tributes and oversight functions. The independence of the Tahirids contributed greatly to the decline of Abbasid supremacy in the east.

In A.H. 224 (838-839) Mazyar ibn Qarin who detested the Tahirids rebelled against them. Previously he had insisted on paying the taxes of his Caspian region directly to al-Mu'tasim's agent instead of to Abdallah ibn Tahir's. Al-Afshin, desiring to replace Abdallah as Khurasan's governor, intrigued with Mazyar. Mazyar imprisoned people from Sariya, demolished Amul's walls and fortified Tamis, causing apprehension in Jurjan.

Abdallah and al-Mu'tasim dispatched forces to quell the uprising. Abdallah's commander Hayyan ibn Jabalah convinced Mazyar's Qarin ibn Shahriyar to betray Mazyar. Qarin sent Hayyan Mazyar's brother and other commanders Qarin had taken by surprise. The people of Sariyah rose against Mazyar. Al-Quhyar ibn Qarin betrayed Mazyar. He was brought, along with his correspondence, some implicating al-Afshin, to al-Mu'tasim. Mazyar's commander al-Durri was defeated, captured and executed.

When Mazyar entered Samarra on a mule, al-Afshin was arrested and killed in May or June 841. The Khurramiyyah were never fully suppressed, although they slowly vanished during the reigns of succeeding Caliphs. Near the end of al-Mu'tasim's life there was an uprising in Palestine. Al-Mu'tasim sent Raja ibn Ayyub al-Hidari to restore order. Al-Hidari defeated the rebels and captured their leader Abu Harb al-Mubarqa.

The great Arab mathematician al-Kindi was employed by al-Mu'tasim and tutored the Caliph's son, al-Kindi had served at the *Bayt al-Hikma*, or *House of Wisdom*. He continued his studies in Greek geometry and algebra under the caliph's patronage.

Ideologically, al-Mu'tasim followed the footstep of his half-brother al-Ma'mun. He continued his predecessors support for heretical (agreed upon by the majority of scholars) Islamic sect of Mu'tazilah, applying his brutal military methods for torturing Imam Ahmad ibn Hanbal.

Death:

Al-Tabari states that al-Mu'tasim fell ill on October 21, 841. His regular doctor had died the previous year and the new physician did not follow the normal treatment and this was the cause of the caliph's illness. Al-Mu'tasim died on January 5, 842 (p. 207). This caliph is described by al-Tabari as having a relatively easy going nature, being kind, agreeable and charitable. He was succeeded by his son, al-Wathiq.

Sunni Islam titles
Preceded by **Caliph of Islam** Succeeded by
Al-Ma'mun 833-842 **Al-Wathiq**

***

Al-Mutawakkil, Ala Allah Ja'far ibn (821-861): Al-Mutawakkil 'Alā Allāh Ja'far ibn al-Mu'tasim (March 821 – December 861) was an Abbasid caliph who reigned in Samarra from 847 until 861. He succeeded his brother al-Wāthiq and is known for putting an end to the Mihna "ordeal", the Inquisition-like attempt by his predecessors to impose a single Mu'tazili version of Islam.

Life:

While al-Wathiq was caliph, the vizier, ibn Abd al-Malik, had poorly treated al-Mutawakkil. On September 22, 847, al-Mutawakkil had him arrested. The former vizier's property was plundered and he was tortured in his own iron maiden. He finally died on November 2. The caliph had others who had mistreated him in the previous reign punished.

In A.H. 235 (849) al-Mutawakkil had the prominent military commander Itakh al-Khazari seized in Baghdad. Itakh was imprisoned and died of thirst on December 21. One Mahmud ibn al-Faraj al-Nayshapuri arose claiming to be a prophet. He and some followers were arrested in Baghdad. He was imprisoned, beaten and on June 18, 850 he died.

In A.H. 237 (851-852) Armenians rebelled and defeated and killed the Abbasid governor. Al-Mutawakkil sent his general Bugha al-Kabir to handle this. Bugha scored successes this year and the following year he attacked and burned Tiblis, capturing Ishaq ibn Isma'il. The rebel leader was executed. That year (A.H. 238) the Byzantines attacked Damietta.

In A.H. 240 (854-855) the police chief in Homs killed a prominent person stirring an uprising. He was driven out. Al-Mutawakkil offered another police chief. When the next year saw a revolt against this new police chief, al-Mutawakkil had this firmly suppressed. As Christians had joined in the second round of disturbances, the caliph had Christians expelled from Homs.

Also in 241 occurred the firm response to the revolt by the Bujah, people of African descent just beyond Upper Egypt. They had been paying a tax on their gold mines. They ceased paying this, drove out Muslims working in the mines and terrified people in Upper Egypt. Al-Mutawakkil sent al-Qummi to restore order. Al-Qummi sent seven ships with supplies that enabled him to persevere despite the very harsh terrain of this distant territory. He retook the mines, pressed on to the Bujah royal stronghold and defeated the king in battle. The Bujah resumed payment of the tax.

On February 23, 856, there was an exchange of captives with the Byzantines. A second such exchange took place some four years later.

Al-Mutawakkil's reign is remembered for its many reforms and viewed as a golden age of the Abbasids. He would be the last great Abbasid caliph; after his death the dynasty would fall into a decline.

Al-Mutawakkil continued to rely on Turkish statesmen and slave soldiers to put down rebellions and lead battles against foreign empires, notably the Byzantines, from who Sicily was captured. His vizier, Al-Fath bin Khaqan, who was Turkish, was a famous figure of Al-Mutawakkil's era.

His reliance on Turkish soldiers would come back to haunt him. Al-Mutawakkil would have his Turkish commander-in-chief killed. This, coupled with his extreme attitudes towards the Shi'a, made his popularity decline rapidly.

Al-Mutawakkil was murdered by a Turkish soldier on December 11, 861 CE. Some have speculated that his murder was part of a plot hatched by his son, al-Muntasir, who had grown estranged from his father. Al-Muntasir feared his father was about to move against him and struck first.

Accomplishments:

Al-Mutawakkil was unlike his brother and father in that he was not known for having a thirst for knowledge, but he had an eye for magnificence and a hunger to build. The Great Mosque of Samarra was at its time, the largest mosque in the world; its minaret is a vast spiraling cone 55 m high with a spiral ramp. The mosque had 17 aisles and its wall were paneled with mosaics of dark blue glass.

The Great Mosque was just part of an extension of Samarra eastwards that built upon part of the walled royal hunting park. Al-Mutawakkil built as many as 20 palaces (the numbers vary in documents). Samarra became one of the largest cities of the ancient world; even the archaeological site of its ruins is one of the world's most extensive. The Caliph's building schemes extended in A.H. 245 (859-860) to a new city, *al-Ja'fariyya*, which al-Mutawakkil built on the Tigris some eighteen kilometers from Samarra. More water, and al-Mutawakkil ordered a canal to be built to divert water from the Tigris, entrusting the project to two courtiers, who ignored the talents of a local engineer of repute and entrusted the work to al-Farghani, the great astronomer and writer. Al-Farghani, who was not a specialist in public works, made a miscalculation and it appeared that the opening of the canal was too deep so that water from the river would only flow at near full flood.

News leaked to the infuriated caliph might have meant the heads of all concerned save for the gracious actions of the engineer, Sind ibn 'Ali, who vouched for the eventual success of the project, thus risking his own life. Al-Mutawakkil was assassinated shortly before the error became public.

Al-Mutawakkil was keen to involve himself in many religious debates, something that would show in his actions against different minorities. His father had tolerated the Shi'a Imam who taught and preached at Medina, and for the first years of his reign al-Mutawakkil continued the policy. Imam 'Ali al-Hadi's growing reputation inspired a letter from the Governor of Medina, 'Abdu l-Lah ibn Muhammad, suggesting that a coup was being plotted, and al-Mutawakkil extended an invitation to Samarra to the Imam, an offer he could not refuse. In Samarra, the Imam was kept under virtual house arrest and spied upon. However, no excuse to take action against him ever appeared. After al-Mutawakkil's death, his successor had the Imam poisoned: al-Hadī is buried at Samarra. The general Shi'a population faced repression and this was embodied in the destruction of the shrine of Hussayn ibn 'Alī, an action that was carried out ostensibly in order to stop pilgrimages to that site and the flogging and incarceration of the Alid Yahya ibn Umar.

Also during his reign, Al-Mutawakkil met the famous Byzantine theologian Constantine the Philosopher, who was sent to tighten the diplomatic relations between the Empire and the Caliphate in a state mission by the Emperor Michael III.

Of his sons, al-Muntasir succeeded him and ruled until his death in 862, al-Mu'tazz ruled from 866 to his overthrow in 869, al-Mu'eiyyad was murdered by Mu'tazz in 866, al-Mu'tamid reigned as Caliph in 870–892, and al-Muwaffaq was effective regent of the realm until his death in 891.

Al-Mutawakkil: Caliph of Baghdad

Reign 847-861
Dynasty Abbasid
Father al-Mu'tasim

Sunni Islam titles
Preceded by **Caliph of Islam** Succeeded by
Al-Wathiq 847-861 **Al-Muntasir**

***

Al-Nimeiri, Gaafar Muhammad (1930-2009): Sudanese statesman. He led campaigns against rebels in the southern Sudan in the 1950s and joined in leftist attempts to overthrow the civilian government. Following a coup he became Prime Minister in 1969 and Chairman of the Revolutionary Command Council. President from 1971 to 1985, in 1972 he ended the civil war in the southern Sudan, granting it local autonomy. A devout Muslim, he proposed a new Islamic Constitution in December 1984 that made Islamic law apply to everyone. This was opposed in southern Sudan, were the majority of the population are not Muslim, and a military coup overthrew him in 1985.

***

Al Quwatli, Shukri (1891-1967): *Syrian politician; president 1943-49, 1955-58* Born into a rich land-owning family in Damascus, Quwalti was active in Arab nationalist politics as a youth, joining the clandestine al Fatat society. Following the Franco-Syrian Treaty of 1936, Quwalti became minister of defense and finance from 1936-39. After a brief exile from 1941-43, when the pro-Nazi French government, based in Vichy, controlled Syria, he returned to Damascus to led the National Bloc. In February 1958, Quwalti resigned, proposing Gamal Abdul Nasser as president of the United Arab Republic.

***

Al Sabah, Abdullah III ibn Salim I (1895-1965): *Ruler of Kuwait, 1950-65* Son of Shaikh Salim I, al Sabah, was ten years younger than his rival in the Jaber branch, Shaikh Ahmad I ibn Jaber II al Sabah, and at odds with the latter's pro-British leanings. Soon after al Sabah's accession to the throne in 1950, the Iranian oil crisis of 1951-53 boosted Kuwait's petroleum output. By 1955 Kuwait had become the leading oil exporter in the Gulf, a position it maintained until the end of al Sabah's rule. As a result of London's complicity in the Suez War in 1956, anti-British feelings arose. Al Sabah demanded greater latitude in home affairs, and Britain met him halfway. In September 1960 Kuwait became a founder member of the Organization of Petroleum Exporting Countries (OPEC). Following abrogation of the 1899 Anglo-Kuwaiti Agreement in June 1961, Britain officially recognized Kuwait as an independent country. in November 1962 al Sabah promulgated a constitution drafted by an assembly nominated by him.

***

Al Sabah, Ahmad I ivn Jabar II (1885-1950): *Ruler of Kuwait, 1921-50* Son of Shaikh Jabar II al Sabah, al Sabah was the first in the Jabar line to reign over the principality. However, there was an improvement in relations with Najd, which became part of Saudi Arabia in 1932. Al Sabah granted the first Oil concession in 1934 to Western-owned Kuwait Oil Company (KOC). But it was not until 1938 that petroleum was found in commercial quantities. In the meantime al Sabah treated the fees and advance royalties paid by the KOC as his personal property. The sudden death in April 1939 or King Ghazi of Iraq, who had backed the opposition, further helped al Sabah. During the Second World War, ignoring the pro-Axis sentiment prevalent among his subjects, al Sabah, sided with Britain as required by the 1899 Anglo-Kuwaiti Agreement.

***

Al Sabah, Jaber III ibn Ahmad I (1926-2006): *ruler of Kuwait, 1977—* Son of Shaikh Ahmad I ibn Jaber II Al Sabah, al Sabah continued the domestic policies of his predecessor, Shaikh Sabah II ibn Salim I al Sabah, and showed no sign of reviving the National Assembly, which had been dissolved in 1976. in early 1980 al Sabah appointed a constitutional committee to recommend amendments to the constitution. Al Sabah's policy of aiding Iraq in its war with Iran, both financially and logistically, was unpopular with the Shi'as, who warned Kuwait to stay neutral. On 25 May 1985 a suicide bomber driving a car packed with explosives made an unsuccessful attempt to assassinate al Sabah. Kuwait's deepening alliance with Iraq in its war with Iran made its oil tankers vulnerable to attacks by Tehran. In the spring of 1987 al Sabah secured the assistance of the U.S. Navy, which protected Kuwaiti oil tankers by transferring them to a U.S.-based company. Once the Iran-Iraq hostilities ended in August 1988, popular pressure built up for the restoration of parliament.

He tried to use the $12-$14 billion Kuwait had loaned to Iraq during the Iran-Iraq War as a lever to settle a border dispute with Iraq that dated back to 1961. He failed. In September he signed a ten-year-defense cooperation agreement with the United States, allowing it to stockpile military supplies and conduct training exercises, as well as granting it access to Kuwait ports and airfields and stationing of American troops. In 1999, due to the recurring conflict between parliamentarians and the cabinet, he dissolved the National Assembly a year earlier. Al Sabah cooperated with the Bush administration in its preparations for invading Iraq in 2003 to the extent of letting U.S. forces take over nearly two-thirds of his country.

***

Al Sabah, Sabah III ibn Salim I (1913-1977): *ruler of Kuwait, 1965-77* Son of Shaikh Salim I ibn Mubarak, al Sabah began his career as commander of the police force, a position he occupied from 1938 to 1959. On becoming ruler in November 1965, al Sabah nominated a new cabinet. In the June 1967 and October 1973 Arab-Israeli Wars, al Sabah joined the Arab oil embargo against Israel's allies. The steep petroleum price rise in 1973-74 benefited al Sabah's regime. the Lebanese Civil War, which started in April 1975 and involved the Palestinians living there, had an impact on Kuwait as it had a quarter of million Palestinian residents.

***

Al Shaabi, Qahtan Muhammad (1920-1981): South Yemeni politician; president, 1967-69 Born into a notable family in the Lahej principality of the Aden Protectorate, al Shaabi received a secular education before joining the Lahej land department. He negotiated South Yemen's independence with the British in Geneva in November 1967. The radical faction deposed al Shaabi in June 1969. He was jailed in April 1970, and after his release he stayed away from public life.

***

Al Sadr, Musa (1928-1978): *Lebanese/Iranian Islamic leader* Born into a religious family of Lebanese origin in Qom, al Sadr was educated in secular and Islamic traditions before being sent to Tehran University where he acquired a postgraduate degree in Islamic studies in 1956. Al Sadr then acquired Lebanese citizenship. In 1967 he formed the Higher Shi'a Communal Council (HSCC) the first of its kind in the country, becoming a leading spokesman of Shi'as. When the Lebanese Civil War erupted in April 1975, al Sadr realized that unlike most other important religious sects, Shi'as did not have their own militia. during a trip to Libya in August 1978, al Sadr "disappeared". Libya insisted that Al Sadr had left by plane for Italy, but his followers alleged that he had been detained or assassinated by his Libya hosts.

***

Al Said, Nuri (1888-1958): *Iraqi military officer and politician; prime minister, 1930-32, 1939-40, 1941-44, 1946-47, 1949, 1950-52, 1954-57, 1958* Born in Baghdad to a Sunni family of mixed Arab-Kurdish origin, in 1914 he joined the clandestine Arab al Ahd, Rashid Ali Gailani, which lasted until January 1941. He declared war against Germany in 1943. Arab League, inspired by the British, had been done before Faisal II came of age in 1953-54. In 1957 he endorsed the Eisenhower Doctrine, which offered help to Middle Eastern countries threatened by world communism or its regional allies. Free Officer's launched a successful coup in July 1958; it assassinated al Said along with the member of the royal family.

***

Al Saud, Saud ibn Abdul Aziz (1902-1969): *King of Saudi Arabia, 1953-64* After the death of his elder brother, Turki ibn Abdul Aziz (b. 1900), in 1919 Saud became the eldest son of King Abdul Aziz ibn Abdul Rahman al Saud. On succeeding his father, Saud retained the premiership and named Faisal crown prince. After the republican coup in North Yemen in 1962, which implicitly threatened the future of the Saudi monarch, Saud ceded his executive powers once again to Faisal, and Saudi Arabia became involved in the North Yemeni Civil War. Saud went into exile in Europe. In 1966, when rivalry between Egyptian president Gamal Abdul Nasser and King Faisal intensified, Nasser allowed Saud to settle in Cairo to strengthen his own anti-Faisal position. But when, following Egypt's defeat in the June 1967 Arab-Israeli War, Nasser sought a rapprochement with Faisal, Saud lost his importance. He died in Athens, Greece, in February 1969, leaving behind fifty-two sons and fifty-five daughters.

***

Al-Shafi'i (767-820): If *Shari'ah* (Islamic law) is a vast and complex subject, then the 'science of Islamic jurisprudence' (or *Usul al-Fiqh*) is even more complex and sophisticated. This important and challenging task was undertaken by al-Shafi'i, who is today widely considered to be the 'father of the science of Islamic jurisprudence'.

Abu Abdullah Muhammad ibn Idris al-Shafi'i was born in the city of Gaza in southern Palestine, and his family claimed to be direct descendants of the Prophet Muhammad. He grew up there and received elementary education in Arabic language and grammar, and committed the entire Qur'an to memory before he was seven.

From the outset, Shafi'i's prodigious memory and sharp intellect endeared him to his teachers. In Madinah, he devoted all his time and energy to the pursuit of *Hadith* and *Fiqh*, and studied the *al-Muwatta* under Malik's personal supervision. His stay in Madinah proved so productive that Malik subsequently asked him to become his teaching assistant. by the time Malik died in 795, Shafi'i had already become recognized throughout Madinah as an eminent Islamic scholar and jurist.

The thirty-six year old Shafi'i was summoned by Harun al-Rashid, the famous Abbasid Caliph, to appear before him, along with the other alleged conspirators to answer the charges. The following day, Shafi'i went to the Caliph's court and, one by one, he refuted all the charges leveled against him. As a great patron of learning and scholarship, the Caliph deeply admired Shafi'i's intellectual brilliance. The Caliph not only spared Shafi'i's life, he also requested that he stay in Baghdad and help him promote learning and scholarship throughout the land. In Baghdad Shafi'i conducted advanced research in *Fiqh* and *Hadith* under the guidance of its leading scholars, and regularly attended the lectures of Muhammad ibn al-Hasan al-Shaybani.

In 804 Shafi'i left Baghdad and moved to Syria, and from there he went to Makkah where he began to deliver regular lectures on *Fiqh* and *Hadith* at the *Haram al-Sharif* (the Sacred Mosque). After six years of teaching and travelling across Syria and Arabia, Shafi'i returned to Baghdad in 810 only to find al-Ma'mun, the son and successor of Caliph Harun al-Rashid, on the Abbasid throne. He quietly left Baghdad in 814 and proceeded to Egypt. Here he came into contact with scores of renowned Islamic scholars and jurists, including Rabi ibn Sulaiman al-Marali and Abu Ibrahim ibn Yahya al-Muzani.

Shafi'i recorded his ideas and thoughts in his celebrated *Kitab al-Umm* (The Book of Essence) and *al-Risalah* (The Treatise). In these two books, he – for the very first time in Islamic history – systematically formulated the fundamental principles of the science of Islamic jurisprudence. He was so successful in his task that a Shafi'i *Madh'hab* (or school of legal thought) subsequently emerged and spread across the Muslim world. Today, this *Madh'hab* is widely followed in

Islamic Leaders

Egypt, Yemen, Indonesia, Malaysia, and parts of South America and East Africa.

Shafi'i died and was buried in al-Fustat, Egypt at the age of fifty-three. Later, in 1211, the Ayyubid ruler Afdal built an impressive mausoleum, which still stands to this day, as a tribute to his memory.

***

Al Sistani, Ali Husseini (1930–   ): *Iraqi religious leader* Born into a Shi'a religious family in Iran Mashhad, Sistani pursued his theological studies in Qom, where he became a student of Ayatollah Muhammad Hussein Borujerdi. Following the death in 1992 of Khoei whose funeral prayer was performed by him, the mantle of the *marja-e Taqlid* (Arabic: source of emulation) passed not to him. After the deposition of Saddam Hussein in April 2003, the followers of al Sadr's grandson, Moqtada al Sadr, demanded that Sistani leave Najaf.

***

Al-Tabari (839-923): After the emergence of Islam in Arabia in the seventh century, the Arabs – for the first time in their history – embraced learning and education with much interest and enthusiasm. The study of history thus became one of the foremost preoccupations of the early Muslim scholars, thinkers and writers. Although Ibn Khaldun is today widely considered to be the most influential Muslim historian of all time, the coveted title of 'father of Islamic history' has rightly been conferred on al-Tabari for his monumental contribution to Islamic historiography.

Abu Ja'far Muhammad ibn Jarir ibn Yazid al-Tabari was born in Amul in the Persian province of Tabaristan, now in eastern Azerbaijan. After learning Arabic and Persian, young al-Tabari successfully committed the entire Qur'an to memory when he was only seven. He then moved to the historic Persian city of Rayy to pursue further education. Unlike Amul, Rayy was a flourishing center of Islamic learning and commercial activity.

Supported financially by his wealthy father, al-Tabari devoted himself to his studies and devoured books and treatises on all aspects of traditional Islamic sciences. From Rayy he went to Baghdad, the capital of the Abbasid Empire, to study under the guidance of the famous Ahmad ibn Hanbal. But when he arrived in Baghdad, at the age of twenty, he discovered than Ahmad ibn Hanbal had already passed away. So he moved to Basrah and eventually settled in Kufah. Shocked and dismayed by the political chaos and confusion which ensued following the murder of Abbasid Caliph Mutawakkil ala Allah by his Turkish bodyguard in 861, the quiet, peaceful and studious al-Tabari left Kufah and moved to Syria.

During this period he was forced to go without any proper meals, surviving on biscuits and water only. In fact, during this period he memorized a large number of Prophetic traditions, collected information about the life and times of the Prophet, and became thoroughly familiar with the views and opinions of the Prophet's companions on all aspects of Islam. As expected, al-Tabari travelled extensively in pursuit of knowledge and studied in Damascus, Makkah and Egypt, before finally returning to Baghdad.

Despite being a strict adherent of the Prophetic *sunnah* (norms and ethos), he never married and remained a confirmed bachelor all his life. He later became one of the most influential Islamic scholars of all time. He led a simple, pious and austere lifestyle, and deliberately shunned the wealth and luxuries of this world, remaining totally focused on his intellectual pursuits.

As a jurist, al-Tabari initially followed the school of Abu Hanifah but, after carrying out a thorough and systematic study of *Maliki*, *shafi'i* and *Hanbali Fiqh*, he became an adherent of *shafi'i* jurisprudence. Based on his interpretation of Islamic jurisprudence, a different school of Islamic legal thought known as the *Jariri Madh'hab* later emerged in the Muslim world. Since he was thoroughly acquainted with all the prominent schools of Islamic jurisprudence, his ideas and thoughts were variously influenced by all of them.

Yet it is true that al-Tabari is today most famous for his contribution in the field of *Tafsir*. He was in his sixties when he vowed to write two large books; one on the Qur'an and the other on history. He used to write more than twenty pages daily for around forty years. His Qur'anic commentary consisted of more than three thousand pages and was published in thirty bulky volumes. It is one of the largest commentaries ever written on the Qur'an. As a commentator on the Qur'an, al-Tabari was a strict traditionalist who relied entirely on the Prophetic traditions. Overall, his commentary is nothing short of a remarkable contribution in the field of *Tafsir*.

Al-Tabari's *Kitab Tarikh al-Rusul wa'l Muluk* (The Book of the History of Prophets and Kings) must be considered one of the greatest works of history ever written. Beginning with an account of creation, the book traced the journey of humanity through the lives and careers of all the prominent Prophets including the final Messenger of God, Muhammad, his four rightly-guided Caliphs and the reign of the Umayyads before concluding with an entry in 915. Its English edition consists of thirty-eight bulky volumes, ten thousand pages in total. Al-

Tabari was very much like Herodotus, the ancient Greek historian, who also recorded his data without critically examining them. He left the task of sifting the wheat from the chaff to his successors such as al-Baladhuri, al-Isfahani, al-Miskawayh, Thabit ibn Sinan and Ibn al-Athir. Al-Tabari passed away at the ripe old age of around eighty.

***

Al-Tahtawi, Rifah (1801-1873): An Egyptian Alim who described his passionate appreciation of European society in his published diary, was responsible for the translation of European books into Arabic and promoted the idea of modernization in Egypt.

***

Al Thani, Ali ibn Abdullah (1894-1976): *ruler of Qatar, 1948-60* Son of Shaikh Abdullah ibn Qasim, al Thani was born in Doha. With the death in 1947 of his elder brother, Hamad, the heir apparent and deputy ruler, al Thani was named to succeed him. made him abdicate in 1960 in favor of his son, Ahmad.

***

Al Thani, Hamad ibn Khalifa (1932-   ): *ruler of Qatar, 1995-* Born in Doha, al Thani was educated there. After graduating from the Royal Military Academy in Sandhurst, Britain, in 1971, he joined the Qatari military as a major. By the early 1990s he was involved in determining major domestic and foreign policies. In June 1995, while his father, Shaikh Khalifa ibn Hamad al Thani, was in Geneva, Switzerland, al Thani mounted a bloodless coup and ascended the throne. al Thani visited Washington to offer condolences to U.S. President George W. Bush after the September 11 2001 terrorist attacks on New York and Washington. The next year he allowed the Pentagon to shift most of its military facilities from Al Kharj air base in Saudi Arabia to al Ubaid air base in Qatar. This base became the operational headquarters of the U.S. Central Command for the launching of the Operation Iraqi Freedom in March 2003 to overthrow the regime of President Saddam Hussein of Iraq.

***

Al Utaiba, Juheiman ibn Saif (1939-1980): *Saudi Arabian Islamic leader* Born in Sajir in Qasim province, al Utaiba was a grandson of an Ikhwan militant who died in 1929 in battle against Abdul Aziz al Saud. Al

Uthaiba left the National Guard in 1972 and enrolled at the Islamic University of Medina, where he became a student of Shaikh Abdul Aziz ibn Abdullah al Baz, who advocated a return to the letter of the Qur'an and the *sunnah*. On return to his native province, al Utaiba began to preach along the lines of the founder of Wahhabi doctrine, Shaikh Abdul Wahhab (1703-87). a popular poet and writer on Islam, al Utaiba set up cells in numerous Bedouin settlements in Qasim. Resorting to clandestine preaching, al Utaiba developed the idea of Mahdi, which he allied to the traditional Wahhabi doctrine. On New Year's Eve, hundreds of al Utaiba's followers converged on the Grand Mosque in Mecca, where they had concealed arms in the cellars and retreats of the vast complex. Qahtani was one of the 117 rebels killed in the operations, and al Utaiba was one of the 67 to be decapitated in January 1980.

***

Al-Zarqali (1028–1087): Was an Andalusian artisan, skilled in working sheet metal, who became a famous maker of astronomical equipment, an astronomer and a mathematician. He developed a new design for a highly accurate astrolabe which was used for centuries afterwards. He constructed a famous water clock that attracted much attention in Toledo for centuries. He discovered that the Sun's apogee moves slowly relative to the fixed stars, and obtained a very good estimate for its rate of change.

***

Al-Zawahiri, Ayman Muhammad Rabie (1951-   ): Aka Abu Muhammad; Muhammad Ibrahim): *Egyptian Islamist ideologue-politician* Son of pharmacology professor at Cairo University, and grandson of Rabiaa Zawahiri, the Grand Shaikh of al Azhar University, Zawahiri graduated as a surgeon from Cairo University's medical school in 1978. He was one of the founders of Al Jihad at Islami, headed by Ismail Tantawi. In 1986 Azwahiri traveled to Pakistan and joined the medical corps in Peshawar to serve the Islamist Mujahedin fighting the Soviets and the Soviet-backed regime in Afghanistan. In 1997, Zawahiri moved to Afghanistan to join bin Laden there.

It was there that in February 1998, Al Jihad, led by Zawahiri, allied with the Al Qaida network of bin Laden to form the World Islamic Front for Jihad against Crusades and Jews, with Al Jihad members concentrating on forging documents. On 4 November 1998 a U.S. Federal grand jury returned a 238-count indictment—covering 227 murders caused by the bombing of the American embassies in Nairobi and Dar as Salam in August 1998 and eleven other charges—against bin Laden and sixteen others, including Zawahiri, and charging them with leading a terrorist conspiracy from 1989 to the present, working in concert with other terrorists to build weapons and attack American military installations.

***

Ali Ibn Abi Talib (599-661): Ali migrated to Medina shortly after Muhammad did. Once there Muhammad told Ali that God had ordered Muhammad to give his daughter, Fatimah, to Ali in marriage. For the ten years that Muhammad led the community in Medina, Ali was extremely active in his service, leading parties of warriors on battles, and carrying messages and orders. Ali took part in the early caravan raids from Mecca and later in almost all the battles fought by the nascent Muslim community.

Ali was appointed Caliph by the Companions of Muhammad (the *Sahaba*) in Medina after the assassination of the third caliph, Uthman ibn Affan. He encountered defiance and civil war during his reign. In 661, Ali was attacked one morning while worshipping in the mosque of Kufa, and died a few days later.

Ali retains his stature as an authority on Qur'anic exegesis, Islamic jurisprudence and religious though. Ali holds a high position in almost all Sufi orders which trace their lineage through him to Muhammad. Ali's influence has been important throughout Islamic history.

In Mecca, Birth and childhood:

Ali's father Abu Talib was the custodian of the Kaaba and a sheikh of the Banu Hashim, an important branch of the powerful Quraysh tribe. He was also an uncle of Muhammad. Ali's mother, Fatima bint Asad, also belonged to Banu Hashim, making Ali a descendant of Ishmael, the son of Ibrahim or Abraham.

Many sources, especially Shi'a ones, attest that during Mohammad's time Ali was born inside the Kaaba in the city of Mecca, where he stayed with his mother for three days. According to a tradition, Muhammad was the first person whom Ali saw as he took the newborn in his hands. Muhammad named him Ali, meaning "the exalted one".

Muhammad had a close relationship with Ali's parents. When Muhammad was orphaned and later lost his grandfather Abdul Muttalib, Ali's father took him into his house. Ali was born two or three years after Muhammad married Khadijah bint Khuwaylid. When Ali was five or six years old, a famine occurred in and around Mecca, affecting the economic conditions of Ali's father, who had a large family to support. Muhammad took Ali into his home to raise him.

Acceptance of Islam:
The second period of Ali's life begins in 610 when he declared Islam at age 10 and ends with the Hijra of Muhammad to Medina in 622. When Muhammad reported that he had received a divine revelation, Ali, then only about ten years old, believed him and professed to Islam. According to Ibn Ishaq and some other authorities, Ali was the first male to embrace Islam. Being the first Muslim in relation to Zayd or Abu Bakr.

Shi'a doctrine asserts that in keeping with Ali's divine mission, he accepted Islam before he took part in any pre-Islamic Meccan traditional religion rites, regarded by Muslims as polytheistic (see shirk) or paganistic. The Sunnis also use the honorific *Karam Allahu Wajhahu*, which means "God's Favor upon his Face." He was known to have broken idols in the mold of Abraham and asked people why they worshipped something they made themselves.

After declaration of Islam:
For three years Muhammad invited people to Islam in secret, then he started inviting publicly. When, according to the Quran, he was commanded to invite his close relatives to come to Islam he gathered the Banu Hashim clan in a ceremony.

According to al-Tabari, Ibn Athir and Abu al-Fida, Muhammad announced at invitational events that whoever assisted him in his invitation would become his brother, trustee and successor. Only Ali, who was thirteen or fourteen years old, stepped forward to help him. This invitation was repeated three time, but Ali was the only person who answered Muhammad. Muhammad declared that Ali was his brother, inheritor and vice-regent and people must obey him. Most of the adults present were uncles of Ali and Muhammad, and Abu Lahab laughed at them and declared to Abu Talib that he must bow down to his own son, as Ali was now his Emir. This event is known as the Hadith of Warning.

During the persecution of Muslims and boycott of the Banu Hashim in Mecca, Ali stood firmly in support of Muhammad.

Migration to Medina:
In 622, the year of Muhammad's migration to Yathrib (now Medina), Ali risked his life by sleeping in Muhammad's bed to impersonate him and thwart an assassination plot so that Muhammad could escape in safety. This night called *Laylat al-Mabit*.

Ali survived the plot, but risked his life against by staying in Mecca to carry out Muhammad's instructions: to restore to their owners all the goods and properties that had been entrusted to Muhammad for safekeeping. Ali then went to Medina with his mother, Muhammad's daughter Fatimah and two other women.

In Medina, During Muhammad's era:
Muhammad in Medina and Military career of Ali

Ali was 22 or 23 years old when he migrated to Medina. When Muhammad was creating bonds of brotherhood among his companions, he selected Ali as his brother. For the ten years that Muhammad led the community in Medina, Ali was extremely active in his service as his secretary and deputy, serving in his armies, the bearer of his banner in every battle, leading parties of warriors on raids, and carrying messages and orders. As one of Muhammad's lieutenants, and later his son-in-law, Ali was a person of authority and standing in the Muslim community.

Family life, *Ali marital life:*

In 623, Muhammad told Ali that God ordered him to give his daughter Fatimah Zahra to Ali in marriage. Muhammad said to Fatimah: "I have married you to the dearest of my family to me." This family is glorified by Muhammad frequently and he declared them as his *Ahl al-Bayt* in events such as Mubahala and Hadith like the Hadith of the Event of the Cloak. They were also glorified in the Quran in several cases such as the "verse of purification".

Ali had four children born to Fatimah, the only child of Muhammad to have surviving progeny. Their two sons (Hasan and Husain) were cited by Muhammad to be his own sons, honored numerous times in his lifetime and titled "the leaders of the youth of Jannah" (Heaven, the hereafter.)

At the beginning they were extremely poor. For several years after his marriage, Fatimah did all of the household work by herself. The shoulder on which she carried pitchers of water from the well was swollen and the hand with which she worked the hand mill to grind corn were often covered with blisters. Fatimah vouched to take care of the household work, make dough, bake bread, and clean the house; in return, Ali vouched to take care of the outside work such as gathering firewood, and bringing food. Their circumstances were akin to many of the Muslims at the time and only improved following the Battle of Khaybar when the wealth of Khaybar was distributed among the poor. When the economic situations of the Muslims become better, Fatimah gained some maids but treated them like her family and performed the house duties with them.

In battles:

With the exception of the Battle of Tabouk, Ali took part in all battles and expeditions fought for Islam. Ali first distinguished himself as a warrior in 624 at the Battle of Badr. He defeated the Umayyad champion Walid ibn Utba as well as many other Meccan soldiers.

Ali was prominent at the Battle of Uhud, as well as many other battles where he wielded a bifurcated sword known as Zulfiqar. He had the special role of protecting Muhammad when most of the Muslim army fled from the battle of Uhud and it was said "There is no brave youth except Ali and there is no sword which renders service except Zulfiqar." He was commander of the Muslim army in the Battle of Khaybar. Following this battle Mohammad gave Ali the name *Asadullah*, which in Arabic means "Lion of Allah" or "Lion of God". Ali also defended Muhammad in the Battle of Hunayn in 630.

Missions for Islam:

Muhammad designated Ali as one of the scribes who would write down the text of the Quran, which had been revealed to Muhammad during the previous two decades. He was instructed to write down the Treaty of Hudaybiyyah, the peace treaty between Muhammad and the Quraysh in 628. Ali was so reliable and trustworthy that Muhammad asked him to carry the messages and declare the orders. In 630, Ali recited to a large fathering of pilgrims in Mecca a portion of the Quran that declared Muhammad and the Islamic community were no longer bound by agreements made earlier with Arab polytheists. During the Conquest of Mecca in 630, Muhammad asked Ali to guarantee that the conquest would be bloodless. He ordered Ali to break all the idols worshipped by the Banu Aus, Banu Khazraj, Tayy, and those in the Kaaba to purify it after its defilement by the polytheism of the pre-Islamic era. Ali was sent to Yemen one year later to spread the teachings of Islam. He was also charged with settling several disputes and putting down the uprisings of various tribes.

The incident of Mubahala:

According to Hadith collections, in 631 an Arab Christian envoy from Najran (currently in northern Yemen and partly in Saudi Arabia) came to Muhammad to argue which of the two parties erred in its doctrine concerning Jesus. Muhammad, to prove to them that he is a prophet, brought his daughter Fatimah, Ali and his grandchildren Hasan and Husayn. Considered it the proof for Ali's right for Caliphate due to Allah made Ali like the self of Muhammad.

Ghadir Khumm;

As Muhammad was returning from his last pilgrimage in 632, he made some statements about Ali that are interpreted very differently by Sunnis and Shi'as. He halted the caravan at Ghadir Khumm, gathered the returning pilgrims for communal prayer and began to address them:

> "O people, I am a human being. I am about to receive a message from my Lord and I, in response to Allah's call, (would bid good-bye to you), but I am leaving among you two weighty things: the one being the Book of Allah (Quran) in which there is right guidance and light, so hold fast to the Book of Allah and adhere to it. He exhorted (us) (to hold fast) to the Book of Allah and then said: The second you are the members of my household I remind you (of your duties) to the members of my family."

Some Sunni and all Shi'a sources report that then he called *Ali ibn Abu Talib* to his sides, took his hand and raised it up declaring:

> For whoever I am a Mawla of, then Ali is his Mawla.

Shi'as regard these statements as constituting the investiture of Ali as the successor of Muhammad and as the first Imam; by contrast, Sunnis take them only as an expression of Muhammad's closeness to Ali and of his wish that Ali, as his cousin and son-in-law, inherit his family responsibilities upon his death. Many Sufis also interpret the episode as the transfer of Muhammad's spiritual power and authority to Ali, whom they regard as the wali par excellence.

Succession to Muhammad;

After uniting the Arabian tribes into a single Muslim religious polity in the last years of his life, Muhammad's death in 632 signaled disagreement over who would succeed him as leader of the Muslim community. While Ali and the rest of Muhammad's close family were washing his body for burial, at a gathering attended by a small group of Muslims at Saqifah, a close companion of Muhammad named Abu Bakr was nominated for the leadership of the community. Others added their support and Abu Bakr was made the first caliph. The choice of Abu Bakr disputed by some of the Muhammad's companions, who held that Ali had been designated his successor by Muhammad himself.

Later when Fatimah and Ali sought aid from the Companions in the matter of his right to the caliphate, they answered, O daughter of the Messenger of God! We have given our allegiance to Abu Bakr. If Ali had come to us before this, we would certainly not have abandoned him. Ali said, 'Was it fitting that we should wrangle over the caliphate even before the Prophet was buried?'

Following his election to the caliphate, Abu Bakr and Umar with a few other companions headed to Fatimah's house to force Ali and his supporters who had gathered there give their allegiance to Abu Bakr. Then, it is alleged that Umar threatened to set the house on fire unless they came out and swore allegiance with Abu Bakr. Ali did not have actively assert his own right because he did not want to throw the nascent Muslim community into strife.

This contentious issue caused Muslims to later split into two groups, Sunni and Shi'a. Sunnis assert that even though Muhammad never appointed a successor, Abu Bakr was elected first caliph by the Muslim community. The Sunnis recognize the first four caliphs as Muhammad's rightful successors. Shi'as believe that Muhammad explicitly named Ali as his successor at Ghadir Khumm and Muslim leadership belonged to him which had been determined by divine order.

Ali himself was firmly convinced of his legitimacy for caliphate based on his close kinship with Muhammad, his intimate association and his knowledge of Islam and his merits in serving its cause. He told Abu Bakr that his delay in pledging allegiance (*Bay'ah*) as caliph was based on his belief of his own prior title.

According to Shi'a historical reports, Ali maintained his right to the caliphate and said:

> I watched the plundering of my inheritance till the first one went his way but handed over the Caliphate to Ibn al-Khattab after himself.

Inheritance:
Hadith of Muhammad's inheritance

After Muhammad died, his daughter Fatimah asked Abu Bakr to turn over their property, the lands of Fadak and Khaybar. Abu Bakr refused and told her that prophets did not have any legacy and that Fadak belonged to the Muslim community. Fatimah became angry and stopped speaking to Abu Bakr, and continued assuming that attitude until she died.

After Fatima's death Ali again claimed her inheritance during Umar's era, but was denied with the same argument. Umar, the caliph who was famous as Umar Sanni (second Umar), did restore the estates in Medina to sons of 'Abbas ibn 'Abd al-Muttalib, as representative of Muhammad's clan, the Banu Hashim. The properties in Khaybar and Fadak were retained as state property.

Life after Muhammad:
Origin and development of the Quran:

Another part of Ali's life started in 632 after death of Muhammad and lasted until assassination of Uthman Ibn Affan, the third caliph in 656. During these years, Ali neither took part in any battle or conquest. Nor did he assume any executive position. He withdrew from political affairs, especially after the death of his wife, Fatima Zahra. He used his time to serve his family and worked as a farmer. Ali dug a lot of wells and planted gardens near Medina and endowed them for public use. These wells are known today as *Abar Ali* ("Ali's wells").

Ali compiled a complete version of the Quran, M*us'haf*, six months after the death of Muhammad. The volume was completed and carried by camel to show to other people of Medina. The order of this *Mus'haf* differed from that which was gathered later during the Uthmanic era. This book was rejected by several people when he showed it to them. Despite this, Ali made no resistance against *standardized Mus'haf*.

Ali and the Rashidun Caliphs:
Rashidun and The election of Uthman

Ali did not give his oath of allegiance to Abu Bakr until sometime after the death of his wife, Fatimah. Ali participated in the funeral of Abu Baks but did not participate in the Ridda Wars.

He pledged allegiance to the second caliph Umar ibn Khattab and helped him as a trusted advisor. Umar particularly relied upon Ali as the Chief Judge of Medina. He also advised Umar to set Hijra as the beginning of the Islamic calendar.

Ali was one of the electoral council to choose the third caliph which was appointed by Umar. Although Ali was one of the two major candidates, but the council's arrangement was against him. Abdur Rahman offered the caliphate to Ali on the condition that he should rule in accordance with the Quran, the example set by Muhammad, and the precedents established by the first two caliphs. Ali rejected the third condition while Uthman accepted it. Most of the electors supported Uthman and Ali was reluctantly urged to accept him.

Siege of Uthman:
Uthman Ibn Affan, expressed generosity toward his kin, Banu Abd-Shams, who seemed to dominate him and his supposed arrogant mistreatment toward several of the earliest companions. Dissatisfaction and resistance openly arose since 650 – 651 throughout most of the empire. When Uthman's kin, especially Marwan, gained control over him, the noble companions including most of the members of elector council, turned against him or at least withdrew their support putting pressure on the caliph to mend his ways and reduce the influence of his assertive kin.

At this time, Ali had acted as a restraining influence on Uthman without directly opposing him. On several occasions Ali disagreed with Uthman in the application of the Hudud. Finally he tried to mitigate the severity of the siege by his insistence that Uthman should be allowed water.

Although pledging allegiance to Uthman, Ali disagreed with some of his policies. He insisted that religious punishment had to be done in several cases such as Ubayd Allah ibn Umar and Walid ibn Uqba. When Uthman declared that he would take whatever he needed from the fey', Ali exclaimed that in the case the caliph would be prevented by force. Therefore, some historians consider Ali one the leading members of Uthman's opposition, if not the main one. Some other sources say Ali had acted as a restraining influence on Uthman without directly opposing him.

Caliphate:
Rashidun Empire and Ali caliphate

Election as Caliph:
Ali was caliph between 656 and 661, during one of the more turbulent periods in Muslim history, which also coincided with the First Fitna.

Uthman's assassination meant that rebels had to select a new caliph. This met with difficulties since the rebels were divided into several groups comprising the *Muhajirun*, *Ansar*, Egyptians, Kufans and Basntes. There were three candidates: Ali, Talhah and al-Zubayr. First the rebels approached Ali, requesting him to accept being the caliph.

In order to resolve the deadlock, the Muslims gathered in the Mosque of the Prophet on June 18, 656 to appoint the caliph. Initially Ali refused to accept simply because his most vigorous supporters were rebels. However, when some notable companions of Muhammad, in addition to the residents of Medina urged him to accept the offer, he finally agreed.

While the overwhelming majority of Medina's population as well as many of the rebels gave their pledge, some important figures or tribes did not do so. Sa'ad ibn Abi Waqqas was absent and Abdullah ibn Umar abstained from offering his allegiance, but both of them assured Ali that they would not act against him.

Reign as Caliph:
But the sources agree that he was a profoundly religious man, devoted to the cause of Islam and the rule of justice in accordance with the Quran and the Sunnah; he engaged in war against erring Muslims as a matter of religious duty. Thus some authors have pointed out that he lacked political skill and flexibility.

Ali inherited the Rashidun Caliphate – which extended from Egypt in the west to the Iranian highlands in the east – while the situation in the Hejaz and the other provinces on the eve of his election was unsettled. Soon after Ali became caliph, he dismissed provincial governors who had been appointed by Uthman, replacing them with trusted aides. Muawiyah I, the kinsman of Uthman and governor of the Levant refused to submit to Ali's orders; he was the only governor to do so.

When he was appointed caliph, Ali stated to the citizens of Medina that Muslim polity had come to be plagued by dissension and discord; he desired to purge Islam of any evil. Ali recovered the land granted by Uthman and swore to recover anything that elites had acquired before his election. Ali refrained from nepotism, including with his brother Aqeel ibn Abu Talib.

Ali succeeded in forming a broad coalition especially after the Battle of Bassorah. His policy of equal distribution of taxes and booty gained the support of Muhammad's companions especially the Ansar who were subordinated by the Quraysh leadership after Muhammad, the traditional tribal leaders, and the Qurra or Quran reciters that sought pious Islamic leadership. The successful formation of this diverse coalition seems to be due to Ali's charismatic character. This diverse coalition became known as *Shi'a Ali*, meaning "party" or "Faction of Ali".

First Fitna:
Aishah, Talhah, Al-Zubayr and Umayyad especially Muawiyah I wanted to take revenge for Uthman's death and punish the rioters who had killed him. They attacked Ali for not punishing the rebels and murderers of Uthman. On the other hand, the rebels maintained that Uthman had been justly killed, for not governing according to Quran and Sunnah, hence no vengeance was to be invoked.

Under such circumstances, a schism took place which led to the first civil war in Muslim history. In their view Ali was the Imam or error leading a party of infidels. Some others, who are known as party of Ali, believed Uthman had fallen into error, he had forfeited the caliphate and been lawfully executed for his refusal to mend his way or step down, thus Ali was the just and true Imam and his opponents are infidels.

The First Fitna, 656 – 661, followed the assassination of Uthman, continued during the caliphate of Ali, and was ended by Muawiyah's assumption of the caliphate. This civil war (often called the *Fitna*) is regretted as the end of the early unity of the Islamic Ummah (nation). Ali was first opposed by a faction led by Talhah, Al-Zubayr and Muhammad's wife, Aisha bint Abu Bakr. This group, known as "the disobedient ones" (*Nakithin*) by their enemies, gathered in Mecca then moved to Basra with the expectation of finding the necessary forces and resources to mobilize people of Iraq. The rebels occupied Basra, killing many people. They refused Ali's offer of obedience and pledge of allegiance. The two sides met at the Battle of Bassorah (Battle of the Camel) in 656, where Ali emerged victorious.

Ali appointed Ibn Abbas governor of Basra and moved his capital to Kufa, the Muslim garrison city in Iraq. Kufa was in the middle of Islamic land and had strategic position. Later he was challenged by Muawiyah I, the governor of Levant and the cousin of Uthman, who refused Ali's demands for allegiance and called for revenge for Uthman. The two armies encamped themselves at Siffin for more than one hundred days, most of the time being spent in negotiations. Although, Ali exchanged several letters with Muawiyah, he was unable to dismiss the latter, nor persuade him to pledge allegiance. Skirmishes between the parties led to the Battle of Siffin in 657. After a week of combat was followed by a violent battle known as *Laylat al-harir* (the night of clamor), Muawiyah's army were on the point of being routed when Amir ibn al-Aas advised Muawiyah to have his soldiers hoist *Mus'haf* (either parchments inscribed with verses of the Quran, or complete copies of it) on their spearheads in order to cause disagreement and confusion in Ali's army.

The two armies finally agreed to settle the matter of who should be Caliph by arbitration. The refusal of the largest bloc in Ali's army to fight was the decisive factor in his acceptance of the arbitration. Finally, Ali was urged to accept Abu Musa. Some of Ali's supporters, later were known as Kharijites (schismatics), opposed arbitration and rebelled and Ali had to fight with them in the Battle of Nahrawan. The arbitration resulted in the dissolution of Ali's coalition and some have opined that this was Muawiyah's intention.

In the following years Muawiyah's army invaded the plundered cities of Iraq, which Ali's governors could not prevent and people did not support him to fight with them. Muawiyah overpowered Egypt, Hijaz, Yemen and other areas. In the last year of Ali's caliphate, the mood in Kufa and Basra changed in his favor as Muawiyah's vicious conduct of the war revealed the nature of his reign.

Policies:

What shows Ali's policies and ideas of governing in his instruction to Malik al-Ashtar, when appointed by him as governor of Egypt. Ali wrote in his instruction to Malik al-Ashtar:

> "Infuse your heart with mercy, love and kindness for your subjects. Be not in face of them a voracious animal, counting them as easy pretty, for they are of two kinds: either they are your brothers in religion or your equals in creation. So grant them your pardon and your forgiveness to the same extent that you hope God will grant you His pardon and His forgiveness. God has sought from you the fulfillment of their requirements and He is trying you with them."

Death:

On the 19th of Ramadan, while worshipping in the Great Mosque of Kufa, Ali was attacked by the Khawarij Abd-al-Rahman ibn Muljam. He was wounded by ibn Muljam's poison-coated sword while prostrating in the Fajr prayer. Ali ordered his sons not to attack the Kharijites, instead stipulating that if he survived, ibn Muljam would be pardoned whereas if he died, ibn Muljam should be given only one equal hit (regardless of whether or not he died, ibn Muljam should be given only one equal hit (regardless of whether or not he dies from the hit).

Burial:

Ali did not want his grave to be desecrated by his enemies and consequently asked his friends and family to bury him secretly. This secret gravesite was resealed later during the Abbasid caliphate by Imam Ja'far al-Sadiq, his descendant and the sixth Shi'a Imam. Most Shi'as accept that Ali is buried at the Tomb of Imam Ali in the Imam Ali Mosque at what is now the city of Najaf, which grew around the mosque and shrine called Masjid Ali.

Aftermath, *Umayyad dynasty and Umayyad tradition of cursing Ali:*
After Ali's death, Kufi Muslims pledged allegiance to his eldest son Hasan without dispute, as Ali on many occasions had declared that just *Ahl al-Bayt* of Muhammad were entitled to rule the Muslim community. At this time, Muawiyah held both the Levant and Egypt and, as commander of the largest force in the Muslim Empire, had declared himself caliph and marched his army into Iraq, the seat of Hasan's caliphate.

War ensued during which Muawiyah gradually subverted the generals and commanders of Hasan's army with large sums of money and deceiving promises until the army rebelled against him. Finally, Hasan was forced to make peace and to yield the caliphate to Muawiyah. Regular public cursing of Imam Ali in the congregational prayers remained a vital institution which was not abolished until 60 years later by Umar ibn Abd al-Aziz. Muawiyah also established the Umayyad caliphate which was a centralized monarchy.

> In the memory of later generations Ali became the ideal Commander of the Faithful. In face of the fake Umayyad claim to legitimate sovereignty in Islam as God's Vice-regents on earth, and in view of Umayyad treachery, arbitrary and divisive government, and vindictive retribution, they came to appreciate his [Ali's] honesty, his unbending devotion to the reign of Islam, his deep personal loyalties, his equal treatment of all his supporters, and his generosity in forgiving his defeated enemies.

Knowledge:
Ali is respected not only as a warrior and leader, but as a writer and religious authority. According to Hadith which is narrated by Shi'a and Sufis, Muhammad told about him "I'm the city of knowledge and Ali is its gate..." Muslims regard Ali as a major authority on Islam.

According to Sayyed Hossein Nasr, Ali is credited with having established Islamic theology and his quotations contain the first rational proofs among Muslims of the Unity of God. Ali's sayings and sermons were increasingly regarded as central sources of metaphysical knowledge, or divine philosophy. Members of Sadra's school regard Ali as the supreme metaphysician of Islam. Ali was also a great scholar of Arabic literature and pioneered in the field of Arabic grammar and rhetoric.

In addition, some hidden or occult sciences such as *jafr*, Islamic numerology, the science of the symbolic significance of the letters of the Arabic alphabet, are said to have been established by Ali through his having studied the texts of al-Jafr and al-Jamia.

Descendants:
Descendants of Ali ibn Abi Talib and Alavi (surname)

Ali initially married Fatimah, who is his most beloved wife. After she died, he got married again. He had four children with Fatimah, Hasan ibn Ali, Husayn ibn Ali, Zaynab bint Ali and Umm Kulthum bint Ali. His other well-known sons were al-Abbas ibn Ali born to Fatima bint Hizam (um al-Banin) and Muhammad ibn al-Hanafiyyah.

Hasan, born in 625 AD, was the second Shi'a Imam and he also occupied the outward function of caliph for about six months. In the year 50 A.H., he was poisoned and killed by a member of his own household who, as has been accounted by historians, had been motivated by Mu'awiyah.

Husayn, born in 626 AD, was the second Shi'a Imam. He lived under severe conditions of suppression and persecution by Mu'awiyah. On the tenth day of Muharram, of the year 680, he lined up before the army of caliph with his small band of followers and nearly all of them were killed in the Battle of Karbala. The anniversary of his death is called the Day of Ashura and it is a day of mourning and religious observance for Shi'a Muslims. In this battle some of Ali's other sons were killed. Al-Tabari has mentioned their names in his history. Al-Abbas ibn Ali, the holder of Husayn's standard, Ja'far, Abdallah and Uthman, the four sons born to Fatima bint Hizam. Muhammad and Abu Bakr. The death of the last one is doubtful. Some historians have added the names of Ali's others sons who were killed in Karbala, including Irahim, Umar and Abdallah ibn al-Asqar.

His daughter Zaynab – who was in Karbala – was captured by Yazid's army and later played a great role in revealing what happened to Husayn and his followers. Ali's descendants by Fatimah are known as *Sharifs, Sayeds* or *Sayyids*. As Muhammad's only descendants, they are respected by both Sunni and Shi'a, though the Shi'as place much more emphasis and value on the distinction.

Muslim views:

Except for Muhammad, there is no one in Islamic history about whom as much has been written in Islamic languages as Ali. Ali is revered and honored by all Muslims. Having been one of the first Muslims and foremost Ulema (Islamic scholars), he was extremely knowledgeable in matters of religious belief and Islamic jurisprudence, as well as in the history of the Muslim community. He was known for his bravery and courage. Muslims honor Muhammad.

Shi'a:
Shi'a view of Ali

The Shi'a regard Ali as the most important figure after Muhammad. According to them, Muhammad suggested on various occasions during his lifetime that Ali should be the leader of Muslims after his death.

According to this view, Ali as the successor Muhammad not only ruled over the community in justice, but also interpreted the Sharia Law and its esoteric meaning. Hence he was regarded as being free from error and sin (infallible), and appointed by God by divine decree (nass) through Muhammad. Ali is known as "perfect man" (*al-insan al-Kamil*) similar to Muhammad according to Shi'a viewpoint.

Shi'a pilgrims usually go to Mashad Ali in Najaf for Ziyarat, pray there and read "Ziyarat Amin Allah" or other *Ziyaratnamehs*. Under the Safavid Empire, his grave became the focus of much devoted attention, exemplified in the pilgrimage made by Shah Ismail I to Najaf and Karbala.

Sunni:
Sunni view of Ali

Sunni Muslims regard Ali with great respect as one of the Ahl al-Bayt and the last Rashidun caliphs, as well as one of the most influential and respected leaders in Islam. Also, he is one of the *Al-Asharatu Mubashsharun*, the Ten Companions of Muhammad whom the Prophet of Islam promised Paradise.

Sufi:

Almost all Sufi orders trace their lineage to Muhammad through Ali, an exception being Naqshabandi, who go through Abu Bakr. Even in this order, there is Ja'far al-Sadiq, the greatest great grandson of Ali. Sufis believe that Ali inherited from Muhammad the saintly power *wilayah* that makes the spiritual journey of God possible. Sufis recite *Manqabat* Ali in the praise of Ali (Maula Ali), after *Hamd* and *Naat* in their *Qawwali*.

As a deity *Ghulat*:

Some groups such as the Alawis believe that Ali is a deity in his own right or he was God incarnate. They are described as *Ghulat* "exaggerators" by the vast majority of Islamic scholars. Ali is recorded in some traditions as having forbidden those who sought to worship him in his own lifetime.

Historiography:
The primary sources for scholarship on the life of Ali are the Quran and the Hadith, as well as other texts of early Islamic history. However, many of the early Islamic sources are colored to some extent by a positive or negative bias towards Ali.

Until the rise of the Abbasid Caliphate, few books were written and most of the reports had been oral. The most notable work previous to this period is *The Book of Sulaym ibn Qays*, written by Sulaym ibn Qays, a companion of Ali who lived before the Abbasid.

Shi'a of Iraq actively participated in writing monographs but most of those works have been lost. On the other hand, in the 8th and 9th century Ali's descendants such as Muhammad al Baqir and Ja'far as Sadiq narrated his quotations and reports which have been gathered in Shi'a Hadith books.

Buried   Imam Ali Mosque, Najaf, Iraq
Wives   Fatimah, Batima bint Hizam al-Qilabiyya ("Ummu l-Banin")
Offspring   Hasan, Husayn, Zaynab (See: Descendants of Ali ibn Talib
Father   Abu Talib
Mother   Fatima bint Asad

***

Ali Khamanei, Hussein (1939-   ): Iranian religious political leader, Leader 1989 Born into a religious family in Mashhad Khomeini pursued his theological studies in Najaf, Iraq, and then Qom where he became a student of Ayatollah Ruhollah Khomeini. His release from jail in 1975 was followed by internal exile In Iranshahr in the distant Baluchistan-Sistan province. This ended during the revolutionary upsurge of 1977-78, and enabled him to return to Masshad and participate in the movement. Khamanei was one of Khomeini's first appointees to the Islamic Revolutionary Council (IRC), which assumed supreme power after the Islamic revolution. Elected to the Majlis in early 1980, he was active in the IRP'S parliamentary wing. In May he became Khomeini's personal representative on the Supreme Defense Council.

He won 88.5 percent of the votes in the August 1985 presidential poll. But when he tried to replace his radical prime minister, Hussein Musavi he found his hands tied. Khamanei, promoted to ayatollah by Khomeini on his deathbed, became a Mujtahid, a constitutional requirement for the Leader. Khamanei endorsed the result of the 1997 presidential poll unhesitatingly even though it resulted in the defeat of

Ali Akbar Nateq Nouri, the favorite of the religious establishment. He endorsed the repeat landslide victory of Khatami in the presidential election in 2001. With the United States extending its 1996 Iran Libya Sanctions Act for another five years in 2001, the chances of Washington-Tehran rapprochement receded, and this suited Khamanei well. After the war he described the American occupation of Iraq as "worse than Saddam's dictatorship." Khamanei is the author of several books on Islam and history.

***

Ali Pasha (1744-1822): Turkish pasha [military governor] of Yannina (now Ioannina, Greece), a province of the Ottoman Empire (Turkey). He was called the Arslan [lion] of Yannaina. His father, governor at Tepelene in S Albanis, was murdered, and Ali went to live with the mountain brigands who infested the country. He soon rose to leadership among them, came to the attention of the Turkish government, and as its agent put down the rebellion of a governor at Scutari in Albani. About 1787 he became governor of Yannina, where his power grew until he ruled as a quasi-independent despot over most of Albania and Epirus. He made war on the French along the Adriatic coast and entered an alliance (1814) with Great Britain. Valuing Ali's services, the sultan let him do as he wished until, in 1820, Ali ordered the assassination of an opponent in Constantinople. Sultan Mahmud II ordered Ali deposed. Ali was assassinated by an agent of the Turks; his head was exhibited at Constantinople.

***

Ali, Salim Rubai (1935-1978): South Yemeni politician, president 1969-78. Born into a middle class family in Zinjibar near Aden, Ali trained as a teacher. Later he studied law and became involved in a militantly anti imperialist movement, the National Liberation Front. In October 1963 he led a guerilla campaign against the British in the Rafdan Mountains. Just as this drama was unfolding in Sanaa, the two rivals clashed in Aden. While Ali used the army to overcome his opponents, Ismail engaged the party's People's Militia. Ali lost and was executed.

***

Amin Dada, Idi (1925-2003) Ugandan head of state. Possessed of only rudimentary education, Amin rose through the ranks of the army to become its commander. In 1971 he overthrew President Obote and seized power. His rule was characterized by the advancing of narrow tribal interests, the expulsion of non-Africans (most notably Uganda Asians), and violence on a huge scale. He was overthrown with Tanzanian assistance in 1979 and went into exile in Saudi Arabia.

***

Amr ibn al-As (-): influential Meccan nobleman who fought against the Muslims in Medina but would later embrace Islam and rise quickly through its ranks. He was appointed by Abu Bakr one of the three commanders that led the first Muslim armies out of Medina for the conquest of the Holy Land. In 640 he led a raid that would lead to the conquest of Egypt, which he would conquer and rule over on three separate occasions. Dismissed by Uthman, he would regain his old position by a political alliance with Muawiya. One of Muhammad's bitter enemies in Mecca; eventually converted to Islam.

***

Antonius, George (1892-1942): Lebanese writer and thinker Born into a Greek Orthodox family in Lebanon and educated in Egypt, Antonius settled in Palestine in 1921 after taking up a job with the education department there. Nine years later he joined the New York based Institute of Current World Affairs headed by Charles Crane, cochairman of a US commission on the Middle East in 1919. He traced the roots of Arab renaissance to a nascent movement in Beirut in the 1880s, composed largely of Arab Christians educated in the Protestant and Catholic mission schools and colleges of Lebanon. In Palestinian politics he allied himself with radical Haajj Muhammad Amin a Hussein.

***

Aoun, Michel Naim (1935-): Lebanese military officer and politician Born to Maronite parents, Aoun graduated from Lebanon's Military Academy as an artillery officer. He underwent further training in France from 1958-59. He rose steadily in the army, which became increasingly fractured along religious lines as the Lebanese Civil War beginning in 1975 dragged on for many years. On October 1990 his troops collapsed when attacked by the joint forces of his Lebanese opponents and Syria. He took refuge in the French Embassy. The following August he left for France, after the Lebanese government had granted him conditional amnesty. His attempts since then to return to Lebanon have failed.

***

Arabi Pasha: The English name of Ahmad Urabi Pasha al-Misri (1839-1911), Egyptian nationalist leader. A conscript in the Egyptian army, he rose to the rank of colonel in the Egyptian-Ethiopian War (1875-76). In 1879 he took part in an officers' revolt against the Turkish governor of Egypt, and led a further revolt in 1881. In 1882, when Britain and France intervened at the request of Khedive Tawfiq, bombarding the city of Alexandria, he organized a nationalist resistance movement. The British defeated him at Tel-el-Kebir, and exiled him to Sri Lanka. He returned to Egypt in 1901.

***

Arafat, Yasir (1929-2004): Born Mahmud Abdul Rahman Abul Rauf Arafat al Qudwa, nicknamed Yasser; leader of the Palestine Liberation Organization (PLO), the coordinating body for Palestinian organizations, and head of Al Fatah, the largest group in the PLO. He was born in Jerusalem. After smuggling arms to Arab forces during the 1948 Arab-Israeli War, Arafat entered Cairo Univ., where he became chair-man of the Palestine Student Federation. He served in the Egyptian army during the Suez campaign (1956) and the following year moved to Kuwait, where he trained Palestinian commandos and edited *Our Palestine* magazine. Arafat joined the Al Fatah commando group and in 1965 returned to Egypt to head Al Assifa, the military arm of Al Fatah. He went on to become leader of Al Fatah, and when the group gained control of the PLO (1969), Arafat was named the larger body's chairman.

In 1983, after an Israeli invasion of Lebanon, the PLO was forced to move its headquarters to Tunisia. In 1988 the PLO, under Arafat's leadership, in effect renounced terrorism and accepted Israel's right to coexist with an independent Palestine. In 1993 he signed a peace accord with Israel, in which Israel agreed to withdraw its troops from the West Bank and the Gaza Strip areas, and the PLO agreed to give up terrorism. Arafat, along with Yitzhak Rabin and Foreign Minister Shimon Peres of Israel, was awarded the Nobel Peace Prize in 1994. He was elected President of the newly formed Palestinian National Authority in 1996.

***

Arif, Abdul Rahman (1916- 2007) Iraqi military leader, president 1966-68 Born into a middle class family in Baghdad, Arif enrolled at the local military academy and became an officer. A nationalist and opposed to the pro western stance of the monarchical regime, he joined the Free

Officers group that overthrew the royalist regime in July 1958. The opposition felt emboldened to demonstrate in the streets, demanding free elections. This paced the way for disaffected Ba'athist officers, led by Ahmad Hassan Bakr and the military intelligence chief, Abdul Rahman Nayif, to overthrow Arif in July 1969, forcing him into exile in Turkey. After many years in Turkey he was allowed to return home.

***

Arif, Abdul Salam (1929-1966): Iraqi military and political leader, president, 1963-66 Born into a middle class family in Baghdad, Arif enrolled at the military academy and became an officer. His experience in the Palestine War, in which the Iraqi troops performed poorly, turned him against the pro Western regime of King Faisal II. Arif embarked on a plan to unite Iraq and Egypt, starting with economic and military coordination and a joint presidential council. He tackled the long running Kurdish problem and was on the verge of signing an accord with Kurdish insurgents when he was killed in an air crash in April 1966.

***

Asbar, Ali Ahmad Said (1930-   ): Syrian poet domiciled in Lebanon. Born of an Alawi family in Kassabin, a village near Latakia, Asbar obtained a philosophy degree from Damascus University in 1954, with special interest in Sufism. A staunch member of the Syrian Social Nationalist Party whose leader Antun Saada named him Adonis, Asbar received a long jail sentence for his subversive politics. In 1956 he escaped to Beirut where he combined further studies with journalism and literary writing, mainly poetry and criticism. He co edited Shiar, a literary magazine from 1956-63.

***

Askia Muhammad I, The Great (1443-1538): Emperor of Songhay (1493-1528) in West Africa. Originally named Muhammad Ture, he was Sonni Ali's best general. He usurped Songhay from Ali's son in 1493, thus founding a new dynasty, and took the title Askia. He was a convert to Islam, but tolerant toward pagans, and made the pilgrimage to Mecca, meeting many notable men, especially the great Muslim teacher al-Maghili.

***

Assad Rifaat (1937-): Syrian politician Born in the family of a rural notable in Qurdaha, an Alawi village near Latakia. Assad joined the Baath party in 1952. He did his military service during the period when Syria was part of the United Arab Republic (1958-61). After the Baathist coup of March 1963, Assad was put through a crash course at the Homs military academy. In late 1999 the government closed down a port in Latakia that had been built illegally by Assad, and warned him that he faced prosecution if he returned home. Following Hafiz Assad's death in 2000, Assad described the accession of Bashar Assad as unconstitutional.

Atef, Muhammad (1944-2001): Aaka Abu Hafs, Abu Khadijah, Tayseer Abdullah, Born Muhammad Sobhi abu Sitta in a poor, religious family in Menoufia, Egypt, Atef grew up to be a tall man of 6'6. A devout Muslim, he trained as a police officer and rose through the ranks during the 1970s. He joined the clandestine Al Jihad group soon after its founding in 1978. In January 2001 Aref caught media attention with the video of the wedding of his daughter, Khadijah to Muhammad, eighteen year old son of Osama bin Laden. Following the terrorist attacks on the US in September, Washington froze his assets along with those of eleven others, Soon after the evacuation of Kabul by the Taliban on 12-13 November. Aref was killed in an air strike by US warplanes

***

Attasi, Nur al Din (1929-1992): Syrian politician president 1966-70, Born into a landlord family of the Attasi clan, based in the countryside around Homs, Attasi acquired a medical degree from Damascus University in 1955. He joined the Baath party as a youth. His trial release in late 1980 when the Assad regime faced a severe Islamist challenge, ended when he failed to cooperate. However his subsequent house arrest soon ended when he agreed to refrain from politics.

***

Awrangzeb Alamgir (1618-1707): The Mughal dynasty endured for more than three hundred years before the British assumed control of India and sent the last Mughal ruler, Bahadur Shah Zafar II, into exile in 1858. The splendor and magnificence of the Mughals rivaled the glorious achievements of the Ottomans, the greatness of the Safavids and the might of the great European nations of the time. The descendants of Timur the World Conqueror ruled a vast stretch of land where people of all faiths, cultures and traditions lived and thrived, producing some of the world's most famous works of art and architecture, including the immortal Taj Mahal. And in so doing they left their indelible marks in the annals of history. The last, equally courageous and most impressive, of all the great Mughal rulers was Awrangzeb Alamgir.

Abul Muzaffar Muhammad Muhyi al-Din Awrangzeb Alamgir Badshah-i-Ghazi, known as Awrangzeb Alamgir for short, was born in Dohud in the province of Deccan during the reign of his grandfather Jahangir. The real love of his life was Mumtaz Mahal (The Chosen One of the Palace), his beloved wife and consort who bore him fourteen children. As Shah Jahan's third son, Awrangzeb received the best education money could buy at the time. Awrangzeb became a devout Muslim who prayed five times a day and refused to engage in any form of un-Islamic activities.

Awrangzeb was barely ten years old when his father ascended the Mughal throne and ruled the country for three decades. Aurangzeb's courage and bravery impressed Shah Jahan who offered him his weight in gold as reward for his heroism. Impressed by his son's good personal qualities and attributes, Shah Jahan appointed him commander of the Mughal army.

Delighted with Aurangzeb's progress, Shah Jahan appointed him Minister of the Deccan province when he was only seventeen. True to form, Awrangzeb came to Deccan and soon established peace and security throughout the province using his carrot-and-stick approach. During this period he also married the daughter of a noble businessman. The futility of worldly power, wealth and possessions prompted him to resign as Minister and become a hermit; he was only twenty-four at the time. With a new sense of mission, he left his hermitage and moved to Agra where his father initially refused to pardon him for apparently disgracing the royal family's name by becoming a hermit, but eventually Shah Jahan relented and appointed him Minister of the province of Gujarat.

Thus, in 1647, Shah Jahan ordered Awrangzeb to take charge of an expeditionary force and set out for Central Asia. Both the ruler and the people of this historic city put up determined resistance, and the Mughals' dream of annexing Samarqand soon faded away before their eyes. Although Shah Jahan's military campaign against the Uzbeks, as well as the Safavids, proved disastrous for the Mughals, Awrangzeb won much acclaim for his bravery and resilience on the battlefield. Nonetheless, to prevent rivalry and ill-feeling within the royal family, Shah Jahan made all his sons Ministers of their own provinces. The intelligent and accomplished Awrangzeb was re-appointed Chief of the Deccan province.

By putting his four sons in charge of four different provinces, Shah Jahan maintained peace and unity within the royal family until he was taken ill in 1657. The news of his illness prompted his four sons to engage in a protracted succession battle. After removing his brothers one by one, from his path Awrangzeb became Emperor of the Mughal dynasty in 1658 at the age of around forty.

Unlike his predecessors who surrounded themselves with much wealth and luxury, Awrangzeb despised pomp and pageantry and lived like a hermit, sleeping on the floor, covered only with a tiger skin, and ate most frugally. The restoration of peace, justice and prosperity across Mughal India was more important to him than satisfying his own personal whims and desires.

During his long reign of fifty years, Awrangzeb face many challenges. A copy of the Qur'an written by Awrangzeb has been preserved in the *dar al-uloom* library in Deoband. In addition to this, Awrangzeb constructed the famous Badshahi mosque in Lahore, which is one of the Muslim world's largest and most beautiful mosques.

Emperor Awrangzeb Alamgir died at the ripe old age of eighty-five and was buried at the mausoleum of Shaykh Zain al-Haq at Khuldabad (located in present-day India). After his death, the Mughal Empire began to decline irreversibly.

***

Ayatullah Khomeini (1902-1989): The word 'Iranian' (meaning 'from the land of the Aryans') referred to those people who had migrated from the Iranian plateau around 1500BC and, over time, they became known as the 'Persians' until the Shah of Iran officially outlawed this term in 1935. Historically speaking, after the collapse of the ancient Persian Empire around 331, the Iranian territories were carved up by the Macedonians, Seleucids and the Parthians until the Muslims emerged from Arabia and conquered Iran in 641 during the reign of Caliph Umar.

With the decline of the once-mighty Abbasid Empire, there then emerged many independent dynasties in the Muslim world (including the Seljuks in the eleventh century; the Mongols in the thirteenth century and the Timurids in the fourteenth century). And they ruled the Iranian people until the Safavids, a native Iranian dynasty, emerged at the beginning of the sixteenth century. They ruled for more than two hundred years before the encroaching Afghans destroyed them in 1722. Thereafter, Iran became a playground for the Turks, Russians and the British who fought each other for control of the country until, in 1906, an independent constitutional monarchy was established in Iran which endured until the Iranian Revolution of 1979. The father of this revolution was Ayatullah Khomeini, who single-handedly brought down the Shah of Iran and established an Islamic theocracy which today plays a significant role in world politics.

Ayatullah Ruhullah al-Musavi Khomeini, known as Imam Khomeini for short, was born in Khomein, a small village in Central Iran located about two hundred miles south of Tehran, the capital of Iran. His ancestors claimed to be descendants of the Prophet, through Musa al-Kazim (the seventh Shi'a Imam). After settling in Nishapur, a town located on the outskirts of Mashhad, they migrated to India at the beginning of the eighteenth century. In India, Khomeini's immediate ancestors settled in Kintur, close to the Indian city of Lucknow, where his grandfather Sayyid Ahmad Musavi was born and raised. Later, he moved to Najaf, the famous Iraqi shrine-city, in around 1830 to pursue higher education.

After completing his education, he decided not to return to India; instead he settled in Khomein, married thrice and became a successful entrepreneur. Born in 1856, Khomeini's father, Mustafa, also became a respected Shi'a cleric but he was murdered during a local dispute; Khomeini was only around five months old at the time. After completing his early education in Arabic, Persian, Shi'ite theology, aspects of literature and poetry at his local village school, at the age of seventeen Khomeini moved to Arak. Here he studied Arabic grammar, literature and the religious sciences before moving to Qom, a famous center of Shi'a learning and scholarship in Iran, along with his mentor Shaykh Ha'eri-Yazdi in 1922.

Although Khomeini was a bright student of the exoteric sciences of Islam, he also became fascinated by poetry, *Tasawwuf* (mysticism) and Shi'a esotericism. Being very fond of mystical poetry, he studied the celebrated *Mathnavi* of Jalal al-Din Rumi and the works of Hafiz of Shiraz and Umar Khayyam. Of all his teachers, it was Shahabadi who profoundly influenced Khomeini's ideas and thoughts on philosophy, ethics, morality and politics. Indeed, he argued, it was the religious obligation of all Muslims, scholars and lay people alike, to oppose the anti-Islamic, oppressive and unjust policies of the Shah.

After completing his formal education in Qom, Khomeini started lecturing there while he was still in his late twenties. The rise of Reza Shah, and the founding of the Pahlavi dynasty during the 1920s, raised the hopes and aspirations of the Iranian people. Following in the footsteps of Mustafa Kemal Ataturk of Turkey, the Shah was determined to Westernize Iran by force, if necessary. During this period Khomeini authored his *Kashf al-Asrar* (The Disclosure of Secrets) in which he severely criticized and lambasted the Shah for presiding over a corrupt Government and for punishing and humiliating the Shi'a luminaries.

Like his father, the new ruler was determined to Westernize Iran, despite protests from the country's religious scholars. Khomeini began to openly criticize the Shah's regime for its heavy-handed tactics and autocratic policies. Khomeini was arrested and imprisoned by the regime in 1963. His rising popularity eventually forced the Shah to release him a year later. The Shah re-arrested Khomeini and in 1964 exiled him to Turkey. He spent the next fourteen years in exile in Turkey, Iraq and France.

After establishing contacts with various Iranian opposition groups in Europe and America, Khomeini openly called on the Iranian people to rise up against the Shah and his cohorts. The Shah, he argued, despised the clergy more than any other sector of Iranian society. But Khomeini and his supported were determined not to allow the Shah to succeed; they argued that it would be disastrous for Iran to adopt Western secular values at the expense of its traditional Islamic culture and norms.

In his book Khomeini developed a blueprint for an Islamic State in Iran. He argued that it was the duty of every Muslim, cleric or layman, to work collectively to establish an Islamic State in Iran along the lines of the seventh century Madinian prototype. This, therefore, provided him with the religious justification for the rule of the clerics in the aftermath of the Iranian Revolution of 1979.

Thereafter, Khomeini published his *Jihad-i Akbar* (The Greater Struggle) in which he argued that the clerics and the masses should spiritually cleanse themselves through regular prayers and fasting which, in his opinion, was an essential pre-requisite for the attainment of success in this world and in the hereafter. While he was busy working on a viable Islamic political system, the Shah's grip on power began to weaken. Indeed, as mass protest against his autocratic rule gathered pace in 1978, Khomeini, who was then living in exile in Paris, urged his supporters to continue their political campaign until the Pahlavis were ousted from power. During this momentous period in modern Iranian history, Khomeini became a powerful symbol of resistance and hope for millions of Iranian people across the world. One group, led by Medhi Bazargan the eminent leader of the Iran Freedom Movement, advocated the need for a gradualist approach to socio-political change because they wanted to establish a moderate Islamic Government in Iran. But their voices were drowned out by the supporters of Khomeini, who opted for a strict, hard-line and clergy-dominated political administration in Tehran.

A triumphant Khomeini returned to Tehran and proclaimed the establishment of the Islamic Republic in 1979. This marked the end of more than fifty years of Pahlavi rule, and the beginning of a new chapter in Iranian history. Khomeini ruled Iran for more than a decade.

There is no doubt that Khomeini's legacy will play a powerful role in Iranian politics, at least for the foreseeable future. Ayatullah Khomeini died at the age of eighty-seven and was buried in the famous cemetery of Behesht-i Zahra in Tehran.

***

Ayub Kahn, Muhammad (1907-1974): Military leader and President of Pakistan (1958-69). A Pathan from the Hazara district, he was a professional soldier who, when the state of Pakistan was created (1947), assumed command of military forces in East Pakistan (now Bangladesh). He was appointed commander-in-chief of the Pakistan Army in 1951. Minister of Defense (1954-56), and Chief Martial Law Administrator after the 1958 military coup.... In March 1968 he suffered a serious illness and thereafter lost political control, being replaced in March 1969 by General Yahya Khan.

***

Azikiwe, (Benjamin) Nnamdi (1904-1996): Nigerian statesman, first President of Nigeria (1963-66). An Ibo (Igbo), he founded the National Council of Nigeria and the Cameroon's (NCNC) and exerted a strong influence throughout the 1940s on emerging Nigerian nationalism. He held a number of political posts before becoming the first governor-general of Nigeria (1960-63). He was deposed by a military coup (1966), which ousted the civilian government, but remained leader of the Nigerian People's Party (until political parties were banned in 1984) and was a member of the Nigerian Council of State (1979-83).

***

Aziz, Tariq (1936-   ): Iraqi politician Born Mikhail Yahunna of a Chaldean Catholic family in Mosul Aziz obtained a postgraduate degree from Baghdad University in the early 1950s. He joined the clandestine Baath party soon after it was established in Iraq in 1950. After the overthrow o the monarchy in July 1958, he joined al Jumhuriya journalist. Following the Ba'athist coup in March 1963 he became editor of the party's mouthpiece, al Jamahir (the peoples). UN security Council Resolution 687 of April 1991 however as the roving ambassador of Saddam Hussein, he succeeded in improving Iraq's relations with the rest of the Arab world as well as China, France and Russia. After the Gulf War III in 2003, he surrendered to the occupying U.S. Forces.

***

Azzam, Abdullah (1941-1989): Palestinian Islamist ideologue Born in Jenin, Palestine Azzam and his parents fled to Jordan during the 1948-49 Arab Israeli war. After graduating in Islamic theology from Damascus University in 1966, he fought in the June 1967 Arab Israeli War. Once the Soviets withdrew completely from Afghanistan in February 1989, Azzam claimed victory for the jihad. Seven months later a car bomb killed Azzam and his two sons as they were entering their mosque for the Friday prayer. This shattered bin Laden who then resolved to continue running Maktab al Khidmat under the new title of Al Qaida, but with a more ambitious aim of creating an international network of those who had participated in the Anti Soviet Jihad.

***

Babur (1483-1530): The first Mogul Emperor of India (1526 – 1530). He was born in Ferghana, Central Asia, in a princely family of mixed Mongol and Turkish blood. Failure to recover his father's lands caused him to turn reluctantly south-east, for India seemed to present the last hope for his ambitions. Defeat of Ibrahim Lodi, the Afghan ruler of Delhi, at the battle of Panipat in 1526 initiated 200 years of strong Mogul rule in India. Having conquered much of northern India, Babur ruled by force, lacking any civil administration. A descendant of Timur, set siege to Samarkand in 1496 at the age of 13. In 1504, he took the city of Kabul, Afghanistan.

***

Bakdash, Khalid(1912-1995): Syrian politician Born into Kurdish family in Damascus, Bakdash obtained a law degree at Damascus University. Politically active while in his teens, Bakdash became the secretary general of the Communist Party of Syria and Lebanon in 1936. He was jailed by the French Mandate. With his election as the party's secretary general in 1974, he resumed his position as the Arab world's most senior communist leader until he was replaced by Yusuf Faisal.

***

Bakhtiar, Shahpur(1914-1991): Iranian politician, prime minister 1979 Born into a family belonging to the powerful Bakhtiar tribe, Bakhtiar finished his higher education at Paris University in 1940 with a doctorate in international law and political science. He enrolled in the French army to fight Nazi Germany. On returning to Iran in 1946, he took up a job with the labor ministry and served for two years. He founded the monarchist National Resistance Movement in 1982 and remained a loyal supporter of the young pretender, Reza Cyrus Pahlavi. After an unsuccessful attempt on his life in 1980, Bakhtiar was given official protection by the French government. Despite the, he was assassinated in August 1991.

***

Bakr, Ahmad Hassan (1912-1982): Iraqi officer and political, president 1968-79. Born into the al Tikriti clan from Tikrit, Bakr enrolled in the army in 1938 and graduated from the Baghdad Military Academy four years later. He secretly joined the Baath party in 1956 when he was colonel. He was a leader of the Free Officers Organization, which staged the republican coup in July 1958. A pan Arabist he wanted a union between Iraq and Egypt and sided with Abdul Karim Qasim. On the eve of the 11th anniversary of the Ba'athist revolution, Saddam Hussein secured Bakr's resignation from all his governmental and party posts on health grounds. Bakr spent his last years under house arrest in ignominy.

***

Banisadr, AbolHassan (1933-   ): Iranian politician, president 1980-81 Born into a religious family in Hamadan, Bani Sadr pursued his university education in Tehran specializing in economics, sociology and Islamic Law. In the Economics of Divine Unity, published before the revolution, Bani Sadr expounded Islamic economics, rejected capitalism and Soviet socialism, and argued that Islamic teachings were a means to a just and equitable society. He encapsulated his later political experiences in My Turn to Speak.

***

Banu Musa brothers: The Ja'far-Muhammad, Ahmad and al-Hasan (ca. early 9th century) were three Persian sons of a colorful astronomer and astrologer. They were scholars close to the court of caliph al-Ma'mun and contributed greatly to the translation of ancient works into Arabic. They elaborated the mathematics of cones and ellipses, and performed astronomic calculations. Most notably, they contributed to the field of automation with the creations of automated devices such as the ones described in their Book of Ingenious Devices.

***

Barakah (-   ) (Also known as Umm Ayman): slave girl whom Muhammad inherited from his father; promised to look after Muhammad after his mother's death. Cherished figure of Muhammad's childhood to whom he gave freedom on the day of his marriage to Khaijah. Many years later she became one of the wives of Zayd ibn Haritha and although she must have been around twenty years older than her husband, they would have a child, Usama.

***

Barbarossa (Turkish, Khayr ad-Din Pasha .1483-1546): A famous Corsair, and later grand admiral of the Ottoman fleet. He and his brother Aruj first came to fame for their success against Christian vessels in the eastern Mediterranean. In 1516 Algier appealed to Aruj to save it from Spain, and made him sultan. Aruj was killed fighting in 1518, and made him sultan. Aruj was diplomatically ceded Algiers and its territory to the Ottoman sultan. He served as viceroy until 1533, when Charles V expelled him in 1535. After a number of minor engagements he retired in 1544.

***

Barzani, Masud (1946-   ) Iraqi Kurdish leader Born during the tumultuous times that followed the collapse of the Kurdish Republic of Mahabad, led military by his father, Mustafa, Barzani grew up in Moscow. After a two year stay in Baghdad following the republican coup of 1958, the family returned to Barzan in northern Iraq. He coordinated his military strategy with Talabani when America, backed by Britain, prepared to invade Iraq in March 2003. After the fall of the Saddam Hussein regime in April, Barzani publicly welcomed the US pro consul, Gen. Jay Rayner when he visited Kurdistan.

***

Barzani, Mustafa (1904-1979): Iraqi Kurdish leader Born into the family of a notable in Barzan, northern Iraq, Barzani grew up to be a leader of the Barzani tribe, which was traditionally opposed to the authority of the government, whether based in Mosul or **Baghdad.** Baghdad and Tehran reached an accord in March 1975, which resulted in Iran cutting off military and logistical aid to Barzani's men. His rebellion failed. After escaping to Iran, Barzani fled to the United States and settled in northern Virginia, where he died in 1979.

***

Barzargan, Mahdi (1905-1995): Iranian politician, prime minister, 1979. Born into a wealthy trading family in Tabriz. Bazargan obtained an engineering degree from Paris University. In 1985 his candidacy for president was rejected by the Guardians Council. Ignoring calls for action against Bazargan, Khomeini allowed him freedom of movement, including foreign travel, while denying him facilities for propagating his consistently critical views. This policy continued after Khomeini's death in 1989.

***

Bayezid I (1347-1403): Ottoman sultan (1389-1402), known as Yildrim ('Thunderbolt'). He succeeded his father Murad I and absorbed rival Turkish principalities in western Asia Minor, took Trnovo in Bulgaria (1393), and Thessaloniki in Greece (1394) blockaded Constantinople (1394-1401) and defeated a Christian army at Nilopolis in 1396. His thrust into eastern Asia Minor, however, brought him to disaster at Ankara in 1402, and he died a captive of his conqueror, Tamerlane.

***

Bayezid II (1447-1512): Ottoman sultan (1481-1512). He wrested the throne from his brother Jem on the death of their father Mehmed II, fought inconclusively with the Mamluks (1485-91), gained Greek and Adriatic territories from Venice, and was faced with the emerging power of Ismail I Safavi. He abdicated a month before his death in favor of his youngest son, Selim. welcomed the expelled Spanish Jews to his dominion.

***

Bello, Alhaji Sir Ahmadu (1906-1966): Nigerian statesman. He became leader of the Northern People's Congress, and, in 1952, the first elected minister in Northern Nigeria, and in 1954 Premier. When Nigeria became independent in 1960, his party combined with Azikiwe's National Council of Nigeria and the Cameroons (NCNC) to control the federal Parliament. Bello's deputy Prime Minister, while Bello himself remained to lead the party in the north. In 1966, when the army seized power, Bello was among the political leaders who were assassinated.

***

Ben Bella, Ahmed (1916- 2012): Algerian revolutionary leader. He served in the French army in World War II, and in 1947 became a leader of the secret military wing of the Algerian nationalist movement. He organized revolutionary activities and was imprisoned by the French (1950-52).

He then founded and directed the National Liberation Front (FLN), which began the Algerian war with France. In 1956, when he was on board a Moroccan airliner he was seized and interned in France. In 1962 he was freed under the Evian Agreements; he became Prime Minister of Algeria (1962-65) and was elected the first President of the Algerian Republic in 1963. In 1965 his government was overthrown in a military coup by Colonel Houari Boumedienne. He was kept in prison until July 1979, and under house arrest until 1980, when he was freed unconditionally. He returned to Algeria from exile in 1990.

***

Berri, Nabih (1938-   ): Lebanese political Born into a Lebanese Shi'a merchant family that settled in Freetown, Sierra Leone, Berri returned to Tibnin in southern Lebanon the town of his ancestors. Following a fresh parliamentary poll in 1992 Berri became speaker of parliament. He was reelected speaker after the 1996 and 200 general elections.

***

Beyazid I (1347-1403): Ottoman sultan (1389-1402), son and successor of Murad I. He besieged the Turkish rulers in E Anatolia and defeated the army of Sigismund of Hungary (see Sigismund, Holy Roman emperor) at Nikopol. Ottoman expansion led to conflict with the conqueror Timur, and the two armies met at Ankara in 1402. Beyazid's troops consisted only of Serbs and the Janissaries, since the Tatars and most of his Turkish vassals had deserted him. His army was routed, and he died as Timur's prisoner. His sons fought (1402-13) each other for the succession; Muhammad I emerged victorious. The name appears in other forms, e.g., Bajazet, Bayazid, and Beyazit.

***

Bhutto, Benazir (1953-2007): Pakistani stateswoman. Prime Minister of Pakistan (1988-90, 1993-96). The daughter of Zulfikar Ali Bhutto, she completed her studies at Harvard and Oxford Universities and went back to Pakistan only a few days before her father was deposed in a coup (1977). She was frequently held under house arrest from 1977 until 1984, when she went into exile. After her father's execution (1979) she led the Pakistan People's Party (PPP) and campaigned for the restoration of democracy. Martial law was lifted in 1986 and Bhutto returned to Pakistan, leading opposition to General Zia Ul-Haq's government.

The PPP won elections in 1988 and Bhutto became Prime Minister until 1990, when her government was dismissed. She was charged with corruption and fraud, but was acquitted of most of the charges in 1994. In 1993 she was elected Prime Minister for the second time, as head of a PPP-led coalition. Her plans to implement social reforms and to liberalize Pakistani society were hampered by economic difficulties, violent social unrest, and rising Islamic fundamentalism. She was again accused of corruption and dismissed from office (1996) and was defeated in elections held in 1997.

***

Bhutto, Zulfikar Ali (1928-1979): Pakistani statesman. Prime minister of Pakistan (1971-77) who made concessions to the Islamists but was overthrown by the more devout Zia ul Haqq. In 1958 he joined Ayub Khan's first military government as Minister of Fuel and Power and subsequently became Foreign Minister (1963). Dismissed from Ayub's cabinet in 1967 he formed the Pakistan People's Party with a policy of Islam, democracy, socialism, and populism. In the elections of 1970 the PPP secured the largest share of the vote in West Pakistan and, after the military government was discredited by the loss of Bangladesh. Bhutto became President (1971), but stepped down in 1973 to become Prime Minister. Bhutto concluded the Simia agreement with India in 1972….Bhutto was subsequently hanged on the charge of complicity in a political murder. His widow, Begum Nusrat Bhutto (1934--), has also been active in politics and his daughter Benazir Bhutto became Prime Minister.

***

Bilal ibn Rabah (579-641): During the early days of Islam, several non-Arabs embraced Islam and became prominent companions of the Prophet Muhammad. They included Salman al-Farisi, Suhaib al-Rumi and Bilal ibn Rabah. Perhaps the most devoted and dedicated non-Arab to embrace Islam, however, was Bilal. Born into slavery, he rose to become one of the Islamic history's most celebrated figures.

Bilal was born to an Abyssinian slave girl of the Banu Jumah tribe of Makkah. When Bilal was in his early twenties, he was sold to Umayyah ibn Khalaf, a powerful Makkan chieftain, as a slave. When Prophet Muhammad started promulgating Islam in Makkah, Bilal was around thirty years old. He was one of the first seven people to embrace Islam. Bilal the Ethiopian continued to defy Umayyah in a heroic manner.

According to the historians, Umayyah used to make Bilal sleep on the scorching desert sand, tie him up, place a heavy stone on his chest and leave him in the desert to suffer. Bilal would not renounce Islam come what may; his faith was as solid as a rock. Moved by his suffering and plight, Abu Bakr, who was a wealthy businessman and early convert to Islam, offered to buy Bilal his freedom. Now for the first time in his life, Bilal was a free man who bowed before none, other than the One True God. When the Prophet eventually left his native Makkah for Madinah in 622, Bilal followed suit.

As a prominent aide and supporter of the Prophet, Bilal discharged his duties scrupulously. Moreover, after the building of the Prophet's mosque was completed, Bilal encouraged his companions to perform their five daily prayers (*Salat*) in congregation (*Jama'ah*) in the mosque, which the Prophet himself led.

Then, one day, a companion called Abdullah ibn Zaid appeared before the Prophet and said he saw in a dream where a person was calling all Muslims to prayer from the roof of the mosque. The Prophet and his companions liked this idea. The *Adhan* (or 'call to prayer') was thus instituted by the order of the Prophet. It consisted of repeating the following formulas:

Allahu Akbar (Allah is great),
Ashadu Allah-ihala illa Allah (I bear witness that there is no god but Allah)
Ashadu ann Muhammadan Rasul Allah (I bear witness that Muhammad is Allah's Messenger),
Haiya alas salah (Hasten to Prayer),
Haiya alal Falah (Hasten to Success),
Allahu Akbar (Allah is great),
La ilaha illa Allah (There is no god but Allah)

Since Bilal had the most beautiful voice, the Prophet asked him to go into the *Masjid al-Nabi* and make the first historic call to prayer. Thus Bilal became the first, and the most famous, *Mu'adhdhin* (or 'caller to prayer') in Islamic history.

Umayyah, Bilal's chief tormentor, is today remembered as a cruel and pathetic man who was put to the sword by Bilal at the Battle of Badr for his unspeakable cruelty and inhumanity toward Bilal.

When the Prophet passed away in 632, Bilal was so devastated that he could no longer bear to live in Madinah, for his memories of happy times with the Prophet made him very sad and lonely. He eventually accompanied a Muslim army, led by Abu Ubaida ibn Al-

Jarrah, to Syria and settled in Damascus permanently. Bilal served as governor of Damascus for a short period and died around sixty.

***

Bin Laden, Osama (or Usama, 1957-2011): Saudi-born leader of Al Qaeda [Arab.,=the base], a terrorist organization devoted to uniting all Muslims and establishing a transnational, strict-fundamentalist Islamic state. The youngest son of a wealthy Yemeni-born businessman, bin Laden was trained as a civil engineer (grad. 1979, King Abdul Aziz Univ., Jidda), but following the Soviet invasion of Afghanistan (see Afghanistan War) he went to Pakistan where he helped to finance the mujahidin and to found Makhtab al Khadimat [services office] (MAK), which recruited and trained non-Afghani Muslims to fight in the war. In 1987 he split with MAK to begin a jihad [holy war] against Israel and Western influence in Islamic countries; he founded Al Qaeda the next year.

Following the Soviet withdrawal from Afghanistan, he returned to his family's construction business in Saudi Arabia. When U.S. troops were stationed (1990) on Saudi soil during Persian Gulf War he became violently opposed to the Saudi monarchy and the United States. After he was caught smuggling arms in 1991, he went to Sudan, where he began financing terrorists training camps while investing in businesses and increasing his fortune. His Saudi citizenship was revoked in 1994. After the attempted assassination (1995) of Egyptian president Mubarak, to which bin Laden was linked, he was expelled (1996) from Sudan and reestablished himself in Afghanistan, where the extreme Islamic fundamentalist Taliban had come to power.

That same year he issued a declaration of war against the United States. In its camps in Afghanistan…1996 car bombing of the U.S. embassies in Kenya and Tanzania, the 2000 attack on the USS *Cole* in Yemen, and in the 2001 attacks on the World Trade Center and the Pentagon. He has been indicted in the United States for the embassy bombings, and the United States launched retaliatory cruise missile attacks against his Afghanistan camps in 1998. Following the 2001 attacks the United States demanded the Taliban hand over bin Laden. When the Afghanis refused, U.S. forces began military action against Afghanistan, and in conjunction with opposition forces there largely defeated Taliban and Al Qaeda forces by Jan., 2002. Bin Laden, however, was not captured, and Al Qaeda continued to function and launch terror attacks on limited scale.

***

Bishara, Azmi (1956-   ): Israeli Arab academic and politician Born into a middle class family in Nazareth, Bishara founded the National Committee of Arab High School Students in 1974. Later while enrolled at Haifa University for a degree in political science he established the Arab Students Union which elected him as its chairman. On the Eve of the 2003 parliamentary poll, the Israeli election commission barred him by 22 votes to nineteen from contesting the election, but the High Court overturned the ban. He retained his seat.

***

Bitar, Salah al Din (1912-1980): Syrian politician Born into a prominent Sunni family in Damascus. Bitar received his higher education at Damascus University, followed by Sorbonne University, Paris Back in the Syrian capital in 1934, he taught mathematics and physics at a prestigious secondary school. In 1940, together with Michel Aflaq a fellow teacher, he established a study circle called the Movement of Arab Renaissance. After his return to Paris, Bitar started publishing a journal. Al Ihya al Arabi (the Arab Revival), which became a mobilizing forum for carious Syrian opposition groups in exile. He was assassinated in Paris in July 1980. Syrian complicity in the killing, though not proven, was widely suspected.

***

Boumedienne, Houari (1925-1978): Algerian statesman. In the early 1950s, he joined a group of expatriate Algerian nationalists in Cairo which included Ben Bella, and in 1955 he joined resistance forces in Algeria operating against the French. He became chief-of-staff of the exiled National Liberation Front in Tunisia (1960-62). In March 1962 his forces occupied Algiers for Ben Bella after which a peace treaty was signed with France. He displaced Ben Bella in a coup in 1965, ruling until his death in 1978. He had close ties with the Communist bloc, but also maintained friendly relations with Western countries.

***

Bourguiba, Habib Ali (1903-2000): Tunisian statesman. A staunch nationalist, he was imprisoned at different times by the French and during World War II by the Germans. He negotiated the agreement which led to the Tunisian autonomy (1954) and when Tunisia became independent (1956), he was elected Prime Minister. In 1957 he deposed the Bey of Tunis, abolished the monarchy, and was himself chosen President of the Republic by the constituent Assembly, and President for life in 1975. A moderate, Bourguiba faced riots in 1978 and 1980. After 1981 he democratized the National Assembly of his one-party state, and recognized the right of opposition by forging a coalition alliance. He was deposed in 1987 and placed under house-arrest.

***

Boutros-Ghali, Boutros (1922-   ): Egyptian diplomat, Secretary-General of the United Nations (1992-96). A Coptic Christian from a distinguished family, he was educated in the USA and France, and lectured in law and political science in Cairo, Boutros-Ghali was a political ally of Anwar Sadat and was instrumental in bringing about the Camp David Accord with Israel in 1977. He served as Egypt's deputy Prime Minister (1991-92). In his first year in office as UN Secretary-General, he supported the ill-fated US-led UN military intervention in Somalia; however, growing antagonism between him and the USA, especially over UN funding and the ethnic conflicts in Bosnia-Herzegovina and Rwanda, led the USA to veto his reappointment for a second term.

***

Chalabi, Ahmad (1944-   ): Iraqi politician Born into a rich banking family in Baghdad, Ahmad Chalabi and his parents fled Baghdad in the wake of the antiroyalist coup in 1958. At the Iraqi open Opposition Conference in London in December 2002, Chalabi's proposal for a transitional government for Iraq in post Saddam Iraq was rejected. He returned to Iraq four months later in the wake of the Anglo American invasion of the country.

***

Chehab, Fuad (1902-1973): Lebanese military leader and politician president 1958-64 Born into Maronite family, Chehab joined the army during the French mandate and rose to the rank of colonel. After the independence of Lebanon in 1946, he was promoted to general and appointed commander of the army. After stepping down in 1964, he continued to wield influence through the parliamentarians and military and intelligence officers who remained loyal to him. But he resisted their pressure to stand for the presidency again in 1970.

***

Darwish, Mahmud (1941-2008): Palestinian writer and poet Born into a landowning Sunni family in Barwa village near Acre Darwish and his family escaped to Lebanon during the 1948-49 Palestine War. Opposed to the Oslo Accord of September 1993, he resigned in protest. In Paris he has continued to edit Al Karmel the Palestinian literary review. His latest volumes of poetry in English include Psalms and the Adam of two Eden's (2001).

***

Dost Muhammad (1798-1863): Amir of Afghanistan. He was ruler of Kabul and Afghanistan (1826-39, 1843-63). Defeated in the first Anglo-Afghan War, he regained power in 1843 and consolidated his rule in Afghanistan through control of Kandahar (1855), northern Afghanistan (1850-59), and Heart (1863), so establishing the territorial outlines of modern Afghanistan.

***

Dowlatabadi, Mahmud (1940-   ): *Iranian writer.* Born in Dowlatabadi in the eastern province of Khorasan, in a poor family, Dowlatabadi moved to Tehran in his mid-teens. After completing a course in acting in 1960, he became a stage actor. *The Unoccupied Place of Solooch (Persian: Jay-e Khali-e Solooch),* the story of the survival of a village woman and her three children after her abandonment by her husband, and *Yusuf's Day and Night,* an equally riveting work of social realism.

***

El Cid (1040-1099) (Campeador) (Arabic *al-Said*, 'the lord' and Spanish *Campeador*, 'champion') Spanish hero. He was Rodrigo Diaz de Bivar, a Castilian nobleman, who was exiled after the war between the brothers Sancho II of Castile and Alfonso VI of Leon, becoming a mercenary captain fighting mainly for the Moors. He captured Valencia on his own behalf but was expelled in 1099, dying shortly afterwards. Many of the legends concerning him bear little relation to historical facts.

***

El-Saadawi, Nawal (1931-   ): *Egyptian writer and feminist campaigner* Born into a middle-class family in the village of Kafr Tahla, el Saadawi trained as a doctor. El Saadawi was among the several hundred dissident Egyptian intellectuals who were arrested in September 1981. Freed three months later by President Hosni Mubarak, she resumed her writing and campaigning for women's rights in the Arab world. Due to her opposition to the U.S.-led war against Iraq following that country's invasion of Kuwait, the authorities closed down the Arab Women's Solidarity Association in 1991.

***

Emin Pasha (Mehmed Eduard Schnitzer) (1840-1992) German explorer and physician. He joined the Ottoman army in 1865 and in 1876 he served under General Gordon in Khartoum. Gordon used him for administrative duties and diplomatic missions and in 1878 appointed him governor of the Upper Nile area of Equatoria, where he surveyed the region and suppressed slavery. Isolated when the Mahdi controlled the Sudan, he was rescued in 1888 by H. M. Stanley. In 1890 he was employed by the German government in East Africa. While engaged in exploration for Germany, Arab slave-raiders murdered him.

***

Enver Pasha (1881-1922): Ottoman Turkish general and statesman. He played a prominent part in the 1908 Young Turk revolution which restored the liberal constitution of 1876, and subsequently led a successful coup in 1913. as Minister of War (1913-18) he played the leading role in determining the entry of the Ottoman empire into World War I on the side of the Central Powers and in the conduct of Ottoman strategy during the war. In 1921 he fled to Turkistan, where he was killed leading opposition to Soviet rule. He fought in the Turko-Italian War (1911-12) in Libya and in the Balkan Wars (1912-13).

***

Fahd ibn Abdul Aziz al Saud (1920-2005): King of Saudi Arabia, 1982, Born in Riyadh to Ibn Saud and Hassa bint Ahmad al Sudairi, Fahd was the eleventh son of Ibn Saud. He received a traditional education. During the rule of Saud ibn Abdul Aziz, Fahd served first as education minister (1953-60) and then, from 1962 as interior minister. In August he appointed a fully nominated sixty member Consultative Council. To silence opposition, Fahd detained 200 political dissidents in 1994. He was distressed when a bomb at the National Guard training center in Riyadh in November 1995 killed seven people, including five American officers. One of the richest men in the world in the mid 1990s Fahd's personal wealth was estimated to be around $20 billion.

***

Faisal I ibn Hussein al Hashem (1885-1933): King of Iraq 1921-33 Third son of Hussein ibn Ali al Hashem, Faisal was born in Ta'if Hijaz but was raised in Istanbul, where his father was kept under surveillance by the Ottoman sultan. In 1908 Faisal returned to Hijaz but was raised in Istanbul, where his father was kept under surveillance by the Ottoman sultan. In 1908 Faisal returned to Hijaz along with his father, who was appointed governor of Mecca by the young Turks after they had succeeded the sultan. In 1950 he signed a treaty with Britain: it required him to coordinate his foreign policy with London and to allow the stationing of British troops in Iraq in exchange for a British guarantee to protect Iraq against foreign attack. Britain ended its mandate in October 1932 and sponsored Iraq's membership of the League of Nations.

***

Faisal I or Feisal (1885-1933): King of Iraq (1921-33). The son of Hussein Ibn Ali, he commanded the northern Arab army in Jordan, Palestine, and Syria in association with T. E. Lawrence in the Arab Revolt of 1916-18. in 1920 Faisal was chosen king of Syria by the Syrian national Congress but was expelled by France, the mandatory power. He was then made King of Iraq by Britain, who held the mandate for that territory. As ruler of Iraq (1921-33) he demonstrated considerable political skill in building up the institutions of the new state.

***

Faisal ibn Abd al-Aziz ibn Saud (1905-1975): King of Saudi Arabia (1964-75), son of Ibn Saud, brother of Saud. Faisal led several military campaigns in the making of Saudi Arabia. In 1958 he became premier and foreign minister in the cabinet of his brother, King Saud. Faisal was removed from office in 1960, but was reinstated as premier in 1962. Due to poor health and domestic opposition, King Saud was forced to abdicate (Nov., 1964) by the ruling family in favor of the more popularly approved Faisal. He joined with other Arab nations against Israel in the 1967 Arab-Israeli War. In 1975, Faisal was shot and killed by one of his nephews; he was succeeded by his brother, Crown Prince Khalid.

***

Faisal II ibn Ghazi al Hashem (1935-1958): King of Iraq 1939-58, The only song of King Ghazi ibn Faisal I al Hashem, Faisal as an infant succeeded his father under the regency of his uncle Abdul Ilah ibn Ali. Following the 1941 coup by the nationalist Rashid Ali Gailani, Faisal and his mother fled, along with Abdul Ilah and other members of the royal family. Gailani was defeated and that ensured the future of Faisal as king. After the formation of the Arab Federation of Iraq and Jordan in February 1958, Faisal became its head. Five months later he was gunned down in the royal courtyard during a coup mounted by republican officers.

***

Fakhr al-Din al-Razi (1149-1209): Under the patronage of Abbasid Caliph Harun al-Rashid and his son al-Ma'mun, ancient Greek scientific, philosophical and medical works were translated into Arabic for the first time during the eighth and early part of the ninth century. At the time Baghdad, the capital of the Abbasid Caliphate, became such a prominent center of intellectual and literary activity that students and scholars from across the Muslim world flocked to the city to study and conduct research. Inspired by influential Islamic scholars like Ahmad ibn Hanbal, the traditionalists launched a blistering attack on the Neoplatonic ideas of the early Muslim philosophers. Al-Ghazali emerged in the eleventh century to defend, like his illustrious predecessor, the cause of Islamic traditionalism. And in so doing, he struck a powerful blow against the Neoplatonic theories of al-Kindi, Abu Bakr al-Razi, al-Farabi and Ibn Sina. His critique of Neoplatonism paved the way for the emergence of Fakhr al-Din al-Razi, who became one of the most celebrated Islamic theologians of the twelfth century.

Abu Abdullah Muhammad ibn Umar ibn Hussain, better known as Fakhr al-Din al-Razi, was born in the northern Persian city of Rayy (located close to modern Tehran) into a distinguished family of Islamic scholars and jurists. Keen to learn more, he left his native Rayy and moved to Maraghah (in present-day Azerbaijan) to study the philosophical sciences of the day under the guidance of Majd al-Din al-Jili.

Inspired no doubt by al-Ghazali's criticism of Neoplatonic thought, al-Razi too developed a skeptical attitude toward philosophy. By the time he had moved to Khwarizm (located in modern Uzbekistan), he was widely recognized as a master of traditional Islamic sciences, speculative theology and philosophy, in addition to being familiar with mathematics, medicine and the natural sciences.

The Caliph's anti Mu'tazilite policies forced the adherents of Mu'tazilism to flee from Baghdad and regroup in and around Khwarizm. Unable to respond to his criticism, al-Razi's Mu'tazilite opponents soon wanted him out of Khwarizm. To this end, they instigated a popular revolt against al-Razi which forced him to leave the region. From Khwarizm, he proceeded to Bukhara and from there he went to Samarqand, and eventually returned to his native Rayy.

However, intense jealousy and incessant rivalry between the Government officials, coupled with rumors of political plots and intrigues, soon forced him to quit his job and move to Ghazna in 1185.

As an outspoken exponent of Islam, al-Razi never shied away from religious or philosophical controversies. His criticisms were robust and incisive and, more often than not, his opponents felt the impact of his intellectual onslaught. The Karramiyyah were one such group who became so incensed by his stinging critique of their beliefs and practices that they even attempted to assassinate him in 1189, but the indomitable al-Razi remained as firm as ever. Author of more than one hundred books and treatises on all the sciences of his time (including Islamic sciences, philosophy, medicine and mathematics), al-Razi was a truly gifted scholar and polymath.

Unlike al-Ghazali, al-Razi was not an opponent of philosophical sciences; rather he was only critical of certain aspects of Neoplatonic thought. But it is his *Tafsir al-Kabir*, that famous and encyclopedic commentary on the Qur'an, which has immortalized his name. Al-Razi died at the age of fifty-eight and was buried in Herat (located in present-day Afghanistan).

***

Farouk (1920-1965): King of Egypt (1936-1952). The son of Faud I, whom the British had installed in 1922, he ruled autocratically, as had his father. His pro-Axis sympathies during world War II resulted in a clash with the British, who imposed on him (1942) the Wafd leader Mustapha an-Nahas Pasha as a Premier who would support the allies. Farouk's defeat in the Arab-Israeli conflict (1948), and the general corruption of his reign led to a military coup in 1952, headed by Nasser. He was forced to abdicate in favors of his infant son, Faud II, in 1952, who was deposed in 1953.

***

Farrakhan, Louis (1933-   ): African-American religious leader, b. New York City, as Louis Eugene Walcott. A former calypso singer known as The Charmer, he joined the Nation of Islam (Black Muslims) in 1955, eventually becoming minister of the Harlem Temple after Malcolm X broke with the religious group. After Elijah Muhammad died and his son steered the Black Muslims toward Sunni Islamic practice, Farrakhan founded (1977) a reorganized Nation of Islam that adhered to the elder Muhammad's teachings.

***

Fatimah bint Muhammad (605-633): Fatimah (Arabic: Fatimah; born c. 605 or 615 – d. 633) was a daughter of Muhammad and Khadijah, wife of Ali and mother of Hasan and Husain, and one of the five members of Ahl al-Bayt. She became the object of great veneration by all Muslims, because she lived closest to her father and supported him in his difficulties and because of historical importance of her husband and her two sons, and that she is the only member of Muhammad's family that gave him descendants, numerously spread through the Islamic world.

She was involved in three significant political actions, each recorded in almost all sources. First, after the conquest of Mecca, she refused her protection to Abu Sufian; Second, after Muhammad's death, she courageously defended Ali's cause, fiercely opposed the election of Abu Bakr, and had violent disputes with him and particularly with Umar; Third, she laid claim to the property rights of her father and challenged Abu Bakr's categorical refusal to cede them, particularly Fadak and a share in the produce of Khaybar.

She died a few months after her father's death, and was buried in Jannat Al-Baqi', but the exact location of her grave is unknown. Most Shi'a Muslims believe that she died as a result of her injury caused by Umar, during defending Ali against Abu Bakr.

Birth (*Genealogy of Khadijah's daughters*):

Fatimah was born in Mecca to Khadijah, the first wife of Muhammad. There are differences of opinion on the exact date of her birth (605 or 615), but the widely accepted view is that she was born five years before the first Qur'anic revelations, during the time of the rebuilding of the Kaaba in 605, although this does imply she was over 18 at the time of her marriage, which was unusual in Arabia. Shi'a sources, however, state that she was born either two or five years after the first Qur'anic revelations, but that timeline would imply her mother was over fifty at the time of her birth.

Fatimah as believed by Sunnis is the fourth of Muhammad's daughters after Zaynab, Ruqayya, and Umm Kulthum. While according to Shi'a scholars, Fatimah was Muhammad's only biological daughter, they further claimed, Ruqayyah and Umm Kulthum are actually, being the daughters of Hala, the sister of Khadijah, who were adopted by Muhammad and Khadijah at her death, however Sunnis accept that Muhammad had four daughters all from Khadijah.

Titles (*List of Shi'a titles for Fatima Zahra*):

Fatimah is given many titles by Muslims to show their admiration of her moral and physical characteristics. The most used title is "*al-Zahra*", meaning "the shining one", and she is commonly referred to as *Fatimah Zahra*. She was also known as *Ummu Abeeha* (Mother of her Father) and "*al-Batul*" (the chaste and pure one) as she spent much of her time in prayer, reciting the Qur'an and in other acts of worship.

Early life:
Following the birth of Fatimah, she was personally nursed, contrary to local customs where the newborn were sent to "wet nurses" in surrounding villages. She spent her early youth under the care of her parents in Mecca in the shadow of the tribulations suffered by her father at the hands of the Quraysh.

According to tradition, on one occasion while Muhammad was performing the *salah* (prayer) in the Kaaba, Amr ibn Hishām (Abu Jahl) and his men poured camel placenta over him. Fatimah, upon hearing the news, rushed to her father and wiped away the filth while scolding the men.

Following the death of her mother, Fatimah was overcome by sorrow and found it very difficult to come to terms with her death. She was consoled by her father, who informed her that he had received word from angel Gabriel that God had built for her a palace in paradise.

Marriage:
Many of Muhammad's companions asked for Fatimah's hand in marriage, including Abu Bakr and Umar. Muhammad turned them all down, saying that he was awaiting a sign of her destiny. Ali, Muhammad's cousin, also had a desire to marry Fatimah but did not have the courage to approach Muhammad due to his (Ali's) poverty. Even when he mustered up the courage and went to see Muhammad, he could not vocalize his intention but remained silent. Muhammad understood the reason for his being there and prompted Ali to confirm that he had come to seek Fatimah in marriage. He suggested that Ali had a shield, which if sold, would provide sufficient money to pay the bridal gift (*mahr*). Muhammad put forward the proposal from Ali to Fatimah, who remained silent and did not protest, which Muhammad took to be a sign of affirmation and consent.

The actual date of the marriage is unclear, but it most likely took place in 623, the second year of the Hijra, although some sources say it was in 622. The age of Fatimah is reported to have been 9 or 19 (due to differences of opinion on the exact date of her birth i.e. 605 or 615) at the time of her marriage while Ali was between 21 and 25. Muhammad told Ali that he had been ordered by God to give his daughter Fatimah to Ali in marriage. Muhammad said to Fatimah: "I have married you to the dearest of my family to me." Ali sold his shield to raise the money needed for the wedding, as suggested by Muhammad.

However, Uthman ibn Affan, to whom the shield was sold, gave it back to Ali saying it was his wedding gift to Ali and Fatimah. Muhammad himself performed the wedding ceremony and two of his wives, Aisha and Umm Salama, prepared the wedding feast with dates, figs, sheep and other food donated by various members of the Medinan community. Their marriage lasted about ten years and ended when Fatimah died. Although polygamy is permitted by Islam, Ali did not marry another woman while Fatimah was alive.

Life before the death of Muhammad:
Poverty:

After her marriage to Ali, the wedded couple led a life of abject poverty in contrast to her sisters who were all married to wealthy individuals. Ali had built a house not too far from Muhammad's residence where he lived with Fatimah. However, due to Fatimah's desire to be closer to her father, a Medinan (Haritha bin al-Numan) donated his own house to them.

At the beginning they were extremely poor. For several years after her marriage, she did all of the work by herself. The shoulder on which she carried pitchers of water from the well was swollen and the hand with which she worked the hand mill to grind corn where often covered with blisters. Fatimah vouched to take care of the household work, make dough, bake bread, and clean the house; in return, Ali vouched to take care of the outside work such as gathering firewood, and bringing food. Ali worked to irrigate other peoples lands by drawing water from the wells which caused him to complain of chest pains. Their circumstances were akin to many of the Muslims at the time and only improved following the Battle of Khaybar when the produce of Khaybar was distributed among the poor. When the economic situations of the Muslims become better, Fatimah gained some maids but treated them like her family and performed the house duties with them.

Life after the death of Muhammad:
Caliphate of Abu Bakr:

For the few months that she survived following the death of her father, Fatimah found herself indirectly at the center of political disunity. Differing accounts of the events surrounding the commencement of the caliphate exist which were the cause of the Shi'a and Sunni split. According to the Sunnis the majority of Muslims at the time of Muhammed's death favored Abu Bakr as the Caliph while a portion of the population supported Fatimah's husband, Ali. Shi'as believe that Ali was appointed by Muhammed to be the new caliph at

Ghadir Al-Khumm. Some Sunnis dispute this claim while others accept the event of Ghadir Al-Khumm but do not accept his caliphate.

Following his election to the caliphate after a meeting in Saqifah, Abu Bakr and Umar with a few other companions headed to Fatimah's house to obtain homage from Ali and his supporters who had gathered there. Then Umar threatened to set the house on fire unless they came out and swore allegiance with Abu Bakr.

According to the Encyclopedia of Islam, some Shi'a sources say that upon seeing them, Ali came out with his sword drawn but was disarmed by Umar and their companions. Fatimah, in support of her husband, started a commotion and threatened to "uncover her hair", at which Abu Bakr relented and withdrew.

Shi'a historians hold that Umar called for Ali and his men to come out and swear allegiance to Abu Bakr. When they did not, Umar broke in, resulting in Fatimah's ribs being broken by being pressed between the door and the wall causing her to miscarry Muhsin which led to her eventual death.

Inheritance (*Fadak*):

After the death of her father, Fatimah approached Abu Bakr and asked him to relinquish her share of the inheritance from Muhammad's estate. Fatimah expected the land of Fadak (situated 30 mi (48 km) from Medina) and a share of Khaybar would be passed onto her as part of her inheritance. However, Abu Bakr rejected her request citing a narration where Muhammad stated that prophets do not leave behind inheritance and that all their possessions become Sadaqah to be used for charity. Fatimah was upset at this flat refusal by Abu Bakr and did not speak to him until her death (however some Sunni sources claim she had reconciled her differences with Abu Bakr before she died). Shi'as contend that Fadak had been gifted to Fatimah by Muhammad and Abu Bakr was wrong in not allowing her to take possession of it.

> Fatimah remained alive for six months after the death of Allah's Apostle.
> —Muhammad al-Bukhari, *Sahih al-Bukhari*

According to the one of the famous scholars, "Kitab al-Tabaqat al-Kabir, (Book of the Major Classes), Volume 2, by Ibn Sa'd, pages 391–394: She did not talk with him till she died. She lived six months after the Apostle of Allah.

Fatimah came to Abu Bakr and demanded her share in the inheritance. Al-Abbas came to him and demanded his share in the inheritance. Ali came with them. Thereupon Abu Bakr said, "The

Apostle of Allah said, "We leave no inheritance, what we leave behind us is Sadaqah." Then they became quiet and retired.

Death:

Following the farewell pilgrimage, Muhammad summoned Fatimah and informed her that he would be dying soon but also informed her that she would be the first of his household to join him. Some days after this discussion, Muhammad died, following which Fatimah was grief stricken and remained so for the remainder of her life until she died less than six months later, in the month of Ramadhan.

There are two distinct views on the manner of her death between the Shi'as and Sunnis. The Sunnis state that on the morning of her death, she took a bath, put on new clothes and lay down in bed. She asked for Ali and informed him that her time to die was very close. Upon hearing this news, Ali began to cry but was consoled by Fatimah who asked him to look after her two sons and for him to bury her without ceremony. After her death, Ali followed her wishes and buried her without informing the Medinan people.

Shi'as, however, maintain that Fatimah died as a result of injuries sustained after her house was raided by Umar ibn al-Khattab who burnt the house and stormed her house by pushing the door to the farthest extent, cracking her rib-cage whilst she was pregnant. Note that this accident also has been affirmed by the Sufi (Nagina mosque order) scholar Maulana Shibli's famous book Al-Farook, but he has described the other reasons for this incident as well. Umar not only murdered her in the process but her unborn child, Mohsen, who was miscarried shortly thereafter as a direct result of Umar's attack.

Her grave is in Jannat Al-Baqi', Medina beside Imam Hasan and other Imams. The single separate grave in the group is of Fatimah as per Dawoodi Bohra and other Shi'as.

Descendants (*Descendants of Ali ibn Abi Talib*):

Fatimah was survived by two sons, Hasan and Husayn, and two daughters, Zaynab and Umm Kulthum.

Modern descendants of Muhammad trace their lineage exclusively through Fatimah, as she was the only surviving child of Muhammad. Muhammad had no sons who reached adulthood. Fatimah's descendants are given the honorific titles *Sayyid* (meaning *lord* or *sir*), *Sharif* (meaning *noble*), and respected by both Sunni and Shi'a, though the Shi'as place much more emphasis and value on the distinction.

Views:

Muslims regard Fatimah as a loving and devoted daughter, mother, wife, a sincere Muslim, and an exemplar for women. It is believed that she was very close to her father and her distinction from other women is mentioned in many Hadith. After Khadijah, Muslims regard Fatimah as the most significant historical figure, considered to be the leader (Arabic: *Sayyidih*) of all women in this world and in Paradise. It is because of her moral purity that she occupies an analogous position in Islam to that Mary occupies in Christianity. She was the first wife of Ali, whom Sunnis consider the fourth *Rashidun* caliph and Shi'as consider the first infallible Imamah, the mother of the second and third Imams, and the ancestor of all the succeeding Imams; indeed, the Fatimid Caliphate is named after her.

Shi'a view (*The Fourteen Infallibles and Fatimid*):

Fatimah, regarded as "the Mother of the Imams", plays a special role in Shi'a piety. She has a unique status as Muhammad's only surviving child, the wife of Ali, their first Imam, and the mother of Hasan and Husayn. Fatimid Caliphate/ Imamate is based on her name. Fatimid faith continue further in Ismaili/Bohras (refer Tree on right). She is believed to have been immaculate, sinless and a pattern for Muslim women. Although leading a life of poverty, the Shi'a tradition emphasizes her compassion and sharing of whatever she had with others.

According to Mahmoud Ayoub, the two main images of Fatimah within the Shi'a tradition is that of "Eternal Weeper" and "the Judge in the hereafter". According to Shi'a tradition, the suffering and death of Fatimah was the first tragedy of Islam. She spent her last days mourning at the death of her father. Fatimah eternally weeps at the death of her two sons, who were murdered by the Umayyads. Shi'as believe they share in Fatimah's suffering by weeping for her sorrows. The tears of the faithful is also believed to console Fatimah. Shi'as hold that Fatimah will play a redemptive role as the mistress of the day of judgment in the hereafter as a reward for her suffering in this world.

***

Franjieh, Suleiman (1910-1993): Lebanese politician, president 1970-76 Born into the Maronite Franjieh clan at the Ihden palace, 12 miles/ 20 km from Zghorta, Franjieh grew up in the shadow of his elder brother, Hamid. Unlike right ring Maronites, his party participated in the 1992 parliamentary elections and won half of the 34 seats reserved for Maronites in a house of 128. With the right wing Maronites ending their boycott of the general election in 1996, the share of his party in the Maronite seats declined

***

Gabriel: Gabriel is the single most important angel in the Islamic tradition. According to Islam, Gabriel appeared before Muhammad while he was meditating in a cave. Gabriel then recited the Quran, verse by verse, commanding Muhammad to memories each line and spread it to others. The Quran is believed to be a series of quotes directly from God to Gabriel and onto Muhammad. This explains the Muslim emphasis on the actual spoken word of the Quran and why all prayers must be said in the original Arabic. In Christianity, Gabriel is believed to be one of God's archangels.

Some writings say there were three such higher-ranking angels, including Michael and Raphael. Other say there were seven. Gabriel makes several appearances in Christian tradition to relay God's messages. Gabriel appears before Zacharias and tells him that John the Baptist, a predecessor of Christ, will be born to Elizabeth. Gabriel also appears before Mary to tell her that she will give birth to Jesus. This interaction with Mary is known as the Annunciation. In Judaism, Gabriel interacts twice with Daniel. The first time, after Daniel has seen a vision from God that he cannot understand, God sends Gabriel to help him interpret. The second time, Gabriel appears before Daniel and predicts the end of the Jews' exile in Babylon.

***

Gailani, Rashid Ali (1892-1965): Iraqi politician, prime minister, 1933, 1940-41. Born into an eminent Sunni family in Baghdad Law School and set up legal practice. During the Second World War, when politicians and military officers split into pro and anti British factions, Gailani headed the anti British, nationalist camp. He became prime minister in March 1940. Three months later, when Italy declared war against Britain and its allies, he refused to cut links with Italy. He also refused to abide by Article 4 of the Anglo Iraqi Treaty which gave landing and transit rights to Britain in the event of a war. After his failed coup attempt in conjunction with the United Arab Republic in December 1958, Gailani was sentenced to capital punishment, but Qasim commuted his sentence and freed him in October 1961. Gailani then stayed away from politics.

***

Gemayel, Bashir (1947- 1982): Lebanese politician, president elect 1982. Born into a notable Maronite family in Beirut. Gemayel started his law and political science studies at St. Joseph University but did not finish them. During the Israeli invasion of Lebanon in June 1982, Gemayel's forces linked up with the Israelis on the outskirts of Beirut. The expulsion of the PLO and the Syrians from Beirut by the Israelis strengthened the Phalange and improved Gemayel's chances of achieving the highest office. On 14 September 1982, eight days before Gemayel was to be installed in office, a bomb explosion at the Phalange headquarters in Beirut killed him and 26 others.

***

Gemayel, Pierre (1905-1984): Lebanese politician. Born into a notable Maronite clan in Bikfaya, Gemayel received his university education in Beirut and Paris and trained as a pharmacist. Interested by the Nazi Youth Movement in Germany and by the Berlin Olympics in the summer of 1936. In July he stepped down as chairman of the Phalange Party, and the following month he died. Lebanon Leader of the Kataeb or Phalange, founded in 1936.

***

Genghis Khan (or Jenghiz Khan (1167-1227): Kahn, Mandarin *Che'ng-chi-ssu-han*, Mongol conqueror, originally named Temujin. He succeeded his father, Yekusai, as chieftain of a Mongol tribe and fought to become ruler of a Mongol confederacy. After subjugating many tribes of Mongolia and establishing his capital at Karakorum, Temujin held (1206) a great meeting, and Khuriltai, at which he accepted leadership of the Mongols and assumed his title. He promulgated a code of conduct and reorganized his armies. He attacked (1213) the Jurchen-ruled Chin empire of N China and by 1215 had occupied most of its territory, including the capital, Yenching (now Beijing). From 1218 to 1224 he conquered Turkistan, Transoxania, and Afghanistan and raided Persia and E Europe to the Dnieper River, Genghis Khan ruled one of the greatest land empires the world has ever known. He died while campaigning against the Jurchen, and his vast domains were divided among his sons and grandsons. His wars were marked by ruthless carnage, but Genghis Khan was a brilliant ruler and military leader. Timur was said to be descended from him.

***

Ghashmi, Ahmad Hussein (1938-1978): Yemeni military officer and politician, president 1977-78 Born in Hamada into a clan of the Hashid tribal confederation. Ghashmi was trained as an officer at the Baghdad Military Academy. A conservative Ghashmi was considered pro Saudi. After the assassination of Hamdi in October 1977 he became commander in chief and chairman of a three man MCC. He was assassinated in June by the blast of a bomb hidden in a briefcase by an emissary of South Yemeni President Salim Rubai Ali.

***

Ghazi ibn Faisal I al Hashem (1912-1939): King of Iraq 1932-39, the only son of Faisal I ibn Hussein al Hashem. Ghazi was born in Hijaz under the Ottoman rule. Following the installation of his father as king of Iraq in 1921, he became heir apparent. Educated partly in Baghdad and partly in Britain. Ghazi succeeded his father in 1933. He died as a result of an alleged car crash.

***

Glubb (Pasha), Sir John Bagot (1897-1986): British military officer in the Middle East Born in Preston, Britain, Glubb was educated at Cheltenham College and the Royal Military Academy in Woolwich, London. During the First World War he was wounded in combat and was awarded the Military Cross. After the war he was sent to Iraq. To offset the rising popular charge that he was a puppet of Britain, King Hussein dismissed Glubb in March 1956, Glubb retired to Britain where he lectured and wrote books mainly about Arab countries and peoples. Golan Heights: Syrian region Also called the Golan Plateau. Area 454 sq miles, 1,176 sq km, pop 33,000, divided equally among Jewish settlers and Syrian equally among Jewish settlers and Syrian Druze.

Part of Syria since the First World War, the western border of the Golan Heights, overlooking the Hula Valley and Lake Tiberius/ Sea of Galilee was fortified after the founding of Israel in 1948. In 1969 Syria gave Palestinian commandos greater freedom of action in the area. Since the US peace plan of June 1970 made no mention of Israel evacuating the Heights, Syria rejected it. In the October 1973 Arab Israeli War, The Syrian offensive, launched on 6 October, limited itself to recovering the Golan Heights. They resumed in 1999 after the election of Ehud Barak as Israel's prime minister. But they failed in March 2000 when Barak insisted on keeping a strip of the Golan along Lake Tiberius, which Syrian President Hafiz Assad refused.

***

Golpaygani, Muhammad Reza Musavi (1899-1993): Iranian leader, Born in Golpaygani of a religious Shi'a family, Golpaygani lost his parents when young and as raised by his sisters. When Khomeini was exiled in 1964, Golpaygani took over the administration of the prestigious Faiyziyya seminary in Qom. He offered the concept of Vilayat e Faqih which assigned spiritual and temporal leadership of an Islamic community to jurisprudents. When Khomeini died in 1989 without having named a successor, the Assembly of Experts reportedly offered the position of leader to Golpaygani. Being in poor health, he turned it down. As a cleric who had been in close contact with all the leading Shi'a personages of the 20th century, Golpaygani was unique.

***

Habash, George (1926-2008): Palestinian leader. Born into a Greek Orthodox family in Lydda, Habash moved to Amman with his parents after the Palestine War (1948-49) While at the AUB in 1952 he co founded the Arab Nationalist Movement.. Under his leadership the ANM's Palestinian members formed a Preparatory Committee for Unified Palestinian Action in early 1966. After the PFLP's expulsion from Amman, Habash relocated it in Beirut. When in 1974 the Palestine National Council accepted the idea of a Palestinian state on the West Bank and the Gaza strip as an intermediate step toward the liberation of Palestine, Habash rejected it and began a boycott of the PLO Executive Committee. During the crisis created by Iraq's invasion of Kuwait in August 1990, Habash backed President Saddam Hussein especially after the latter tried to link the Kuwaiti issue to Israel's occupation of the Arab territories. Afflicted with cancer, he gave up his leadership of the PFLP to his deputy, Mustafa Zifri, also known as Abu Alo Mustafa in 2000.

***

Habibi, Emile Shukri (1921-1996): Palestinian writer and political Born into a Christian family in Haifa. Habibi received his secondary school education in Haifa and Acre. He was elected to parliament in 1951, 1955 and 1961. Four years later, together with Emile Touma and Meir Vilner, Habibi left Maki and established Rakah. He failed to get reelected to parliament in 1965 and 1969 but was unsuccessful in 1973. Then followed Lukaa bin Lukaa (Lukaa, son of Lukaa) (1980) Ikhtiyaa (1985) and Suraya bint al Ghoul (1991) He won the Israel prize for literature in 1992, the first Israeli Arab to do so.

***

Hafiz, Amin(1921-   ) Syrian politician, president 1963-66. The son of a Sunni policeman in Aleppo. Hafiz became a noncommissioned officer in the French Syrian Social Forces during the Second World War.

After his release from jail in June 1967 he went into exile in Lebanon. When the Afaw led faction of the Baath party seized power in Iraq about a year later, he moved to Baghdad.

Hafiz continued his anti Assad activities, later heading the National Alliance of the Liberation of Syria, an umbrella body of various anti Assad factions.

***

Hafsah: fourth wife of the Prophet and daughter of Umar. Hafsah's first husband died at the battle of the wells of Badr, leaving her an eighteen year old widow. Known to be fiery tempered, literate and independent minded. She possessed the first written prototype of the Koran, the basis for the great compilation later achieved by Uthman. Omar's daughter, Muhammad's wife-18

***

Hagar: Abraham's second wife; Ishmael's mother; and Egyptian maiden. In the Bible, she is the wife of Abraham and the mother of Abraham's son Ishmael (in Arabic Ismail), who became the father of the Arab peoples. Hence Hagar is revered as one of the matriarchs of Islam and remembered with especial reverence in the ceremonies of the hajj pilgrimage to Mecca.

***

Hamad ibn Isa Al Khalifa **(1950-   ):** ruler of Bahrain, 1999 Born in Riffa al Khalifa was educated in Bahrain. In 2000 when the Supreme National Committee appointed by Al Khalifa, drafted a National Action Charter, recommending a constitutional monarchy and a bicameral parliament, he held a referendum in early 2001.

***

Hamdi, Ibrahim (1943-1977): North Yemeni political, president 1974-77 born of a religious Zaidi Shi'a father and a Shafii Sunni mother in Dhamar. Hamdi trained as an Islamic judge. But two days before Hamdi's departure for Aden in October 1977 to sign a mutual defense pact he was assassinated along with his brother Lt. Col. Abdullah Hamdi, commander of an elite brigade. These killings were widely believed to have been inspired by Riyadh.

***

Hariri, Rafiq (1944-2005): Lebanese politician; prime minister 1992-98, 2000 Born into a Sunni family in Sidon, Hariri enrolled as a student of business administration as Beirut Arab University in 1965. Following the Israeli invasion of Lebanon in 1982, he offered the services of his firms to counter the effects of the long Israeli siege of Beirut. After the general election held in August October 1992, followed by a government led by Omar Karami, public attention focused on reconstruction and rehabilitation. Frustrated by the parliament's resistance to his reconstruction plans, he resigned again in May 1995, but was recalled.

***

Harun al-Rashid (766-809): The Abbasid Empire was one of the foremost political dynasties to have ruled the Islamic world. The Umayyad era came to an abrupt end following the Abbasid revolution of 750 when Marwan II, the last Umayyad ruler, was resoundingly defeated by the supporters of Abul Abbas Abdullah ibn Muhammad ibn Ali ibn Abdullah ibn Abbas (otherwise known as Abul Abbas al-Saffah), after which the Abbasids went on to rule the Muslim world until the Mongol hordes emerged from Asia in the thirteenth century.

Though al-Saffah is generally considered to be the founder of the Abbasid Empire, it was his brother Abdullah ibn Muhammad ibn Ali ibn Abdullah ibn Abbas (better known as Abu Ja'far al-Mansur) who played a pivotal role in consolidating Abbasid rule across the Islamic world. After the death of al-Saffah, al-Mansur not only swiftly established his authority as Caliph, but also founded the city of Baghdad in 762.

Abu Abdullah Muhammad ibn al-Mansur (better known as al-Mahdi) succeeded his father, al-Mansur, and ruled for a decade. He had seven sons including Musa and Harun. After al-Mahdi's death, his son Musa ascended the Abbasid throne, but his rule only lasted a year. He was succeeded by Prince Harun al-Rashid who went on to become one of the Muslim world's most famous and influential rulers.

Born in the central Iranian city of Rayy, Harun soon became well-known for his bravery, intelligence and loyalty to the Abbasid clan. Like his grandfather al-Mansur, his father al-Mahdi was very fond of the people of Makkah and Madinah. As a youngster, Harun accompanied his father to Makkah and Madinah during the *hajj* season, and instantly fell in love with the people of the two sacred cities. On their return to Baghdad, al-Mahdi entrusted Harun's educational needs to Yahya ibn Khalid al-Barmaki, his talented Persian political advisor and administrator.

Harun was barely fifteen when his knowledge of military strategy and tactics was put to a severe test. Appointed commander of the Abbasid army in 780, his orders were to go and neutralize the Byzantine forces which had become a persistent thorn in the side of the Abbasid army. Harun's military campaign against the Byzantines proved very successful, and he acquired first-hand experience of leading an army on the battlefield. Two years later, Harun was commissioned to lead another large scale military campaign against the Byzantines and again he returned home triumphant. This was a remarkable achievement for the sixteen-year-old Harun whose efforts earned him the title of *al-Rashid*, meaning 'the rightly-guided one'.

When al-Mahdi died in 785, Harun was the governor of the Western region of Abbasid Empire which extended all the way from Tunisia at one end, to Anbar on the outskirts of Baghdad at the other. Only twenty-one at the time, the young Caliph appointed the aged Yahya ibn Khalid as his personal advisor and guide, the highest ranking Government post in the land. Harun soon established himself as the undisputed ruler of the Muslim world. However, it was Yahya's younger son, Ja'far, who forged a close friendship with the young Caliph. They had so much in common that Ja'far subsequently became famous as Harun's loyal companion in the world-famous adventure tale *The Thousand and One Nights* (*alf laylah wa laylah* – also known as *The Arabian Nights*).

As a devout Muslim, Harun became the first and only Caliph to have had performed the *hajj* no fewer than eight times together with his beloved wife Zubaida. During his reign as Caliph, he also radically reformed the civil and administrative systems of the State. Harun's greatness lay in the fact that he not only preached, but also led his people by his personal example. In fact, during his reign as Caliph, Harun sent military expeditions against the Byzantines every year. His reign thus represented the zenith of Abbasid glory and achievement. He founded the first fully-operational hospital in Baghdad. He also established a library and research center, which became known as *bait al-Hikmah* (or the 'House of Wisdom'), where Muslim scientists, astronomers and philosophers pursued pioneering studies and research in all the sciences of the day.

Harun's reign became known as the Golden Age of Abbasid rule, and echoes of this period naturally found their way into the stories of the famous *Thousand and One Nights*. Being the main hero of this epic tale, Harun is depicted roaming around Baghdad. The *Thousand*

and One Nights is a fictional account of Caliph Harun al-Rashid's supposed exploits.

Caliph Harun transformed Baghdad into one of the world's most advanced and dazzling cities. After a long quest for his ideal location, he finally settled in the ancient Roman city of Callinicum, which had been transformed by his grandfather al-Mansur into a thriving metropolis. Later renamed al-Rafiqa, it is today located in Syria. In 802, Harun went to perform yet another *hajj* and this time he took his sons Muhammad (who later became known as Caliph al-Amin) and Abdullah (who took the title of Caliph al-Ma'mun) with him. The Caliph was only thirty-six at the time.

During the final years of his reign, Harun became preoccupied with military campaigns against the Byzantines and his political opponents at home. He died of illness at the age of forty-three, during a military expedition to Persia, and was buried in the ancient city of Tus. With the death of Caliph Harun al-Rashid, a glorious chapter in Islamic history came to an abrupt end.

(literally, 'Aaron the rightly guided') (c 763-809) The fifth Abbasid caliph (786-809). Under him Baghdad reached its greatest brilliance, partly thanks to the ability of the Persian Viziers of the house of Barmak (until their fall I 803). He was a competent commander and a patron of learning and the arts. His court and capital provided the setting for many of the stories in the *Thousand and One Nights*. His division of the empire among his heirs led to conflict after his death (809-18). According to French chronicles, there was an exchange of embassies between Harun and Charlemagne. Aaron the Upright, c.764-809, 5th and most famous Abbasid caliph (786-809). He succeeded his brother Musa al-Hadi, fourth caliph. In his youth he had been very successful as a general in invasions of Asia Minor; on one of these he reached the Bosporus. Harun's empire included all SW Asia and the northern part of Africa, but by the end of his caliphate much of Africa had withdrawn from all but nominal obedience.

Harun was repeatedly faced with insurrections in his empire. These grew more frequent after the fall of the Barmakids, who were adroit statesmen. After this Harun's prime minister was Fazl ibn-Rabi. Harun was a munificent patron of letters and of arts, and under him Baghdad was at its apogee. He became a great figure to the Arabs, who tell about him in many of the stories of the *Thousand and One Nights*. The best in Baghdad Abbasid caliph of Baghdad; founder of Bayt Al Hikmah School. A caliph of Baghdad; son of Caliph Al-Mansur (the founder of Baghdad), the Golden Age of the Islamic caliphate; sponsored the translations of Greek philosophy and European sciences.

***

Hasan Al-Banna (1906-1949): During the nineteenth and early twentieth century's, a significant part of the Muslim world was colonized by prominent European powers such as France, Britain, Holland and Italy. And although Egypt has been a bastion of Islamic culture and tradition since the beginning of the seventh century, in 1882 the British invaded and colonized this important Muslim country. The Egyptian masses considered the British attempt to liberalize and westernize their country as an open attack on their Islamic identity, culture and heritage. Faced with mass opposition and resentment, in 1922 the British were forced to grant limited autonomy to Egypt, although the Egyptian people continued to campaign for their full independence. Their campaign eventually forced the British authorities to withdraw their forces and quit Egypt.

Though the British occupation of Egypt formally ended in 1936, they continued to exercise considerable political, economic and cultural influence in the country. The main mission of the Egyptian liberation movement (led by prominent leaders like Sa'd Zaghlul) was to throw the British out of their country. The *jami'yat al-Ikhwan al-muslimun* (or 'the Muslim Brotherhood') was destined to fill this moral and spiritual vacuum. Founded by Hasan al-Banna, this mass-Islamic movement attempted to arrest the spread of secularism and westernization in Egypt by rejuvenating the Islamic ethos, morals and values across the country. And in the process, the Muslim Brotherhood became one of the twentieth century's most powerful and influential Islamic movements.

Hasan ibn Ahmad ibn Abd al-Rahman ibn Muhammad al-Banna al-Sa'ati was born in the Egyptian village of Mahmudiyyah. His father, Ahmad ibn Abd al-Rahman al-Banna, hailed from a lower-middle class Egyptian family and attended al-Azhar University, one of the Muslim world's most famous seats of Islamic learning and scholarship. Ahmad's personal piety and love of books (he had a large personal library of traditional Islamic literature), inspired young Hasan al-Banna to commit the entire Qur'an to memory as a child. After completing his elementary education at home under the care of his learned father, he enrolled at a local Government funded Teachers' Training Center, where he successfully completed a three-year course. He then applied to join the *dar al-uloom* (Cairo University) to pursue higher education. Thus, at the age of twenty-one, he took up his post as a teacher at a Government school in Ismailiyyah.

The masses began to succumb to the lures of modernity and westernization, leading to a flagrant disregard for, and violation of, Islamic principles and practices across urban Egypt. Being neither a theoretician nor an academic, al-Banna propagated the message of Islam through personal contact. The people, in return, came to profoundly admire and respect him for his unflinching devotion to Islam.

Al-Banna formally inaugurated the *Ikhwan al-muslimun* in 1928 to revive traditional Islamic principles and practices in and around Ismailiyyah. His experiment proved so successful that people from all walks of life flocked to the Brotherhood.

Al-Banna was neither a political theorist/activist, nor a religious thinker. Rather he was a community activist. The Islamic concept of *Tawhid* (Divine Unity), he felt, provided the basis for a moral, spiritual, political, economic and social transformation of society for the betterment of the people. Al-Banna urged his followers and supporters to engage in devotional activities during the night time and strive hard to reform their society in accordance with Islamic teachings during the daytime. He encouraged his followers to work collectively under the banner of the Brotherhood.

Indeed, al-Banna's practical and down-to-earth approach proved hugely successful in Ismailiyyah. Six years after its inception, the Brotherhood became one of the most powerful and active Islamic organizations in and around Ismailiyyah. Al-Banna wrote scores of articles on different aspects of Islam which were later published under the title of *Maqalat al-Hasan al-Banna* (Articles of Hasan al-Banna).

Al-Banna stayed in Ismailiyyah until 1933, when he was transferred to a teaching post in Cairo. He abandoned his teaching career and became a full-time Islamic activist. New branches of the Brotherhood were soon established across Cairo so that by 1934 it had established its presence in no fewer than fifty suburbs of Cairo. As a successful grassroots-based organization, the Brotherhood soon spread across Egypt and won the hearts and minds of the Egyptian people (including farmers, students, teachers, doctors, engineers and lawyers).

In 1938, al-Banna prepared a comprehensive program for the Brotherhood and called for reform in all spheres of Egyptian society in the light of the Qur'an and Prophetic *sunnah*. During the period from 1939 to 1945, the Brotherhood became one of the largest and most influential Islamic organizations in Egypt. By establishing their own mosques, schools, medical clinics, shops, community centers, women's groups, newspapers, magazines and recreational facilities (without any support or assistance from the Egypt Government), the Brotherhood effectively became a State within a State.

Wrongly accused of spreading anti-State propaganda, the authorities first outlawed the Brotherhood's newspapers and journals, including the famous *al-Manar* (The Lighthouse) magazine, leading to the forced dispersal of its prominent leaders and activists from Cairo. Then, in 1948, the State of Israel was founded in Palestine and this prompted some members of the Brotherhood to spearhead a military campaign against the new country. A year later, the Brotherhood was outlawed by the Egyptian Government which led to widespread rioting, as well as the murder of the Egyptian police chief, allegedly by a member of the Brotherhood. In response, the Government arrested all the prominent members of the Brotherhood and curtailed its activities across the country. The ensuing crisis eventually spiraled out of control when Mahmud Fahmi al-Nuqrashi, the Egyptian Prime Minister, was assassinated, allegedly by a member of the Brotherhood.

A month later, al-Banna himself was gunned down on the streets of Cairo, allegedly by the Egyptian secret police; he was forty-three at the time. Al-Banna's religious ideas and thoughts have influenced some of the most prominent Islamic scholars and reformers of the twentieth century, including Sayyid Qutb, the influential author of *Fi Zilal al-Qur'an* (In the Shade of the Qur'an); Taqi al-Din al-Nabhani, the founder of H*izb ut-tahrir* (the Party of Liberation), and Shaykh Ahmad Yasin, the founder of *hamas* (the popular Palestinian Islamic Resistance Movement) among others.

***

Hasan al-Basri (642-728): Following the assassination of Caliph Uthman in 656, the early Muslim community became bitterly divided, which led to considerable political infighting and rivalry during the Caliphate of Ali. And after the latter was brutally murdered in 661, Muawiyah ibn Abi Sufyan not only became the ruler of the Islamic world, but also established the first political dynasty in Islamic history. The formation of the Umayyad dynasty shattered the balance struck by the *al-khulafa al-Rashidun* (the four 'rightly-guided Caliphs') between the religious and political dimensions of Islam. After Muawiyah's death, the gulf between the Umayyad rulers and the masses continued to widen as the ruling elite indulged themselves in excessive pleasure-seeking and hedonism. This prompted a number of prominent Islamic scholars to warn both the Umayyad rulers and the people of the dangers of excessive materialism and hedonism. One such influential Islamic scholar and sage was Hasan al-Basri.

Abu Sa'id Hasan ibn Abi'l Hasan Yasar al-Basri, better known as Hasan al-Basri, was born in Madinah during the reign of Caliph Umar. Of Persian origin, his father, Yasar, was captured in the Iraqi province of Maisan by the Muslim army and sent to Madinah in 635 where he became a close associate of Zaid ibn Thabit, the famous companion and scribe of the Prophet. After embracing Islam, he gained his freedom and married Khaira, a freedwoman of Umm Salama, the widow of the Prophet, and settled in Wadi al-Qura. It was here that

Hasan al-Basri was born and brought up, before migrating to Basrah when he was a young man. It was Imram ibn Hussain, a noted companion, *Qadi* (judge) and prolific narrator of *Hadith* (Prophetic tradition), who influenced Hasan the most.

Hasan became very knowledgeable regarding Islam and Islamic spirituality. From 663 to 665, he volunteered for military service and actively participated in expeditions led by the Muslims in many distant lands, including as far away as modern Afghanistan. For a period he also served as secretary to the governor of the Persian province of Khurasan. He resigned from his job as political secretary and became a champion of Islamic morality, ethics and spirituality, at a time when both the rulers and he masses were openly embracing a hedonistic lifestyle.

Although the exact date of Hasan's move from Khurasan to Basrah is not known, it probably took place during the final years of Muawiyah's reign, because Hasan was in Basrah when Muawiyah decided to nominate his son, Yazid, as his successor. As a distinguished Islamic scholar and sage of Basrah, Hasan also refused to pledge loyalty to Yazid. And despite his protests against Muawiyah's choice of successor, Hasan did not directly participate in any political rebellion or military uprisings against Yazid.

A contemporary of such Islamic luminaries as Ata ibn Rabah, Ibn Sirin and al-Sha'bi, Hasan stood over and above them by virtue of his great character, courage, learning and uncompromising defense of Islam. His regular lectures on Islam became so popular that students and scholars flocked to Basrah from across the Muslim world to listen to his inspirational talks on the Qur'an, *Hadith*, *Fiqh* and aspects of Islamic spirituality. Even the military strongman Hajjaj ibn Yusuf never dared to cross his path.

Hasan vehemently opposed any form of armed rebellion against the rulers of his time – even the tyrannical ones – especially if he felt such actions could lead to a greater *Fitna* (chaos and bloodshed). His views on this issue remained unchanged all his life. He argued that all human actions and behavior must be motivated by a concern for the hereafter. Hasan was reportedly appointed *Qadi* of Basrah during the reign of Caliph Umar ibn Abd al-Aziz; he was in his late seventies at the time.

Thus prominent Sufis like Habib al-Ajami, Rabi'a al-Adawiyyah, Dawud al-Ta'i and Abul Qasim al-Junayd al-Baghdadi among others were directly influenced by Hasan's spirituality. Hasan died at the advanced age of eighty-six and was buried in Basrah.

***

Hasan Ibn Ali (625-669): (sometimes spelled Hassan): first son of Ali and Fatima, grandson of Muhammad, fourth caliphate of Islam. A heroic practitioner of Islam as the true religion of peace. The son of Ali ibn Abi Talib and the grandson of the Prophet Muhammad. He is revered by Shiis as the Second Shii Imam. After the murder of his father, Shiis acclaimed him as caliph, but Hasan agreed to retired from politics and lived a quiet and somewhat luxurious life in Medina.

***

Hasan Muhammad Abdille Sayyid (1864-1920): Somali nationalist leader, known to the British as the 'Mad Mullah'. After a visit to Mecca he joined the Salihiya, a militant and puritanical Islamic fraternity. He traveled to the Sudan, KIenya, and Palestine before coming to Berbera on the Gulf of Aden. He believed that Christian colonization was destructive of Islamic faith in Somaliland and in 1989 he proclaimed a *jihad* (holy war) on all colonial powers. Between 1900 and 1904 four major expeditions by the British, Italians, and Ethiopians failed to defeat him. After a truce (1904 – 20) he resumed war again and was routed and killed by a British attack in 1920.

***

Hashim: Muhammad's great grandfather, whose numerous descendants would form the Beni Hashim clan-hereditary guardians of the Kaaba in Mecca for centuries and from whom the Hashemite dynasty would emerge.

***

Hawatmeh, Nayif (1934-   ): Palestinian leader Born into a Greek Catholic family in Salt, Jordan, Hawatmeh was a cofounder of the Arab Nationalist Movement in Beirut with the Arab defeat in the 1967 Six Day War he became disillusioned with Egyptian President Gamal Abdul Nasser who he had seen as the leader to liberate Palestine through a conventional war with Israel. After his expulsion from Beirut. Hawatmeh relocated the DFLP in Damascus. He began to cooperate with the PFLP leader, George Habash.

***

Heikal, Muhammad Hassanein (1923-   ): *Egyptian journalist and politician.* Born into a middle-class family in Cairo, Heikal secured a degree in law and economics from Cairo University. After a year at the *Egyptian*

Gazette in 1943 as a reporter, he joined the weekly *Rose at Yussuf* and then the *Akhbar al Yom* (The Daily News), covering the second World War, the Greek Civil War, and the Palestine Ware (1948-49). In 1968 Heikal was appointed to the central committee of the Arab Socialist Union, where he advocated less reliance on the Soviet Union and political liberalization at home. Following Heikal's opposition to Sadat's dramatic peace moves with Israel in late 1978, he was harassed by the police and deprived of his passport.

***

Helou, Charles (1913-2001): *Lebanese politician; president, 1964-70* Also spelled Helou. Born into a middle-class Maronite family in Beirut, Helou studied law and practiced as a lawyer and journalist. From 1935 to 1946 he was the managing editor of the daily *L'Orient le Jour (French: The Oriental Morning)*. Helou approved the Cairo Agreement of 1969, by which Lebanon allowed the Palestine Liberation Organization control of the Palestinian refugee camps. During the 1975-90 Lebanese Civil War, Helou was consulted as someone whose mediation might help to end the conflict.

***

Himayun (1508-1556): The second Mogul emperor of India (1530-40, 1554-55). His name means 'fortunate', yet after ten years of precarious rule he was driven into exile in Persia, recovering his empire only shortly before his death in an accident. His reign is significant mainly because of the introduction of Persian influences into India when he returned from exile accompanied by Persian scholars and artists. Persian became the court language, and pockets of Shiite religious influence grew up in India.

***

Hoss, Salim (1929-   ): Lebanese Politician; prime minister, 1976-78, 1979-80, 1987-90 1998-2000 Born into a Sunni family in Beirut, Hoss received his postgraduate degree in economics and business administration at the American University in Beirut and capped it with a doctorate in economics at a university in the United States in 1961. Following the election of Elias Hrawi as president on 24 November 1989, Hoss was called to form the next government. He announced a cabinet of fourteen, divided equally between Christians and Muslims.

***

Hoveida, Amir Abbas (1919-1979): Iranian political leader, prime minister of Iran (1965-77). After serving (1958-64) with the National Iranian Oil Company, he became (1964) minister of finance in the liberal government of Hassan Ali Mansur. When Mansur was killed by right-wing Muslim extremists, Hoveida was named (1965) prime minister. Hoveida was reelected in 1967 and 1971. He fell out of favor with the Shah in 1977, surrendered to the Ayatollah Khomeini in 1979, and was shot.

***

Hrawi, Elias (1925-2006): Lebanese politician, president, 1990-98, Born into a landowning Maronite family in the Zahle region. Hrawi obtained a degree in business administration at a Beirut university. He then managed the family lands. He became a parliamentary deputy in 1972, representing Zahle. His supporters' success in the general election of 1992, which was boycotted by right-wing Maronites, strengthened Hrawi's hands. In 1995 the parliament extended his presidency by three years.

***

Hulagu Khan (1217-1265): Mongol conqueror, grandson of Jenghiz Khan. His brother Mangu, grand khan of the Mongols directed him to quell a revolt in Persia. In 1256, in the course of his successful campaign, his forces virtually exterminated the powerful Assassin sect. Moving went to enlarge his conquests, he sacked and burned Baghdad in 1258 (executing the last Abbasid caliph) and captured Aleppo and Damascus in 1260. Further advances were checked by the Mamluks, who defeated him (Sept., 1260) at the decisive battle of Ayn Jalut (Goliath's Well) in Syria.

Hulagu withdrew to Azerbaijan, adopted Islam, and founded the Il-khan dynasty. His khanate, which included all of Persia, endured until 1335, when it was divided into five parts. Mongol devastator of Baghdad Mongol Khan; grandson of Genghis Khan; invaded the Islamic lands in 1255, sacked Baghdad in 1258 and massacred its inhabitants and the Abbasid caliph, Al-Musta'sim, and every member of his family. Grandson of Genghis Khan, destroyed Baghdad in 1258, tens of thousands were massacred.

***

Hunayn ibn Ishaq (809-871): Was one of the most important translators of the ancient Greek works into Arabic. Hunayn also translated the famous Hippocratic Oath, which became obligatory for Muslim physicians. He was also a physician and a writer on medical subjects. His translations interpreted, corrected and extended the ancient works. Some of his translations of medical works were used in Europe for centuries. He wrote no fewer than 29 medical books of his own, including the most important of these is a collection of ten essays on ophthalmology which cover in systematic fashion the anatomy and physiology of the eye and the treatment of various eye diseases. It is the first Arabic medical work to include anatomical drawing. It was translated into Latin and for centuries remained the most authoritative work on the subject. His book *Ten Treatises on the Eye* was influential in the West until the 17th century.

***

Husain ibn Ali (-): the second son of Ali ibn Abi Talib and the grandson of the Prophet Muhammad. He is revered by Shiis as the Third Imam and his death at the hands of Caliph Yazid is mourned annually during the month of Muharram. After the death of his elder brother Hasan, he took on the mantle of the Alid cause and would respond to the call of the people of Kufa to lead them back into freedom. Abandoned by his own supporters, he chose martyrdom at Karbala rather than dishonor.

***

Husayn ibn Ali (1856-1931): Political and religious leader. In 1908 he succeeded as grand sheriff of Mecca and thus became ruler of the Hejaz under the Ottoman Empire. In World War I, after receiving British assurances that all Arab lands not under French control would be liberated, he began (1916) a successful revolt against the Turks in Arabia and proclaimed himself king of the Hejaz and all of Arabia. Believing that the British had not kept their promises, he refused to sign the Treaty of Versailles. Great Britain lent him no support in his struggle with the Ibn Saud, who defeated him in 1924, forcing him to abdicate and renounce his claim to be caliphate. That claim, advanced after the Turkish Husayn's membership in the Hashemite family, a branch of the Quraysh tribe, to which Muhammad the Prophet had belonged. In 1925, Ibn Saud took Husayn's domain, and Husayn lived (1924-30) in exile on Cyprus. He died in Amman, the capital of Transjordan (now Jordan). He abdicated in favor of his son Ali in October 1924. His son Abdullah became ruler of Trans-Jordan thus founding the royal line o Jordan, and another son Faisal I, became king of Iraq.

***

Husayn ibn Mansur al-Halaj (858-922): Leader and founder of the Sufi sect. Expounded ecstatically on the annihilation of one's being in the divine will. He declared "I am both the lover and the beloved," that is, both God and the worshipper. Jailed for 8 years in Baghdad, then executed.

***

Husayn (-): Muhammad's grandson, son of Ali and Fatima; who was beheaded. Grandson of the prophet Muhammad and son of Ali, martyred in a seventh century clash with the Umayyad Dynasty at Karbala.

***

Hussain ibn Ali (625-680): He was braver than a lion, an angel among men and the prince of all martyrs. That was Hussain, the grandson of the Prophet Muhammad.

Hussain ibn Ali ibn Abi Talib was born in Madinah into the most noble and respected family of Arabia. His father was Ali ibn Abi Talib, the fourth Caliph of Islam, and his mother was Fatimah, the youngest daughter of Prophet Muhammad. As far as family background and nobility of origin was concerned, no one was superior to Hussain; he was beyond comparison in this respect. Above all, Hussain grew up to be a man of sound beliefs and uncompromising principles. Being very fond of his two grandsons, the Prophet visited them daily and spent quality time with them

Hussain was only seven when the Prophet passed away in 632. Six months later he suffered another shock when his beloved mother Fatimah also died, leaving him in the care of his father, Ali. When Uthman became Caliph, Hussain was about twenty years old and had become well known for his versatility, military skills and bravery. As an accomplished soldier, he participated in a number of battles against the adversaries of Islam, including the one that led to the conquest of Tabaristan. It was Hussain and his brother who stood at the front gate of the Caliph's house to protect him from his opponents. Unfortunately, the insurgents managed to enter Caliph Uthman's house through the back door and brutally murdered him. Ali was then elected the fourth Caliph, in 656.

Four and a half years into his Caliphate, Ali died of a stab wound inflicted by a member of the *khawarij* sect. Before his death, he called his sons Hasan and Hussain and told them: 'I want you to fear God always. Don't feel sorry for what you cannot get. Be good to the people. Help the weak against the oppressor.' Hasan was naturally a gentle and peace-loving man who disliked conflict and bloodshed. Though immediately after his father's death he was elected Caliph, he abdicated in favor of his rival Muawiyah ibn Abi Sufyan to avoid yet another leadership contest. Hussain's stance on the issue of political leadership put him on a collision course with Yazid, the son of Muawiyah, who succeeded his father as the ruler of the Islamic State in 680.

Muawiyah ignored all friendly advice and insisted on nominating Yazid as his successor. Devoid of tact and intelligence, Yazid created chaos and disorder across the Islamic State. Against this backdrop, Hussain and Abdullah ibn Zubair emerged to challenge Yazid's right to rule the Islamic State. During his stay in Makkah, Hussain received countless letters from the people of Kufah, urging him to move to their city and spearhead the opposition against Yazid from there. As soon as Ibn Ziyad was informed that Hussain was on his way to Kufah, he stationed guards on the outskirts of the city to capture him on his arrival.

Ibn Ziyad then wrote to his commander to force Hussain to camp in a barren place where there was no water. That fateful place was Karbala. After Hussain settled at Karbala, Ibn Ziyad sent Umar ibn Sa'd with a large contingent to confront Hussain and his men. After much discussion, both parties agreed to a peace plan. Instead, the governor urged Umar to fight Hussain and force him to pledge loyalty to Yazid.

The bloodthirsty Shimar was keen to fight and shed innocent blood. That evening Hussain spoke to his family and friends and asked them to prepare for battle. This conflict was destined to become one of the most heartbreaking tragedies in the annals of Islam. On the tenth of Muharram, sixty one years after the *Hijra*, Hussain, his family and friends took a stand against political tyranny and oppression. Attacked by Ibn Ziyad's forces, Hussain and his followers fought like lions – and one by one they fell on the battlefield – except the indomitable Hussain who continued to fight. No one dared to touch the man who was the apple of the Prophet's eye. In desperation, as arrows pierced his body and neck, Hussain searched for water to drink by his heartless pursuers refused him relief. The cursed Malik then landed a blow on his head.

Hussain picked up his sword and marched toward the enemy and they fell upon him from all directions. His body was mutilated and the wretched Shimar cut off his head, and it was carried to the governor of

Kufah who, in turn, sent it to Yazid in Damascus. According to the historians, Hussain's body was buried in Karbala. He was brutally martyred at the age of fifty-five.

Hussain's uncompromising stance against Yazid earned him the title of 'prince of martyrs', while Yazid became known to posterity as the 'king of hatred', the most despised man in Islamic history. The House of Umayyah (the Umayyad dynasty) soon crumbled and the butchers of Karbala were caught and punished in an exemplary fashion by the Abbasids.

***

Hussein ibn Talal al Hashem (1935-1999): King of Jordan 1952-99 Born in Amman, Hussein was educated at Victoria college, Alexandria and then at a private college in Harrow and at Sandhurst Military Academy in Britain. When the government headed by Premier Suleiman Nabulsi abrogated the 1948 Anglo Jordanian Treaty which entitled Britain to maintain military bases in Jordan, Hussein acquiesced. In the charged atmosphere in the buildup to the June 1967 Arab Israeli War, Hussein joined the Egyptian Syrian defense pact. During the October 1973 Arab Israeli War Hussein rejected calls by Egypt, Syria and Saudi Arabia to open a third front against Israel and accepted Washington's advice to stay out of the conflict. he continued to press for Israel's evacuation of the West Bank. By receiving a PLO delegation to Amman in February 1977, Hussein enhanced his standing in the Arab world. He refused to join the peace process initiated by the Camp David Accords between Egypt and Israel in September 1978. In the Iran Iraq War 1980-88, Hussein sided with Iraq.

This accelerated Jordan's economic integration with Iraq Emulating Iraqi President Saddam Hussein's example of giving his regime a parliamentary veneer, Hussein revived the suspended Jordanian parliament in January 1984. He actively backed a move to establish the Arab Cooperation Council an alliance of Jordan, Egypt, Iraq and North Yemen. Following Iraq's invasion of Kuwait in August 1990, Hussein worked hard to provide an Arab solution for the crisis but failed. After the end of the Second Gulf War, he tried to repair the damage by distancing himself from Saddam Hussein. He continues to coordinate Jordan's position with Syria and Lebanon in his peace talks with Israel. Just before his death due to lymph cancer to the dismay and shock of Crown Prince Hassan, who had been acting as the monarch during Hussein's extended medical treatment in the US, Hussein named his eldest son Abdullah as his heir.

***

Hussein, Qusay Saddam (1966-2003): Iraqi politician. Born to Saddam Hussein and Sajida Talfa in Baghdad, Hussein attended Exemplary Kharkh School run by his mother until 1979 when his father became president. In 2001 when Hussein was elected to the Baath Party Regional Command, he held the rank of major general. During the Gulf War III, Hussein directed the Republican Guard until its top commanders, unable to communicate with him, made a secret deal with US intelligence officials, and deserted. Having reportedly collected 1,000 million from the Central Bank on his father's behalf he and Saddam went underground on 9 April.

***

Hussein, Saddam (1937-2005): Iraqi politician: president 1979. Born into the Begat clan of the al Bu Nasir tribe in Auja, a village near Tikrit, the son of Hussein Abd al Majid, a landless peasant and Subha Talfa al Massallat, Hussein was raised by his maternal uncle, Khairallah Talfa, due to the death of his father before his birth. A member of the team that tried, unsuccessfully, to assassinate Qasim in October 1959, Hussein was injured in the leg. He escaped to Syria and then to Egypt, where he studied law at Cairo University. After the Ba'athist seizure of power in 1963, Hussein returned to Iraq. When Abdul Salam Arif usurped power from the Ba'athists, Hussein was involved in an abortive attempt to overthrow Arif.

He was imprisoned but managed to escape in July 1966. By the mid 1970s, Hussein had outstripped Bakr in leadership, cunning, ruthlessness, and organizational ability. It was he who signed the Algiers Accord with Muhammad Reza Shah Pahlavi of Iran in 1975, thus ending a bitter feud with Tehran. By the late 1970s, he felt powerful enough to overrule Bakr's strategy of conciliating Shi'a dissidents, inspired by the Islamic revolution in Shi'a majority Iran. In September 1980 Hussein invaded Iran to recover the eastern half of the Shatt al Arab which he had conceded to Tehran in the 1975 Algiers Accord. But as his troops made inroads into Iran, he expanded his war aim to include the incorporation of captured areas into Iraq on the basis that the majority of its inhabitants were ethnic Arabs.

Against this background in the spring of 1988, Iraq making extensive use of chemical weapons staged a series of successful offensives to regain territory that had been lost to Iran from 1984-86. This compelled Tehran to accept unconditionally UN Security Council Resolution 598 of July 1987. The truce came into effect on 20 August 1988. In the course of the eight year Iran Iraq War Hussein enlarged his military from 250,000 to 1,250,000 vastly expanded the industrial military complex and made much progress in developing or producing chemical biological and nuclear arms. In August 1990 Hussein invaded Kuwait a neighbor that had aided Iraq materially and logistically during its war with Iran.

US President George Bush took a lead in rallying the support of the international community to reverse the Iraqi aggression and cobbled together an alliance of twenty nine Western and Arab nations. Despite intense efforts by the leading Western powers, Israel, and Saudi Arabia to have Hussein assassinated or his regime overthrown by a coup he survived. But his elation at Bush's defeat in the US presidential election in November 1992 proved premature when President Bill Clinton continued Bush's hard-line policy toward Hussein.

By October 1994, having complied with all the conditions of UN Security Resolution 687 and Resolution 715, Hussein felt that it was time for the UN to lift the economic sanctions. In February 1996 after the return of Hussein Kamil Hassan and his family to Baghdad the erstwhile defector was killed in a gun battle by his uncle, Gen. Ali al Majid. He backed the Palestinian al Aqsa Intifada by sending food and medical aid to the Palestinian Territories and paying generous compensation to the families of the Palestinian killed in the uprising. 9 April when Baghdad fell to the invading forces. He disappeared, reportedly carrying 1,000 million in cash collected from the Central Bank by his son Qusay. In May in an Audi taped statement he called on Iraqis to resist the foreigners.

***

Hyder Ali (1722- 1782): Sultan of Mysore, south India (1761-82) Born in relative obscurity, he managed to supplant the Hindu ruler of Mysore. However, he soon had to face the expanding East India Company armies, aided by Indian allies. In wars with the Company (1767-69 and 1780-84) he proved himself one of its most formidable obstacles, winning, with some French mercenary assistance, a series of remarkable victories. But heavy defeats in 1781 persuaded him that further struggle was pointless, and he urged his son, Tipu Sultan, to seek terms with the Company.

***

Ibn Abd al-Wahhab, Muhammad (1703-1792): Muhammad ibn Abd al-Wahhab (1703 – 22 June 1792) was an Arabian Islamic theologian and founder of the Salafi movement whose pact with Muhammad bin Saud helped to establish the first Saudi state and began a dynastic alliance and power-sharing arrangement between their families which continues to the present day. The descendants of Ibn Abd al-Wahhab, the Al ash-

Sheikh, have historically led the ulama in the Saudi state, dominating the state's clerical institutions.

Background:

Ibn Abd al-Wahhab is generally acknowledged to have been born in 1703 into the Arab tribe of Banu Tamim in 'Uyayna, a village in the Najd region of the modern Saudi Arabia.

He was thought to have started studying Islam at an early age, primarily with his father, Abd al-Wahhab as his family was from a line of scholars of the Hanbali school of jurisprudence

Ibn Abd al-Wahhab spent some time studying with Muslim scholars in Basra (in southern Iraq and it is reported that he traveled to the Muslim holy cities of Mecca and Medina to perform Hajj and study with the scholars there.
In Medina, he studied under Mohammad Hayya Al-Sindhi, to whom he was introduced by an earlier tutor. It was Muhammad Hayya who taught Ibn Abd al-Wahhab to reject the popular veneration of saints and their tombs. Nonetheless, almost all sources agree that his reformist ideas were formulated while living in Basra. He returned to 'Uyayna in 1740.

After his return home, Ibn Abd al-Wahhab began to attract followers, including the ruler of 'Uyayna, Uthman ibn Mu'ammar. With Ibn Muhammad's support, Ibn Abd al-Wahhab began to implement some of his ideas for reform. First, citing Islamic teachings forbidding grave worship, he persuaded Ibn Mu'ammar to level the grave of Zayd ibn al-Khattab, a companion of Muhammad, whose grave was revered by locals. Secondly, he ordered that all adulterers be stoned to death, a practice that had become uncommon in the area. Indeed, he personally organized the stoning of a woman who confessed that she had committed adultery.

Pact with Muhammad bin Saud:

Upon his expulsion from 'Uyayna, Ibn Abd al-Wahhab was invited to settle in neighboring Diriyah by its ruler Muhammad bin Saud. Upon arriving in Diriyah, Muhammad bin Saud and Muhammad ibn Abd al-Wahhab concluded an agreement that, together, they would bring the Arabs of the peninsula back to the "true" principles of Islam as they saw it. According to one source, when they first met, bin Saud declared:

"This oasis is yours; do not fear your enemies. By the name of God, if all Nejd was summoned to throw you out, we will never agree to expel you." Muhammad ibn Abd al-Wahhab replied, "You are the settlement's chief and wise man. I want you to grant me an oath that you will perform jihad (holy war) against the unbelievers. In return you will be imam, leader of the Muslim community and I will be leader in religious matters".

The agreement was confirmed with an oath in 1744. This agreement became a "mutual support pact"[1] and power-sharing arrangement between the Al Saud and the Al ash-Sheikh, which has remained in place for nearly 300 years, providing the ideological impetus to Saudi expansion.

Emirate of Diriyah:

The 1744 pact between Muhammad bin Saud and Muhammad ibn Abd al-Wahhab marked the emergence of the first Saudi state, the Emirate of Diriyah. By offering the Al Saud a clearly defined religious mission, the alliance provided the ideological impetus to Saudi expansion. First conquering Najd, Saud's forces expanded the Salafi influence to most of the present-day territory of Saudi Arabia, eradicating various popular and Shi'a practices and propagating the doctrines of Abd al-Wahhab.

Muhammad bin Saud died in 1765 but his son, Abd al Aziz, continued the Salafi cause. Ibn Abd al-Wahhab in turn died in 1792.

Teachings, Wahhabi and Salafi:

Muhammad ibn Abd al-Wahhab considered his movement an effort to purify Islam by returning Muslims to what he believed were the original principles of that religion, as typified by the Salaf and rejecting what he regarded as corruptions introduced by Bid'ah and Shirk.

Although all Muslims pray to one God, Ibn Abd al-Wahhab was keen on emphasizing that no intercession with God was possible without God's permission, which God only grants to whom He wills and only to benefit those whom He wills, certainly not the ones who invoke anything or anyone except Him, as these would never be forgiven.

Family, Al ash-sheikh:

While in Baghdad, Ibn Abd al-Wahhab married an affluent woman. When she died, he inherited her property and wealth. Muhammad ibn 'Abd Al-Wahhab had six sons; Hussain, Abdullah, Hassan, Ali and Ibrahim and Abdul-Aziz who died in his youth. All his surviving sons established religious schools close to their homes and taught the young students from Diriyah and other places.

The descendants of Ibn Abd al-Wahhab, the Al ash-Sheikh, have historically led the ulama in the Saudi state, dominating the state's religious institutions. Within Saudi Arabia, the family is held in prestige similar to the Saudi royal family, with whom they share power, and has included several religious scholars and officials. The arrangement between the two families, which persists to this day, is based on the Al Saud maintaining the Al ash-Sheikh's authority in religious matters and upholding and propagating Salafi doctrine. In return, the Al ash-Sheikh supports the Al Saud's political authority thereby using its religious-moral authority to legitimize the royal family's rule. Consequently, each legitimizes the other.

Assessment:

As with the early Salafi's, Ibn Abd al-Wahhab was criticized for disregarding Islamic history, monuments, traditions and the sanctity of Muslim life. His own brother, Sulayman, was particularly critical, claiming he was ill-educated and intolerant, classing Ibn Abd al-Wahhab's views as fringe and fanatical. Both Sulayman and Ibn Humaydi (the Hanbali mufti in Mecca) suggested Ibn Abd al-Wahhab was even selective with the works of Ibn Taymiyyah, whose views otherwise closely influenced the Wahhabis.

Ibn Abd al-Wahhab is accepted by Salafi scholars as an authority and source of reference.

Works:
- *Kitab at-Tawhid* (The Book of the Unity of God)
- *Kashf ush-Shubuhaat* (Clarification Of The Doubts)
- *Thalaathat-Ul-Usool* (The Three Fundamental Principles)
- *Al-Usool-uth-Thalaatha*
- *Al Qawaaid Al 'Arbaa' (The Four Foundations of Shirk)*
- (The Six Fundamental Principles)
- *Adab al-Mashy Ila as-Salaa* (Manners of Walking to the Prayer)
- *Usul al-Imam* (Foundations of Faith)
- *Fada`il al-Islam* (Excellent Virtues of Islam)
- *Fada`il al-Qur'an* (Excellent Virtues of the Qur'an)
- *Majmu'a al-Hadith 'Ala Abwab al-Fiqh* (Compendium of the Hadith on the Main Topics of the Fiqh)
- *Mukhtasar al-Iman* (Abridgement of the Faith; i.e. the summarized version of a work on Faith)
- *Mukhtasar al-Insaf wa`l-Sharh al-Kabir* (Abridgement of the Equity and the Great Explanation)
- *Mukhtasar Seerat ar-Rasul* (Summarized Biography of the Prophet)
- *Kitaabu l-Kabaair* (The Book of Great Sins)

- *Kitaabu l-Imaan* (The Book of Trust)

Muhammad ibn 'Abd al-Wahhab

School/tradition	Hanbali
Notable ideas	Views on innovations within Islam (bid'ah), Islamic Monotheism (Tawhid) and Polytheism (shirk)

***

Ibn al Arabi (1165-1240): the Greatest Master of Sufi teachings, famous among other things for elaborate discussions of the Oneness of Being and the Perfect Man. Muid ad Din (d. 1240): a Spanish mystic and philosopher, who traveled extensively in the Muslim empire. A prolific and highly influential writer, he preached a punitive and pluralistic theological vision, in which spirituality is fused indissolubly with his philosophy. Spanish Islamic scholar; died in Damascus. He dealt with the principle of the unity of all beings; Jews, Christians and Muslims all pray to the same God.

***

Ibn Al-Haytham, Alhazen (965-1040): Abu ʿAli al-Hasan ibn al-Hasan ibn al-Haytham Latinized: Alhacen or (deprecated) Alhazen) (965 in Basra – c. 1040 in Cairo) was a Muslim scientist and polymath described in various sources as either Arab or Persian. Alhazen made significant contributions to the principles of optics, as well as to physics, astronomy, mathematics, ophthalmology, philosophy, visual perception, and to the scientific method. He also wrote insightful commentaries on works by Aristotle, Ptolemy, and the Greek mathematician Euclid.

He is frequently referred to as Ibn al-Haytham, and sometimes as al-Basri, after his birthplace in the city of Basra. He was also nicknamed *Ptolemaeus Secundus* ("Ptolemy the Second") or simply "The Physicist" in medieval Europe.

Born circa 965, in Basra, present-day Iraq, he lived mainly in Cairo, Egypt, dying there at age 74. Overconfident about practical application of his mathematical knowledge, he assumed that he could regulate the floods of the Nile. After being ordered by Al-Hakim bi-Amr Allah, the sixth ruler of the Fatimid caliphate, to carry out this operation, he quickly perceived the impossibility of what he was attempting to do, and retired from engineering. Fearing for his life, he feigned madness and was placed under house arrest, during and after which he devoted himself to his scientific work until his death.

Biography:
Alhazen was born in Basra, in the Iraq province of the Buyid Empire . Many historians have different opinions about his ethnicity whether he was Arab or Persian. He probably died in Cairo, Egypt. During the Islamic Golden Age, Basra was a "key beginning of learning", and he was educated there and in Baghdad, the capital of the Abbasid Caliphate, and the focus of the "high point of Islamic civilization". During his time in Buyid Iran, he worked as a civil servant and read many theological and scientific books.

One account of his career has him called to Egypt by Al-Hakim bi-Amr Allah, ruler of the Fatimid Caliphate, to regulate the flooding of the Nile, a task requiring an early attempt at building a dam at the present site of the Aswan Dam. After his field work made him aware of the impracticality of this scheme, and fearing the caliph's anger, he feigned madness. He was kept under house arrest from 1011 until al-Hakim's death in 1021. During this time, he wrote his influential *Book of Optics*. After his house arrest ended, he wrote scores of other treatises on physics, astronomy and mathematics. He later traveled to Islamic Spain.

Some biographers have claimed that Alhazen fled to Syria, ventured into Baghdad later in his life, or was in Basra when he pretended to be insane. In any case, he was in Egypt by 1038. During his time in Cairo, he became associated with Al-Azhar University, as well the city's "House of Wisdom", known as *Dar al-`Ilm* (House of Knowledge), which was a library "first in importance" to Baghdad's House of Wisdom.

Among his students were *Sorkhab (Sohrab)*, a Persian student who was one of the greatest people of Iran's Semnan and was his student for over 3 years, and *Abu al-Wafa Mubashir ibn Fatek,* an Egyptian scientist who learned mathematics from Alhazen.

Legacy:
Alhazen made significant improvements in optics, physical science, and the scientific method. Alhazen's work on optics is credited with contributing a new emphasis on experiment

The Latin translation of his main work, *Kitab al-Manazir* (*Book of Optics*), exerted a great influence on Western science: for example, on the work of Roger Bacon, who cites him by name, and on Johannes Kepler. His research in catoptrics (the study of optical systems using mirrors) centered on spherical and parabolic mirrors and spherical aberration. He made the observation that the ratio between the angle of incidence and refraction does not remain constant, and investigated the magnifying power of a lens. His work on catoptrics also contains the problem known as "Alhazen's problem".

Meanwhile in the Islamic world, Alhazen's work influenced Averroes' writings on optics, and his legacy was further advanced through the 'reforming' of his *Optics* by Persian scientist Kamal al-Din al-Farisi (d. ca. 1320) in the latter's *Kitab Tanqih al-Manazir* (*The Revision of* [Ibn al-Haytham's] *Optics*). The correct explanations of the rainbow phenomenon given by al-Farisi and Theodoric of Freiberg in the 14th century depended on Alhazen's *Book of Optics*. The work of Alhazen and al-Farisi was also further advanced in the Ottoman Empire by polymath Taqi al-Din in his *Book of the Light of the Pupil of Vision and the Light of the Truth of the Sights* (1574).

He wrote as many as 200 books, although only 55 have survived, and many of those have not yet been translated from Arabic. Even some of his treatises on optics survived only through Latin translation. During the Middle Ages his books on cosmology were translated into Latin, Hebrew and other languages. The crater Alhazen on the Moon is named in his honor as was the asteroid 59239 Alhazen. In honor of Alhazen, the Aga Khan University (Pakistan) named its Ophthalmology endowed chair as "The Ibn-e-Haitham Associate Professor and Chief of Ophthalmology".

Alhazen (by the name Ibn al-Haytham) is featured on the obverse of the Iraqi 10,000 dinars banknote issued in 2003, and on 10 dinar notes from 1982.

Book of Optics:

Alhazen's most famous work is his seven volume Arabic treatise on optics, *Kitab al-Manazir* (*Book of Optics*), written from 1011 to 1021.

Optics was translated into Latin by an unknown scholar at the end of the 12th century or the beginning of the 13th century. This work enjoyed a great reputation during the Middle Ages. Works by Alhazen on geometric subjects were discovered in the Bibliothèque Nationale in Paris in 1834 by E. A. Sedillot. Other manuscripts are preserved in the Bodleian Library at Oxford and in the library of Leiden.

Theory of Vision:

Two major theories on vision prevailed in classical antiquity. The first theory, the emission theory, was supported by such thinkers as Euclid and Ptolemy, who believed that sight worked by the eye emitting rays of light. The second theory, the intromission theory supported by Aristotle and his followers, had physical forms entering the eye from an object. Alhazen argued that the process of vision occurs neither by rays emitted from the eye, nor through physical forms entering it. He reasoned that a ray could not proceed from the eyes and reach the distant stars the instant after we open our eyes. He also appealed to common observations such as the eye being dazzled or even injured if we look at a very bright light. He instead developed a highly successful theory which explained the process of vision as rays of light proceeding to the eye from each point on an object, which he proved through the use of experimentation. His unification of geometrical optics with philosophical physics forms the basis of modern physical optics.

Alhazen proved that rays of light travel in straight lines, and carried out various experiments with lenses, mirrors, refraction, and reflection. He was also the first to reduce reflected and refracted light rays into vertical and horizontal components, which was a fundamental development in geometric optics.

Alhazen also gave the first clear description and correct analysis of the camera obscura and pinhole camera. While Aristotle, Theon of Alexandria, Al-Kindi (Alkindus) and Chinese philosopher Mozi had earlier described the effects of a single light passing through a pinhole, none of them suggested that what is being projected onto the screen is an image of everything on the other side of the aperture. Alhazen was the first to demonstrate this with his lamp experiment where several different light sources are arranged across a large area. He was thus the first to successfully project an entire image from outdoors onto a screen indoors with the camera obscura.

In addition to physical optics, *The Book of Optics* also gave rise to the field of "physiological optics". Alhazen discussed the topics of medicine, ophthalmology, anatomy and physiology, which included commentaries on Galenic works. He described the process of sight, the structure of the eye, image formation in the eye, and the visual system. He also described what became known as Hering's law of equal innervations, vertical horopters and binocular disparity and improved on the theories of binocular vision, motion perception and horopters previously discussed by Aristotle, Euclid and Ptolemy.

His most original anatomical contribution was his description of the functional anatomy of the eye as an optical system. It was his comparison between the eye and the camera obscura which brought about his synthesis of anatomy and optics, which forms the basis of physiological optics.

Scientific method:

Some historians state that Alhazen developed rigorous experimental methods of controlled scientific testing to verify theoretical hypotheses and substantiate inductive conjectures.

Moreover, his experimental directives rested on combining classical physics (*'Ilm tabi'i*) with mathematics (*Ta'alim*; geometry in particular) in terms of devising the rudiments of what may be designated as a hypothetico-deductive procedure in scientific research. His legacy was further advanced through the 'reforming' of his *Optics* by Kamal al-Din al-Farisi (d. ca. 1320) in the latter's *Kitab Tanqih al-Manazir* (*The Revision of* [Ibn al-Haytham's] *Optics*).

The concept of Occam's razor is also present in the *Book of Optics*. For example, after demonstrating that light is generated by luminous objects and emitted or reflected into the eyes, he states that therefore "the extra mission of [visual] rays is superfluous and useless."

Alhazen's problem:

His work on catoptrics in Book V of the Book of Optics contains a discussion of what is now known as Alhazen's problem, first formulated by Ptolemy in 150 AD. It comprises drawing lines from two points in the plane of a circle meeting, at a point on the circumference and making equal angles with the normal at that point, thus, its main application in optics is to solve the problem, "Given a light source and a spherical mirror, find the point on the mirror where the light will be reflected to the eye of an observer." This leads to an equation of the fourth degree. This eventually led Alhazen to derive the earliest formula for the sum of fourth powers; by using an early proof by mathematical induction, he developed a method that can be readily generalized to find the formula for the sum of any integral powers.

He applied his result of sums on integral powers to find the volume of a paraboloid through integration. He was thus able to find the integrals for polynomials up to the fourth degree. Alhazen eventually solved the problem using conic sections and a geometric proof, though many after him attempted to find an algebraic solution to the problem, which was finally found in 1997 by the Oxford mathematician Peter M. Neumann. Alhazen's problem can also be extended to multiple refractions from a spherical ball. Given a light source and a spherical ball of certain refractive index, the closest point on the spherical ball where the light is refracted to the eye of the observer can be obtained by solving a tenth degree equation.

Other contributions:

He also used this result to explain how intense, direct light hurts the eye, using a mechanical analogy: "Alhazen associated 'strong' lights with perpendicular rays and 'weak' lights with oblique ones.

Chapters 15–16 of the *Book of Optics* covered astronomy. Alhazen was the first to discover that the celestial spheres do not consist of solid matter. He also discovered that the heavens are less dense than the air. These views were later repeated by Witelo and had a significant influence on the Copernican and Tychonic systems of astronomy.

Sudanese psychologist Omar Khaleefa has argued that Alhazen should be considered be the "founder of experimental psychology", for his pioneering work on the psychology of visual perception and optical illusions. Khaleefa has also argued that Alhazen should also be considered the "founder of psychophysics", a sub discipline and precursor to modern psychology.

Alhazen offered an explanation of the Moon illusion, an illusion that played an important role in the scientific tradition of medieval Europe. Many authors repeated explanations that attempted to solve the problem of the Moon appearing larger near the horizon than it does when higher up in the sky, a debate that is still unresolved. Alhazen argued against Ptolemy's refraction theory, and defined the problem in terms of perceived, rather than real, enlargement. He said that judging the distance of an object depends on there being an uninterrupted sequence of intervening bodies between the object and the observer. When the Moon is high in the sky there are no intervening objects, so the Moon appears close. The perceived size of an object of constant angular size varies with its perceived distance. Therefore, the Moon appears closer and smaller high in the sky, and further and larger on the horizon. Although Alhazen is often credited with the perceived distance explanation, he was not the first author to offer it. Cleomedes (2nd century) gave this account (in addition to refraction), and he credited it to Posidonius (135-50 BC).

Optical treatises:

Besides the *Book of Optics*, Alhazen wrote several other treatises on optics. His *Risala fi l-Daw'* (*Treatise on Light*) is a supplement to his *Kitab al-Manazir* (*Book of Optics*). He also carried out further examinations into anatomy of the eye and illusions in visual perception. He built the first camera obscura and pinhole camera.

In his treatise, *Mizan al-Hikmah* (*Balance of Wisdom*), Alhazen discussed the density of the atmosphere and related it to altitude. He also studied atmospheric refraction. He discovered that the twilight only ceases or begins when the Sun is 19° below the horizon and attempted to measure the height of the atmosphere on that basis.

Astrophysics:

In astrophysics and the celestial mechanics field of physics, Alhazen, in his *Epitome of Astronomy*, discovered that the heavenly bodies "were accountable to the laws of physics". Alhazen's *Mizan al-Hikmah* (*Balance of Wisdom*) covered statics, astrophysics, and celestial mechanics. He discussed the theory of attraction between masses, and it seems that he was also aware of the magnitude of acceleration due to gravity at a distance. His *Maqala fi'l-qarastun* is a treatise on centers of gravity. In this treatise, Alhazen formulated the theory that the heaviness of bodies varies with their distance from the centre of the Earth.

He disproved the universally held opinion that the Moon reflects sunlight like a mirror and correctly concluded that it "emits light from those portions of its surface which the sun's light strikes."

Mechanics:

In the dynamics and kinematics fields of mechanics, Alhazen's *Risala fi'l-makan* (*Treatise on Place*) discussed theories on the motion of a body. He maintained that a body moves perpetually unless an external force stops it or changes its direction of motion. Alhazen's concept of inertia was not verified by experimentation, however. Galileo Galilei repeated Alhazen's principle, centuries later, but introduced the concept of frictional force and provided experimental results.

In his *Treatise on Place*, Alhazen disagreed with Aristotle's view that nature abhors a void, and he thus used geometry to demonstrate that place (*al-Makan*) is the imagined three-dimensional void between the inner surfaces of a containing body.

Astronomical works, *Doubts Concerning Ptolemy:*

Alhazen criticized many of Ptolemy's works, including the *Almagest*, *Planetary Hypotheses*, and *Optics*, pointing out various contradictions he found in these works and wrote a scathing critique of the physical reality of Ptolemy's astronomical system, noting the absurdity of relating actual physical motions to imaginary mathematical points, lines and circles.

Unlike some later astronomers who criticized the Ptolemaic model on the grounds of being incompatible with Aristotelian natural philosophy, Alhazen was mainly concerned with empirical observation and the internal contradictions in Ptolemy's works.

The duty of the man who investigates the writings of scientists, if learning the truth is his goal, is to make himself an enemy of all that he reads, and, applying his mind to the core and margins of its content, attack it from every side. He should also suspect himself as he performs his critical examination of it, so that he may avoid falling into either prejudice or leniency.

On the Configuration of the World:

In his *On the Configuration of the World*, despite his criticisms directed towards Ptolemy, Alhazen continued to accept the physical reality of the geocentric model of the universe, presenting a detailed description of the physical structure of the celestial spheres in his *On the Configuration of the World*.

While he attempted to discover the physical reality behind Ptolemy's mathematical model, he developed the concept of a single orb (*falak*) for each component of Ptolemy's planetary motions. This work was eventually translated into Hebrew and Latin in the 13th and 14th centuries and subsequently had an influence on astronomers such as Georg von Peuerbach during the European Middle Ages and Renaissance.

Model of the Motions of Each of the Seven Planets:

Alhazen's *The Model of the Motions of Each of the Seven Planets*, written in 1038, was a book on astronomy. The surviving manuscript of this work has only recently been discovered, with much of it still missing, hence the work has not yet been published in modern times. Following on from his *Doubts on Ptolemy* and *The Resolution of Doubts*, Alhazen described the first non-Ptolemaic model in *The Model of the Motions*. His reform was not concerned with cosmology, as he developed a systematic study of celestial kinematics that was completely geometric. This in turn led to innovative developments in infinitesimal geometry.

His reformed empirical model was the first to reject the equant and eccentrics, separate natural philosophy from astronomy, free celestial kinematics from cosmology, and reduce physical entities to geometric entities. The model also propounded the Earth's rotation about its axis, and the centers of motion were geometric points without any physical significance, like Johannes Kepler's model centuries later.

Other astronomical works:

Alhazen distinguished astrology from astronomy, and he refuted the study of astrology, due to the methods used by astrologers being conjectural rather than empirical, and also due to the views of astrologers conflicting with that of orthodox Islam.

Alhazen also wrote a treatise entitled *On the Milky Way*, in which he solved problems regarding the Milky Way galaxy and parallax and "determined that because the Milky Way had no parallax, it was very remote from the earth and did not belong to the atmosphere." He wrote that if the Milky Way was located around the Earth's atmosphere, "one must find a difference in position relative to the fixed stars." He made the first attempt at observing and measuring the Milky Way's parallax, and determined that since the Milky Way had no parallax, then it does not belong to the atmosphere.

Mathematical works:

In mathematics, Alhazen built on the mathematical works of Euclid and Thabit ibn Qurra. He systemized conic sections and number theory, carried out some early work on analytic geometry, and worked on "the beginnings of the link between algebra and geometry." This in turn had an influence on the development of Descartes' geometric analysis and Isaac Newton's calculus.

Geometry:

In geometry, Alhazen developed analytical geometry and established a link between algebra and geometry. He discovered a formula for adding the first 100 natural numbers, using a geometric proof to prove the formula.

Alhazen made the first attempt at proving the Euclidean parallel postulate, the fifth postulate in Euclid's *Elements*, using a proof by contradiction, where he introduced the concepts of motion and transformation into geometry. His work had a considerable influence on its development among the later Persian geometers Omar Khayyam and Nasir al-Din al-Tusi and the European geometers Witelo, Gersonides, Alfonso, John Wallis, Giovanni Girolamo Saccheri and Christopher Clavius.

The two lines formed from a right triangle by erecting a semicircle on each of the triangle's sides, inward for the hypotenuse and outward for the other two sides, are known as the lines of Alhazen; they have the same total area as the triangle itself.

Number theory:

His contributions to number theory includes his work on perfect numbers. In his *Analysis and Synthesis*, Alhazen was the first to realize that every even perfect number is of the form $2^{n-1}(2^n - 1)$ where $2^n - 1$ is prime, but he was not able to prove this result successfully (Euler later proved it in the 18th century). Alhazen solved problems involving congruences using what is now called Wilson's theorem.

Other works, *Influence of Melodies on the Souls of Animals*:

In psychology and musicology, Alhazen's *Treatise on the Influence of Melodies on the Souls of Animals* was the earliest treatise dealing with the effects of music on animals. Through to the 19th century, a majority of scholars in the Western world continued to believe that music was a distinctly human phenomenon, but experiments since then have vindicated Alhazen's view that music does indeed have an effect on animals.

Engineering:

In engineering, one account of his career as a civil engineer has him summoned to Egypt by the Fatimid Caliph, Al-Hakim bi-Amr Allah, to regulate the flooding of the Nile River. He carried out a detailed scientific study of the annual inundation of the Nile River, and he drew plans for building a dam, at the site of the modern-day Aswan Dam. His field work, however, later made him aware of the impracticality of this scheme, and he soon feigned madness so he could avoid punishment from the Caliph.

According to Al-Khazini, Alhazen also wrote a treatise providing a description on the construction of a water clock.

Philosophy:

In early Islamic philosophy, Alhazen's *Risala fi'l-makan* (*Treatise on Place*) presents a critique of Aristotle's concept of place (Topos). Aristotle's *Physics* stated that the place of something is the two-dimensional boundary of the containing body that is at rest and is in contact with what it contains. Alhazen disagreed and demonstrated that place (al-Makan) is the imagined three-dimensional void between the inner surfaces of the containing body. He showed that place was akin to space, foreshadowing René Descartes' concept of place in the *Extensio* in the 17th century. Following on from his *Treatise on Place*, Alhazen's *Qawl fi al-Makan* (*Discourse on Place*) was a treatise which presents geometric demonstrations for his geometrization of place, in opposition to Aristotle's philosophical concept of place, which Alhazen rejected on mathematical grounds.

Theology:

Alhazen was a devout Muslim, though it is uncertain which branch of Islam he followed. Alhazen wrote a work on Islamic theology, in which he discussed prophethood and developed a system of philosophical criteria to discern its false claimants in his time. He also wrote a treatise entitled *Finding the Direction of Qibla by Calculation*, in which he discussed finding the Qibla, where Salah prayers are directed towards, mathematically.

He wrote in his *Doubts Concerning Ptolemy*:

"Truth is sought for its own sake ... Finding the truth is difficult, and the road to it is rough. For the truths are plunged in obscurity. ... God, however, has not preserved the scientist from error and has not safeguarded science from shortcomings and faults. If this had been the case, scientists would not have disagreed upon any point of science... "

Alhazen described his theology:

I constantly sought knowledge and truth, and it became my belief that for gaining access to the effulgence and closeness to God, there is no better way than that of searching for truth and knowledge.

Works:
Alhazen was a pioneer in many areas of science, making significant contributions in varying disciplines. His optical writings influenced many Western intellectuals such as Roger Bacon, John Pecham, Witelo and Johannes Kepler. His pioneering work on number theory, analytic geometry, and the link between algebra and geometry, also had an influence on Descartes' geometric analysis and Isaac Newton's calculus.

According to medieval biographers, Alhazen wrote more than 200 works on a wide range of subjects, of which at least 96 of his scientific works are known. Most of his works are now lost, but more than 50 of them have survived to some extent. Nearly half of his surviving works are on mathematics, 23 of them are on astronomy, and 14 of them are on optics, with a few on other subjects. Not all his surviving works have yet been studied.

Alhazen
Alhazen (Ibn al-Haytham)

Fields	Physicist and Mathematician
Known	*Book of Optics, Doubts Concerning Ptolemy, On the Configuration of the World. The*

Model of the Motions, Treatise on Light, Treatise on Place, scientific method, experimental science, experimental physics, experimental psychology, visual perception, analytic geometry, non-Ptolemaic astronomy, celestial mechanics

Influenced   Averroes, Witelo, Roger Bacon, Kepler

***

Ibn Al-Nafis (1213–1288): was a physician who was born in Damascus and practiced medicine as head physician at the al-Mansuri hospital in Cairo. He wrote an influential book on medicine, believed to have replaced ibn-Sina's *Canon* in the Islamic world – if not Europe. He wrote important commentaries on Galen and ibn-Sina's works. One of these commentaries was discovered in 1924 and yielded a description of pulmonary transit, the circulation of blood from the right to left ventricles of the heart through the lungs.

***

Ibn Arabi (1165-1240): Following the establishment of the Umayyad rule in Spain in the beginning of the eighth century, towering Umayyad rulers like Abd al-Rahman III and al-Hakam transformed the fortunes of *al-Andalus*. Though their rule represented one of the most glorious periods in the history of Western Islam, the Umayyads were eventually ousted from power in 1031. Ruler Yusuf ibn Tashfin marched into Spain and reunited the country under his leadership. Peace and security was restored across Spain until the al-Moravids lost their grip on power in 1145. Amidst the prevailing political chaos and disorder, one of the Muslim world's most influential mystical philosophers emerged to develop a powerful and equally controversial metaphysical theory. This remarkable thinker and writer was none other than Ibn al-Arabi.

Muhyi al-Din Abu Abdullah Muhammad ibn Ali ibn Muhammad ibn al-Arabi al-Hatimi al-Ta'i, known as *Shaykh al-akbar* ('the Great Master'), was born in Murcia (*mursiyah*) in Islamic Spain. As the son of a respected civil servant and Sufi sage, Ibn al-Arabi grew up to be a sensible, intelligent and disciplined young man. According to Ibn al-Arabi, he was fifteen when he met Ibn Rushd (Averroes), the famous Muslim philosopher and jurist of Spain, and the latter was apparently impressed by his grasp of Islamic teachings and spirituality. After marrying at a young age, he worked as a clerical assistant to the governor of Seville. During the next decade he pursued advanced education in Islamic studies. Then, at the age of thirty, he left Spain and moved to North Africa. In 1200 he journeyed to the Islamic East where he remained for the rest of his life.

For the next two decades Ibn al-Arabi travelled extensively in pursuit of knowledge, and received advanced training in all aspects of Islamic spirituality and gnosis. After visiting Baghdad, Makkah, Madinah, Aleppo, Mosul, parts of Central Asia and Turkey, he eventually settled in Damascus in 1223 with his small band of disciples.

What set Ibn al-Arabi apart from his peers were his inner qualities, spiritual attainments and powerful imagination. He established his reputation as one of the Muslim world's most gifted metaphysicians and writers. The Sufis (or mystics) long for the 'unveiling' (*Kashf*) of the Ultimate Reality before the eye of the heart in order to attain spiritual illumination. Unlike Abd al-Qadir al-Jilani, Jalal al-Din Rumi, Baha al-Din Naqshband, Mu'in al-Din Chishti or Najm al-Din al-Kubra, he did not initiate a Sufi *Tariqah* (Order), nor did he establish a specific *Madh'hab* (school of thought). His main objective, it seems, was to formulate a comprehensive mystical philosophy so that the masses could draw on it as and when they needed, in order to quench their intellectual and spiritual needs.

Writing was an effortless process for him. According to some of his biographers, he authored as many as eight hundred books and treatises on all aspects of Islamic mystical thought. Of his published works, the most famous ar *Al-Futuhat al-Makkiyyah* (The Makkan Revelations), which as the title suggests was written during his stay in Makkah; the *Fusus al-Hikam* (The Bezels of Wisdom) was written in Damascus, while *Tarjuman al-Ashwaq* (The Interpreter of Desires) was also written in Makkah. He explored the meaning of the ninety-nine Divine Names and the Attributes (*al-asma wa'l Sifat*) as mentioned in the Qur'an. In his *Fusus al-Hikam* he claimed to have presented a systematic interpretation of Islamic mystical philosophy as revealed to twenty-seven Prophets, beginning with Adam and concluding with Muhammad, the Seal of the Prophets (*khatm al-Anbiya*).

Ibn al-Arabi's entire metaphysical theory revolved around the notion that, at a certain level, all Being is fundamentally One (*wahdat al-Wujud*), while, at another level, everything is only a manifestation of the Divine Substance. In fact, his concept of Oneness of Being, or monism (*wahdat al-Wujud*), coupled with his mystical interpretation of Divine Names and Attributes (*al-asma wa'l Sifat*) along with his notion of Perfect Man (*al-insan al-Kamil*), not to mention his claim to have been the Seal of Muhammadan Sanctity, proved hugely controversial.

Ibn al-Arabi's mystical philosophy has been hugely influential in the Muslim world. He died at the age of seventy-five and was buried in Damascus.

***

Ibn Batuttah (1332-1406): Muhammad ibn Ahmad ibn Jubayr was not only one of the Muslim world's most prominent globetrotters, he was also one of the great travelers of medieval Europe. He left Islamic Spain and travelled across the Islamic East (including Egypt, Arabia and Syria). Both Ibn Jubayr and Marco Polo were great travelers who undertook their journeys at a time when long distance travelling was far from being the norm. A year after Marco Polo's death, a young North African Muslim set out to discover the world, travelling on foot, riding on mules and sailing on boats, and in so doing he became arguably the greatest traveler in human history. This fearless, indomitable and inspirational globetrotter was none other than the influential Ibn Battutah.

Abu Abdullah Muhammad ibn Abdullah ibn Muhammad ibn Ibrahim al-Luwati, better known as Ibn Battutah, was born in Tangier (in present-day Morocco) into a distinguished family of Islamic scholars and judges. He studied Arabic language, literature and traditional Islamic sciences during his early years. Only twenty-one at the time, he was nonetheless very keen to undertake the long and arduous journey to Makkah in order to accomplish the fifth pillar of Islam and also pursue higher education in Islamic jurisprudence.

In 1325, he bade farewell to his family and set out for Makkah. From Tangier he travelled to Tilimsan and from there he went to Algiers in the company of a group of merchants. Passing by Constantinople, he reached Tunis just in time for the Islamic festival of *Eid al-Fitr* (or the feast which marks the end of the sacred month of Ramadan). In April 1326, he arrived in Alexandria with the pilgrim caravans and met a Sufi dervish (Islamic mystic) who apparently prophesied that he would one day travel across the world.

Keen to complete the pilgrimage, Ibn Battutah left Alexandria by boat and arrived in Cairo in July 1326. From Cairo, he travelled across the barren desert and visited Gaza, Hebron, Bethlehem and Jerusalem. During his stay in Jerusalem, he visited *Masjid al-Aqsa* and the Dome of the Rock (*Qubbat al-Sakhra*), which is the Muslim world's third holiest site. After touring Palestine, he proceeded to Syria, visiting Aleppo and Antioch, before finally arriving in Damascus in August 1326. Here he claimed to have encountered the city's most distinguished citizens, namely *Shaykh al-Islam* Ibn Taymiyyah, the great Islamic thinker and reformer. As a keen student of Islam, he soon obtained certification (*Ijazah*) in the traditional Islamic sciences. Here he also married for the third time. But a month later, he left Damascus and set out for Madinah, the city of the Prophet, via Tabuk. After four days of prayer and devotion, he went to Makkah to perform another pilgrimage. Then, in November 1326, he left Makkah by caravan and soon reached Iraq.

A year later, he performed his fourth pilgrimage and obtained certification in advanced Islamic studies. Having chosen not to return home to Tangier, Ibn Battutah decided to travel around the world. After completing the pilgrimage, he decided to go to India and see the land of Sultan Muhammad ibn Tughluq for the very first time. He eventually arrived in Anatolia, where he received a warm welcome from the locals, despite not being able to speak a word of Turkish.

From Anatolia, Ibn Battutah proceeded to Konya, where the mausoleum of Mawlana Jalal al-Din Rumi, the great Sufi thinker and poet, had become an important center of Sufi activities. Then he headed in the direction of the Caucasus, the land of Sultan Muhammad Uzbeg Khan of the Golden Horde. In September 1333, at the age of twenty-nine, he finally reached the borders of India. He stayed in India for a long time and travelled extensively across the country.

After almost a decade in India, just as Ibn Battutah finally decided to return to Makkah, the reigning Sultan summoned him to his court and requested him to head a diplomatic mission to the Mongol ruler of China. Keen to undertake yet another adventure, he accepted the Sultan's offer and set out for the Far East. From East Bengal, he travelled to the Indonesian island of Sumatra and there boarded a vessel which took him on to China.

Travelling along the Persian Gulf, Ibn Battutah reached Baghdad and from there he went to Syria where, for the first time, he witnessed the havoc wreaked by the deadly plague known as 'the Black Death'. After travelling around the world, in 1352, at the age of forty-eight, he embarked on yet another adventure. He crossed the Strait of Gibraltar and arrived in Granada. He eventually returned to Fez at the age of fifty and by royal order he dictated his *Rihla* (Accounts of Travel) to Sultan Abu Inan's personal secretary.

Ibn Battutah spent the next twenty-four years of his life in Fez. During this period he also served as a judge and eventually died at the age of seventy-four. Known widely as the 'Traveler of Islam', he travelled more than seventy-five thousand miles and did so all on his own. Thanks to Sir Hamilton A.R. Gibb, the renowned British Arabist, Ibn Battutah's entire *Rihla* is now available in English.

A famous Maghribi traveler whose Travels all over the lands of Islam are a prime source for Islamic archaeology. The approximate chorology is as follows: 1325 N Africa, Egypt and Syria; 1326 Hijaz, Iraq, Tabriz, W Persia and Baghdad; 1137-30 Arabia with three pilgrimages, by 1332 the Red Sea and the Persian Gulf by 1334 Constantinople, the Lands of the Golden Horde, Transoxania, Afghanistan and India, then far east return to the Maghreb by 1349 and a journey across the Sahara to central Africa from which he returned in 1353.

***

Ibn Hanbal, Ahmad (780-855): Muslim jurist and theologian. His disciples founded the fourth of the four major Sunni schools of jurisprudence, the Hanzah. Ibn Hanbal's conception of law was principally influenced by Hadith which led him to reject the officially sanctioned theology that promoted the dogma of the creation of the Qur'an. He held the view, for which he was imprisoned, that the Qur'an was uncreated and largely abstained from teaching until the revival of Sunnism in 847…as the imam of Baghdad…Belief in God, according to Ibn Hanbal, should leave to God the understanding of the Divine mystery. A derivative of his axiomatic acceptance of the Qur'an as the uncreated Word of God was to stress the dominance of the Qur'an and Sunnah. He even objected to the codifying of his thought, for fear of infringing on the authority of these two sources.

***

Ibn Harith, Muthana: chief of the Beni Bekr who had fought against the Persians as a young man and became military ally of Khalid in the first raids on Iraq. Fought at battles of Ullais, Al Jisr and Buwayba. A pure-blooded Bedouin Arab chieftain.

***

Ibn Hazm al-Andalusi (994-1064): The period from the eighth to the thirteenth century may have been a period of intellectual stagnation in Europe, but it was far from being this for the Muslims. Indeed, it was the Golden Age of Islamic civilization – a time when Muslims reigned supreme politically, economically and intellectually. Less than half a century after the death of the Prophet, Muslims reached North Africa and within a few more years would overwhelm the Visigothic Kingdom of Iberia. *Al-Andalus* (or Islamic Spain) thus became a beacon of light for the rest of Europe.

When Islamic Spain reached its zenith in the tenth century, under the stewardship of Caliph Abd al-Rahman III, Cordova alone housed more than seventy public libraries, containing more than half a million books on all the sciences of the day. But following the mass expulsion of Muslims from Spain by Ferdinand and Isabella in 1492 Spain began to lose its former glory, to the extent that in the eighteenth century there was not a single public library in Madrid. Spain had produced some of Europe's most influential scholars and thinkers. One such scholar was Ibn Hazm al-Andalusi who was one of the great writers and thinkers of medieval Europe.

Abu Muhammad Ali ibn Ahmad ibn Sa'id ibn Hazm ibn Ghalib ibn Salih ibn Khalaf ibn Ma'dan ibn Sufyan ibn Yazid, known as Ibn Hazm al-Andalusi for short, was born in Cordova during the reign of Caliph Hisham II. It was in these roles that Ibn Hazm's father served both Caliph al-Hakam II and his successor Hisham II as an advisor.

As a gifted student, Ibn Hazm was able to memorize and retain vast quantities of information. Unlike Caliphs Abd al-Rahman III and al-Hakam II, the reign of Hisham II was marred by considerable political instability and social upheaval. But, like his father, Ibn Hazm remained loyal to the royal family and served them in the capacity of a Minister of State, a post which he held at three different occasions during the reigns of Caliphs al-Murtada, al-Mustazhir and al-Mu'tadd.

The scope and breadth of Ibn Hazm's learning was nothing short of encyclopedic. Exasperated by the never-ending cycle of violence and political rivalry, he finally turned his back on public life at the age of about forty, and entered a new phase where he focused all his time and energy on research and literary activities. He devoted the next thirty years of his life to the pursuit of knowledge, as well as writing books on a wide range of subjects. It was during this period that he authored some of his most influential works.

One such work was *Tawq al-Hamamah* (The Dove's Necklace). Consisting of both prose and poetry, in this book Ibn Hazm recorded his ideas and thoughts on the subject of love and lovers. His psychological observation of human behavior revealed an inherent contradiction between language, thought and action. He argued that all human actions can be classified into one of the five following juridical categories: F*ard* (compulsory), M*ustahhab* (commended), M*akruh* (disliked), *Haram* (outlawed) and *Halal* (permissible).

Perhaps Ibn Hazm's most influential work was his *Kitab al-Fasl*. Consisting of five bulky volumes in Arabic, this is a truly monumental work of scholarship and one of the first books to be written by a Muslim on comparative religion. He considered the Word of God (*kalam Allah*) to be the most reliable and authoritative source of knowledge. He emphasized the superiority of revelation over rationality; indeed, he considered both revelation and reason to be complementary rather than contradictory.

The sheer quality and quantity of Ibn Hazm's works (consisting of more than four hundred books and treatises, that is, around eighty thousand pages in total) proves, if proof is required, that he was a scholar and writer of indefatigable energy. Recently, European scholars have rediscovered the vast treasures of knowledge and wisdom he has bequeathed to posterity. Ibn Hazm died in exile at the age of seventy and was buried in Niebla (located in the Spanish province of Seville).

***

Ibn Ishaq (704-767): Keen to preserve and protect the Qur'anic revelation and the Prophetic traditions (*Hadith*), the close companions of the Prophet Muhammad began to memorize and meticulously record the Divine revelation and his sermons and exhortations for their own guidance, and for the benefit of future generations. Following the death of the Prophet in 632, written information about his life and Prophetic career began to proliferate. One of al-Zuhri's favorite students, and arguably the most influential biographer of the Prophet, was Ibn Ishaq.

Abu Abdullah Muhammad ibn Ishaq ibn Yasar ibn Khiyar was born in Madinah during the Caliphate of Abu Bakr. His early education began at home under the supervision of his learned who taught him the basics of Islam. It was not necessary for young Ibn Ishaq to travel to other prominent centers like Makkah or Kufah to acquire higher education. He was fortunate to have met and acquired *Hadith* from the famous companion, Anas ibn Malik.

Ibn Ishaq was not only a T*abi* (successor of the Prophet's companions); he also became a renowned scholar by virtue of his vast knowledge of *Hadith* and the Prophet's military campaigns. His contributions in this field made him famous throughout the Muslim world. After completing his higher education, he left Madinah for Egypt where he studied *Hadith* under the guidance of a number of leading scholars of *Hadith*.

The methodology pursued by Ibn Ishaq was, first and foremost, that of a historian and biographer. Rightly considered to be one of the greatest scholars of *Hadith*, M*aghazi*, and *Sirah* by the leading scholars of his day, he became an indefatigable collector of Prophetic traditions.

Ibn Ishaq stayed in Egypt for a short period before moving to Kufah, where he settled down and began to teach *Hadith*, *Maghazi* and *Sirah*. It was his voluminous biography of the Prophet which represented the very first systematic and substantial study of the life and career of the Prophet. Based on his lectures on the Prophet's *Sirah*, Ibn Ishaq's *Kitab Sirat Rasul Allah* (The Biography of God's Messenger) proved a detailed exposition of the Prophet's life and times, focusing especially on his military campaigns. He completed his monumental biography of the Prophet during his stay in Kufah and Rayy, before he eventually settled in Baghdad at the behest of the Abbasid Caliph Abu Ja'far al-Mansur.

After completing his biography of the Prophet, Ibn Ishaq presented a copy to the Abbasid Caliph Abu Ja'far al-Mansur who reportedly rewarded him handsomely for his efforts. Muhammad ibn Ishaq died and was buried in the cemetery of Khayzuran in Baghdad, the capital of the Abbasid dynasty, at the age of sixty-three.

***

Ibn Jubayr (1145-1217): Andalusia traveler, who to expiate the sin of drinking wine, made the pilgrimage to Mecca and described it in his travels which are the most graphic and useful account of the shrines of medieval Mecca and Medina and the rites observed there. His decryption of Mesopotamia is similarly graphic and rewarding.

***

Ibn Khaldun (1332-1406): The Qur'an constantly exhorts Muslims to study history and explore the past. The Qur'anic exhortations inspired the early Muslims to record historical information in a meticulous way. As ancient Greek historians like Herodotus of Halicarnassus considered history to be a mere sequence of events, they did not conduct a rigorous scrutiny of their data. The father of the philosophy of history, and one of the most influential historians of all time, was Ibn Khaldun.

Abd al-Rahman ibn Muhammad ibn Muhammad ibn Khaldun was born in Tunis (in present-day Tunisia) into a family of distinguished politicians and civil servants. Of Yemeni origin, Ibn Khaldun's family members settled in Tunis in 1248. He then studied Arabic grammar and literature, before pursuing traditional Islamic sciences. He excelled in his studies. His extensive training in both the Islamic and philosophical sciences not only expanded his intellectual horizon, it also sharpened his mind in a powerful way. He became one of the most profound and insightful observers of human behavior and society in the annals of history. He turned down an offer of a civil service job and went to Fez, which at the time was one of North Africa's most prosperous and thriving cities.

Sultan Abu Inan was so impressed with Ibn Khaldun's performance that he promoted him to a position of considerable political eminence. He continued to serve Sultan Abu Inan conscientiously until he was accused of disloyalty and subsequently incarcerated. After Abu

Inan's death in 1358, Ibn Khaldun was released by his successor and again he returned to political life. This prompted him to leave North Africa and move to Granada. After he moved to Granada in 1362, he received a warm reception from its ruling elites including Lisan al-Din ibn al-Khatib, the learned Chief Minister of the State, who subsequently became one of his closest allies. Ibn al-Khatib had nominated Ibn Khaldun – who had become a scholar of repute and a politician in his own right.

In the end, Ibn Khaldun had no choice but to leave Granada and return to North Africa. He was the ultimate survivor, in the sense that one day he would be sitting next to the Sultan, while on another day he would find himself locked in a prison. He was around forty-five when he settled with his family in a quiet location in the district of Bani Arif, and spent the next four years living like a hermit.

Being a brilliant intellectual, Ibn Khaldun understood the nature of social trends and the factors which influenced historical change better than anyone else. He was determined to investigate, decipher and demonstrate the relationship between the external (*Zahiri*) and internal or invisible (*batini*) factors which contributed to the rise and decline of cultures and civilizations. There was an underlying rational structure behind all social and historical events. Ibn Khaldun was able to demonstrate that a combination of factors – some of which were external, while others were internal – contributed to the rise and decline of human culture, society and civilization. This, in turn, led to the formation of urbanized towns and cities where cultural, artistic and scientific pursuits flourished, until the people began to succumb to the lures of luxuries and pleasure, which precipitated the age of decline and disintegration. No other historian or social philosopher before or after him had been able to analyze human culture and history in such a thoroughly modern, scientific and innovative manner. He is today widely considered to be the founding father of both the sociology and philosophy of history.

Ibn Khaldun completed his *Kitab al-Ibar* in 1382 at the age of fifty; it is known as the *Muqqadimah fi'l Tarikh* (Introduction to History). His autobiography, entitled *al-Ta'rif*, also appears at the end of the third book. Experts in Arabic literature have rated this autobiography very highly for its literary merit and eloquence. His vast knowledge of Islamic law and jurisprudence subsequently prompted the Mamluk Sultan al-Zahir Barquq, the reigning monarch of Egypt, to make him a judge but soon he became embroiled in yet another political coup and more intrigue.

During this period Ibn Khaldun suffered a great shock when his wife and seven children perished in a shipwreck en route to Cairo. This prompted him to go to Makkah and perform the *hajj* in 1387. At the same time he also visited Damascus and Palestine, including the historic city of Jerusalem. He then volunteered to go and meet Amir Timur, who is better known in the West as Tamerlane, in order to dissuade the fearsome Mongol conqueror from attacking Damascus. Ibn Khaldun died at the age of seventy-four and was buried in the Sufi Cemetery on the outskirts of Cairo.

***

Ibn Rushd (Averroes; 1126-1198): When Tariq ibn Ziyad crossed the sea and landed in Gibraltar in 711, he found Europeans were still living in the Dark Ages. For nearly eight centuries, the Muslims of *al-Andalus* (or Islamic Spain) became the pioneers of a new European civilization. Through Islamic Spain, Muslims not only introduced Plato, Aristotle, Algebra and paper-making to Europe, they also built magnificent works of art and architecture, and established some of Europe's first schools, colleges, libraries and hospitals. Moreover, it was during this period that the Spanish roads and streets became some of Europe's first to be lit by lamps. Thus great European Muslim philosophers and thinkers like Ibn Hazm, Ibn Massarrah, Ibn Bajjah, Ibn Tufayl and Ibn al-Arabi blazed a trail which captured the European imagination. However, one man exerted more influence on medieval European philosophy and thought than probably any other; he was none other than Ibn Rushd.

Abul Walid Muhammad ibn Ahmad ibn Muhammad ibn Rushd, known in the Western world as Averroes, was born in Cordova, the capital of Muslim Spain, which at the time was one of the most famous centers of learning and higher education in Europe. During his early years he studied Arabic, the Qur'an and aspects of *Fiqh*. He then received advanced training in Islamic jurisprudence and mastered *Maliki* legal thought. He was also familiar with both Greek and Hebrew.

After the Umayyad rule of Spain came to an end in 1031, political in-fighting and ethnic rivalry broke out until the Moroccan-based al-Moravids (*al-Murabitun*) marched into Spain under the able leadership of Yusuf ibn Tashfin and reunited the warring factions. In 1146, when Ibn Rushd was only twenty, the al-Moravids were overthrown by the al-Mohads (*al-Muwahhidun*), another powerful politico-religious movement, founded by Abu Abdullah Muhammad ibn Abdullah ibn Tumart in Morocco, which went on to rule Islamic Spain for nearly a century.

Soon after becoming Caliph, Abu Yaqub Yusuf transferred the capital of Islamic Spain to Seville and appointed Ibn Rushd a *Qadi* (judge) in 1169. Ibn Rushd's profound knowledge of Islamic law, coupled with his qualities of honesty, fair play and impartiality in legal matters, soon won him much acclaim and endeared him to Caliph Abu Yaqub Yusuf.

If Ibn Rushd's achievements in Islamic jurisprudence were considerable, then his contributions in the fields of science and philosophy were nothing short of remarkable. In addition to studying astronomy and mathematics, he excelled in medicine and, after Ibn Tufayl's retirement in 1182, Caliph Abu Yaqub Yusuf called him to Marrakesh and appointed him to be his own personal physician.

Ibn Rushd wrote more than twenty books and treatises on all aspects of medicine, including his famous *Kitab al-Kulliyyat fi al-Tibb* (The Book of Universal Rules of Medicine), which was a medical encyclopedia written at the request of Caliph Abu Yaqub Yusuf. In 1194, when at the age of around sixty-eight, he was ordered by the Caliph to leave Marrakesh in order to appease the conservative U*mala* (religious scholars) who considered Ibn Rushd's philosophical and theological ideas to be unorthodox and heretical. During this period his books were publicly burnt by the conservative *ulama*. Wrongly accused of heresy, the beleaguered Caliph ordered him to flee to Lucena, a town located towards the south east of Cordova.

In addition to being an eminent jurist, a distinguished physician and an outstanding theologian, Ibn Rushd was also one of the greatest Muslim philosophers of all time. According to him, there was no conflict between reason and revelation, and therefore religion and philosophy were not incompatible in Islam, despite al-Ghazali's stinging critique of philosophy in his *Tahafut al-Falsafah* (The Refutation of Philosophy). In this acclaimed treatise, al-Ghazali accused the philosophers of heresy, but Ibn Rushd repudiated his views and defended the ideas and thoughts of the philosophers with great wit and eloquence. However, Ibn Rushd's critics refused to accept his philosophical interpretation of Islam because he was heavily influenced by Aristotle. His religious rationalism, they argued, represented nothing more than the Aristotelianization of Islam. Their charge of heresy leveled against him was both unfair and unjustified.

In addition to numerous works on philosophy, law and medicine, Ibn Rushd published scores of books and treatises on logic, astronomy, physics and cosmology. Considered to be Europe's greatest authority on Aristotle, his commentaries were read and studied widely; he was also revered throughout medieval Europe as a philosopher *par excellence*. Indeed, he acquired such a large following in Europe that his followers became known as the 'Latin Averroist' and his works were avidly studied at universities across Europe.

Ibn Rush became an intellectual trail-blazer in medieval Europe, thus paving the way for the Renaissance. The great European Muslim philosopher died in Marrakesh (in present-day Morocco) at the age of seventy-two. His remains were later transferred to his native Cordova.

***

Ibn Sinna, Abu Ali Husayn (Avicenna) (980–1037): Was a Persian physician, astronomer, physicist, mathematician and polymath, who was said to have dominated the field of philosophy and medicine more than probably anyone else in the history of human thought. Great as Razi was, he was at least equaled in stature by another Arabic-speaking Persian Muslim, Ibn Sina, better known in the West by his Latin name, Avicenna. Called "The Prince of Philosophers" by his contemporaries, he is still recognized as one of the great minds of all time and wrote some 170 books on philosophy, medicine, mathematics and astronomy, as well as poems and religious works. Also, he wrote almost 450 treatises on a wide range of subjects, of which around 240 have survived. In particular, 150 of his surviving treatises concentrate on philosophy and 40 of them concentrate on medicine. He is said to have memorized the entire Koran when he was only 10 years old, and at 18 he was personal physician to the Sultan of Bukhara, in Turkestan.

Ibn Sina's philosophy maintained the ontological theme of God's transcendence, but he distinguished between essence and existence. This distinction allowed him to explain in philosophical terms how the universe came into existence within an Islamic framework.

Abu Ali Hussain ibn Abdullah ibn Hasan ibn Ali ibn Sina was born in Afshanah, a small town located close to Bukhara (in present-day Uzbekistan). Originally from Balkh, Ibn Sina's father, Abdullah, moved to Afshanah where he met his Persian wife, Sitara and became a prominent member of the Samanid civil service. His second son, Hussain (better known as Ibn Sina), was born a few years later. Young Ibn Sina committed the whole Qur'an to memory before he was ten. Such was his thirst for knowledge that he read, and became thoroughly familiar with, al-Farabi's voluminous commentary on Aristotle's metaphysics, before he was eighteen. In addition to a treatise on mathematics, Ibn Sina authored a book on ethics and also compiled an encyclopedia of all the sciences of this time. Astonishingly, he was only twenty-one when he composed these books.

Adulthood:

Ibn Sina's first appointment was that of physician to the emir, who owed him his recovery from a dangerous illness (997). Ibn Sina's chief reward for this service was access to the royal library of the Samanids, well-known patrons of scholarship and scholars. When the library was destroyed by fire not long after, the enemies of Ibn Sina accused him of burning it, in order for ever to conceal the sources of his knowledge.

When Ibn Sina was 22 years old, he lost his father. The Samanid dynasty came to its end in December 1004. Ibn Sina seems to have declined the offers of Mahmud of Ghazni, and proceeded westwards to Urgench in modern Turkmenistan, where the vizier, regarded as a friend of scholars, gave him a small monthly stipend. Qabus, the generous ruler of Dailam and central Persia, himself a poet and a scholar, with whom Ibn Sina had expected to find asylum, was on about that date (1012) starved to death by his troops who had revolted. Ibn Sina himself was at this time stricken by a severe illness. Finally, at Gorgan, near the Caspian Sea, Ibn Sina met with a friend, who bought a dwelling near his own house in which Ibn Sina lectured on logic and astronomy. Several of Ibn Sina's treatises were written for this patron; and the commencement of his Canon of Medicine also dates from his stay in Hyrcania.

Ibn Sina subsequently settled at Rai, in the vicinity of modern Tehran, (present day capital of Iran), the home town of Rhazes; where Majd Addaula, a son of the last Buwayhid emir, was nominal ruler under the regency of his mother (Seyyedeh Khatun). About thirty of Ibn Sina's shorter works are said to have been composed in Rai. After a brief sojourn at Qazvin he passed southwards to Hamadan where Shams al-Daula, another Buwayhid emir, had established himself. Ibn Sina was even raised to the office of vizier. The emir decreed that he should be banished from the country. Ibn Sina persevered with his studies and teaching. Every evening, extracts from his great works, the Canon and the Sanatio, were dictated and explained to his pupils.

Meanwhile, he had written to Abu Ya'far, the prefect of the dynamic city of Isfahan, offering his services. Ibn Sina returned with the emir to Hamadan, and carried on his literary labors. Ibn Sina escaped from the city in the dress of a Sufi ascetic. After a perilous journey, they reached Isfahan, receiving an honorable welcome from the prince.

Later life and death:

The remaining ten or twelve years of Ibn Sinna's life were spent in the service of Abu Ja'far 'Ala Addaula, whom he accompanied as physician and general literary and scientific adviser, even in his numerous campaigns.

His friends advised him to slow down and take life moderately. He refused, however, stating that: *"I prefer a short life with width to a narrow one with length"*. On his deathbed remorse seized him; he bestowed his goods on the poor, restored unjust gains, freed his slaves, and read through the Qur'an every three days until his death. He died in June 1037, in his fifty-eighth year, after treating himself unsuccessfully for an illness, in the month of Ramadan and was buried in Hamadan, Iran. His enemies, jealous of his vast knowledge and great fame, maliciously observed that his medicine could not save his body, nor his metaphysics his soul.

Avicennian philosophy:

Ibn Sinna wrote extensively on early Islamic philosophy, especially the subjects logic, ethics, and metaphysics, including treatises named *Logic and Metaphysics*. Most of his works were written in Arabic - which was the de facto scientific language of the time in the Middle East, and some were written in the Persian language. Ibn Sinna's commentaries on Aristotle often corrected the philosopher, encouraging a lively debate in the spirit of Ijtihad. Avicennism eventually became the leading school of Islamic philosophy by the 12th century, with Avicenna becoming a central authority on philosophy.

Avicennism was also influential in medieval Europe, particular his doctrines on the nature of the soul and his existence-essence distinction, along with the debates and censure that they raised in scholastic Europe. This was particularly the case in Paris, where Avicennism was later proscribed in 1210.

Metaphysical doctrine:

Early Islamic philosophy and Islamic metaphysics, imbued as it is with Islamic theology, distinguishes more clearly than Aristotelianism the difference between essence and existence. Whereas existence is the domain of the contingent and the accidental, essence endures within a being beyond the accidental. The philosophy of Ibn Sinna, particularly that part relating to metaphysics, owes much to al-Farabi.

Following al-Farabi's lead, Avicenna initiated a full-fledged inquiry into the question of being, in which he distinguished between essence (Mahiat) and existence (Wujud). Existence must, therefore, be due to an agent-cause that necessitates, imparts, gives, or adds existence to an essence. To do so, the cause must be an existing thing and coexist with its effect.

Avicenna's consideration of the essence-attributes question may be elucidated in terms of his ontological analysis of the modalities of being; namely impossibility, contingency, and necessity. Avicenna argued that the impossible being is that which cannot exist, while the contingent in itself (Mumkin bi-dhatihi) has the potentiality to be or not to be without entailing a contradiction. Thus, contingency-in-itself is potential bigness that could eventually be actualized by an external cause other than itself. The metaphysical structures of necessity and contingency are different. The necessary is the source of its own being without borrowed existence. It is what always exists. The Necessary exists 'due-to-Its-Self', and has no quiddity/essence (Mahiyya) other than existence (Wujud).

Natural philosophy;

Ibn Sina and Abu Rayhan al-Bīrūnī engaged in a written debate, with Abu Rayhan Biruni mostly criticizing Aristotelian natural philosophy and the Peripatetic school, while Avicenna and his student Ahmad ibn 'Ali al-Ma'sumi respond to Biruni's criticisms in writing. Abu Rayhan began by asking Avicenna eighteen questions, ten of which were criticisms of Aristotle's On the Heavens.

Theology:

Ibn Sinna was a devout Muslim and sought to reconcile rational philosophy with Islamic theology. His aim was to prove the existence of God and His creation of the world scientifically and through reason and logic.

Ibn Sinna memorized the Qur'an by the age of seven, and as an adult, he wrote five treatises commenting on suras from the Qur'an. Avicenna argued that the Islamic prophets should be considered higher than philosophers.

Thought experiments:

While he was imprisoned in the castle of Fardajan near Hamadhan, Avicenna wrote his famous "Floating Man" thought experiment to demonstrate human self-awareness and the substantiality and immateriality of the soul. Avicenna believed his "Floating Man" thought experiment demonstrated that the soul is a substance, and claimed humans cannot doubt their own consciousness, even in a situation that prevents all sensory data input. Because it is conceivable that a person, suspended in air while cut off from sense experience, would still be capable of determining his own existence, the thought experiment points to the conclusions that the soul is a perfection, independent of the body, and an immaterial substance. However, Avicenna posited the brain as the place where reason interacts with sensation. Sensation prepares the soul to receive rational concepts from the universal Agent Intellect. Avicenna thus concluded that the idea of the self is not logically dependent on any physical thing, and that the soul should not be seen in relative terms, but as a primary given, a substance. The body is unnecessary; in relation to it, the soul is its perfection. In itself, the soul is an immaterial substance.

The Canon of Medicine:

About 100 treatises were ascribed to Ibn Sina. Some of them are tracts of a few pages. Others are works extending through several volumes. His 14-volume The Canon of Medicine (Al-Qanoon fi al-Tibb, The Laws of Medicine) was a standard medical text in Europe and the Islamic world until the 18th century.

Medicine and pharmacology:

The book is known for its description of contagious diseases and sexually transmitted diseases, quarantine to limit the spread of infectious diseases, and testing of medicines. Ibn Sinna adopted, from the Greeks, the theory that epidemics are caused by pollution in the air (miasma). The Canon agrees with Aristotle (and disagrees with Hippocrates) that tuberculosis was contagious, a fact which was not universally accepted in Europe until centuries later. It also describes the symptoms and complications of diabetes. Both forms of facial paralysis were described in-depth.

An Arabic edition of the Canon appeared at Rome in 1593, and a Hebrew version at Naples in 1491. Of the Latin version there were about thirty editions, founded on the original translation by Gerard de Sabloneta. In the 15th century a commentary on the text of the Canon was composed.

It was mainly accident which determined that from the 12th to the 18th century, Ibn Sinna should be the guide of medical study in European universities, and eclipse the names of Rhazes, Ali ibn al-Abbas and Averroes.

The work has been variously appreciated in subsequent ages, some regarding it as a treasury of wisdom, and others, like Averroes, holding it useful only as waste paper. The vice of the book is excessive classification of bodily faculties, and over-subtlety in the discrimination of diseases. It includes five books; of which the first and second discuss physiology, pathology and hygiene, the third and fourth deal with the methods of treating disease, and the fifth describes the composition and preparation of remedies. This last part contains some personal observations.

He introduced into medical theory the four causes of the Peripatetic system. Of natural history and botany he pretended to no special knowledge. Up to the year 1650, or thereabouts, the Canon was still used as a textbook in the universities of Leuven and Montpellier.

Ibn Sinna was interested in the effect of the mind on the body, and wrote a great deal on psychology, likely influencing Ibn Tufayl and Ibn Bajjah. He also introduced medical herbs.

Avicenna extended the theory of temperaments in The Canon of Medicine to encompass "emotional aspects, mental capacity, moral attitudes, self-awareness, movements and dreams."

Physical Exercise: the Key to Health:
The Canon of Medicine: Volume 1 of 5, Part 4 of 5: The Preservation of health Of Ibn Sina's Canon of Medicine which is written in 5 volumes, only the first volume has appeared in the English Language. In the first volume, Ibn Sina divides medicine into two parts as he explains it throughout the first book: the theoretical and the practical.

Theoretical and Practical Medicine:
Ibn Sina goes on to say that you do not get any benefit from just knowing how your body works, but rather the true benefit of medicine itself is in its practical aspect, since medicine is for the preservation of health.

The Benefits of Exercise:
"Since the regimen of maintaining health consists essentially in the regulation of: (1) exercise (2) food and (3) sleep, we may begin our discourse with the subject of exercise". (Avicenna 1999, p. 377)

Exercise itself is divided into three main parts: The Massage (which is equivalent to massaging your muscles before you start to exercise); The Exercise itself; and lastly the Cold Bath.

> "Once we direct the attention towards regulating exercise as to amount and time, we shall find there is no need for such medicines as are ordinarily required for remedying diseases"

> "Vigorous exercise invigorates the muscular and nervous system." (Avicenna 1999, p. 379)

The Purpose of Exercise and the Dangers of its negligence:
Continuing on the proof to why exercise should be so beneficial Ibn Sina says "We know that this must be so when we reflect how in regard to nutriment, our health depends on the nutriment being appropriate for us and regulated in quantity and quality. For not one of the aliments which are capable of nourishing the body is converted into actual nutriment in its entirety. In every case digestion leaves something untouched, and nature takes care to have that evacuated. Nevertheless, the evacuation which nature accomplishes is not a complete one. Hence

at the end of each digestion there is some superfluity left over. As a result, harmful effete substances would form and injure various parts of the body. When they undergo decomposition, putrefactive diseases arise [bacterial infections]. That is the reason why we must be careful to evacuate these substances. Their evacuation is usually not completely accomplished without the aid of toxic medicines, for these break up the nature of the effete substances. This can be achieved only by toxic agents. As Hippocrates says: "Medicine purges and ages". Thus to make his pint very clear, and show the extreme necessity of daily exercise for health…

"Now exercise is that agent which most surely prevents the accumulation of these matters, and prevents plethora. The other forms of regiment assist it. It is this exercise which renews and revives the innate heat, and imparts the necessary lightness to the body, exercise causes the innate heat to flourish and keeps the joints and ligaments firm, so as to be always ready for service, and also free from injury".

Massage:
Before you begin to exercise it is important that you massage your muscles; as Ibn Sina says on page 385:

> "Massage as a preparatory to athletics. The massage begins gently, and then becomes more vigorous as the time approaches for the exercise." (Avicenna 1999, p. 385)

There are certain important things to note once you start exercising, one is the amount, the other consistency; Ibn Sina states about the amount:

> "(1) the color - as long as the skin goes on becoming florid, the exercise may be continued. After it ceases to do so, the exercise must be discontinued." (Avicenna 1999, p. 384)

Bathing in Cold Water:
Once you have finished exercising; it is often that the person will feel tired and fatigued; to combat this problem Ibn Sina says on page 388:

> "The beneficial Effects of Baths: The benefits are (1) induction of sleep (2) dilation of pores (3) cleansing of skin (4) dispersal of the undesirable waste matters (5) maturation of abscesses (6) drawing of nutriment towards the surface of the body (7) assistance to the physiological

dispersion and excretion of poisonous matters (8) prevention of diarrhea and (9) removal of fatigue effects." (Avicenna 1999, p. 388)

Most importantly you should remember:

"A person should not go into the bath immediately after exercise. He should rest properly first." (Avicenna 1999, p. 387)

"Cold Bathing should not be done after exercise except in the case of the very robust.

Diet:
Once Ibn Sina has laid the foundation of exercise being central to health, he names many exercises as running, swimming, weight lifting, polo, fencing, boxing, wrestling, long jumping, high jumping, etc. He also gives a diet to go along with the exercise:

"The meal should include: (1) meat especially kid of goats; veal, and year-old lambs [this means white meat in today's terms] (2) wheat, which is cleaned of extraneous matter and gathered during a healthy harvest without ever being exposed to injurious influences (3) sweets (fruits) of appropriate temperament." (Avicenna 1999, p. 390)"

Lastly, the third thing mentioned is sleep; to make sure that you do not sleep during the days, and do not stay awake during the nights. From the above reading, it is clear that Ibn Sina gave advice in his book which is still the same advice medical doctors give to their patients. Daily Physical Exercise; and to defeat diseases such as type 2 diabetes, high blood pressure, the prescription of a diet which contains high amounts of Whole Grains and little to no amounts of Refined Carbohydrates.

Psychology:
In The Canon of Medicine, Avicenna described a number of conditions, including melancholia. He described melancholia as a depressive type of mood disorder in which the person may become suspicious and develop certain types of phobias.

Philosophy of science:

In the *Al-Burhan* (*On Demonstration*) section of *The Book of Healing*, Avicenna discussed the philosophy of science and described an early scientific method of inquiry.

Physics:

In mechanics, Ibn Sinna, in The Book of Healing, developed an elaborate theory of motion, in which he made a distinction between the inclination (tendency to motion) and force of a projectile, and concluded that motion was a result of an inclination (Mayl) transferred to the projectile by the thrower, and that projectile motion in a vacuum would not cease. He viewed inclination as a permanent force whose effect is dissipated by external forces such as air resistance.

In optics, Ibn Sina was among those who argued that light had a speed, observing that "if the perception of light is due to the emission of some sort of particles by a luminous source, the speed of light must be finite. Avicenna says in his book of heaven and earth, that heat is generated from motion in external things.

Psychology:

Avicenna's legacy in classical psychology is primarily embodied in the Kitab al-nafs parts of his Kitab al-Shifa' (The Book of Healing) and Kitab al-Naat (The Book of Deliverance). These were known in Latin under the title De Anima (treatises "on the soul"). The main thesis of these tracts is represented in his so-called "flying man" argument, which resonates with what was centuries later entailed by Descartes' cogito argument (or what phenomenology designates as a form of an "epoch."

Avicenna's psychology requires that connection between the body and soul be strong enough to ensure the soul's individuation, but weak enough to allow for its immortality. Avicenna grounds his psychology on physiology, which means his account of the soul is one that deals almost entirely with the natural science of the body and its abilities of perception. In sense perception, the perceiver senses the form of the object; first, by perceiving features of the object by our external senses. This sensory information is supplied to the internal senses, which merge all the pieces into a whole, unified conscious experience. This process of perception and abstraction is the nexus of the soul and body, for the material body may only perceive material objects, while the immaterial soul may only receive the immaterial, universal forms.

The soul completes the action of intellection by accepting forms that have been abstracted from matter. This process requires a concrete particular (material) to be abstracted into the universal intelligible (immaterial). The material and immaterial interact through the Active Intellect, which is a "divine light" containing the intelligible forms. The Active Intellect reveals the universals concealed in material objects much like the sun makes color available to our eyes.

Astronomy and astrology:

The practice of judicial astrology was refuted by Avicenna. His reasons were due to the methods used by astrologers in judicial astrology being conjectural rather than empirical and also due to the principles of this type of astrology conflicting with orthodox Islam. He also cited passages from the Qur'an in order to justify his refutation of astrology on both scientific and religious grounds. He stated that it was true that each planet had some influence on the earth, but his argument was the difficulty of astrologers being able to determine the exact effect of it. In essence, Avicenna did not refute astrology, but denied man's limited capacity to be able to know the precise effects of the stars on the sub lunar matter. With that, he did not refute the essential dogma of astrology, but only refuted our ability to fully understand it.

In astronomy, he criticized Aristotle's view of the stars receiving their light from the Sun. Ibn Sinna stated that the stars are self-luminous, and believed that the planets are also self-luminous. He claimed to have observed the transit of Venus across the Sun on May 24, 1032. He used his transit observation to demonstrate that Venus was, at least sometimes, below the Sun in the Ptolemaic cosmology.

Avicenna concluded that Venus is closer to the Earth than the Sun. In 1070, Abu Ubayd al-Juzjani, a pupil of Ibn Sinna, claimed that his teacher Ibn Sīnā had solved the equant problem in the Ptolemaic model.

Chemistry:

Ibn Sīnā used distillation to produce essential oils such as rose essence, forming the foundation of what later became aromatherapy. Ibn Sīnā discredited the theory of the transmutation of substances commonly believed by alchemists:

> "Those of the chemical craft know well that no change can be effected in the different species of substances, though they can produce the appearance of such change".

Ibn Sina proposed a four-part classification of inorganic bodies, which was a significant improvement over the two-part classification of Aristotle (into orycta and metals) and three-part classification of Galen (into terrae, lapides and metals). The four parts of Ibn Sina's classification were: lapides, sulfur, salts and metals.

Poetry:
   Almost half of Ibn Sina's works are versified. His poems appear in both Arabic and Persian:

Up from Earth's Centre through the Seventh Gate,
I rose, and on the Throne of Saturn sate,
And many Knots unraveled by the Road,
But not the Master-Knot of Human Fate.

Legacy:
   As early as the 14th century when Dante Alighieri depicted him in Limbo alongside the virtuous non-Christian thinkers in his Divine Comedy such as Virgil, Averroes, Homer, Horace, Ovid, Lucan, Socrates, Plato, and Saladin, Avicenna has been recognized by both East and West, as one of the great figures in intellectual history.

   George Sarton, the author of *The History of Science*, described Ibn Sīnā as "one of the greatest thinkers and medical scholars in history" and called him "the most famous scientist of Islam and one of the most famous of all races, places, and times." He is remembered in the Western history of medicine as a major historical figure who made important contributions to medicine and the European Renaissance. His influence following translation of the *Canon* was such that from the early fourteenth to the mid-sixteenth centuries he was ranked with Hippocrates and Galen as one of the acknowledged authorities, *princeps medicorum* (prince of physicians).

   In Iran, he is considered a national icon, and is often regarded as one of the greatest Persians to have ever lived. his portrait hangs in the Hall of the Avicenna Faculty of Medicine in the University of Paris. There is also a crater on the Moon named *Avicenna*. In 1980, the former Soviet Union, which then ruled his birthplace Bukhara, celebrated the thousandth anniversary of Avicenna's birth by circulating various commemorative stamps with artistic illustrations, and by erecting a bust of Avicenna based on anthropological research by Soviet scholars.

   In March 2008, it was announced that Avicenna's name would be used for new Directories of education institutions for health care professionals, worldwide. He has had a lasting influence on the development of medicine and health sciences. The use of Avicenna's name symbolizes the worldwide partnership that is needed for the promotion of health services of high quality."

Works:
The treatises of Ibn Sīnā influenced later Muslim thinkers in many areas including theology, philology, mathematics, astronomy, physics, and music. Ibn Sīnā's works numbered almost 450 volumes on a wide range of subjects, of which around 240 have survived. In particular, 150 volumes of his surviving works concentrate on philosophy and 40 of them concentrate on medicine. His most famous works are The Book of Healing, a vast philosophical and scientific encyclopedia, and The Canon of Medicine,

Ibn Sīnā wrote at least one treatise on alchemy, but several others have been falsely attributed to him.

The Logic and Metaphysics have been extensively reprinted, the latter, e.g., at Venice in 1493, 1495, and 1546. Some of his shorter essays on medicine, logic, etc., take a poetical form (the poem on logic was published by Schmoelders in 1836). Two encyclopedic treatises, dealing with philosophy, are often mentioned.

***

Ibn Taymiyyah (1263-1328): Muslim belief is that the Qur'an is God's final communication to mankind. Muslim scholars and reformers have been able to repeatedly utilize this slogan with much success throughout Islamic history. *Shaykh al-Islam* Ibn Taymiyyah was one such extraordinary scholar and reformer.

Taqi al-Din Abul Abbas Ahmad ibn Abd al-Halim ibn Taymiyyah was born in Harran, a city located on the outskirts of Damascus, into a distinguished family of writers, scholars and theologians. Brought up in an intellectually friendly environment, Ibn Taymiyyah memorized the entire Qur'an. When he was barely seven, his entire family was forced to flee from Harran in the face of an imminent threat of a Mongol onslaught on the city. The Mongol hordes stormed out of Asia like a thunderbolt from the heavens, and inflicted a crushing blow on the Muslim world by invading Baghdad, the seat of the Abbasid Caliphate, and destroying everything before them with unspeakable brutality; at the time the entire Muslim world was gripped by fear and trepidation. Although the Mongol invasion of Baghdad represented one of the most destructive periods in Islamic history, it was the valiant Egyptian Mamluk soldiers who finally stopped them in 1260 at the Battle of *Ayn Jalut* (or the 'Spring of Goliath'). The Mamluk victory at *Ayn Jalut* saved Egypt, Arabia and the neighboring Islamic lands from Mongol invasion and pillage. Despite suffering a crushing defeat at *Ayn Jalut*, the Mongols remained a serious threat.

Ibn Taymiyyah's family moved to the safety of Damascus, which was then controlled by the victorious Mamluks. Like his father and grandfather, young Ibn Taymiyyah was an exceptionally bright student who was blessed with a sharp intellect and retentive memory. His thirst for knowledge was such that he claimed to have studied under no fewer than two hundred eminent Islamic scholars of his day, including Shaykh Ahmad ibn Abu al-Khair, Yahya ibn al-Sairafi, Ibn Abu a-Yusr, and Shams al-Din al-Maqdisi, who was the Chief Justice of Damascus. Shams al-Din, the Chief Justice, considered Ibn Taymiyyah to be competent enough to issue juristic rulings (*fatawa*) when he was barely seventeen years old.

Though Ibn Taymiyyah's formal education was that of a *Hanbali* theologian and jurist, he was very fond of the Qur'an from the outset. Following the death of his father, he was appointed professor of Islamic Thought at the same institution where his father once taught; he was only twenty at the time. He remained a confirmed bachelor all his life.

Not keen on only preaching, Ibn Taymiyyah went out of his way to issue legal edicts (*fatawa*) on several controversial theological issues. This infuriated the established scholars of Damascus, who called on the local authorities to punish him for alleged heresy. Eager to quell the uproar, the authorities complied with the scholars' demands and imprisoned Ibn Taymiyyah.

Theologically speaking, neither Ash'arism nor Mu'tazilism appealed to Ibn Taymiyyah. Despite being a *Hanbali* jurist, he refused to adhere exclusively to any one of the four prominent schools of Islamic legal thought (M*adhahib*), thus leaving himself wide open to accusations of heresy and religious innovation (B*ida*). As a *Mujtahid* (one who was competent to exercise *Ijtihad*), he felt he was not duty-bound to follow any one of the existing schools of law.

Ibn Taymiyyah rarely backed down in a confrontation with his opponents. In 1300, the Mongol hordes unexpectedly breached the heavily fortified defenses erected by the Mamluks and occupied Syria. In response, Ibn Taymiyyah urged the people of Damascus to engage in *jihad* (military struggle) and liberate their country from Mongol occupation. Thanks to him, a combined Egyptian-Syrian army confronted the Mongols in 1302 and in the ensuing battle he fought like a lion until the enemy was driven out of Mamluk territories. His role in the war against the Mongols won him national recognition in Syria.

Ibn Taymiyyah went out of his way to expose what he considered to be the unorthodox beliefs and practices of the Sufis, especially the metaphysical thought of Ibn al-Arabi. He also attacked the philosophical and speculative discourse of al-Farabi, Ibn Sina, Fakhr al-Din al-Razi, al-Shahrastani and even called into question aspects of al-Ghazali's theological views. His stance on various religious issues led to his imprisonment on more than one occasion, including once in 1306, again in 1309, yet again in 1318 and finally in 1326. It was during these periods that he wrote most of his books. He authored around one hundred books and treatises on Islamic sciences, comparative religion and aspects of philosophy, and logic and mysticism. According to his other biographers, he authored as many as five hundred books, treatises and essays on a wide range of subjects.

Ibn Taymiyyah died in prison at the age of sixty-five. He is widely considered to be one of the Muslim world's greatest thinkers.

Declared total war on Sufism, Shi'ism and the study of Greek philosophy. He encouraged jihad. He encouraged the ruler of Syria, al-Nasir, to wage war against the Mongol Ghazan Khan.

***

Ibn Tufayl (1101-1185): Ancient Greek, Persian and Indian science and philosophy first entered the Muslim world during the eighth century and found their finest expression in the works of al-Kindi and al-Razi in the ninth century and in that of al-Farabi and *Ikhwan al-Safa* (The Brethren of Purity) in the tenth, culminating in the works of the great Neo-Platonist Ibn Sina in the eleventh century. When philosophy was in full retreat in the Islamic East, it found a warm welcome in *al-Andalus* in the Islamic West. As a result, Islamic philosophy flourished in Muslim Spain during the twelfth century, thanks largely to the efforts of great European Muslim philosophers like Ibn Bajjah (Avempace) and Ibn Rushd (Averroes). But it was in the works of Ibn Tufayl that Islamic philosophy found a refreshing, innovative and powerful expression.

Abu Bakr Muhammad ibn Abd al-Malik ibn Muhammad ibn Tufayl, known as Abubacer in the Western world, was born at Guadix (in present-day Wadi Ash) in Islamic Granada. By the time Ibn Tufayl was born, the al-Moravids had reunited the entire country under their leadership and established much-needed peace and prosperity there.

As a student prodigy, Ibn Tufayl excelled in both the scientific and philosophical sciences and received instant recognition for his mastery of mathematics, medicine and philosophy. To a great extent he is considered to be unnatural successor of Ibn Bajjah, in the same way that Ibn Rushd is regarded, in turn, as his successor in the intellectual history of Islamic Spain.

Following the death of the al-Moravid ruler Ali ibn Yusuf in 1143, political chaos and social anarchy again returned to Islamic Spain, prompting the neighboring Christian principalities to reorganize their forces and launch fresh incursions into the Islamic territories. After Abu Yaqub Yusuf al-Mansur ascended the al-Mohad throne, he came to hear about Ibn Tufayl's skills as a medical practitioner and arranged for him to be brought to the al-Moravid court. Ibn Tufayl was one such intellectual who served Abu Yaqub as a physician, secretary and advisor.

Like Abu Yaqub, Ibn Tufayl was also in the habit of recruiting some of the finest scholars and thinkers of the time to the court in Marrakesh. One of Ibn Tufayl's star recruits was Ibn Rushd.

Whether the universe was eternal of a finite creation of God was a contentious philosophical point, which was hotly debated by the Muslim philosophers and theologians alike.

Unlike Ibn Bajjah, Ibn Tufayl was not a pure rationalist, nor did he subscribe to the philosophical theology of al-Ghazali, even though he was well-acquainted with both points of view. The philosophical synthesis he formulated between the Peripatetic thought of al-Farabi and Ibn Sina on the one hand, and al-Ghazali's mystical philosophy on the other found its most profound and enduring expression in his world famous novel *Risalah Hayy ibn Yaqdhan* (The Tale of Living Son of Vigilant). All the believers, irrespective of whether they worshipped in the mosques, lodges or sanctuaries, were, in Ibn Tufayl's opinion, seeking the One and the same Truth. He believed that in reality there was no conflict between reason and revelation; thus, in his *Risalah*, he attempted to reconcile some of the most complex and intractable philosophical, mystical and theological controversies which had been raging in the Muslim world for many centuries.

The *Risalah* was first translated into Hebrew (with an explanatory commentary) in 1349 by Moses Ben Joshua of Narbonne; the Englishman Edward Pococke then published a Latin version under the title of *Philosophus Autodidactus* (or 'the self-taught philosopher') along with the original Arabic text in 1671 at Oxford. This book was then translated into English, Dutch, Russian, Spanish, German and other Western languages.

After serving as a royal physician to Abu Yaqub Yusuf for nearly two decades, Ibn Tufayl finally retired in 1182. Three years later, this great European Muslim philosopher died at the age of eighty-four and was buried in Marrakesh (in present-day Morocco).

***

Ibn Tulun, Ahmad (835-884): Ahmad ibn Tulun (September 835 – March 884) was the founder of the Tulunids dynasty that ruled Egypt briefly between 868 and 905 AD. Originally sent by the Abbasid caliph as governor to Egypt, ibn Tulun established himself as an independent ruler.

Biography:

Ibn Ṭūlūn was born in Baghdad during the month of Ramadan 220 AH (September 835). His father, Ṭūlūn, was one of the Turkic slaves included with a tribute sent by the governor of Bukhara to the Abbasid Caliph al-Ma'mun around the year 815-16. The Abbasid court recruited Turkish slaves to serve as military officers, and Tulun did well for himself, eventually coming to command the Caliph's private guard.

The family moved to Samarra in 850, and ibn Tulun received his military training there, and also studied theology. He was appointed commander of special forces for the Caliph al-Mutawakkil in 855. Tulun died around this time, and his widow married an influential Turkish commander in the palace, Bayik Bey (*Bākbāk* in some of the Arabic sources). Ibn Ṭūlūn married Hatun, the daughter of another influential Turkish general in the palace guard, who bore him two children: 'Abbes and Fatimah.

After serving in military campaigns against the Byzantine Empire in Tarsus, ibn Tulun gained the favor of the Caliph al-Musta'in. On returning to Baghdad in 863, the Caliph presented him with a concubine, Meyyaz, with whom he had Khumarawaih, the son who eventually succeeded him as ruler of Egypt.

In 868, the Caliph al-Mu'tazz appointed Bayik Bey as the governor of Egypt; Bayik Bey in turn sent Ahmad ibn Ṭūlūn as his regent. Ibn Ṭūlūn arrived in Egypt in September 868.

On arriving in Egypt, ibn Ṭūlūn found that the existing capital of Egypt, al-Fustat, founded by Amr ibn al-'As in 641, was too small to accommodate his armies. He founded a new city to serve as his capital, Madinat al-Qatta'i, or *the quartered city*. Al-Qatta'i was laid out in the style of grand cities of Persia and the Byzantine Empire, including a large public square, hippodrome, a palace for the governor, and a large ceremonial Mosque of Ibn Tulun, which was named for ibn Ṭūlūn. The city was razed in 905 AD, and the mosque alone has survived.

Initially, ibn Ṭūlūn's rule in Egypt was marked by a struggle for control with the existing head of the council of financial affairs, Ibn al-Mudabbir. Ibn al-Mudabbir was disliked by the local population because of high rates of taxation (particularly against non-Muslim citizens, which comprised over half of Egypt's population) and greed. Ibn al-Mudabbir reported directly to the Caliph, not to the governor of Egypt, and as such ignored ibn Ṭūlūn entirely. Ibn Ṭūlūn used his influence at the Abbasid court to work against Ibn al-Mudabbir, and finally was able to have him removed after four years.

Bayik Bey was murdered around 870, and governorship passed to Yarjukh al-Turki, father of ibn Tulun's wife, Hatun. Yarjukh retained ibn Ṭūlūn as his regent in Egypt, and increased his power by granting him authority over Alexandria and other territories in the region. Ibn Ṭūlūn led a campaign against the rebellious governor of Syria, 'Īsā ibn Shaykh ash-Shaybanī, which allowed him to amass an army of 100,000 men.

In 871, the Caliph al-Mu'tamid appointed his brother Al-Muwaffaq as governor of Damascus, and his son, later the Caliph Al-Mu'tadid, to succeed Yarjukh as governor of Egypt. The rebellion of the Zanji, a group of black slaves who seized control of Basra and much of southern Iraq during this decade, siphoned much of the caliphate's resources away from the provinces. In 874, ibn Ṭūlūn took advantage of the chaos in Iraq to sever relations with Baghdad and declare independence.

It was not until 877 that Al-Mu'tadid sent armed forces under Musa ibn Bugha to retake control of Egypt. But the attempted invasion was a rout, with most of Musa's army scattering before the larger forces led by ibn Ṭūlūn. Ibn Ṭūlūn's forces followed and took control of large portions of Syria, but the campaign was cut short when ibn Ṭūlūn had to return to Egypt to deal with a revolt led by his own son, 'Abbes.

Following his return from Syria, ibn Ṭūlūn added his own name to coins issued by the dynasty, along with those of the Caliph and heir apparent. In 882, ibn Ṭūlūn invited the nearly powerless Caliph al-Mu'tamid to Egypt to offer him protection against his brother, Al-Muwaffaq, who was trying to remain in power as regent. Al-Muta'mid was intercepted *en route* to Egypt, and ibn Ṭūlūn and Al-Muwaffaq began an endless campaign against each other. Ibn Ṭūlūn was able to have a group of prominent jurists declare Al-Muwaffaq a usurper, and both leaders had the other cursed during Friday prayers.

Military skirmishes followed. After leading the siege of Tarsus under Yazaman al-Khadim in 883, ibn Ṭūlūn fell ill on his return to Egypt and died on May 10, 884. He was succeeded by his 20-year old son, Khumarraweh, who lacked much of the charisma and cunning that kept ibn Ṭūlūn in power. The Tulunids dynasty was short-lived, and Egypt was preoccupied by Abbasid forces in the winter of 904–05.

***

Ibrahim Pasha (1789-1848): Egyptian general. He was the eldest son of Muhammad Ali, governor of Egypt under the Ottoman Empire. Ibrahim conducted (1816-19) largely successful campaigns against the Wahhabis in Arabia. He fought (1825-28) against the insurgent Greeks, but the landing of French troops forced him to withdraw from the country. After Muhammad Ali turned against the Ottoman sultan, Ibrahim conquered (1832-33) Syria. His attempts to apply to Syria the reforms that his father had introduced in Egypt caused a series of disorders. Warfare with the Turks was resumed in 1838, but British and Austrian military intervention on Turkey's behalf compelled Ibrahim to evacuate to Egypt. In 1848 he was regent of Egypt during his father's insanity. Was sent to cleanse Syria, Iraq and Kuwait of the Wahhabis.

***

Idris, Yusuf (1927-1991): Egyptian writer Born in a village near Zagazig in the Nile delta, Idris obtained a medical degree from Cairo University in 1951. Dissatisfied with the Western dramatic structure, Idris turned to the forms used by popular entertainers in the Arab world-shadow plays and puppet theatre. Now his main character, instead of being an heroic failure was often enigmatic and miraculous, who operated in a world that hovered between illusion and reality. Some of his stories were translated into foreign languages.

***

Inn, Ismet (1884-1973): Turkish statesmen and solider, president of Turkey (1938-50). He served in the Balkan Wars and World War I and became (1920) chief of staff to Mustafa Kemal, later known as Kemal Ataturk. He played an important part in the establishment of the Turkish republic and in Kemal's victory over the Greeks, and he represented Turkey at the Conference over Lausanne (see Lausanne, Treaty of, 1922-23). As prime minister (1923-24, 1925-37) he able seconded the reforms of Ataturk, whom he succeeded (1938) as president of the republic. Inonu instituted free general elections for the first time in 1950; his party was defeated, and he was succeeded by Celal Bayar. After a military coup (1960; see Turkey) and the promulgation of a new constitution, Inonu's Republican People's party won a parliamentary plurality in the elections of 1961. He again became premier, heading successive coalition cabinets until 1965, when his government fell.

***

Iqbal, Muhammad (1876-1938): Indian philosopher poet, and political leader. He took an active part in politics in the Punjab and was President of the Muslim League in 1930 when he advanced the idea of a separate Muslim state in north-west India, the beginning of the concept of Pakistan.

***

Isa II ibn Salman (1933-1999): ruler of Bahrain 1961-99 Born in Manama, al Khalifa was named heir apparent at twenty four. Bahrain, with a Shi'a majority was affected by the Islamic revolution in Shi'a majority Iran. When the Islamic opposition demanded that Bahrain be declared an Islamic republic, al Khalifa, a Sunni reacted with a heavy hand. To meet the rising demand for reform, he appointed a thirty member advisory council in 1993, but kept the 1973 constitution suspended.

***

Ismail: The prophet who is known as Ishmael in the Bible, the eldest son of Abraham, who was cast out into the wilderness at God's command with his mother, Hagar, but saved by God. Muslim tradition has it that Hagar and Ismail in Mecca, that Abraham came to visit them there and that Abraham and Ismail rebuilt the Kabah (which had been originally constructed by Adam, the first prophet and father of mankind). Also: **Ismail:** The seventh Imam in Shi'ism, who was "the expected one" (messiah); his followers are the "Ismailis".

***

Ismail, Abdul Fattah (1936-1986): South Yemeni politician, president 1978-80, Born into a peasant family in the Hujairiah region of North Yemen, Ismail traveled to Aden for further education. The radical policies of Ismail alienated Muhammad, who espoused a more pragmatic approach. In April 1980 Ismail was forced to resign his position and go into exile in Moscow. In the subsequent violence Muhammad was defeated but Ismail lost his life.

***

Ismail I Safavi (1487-1524): First ruler of the Safavid dynasty in Persia (1501-24). His ancestor Safe ud-Din (1252-1334) was a Sufi holy man and founder of the Safaviyya the mystic brotherhood after which the dynasty is named. Supported by Turcoman tribesmen, he established his rule over Persia, extending it into Kurdistan and driving the Uzbeks from Khurasan in the north-east. His expansion was checked in the west by the Ottoman sultan Selim I at Chaldiran in 1514. His most enduring achievement was to convert his realm from Sunni to Shiite Islam.

***

Ismail ibn Ja'far: He was appointed the Seventh Imam of the Shiah by his father Ja'far as Sadiq. Some Shiis (known as Ismailis or Seveners) believe that he was the last of the direct descendants of Ali ibn Abi Talib to succeed to the imamate, and do not recognize the imamate of Musa al Kazim, the younger son of Ja'far as Sadiq, who is revered by Twelver Shiis as the Seventh Imam.

***

Ismail Pasha (1830-1895): ruler of Egypt (1863-79), son of Ibrahim Pasha. He succeeded his uncle Said Pasha as ruler, Ismail used the Egyptian cotton crop, enormously enhanced in value by the American Civil War, to obtain credits for grandiose schemes, including irrigation projects, schools, palaces, the construction of the Suez Canal, and the extension of Egyptian rule in Sudan. Much of the money was wasted, and the country was seriously involved in debt. In 1875, Ismail was forced to sell to Great Britain his stockholdings (some 44%) in the Suez Canal, and in 1876 he was obliged to place the finances of Egypt under the control of a debt commission that represented the French and British bondholders. His attempt to throw off foreign control in 1879 was answered by the Ottoman sultan's deposing him in favor of his son Tewfik Pasha. In 1866, Ismail received the title khedive (viceroy), which his successors also enjoyed.

***

Jadid, Salah (1926-1993): Syrian military leader and politician Born into a notable Alawi family in Duwair Baabda a village near Jablah port, Jadid trained as an officer at the Homs Military Academy. Angered at President Gamal Abdul Nasser's decision to dissolve the Baath party in Syria, he joined Hafiz Assad and two other Ba'athist officers to form, secretly the Military Committee n 1959. In October, promoted to major general Jadid was named chief of staff. The Syrian defeat in the June 1967 Arab Israeli War involving the loss of the Golan Heights was a strong blow to Jadid's regime. Among other things it created a rift between Jadid and Assad who advocated pragmatic policies. He was held in the Mezze fortress prison until 1983. After his release he was kept under surveillance and barred from public life until after a brief period of freedom he was again detained at the Mezze prison where he died of illness.

***

Ja'far: Young cousin of Muhammad, son of Abu Talib and one of the early believers who took refuge in Christian Abyssinia and who would be killed alongside Zayd at the battle of Mutah in 629.

***

Ja'far al-Sadiq (700-765): One man who attained this exalted ability through his single-minded devotion and dedication to Islamic principles and practices, notwithstanding all the obstacles that were placed in his path by his enemies and detractors, was the celebrated Ja'far al-Sadiq.

Ja'far ibn Muhammad ibn Ali Zain al-Abideen ibn Hussain ibn Ali was born in the sacred city of Madinah (in present-day Saudi Arabia) into the most illustrious and noble family of Arabia. Ja'far was a direct descendant of the Prophet Muhammad through his youngest and most beloved daughter, Fatimah. Ja'far's mother, Umm Farwa, was the great-granddaughter of Caliph Abu Bakr, through his son Muhammad. Ja'far developed an instant affinity with Islam as a religion and a way of life. He pursued his advanced Islamic education under the tutelage of his maternal grandfather, al-Qasim ibn Muhammad, who was one of the greatest Islamic scholars of his generation and a pre-eminent *Tabi* (successor of the Prophet's companions).

Ja'far shunned frivolous and time-consuming activities, and instead devoted all his spare time to prayers, recitation of the Qur'an and other devotional activities. His lectures were attended by some of the Muslim world's greatest scholars, thinkers and historians, including Abu Hanifah, Malik ibn Anas, Muhammad ibn Ishaq, Yahya ibn Sa'id, Sufyan al-Thawri, Shuba ibn al-Hajjaj, Sufyan ibn Uyayna, Abd al-Malik ibn Juraij and Jabir ibn Hayyan among others. Many of his students were his contemporaries. His peers conferred the title of *al-Sadiq* (or 'the truthful') on him due to his scrupulousness as a *Hadith* narrator. Indeed, his interpretation of the Qur'an and *Hadith* was so refreshing and wide-ranging that a new school of Islamic legal thought, the *Ja'fari Madh'hab*, later emerged and spread to different parts of the Muslim world. Like the *Hanafi, shafi'i, Maliki, Hanbali* and *Zaydi Madhahib*, it also originated and evolved during this formative period of Islamic legal thought.

Despite the tyranny of some Umayyad rulers, Ja'far remained politically neutral. Since political rivalry between the ruling Umayyads and their Abbasid counterparts became very intense then, Ja'far chose to tread the path of political neutrality. Notwithstanding his political neutrality, Ja'far was summoned to Baghdad on several occasions by the Abbasid ruler Abu Ja'far al-Mansur, who accused him of taking part in political intrigues and fanning the flames of civil unrest and social disturbance.

Whenever Ja'far visited Baghdad, the people of that city always gave him a warm reception. According to him, the most learned person is the one who is most acquainted with the differences of opinion (I*khtilaf*) among the scholars. On a personal level, he led a simple and austere lifestyle, devoted solely to the service of Islam. However, within the *Ithna 'Ashari* (Twelver) Shi'a branch, Ja'far occupies the position of the sixth Imam. The other five Shi'a Imams include Caliph Ali, his sons Hasan, Hussain, Ali Zain al-Abideen and Muhammad al-Baqir, the father of Ja'far al-Sadiq. By contrast, the Sunnis, who form the vast majority of the world's Muslim population, do not subscribe to the doctrine of Imamate; they consider Ja'far to be one of the Muslim world's most gifted scholars and sages.

Ja'far al-Sadiq died at the age of around sixty-five and was buried in the famous cemetery of Jannat al-Baqi in Madinah.

***

Jabir ibn Hayyan (738-813): The origin of the word 'chemistry' can be traced back to its Arabic root *al-Kimiya*, which was also translated as alchemy. Perhaps the word *al-Kimiya* originated from the Egyptian K*hem*, meaning 'black'; both the ancient Egyptians and Greeks considered chemistry to be the 'art of *Khem*'. Among the early Muslim practitioners of alchemy were Khalid ibn Yazid, the grandson of Caliph Muawiyah, and Ja'far al-Sadiq, the prominent Islamic scholar of Madinah who acquired knowledge of this subject from a combination of religious and Syriac sources. This state of affairs prevailed until Jabir ibn Hayyan, known in the Latin West as Geber, emerged to pave the way for the emergence of alchemy as an independent branch of science.

Jabir ibn Hayyan ibn Abdullah al-Kufi al-Sufi was born in Tus in the Persian province of Khurasan. Hailing from the southern Arabian tribe of Azd, his ancestors moved to Kufah during the early years of Islamic expansion. Perhaps it was his political links with the Abbasids which prompted him to leave Kufah for Khurasan, where he continued to support the Abbasid insurgency against the Umayyads. While Jabir was a child his father was captured and sentenced to death by the Umayyad judiciary for supporting politically subversive activities. Thereafter, Jabir studied astrology, cosmology and further aspects of medicine and alchemy.

As a practicing Sufi, Jabir was also in the habit of going into spiritual retreats but his Sufism was far from being other-worldly, for he found time to learn and master the experimental sciences too. An adherent of the Sufi *Tariqah* (or Order) founded by Abul Hashim of Kufah, Jabir successfully combined spiritualism with physical and intellectual activism. When Harun al-Rashid, the celebrated Abbasid Caliph, came to hear about Jabir, he went out of his way to recruit him to his research center in Baghdad. Jabir thus became associated with the Abbasids, especially the Barmakids who at the time served as chief advisors to the Caliph.

Although Jabir continued to live in Kufah, he travelled regularly to Baghdad to collaborate with the leading Muslim scholars and scientists of the day. However, it was in the field of alchemy, or chemistry, that he made his lasting contribution. Before his own time, alchemy was widely considered to be a spiritual rather than an experimental science, but post-Jabir it became an experimental science, detached from its spiritual roots. Had it not been for Jabir's bold and innovative experimental scientific methodology, the development of chemistry as a separate scientific discipline would no doubt have been delayed by at least a few centuries. For this reason, today he is widely considered to be the 'father of Islamic alchemy' and one of the pioneers of chemistry. His experimental approach to alchemy, coupled with the discovery of his private chemical laboratory in Kufah two centuries after his death, proved, if proof was required, that he was a great alchemist and pioneering chemist.

Using his experimental approach to chemistry, Jabir named and classified chemicals and minerals into three broad categories. The first category consisted of spirits (such as sulpher, mercury, camphor and arsenic compounds) which, he argued, could be refined through the application of heat. The second category included metals like gold, silver, lead, tin, copper, iron and zinc. The final category consisted of pulverized substances, even though he pointed out that some pulverized substances, such as living creatures, were made of both spirit and matter. Jabir made a number of remarkable discoveries. For instance, by developing a special acidic powder, he was able to dissolve solid gold, and also produced a chemical substance which enabled him to separate gold from silver. Likewise, he coined scores of technical terms such as *alkali*, *antimony*, *alembic*, and *cinnabar* which have today become commonplace around the world.

Jabir led a very simple, pious and productive life, devoted entirely to the pursuit of knowledge. He had free access to all the royal libraries in Baghdad. Jabir died at the age of seventy-one and was buried in Kufah. He was not only an outstanding chemist, he was also a prolific writer who authored more than one hundred books and treatises on aspects of alchemy. Most of his books perished in 1258 during the Mongol sack of Baghdad.

After his works were translated into Latin and other European languages during the thirteenth and fourteenth centuries, Jabir's ideas and thoughts had a profound impact on medieval European thinkers and scientists.

***

Jalal ad-Din Rumi, Muhammad Balkhi (1207-1273): Also known as Jalal ad-Din Muhammad and popularly known as Mevlana in Turkey and Mawlana in Iran and Afghanistan but known to the English-speaking world simply as **Rumi** (30 September 1207 – 17 December 1273) was a 13th-century Persian Muslim poet, jurist, theologian, and Sufi mystic. *Rūmī* is a descriptive name meaning "Roman" since he lived most of his life in an area called "Rûm" (then under the control of Seljuq dynasty) because it was once ruled by the Eastern Roman Empire. He was one of the figures who flourished in the Sultanate of Rum.

His birthplace and native language both indicate a Persian heritage. His family claimed descent from Abu Bakr, the first Caliph of Islam. His father decided to migrate westwards due to quarrels between different dynasties in Khorasan, opposition to the Khwarizmid Shahs, who were considered deviant by Bahā ad-Din Walad, or fear of the impending Mongol cataclysm. Rumi's family traveled west, first performing the Hajj and eventually settling in the Anatolian city Konya (capital of the Seljuk Sultanate of Rum, in present-day Turkey). This was where he lived most of his life, and here he composed one of the crowning glories of Persian literature which profoundly affected the culture of the area.

He lived most of his life under the Sultanate of Rum, where he produced his works and died in 1273 AD. He was buried in Konya and his shrine became a place of pilgrimage. Following his death, his followers and his son Sultan Walad founded the Mevlevi Order, also known as the Order of the Whirling Dervishes, famous for its Sufi dance known as the Sama ceremony.

Rumi's works are written in the New Persian language. A Persian literary renaissance (in the 8th/9th century) started in regions of Sistan, Khorasan and Transoxiana and by the 10th/11th century, it reinforced the Persian language as the preferred literary and cultural language in the Persian Islamic world. Rumi's importance is considered to transcend national and ethnic borders. His original works are widely read in their original language across the Persian-speaking world. Translations of his works are very popular in other countries. His poetry has influenced Persian literature as well as Urdu, Punjabi and other Pakistani languages written in Perso/Arabic script e.g. Pashto and

Sindhi. His poems have been widely translated into many of the world's languages and transposed into various formats. In 2007, he was described as the "most popular poet in America."

Life:
Rumi was probably born on 30 September 1207 in the province of Balkh in the district of Wakhsh in Khorasan (now in modern Afghanistan/Tajikistan). He died on 17 December 1273 in Konya in Seljuqid Rum (now modern Turkey). He was laid to rest beside his father and over his remains a splendid shrine was erected. A hagiographical account of him is described in Shams ud-Din Ahmad Aflākī's *Manāqib ul-Ārifīn* (written between 1318 and 1353).

Rumi's father, who, at home, taught Rumi Arabic, Persian, traditional Islamic sciences and poetry during his early years, was Bahā ud-Din Walad, a theologian, jurist and a mystic from Wakhsh, who was also known by the followers of Rumi as Sultan al-Ulama or "Sultan of the Scholars". The most complete genealogy offered for the family stretches back to six or seven generations to famous Hanafi Jurists.

We do not learn the name of Baha al-Din's mother in the sources, but only that he referred to her as "Māmī" (Colloquial Persian for Māma) and that she was a simple woman and that she lives in 13th century. The mother of Rumi was Mu'mina Khatun. The profession of the family for several generations was that of Islamic preachers of the liberal Hanafi rite.

When the Mongols invaded Central Asia sometime between 1215 and 1220, Baha ud-Din Walad, with his whole family and a group of disciples, set out westwards. Rumi encountered one of the most famous mystic Persian poets, 'Attar, in the Iranian city of Nishapur, located in the province of Khorasan. 'Attar immediately recognized Rumi's spiritual eminence. He saw the father walking ahead of the son and said, "Here comes a sea followed by an ocean." He gave the boy his *Asrārnāma*, a book about the entanglement of the soul in the material world. This meeting had a deep impact on the eighteen-year-old Rumi and later on became the inspiration for his works.

From Nishapur, Walad and his entourage set out for Baghdad, meeting many of the scholars and Sufis of the city. From there they went to Baghdad and Hejaz and performed the pilgrimage at Mecca. The migrating caravan then passed through Damascus, Malatya, Erzincan, Sivas, Kayseri and Nigde. They finally settled in Karaman for seven years; Rumi's mother and brother both died there. In 1225, Rumi married Gowhar Khatun in Karaman. They had two sons: Sultan Walad and Ala-eddin Chalabi. When his wife died, Rumi married again and had a son, Amir Alim Chalabi, and a daughter, Malakeh Khatun.

On 1 May 1228, most likely as a result of the insistent invitation of 'Alā' ud-Din Key-Qobād, ruler of Anatolia, Baha' ud-Din came and finally settled in Konya in Anatolia within the westernmost territories of the Seljuk Sultanate of Rûm.

Baha' ud-Din became the head of a madrasah (religious school) and when he died, Rumi, aged twenty-five, inherited his position as the Islamic Molvi. One of Baha' ud-Din's students, Sayyed Burhan ud-Din Muhaqqiq Termazi, continued to train Rumi in the Shariah as well as the Tariqa, especially that of Rumi's father. For nine years, Rumi practiced Sufism as a disciple of Burhan ud-Din until the latter died in 1240 or 1241. Rumi's public life then began: he became an Islamic Jurist, issuing fatwas and giving sermons in the mosques of Konya. He also served as a Molvi (Islamic teacher) and taught his adherents in the madrasah.

During this period, Rumi also traveled to Damascus and is said to have spent four years there.

It was his meeting with the dervish Shams-e Tabrizi on 15 November 1244 that completely changed his life. From an accomplished teacher and jurist, Rumi was transformed into an ascetic. Shams had traveled throughout the Middle East searching and praying for someone who could "endure my company". A voice said to him, "What will you give in return?" Shams replied, "My head!" The voice then said, "The one you seek is Jalal ud-Din of Konya." On the night of 5 December 1248, as Rumi and Shams were talking, Shams was called to the back door. He went out, never to be seen again. It is rumored that Shams was murdered with the connivance of Rumi's son, 'Ala' ud-Din; if so, Shams indeed gave his head for the privilege of mystical friendship.

Rumi's love for, and his bereavement at the death of, Shams found their expression in an outpouring lyric poems, *Divan-e Shams-e Tabrizi*. He himself went out searching for Shams and journeyed again to Damascus. There, he realized:

> Why should I seek? I am the same as He.
> His essence speaks through me.
> I have been looking for myself!

Mewlana had been spontaneously composing *ghazals* (Persian poems), and these had been collected in the *Divan-i Kabir* or Diwan Shams Tabrizi. Rumi found another companion in Salaḥ ud-Din-e Zarkub, a goldsmith. After Salah ud-Din's death, Rumi's scribe and favorite student, Hussam-e Chalabi, assumed the role of Rumi's companion. Rumi smiled and took out a piece of paper on which were written the opening eighteen lines of his *Masnavi*, beginning with:

> Listen to the reed and the tale it tells,
> how it sings of separation...

Rumi spent the next twelve years of his life in Anatolia dictating the six volumes of this masterwork, the *Masnavi*, to Hussam.

In December 1273, Rumi fell ill; he predicted his own death and composed the well-known *ghazal*, which begins with the verse:

> How doest thou know what sort of king I have within me as companion?
> Do not cast thy glance upon my golden face, for I have iron legs.

Rumi died on 17 December 1273 in Konya; his body was interred beside that of his father, and a splendid shrine, the *Yeşil Türbe* (Green Tomb; today the Mevlana Museum), was erected over his place of burial. His epitaph reads:

> When we are dead, seek not our tomb in the earth,
> but find it in the hearts of men.

The 13th century Mawlana Mausoleum, with its mosque, dance hall, dervish living quarters, school and tombs of some leaders of the Mevlevi Order, continues to this day to draw pilgrims from all parts of the Muslim and non-Muslim world. Jalal al-Din, who is also known as Rumi, was a philosopher and mystic of Islam. His doctrine advocates unlimited tolerance, positive reasoning, goodness, charity and awareness through love. To him and to his disciples all religions are more or less truth. Looking with the same eye on Muslim, Jew and Christian alike, his peaceful and tolerant teaching has appealed to people of all sects and creeds.

Teachings:
The general theme of Rumi's thought, like that of other mystic and Sufi poets of Persian literature, is essentially that of the concept of *Tawhid* – union with his beloved (the primal root) from which/whom he has been cut off and become aloof – and his longing and desire to restore it

Rumi believed passionately in the use of music, poetry and dance as a path for reaching God. For Rumi, music helped devotees to focus their whole being on the divine and to do this so intensely that the soul was both destroyed and resurrected. It was from these ideas that the practice of whirling Dervishes developed into a ritual form. His teachings became the base for the order of the Mevlevi which his son Sultan Walad organized. Rumi encouraged Sama listening to music and turning or doing the sacred dance. In the Mevlevi tradition, Samā' represents a mystical journey of spiritual ascent through mind and love to the Perfect One. In this journey, the seeker symbolically turns towards the truth, grows through love, abandons the ego, finds the truth and arrives at the Perfect. The seeker then returns from this spiritual journey, with greater maturity, to love and to be of service to the whole of creation without discrimination with regard to beliefs, races, classes and nations.

In other verses in the *Masnavi*, Rumi describes in detail the universal message of love:
The lover's cause is separate from all other causes.
Love is the astrolabe of God's mysteries.

Major works:
Rumi's poetry is often divided into various categories: the quatrains (*rubayāt*) and odes (*ghazal*) of the *Divan*, the six books of the *Masnavi*. The prose works are divided into The Discourses, The Letters, and the *Seven Sermons*.

Poetic works:
- Rumi's major work is the *Maṭnawīye Ma'nawī* (*Spiritual Couplets*), a six-volume poem regarded by some Sufis as the Persian-language Qur'an. It is considered by many to be one of the greatest works of mystical poetry. It contains approximately 27,000 lines of Persian poetry.

- Rumi's other major work is the *Dīwān-e Kabir* (*Great Work*) or *Diwan-e Shams-e Tabrizi|Dīwān-e Shams-e Tabrizi* (*The Works of Shams of Tabriz*; named in honor of Rumi's master Shams. Besides approximately 35000 Persian couplets and 2000 Persian quatrains, the Divan contains 90 Ghazals and 19 quatrains in Arabic, a couple of dozen or so couplets in Turkish (mainly macaronic poems of mixed Persian and Turkish) and 14 couplets in Greek (all of them in three macaronic poems of Greek-Persian).

Philosophical outlook:

Rumi was an evolutionary thinker in the sense that he believed that the spirit after devolution from the divine Ego undergoes an evolutionary process by which it comes nearer and nearer to the same divine Ego. All matter in the universe obeys this law and this movement is due to an inbuilt urge (which Rumi calls "love") to evolve and seek enjoinment with the divinity from which it has emerged. Evolution into a human being from an animal is only one stage in this process. The doctrine of the Fall of Adam is reinterpreted as the devolution of the Ego from the universal ground of divinity and is a universal, cosmic phenomenon. Rumi believes that there is a specific *goal* to the process: the attainment of God. For Rumi, God is the ground as well as the goal of all existence.

However Rumi need not be considered a biological evolutionary creationist. In view of the fact that Rumi lived hundreds of years before Darwin, and was least interested in scientific theories, it is probable to conclude that he does not deal with biological evolution at all. Rather he is concerned with the spiritual evolution of a human being: Man not conscious of God is akin to an animal and true consciousness makes him divine.

> "I died as a mineral and became a plant,
> I died as plant and rose to animal,
> I died as animal and I was Man.
> Why should I fear? When was I less by dying?
> Yet once more I shall die as Man, to soar
> With angels bless'd; but even from angelhood
> I must pass on: all except God doth perish.
> When I have sacrificed my angel-soul,
> I shall become what no mind e'er conceived.
> Oh, let me not exist! for Non-existence
> Proclaims in organ tones,
> To Him we shall return."

Universality:

It is often said that the teachings of Rumi are ecumenical in nature. For Rumi, religion was mostly a personal experience and not limited to logical arguments or perceptions of the senses. Creative love, or the urge to rejoin the spirit to divinity, was the goal towards which everything moves. The dignity of life, in particular human life (which is conscious of its divine origin and goal), was important.

Islam:

A number of Rumi poems suggest the importance of outward religious observance, the primacy of the Qur'an.

Flee to God's Qur'an, take refuge in it,
there with the spirit of the prophets merge.
The book conveys the prophet's circumstances,
those fish of the sea of majesty.

Legacy:

Rumi's poetry forms the basis of much classical Iranian and Afghan music (Eastern-Persian, Tajik-Hazara music. To many modern Westerners, his teachings are one of the best introductions to the philosophy and practice of Sufism.

Today Rumi's poems can be heard in churches, synagogues, Zen monasteries, as well as in the downtown New York art/performance /music scene." According to Professor Majid M. Naini, "Rumi's life and transformation provide true testimony and proof that people of all religions and backgrounds can live together in peace and harmony.

Rumi's visions, words, and life teach us how to reach inner peace and happiness so we can finally stop the continual stream of hostility and hatred and achieve true global peace and harmony."

Rumi's work has been translated into many of the world's languages, including Russian, German, Urdu, Turkish, Arabic, Bengali, French, Italian, and Spanish, and is being presented in a growing number of formats, including concerts, workshops, readings, dance performances, and other artistic creations. The English interpretations of Rumi's poetry by Coleman Barks have sold more than half a million copies worldwide, and Rumi is one of the most widely read poets in the United States.

Recordings of Rumi poems have made it to the USA's Billboard's Top 20 list. A selection of American author Deepak Chopra's editing of the translations by Fereydoun Kia of Rumi's love poems has been performed by Hollywood personalities such as Madonna, Goldie Hawn, Philip Glass and Demi Moore.

Rumi and his mausoleum were depicted on the reverse of the 5000 Turkish lira banknotes of 1981-1994.

Iranian world:

Rumi's poetry is displayed on the walls of many cities across Iran, sung in Persian music, and read in school books.

Islamic Leaders

Mewlewī Sufi Order:

The Mewlewī Sufi order was founded in 1273 by Rumi's followers after his death. His first successor in the rector ship of the order was "Husam Chalabi" himself, after whose death in 1284 Rumi's younger and only surviving son, Sultan Walad (died 1312), favorably known as author of the mystical *Maṭnawī Rabābnāma*, or the *Book of the Rabab* was installed as grand master of the order. The leadership of the order has been kept within Rumi's family in Konya uninterruptedly since then. The Mewlewī Sufis, also known as Whirling Dervishes, believe in performing their *dhikr* in the form of Sama. During the time of Rumi (as attested in the *Manāqib ul-Ārefīn* of Aflākī), his followers gathered for musical and "turning" practices.

According to tradition, Rumi was himself a notable musician who played the *Robb*, although his favorite instrument was the *ney* or reed flute. The music accompanying the *Samā'* consists of settings of poems from the *Maṭnawī* and *Dīwān-e Kabir*, or of Sultan Walad's poems. The Mawlawīyah was a well-established Sufi order in the Ottoman Empire, and many of the members of the order served in various official positions of the Caliphate. The center for the Mevlevi was in Konya. The Mewlewī order issues an invitation to people of all backgrounds:

> "Come, come, whoever you are,
> Wander, idolater, worshipper of fire,
> Come even though you have broken
> Your vows a thousand times,
> Come, and come yet again,
> Ours is not a caravan of despair."

With the foundation of the modern, secular Republic of Turkey, Mustafa Kemal Ataturk removed religion from the sphere of public policy and restricted it exclusively to that of personal morals, behavior and faith. On 13 December 1925, a law was passed closing all the *tekke*s (or *tekeyh*) (dervish lodges) and *Ziwiyas* (chief dervish lodges), and the centers of veneration to which pilgrimages (*ziyārat*) were made. Istanbul alone had more than 250 *tekke*s as well as small centers for gatherings of various fraternities; this law dissolved the Sufi Orders, prohibited the use of mystical names, titles and costumes pertaining to their titles, impounded the Orders' assets, and banned their ceremonies and meetings. The law also provided penalties for those who tried to re-establish the Orders.

In the 1950s, the Turkish government began allowing the Whirling Dervishes to perform once a year in Konya. In 1974, the

Whirling Dervishes were permitted to travel to the West for the first time. In 2005, UNESCO proclaimed the "The Mevlevi Sama Ceremony" of Turkey as one of the Masterpieces of the Oral and Intangible Heritage of Humanity (the introduction of Twelver Shi'a as the state religion in the Safavid Empire in 1501.)

Eight hundredth anniversary celebrations:
In Afghanistan, Rumi is known as "Mewlana" and in Iran as "Mevlevi".
UNESCO was associated with the celebration, in 2007, of the eight hundredth anniversary of Rumi's birth. The commemoration at UNESCO itself took place on 6 September 2007;
On 30 September 2007, Iranian school bells were rung throughout the country in honor of Mewlana. Also in that year, Iran held a Rumi Week from 26 October to 2 November. Scholars from twenty-nine countries attended the events, and 450 articles were presented at the conference. 2007 was declared as the "International Rumi Year" by UNESCO.
Also on 30 September 2007, Turkey celebrated Rumi's eight-hundredth birthday with a giant Whirling Dervish ritual performance of the *Samā'*, which was televised using forty-eight cameras and broadcast live in eight countries, making it the largest performance of sama in history."

See also

Rumi experts
- William Chittick
- Badiozzaman Forouzanfar
- Hossein Elahi Ghomshei
- Shahram Shiva
- Hamid Algar
- Rahim Arbab
- Kabir Helminski
- Fatemeh Keshavarz
- Majid M. Naini
- Seyyed Hossein Nasr
- Franklin Lewis
- François Pétis de la Croix
- Annemarie Schimmel
- Abdolkarim Soroush
- Dariush Shayegan
- Abdolhossein Zarinkoob

English translators of Rumi poetry
- William Chittick
- Ravan A. G. Farhadi
- Shahram Shiva
- Nader Khalili
- Franklin Lewis
- Majid M. Naini
- Reynold A. Nicholson
- James W. Redhouse

Interpreters of Rumi
- Coleman Barks
- Shahram Shiva
- Omer Tarin

***

Jamal al-Din al-Afghani (1838-1897): The leading European nations subsequently made their way into the heart of the Muslim world during the eighteenth and nineteenth centuries, and in so doing they colonized a large part of the Muslim world. This inspired scores of influential Muslim scholars, thinkers and reformers to arise in order to reawaken the Muslim world from its slumber. Jamal al-Din al-Afghani was arguably the most charismatic and influential of them all.

Sayyid Muhammad ibn Safdar, better known as Jamal al-Din al-Afghani, was born into a noble Muslim family which traced its lineage all the way back to the Prophet of Islam, through his grandson Hussain. Al-Afghani was born in Hamadan in Persia and was therefore of Iranian origin – even though he has become popularly known as 'al-Afghani'. Assuming that he was indeed born in Persia, his family must have migrated to Afghanistan soon after his birth. Such was his eagerness to learn that he subsequently gained proficiency in aspects of medicine, mathematics, chemistry and other physical sciences.

Al-Afghani returned to India for a second time in 1869. Following the abortive mutiny of 1857, the British assumed full political and military control of India. Thus, on his arrival in India in 1869, the British initially allowed him to move around freely in the country. But, as the failed mutiny of 1857 was a disturbing and frightening experience for the British, they closely monitored the activities of everyone who was associated with the Indian liberation movement. The British authorities granted al-Afghani a pass to board a British vessel bound for Egypt. On his arrival in Cairo, he went straight to al-Azhar University, the ancient seat of Islamic learning and scholarship. Here he delivered regular lectures on all aspects of Islam, philosophy, history and politics. His erudition, versatility, charisma and electrifying oratory skills created a huge stir at al-Azhar, and during his short stay at Cairo, al-Afghani left a deep impression on all the scholars, teachers and students he met at al-Azhar.

From Cairo, al-Afghani proceeded to Istanbul, the political capital of the Ottoman Empire, in 1870. After his name and fame spread across Istanbul, he was appointed a member of the Ottoman Educational Council. Invited to deliver regular lectures at the famous Aya Sofia (Hagia Sophia) and other mosques across Istanbul, al-Afghani's inspiring lectures moved his audiences wherever he went. When Hasan Fahmi's diatribes against al-Afghani intensified, the latter was forced to leave Istanbul and return to Cairo.

Al-Afghani was offered a generous stipend by the Egyptian Government to teach at al-Azhar. During this period he also gathered around him a small band of disciples, which included the influential Islamic thinker and reformer Muhammad Abduh. This prompted al-

Afghani to highlight and emphasize the importance of the political and social dimensions of Islam. He therefore urged the Egyptian Muslim intelligentsia to engage in political and social activism in order to liberate their land from British hegemony. Accused of spreading anti-British propaganda, the Egyptian ruler, Tewfiq Pasha, demanded that al-Afghani leave the country forthwith. In 1879, at the age of forty-one, he was forced to leave Egypt for India.

In India, al-Afghani settled in Hyderabad where, along with Rafat Yar Jung, he became the co-founder of the Osmani University, which became one of the first institutions of higher education in the country.

Through their journal, *al-Urwa al-Wuthqa*, al-Afghani and Muhammad Abduh sought to awaken the Muslim world from its deep sleep. They urged their Muslim readers to unite under the banner of Islam and liberate the Muslim world from foreign political and military occupation. Considered to be highly inflammatory, this journal was banned by the British authorities in Egypt and India.

From Paris, al-Afghani moved to Russia where he lived for four years and helped the Russian Muslims to publish the Qur'an there for the first time. At the invitation of the Ottoman Sultan Abd al-Hamid II, he then moved to Istanbul in 1892 where the Sultan offered him a generous monthly stipend and a furnished cottage. He spent the last five years of his life in Istanbul.

Indeed, as the 'father of modern pan-Islamism', al-Afghani was responsible for initiating one of the most powerful political movements of modern times. The European colonial powers were, one-by-one, driven out from the Muslim world. Al-Afghani was not only a political revolutionary, he was also an outstanding intellectual and a linguist who knew more than seven languages (including Arabic, Persian, French, English and Russian). Being too occupied with political and social activism, he had no time to marry and therefore remained a confirmed bachelor all his life.

The indomitable al-Afghani died at the age of fifty-nine and was laid to rest in Istanbul, Turkey. Then, on January 2nd 1945, his remains were transferred to Afghanistan and reburied at Aliabad, located on the outskirts of Kabul.

***

Jibran, Khalil (1883-1931): also spelled Gibran Khalil. Lebanese writer Born into a Maronite family in the village of Bishari, Jibran received his schooling in Beirut until 1895 when he left with his parents for Boston, USA. Three years later, he traveled to Beirut to study Arabic and French at the Maronite al Hikma Institute. After his return to Boston, he took to writing and painting. He published his volume of Arabic poems The Processions in 1923. But far more important was his volume in English, The Prophet(1923) in which he discussed relations between man and man in a mystical fashion, an approach that won him critical acclaim and riches.

***

Jibril, Ahmad (1938-   ): Palestinian leader Born of a Palestinian father and a Syrian mother in Yazour, a village near Jaffa Jibril and his family fled to Syria during the Palestine War (1948-49). After finishing his education, he joined the Syrian army and rose to be captain. Following the expulsion of the PLO from Beirut in 1982, Jibril made Damascus the base of his group. He joined an anti-Yasser Arafat rebellion masterminded by Syrian President Hafiz Assad. In May 1985 Israel released 1,150 Palestinian prisoners in exchange for three Israeli soldiers whom Jibril's group had captured during the 1982 Israeli invasion of Lebanon. Though Jibril's party was secular, socialist, and nationalist, in the late 1980s he started to form links with Iran and visited Tehran periodically. He rejected the Israeli PLO Accord of September 1993. His continues opposition to the peace process led to a split in his party in 1999.

***

Jumblat, Kamal (1917-1977): Lebanese politician. Born into a notable Druze family in Mukhtara village, Jumblat studied law and sociology at universities in Beirut and Paris. He was elected to parliament in 1947. The next year he became head of his clan, and in 1949 he established the Progressive Socialist Party. In the Lebanese Civil War, which erupted in April 1975, Jumblat led the LNM against its opponent the rightist Maronite coalition allied the Lebanese Front. Jumblat formed an alliance with the Palestine Liberation Organization. It was friendly with Syria. But when the LNM-PLO alliance captured two thirds of Lebanon by April 1976, Syrian President Hafiz Assad revised his stance, fearing that total victory by the radical LNM-PLO alliance would result in Israeli military intervention and destabilization of the whole region, including Syria. In June Syria attacked LNM-PLO positions and spared the Lebanese Front a humiliating defeat.

***

Jumblat, Walid (1949-   ): Lebanese politician. Born into a notable Druze family in Mukhtara village, Jumblat went to the American University in

Beirut and then to a university in Paris. He was active with the militia of the Progressive Socialist Party. After the initialing of a peace treaty between Israel and Lebanon in May 1983, Jumblat joined an alliance that had formed to overturn it. In late 1985 Jumblat was one of the three militia leaders who signed the "National Agreement to Solve the Lebanese Crisis," a detailed document outlining political reform and Lebanese Syrian relations. Following the end of the Lebanese Civil War in October 1990 when a national reconciliation government was formed under Omar Karami, Jumblat was made a minister without portfolio, and the following June he was nominated to the expanded parliament.

***

Junaid of Baghdad (d. 910): The first of the "Sober Sufis" who insisted that the experience of God lay in enhanced self possession and that the wild exuberance of the "drunken Sufis" were merely a stage that the true mystic should transcend.

***

Ka'b bin Al Ashraf: A Jewish poet who mocked Muhammad in his verses and was assassinated on Muhammad's orders. A Jewish poet of the Bani Nadir Tribe. Muhammad had him assassinated.

***

Kabir (1440-1518): Indian mystic and poet, who preached the unity of all religions. There is uncertainty about his origins, but it is believed that he was adopted by a Muslim weaver after being abandoned by his Brahmin Hindu mother. His borrowings from both Hinduism and Islam resulted in the preaching of a new mystic path, the *Kabir panth*, and the founding, by one of his disciples, of the Sikh religion. His mystical poems, stressing the oneness of God, together with his rejection of caste, have made Kabir one of the most popular religious figures in his country's history.

***

Karami, Rashid (1921-1987): Lebanese politician: prime minister. 1955-60, 1961-64, 1965-66, 1966-68, 1969-70, 1975-76 and 1984-87 Born into a religious Sunni family in Tripoli, Karami secured a law degree from Cairo University. He set up legal practice in Tripoli. In the May 1968 election Karami led the Democratic Parliamentary Forum, which emerged slightly behind its rival, the Triple Alliance of Camille Chamoun, Pierre Gemayel and Raymond Edde. After the election of Suleiman Franjieh as president in 1970, Karami failed to win a further mandate for his premiership. Soon after the start of the Lebanese Civil War in April 1975. Following the Israeli invasion of Lebanon in June 1982, Karami joined the anti Israeli camp and called for deferment of the presidential poll until after Israel's evacuation.

***

Kashani, Abol Qasim (1884-1962): Iranian religious political leader. Born into a religious Shi'a family in Tehran, Kashani grew up in Najaf Iraq, where he studies Islam. He returned to Iran in 1921 after Iraq had been placed under British mandate. Kashani was sent into exile in the northern city of Qazvin until late 1947. His third arrest followed by banishment to Lebanon came in the wake of a failed attempt on the life of Muhammad Reza Shah Pahlavi (1941-79) on 4 February 1949. He was permitted to return home after a year. At Kashani's intercession, Mussadiq released twenty eight members of the Fedaiyan e Islam including the assassin of a prime minister. But the Kashani Mussadiq alliance broke down when in order to survive politically Mussadiq began to rely increasingly on secular leftists. After his death his mantle of radical religious opposition to the shah was taken over by Khomeini.

***

Kassem, Abdul Karim (1914-1963): Iraqi general and politician. A graduate (1934) of the Iraqi military academy, he attended the army staff college. His outstanding bravery, shown in campaigns against the Kurds and in the Palestinian war of 1948, won him many military decorations. He organized the military coup that in July, 1958, overthrew the Iraqi monarchy and established Kassem as premier of the new republic. An Arab nationalist, he quelled a pro-Communist uprising in 1959. After this, Kassem's power and influence steadily deteriorated. He was overthrown and executed by military and civilian members of the Ba'ath party in Feb., 1963.

***

Khaddam, Abdul Halim (1932-   ): Syrian politician, first vice president 1984, Born into a poor Sunni Family in Banias, Khaddam obtained a law degree at Damascus University where he joined the Baath party. A friend of Hafiz Assad since their senior school days (1949-51), Khaddam's career advanced in line with Assad's. His moment of glory came a year later when the Lebanese Civil War ended on Syria's terms. He was confirmed in his post in 2000 by President Basah Assad.

***

Khadijah bint Khuwailid (555-619): As a symbol of honesty, faithfulness, integrity and unflinching steadfastness, Khadijah has no equals in Islamic history. Her remarkable contribution to the cause of Islam was acknowledged by the Prophet himself.

Khadijah bint Khuwailid ibn Asad was born and brought up in Makkah. Her father Khuwailid ibn Asad was an immensely wealthy merchant and an eminent leader of the Qurayshi tribe of Makkah. After the death of her father, she inherited the family business and became one of the wealthiest women in Makkah. After the untimely death of her first husband, Abu Halah ibn al-Nabbash (by whom she had two children), Khadijah married Atiq ibn Abid and they had one child. Her second marriage, too, did not last long; it was terminated on the grounds of incompatibility.

Khadijah was an unusually gifted lady who defied the socio-cultural taboos of her society by becoming very successful. She traded in all types of goods and merchandise, and in so doing established a thriving import and export business. Her generosity was such that she often divided the profits in half, giving one half to her managers while retaining the other portion for herself.

When she was informed about the sublime qualities and attributes of the twenty-five year old Muhammad, the son of Abdullah, she went out of her way to recruit him into her expanding business. Unbeknown to both Muhammad and Khadijah, this was to mark the beginning of a relationship which was destined to last a quarter of a century, and go down in the annals of Islam as a great partnership.

One day Khadijah went to consult her cousin Waraqa ibn Nawfal, a blind man who was well versed in ancient scriptures, about a dream where she saw the sun descending into her courtyard. Waraqa told Khadijah that Muhammad was special.

One could not find a better woman in all Arabia at the time. At the time of their marriage, Muhammad was twenty-five while Khadijah was forty. It proved to be an immensely blissful marriage and they were blessed with six beautiful children, four girls and two boys. The sons died in their infancy.

One night, while Muhammad was meditating on the Mount of Light, he was visited by archangel *Jibrail* (Gabriel) and the first verses of the Qur'an were revealed to him. Angel *Jibrail* confirmed that he was God's last Prophet to mankind and that his mission in life was to propagate Islam, a religion and way of life chosen for all humanity by the Creator of the universe. Khadijah's unshakeable faith in her husband reassured the Prophet. She not only became the first person to embrace Islam, she also threw all her weight behind her husband and his new mission.

Khadijah was fifty-four when her husband became the Prophet and for the next ten years of her life she freely spent all her wealth, and devoted all her time and energy, for the cause of Islam. As more and more people continued to embrace Islam, in utter desperation the Prophet's opponents imposed a total boycott on *Banu Hashim*, the Prophet's tribe.

The Prophet himself acknowledged the pivotal role played by Khadijah in those early days of Islam, 'She converted to Islam, spent all her wealth and worldly goods to help me spread this faith...'

Khadijah was a symbol of hope in the face of adversity; a paragon of virtue and steadfastness. Khadijah, the 'mother of the believers' (*ummul Mu'minin*), passed away during the tenth year of Muhammad's Prophethood and was buried in Hajun, located on the outskirts of Makkah; she was sixty-five at the time of her death.

Muhammad's first wife and first convert; the first wife of the Prophet Muhammad and the mother of all his surviving children. She was also the first convert to Islam and died before the Hijra during the persecution of the Muslim by the Quraysh in Mecca (616-19), possibly as a result of the privations she suffered. First wife of Muhammad, his senior in wealth and years. Mother of four daughters (Zaynab, Ruqayyah, Umm Kulthum, and Fatimah) and two boys (both of whom died in their infancy). Chief confidante and colleague in Muhammad's early search for religion and the first person to recognize him as a Prophet of God.

***

Khalaf, Salah (1932- 1991): Palestinian leader. Born into a middle class household in Jaffa, Khalaf and his family became refugees in al Bureij camp in the Gaza Strip in 1948. In March 1959 Arafat then working in Kuwait secured him an entry permit for Kuwait. That summer together with Arafat and Khalil Wazir he became a cofounder of Fatah. Helped by the Ba'athist government in Syria and Khalaf began to recruit for Fatah in Gaza and Jordan. In 1969 Khalaf and other Fatah leaders assumed control of the Palestine Liberation Organization PLO. Following the banishment of the PLO from Beirut to Tunis and other setbacks that followed in the mid 1980s Khalaf mellowed. He was assassinated in January 1991 at the PLO headquarters in Tunis by his body guard, described by PLO sources as Abu Nidal's agent.

***

Khalifa, Abdallah Muhammad (1846-1899): Al-Ta'a'ishi). The successor of the Sudanese Mahdi. In 1883 the Mahdi made Khalifa commander of the army and he was largely responsible for the victory over the British at Khartoum in 1885. When the Mahdi died Khalifa eliminated the remaining Egyptian garrisons, and waged war on Ethiopia until 1889. After his defeat by Kitchener at Omdurman he fled to Kordofan, where he died in battle.

***

Khalid ibn al-Walid (584-642): Khalid ibn al-Walid, 'the thunder from Arabia', was an incomparable military genius who single-handedly humbled two of the greatest empires of his time. The of al-Walid, he was a natural-born talent, a military genius who read his adversaries' weaknesses. Even today, children throughout the Muslim world grow up listening to his heroic feats.

Khalid ibn al-Walid ibn al-Mughirah was born into the respected Qurayshi tribe of Makkah. He was around twenty-four when Muhammad received his first revelation. Khalid's father, Walid ibn al-Mughirah, was a highly respected individual who was most considered to be one of the wisest and most clever men of his generation.

The Prophet's success frightened the Makkans more than anything else, so they resolved to take direct action against the nascent Muslim community. When a large Makkan army set out to obliterate the Muslims, the Prophet and his followers met the advancing Makkan army at Badr and inflicted a crushing defeat on them.

In 630, during the eighth year of the Prophet's migration to Madinah, the forty-six year old Khalid received a letter from his brother al-Walid ibn Walid, who had already embraced Islam. '...The Messenger of God also asked me: 'Where is Khalid?' He remarked, 'How is a man like Khalid ignorant of Islam? It would be good for him if he devoted his capabilities for the cause of the Muslims'...'

This letter shook Khalid to his core and suddenly the ray of Islam began to shine all over his being. Along with Amr ibn al-As, another brilliant Muslim general, Khalid left Makkah for Madinah and presented himself before the Prophet. 'O Messenger of God!' cried Khalid, 'I remember all the scenes of fighting with you, and my animosity with the Truth. Please pray to God to forgive me.' After embracing Islam, he became an almighty hammer which helped crush Islam's opponents. The very mention of his name was enough to send shivers down his enemy's spine.

Given Khalid's abilities as a soldier and military tactician, the Prophet asked him to accompany the Muslim army and face the subversive Byzantines who had camped along the northern borders of

Arabia. Only three thousand Muslims fought more than fifty thousand well-equipped and highly-trained Byzantine soldiers. Khalid withdrew some of his forces from the battlefield and instructed them to attack from the rear to divert the enemy's attention. This stroke of genius by Khalid enabled the Muslim army to create a buffer zone between them and their enemies. From that day on, Khalid became known as *Saifullah* or the 'Sword of God'.

With great foresight and profound understanding of Khalid's unusual military abilities, Caliph Abu Bakr sent him to face the battle-hardened Persian army in 633. Not willing to tolerate Persian interference in the affairs of the Muslims, Caliph Abu Bakr summoned Khalid and told him to go and teach the Persians a good lesson in warfare. He marched out of Arabia and came in direct contact with the Persian army. He then wrote a letter to Hurmuz, the famous Persian military general, in which he spelled out his objective:

'Our aim is not to fight you. Accept Islam, the peaceful way, and you will be safe. If not then clear our way to the people so that we may explain this beautiful way of life to them... if you do not accept any of these conditions then the only alternative is the use of the sword. Before deciding on the third alternative you should keep in mind that I am bringing against you a people who love death more than you love your life.'

Hurmuz dismissed Khalid's letter and challenged him to fight one-on-one. Khalid accepted the challenge and put the most famous Persian general to the sword before he could even make a move. In total, Khalid fought fifteen battles against the Persians and on each and every occasion he brought them to their knees. The Persians feared Khalid more than anyone else.

After subduing the Persians, Khalid turned his attention to the infiltrative activities of the Byzantine army. They, too, feared the growing power of the Islamic State and indirectly encouraged the neighboring states to rise up against the Muslims. Caliph Abu Bakr resolved to deal with the looming danger presented by the Byzantines. In July 634, Khalid met up with the Muslim army at Ajnadayn. He held a council of all the Muslim commanders and suggested that one of them should take overall command of the army. The decisive battle of Yarmuk was now looming in the horizon.

During the battle, Khalid received a letter from Madinah informing him of the death of Caliph Abu Bakr. Under Khalid's able leadership, forty-five thousand Muslims crushed the mighty Byzantine forces.

Although Khalid became a Muslim only a few years before the conquest of Makkah in 630, he became one of the greatest champions of Islam immediately upon embracing the new faith. Khalid died of prolonged illness at the age of fifty-eight and was buried in Hims, in Syria; his desire to attain martyrdom was not realized.

One of Muhammad's bitter enemies in Mecca; eventually converted to Islam. pagan Meccan nobleman who fought against Muslims in Medina before converting and taking his place as the most talented general of early Islam, saluted and promoted by even the Prophet himself. A succession of three victories during the Ridda Wars culminated in his inspired maneuvers during the conquest of the Holy Land which led to his ultimate achievement, the decisive victory at Yarmuk. He would later be reduced to the ranks by Omar and prosecuted into disgrace.

***

Khatami, Muhammad (1943-   ): Born in a religious family in Yazd, his father being a Sayyid, a descendant of Prophet Muhammad, he pursued religious education in Qom where he obtained a degree in advanced theology. At home his government accorded greater freedoms to citizens. The crisis caused by the student rioting in Tehran in July 1999 brought Khatami and leader Ali Khamanei together. In the June 2001 presidential election, Khatami won 78 percent of the vote on a lower turnout of 67 percent, with his nearest rival getting a mere 16 per cent of the ballots. Khatami was quick to condemn the terrorist attacks on the US and his government was glad to see the downfall of the Taliban regime in Afghanistan with which it nearly went to war in September 1998. As the US began its military buildup in the Gulf region, Khatami warned against attacking Iraq. And after the Anglo American forces had occupied Iraq in April 2003, Khatami demanded that they leave the country.

***

Khatib, Ahmad (1940-   ): Kuwaiti political. Born into a middle class family in Kuwait, Khatib studied medicine at the American University of Beirut, where he came under the influence of George Habash. Khatib was a cofounder of the Arab Nationalist Movement based in Beirut. Once the Iran Iraq War in which Kuwait sided with Iraq, had ended in August 1988, Khatib joined the movement for the restoration of the National Assembly. Following the Iraqi occupation of Kuwait in August 1990, Baghdad tried to co opt Khatib, but he refused. He went into exile. He returned to Kuwait after the Second Gulf War. In the poll to the restored National Assembly in October 1992, Khatib was elected a deputy.

***

Islamic Leaders

Khoei, Abol Qasim (1899-1992): Iraqi Islamic leader. Born into a religious Shi'a family in Khoy, Iranian Azerbaijan. Khoei emigrated with his parents to Najaf, Iraq in 1912. He kept up his teaching and a steady output of books on the Sharia religious biography and Qur'anic commentary. On the death in 1970 of Ayatollah Muhsin Hakim, the status of marja-e Taqlid (Arabic: source of emulation) passed to Khoei, who also acquired the title of grand ayatollah. Following his invasion of Iran, President Saddam Hussein sought Khoei's approval for his action, but Khoei maintained a studied silence. After the collapse of the Shi'a uprising in southern Iraq in the wake of the Second Gulf War, Khoei, then seriously ill, was put under house arrest and coerced into appearing on television with Saddam Hussein. He was then moved to Kufa where he died in August 1992. He left behind some ninety books and pamphlets.

***

Khosrau I (d. 579): King of Persia (531-79), whose reign, after a long period of turbulence, marked the highest point of the Sassanian Empire. Khosrau I restored royal authority over the army, bureaucracy, and lower nobility, reformed taxation, and restored defenses and public works. He invaded Byzantine Syria in 540 and took Antioch. In 565, in alliance with the western Turks, he destroyed the Hephthalite empire on his eastern frontier. He also annexed Yemen and died during negotiations with Byzantium over his invasion of Mesopotamia.

***

Khosrau II (d. 628): King of Persian (590-628) who succeeded to the throne after the deposition of his father, Hormidz. After being unseated by a coup, he accepted Byzantine aid to regain his throne in return for most of Armenia. He recovered his territory, with Edessa and Caesarea, in 610. in 611 Jerusalem was taken and several thousand Christians massacred. In 616 Khosrau II simultaneously invaded Egypt, captured Ankara, and besieged Constantinople. A Byzantine counter-attack drove him back to Ctesiphon, where he was assassinated. He had overtaxed the resources of his empire, which fell to Arab conquest within a decade of his death.

***

Khosrow I (531-579): (Khosrow Anushirvan), d. 579, king of Persia, greatest of the Sassanid or Sassanian monarchs. He is also known as Chosroes I. He succeeded his father, Kavadh I, but before becoming king, Khosrow was responsible for a great massacre (528) of the communistic Mazdakites. He extended Persian rule E to the Indus River with the capture (560) of Bactria, W across Arabia by establishing (570) at least nominal rule over Yemen, and north and northwest by taking part of Armenia and Caucasia from the Byzantine Empire. He fought against Belisarius and the other generals of Justinian I and against Justin II. Khosrow is revered by the Persians as a just though despotic ruler who encouraged learning, stimulated commerce, rebuilt cities, and set up a reformed system of taxation.

***

Khouri, Bishara (1890-1964): Lebanese politician, President 1943-52. Born into a Maronite family in Beirut, Khouri went to Paris to pursue his law studies. Returning home in 1911, he set up a legal practice. Khouri led the Christian camp in its dispute with the Muslim side about sharing parliamentary seats. At home Khouri co-opted urban Muslim leaders in administering the state; and he aligned his foreign policies with those of the Arab hinterland and participated in the Palestine War (1948-49.)

***

Khwajah Naqshband (1317-1389): Although Muslims first entered Central Asia during the reign of Caliph Umar, the Islamic presence in that region was not consolidated until the time of Caliph Uthman. Central Asia produced some the Muslim world's most influential scholars, thinkers and personalities, like al-Bukhari, al-Khwarizmi, al-Maturidi, Ibn Sina and Ulugh Beg. Amir Timur (Tamerlane), who was one of the most successful conquerors in history, was also born and raised on the cold, harsh and intimidating steppes of Central Asia. Sufism became part and parcel of the Central Asian religious landscape during the early days of Islam. One such Sufi tradition was the N*aqshbandiyyah Tariqah*, which was championed by Khwajah Naqshband, and it is today widely considered to be one of the Muslim world's most influential Sufi traditions.

Muhammad ibn Muhammad Baha al-Din al-Bukhari, better known as Khwajah Naqshband, was born in the village of Qasr-I Hinduwan, not far from Bukhara in modern Uzbekistan in Central Asia. He traveled to Bukhara to pursue higher education. During his stay in Bukhara, he married and eventually returned home after completing his formal education. Under Sayyid Kulal's guidance, Khwajah Naqshband mastered Sufi thought and practices. He went to Samarqand where he entered the service of the reigning Sultan Khalil. He served him for twelve years, until the Sultan was ousted from power in 1347.

Although Khwajah Naqshband led a life of renunciation, sacrifice and single-minded devotion to the ideals and practices of Islam, he knew more than anyone else that one cannot attain success in any sphere of human endeavor without a measure of Divine grace and favor. He was an uncompromising exponent of the Islamic concept of Divine Unity (*Tawhid*).

There is no doubt that Khwajah Naqshband believed that he was chosen by Providence to pursue and disseminate Islamic spirituality and gnosis in the light of the Qur'an and the Prophetic *sunnah*. "...do not hear too much mystic music...do not condemn mystic music...eat only what is permitted...so far as you can, do not marry a woman who wants material comforts...laughter kills one's heart. Your heart should be full of grief, your body as if of an ailing person, your eyes wet, your actions sincere, your prayers earnest, your dress tattered, your company dervishes, your wealth poverty, your house the mosque and your friend God."

After some deliberation, Khwajah Naqshband initiated a mass Islamic spiritual movement which subsequently became known as the *Naqshbandiyyah* Sufi Order. The Khwajah did not write much; rather he became a religious-cum-spiritual reformer *par excellence*. Over time the movement became one of the most influential of all Sufi traditions, along with the Q*adiriyyah Tariqah* founded by Abd al-Qadir al-Jilani. The *Naqshbandiyyah Tariqah* has today gained thousands of followers in both Europe and America.

The Islamic spiritualist movement initiated by Khwajah Naqshband has few parallels in the history of Islam. He breathed his last at the age of seventy-two and was buried in his native village, where a mausoleum was later erected in his memory.

***

Kublai Kahn (1214-1294): First Yuan emperor of China (1279-1294), a grandson of Genghis Khan. Elected Kahkhad (Great Kahn) in 1260 on the death of his brother Mangu he completed the conquest of China. In 1276 Hangzhou fell and in 1279 the Song fleet was defeated off southern China. Contrary to Mongol practice, he did not entirely lay waste the country. In 1267 he made Khanbaligh (Beijing) the Mongol capital. His rule, according to Chinese historians, was harsh, though Marco Polo, who served him from 1275 to 1292, described it as mild. He followed Chinese precedents of government, though civil service examinations were temporarily abandoned. Many foreigners, particularly Muslims from Central Asia, were appointed to civil and military posts. Campaigns against Japan (1274 and 1281) failed dismally.

Kublai Khan, 1215-1294, Mongol emperor, founder of the Yuan dynasty of China. From 1251 to 1259 he led military campaigns in S China. He succeeded (1260) his brother Mongke (Mangu) as khan of the empire that their grandfather Jenghiz Khan had founded. The empire reached its greatest territorial extent with Kublai's final defeat (1279) of the Sung dynasty of China; however, his campaigns against Japan (see kamikaze), Myanmar, Vietnam, and Indonesia failed. Kublai's rule as the overlord of the Mongol empire was nominal except in Mongolia and China. He recruited men of all nations for his civil service, but only Mongols were permitted to hold the highest government posts. He fostered Chinese scholarship and arts. Although he favored Tibetan Buddhism (Lamaism), other religions (except Taoism) were tolerated. Kublia encouraged foreign commerce, and his magnificent capital at Cambuluc (now Beijing) was visited by several Europeans, notably Marco Polo, who described it.

***

Lahoud, Emile (1936-   ): Lebanese military and political leader, president 1988-Son of General Jamil Lahoud and Adrenee Bajakian in Baabdate, Lahoud was educated locally. After joining the Beirut Military Academy as a cadet in 1956, he graduated with the rank of lieutenant four years later after passing a naval engineering course in Britain. He became commander of the Second Fleet in 1966. Lahoud led the campaigns against Aoun in October 1990, which ended the civil war. When the pro Rafiq Hariri groups did well in the 2000 parliamentary poll, Lahoud called on Hariri to head the next cabinet. While Hariri agreed to focus on the economy Lahoud took charge of defense and security.

***

Lawrence of Arabia (Thomas Edward 1888-1935): Son of an Anglo Irish baronet, Sir Thomas Chapman, Lawrence grew up in Oxford, Britain, and graduated from the city's Jesus College specializing in medieval military architecture. Following the outbreak of the First World War, Lawrence was sent to Cairo where he was assigned to military intelligence and then in January 1916 to the Arab Bureau of Intelligence and diplomatic officers established to define and implement Britain's role in the Arab revolt against Ottoman Turkey.

In September 1918 Lawrence, now promoted to lieutenant colonel entered Damascus with the Arab forces. As a member of the British delegation to the Paris Peace Conference of the Council of Four in March 1919, he liaised with the Arabs and acted as adviser to Faisal ibn Hussein. His lobbying for Arab independence failed. When Colonial Secretary Winston Churchill set up the Middle East department in March 1921, he appointed Lawrence as his Arab affairs adviser. finished his long memoirs, recounting his wartime experiences (Seven Pillars of Wisdom 1922). He retired from the RAF in 1935 and died in a motorcycle accident soon after.

***

Liaqat Ali Khan, Nawabzada (1895-1951) First Prime Minister of Pakistan (1947-51). He began his political career in British India as a Muslim leader in the United Provinces, and from 1933 became Jinnah's right-hand man in the Muslim League. In 1946 he became Finance Minister in the Interim Government. Between the death of Jinnah in 1948 and his own assassination in 1951. He was the most powerful politician in Pakistan, when he endeavored to achieve a reconciliation with India via the Delhi Pact (1950).

***

Mahdi, the: the Islamic spiritual and temporal savior. According to Islamic teaching he will be sent by divine command to prepare human society for the end of earthly time by means of perfect and just government (Millenarianism). Many have claimed to be the Mahdi at different times.

Best known was Muhammad Ahmad bin Abdallah (1843-85). Of Nubian origin, he claimed descent from Muhammad. Feeling called to purify the world from wantonness and corruption; he gathered many followers and proclaimed himself Mahdi in 1881. In 1882 he Egyptian government sent expeditions against him, but by 1884, with the capture of Khartoum, he made himself master of Sudan. General Gordon was killed in Khartoum on 30 January 1885; the Mahdi himself died, probably of typhus, five months later. Politically his struggle was carried on by the Khalifa Abdallah until Kitchener defeated him at Omdurman in 1898. "a guide". More specifically al Mahdi (the guide) is a figure who will appear with Prophet Jesus before the end of time, when God allows it, to bring world peace, order and justice, after it has been overcome with injustice and aggression. The Sunnis regard someone else as the Mahdi. According to Shiite belief, the 12th and last

Imam, who has been hidden from humanity's view for centuries but will reappear to usher in a period of justice before Judgment Day.

An Arabic term literally meaning "the rightly guided one," that is to say, "guided by God." According to a Muslim belief that is widely held though not grounded in the Koran, the Mahdi is a Messianic figure who will come at the end of time to establish justice and restore the faith. There have been many claimants to this title and office in the course of Muslim history. Awaited one, a Messiah and reformist leader who aims to restore the original purity of the Islamic faith and polity. In Shi'ite tradition the Twelfth Imam. Messiah who will come to restore religion and justice: twelfth imam expected by the Shiites

***

Mahdi of Sudan, The (1844-1885): Sudan is an enormous African country; it borders eight other countries, is about half the size of Europe, and links the Arab world with the continent of Africa, making it an attractive target for foreign colonial powers. Due to its geo-strategic importance, the forces of Muhammad Ali Pasha, the Ottoman viceroy of Egypt, established their politico-economic hegemony over Sudan during the 1870s. Southern Sudan is inhabited mainly by tribal people, some of whom are either converts to Christianity or Islam, while the majority are pagans who speak Sudanic languages and observe traditional African customs and traditions. However, as a strategically important country, Sudan became the centre of a global power struggle between the Ottomans, the Egyptians and the British during the nineteenth century as they fought each other to establish their politico-economic control in that country. The towering figure of the Mahdi emerged to free Sudan from the grip of imperial powers and return that country to its people.

Muhammad Ahmad ibn Abdullah, better known as the Mahdi of Sudan, was born on Labab Island, located in the province of Dongola in northern Sudan. His family claimed to be the descendants of the Prophet through his grandson Hasan, the eldest son of Caliph Ali. Since both his parents were practicing Muslims, Muhammad Ahmad grew up in a religious atmosphere. After his father's death, his oldest brother assumed responsibility for the entire family and he encouraged Muhammad Ahmad to continue his studies. As a gifted student, he not only learned Arabic but also committed the entire Qur'an to memory before he was ten.

After completing his formal studies at the age of seventeen, he was initiated into the *Sammaniyyah* Sufi Order by its influential exponent, Shaykh Muhammad Sharif Nur al-Da'im. As the renowned Persian Sufi Abu Yazid al-Bistami (who is also known as Bayezid

Bistami) once remarked, 'One who has no guide has taken S*haytan* (Satan) as his guide.' Muhammad Ahmad attained the rank of a Shaykh himself; he was only twenty-two at the time.

Muhammad Ahmad married and set up his own family. He was only twenty-four when he built a new mosque and Sufi *Zawiyyah* (lodge). He decided to stay in Sudan and help revive Islamic principles and practices in that country. He then established a Sufi lodge and gathered around him a small band of followers. Muhammad Ahmad went and pledged allegiance to Shaykh Qurayshi Wad al-Zain, who was a master of another branch of *Sammaniyyah* Sufi Order, and strengthened his ties with the latter by marrying his daughter. Following Shaykh Quraishi's death in 1878, Muhammad Ahmad succeeded him as the leader of this Sufi branch and his reputation began to spread across the wider region.

Since Sudan was an Ottoman-Egyptian colony at the time, the country's colonial rulers not only failed to exercise proper political leadership, they also did not seem to have any plans to improve the Sudanese people's socio-economic condition. A man named Abdullahi ibn Muhammad Adam (who hailed from the province of Kordofan) came to visit Muhammad Ahmad in 1880. The two men instantly became close friends and resolved to work together for the political, economic and spiritual betterment of their people. Even before Abdullahi's arrival, Muhammad Ahmad told some of his close disciples that he was the long-awaited Mahdi (or the 'centenarian renewer of faith') whom the East Africans expected to arrive during the thirteenth century of Islam and help them to liberate their land from foreign occupation. After his arrival, Abdullahi convinced Muhammad Ahmad that he was indeed that 'renewer of faith' long expected by his countrymen. Muhammad Ahmad reinforced his claim to Mahdihood by reinterpreting the Prophetic traditions (*Hadith*) concerning the emergence of Imam Mahdi towards the end of time.

As his followers began to increase rapidly, Muhammad Ahmad lambasted the oppressive policies of the colonial rulers. Like the Prophet, he asked his followers to pledge loyalty (B*ay'ah*) to him; he also performed a migration (*Hijra*) from Aba Island to Jabal Qadir in the same way the Prophet migrated from Mecca to Medina, and finally he named his supporters *al-Ansar* (the helpers) just as the Prophet had.

The Khartoum-based Ottoman-Egyptian rulers became very alarmed. In 1882, two successive military expeditions were sent by the Egyptian forces against the *Mahdiyah* in which the latter inflicted a crushing defeat on the Egyptian army.

As a charismatic leader and an electrifying orator, Muhammad Ahmad inspired his followers to pursue *jihad* (military struggle) against their enemies; he promised to lead them all the way to Mecca and Medina, two of Islam's most sacred cities, via Cairo. He and his forces went on to reunite the whole country under his leadership. He also forced out the combined might of the Ottoman, Egyptian and the British armies from his country. However, six months after establishing himself in Omdurman, which became the new capital of Sudan, he suddenly died of fever at the age of forty-one.

Though the *Mahdiyah* State established by Muhammad Ahmad was destroyed by an Anglo-Egyptian army barely fourteen years after its inception, his influence and legacy continues to play a powerful role in Sudanese politics to this day. He deserves to be recognized as one of the most influential Islamic warriors (M*ujahid*) of modern times. Muhammad Ahmad's heroic struggle against the colonial powers turned him into a powerful symbol of pride and prestige among Black nationalists across Africa, Europe and the United States.

***

Mahfouz, Naguib (1911-2006): Egyptian writer: winner of the Nobel Prize for Literature. 1988 Born into a merchant family in Cairo, Mahfouz graduated in philosophy from Cairo University in 1934. The next three novels-Khan al Khalili (1945), Midaqq Alley (1974), and The Beginning and the End (1949) revolved around the lower middle classes in Cairo. Next followed his most mature work. The Trilogy (1956-57): Bayn al Qasryn (The Palace Walk), Qasr al Shawq (The Palace of Desire), and Al Sukkariyya (The Sugar Street) named after Cairo streets.

In its length and scale The Trilogy remains unrivaled in Arabic literature. Adrift in the Nile was published in 1993, followed by the Harafish in 1994 a story of an Egyptian family living in an alley over several centuries. Among his later publications are Arabian Nights and Days (1995); The Honeymoon (1995); The Beggar, the Thief and the Dogs (2000); The Day the Leader was Killed (2001); Naguib Mahfouz at Sidi Gaber; Reflections of a Nobel Laureate, 1994-2001 (2001); and Voices from the Arab World: Ancient Egyptian Tales (2003) capped by The Complete Mahfouz Library (2002.)

***

Mahmud II (1784-1839): Ottoman sultan (1808-1839), younger son of Abd al-Hamid I. He was raised to the throne of the Ottoman Empire (Turkey) upon the deposition of his brother. Mustafa IV, and continued the reforms of his cousin, Selim III. During his reign, the Eastern Question assumed increasing importance. Mahmud inherited the Russo-Turkish War of 1806-1812, which ended with Turkey's loss of Bessarabia. However, Russia was obliged to end its support of the Serbian rebels under Karageorge, and Serbia returned (1813) to Turkish control. In 1817, Mahmud recognized Milos as prince of Serbia, a Turkish vassal. He suppressed (1822) the rebellion of Ali Pasha and defeated the Greeks in the first phase of the Greek War of Independence.

At the height of his power he ruthlessly carried out (1826) a long-cherished project-the destruction of the Janissaries. The Turkish successes in Greece were largely due to the troops sent by the viceroy of Egypt, Muhammad Ali, under the command of Ibrahim Pasha. British, Russian, and French intervention led to the destruction (1827) of the Egyptian fleet at Navarino, the Russo-Turkish War of 1828-29, a humiliating peace (see Adrianople, Treaty of), and the independence of Greece. The sequel of the Greek war was the invasion of Turkey by Ibrahim Pasha after Mahmud had refused to give Syria to Muhammad Ali as reward for his aid against the Greeks.

At Konya, the Turkish army was completely rounded (1832), and Constantinople was saved only by the intervention of a Russian fleet. Mahmud was obliged to accede (1833) to Muhammad Ali's demands and, by a secret agreement with Russia, promised to close the Dardanelles to all warships hostile to Russia. In 1839, war with Egypt was resumed, and on the day of Mahmud's death, news came of the ignominious surrender of the Turkish fleet in the harbor of Alexandria. He came to the throne on the deposition of his brother, Mustafa IV, and continued the reforming policies of his cousin, Selim III (1789-1807) he rid himself of the Janissaries, the traditional military corps that had become unruly and inefficient, by having hem massacred, and established a new, European-style army. He curbed the power of the religious classes, centralized government, and reduced provincial autonomy. He was attacked by Mehemet Ali of Egypt, and his army defeated in the battle of Nizip (1839) in Syria.

***

Mahmud of Ghazna (967-1030): After the overthrow of the Umayyads in 750, the Abbasids assumed political leadership of the Muslim world. At that time the Muslim world extended from Spain in the West, to the banks of the Indus in the East. The vast Abbasid Empire broke up into a series of regional political entities during the tenth century.

Sebuktekin was a fearless military commander and a wise political administrator who, during his reign of two decades, not only consolidated Ghaznavid rule, but also established peace, order and security across his kingdom. Following his death in 997, his young son Ismail ascended the throne but he proved to be inexperienced and incompetent, and was therefore succeeded by his older brother, Mahmud. It was under Mahmud's stewardship that the Ghaznavids became one of Asia's most prominent political powers, as well as generous patrons of learning and education.

Mahmud ibn Sebuktekin al-Ghaznavi was born into a prominent Turkish family of soldiers and military leaders. Their bravery, courage and loyalty soon won them the favor of their Abbasid rulers, who promoted them to the highest echelons of their armed forces.

Mahmud committed the entire Qur'an to memory during his early years. After his father's death, he overthrew his younger brother from power, and ascended the Ghaznavid throne at the age of around twenty-eight. Within the first year of his reign he overthrew the Samanids and conquered all their territories up to the Oxus; it had been hitherto restricted to the province of Ghazna in eastern Afghanistan (including parts of North-eastern Iran). A year later, Mahmud marched into Kohistan and added this territory to his rapidly expanding empire. He then turned his attention towards India, and in 1001 launched his first military campaign against the Hindu ruler Jaipal I of Punjab. The two armies clashed near Peshawar (in present-day Pakistan) and after a fierce battle, Sultan Mahmud's forces inflicted a crushing defeat on their enemies; Jaipal I was also captured during the battle. Distressed and devastated by his defeats, Jaipal I abdicated and committed suicide; the victorious Sultan Mahmud, however, went on to extend his territorial control all the way to the banks of the Indus. Only thirty at the time, he became the ruler of an empire which now extended all the way from Central Asia to the Indus Valley.

Worried that the Sultan was getting too close to their territories for their comfort, the Hindu rulers came together to create a confederation of Hindu principalities in order to confront the advancing Ghaznavid conqueror. The combined might of the Hindu forces clashed with the Sultan's army in 1008, close to modern Hazro, led by Anand Pal, the son and successor of Jaipal I. In the ensuing battle, the Sultan's forces gained the upper hand and forced their adversaries to flee in disorder. Keen to press home his advantage, he quickly reorganized his forces and marched into Punjab in 1009 in order to teach the treacherous Anand Pal a lesson for violating his agreement to pay an annual tribute to the Ghaznavids. Mahmud extended Ghaznavid rule into mainland India.

Subsequently, in 1018, the Sultan turned his attention toward the West and swiftly overthrew the Khwarizmshahs of Central Asia. Indeed, he dominated Central Asia to such an extent that he became the undisputed ruler of that whole region. As a result, he became one of the most powerful and influential Muslim rulers of the eleventh century. He went on to establish an empire which would dominate Asian history for more than two hundred years.

As a practicing Muslim, he considered the Hindu practice of worshipping and adoring idols an abomination. Furthermore, a third of his army consisted of Hindus, while five out of his twelve senior generals were of Hindu background. His Hindu opponents regularly stored gold as well as arms and ammunition inside their temples.

Mahmud was not only a great conqueror; he was also one of Asia's most educated and articulate rulers. He transformed Ghazna, the capital of his vast empire, into one of Asia's most prominent centers of learning and culture of the time. The poets who lived in his court regularly competed with each other to compose verses in praise of the Sultan in order to win his favor. Firdawsi was one such poet and composed his monumental *Shahnama* (The Book of Kings) during Sultan Mahmud's reign, and dedicated it to him. Today, the *Shahnama* is widely considered to be one of the greatest epic poems of all time.

During his thirty-one year reign the Sultan completely rewrote the history of not only Asia, but also the Muslim world as a whole. He died at the age of sixty-three and was buried in Ghazna (located in present-day Afghanistan).

(969-1030) Muslim ruler of the Ghaznavid dynasty of Afghanistan and Khurasan (999-1030). He led 17 raids into northern India in the name of Islam. Sapping Hindu power in the process, he paved the way for Muslim conquest of the subcontinent. He also extended his power into Transoxania, Persia, and Mesopotamia.

***

Malaika, Nazik (1923-2001): Iraqi poet Born in Baghdad into a literary family with both her parents being poets Malaika composed her first poem in classical Arabic at ten. Her first collection of poems, Aashiqat Al Layl (Lover of Night), appeared in 1947. In 1962 she published a collection of essays on the merits and demerits of free verse and metrical poetry Qadaya l Shiar al Muaasir (The Contemporary Poetry Issues). Following the invasion of Kuwait by Iraq in August 1990, she returned to Baghdad. Then she moved to Cairo. There a collection of her poems, Youghiyar Alouanah Al Bahr (Leaving the Sea of Sorrow), most of them written a quarter century ago appeared in 1999.

***

Malcolm X (1925-1965): The enslavement of black Africans (in the British colonies of North America) began as early as the 1640s and this state of affairs persisted until Abraham Lincoln, the sixteenth President of the United States, formally abolished slavery (in the Northern States) by signing the Emancipation Proclamation in 1863. The Depression years of the 1930s only helped exacerbate racial strife and tension across America, which led to widespread rioting and racial violence between the whites and blacks in both the Northern and Southern States.

Born Malcolm Little in Omaha in the State of Nebraska, Malcolm X was the son of a Baptist Minister. His father, Reverend Earl Little, and his mother, Louise, were active members of Marcus Garvey's Universal Negro Improvement Association (UNIA). The Ku Klux Klan (a white supremacist group) forced his family to leave Omaha and settle in Lansing, Michigan; Malcolm was only a youngster at the time. When Malcolm was six his father died, and this again forced his family to experience more difficulties. Like his brothers and sisters, Malcolm was brought up in foster homes before he enrolled at Mason Junior High school in Lansing, where he completed the eighth grade. Malcolm quit formal education in disgust. From Lansing he travelled to Boston. Happy with their share of material benefits and comforts, Malcolm thought these people were no longer willing to fight for the cause of Black Nationalism like the previous generations.

Sucked into the murky world of drugs, prostitution and crime, Malcolm soon became a seasoned street hustler and the leader of a gang of thieves, and thereby established his reputation as a fearsome leader of the local criminal fraternity. Imprisoned for six years, he soon experienced a life-changing transformation. Keen to explore these issues, he read books on history, philosophy, culture and religion. So it was, whilst still in prison, his brother introduced him to the teachings of Elijah Muhammad and the Nation of Islam.

Inspired by Fard Muhammad, Elijah (who was the son of a Baptist preacher from Georgia) established the Nation of Islam, a religious-cum-black-nationalist movement, during the 1930s. According to Elijah, the white people were devils who were created by black scientists, and Fard Muhammad was incarnation of God. Malcolm found the tone and confidence of his message irresistible. Having experienced much racism and hardship at the hands of the white supremacists, in the Nation of Islam Malcolm found a socio-religious movement which was not afraid to speak up for the rights of black people.

As expected, on his release from prison in 1952, Malcolm became an active member of the Nation. As an eloquent orator and great motivator of people, he took the message of the Nation directly to the people. His hard work, coupled with his indefatigable energy and commitment to his tank, soon saw him rise from being an obscure assistant Minister of the Nation's Detroit Temple Number One, to its national spokesman within a short period. Under his able leadership the Nation of Islam became a powerful mass-movement with more than a hundred thousand loyal followers. By the 1960s the Nation of Islam had more than forty temples in various cities. The Nation of Islam's image of being a fringe fundamentalist group soon changed for good.

Malcolm's frank and outspoken attack on the ruling classes began to anger the Establishment. According to his critics, Malcolm was a racist who preached a concocted, confused message of racial supremacy, religious hatred and cultural separatism. Unlike Martin Luther King Jr. (whom he considered to be a 'chump, not a champ'), Malcolm became a voice for millions of voiceless African-Americans. Indeed, under his stewardship, the Nation of Islam became a very powerful and influential voice for America's black proletariat.

As Malcolm's popularity continued to rise, Elijah Muhammad became concerned by the increasing politicization of the Nation of Islam. Malcolm's fusion of religious fervor with political activism horrified a laidback Elijah, who now began to see him as more of a liability than an asset. During this period Malcolm became aware of Elijah's mismanagement of the Nation's finances, as well as his amoral sexual practices (such as his involvement in extra-marital affairs), which of course shocked and horrified him. This prompted Malcolm to leave the Nation of Islam in 1964. After leaving the Nation, he and his supporters inaugurated two separate organizations, namely the Muslim Mosque, Inc., and the Organization of Afro-American Unity (OAAU).

Thereafter, Malcolm travelled across Africa and the Middle East, and also performed the sacred *hajj* (pilgrimage to Makkah) where he experienced yet another life-changing transformation. In response, he openly renounced Elijah's distorted and racialistic interpretation of Islam and became an orthodox Muslim; from then on he became known by his new Muslim name, al-Hajj Malik al-Shabazz.

Malcolm fell prey to an assassin's bullet on February 21 1965, three months short of his fortieth birthday (although according to another source, he was assassinated on his fortieth birthday). As a result, three Nation of Islam loyalists were arrested and found guilty of his murder, although it is not clear whether the Central Intelligence Agency (CIA) or the Federal Bureau of Investigation (FBI) had played a role in his assassination. Just before his death, Malcolm had completed his autobiography with the assistance of Alex Haley.

(1925-65) US Black leader, Born Malcolm Little, he renounced his surname (in common with other Black Muslims) in favor of 'X', a sign indicating the lost tribal names that had been taken from his ancestors on their capture and transportation as slaves. He rejected the co-operation with White liberals that had marked the Civil Rights movement. He became a leading spokesman for the Black Muslims in the 1950s but was suspended by the movement's leader, Elijah Muhammad, for a controversial speech delivered after the assassination of President Kennedy. In 1964, after conversion to orthodox Islam, he preached brotherhood between Black and White people and formed the Organization of Afro-American Unity. He was assassinated in 1965. Militant black leader in the United States, also known as EL-Hajj Malik El-Shabazz, B. Malcolm Little in Omaha, Neb. He was introduced to the Black Muslims while serving a prison term and become a Muslim minister upon his release in 1952.

He quickly became very prominent in the movement with a following perhaps equaling that of its leader, Elijah Muhammad. In 1963, Malcolm was suspended by Elijah after a speech in which Malcolm suggested that President Kennedy's assassination was a matter of the chickens coming home to roost. He then formed a rival organization of his own, the Muslim Mosque, Inc. In 1964, after a pilgrimage to Mecca, he announced his conversion to orthodox Islam and his new belief that there could be brotherhood between black and white. In Feb., 1965, he was shot and killed in a public auditorium in New York City. His assassins were vaguely identified as Black Muslims, but his is a matter of controversy. Leader of the Nation of Islam. After his hajj to Mecca, he changed his name to El Hajj Malik Shabazz; was assassinated by his own people.

***

Malik ibn Anas (711-795): As Islam is not only a religion but also a complete way of life, the Holy Qur'an and the normative practice (*sunnah*) of the Prophet provide detailed and comprehensive guidance for Muslims, covering every sphere of their life. After preaching and propagating Islam in Makkah for more than a decade, the Prophet migrated to Madinah in 622, where he established the first Islamic State in history.

Abu Abdullah Malik ibn Anas ibn Malik ibn Abi Amir al-Asbahi, known as Imam Malik, was born in Madinah during the reign of the Umayyad Caliph al-Walid ibn Abd al-Malik. Hailing from the Yemeni province of Himyar, Malik's grandfather came to Madinah and settled there with his family during the reign of Caliph Umar. After memorizing the whole Qur'an, Malik received instruction in Arabic grammar and traditional Islamic teachings at home. His love for learning remained with him for the rest of his life, as he went on to become one of the Muslim world's most celebrated scholars and jurists. The study of Prophetic *Hadith* (or tradition) became his favorite preoccupation in life. He insisted on visiting all the luminaries of Madinah including Muhammad ibn Yahya al-Ansari, Abu Hazim Salmah ibn Dinar and Yahya ibn Sa'id in order to learn *Hadith* from them.

Malik began to attend the class of Rabi'ah ibn Abd al-Rahman and Sa'id ibn Musayyib, two of the greatest Islamic scholars of their generations. Not content with what he had learned so far, Malik then mastered *Hadith* under Hisham ibn Urwa, Abd al-Rahman ibn Hurmuz and Sa'id ibn Musayyib. Malik then attended Ja'far al-Sadiq's lectures on the Qur'an, *Hadith* and *Fiqh* at the *Masjid al-Nabi*. As well as being a direct descendant of the Prophet, Ja'far was a great Islamic scholar and sage of his time.

After the emergence of various religious groups like the S*hi'at Ali*, *khawarij*, M*u'tazilah* and the M*urijah*, political rivalries and religious schisms began to spread across the Islamic dominion.

By the time Malik reached his fortieth birthday, he was already widely recognized as an eminent Islamic scholar and jurist throughout Madinah. He chose to live in virtual poverty, far removed from the wealth and pleasures of this life. After the death of his beloved teacher Babi'ah in 755, he came to be regarded as one of Madinah's most learned scholars. Malik began to deliver daily lectures on *Hadith* and *Fiqh* in the *Masjid al-Nabi.* al-Zuhri, who was also a great scholar of *Hadith* and a contemporary of Malik, referred to him as a 'great vessel of knowledge'.

According to some scholars, Abu Hanifah, Abbasid Caliphs Abu Ja'far al-Mansur, sons (who later became Caliphs al-Amin and al-Ma'mun) has also attended Malik's lectures. This style of teaching proved so successful that later it became institutionalized in the form of *madrasah* (Islamic seminaries) across the Islamic world. His famous *Kitab al-Muwatta* (The Book of the Beaten Path), composed at the behest of Abbasid Caliph Abu Ja'far al-Mansur, became o ne of the first and most important anthologies of *Hadith* ever produced.

Caliph Harun al-Rashid asked Malik for his permission to make his book the law of the land. this pioneering work later inspired generations of Islamic scholars like al-Burkari, Muslim ibn al-Hajjaj, Abu Dawud, al-Tirmidhi and others to compose their own voluminous collections of *Hadith*. Malik was not only a great scholar of *Hadith, Fiqh* and theology; he was also a fearless defender of traditional Islam. Malik died in Madinah at the advanced age of around eighty-five and was buried in the city's famous cemetery, Jannat al-Baqi. Named after Malik, the *Maliki Madh'hab* (school of legal thought) later emerged and spread across the Muslim world.

***

Mansa Musa (ruled 1307-1337) the most celebrated of the rulers (Kankans) of Mali, chiefly because of his spectacular pilgrimage to Mecca in 1324. He caused a sensation in Cairo with his 500 slaves and 80-100 camels carrying gold. In his absence one of his generals acquired Gao, the capital of the neighboring Songhay state for him. He returned from Mecca with the Andalusian poet-architect Es-Saheli, who built the palace and Great Mosque of Timbuktu. He greatly expanded the commerce and prosperity of Mali, and gave encouragement to Islamic learning and culture.

***

Mansur, Husain al (also known as al Hallaj, the Wool Carder): one of the most famous of the Drunken Sufis, who is said in ecstasy to have cried "Ana al Haqq!" (I am the truth!!) so convinced was he of his total union with God. He was executed for heresy in 922.

***

Mariyah or Marya or Meriem (....-....): Coptic concubine sent to Medina as a gift to the Prophet from Muqaqis, a ruler of Egypt. She was given her freedom after she gave birth to Muhammad's son Ibrahim, though she was never given the honor of being addressed like the Prophet's other wives as a Mother of the Faithful.

***

Marwan II (684-750): last of the Umayyad caliphs. He served as governor of Armenia before his short-lived rule as caliph (744-50). Marwan reorganized his army, taking Syria by 746. Soon afterward, the Umayyad army was defeated (750) by a combined force of Iraqi, Persian, Shiite, and Abbasid soldiers. Marwan fled, only to be killed by troops under the first caliph of the subsequent Abbasids.

***

Masudi, Abd al-Hasan Ali ibn al-Hussyn, (896-956): Arab historian, geographer, and philosopher, b. Baghdad. He traveled in Spain, Russia, India, Sra Lanka, and China and spent his last years in Syria and Egypt. His *Muruj adh-Dhahab* [meadows of gold], and epitome of a longer history of the world from creation to A.D. 947, is a compilation of his travel observations and studies. It embraces social and literary history, discussions of religions, and geographic descriptions. A French version of this work was published between 1861 and 1878. The first volume has been translated into English.

***

Mehmed II (Muhammad II, the Conqueror 1430-1481): Ottoman sultan (1451-81). He was frustrated while ruling briefly (1444-46) during the retirement of his father, Murad II, but on coming to power backed expansionist factions, and by 1453 had achieved the long-standing Ottoman objective of taking Constantinople and thus uniting the European and Asian parts of the empire. Ceaseless campaigns brought further gains in the Balkans, consolidated control of Asia Minor, and took Otranto in Apulia, but failed to wrest Rhodes from the Knights of St John. He modernized his forces by equipping them with firearms and artillery, and created the institutional framework of the developed Ottoman state. Ottoman sultan (1451-61) who is known as "the Conqueror" because he achieved the conquest of Byzantine Constantinople in 1453.

***

Mehemet Ali (1769–1849): Pasha (or viceroy) of Egypt (1805–1849). An Albanina by birth, he rose from the ranks to command an Ottoman army in an unsuccessful attempt to drive Napoleon from Egypt. In 1801 he returned to Egypt in command of Albanian troops and ruled Egypt almost without interruption since 1250. Technically viceroy of the Ottoman sultan, Mahmud II, he was effectively an independent ruler and reorganized the administration, agriculture, commerce, industry, education, and the army, employing chiefly French advisers, making Egypt he leading power in the eastern Mediterranean.

He occupied the Sudan (1821-23), and campaigned for the Ottoman government in Arabia (1811-18) against the Wahhabis, and in Greece (1822-28), when his fleet was destroyed by a combination of British French, and Russian navies at the Battle of Navarino (1827). He took Syria (1831-33) and defeated the Ottoman troops at the battle of Nizip (1839). Threatened by European opposition he agreed to accept the suzerainty of the Ottoman sultan in 1841 and in return was granted a request that his family be hereditary pashas of Egypt.

***

Midhat Pasha (1822-1883): Turkish politician. As governor of Bulgaria he succeeded within the few years of his tenure (1864-69) in raising the country from misery to relative prosperity. Schools, roads, and granaries were built from funds obtained by local taxation. His hostility to Pan-Slavism caused the Russian ambassador of Constantinople to secure his transfer to Baghdad. He was briefly grand vizier (chief executive officer) in 1872. In 1876, at the head of the reforming party, he led the revolution that deposed Sultan Abd al-Aziz. The new sultan, Murad V, was in turn shortly deposed because of his insanity, and Abd al-Hamid II succeeded. Late in 1876, as grand vizier, Midhat secured the promulgation of the first Turkish constitution, but as soon as Abd al-Hamid regained control over the situation he sent Midhat into exile. After being recalled as governor of Syria, Midhat was charged with the murder of Abd al-Aziz, imprisoned, and strangled.

***

Mimar Sinan (1489-1588): Some of the world's most beautiful and historic buildings were constructed by the Muslims under the patronage of influential rulers like Abd al-Malik ibn Marwan, Abd al-Rahman III, Sulaiman the Magnificent and Emperor Shah Jahan. Great works of architecture are produced by great architectural minds and the Muslim world has produced some of the world's great architectural geniuses including Muhammad Tahir Agha and Mahmud Agha, the two brothers who built the magnificent Blue Mosque in Istanbul, and Fazlur Rahman Khan, the brains behind the Sears Tower in Chicago, which was once the world's tallest building. But the greatest Muslim architect, and arguably the most prolific builder of all time, was Sinan.

Mimar Sinan was born in the central Anatolian province of Qaisariyyah (in present-day Turkey). Of Greek origin, his father, Abd al-Mannan, embraced Islam and became a notable member of the Ottoman civil and administrative service. After completing his early education, Sinan followed in his father's footsteps and joined the Janissaries – derived from the Turkish *Yeni Cheri* (meaning 'new troops') – in order to serve the powerful Ottoman army.

Founded by the Ottomans in the fourteenth century to strengthen their army, the Janissaries were an elite military force. They were professionally trained soldiers, recruited from across the Ottoman Empire, but especially from the Balkans. The recruits were given Turkish names, offered tutorials in Islam and trained in all aspects of warfare before they graduated with military honors.

Thanks to his physical prowess, sharp intellect and organizational ability, Sinan won instant recognition within the Ottoman army. During the reign of Sultan Salim I, he helped build more than one hundred and fifty warships to give the Ottoman's navy superiority over their rivals. After Sulaiman the Magnificent succeeded Salim I in 1520, the Ottomans launched a large-scale military operation against the Hungarians and subdued Belgrade after seven days of intensive bombardment. Sinan and the Janissaries played a pivotal role in the fall of Belgrade. Then, in 1522, Sultan Sulaiman led a campaign against the island of Rhodes and again Sinan played an important role in the fight against the fanatical Knights of St. John. During this battle he devised and developed a formidable artillery system which enabled the Janissaries to outflank their opponents and capture the island. Able to think and act quickly, and do so often in the middle of battle, he built bridges, fixed damaged roads and constructed war vessels at short notice.

After he polished his design and architectural skills in the Ottoman army, in 1538 at the age of around forty-nine, Sinan was promoted by Sultan Sulaiman to one of the highest posts within the Ottoman imperial court; that is to say, he became the Sultan's chief architect and builder. Under Sultan Sulaiman's patronage, he constructed some of the Muslim world's most dazzling and inspirational works of architecture. Following the Ottoman conquest of the ancient city of Constantinople under the leadership of Sultan Muhammad II, this historic city was renamed Istanbul (or the 'city of Islam') by its new conqueror. As one of the oldest buildings in Istanbul, the Hagia Sophia (Aya Sofia) had been neglected by the Byzantines. Originally built by Geek architects for Emperor Justinian, this historic building was thoroughly repaired and restored to its former glory by the Ottomans. This mammoth task was entrusted to none other than Sinan, who refurbished the entire building and added beautiful new minarets to it to symbolize the Ottoman's victory over their old Byzantine rival.

For more than half a century, Sinan worked full-time for three different Ottoman rulers, Sulaiman I, Salim II and Murad III, and during this period he built scores of magnificent mosques, palaces, mausoleums, libraries, schools and bridges throughout the Ottoman Empire. In addition to designing and constructing the mausoleums of Abu Hanifah (located in Baghdad) and Jalal al-Din Rumi (in Konya, in present-day Turkey), he designed and built the seven-hilled city close to the Bosphorus. But his first major architectural project was the Sehzade Mosque Complex in Istanbul. Sinan set himself very high standards and always tried to surpass the Sultan's expectations.

Sinan's second major project was the magnificent Sulaimaniyyah Mosque Complex in Istanbul. The Sultan wanted the Sulaimaniyyah Mosque Complex to be one of the world's most impressive and elegant buildings. Sinan worked on this massive project round-the-clock for seven years. In 1557, the Sulaimaniyyah Mosque Complex was formally opened by the Sultan and in so doing helped to completely transform the skyline of Istanbul for good. But, being a perfectionist, Sinan felt he could do even better in the future.

The Salimiyyah Mosque was the largest of all the Ottoman buildings and is today considered to be one of the world's most beautiful works of architecture.

Sinan was a unique architect and builder, who understood the need for space, but not at the expense of beauty, elegance, and grandeur. He actually planned, supervised and built more than three hindered and fifty construction projects in total, including eighty-one mosques, fifty-five schools, thirty-four palaces, eight bridges and nineteen mausoleums. He died at the advanced age of ninety-nine and was buried in a mausoleum he had built close to the Sulaimaniyyah Mosque Complex in Istanbul. Sinan's achievements are second-to-none in the annals of Islamic art and architecture.

***

Montazeri, Hussein-Ali (1922-2009): Iranian religious political leader. Born into a poor peasant family in Najafabad, Montazeri had his early theological education in Isfahan. He then went to Qom where he became a student of Ayatollah Ruhollah Khomeini. Instead of following Khomeini's example of intermittently backing one or other faction within the ruling establishment, Montazeri consistently advocated moderate policies, such as allowing a fair degree of opposition and liberalizing the economy, thus alienating centrist and radicals. When he publicly questioned the religious learning and standing of Khomeini's successor Ayatollah Ali Khamanei he was put under house arrest. In the late 1990s he set up his own web site to express his views and communicate with others. In early 2003 the authorities lifted the restrictions on his movements.

***

Moussa, Amr (1936-   ): Egyptian diplomat and politician, secretary general of the Arab League 2001, Born into a middle class family in Cairo, Moussa graduated in law from Cairo University in 1957. He and president Hosni Mubarak were active in advising the Palestinian leadership during its secret talks with Israel that led to the Oslo I Accord in September 1993.

***

Muawiya ibn Abi Sufyan (605-680): The reign of the first four Caliphs of Islam became known as the period of the 'rightly-guided Caliphs' (*al-*

khulafa al-Rashidun) because they ruled in accordance with the teachings of the Qur'an and the Prophetic *sunnah* (norms and practices). After the death of Uthman, the third rightly-guided Caliph in 656, the Muslim world was plunged into serious political and social turmoil. The death of Caliph Uthman shattered the political unity of Islam. Although Ali, the cousin and son-in-law of the Prophet, succeeded Uthman as the fourth Caliph, he was not able to put an end to the political rivalry and tribal infighting. Amidst the prevailing chaos and disorder, Muawiyah ibn Abi Sufyan emerged to establish the Umayyad dynasty, which subsequently became one of the most powerful dynasties to rule the Muslim world.

Muawiyah ibn Abi Sufyan ibn Harb was born into the powerful Makkan clan of Banu Umayyah. His father, Abu Sufyan, was a wealthy and powerful Makkan chieftain. Muawiyah grew up to be an intelligent, wise and pleasant young man. The Prophet's message of unity, brotherhood, justice and equality clearly threatened Abu Sufyan and his like.

During the next thirteen years, Abu Sufyan – actively encouraged by his wife Hind bint Utba – opposed the Prophet and his small band of followers with great determination. After the Prophet migrated (*Hijrah*) to the nearby oasis of Madinah, Abu Sufuyan spearheaded a series of military expeditions against the nascent Muslim community but on each and every occasion he failed to breach the strong defense put up by the Muslims. Eventually, in 630, the Prophet, accompanied by his companions, returned to Makkah unopposed and it was then that Abu Sufyan embraced Islam but Muawiyah had already become a Muslim a year earlier. Umm Habibah, the daughter of Abu Sufyan, had embraced Islam much earlier, and she was married to the Prophet. Muawiyah was around twenty-five when he embraced Islam. He volunteered to be one of the Prophet's secretaries (*Kuttab al-Wahy*).

After the Prophet's death in 632, Muawiyah played an active part in the affairs of the early Islamic State. His services to the Prophet and early Muslim community prompted Umar, the second Caliph, to appoint Muawiyah governor of Syria in 639, following the death of Abu Ubaida ibn al-Jarrah. Muawiyah appointed some of his most trusted and loyal lieutenants to key positions in Government. Syria became one of the most politically stable and economically prosperous provinces of the Islamic State. Following Umar's assassination in 644, Uthman became Caliph and he ruled for twelve years before he, too, was assassinated by a group of insurgents in 656. By the time Ali became Caliph, Muawiyah was already considered the undisputed ruler of Syria in all but name.

Ali, the new Caliph, found himself in an extremely difficult position. Unable, in the circumstances, to hunt down Uthman's assassins or restore peace and security across the Islamic State, the new

Caliph was now fighting a losing battle. To make matters worse, a group of Uthman's close relatives, led by his widow Nailah bint Farafisah, then proceeded to Syria and provocatively paraded the bloodstained robes of Uthman before Muawiyah and the people of Syria. Since Muawiyah and Uthman belonged to the same Umayyah clan, Caliph Ali now found himself in conflict with yet another group of Uthman's supporters in Syria who openly refused to pledge allegiance (*Bay'ah*) to him.

Muawiyah then sent a letter to Caliph Ali with simply the words *bismillah al-Rahman al-Rahim* (In the name of God, Most Gracious, Most Merciful) inscribed on it. To Ali, this represented an open refusal to acknowledge his Caliphate. The Caliph, on the other hand, demanded an unconditional pledge of loyalty, but Muawiyah refused this. Not willing to tolerate open rebellion, Ali marched to Syria with a fifty thousand strong force and camped at Siffin. Muawiyah came out with his forces to meet the Caliph's army. When the two Muslim armies were about to clash, the Caliph decided to give peace another chance. When the deadlock could not be broken, the two armies clashed on the field of battle at Siffin. As the Caliph's army was about to inflict a crushing defeat on Muawiyah's forces, the latter called for arbitration (T*ahkim*). Ali stopped the fight and agreed to resolve their differences through arbitration. The decision to engage in arbitration proved fatal for Ali because it led to considerable political tension and dissension within his camp. Ali's reign came to abrupt end in 661, when he was fatally stabbed by a member of the extremist *khawarij* sect.

Following Ali's assassination his oldest son, Hasan, was elected Caliph but he subsequently abdicated. But after Muawiyah became the ruler of the Muslim world in 661, he rewarded Hasan with a generous State pension for stepping out of his way. After being crowned Caliph, Muawiyah swiftly restored Islamic political unity and actively promoted peace and prosperity across the Islamic dominion. Having lived and worked under the supervision of the Prophet and the first three "rightly-guided Caliphs" of Islam, he developed a thorough understanding of Islamic principles and practices. The brother of Umm Habibah, the Prophet's widow, Muawiyah simply made a mistake in his exercise of juristic discretion (*Ijtihad*) in his dispute with Caliph Ali.

Muawiyah's well-known motto was, 'I do not use my sword where my stick is sufficient, and I do not use my stick where my words are sufficient; and if there is only a hair (of understanding) between me and the people, I will not allow it to be cut.' After transferring the capital of the Islamic world from Kufah to Damascus, he transformed the city into a prominent center of Islamic learning, culture and civilization. During his reign, the Islamic dominion also expanded rapidly both in the East and the West. Under the command of Uqba ibn Nafi, the Muslim forces not only reasserted their authority in North Africa, but also mounted naval expeditions to Sicily and laid unsuccessful siege to Constantinople. Likewise, in the East, Muslims successfully captured Kabul, Khurasan, Bukhara and Samarqand, thanks to Muawiyah's outstanding and inspirational leadership.

Muawiyah served as a governor for twenty years, and as a Caliph for almost another two decades. After nearly four decades of continuous service to his people, he surprised everyone with his nomination of Yazid as his successor, even though the latter was not fit for the post of Caliphate. Muawiyah died at the age of about seventy-five and was buried in Damascus. But, by nominating his son as his successor, Muawiyah became the founder of the first, and one of the Muslim world's most powerful, political dynasties. The Umayyads ruled the Muslim world for nearly a century before the Abbasids overthrew them in 750.

Governor of Syria who opposed the selection of Ali as caliph after the murder of Uthman.

***

Muawiya II, ibn Yazid (661-684): Muawiyah II (or Mu'awiya ibn Yazīd) (661–684) was an Umayyad caliph for about four months after the death of his father Yazīd. The empire he inherited was in a state of disarray with Abdullah bin Zubayr claiming to be the true caliph and holding the Hejaz as well as other areas.

Birth and early years:
Muawiya II was born on the 28th March 661 and was the son of Yazid I of the Umayyad dynasty and on his mother's side a descendent of the Quraysh tribe in the Hejaz. His mother's father, Abu Hashim ibn Utbah ibn Rabi'ah was appointed Governor of Basra and his mother married Yazid I in 660. Mu'awiya was the eldest son to be born, out of six brothers and many (uncounted) daughters. When Mu'awiya I became Caliph in 661, it is said that on his day of accession he heard the news that his son had given birth to a son. The account is related in Al Nasab (890-949) in his History of the Wars:

At the same time as the birth (of Mua'wiya II), his grandfather had met with the Islamic Elders (i.e. the Shura) and when he heard that he had a grandson he said, "Surely this is a blessing from God and a sure sign, if there is any, that I am the true Caliph. For I shall establish a dynasty that shall be well-remembered. My son shall follow me, and his son shall follow him." And the child was named Mua'wiya in his honor.

According to al-Tabari, Mu'awiya II was 13 years old when he died. This means Mu'awiya must have been born in 671 when Yazid I his father was 25 years old.

Mu'awiya was the first prince of the Umayyads to grow up entirely at the court of the Caliph, being kept there to protect him from potential assassins. He was the first to be given private scholars and teachers as is recorded in Al-Hahah (854-905)'s Court of the Righteous Caliphs.

The fact that Mu'awiya was not sent to Mecca and Medina was also unpopular with Muslims. This growing unpopularity became worse with the campaigns against Husayn ibn Ali and Ibn al-Zubayr. The latter was, leading to the capture of Medina and the siege of Mecca, was even more unpopular. Fortunately for the Arab Empire, Yazid I died soon afterwards in 683 and his son succeeded him.

Accession:

The accession of Mu'awiya II was met first with indifference and trepidation by Muslims, for they didn't know anything about him as he had been kept away in the home of the Caliphs. Yet, when Mu'awiya declared that a truce would be made, it was met with almost universal acclamation, for it had ended the war in the Holy Places. Mu'awiya II declared that the war in Medina and Mecca had been foolish and blasphemous and that the damage to the Ka'aba was sacrilege.

But the followers of Ibn al-Zubayr urged the rebel to break the truce and declare war, stating that the Caliph was a beardless boy and a coward, afraid to fight and so easy to defeat. Yet the truce held officially for many months, though there was sporadic fighting in Mecca.

Personality and family:

In the primary sources and modern histories, Mu'awiya II's reign is usually passed over quickly. The caliph is portrayed as being weak-willed but with a good-nature. He is said to have declared when news came of his father's death, that this is the news he dreaded for now he was Caliph and did not wish to be. Mu'awiya was even prepared to summon the Shura and call on them to choose a Caliph of their own, and thus restore the non-hereditary traditions of the Caliphate. Many stories have been written in the sources of Mu'awiya's weak but good-willed nature, not all of them true.

The marriage of Mu'awiya was deemed contentious and problematic. His grandfather Mu'awiya I wished him to marry into another tribe and thus strengthen the power of the dynasty. This, Mu'awiya did but his wife died in 677. He then married again in 678 and 680, having two wives, but he divorced both by 682 for providing no children. Yazid now forced him to marry a fourth wife in 683, a foreign princess, to extend the power of the Caliphate. It is said that Mu'awiya despised this woman, and as soon as Yazid had died, she was divorced.

Government acts:
Traditionally, Mu'awiya is shown to have had no interest in politics, perhaps with justification. He is said to have claimed that only by mistake of the hereditary principle was he Caliph and under no other means would he have ever been chosen. Yet it is said that his courtiers persuaded him to remain Caliph as he was kind and would do some virtuous deeds. Some say they did this to prolong their own power or because it was ungrateful for Mu'awiya to give back the power given to him by God.

Once a truce had been made in 683, Mu'awiya turned to domestic affairs. He did not involve himself for many months with Zubayr, even when fighting continued and when the truce had obviously been broken in all but name. Mu'awiyya passed three laws which he said were necessary. Firstly, he said that the rights of women should be protected, secondly that no man should be put to death because of a crime, and thirdly that the charity tax should be made compulsory. These laws were removed once he had died. According to al-Tabari, Mu'awiya II reigned only 40 days before he died.

Conflict with Abdullah ibn al-Zubayr:
By the beginning of 684, the problem of Ibn al-Zubayr had worsened, and Mu'awiya was forced to turn his attention back to southern Arabia. He rejected any attempts to launch an attack, declaring that Medina and Mecca were sacred.

Instead he sent an embassy to Ibn al-Zubayr and declared that as he himself had no son, that Ibn al-Zubayr could be his heir. Zubayr rejected this for he knew that Mu'awiya was young and could have many children. "I shall not be a nursemaid", Ibn al-Zubayr is said to have answered.

The embassy was imprisoned and Ibn al-Zubayr continued the conflict.

It seems this embassy was rejected as well. Two weeks before his death, Mu'awiya declared he would abdicate, saying he would rather lose his life than have many lose their lives for him in a civil war.

Shi'a view of his abdication and death. In June 684, Mu'awiya abdicated. Shi'a Muslims believe that he converted to Shi'ism and abdicated, by saying that he could "smell the blood of Ahl ul-Bayt" from the throne. By this they mean that he considered his forefathers to be the murders of the *Ahl ul-Bayt* (the household of prophet Muhammad).

It is generally believed that he abdicated and died a month later.

***

Mubarak, Muhammad Hosni (1928-   ): Egyptian military leader and political, president 1981- Son of a court functionary and born in the Nile delta village of Kafr al Musaliha, Mubarack graduated from the air force academy in 1950. After Egypt's debacle in the June 1967 Arab Israeli War, Mubarak was returned to his earlier job of director general of the air force academy. Two years later he was appointed chief of staff of the air force and promoted to air vice marshal. In the October 1973 Arab Israeli War under his command the air force performed well during the crucial initial hours, and he was promoted the next year to air marshal. In April 1975 President Anwar Sadat appointed Mubarak vice president. Following Sadat's assassination in October 1981 Mubarak took over as President. He also became leader of the NDP.

After the final expulsion of Yasser Arafat from Lebanon in 1983, Mubarak helped him to reassemble his scattered forces. In February 1986 a riotous mutiny by 17,000 conscripts of the Central Security Forces in Cairo threatened Mubarak's regime. Its suppression by Defense Minister Field Marshal Abdul Halim Abu Ghazala so enhanced Ghaala's prestige that Mubarak sacked him in April to get rid of a serious potential rival to his own authority. As the sole candidate Mubarak was reelected president in 1987. When Iraqi President Saddam Hussein occupied Kuwait in August 1990, Mubarak condemned his action. Militant Islamist groups such as Gamaat a Islamiya and Jihad al Islamic intensified their campaign against his regime in 1992.

Nonetheless he was reelected president in 1993. An attempt by al Gamaat al Islamiya to assassinate Mubarak during his visit to Addis Ababa to attend the Organization of African Union summit in June 1995 failed. In July 2000 he advised Yasser Arafat not to compromise on the future status of Jerusalem by conceding the sovereignty of the Dome of the Rock to Israel in his talks with Israeli Prime Minister Ehud Barak at Camp David. Following the terrorist attacks on the US in September 2001, Mubarak's calls for an international convention to define terrorism as a preamble to a worldwide campaign against it went unheeded by the administration of President George W. Bush. Nor were his repeated warnings against invading Iraq heeded.

***

Mughira ibn Shuba: renegade from the Thaqif tribe of Ta'if who greatly benefited from a timely early conversion to Islam. Despite his moral failings his political insights made him an indispensable adviser who served both the Prophet and Omar and would seek to serve Ali before defecting to Muawiya's camp during the Civil War. He would die in office as Muawiya's feared governor of Kufa.

***

Muhammad Abduh (1849-1905): The nineteenth century was one of the most politically traumatic and intellectually degenerative periods in the annals of Islam. During the Umayyad period, Hasan al-Basri and Umar ibn Abd al-Aziz emerged to warn the masses of the dangers of unbridled power, greed and hedonism. Ahmad ibn Hanbal and his successors did the same thing during the Abbasid period. Amidst the chaos wrought by the Mongols in the thirteenth century, Ibn Taymiyyah and al-Nawawi attempted to revive the Prophetic norms, practices and methodology (*Minhaj al-sunnah*). It paved the way for Muhammad Abduh, an eminent disciple of al-Afghani and the 'father of Islamic modernism' to emerge and become one of the most influential Islamic thinkers and reformers of the nineteenth century.

Born in a village in northern Egypt close to the Nile, Abduh's father was a relatively well-off trader of some standing in his locality. Impressed by his rapid progress, Abduh's family enrolled him at the noted Ahmadi mosque-cum-seminary in Tanta at the age of thirteen. During his time at this institute, Abduh developed keen interest in the speculative sciences, including philosophy and mysticism. He then enrolled at al-Azhar University in Cairo to pursue higher education in Arabic literature, logic, philosophy and mysticism. Originally founded by the Fatimids in the tenth century, al-Azhar is not only one of the world's oldest institutions of higher education, it is also one of the Muslim world's most famous seats of Islamic learning and scholarship. For the next two years Abduh lectured at al-Azhar and became a popular figure due to his great learning and refreshing approach to Islam.

It was during his tenure as a lecturer at al-Azhar that Abduh first met Jamal al-Din al-Afghani, the famous Muslim thinker and pan-Islamist politician of the nineteenth century. Since a large part of the Muslim world was suffering under European colonial rule at the time, Abduh was convinced that al-Afghani's rallying call for Islamic unity and solidarity was the only way the Muslims could liberate their lands from foreign occupation. Alarmed by al-Afghani's ideological interpretation of Islam, the British, who exercised real political power in

Egypt at the time, expelled him from the country in 1879. Abduh would continue to oversee the development of pan-Islamism in that country.

Following al-Afghani's expulsion from Egypt, Abduh returned to his native village. But the voices of nationalism became louder by the day after the formal British military occupation of Egypt in 1882, and it was during this period that Abduh fell out with the British authorities for supporting the nationalists, and he was forced to live in exile for about six years. Combining the traditional methods of teaching Islamic sciences with a modern approach was the only viable alternative, argued Abduh. A few years later, he left Beirut for Paris where he joined forced with al-Afghani, his former mentor and guide, to bring about political change and reform in the Muslim world.

In Paris, they established an institute for socio-political reform in the Muslim world and published their famous journal *al-Urwa al-Wuthqa* (The Unbreakable Bond) – a phrase which appears twice in the Qur'an and refers to those people who place their absolute trust in Divine power and judgment. Their call for the masses to rise against the colonial powers and liberate their lands from Western domination, instantly turned Abduh and al-Afghani into heroic figures in many parts of the Muslim world. In response, the British authorities in Egypt imposed a ban on their journal, but it was regularly smuggled into the country where it acquired a large following. After publishing only eighteen issues, the journal became defunct due to lack of funding, censorship and political restrictions.

After the demise of *al-Urwa al-Wuthqa* in 1884, Abduh left Paris and returned to Beirut where he gathered around him a number of talented young intellectuals and activists, including Muhammad Rashid Rida who became one of his most able and trusted disciples. The British authorities allowed Abduh to return to Cairo in 1888.

Abduh's most famous book was *Risalat al-Tawhid* (A Treatise on Divine Unity) in which he developed a fresh and challenging exposition of Islamic philosophy and theology in the light of Western modernity. Abduh was of the opinion that the universal principles of Islam are timeless and unchangeable, but our existential condition constantly changes and evolves; thus the principles of Islam must always underpin our personal as well as collective actions.

After working as a judge for about a decade, in 1899 Abduh was appointed Grand Mufti of Egypt, which was the highest judicial post in the country; he also became a member of the Egyptian Legislative Council. Six years after becoming the Grand Mufti, Abduh died at the age of fifty-four and was buried in Cairo. As the 'father of Islamic modernism', his reformist ideas and thoughts have influenced generations of Islamic scholars, thinkers and reformers across the Muslim world, especially in Egypt and Indonesia.

***

Muhammad Ali (1769-1849): Pasha of Egypt after 1805. He was a common soldier who rose to leadership by his military skill and political acumen. In 1799 he commanded a Turkish army in an unsuccessful attempt to drive Napoleon from Egypt. As pasha he was virtually independent of his nominal overlord, the Ottoman sultan. He modernized his armed forces and administration, created schools, and began many public works, particularly irrigation projects. The cost of these reforms bore heavily on the peasants and brought them few benefits. In 1811 he exterminated the leaders of the Mamluks, who had ruled Egypt almost uninterruptedly since 1250.

With his son, Ibrahim Pasha, Muhammad Ali conducted successful campaigns in Arabia against the Wahhabis. In 1820 he sent armies to conquer Sudan. He scored great successes fighting for the Ottoman sultan in Greece until the British, French, and Russians combined to defeat his fleet at Navarino in 1827. The sultan, Mahmud II, to win his intervention in the Greek revolt, had promised to make him governor of Syria. When the sultan refused to hand over the province, Muhammad Ali invaded Syria with great success. In 1839 he attacked his overlord in Asia Minor, but was forced to desist when the he lost the support of France and was threatened by united European opposition. In a compromise arrangement the Ottoman sultan made the governorship of Egypt hereditary in Muhammad Ali's line. He retired from office in 1848. Muhammad Ali is credited for his many domestic reforms, which hastened the foundations for an independent Egypt.

***

Muhammad Ali (Cassius Marcellus Clay 1942-   ): Muhammad Ali, the legendary American boxer and philanthropist became, during his career, the undisputed king of the ring. He is widely considered to be the most famous sportsman of all time, and one of the most influential boxers in history.

Muhammad Ali was born Cassius Marcellus Clay Jr., in Louisville, Kentucky into a working-class African American family. Ali and his brother Rudy grew up in the happy but conservative environment of Western Louisville.

According to Ali, when he was about twelve, his father bought him a new bike for Christmas, but it was stolen from him by thieves. A tall, slim and shy Ali went to the gym and put on his boxing gloves for the first time. If Joe Martin introduced Ali to boxing, then Fred Stoner became his first serious boxing instructor. As a respected black boxer himself, Stoner taught Ali the art of boxing in a rigorous and systematic way. Ali confirmed Stoner's prediction when he was barely sixteen by winning the Louisville Golden Gloves lightweight tournament. Whilst still at high school, he progressed to the quarter-finals of the regional boxing championship in Chicago. Then, after graduating from Louisville's Central High school at the age of eighteen, he won the National Golden Gloves tournament and also the Amateur Athletic Union competition.

Thanks to his success, Ali was chosen to represent his country at the Olympics in Rome in 1960, where he won a Gold Medal and of course this made him instantly famous. After returning home from Rome with an Olympic Gold Medal, a group of white millionaire businessmen came together and formed the Louisville Sponsoring Group. Ali signed a lucrative contract with this consortium and began his professional boxing career at the age of eighteen. He then approached Angelo Dundee, a renowned boxing trainer, to join his team and supervise his training needs and requirements.

In 1962, Ali thoroughly mesmerized and out-fought Archie Moore. His convincing victory over Moore paved the way for him to challenge Sonny Liston, the then-reigning heavyweight champion of the world. Ali, the challenger, entered the ring with Liston in 1964. Chanting 'Float like a butterfly, sting like a bee', he demolished the feared and revered Liston. Ali stunned the American public by becoming the heavyweight champion of the world. After soundly beating the world heavyweight boxing champion, he emerged to proclaim, 'I am the greatest!'

Even before the dust of his victory over Liston could settle, Ali announced his conversion to the Nation of Islam. As expected, soon after his conversion to the Nation of Islam, Ali's career and public image took a battering from the American press. Taught and mentored by none other than Malcolm X (al-Hajj Malik al-Shabass), he closely studied the Nation's religious thoughts and methodology for more than a year before formally becoming a member. Encouraged by Malcolm X and Elijah Muhammad, he then changed his name to Muhammad Ali, for he no longer wished to be known by his 'slave name'. Like him, tens of thousands of other African-Americans found true freedom, liberation and self-respect in the fold of the Nation of Islam. During this period Ali married for the first time and continued to box.

Ali not only retained his heavyweight championship title by defeating Liston for the second time in 1965, but also successfully defended the title another six times in 1966, with five knockouts. A year later, another public outcry arose when Ali refused to sign up for military duties in Vietnam. Found guilty of draft evasion by an all-white jury, he was fined ten thousand dollars and sentenced to five years in prison. Although freed on appeal, his boxing license was suspended, and he was also stripped of his World Boxing Association (WBA) title. During this period he married for the second time, and three years later the Supreme Court quashed his conviction for draft evasion. Ali regained his title in 1974 and successfully defended it against Frazier a year later in the 'Thrilla in Manilla'.

Two years later, Ali married for the third time and in the following year fought one of his most memorable bouts against George Foreman in the famous 'Rumble in the Jungle' in Zaire, which earned him five million dollars. He then lost against Leon Spinks, but regained his title for the third time and in so doing he became the only man to have won the world heavyweight championship three times. After two more fights – one against Larry Holmes in 1980 and the other against Trevor Burbick in 1981 – Ali finally retired from boxing in 1981 at the age of forty-one, having fought a total of sixty-one bouts. A few years later, he told the New York Times Magazine that he was suffering from Perkinson's syndrome, probably as a result of repeated blows to the head. Ali made more than fifty million dollars from boxing, and gave away a substantial amount to fund charitable activities.

Moreover, as a sporting legend and a distinguished statesman, Ali went to Lebanon in 1985 and Iraq in 1990 to secure the release of hostages from those countries. Ali was honored by the Kings of Saudi Arabia and Morocco for his services to Islam.

Ali lives in Michigan with Lonnie Williams, his fourth wife.

***

Muhammad, Ali (1952-   ): Egyptian military officer: Al Qaida leader Born into a well to do family in Alexandria. Muhammad enrolled at the military academy in Heliopolis, a suburb of Cairo. After an honorable discharge from the US Defense department, Muhammad started a leather import export business. During his visits to New York, he imparted weapons training to the American Muslim militants attending Al Khifa Refugee Center. He found time and inclination to pursue a doctorate in Islamic studies. In 1993 he applied unsuccessfully for a translator's job at the Federal Bureau of Investigation, After the failed attempt on Osama bin Laden's life in Sudan in 1994, Muhammad retrained his bodyguards. After his arrest in 1998 he chose a plea bargain and turned a state witness in the US case against bin Laden. Still in jail in early 2003, Muhammad expected to receive a light sentence.

***

Muhammad Ali Jinnah (1876-1948): Inaugurated in 1526 by Zahir al-Din Babar (Babur) and abolished by the British in 1857, the Mughal Empire was one of the foremost political dynasties to have ruled Muslim India. After more than three centuries of Mughal rule, the British arrived in India during the eighteenth century in the guise of the East India Company and began to exert its influence in that country. As Mughal political authority rapidly deteriorated, the British tightened their grip on India during the first half of the nineteenth century and assumed full military control in 1857.

Being once the masters of their own destinies, they now became the subjects of a foreign power. A mass uprising took place in 1857; better known as the Indian Mutiny, it thoroughly shook the Indian consciousness and body politic, and led to the birth of the Indian liberation movement. As a champion of the Indian liberation movement, a valiant fighter for the rights of Indian Muslims and the founder of Pakistan, now one of the world's most populous and powerful Muslim countries, Muhammad Ali Jinnah was undoubtedly one of the most influential Muslim political leaders of modern times.

Born in the historic Pakistani port city of Karachi, Jinnah's ancestors were originally Hindus, who hailed from the Indian province of Gujarat. At the age of fifteen, while he was still at high school, Jinnah married a local girl at the behest of his parents. Thereafter, he sailed to England to study law. He passed all his law exams with flying colors within two years. A staunch supporter of Dadabhai Naoroji, the first Indian to be elected to the British Parliament, he assisted the latter with his election campaign. After nearly four years in England, he returned to Karachi in 1896. In 1900, he was offered the vacant post of the Presidency Magistrate of Bombay. As a talented lawyer, Jinnah pursued his legal duties with great skill, confidence and authority. Being a Muslim member of the Hindu-dominated Indian National Congress, he increasingly became involved in the political affairs of his country.

Keen to unite the Hindus and Muslims – and work collectively to drive out the British from India – Jinnah attended the 1906 session of the Indian National Congress in Calcutta. During this period he became a prominent defender of the rights and liberties of Indian Muslims, which made him very popular in the Muslim community. As his popularity continued to increase he was elected president of the Lucknow Muslim League in 1916. Under Jinnah's guidance and stewardship, the Indian National Congress and the Muslim League signed the Lucknow Pact and India's Hindus and Muslims became united for the first time.

Jinnah's political strategy worked well until Mahatma Gandhi left South Africa and moved to India during the 1920s. Couched in the language of Hinduism, Gandhi's philosophy of non-violence soon captured the imagination of his Hindu followers, even if it did not go down too well with the Muslims. Jinnah's personal life was devastated when his wife Ruttie suddenly died in 1929. Her death was a major blow to Jinnah, who promptly left Bombay for London where he lived with his daughter Dina and sister Fatimah. Then Liaquat Ali Khan, the future Prime Minister of Pakistan, visited him in 1934 and persuaded him to return to India to lead the Muslim League. The Jinnah-Liaquat partnership thus became one of the most decisive alliances to be formed in modern Indian political history.

Back in India, Jinnah revitalized the Muslim League which once more became a powerful force in Indian politics. So it was, between 1936 and 1937, that one of the major turning-points of his life took place: he exchanged several letters with Sir Muhammad Iqbal, the influential Muslim poet-philosopher of India, who urged him to take a unilateral stand and fight for the rights of the Indian Muslims. Inspired by Iqbal's visionary call for a separate homeland for the Muslims of India, Jinnah now became an indefatigable champion of Pakistan. Thereafter, the creation of a separate homeland for the Muslims of the subcontinent became his main preoccupation in life. Following the passage of the Lahore Resolution in 1940 by the Indian Muslim leaders, Jinnah's quest for Pakistan moved a step closer.

After a long and hard struggle, Jinnah's vision eventually became a reality in 1947. A year after Pakistan appeared on the world map the inspirational *quaid-i-Azam* (or 'the great leader'), as he now came to be known, died at the age of seventy-two and was buried in Karachi. If Jinnah had lived for another five years, there is no doubt that he would have transformed Pakistan into a formidable political and economic power.

Pakistan may be a great military power (it is the only Muslim country to have developed nuclear weapons' capability), but its economy is in tatters. Likewise, more than forty per cent of Pakistanis are illiterate and the vast majority continue to live in abject poverty. In short, today's Pakistan is not the kind of Pakistan Jinnah had in mind.

***

Muhammad, Ali Masser (1939-   ): South Yemeni politician, president 1978, 1980-86. Born in the Dathina tribal region of South Yemen, Muhammad trained as a teacher in Aden. In 1996, Muhammad was allowed to return to Yemen.

***

Muhammad Ali Pasha: Ottoman governor of Egypt from 1805 to 1848. He massacred the Mamluks and fought against the Sudan and the Wahhabis in Arabia. Governor of Egypt, an Albanian born in the heart of the Balkans. He liberated Mecca and Medina from Wahhabi dictatorship.

***

Muhammad of Ghor (1150-1206): Afghan conqueror of N India. A brother of the sultan of Ghor, he was made governor of Ghazni in 1173 and from there launched a series of invasions of India. By 1186 he had conquered the Muslim principalities in the Punjab. He was severely defeated by the Rajputs under Prithvi Raj in 1191, but the following year he routed their army, and Delhi was captured. Muhammad's generals then overran Bihar and Bengal. He succeeded his brother as sultan in 1202 but was murdered in 1206. After his death his empire in N India fell apart and passed to his generals, one of whom founded the Delhi Sultanate.

***

Muhammad I (or Mehmet I, Muhammad the Restorer, 1389-1421): Ottoman sultan (1413-1421), son of Beyazid I. By defeating his brothers he reunited most of his father's empire. He consolidated his authority and thus renewed Ottoman power. His son, Murad II, succeeded him.

***

Muhammad Ibn Abdallah ibn al-Muttalib (Prophet of Islam 570-632): Muhammad (26 April 570 – 8 June 632; also spelled **Mohammad** or **Mohammed**; (full name: Muhammad Ibn `Abd Allāh Ibn `Abd al-Muttalib was the founder of the religion of Islam. He is considered by Muslims and Bahá'ís to be a messenger and prophet of God, and by Muslims the last law-bearer in a series of Islamic prophets. Most Muslims consider him to be the last prophet of God as taught by the Quran. Muslims thus consider him the restorer of an uncorrupted original monotheistic faith (*Islam*) of Adam, Noah, Abraham, Moses, Jesus and other prophets.

Born in 570 CE in the Arabian city of Mecca, he was orphaned at an early age and brought up under the care of his uncle Abu Talib. He later worked mostly as a merchant, as well as a shepherd, and was first married by age 25. Discontented with life in Mecca, he retreated to a cave in the surrounding mountains for meditation and reflection. According to Islamic beliefs it was here, at age 40, in the month of Ramadan, where he received his first revelation from God. Three years after this event Muhammad started preaching these revelations publicly, proclaiming that "God is One", that complete "surrender" to Him (lit. *Islam*) is the only way (D*in*) acceptable to God, and that he himself was a prophet and messenger of God, in the same vein as other Islamic prophets.

Muhammad gained few followers early on, and was met with hostility from some Meccan tribes; he and his followers were treated harshly.

To escape persecution, Muhammad sent some of his followers to Abyssinia before he and his remaining followers in Mecca migrated to Medina (then known as Yathrib) in the year 622. This event, the Hijra, marks the beginning of the Islamic calendar, which is also known as the Hijri Calendar. In Medina, Muhammad united the conflicting tribes, and after eight years of fighting with the Meccan tribes, his followers, who by then had grown to 10,000, conquered Mecca. In 632, a few months after returning to Medina from his Farewell pilgrimage, Muhammad fell ill and died. By the time of his death, most of the Arabian Peninsula had converted to Islam, and he had united the tribes of Arabia into a single Muslim religious polity.

The revelations (or *Ayah*, lit. "Signs of God") — which Muhammad reported receiving until his death — form the verses of the Quran, regarded by Muslims as the "Word of God" and around which the religion is based. Besides the Quran, Muhammad's life (S*ira*) and traditions (*sunnah*) are also upheld by Muslims. They discuss Muhammad and other prophets of Islam with reverence, adding the phrase *peace be upon him* whenever their names are mentioned. His life and deeds have been debated and criticized by followers and opponents over the centuries.

Names and appellations in the Quran:

The name *Muhammad* means "Praiseworthy" and occurs four times in the Quran. The Quran addresses Muhammad in the second person not by his name but by the appellations prophet, messenger, servant of God ('*Abd*), announcer (*Bashir*)[Quran 2:119] witness (*Shahid*), [Quran 33:45] bearer of good tidings (M*ubashshir*), Warner (N*athir*), [Quran 11:2] reminder (M*udhakkir*), [Quran 12:108] one who calls [unto God] (*dā'ī*), [Quran 12:108] light personified (*noor*) [Quran 05:15], and the light-giving lamp (S*iraj Munir*) [Quran 73:1]. He is referred to as the enwrapped (*al-Muzzammil*) in **Quran 73:1** and the shrouded in **Quran 74:1**. In the Quran, believers are not to distinguish between the messengers of God and are to believe in all of them (Sura Al-Baqara 2:285). God has caused some messengers to excel above others 2:253 and in Sura Al-Ahzab 33:40 He singles out Muhammad as the "Seal of the Prophets". The Quran also refers to Muhammad as *Aḥmad* "more praiseworthy" (Arabic: Sura As-Saff **61:6**

Sources for Muhammad's life, Quran:
The Quran is the central religious text of Islam and Muslims believe that it represents the words of God revealed to Muhammad through the archangel Gabriel. The Quran however provides little assistance for a chronological biography of Muhammad, and many of the utterances recorded in it lack historical context.

Early biographies:
Next in importance are historical works by writers of the 3rd and 4th centuries of the Muslim era.

The earliest surviving written *Sira* (biographies of Muhammad and quotes attributed to him) is Ibn Ishaq's *Life of God's Messenger* written ca. 767 (150 AH). The work is lost, but was used verbatim at great length by Ibn Hisham and Al-Tabari. Another early source is the history of Muhammad's campaigns by al-Waqidi (death 207 of Muslim era), and the work of his secretary Ibn Sa'd al-Baghdadi (death 230 of Muslim era).

Hadith:
In addition, the Hadith collections are accounts of the verbal and physical traditions of Muhammad that date from several generations after his death. Hadith compilations are records of the traditions or sayings of Muhammad. They might be defined as the biography of Muhammad perpetuated by the long memory of his community for their exemplification and obedience.

Western academics view the Hadith collections with caution as accurate historical sources. Although usually discounted by historians, oral tradition plays a major role in the Islamic understanding of Muhammad.

Non-Arabic sources:
The earliest documented Christian knowledge of Muhammad stems from Byzantine sources. They indicate that both Jews and Christians saw Muhammad as a "false prophet".

Pre-Islamic Arabia, Jahiliyyah, and Arabian mythology :
The Arabian Peninsula was largely arid and volcanic, making agriculture difficult except near oases or springs. The landscape was

thus dotted with towns and cities, two prominent ones being Mecca and Medina. Medina was a large flourishing agricultural settlement, while Mecca was an important financial center for many surrounding tribes. Communal life was essential for survival in the desert conditions, as people needed support against the harsh environment and lifestyle. Tribal grouping was encouraged by the need to act as a unit, this unity being based on the bond of kinship by blood. Nomadic survival was also dependent on raiding caravans or oases, the nomads not viewing this as a crime.

In pre-Islamic Arabia, gods or goddesses were viewed as protectors of individual tribes, their spirits being associated with sacred trees, stones, springs and wells. As well as being the site of an annual pilgrimage, the Kaaba shrine in Mecca housed 360 idol statues of tribal patron deities. Aside from these gods, the Arabs shared a common belief in a supreme deity called Allah (literally "the god"), who was remote from their everyday concerns and thus not the object of cult or ritual. Three goddesses were associated with Allah as his daughters: Allāt, Manāt and al-'Uzzá. Monotheistic communities existed in Arabia, including Christians and Jews. Hanifs – native pre-Islamic Arab monotheists – are also sometimes listed alongside Jews and Christians in pre-Islamic Arabia, although their historicity is disputed amongst scholars. According to Muslim tradition, Muhammad himself was a Hanif and one of the descendants of Ishmael, son of Abraham.

Life in Mecca: Muhammad in Mecca:
Muhammad was born and lived in Mecca for the first 52 years of his life (570–622). This period is generally divided into two phases, before and after declaring the prophecy.

Childhood and early life: Mawlid and Family tree of Muhammad:
Muhammad was born in the month of Rabi' al-awwal in 570. He belonged to the Banu Hashim clan, one of the prominent families of Mecca, although it seems not to have been prosperous during Muhammad's early lifetime. The Banu Hashim clan was part of the Quraysh tribe. Tradition places the year of Muhammad's birth as corresponding with the Year of the Elephant, which is named after the failed destruction of Mecca that year by the Aksumite king Abraha who had in his army a number of elephants. 20th-century scholarship has suggested alternative dates for this event, such as 568 or 569.

Muhammad's father, Abdullah, died almost six months before he was born. According to Islamic tradition, soon after Muhammad's birth he was sent to live with a Bedouin family in the desert, as the desert life was considered healthier for infants. Muhammad stayed with his foster-mother, Halimah bint Abi Dhuayb, and her husband until he was two years old. At the age of six, Muhammad lost his biological mother Amina to illness and he became fully orphaned. For the next two years, he was under the guardianship of his paternal grandfather Abd al-Muttalib, of the Banu Hashim clan, but when Muhammad was eight, his grandfather also died. He then came under the care of his uncle Abu Talib, the new leader of Banu Hashim. While still in his teens, Muhammad accompanied his uncle on trading journeys to Syria gaining experience in commercial trade, the only career open to Muhammad as an orphan.

Marriage:
It is known that he became a merchant and "was involved in trade between the Indian ocean and the Mediterranean Sea." Due to his upright character he acquired the nickname "al-Amin", meaning "faithful, trustworthy" and "al-Sadiq" meaning "truthful" and was sought out as an impartial arbitrator. His reputation attracted a proposal in 595 from Khadijah, a 40-year-old widow who was 15 years older than he. Muhammad consented to the marriage, which by all accounts was a happy one.

Beginnings of the Quran: Muhammad's first revelation:
Muhammad adopted the practice of meditating alone for several weeks every year in a cave on Mount Hira near Mecca. Islamic tradition holds that during one of his visits to Mount Hira, the angel Gabriel appeared to him in the year 610 and commanded Muhammad to recite the following verses:

> Proclaim! (or read!) in the name of thy Lord and Cherisher, Who created-
> Created man, out of a (mere) clot of congealed blood:
> Proclaim! And thy Lord is Most Bountiful,-
> He Who taught (the use of) the pen,-
> Taught man that which he knew not.
> —**Quran, Sura 96** (Al-Alaq), ayat 1-5

After returning home, Muhammad was consoled and reassured by Khadijah and her Christian cousin, Waraqah ibn Nawfal. Upon receiving his first revelations, he was deeply distressed and resolved to commit suicide. He also feared that others would dismiss his claims as being possessed. The initial revelation was followed by a pause of three years during which Muhammad further gave himself to prayers and spiritual practices. When the revelations resumed he was reassured and commanded to begin preaching: "Thy Guardian-Lord hath not forsaken thee, nor is He displeased."

Role of a prophet:

According to the Quran, one of the main roles of Muhammad is to warn the unbelievers of their eschatological punishment (**Quran 38:70, Quran 6:19**). Sometimes the Quran does not explicitly refer to the Judgment day but provides examples from the history of some extinct communities and warns Muhammad's contemporaries of similar calamities (**Quran 41:13–16**). Muhammad is not only a Warner to those who reject God's revelation, but also a bearer of good news for those who abandon evil, listen to the divine word and serve God. Muhammad's mission also involves preaching monotheism: The Quran commands Muhammad to proclaim and praise the name of his Lord and instructs him not to worship idols or associate other deities with God.

The key themes of the early Qur'anic verses included the responsibility of man towards his creator; the resurrection of dead, God's final judgment followed by vivid descriptions of the tortures in hell and pleasures in Paradise; and the signs of God in all aspects of life. Religious duties required of the believers at this time were few: belief in God, asking for forgiveness of sins, offering frequent prayers, assisting others particularly those in need, rejecting cheating and the love of wealth (considered to be significant in the commercial life of Mecca), being chaste and not to kill newborn girls.

Opposition, Persecution of Muslims by the Meccans and Migration to Abyssinia:

According to Muslim tradition, Muhammad's wife Khadijah was the first to believe he was a prophet. She was soon followed by Muhammad's ten-year-old cousin Ali ibn Abi Talib, close friend Abu Bakr, and adopted son Zaid. Around 613, Muhammad began his public preaching (**Quran 26:214**). Most Meccans ignored him and mocked him, while a few others became his followers. There were three main groups of early converts to Islam: younger brothers and sons of great merchants; people who had fallen out of the first rank in their tribe or failed to attain it; and the weak, mostly unprotected foreigners.

As the number of followers increased, he became a threat to the local tribes and the rulers of the city, whose wealth rested upon the Kaaba, the focal point of Meccan religious life, which Muhammad threatened to overthrow. Muhammad's denunciation of the Meccan traditional religion was especially offensive to his own tribe, the Quraysh, as they were the guardians of the Ka'aba.

Tradition records at great length the persecution and ill-treatment of Muhammad and his followers. Sumayyah bint Khabbab, a slave of a prominent Meccan leader Abu Jahl, is famous as the first martyr of Islam, having been killed with a spear by her master when she refused to give up her faith. Bilal, another Muslim slave, was tortured by Umayyah ibn Khalaf who placed a heavy rock on his chest to force his conversion. Apart from insults, Muhammad was protected from physical harm as he belonged to the Banu Hashim clan.

In 615, some of Muhammad's followers emigrated to the Ethiopian Aksumite Empire and founded a small colony there under the protection of the Christian Ethiopian emperor Aṣhama ibn Abjar.

Satanic verses:
Muhammad desperately hoping for an accommodation with his tribe, either from fear or in the hope of succeeding more readily in this way, pronounced a verse acknowledging the existence of three Meccan goddesses considered to be the daughters of Allah, and appealing for their intercession. Muhammad later retracted the verses at the behest of Gabriel, claiming that the verses were whispered by the devil himself. This episode known as "The Story of the Cranes" (transliteration: Qissat al Gharaneeq) is also known as "Satanic Verses".

In 617, the leaders of Makhzum and Banu Abd-Shams, two important Quraysh clans, declared a public boycott against Banu Hashim, their commercial rival, to pressure it into withdrawing its protection of Muhammad. During this, Muhammad was only able to preach during the holy pilgrimage months in which all hostilities between Arabs were suspended.

Isra and Mi'raj (The Night Journey):
Islamic tradition relates that in 620, Muhammad experienced the *Isra and Mi'raj*, a miraculous journey said to have occurred with the angel Gabriel in one night. In the first part of the journey, the *Isra*, he is said to have travelled from Mecca on a winged steed (*Buraq*) to "the farthest mosque" (in Arabic: *Masjid al-Aqsa*), which Muslims usually identify with the Al-Aqsa Mosque in Jerusalem. In the second part, the *Mi'raj*, Muhammad is said to have toured heaven and hell, and spoken with earlier prophets, such as Abraham, Moses, and Jesus. Ibn Ishaq, author of the first biography of Muhammad, presents this event as a spiritual experience whereas later historians like Al-Tabari and Ibn Kathir present it as a physical journey.

Last years in Mecca before Hijra:
Muhammad's wife Khadijah and his uncle Abu Talib both died in 619, the year thus being known as the "year of sorrow". With the

death of Abu Talib, the leadership of the Banu Hashim clan was passed to Abu Lahab, an inveterate enemy of Muhammad. Soon afterwards, Abu Lahab withdrew the clan's protection from Muhammad. This placed Muhammad in danger of death since the withdrawal of clan protection implied that the blood revenge for his killing would not be exacted.

Many people were visiting Mecca on business or as pilgrims to the Kaaba. Muhammad took this opportunity to look for a new home for himself and his followers. After several unsuccessful negotiations, he found hope with some men from Yathrib (later called Medina). The Arab population of Yathrib were familiar with monotheism and prepared for the appearance of a prophet because a Jewish community existed there. Converts to Islam came from nearly all Arab tribes in Medina, such that by June of the subsequent year there were seventy-five Muslims coming to Mecca for pilgrimage and to meet Muhammad. Meeting him secretly by night, the group made what was known as the *"Second Pledge of al-`Aqaba"*, or the *"Pledge of War"* Following the pledges at Aqabah, Muhammad encouraged his followers to emigrate to Yathrib. As with the migration to Abyssinia, the Quraysh attempted to stop the emigration. However, almost all Muslims managed to leave.

Hijra:

The Hijra is the migration of Muhammad and his followers from Mecca to Medina in 622 CE. In September 622, warned of a plot to assassinate him, Muhammad secretly slipped out of Mecca, moving with his followers to Medina, 320 kilometers (200 mi) north of Mecca. The Hijra is celebrated annually on the first day of the Muslim year.

Migration to Medina: Muhammad in Medina:

A delegation consisting of the representatives of the twelve important clans of Medina, invited Muhammad as a neutral outsider to Medina to serve as chief arbitrator for the entire community. There was fighting in Yathrib mainly involving its Arab and Jewish inhabitants for around a hundred years before 620. The delegation from Medina pledged themselves and their fellow-citizens to accept Muhammad into their community and physically protect him as one of themselves.

Muhammad instructed his followers to emigrate to Medina until virtually all his followers left Mecca. Being alarmed at the departure of Muslims, according to the tradition, the Meccans plotted to assassinate Muhammad. With the help of Ali, Muhammad fooled the Meccans who were watching him, and secretly slipped away from the town with Abu Bakr. By 622, Muhammad emigrated to Medina, a large agricultural oasis. Those who migrated from Mecca along with Muhammad became known as *Muhajirun* (emigrants).

Establishment of a new polity: Constitution of Medina:

Among the first things Muhammad did to settle down the longstanding grievances among the tribes of Medina was drafting a document known as the Constitution of Medina, "establishing a kind of alliance or federation" among the eight Medinan tribes and Muslim emigrants from Mecca, which specified the rights and duties of all citizens and the relationship of the different communities in Medina (including that of the Muslim community to other communities, specifically the Jews and other "Peoples of the Book"). The community defined in the Constitution of Medina, *Ummah*, had a religious outlook but was also shaped by practical considerations and substantially preserved the legal forms of the old Arab tribes. It effectively established the first Islamic state.

Several ordinances were proclaimed to win over the numerous and wealthy Jewish population. But these were soon rescinded as the Jews insisted on preserving the entire Mosaic law, and did not recognize him as a prophet because he was not of the race of David.

The first group of pagan converts to Islam in Medina were the clans who had not produced great leaders for themselves but had suffered from warlike leaders from other clans. This was followed by the general acceptance of Islam by the pagan population of Medina. Those Medinans who converted to Islam and helped the Muslim emigrants find shelter became known as the *Ansar* (supporters). Then Muhammad instituted brotherhood between the emigrants and the supporters and he chose Ali as his own brother.

Beginning of armed conflict: Military career of Muhammad and Battle of Badr:

Following the emigration, the Meccans seized the properties of the Muslim emigrants in Mecca. Economically uprooted and with no available profession, the Muslim migrants turned to raiding Meccan caravans, initiating armed conflict with Mecca. Muhammad delivered Qur'anic verses permitting the Muslims to fight the Meccans (see **Sura Al-Hajj, Quran 22:39–40**). These attacks allowed the migrants to acquire wealth, power and prestige while working towards their ultimate goal of conquering Mecca.

On 11 February 624 according to the traditional account, while praying in the Masjid al-Qiblatain in Medina, Muhammad received a revelation from God that he should be facing Mecca rather than Jerusalem during prayer. As he adjusted himself, so did his companions praying with him, beginning the tradition of facing Mecca during prayer. (**2:136–2:147**)

In March 624, Muhammad led some three hundred warriors in a raid on a Meccan merchant caravan. The Muslims set an ambush for them at Badr. Aware of the plan, the Meccan caravan eluded the Muslims. Meanwhile, a force from Mecca was sent to protect the caravan, continuing forward to confront the Muslims upon hearing that the caravan was safe. The Battle of Badr began in March 624. Though outnumbered more than three to one, the Muslims won the battle, killing at least forty-five Meccans with only fourteen Muslims dead. They also succeeded in killing many Meccan leaders, including Abu Jahl. Seventy prisoners had been acquired, many of whom were soon ransomed in return for wealth or freed. Muhammad and his followers saw in the victory a confirmation of their faith.

The victory strengthened Muhammad's position in Medina and dispelled earlier doubts among his followers. As a result the opposition to him became less vocal. Pagans who had not yet converted were very bitter about the advance of Islam. Two pagans, Asma bint Marwan and Abu 'Afak, had composed verses taunting and insulting the Muslims. They were killed by people belonging to their own or related clans, and no blood-feud followed.

Muhammad expelled from Medina the Banu Qaynuqa, one of three main Jewish tribes. Although Muhammad wanted them executed, Abd-Allah ibn Ubaiy chief of the Khazraj tribe did not agree and they were expelled to Syria but without their property. Following the Battle of Badr, Muhammad also made mutual-aid alliances with a number of Bedouin tribes to protect his community from attacks from the northern part of Hijaz.

Conflict with Mecca: Battle of Uhud:

The Meccans were now anxious to avenge their defeat. To maintain their economic prosperity, the Meccans needed to restore their prestige, which had been lost at Badr. In the ensuing months, the Meccans sent ambush parties on Medina while Muhammad led expeditions on tribes allied with Mecca and sent out a raid on a Meccan caravan. Abu Sufyan subsequently gathered an army of three thousand men and set out for an attack on Medina.

A scout alerted Muhammad of the Meccan army's presence and numbers a day later. The next morning, at the Muslim conference of war, there was dispute over how best to repel the Meccans. Muhammad and many senior figures suggested that it would be safer to fight within Medina and take advantage of its heavily fortified strongholds. Younger Muslims argued that the Meccans were destroying their crops, and that huddling in the strongholds would destroy Muslim prestige. Muhammad eventually conceded to the wishes of the latter, and readied the Muslim force for battle. Thus, Muhammad led his force outside to the mountain of Uhud (where the Meccans had camped) and fought the Battle of Uhud on March 23.

Although the Muslim army had the best of the early encounters, indiscipline on the part of strategically placed archers led to a Muslim defeat, with 75 Muslims killed including Hamza, Muhammad's uncle and one of the best known martyrs in the Muslim tradition. Muhammad was wounded and thought to be dead. The Muslims buried the dead, and returned to Medina that evening. Questions accumulated as to the reasons for the loss, and Muhammad subsequently delivered Qur'anic verses 3:152 which indicated that their defeat was partly a punishment for disobedience and partly a test for steadfastness.

Abu Sufyan now directed his efforts towards another attack on Medina. He attracted the support of nomadic tribes to the north and east of Medina, using propaganda about Muhammad's weakness, promises of booty, memories of the prestige of the Quraysh and use of bribes. Muhammad's policy was now to prevent alliances against him as much as he could. When Muhammad heard of men massing with hostile intentions against Medina, he reacted with severity. One example is the assassination of Ka'b ibn al-Ashraf, a chieftain of the Jewish tribe of Banu Nadir who had gone to Mecca and written poems that helped rouse the Meccans' grief, anger and desire for revenge after the Battle of Badr. Around a year later, Muhammad expelled the Banu Nadir from Medina to Syria allowing them to take some of their possessions because he was unable to subdue them in their strongholds. The rest of their property was claimed by Muhammad in the name of God because it was not gained with bloodshed. Muhammad surprised various Arab tribes, one by one, with overwhelming force which caused his enemies to unite to annihilate him.

Siege of Medina: Battle of the Trench:

With the help of the exiled Banu Nadir, the Quraysh military leader Abu Sufyan had mustered a force of 10,000 men. Muhammad prepared a force of about 3000 men and adopted a new form of defense unknown in Arabia at that time: the Muslims dug a trench wherever Medina lay open to cavalry attack. The idea is credited to a Persian convert to Islam, Salman the Persian. The siege of Medina began on March 31 627 and lasted for two weeks. Abu Sufyan's troops were unprepared for the fortifications they were confronted with, and after an ineffectual siege lasting several weeks, the coalition decided to go home. The Quran discusses this battle in Sura Al-Ahzab, ayat (verses) **9-27, 33:9–27.**

During the battle, the Jewish tribe of Banu Qurayza, located at the south of Medina, had entered into negotiations with Meccan forces to revolt against Muhammad. Although they were swayed by suggestions that Muhammad was sure to be overwhelmed, they desired reassurance in case the confederacy was unable to destroy him. No agreement was reached after the prolonged negotiations, in part due to sabotage attempts by Muhammad's scouts. After the coalition's retreat, the Muslims accused the Banu Qurayza of treachery and besieged them in their forts for 25 days. The Banu Qurayza eventually surrendered; according to Ibn Ishaq, all the men apart from a few who converted to Islam were beheaded, while the women and children were enslaved.

In the siege of Medina, the Meccans exerted their utmost strength towards the destruction of the Muslim community. Their failure resulted in a significant loss of prestige; their trade with Syria was gone. Following the Battle of the Trench, he made two expeditions to the north which ended without any fighting. Directing that charges of adultery be supported by four eyewitnesses (**Sura 24, An-Nur**).

Truce of Hudaybiyyah:

Although Muhammad had already delivered Qur'anic verses commanding the Hajj, the Muslims had not performed it due to the enmity of the Quraysh. In the month of Shawwal 628, Muhammad ordered his followers to obtain sacrificial animals and to make preparations for a pilgrimage (Umrah) to Mecca. Upon hearing of the approaching 1,400 Muslims, the Quraysh sent out a force of 200 cavalry to halt them. Muhammad evaded them by taking a more difficult route, thereby reaching al-Hudaybiyya, just outside of Mecca.

Negotiations commenced with emissaries going to and from Mecca. While these continued, rumors spread that one of the Muslim negotiators, Uthman bin al-Affan, had been killed by the Quraysh. Muhammad responded by calling upon the pilgrims to make a pledge not to flee (or to stick with Muhammad, whatever decision he made) if the situation descended into war with Mecca. This pledge became known as the "Pledge of Acceptance" (Arabic: , bay'at al-ridhwān) or the "Pledge under the Tree". News of Uthman's safety, however, allowed for negotiations to continue, and a treaty scheduled to last ten years was eventually signed between the Muslims and Quraysh. The main points of the treaty included the cessation of hostilities; the deferral of Muhammad's pilgrimage to the following year; and an agreement to send back any Meccan who had gone to Medina without the permission of their protector.

Many Muslims were not satisfied with the terms of the treaty. However, the Qur'anic Sura "Al-Fath" (The Victory) (**Quran 48:1–29**) assured the Muslims that the expedition from which they were now returning must be considered a victorious one.

After signing the truce, Muhammad made an expedition against the Jewish oasis of Khaybar, known as the Battle of Khaybar. This was possibly due to it housing the Banu Nadir, who were inciting hostilities against Muhammad, or to regain some prestige to deflect from what appeared to some Muslims as the inconclusive result of the truce of Hudaybiyya. According to Muslim tradition, Muhammad also sent letters to many rulers of the world, asking them to convert to Islam (the exact date is given variously in the sources). In the years following the truce of Hudaybiyya, Muhammad sent his forces against the Arabs on Transjordanian Byzantine soil in the Battle of Mu'tah, in which the Muslims were defeated.

Final Years: Conquest of Mecca:

The truce of Hudaybiyyah had been enforced for two years. The tribe of Banu Khuza'a had good relations with Muhammad, whereas their enemies, the Banu Bakr, had an alliance with the Meccans. A clan of the Bakr made a night raid against the Khuza'a, killing a few of them. The Meccans helped the Banu Bakr with weapons. After this event, Muhammad sent a message to Mecca with three conditions, asking them to accept one of them. These were that either the Meccans paid blood money for those slain among the Khuza'ah tribe; or, that they should disavow themselves of the Banu Bakr; or, that they should declare the truce of Hudaybiyyah null. The Meccans replied that they would accept only the last condition.

Muhammad began to prepare for a campaign. In 630, Muhammad marched on Mecca with an enormous force, said to number more than ten thousand men. With minimal casualties, Muhammad took control of Mecca. He declared an amnesty for past offences, except for ten men and women who had mocked and ridiculed him in songs and verses. Some of these were later pardoned. Most Meccans converted to Islam and Muhammad subsequently had destroyed all the statues of Arabian gods in and around the Kaaba. There are traditional reports that Muhammad personally spared paintings or frescos of Mary and Jesus.

A year after the Battle of Tabuk, the Banu Thaqif sent emissaries to Medina to surrender to Muhammad and adopt Islam. Many Bedouins submitted to Muhammad to be safe against his attacks and to benefit from the booties of the wars. However, the Bedouins were alien to the system of Islam and wanted to maintain their independence, their established code of virtue and their ancestral traditions. Muhammad thus required of them a military and political agreement according to which they "acknowledge the suzerainty of Medina, to refrain from attack on the Muslims and their allies, and to pay the Zakat, the Muslim religious levy."

Farewell pilgrimage:

In 632, at the end of the tenth year after the migration to Medina, Muhammad carried through his first truly Islamic pilgrimage, thereby teaching his followers the rites of the annual Great Pilgrimage (Hajj). After completing the pilgrimage, Muhammad delivered a famous speech known as The Farewell Sermon, at Mount Arafat east of Mecca. In this sermon, Muhammad advised his followers not to follow certain pre-Islamic customs. He declared that an Arab has no superiority over a non-Arab nor a non-Arab has any superiority over an Arab; also a white has no superiority over black nor a black has any superiority over white except by piety and good action. He abolished all old blood feuds and disputes based on the former tribal system and asked for all old pledges to be returned as implications of the creation of the new Islamic community. Commenting on the vulnerability of women in his society, Muhammed asked his male followers to "Be good to women; for they are powerless captives (Awwan) in your households. You took them in God's trust, and legitimated your sexual relations with the Word of God, so come to your senses people, and hear my words ..."

He told them that they were entitled to discipline their wives but should do so with kindness. He addressed the issue of inheritance by forbidding false claims of paternity or of a client relationship to the deceased, and forbade his followers to leave their wealth to a testamentary heir. According to Sunni Tafsir, the following Qur'anic verse was delivered during this event: "Today I have perfected your religion, and completed my favors for you and chosen Islam as a religion for you."(**Quran 5:3**) According to Shi'a Tafsir, it refers to the appointment of Ali ibn Abi Talib at the pond of Khumm as Muhammad's successor, this occurring a few days later when Muslims were returning from Mecca to Medina.

Death and tomb:

A few months after the farewell pilgrimage, Muhammad fell ill and suffered for several days with a fever, head pain, and weakness. He died on Monday, June 8, 632, in Medina, at the age of 63, in the house of his wife Aisha. With his head resting on Aisha's lap he murmured his final words soon after asking her to dispose of his last worldly goods, which were seven coins.

He was buried where he died, in Aisha's house. During the reign of the Umayyad caliph al-Walid I, the Al-Masjid al-Nabawi (the Mosque of the Prophet) was expanded to include the site of

Muhammad's tomb. The Green Dome above the tomb was built by the Mamluk sultan Al Mansur Qalawun in the 13th century, although the green color was added in the 16th century, under the reign of Ottoman sultan Suleiman the Magnificent. When bin Saud took Medina in 1805, Muhammad's tomb was stripped of its gold and jewel ornaments. Adherents to Wahhabism, bin Sauds' followers destroyed nearly every tomb dome in Medina in order to prevent their veneration, and the one of Muhammad is said to have narrowly escaped. Similar events took place in 1925 when the Saudi militias retook—and this time managed to keep—the city. In the Wahhabi interpretation of Islam, burial is to take place in unmarked graves. Although frowned upon by the Saudis, many pilgrims continue to practice a Ziyarat—a ritual visit—to the tomb. Among tombs adjacent to Muhammad's are those of his companions (Sahabah)—the first two Muslim Caliphs Abu Bakr and Umar—, and an empty one that Muslims believe awaits Jesus.

Aftermath: Rashidun, Muslim conquest, and Succession to Muhammad:

Muhammad united the tribes of Arabia into a single Arab Muslim religious polity in the last years of his life. With Muhammad's death, disagreement broke out over who would succeed him as leader of the Muslim community. Umar ibn al-Khattab, a prominent companion of Muhammad, nominated Abu Bakr, Muhammad's friend and collaborator. Others added their support and Abu Bakr was made the first caliph. This choice was disputed by some of Muhammad's companions, who held that Ali ibn Abi Talib, his cousin and son-in-law, had been designated the successor by Muhammad at Ghadir Khumm. Abu Bakr's immediate task was to make an expedition against the Byzantine (or Eastern Roman Empire) forces because of the previous defeat, although he first had to put down a rebellion by Arab tribes in an episode referred to by later Muslim historians as the Ridda wars, or "Wars of Apostasy".

The pre-Islamic Middle East was dominated by the Byzantine and Sassanian empires. The Roman-Persian Wars between the two had devastated the region, making the empires unpopular amongst local tribes. Furthermore, in the lands that would be conquered by Muslims many Christians (Nestorians, Monophysites, Jacobites and Copts) were disaffected from the Christian Orthodoxy which deemed them heretics. Within only a decade, Muslims conquered Mesopotamia and Persia, Roman Syria and Roman Egypt. and established the Rashidun empire.

Early reforms under Islam:

Historians generally agree that Islamic social reforms in areas such as social security, family structure, slavery and the rights of women and children improved on the status quo of Arab society. Islam "from the first denounced aristocratic privilege, rejected hierarchy, and adopted a formula of the career open to the talents". Muhammad's message transformed the society and moral order of life in the Arabian Peninsula through reorientation of society as regards to identity, world view, and the hierarchy of values. Economic reforms addressed the plight of the poor, which was becoming an issue in pre-Islamic Mecca. The Quran requires payment of an alms tax (zakat) for the benefit of the poor.

Household: Muhammad's wives and Ahl al-Bayt:

Muhammad's life is traditionally defined into two periods: pre-Hijra (emigration) in Mecca (from 570 to 622), and post-Hijra in Medina (from 622 until 632). Muhammad is said to have had thirteen wives or concubines. All but two of his marriages were contracted after the migration to Medina.

At the age of 25, Muhammad married the wealthy Khadijah bint Khuwaylid who was 40 years old at that time. The marriage lasted for 25 years and was a happy one. Muhammad relied upon Khadijah in many ways and did not enter into marriage with another woman during this marriage. After the death of Khadijah, it was suggested to Muhammad by Khawla bint Hakim that he should marry Sawda bint Zama, a Muslim widow, or Aisha, daughter of Um Ruman and Abu Bakr of Mecca. Muhammad is said to have asked her to arrange for him to marry both.

Traditional sources dictate that Aisha was six or seven years old when betrothed to Muhammad, but the marriage was not consummated until she was nine or ten years old. After migration to Medina, Muhammad (who was now in his fifties) married several women. These marriages were contracted mostly for political or humanitarian reasons. The women were either widows of Muslims who had been killed in battle and had been left without a protector, or belonging to important families or clans whom it was necessary to honor and strengthen alliances with.

Khadijah is said to have had four daughters with Muhammad—(Ruqayyah bint Muhammad, Umm Kulthum bint Muhammad, Zainab bint Muhammad, Fatimah Zahra)—and two sons—(Abd-Allah ibn Muhammad and Qasim ibn Muhammad)—who both died in childhood. All except two of his daughters, Fatimah and Zainab, died before him. Some Shi'a scholars contend that Fatimah was Muhammad's only daughter. Maria al-Qibtiyya bore him a son named Ibrahim ibn Muhammad, but the child died when he was two years old.

Nine of Muhammad's wives survived him. Aisha, who became known as Muhammad's favorite wife in Sunni tradition, survived him by many decades and was instrumental in helping bring together the scattered sayings of Muhammad that would form the Hadith literature for the Sunni branch of Islam.

Muhammad's descendants through Fatimah are known as *Sharifs, syeds* or *Sayyids*. These are honorific titles in Arabic, *Sharif* meaning 'noble' and *Sayed* or *Sayyid* meaning 'lord' or 'sir'. As Muhammad's only descendants, they are respected by both Sunni and Shi'a, though the Shi'a place much more emphasis and value on their distinction. Zayd ibn Harith was a slave that Muhammad bought, freed, and then adopted as his son. He also had a wet-nurse. Muhammad owned other slaves as well, whom he bought usually to free.

Muslim views: Islamic views of Muhammad:

Following the attestation to the oneness of God, the belief in Muhammad's prophethood is the main aspect of the Islamic faith. Every Muslim proclaims in the Shahadah that "I testify that there is none worthy of worship except God, and I testify that Muhammad is a Messenger of God". The Shahadah is the basic creed or tenet of Islam. Muslims must repeat the Shahadah in the call to prayer (Adhan) and the prayer itself. Non-Muslims wishing to convert to Islam are required to recite the creed.

According to the Quran, Muhammad is only the last of a series of Prophets sent by God for the benefit of mankind, and commands Muslims to make no distinction between them. **Quran 10:37**. While 2:136 commands the believers of Islam to "Say: we believe in God and that which is revealed unto us, and that which was revealed unto Abraham and Ishmael and Isaac and Jacob and the tribes, and that which Moses and Jesus received, and which the prophets received from their Lord. We make no distinction between any of them, and unto Him we have surrendered."

Sunnah:

The Sunnah represents the actions and sayings of Muhammad (preserved in reports known as Hadith), and covers a broad array of activities and beliefs ranging from religious rituals, personal hygiene, burial of the dead to the mystical questions involving the love between humans and God. The Sunnah is considered a model of emulation for pious Muslims and has to a great degree influenced the Muslim culture. Many details of major Islamic rituals such as daily prayers, the fasting and the annual pilgrimage are only found in the Sunnah and not the Quran.

Muslim mystics, known as Sufis, who were seeking for the inner meaning of the Quran and the inner nature of Muhammad, viewed the prophet of Islam not only as a prophet but also as a perfect saint. Sufi orders trace their chain of spiritual descent back to Muhammad. Muslims have traditionally expressed love and veneration for Muhammad. The Quran refers to Muhammad's as "a mercy (*rahmat*) to the worlds: (**Quran 21:107**).

Muhammad's birthday is celebrated as a major feast throughout the Islamic world, excluding Wahhabi-dominated Saudi Arabia where these public celebrations are discouraged. When Muslims say or write the name of Muhammad or any other prophet in Islam, they usually follow it with *Pease be upon him* (Arabic: *sallAllahu 'alayhi wa sallam*).

Islamic depictions of Muhammad:

In line with the Hadith prohibition against creating images of sentient living beings, which is particularly strictly observed with respect to God and the Prophet, Islamic religious art is focused on the word. Muslims generally avoid depictions of Muhammad, and mosques are decorated with calligraphy and Qur'anic inscriptions or geometrical designs, not images or sculptures. Today, the interdiction against images of Muhammad – designed to prevent worship of Muhammad, rather than God – is much more strictly observed in Sunni Islam (85%–90% of Muslims) than among Shi'as (10%–15%).

During the Ilkhanid period, when Persia's Mongol rulers converted to Islam, competing Sunni and Shi'a groups used visual imagery, including images of Muhammad. In the Persian lands, this tradition of realistic depictions lasted through the Timurid dynasty until the Safavids took power in the early sixteenth century. The Safavids, who made Shi'i Islam the state religion, initiated a departure from the traditional Ilkhanid and Timurid artistic style by covering Muhammad's face with a veil to obscure his features and at the same time represent his luminous essence. Later images were produced in Ottoman Turkey and elsewhere, but mosques were never decorated with images of Muhammad.

European and Western views: Medieval Christian views on Muhammad:

A few learned circles of Middle Ages Europe—primarily Latin-literate scholars—had access to fairly extensive biographical material about Muhammad. They interpreted that information through a

Christian religious filter that viewed Muhammad as a charlatan driven by ambition and eagerness for power, and who seduced the Saracens into his submission under a religious guise. Popular European literature of the time portrayed Muhammad as though he were worshipped by Muslims in the manner of an idol or a heathen god. Some medieval Christians believed he died in 666, alluding to the number of the beast, instead of his actual death date in 632; others changed his name from Muhammad to Mahound, the "devil incarnate". Dante's *Divine Comedy* (Canto XXVIII), puts Muhammad, together with Ali, in Hell "among the sowers of discord and the schismatics, being lacerated by devils again and again."

After the reformation, Muhammad was often portrayed as a cunning and ambitious impostor. Friedrich Martin von Bodenstedt (1851) described Muhammad as "an ominous destroyer and a prophet of murder."

Michael H. Hart in his first book *The 100: A Ranking of the Most Influential Persons in History* (1978), a ranking of the 100 people who most influenced human history, chose Muhammad in both the religious and secular realms.

Prophet Muhammad:
Prophet, Messenger, Apostle, Witness, Bearer of Good:
Cause of death:
Illness (high fever)
Resting place:
Tomb under the Green Dome of Al-Masjid al-Nabawi in Medina, Hejaz, Saudi Arabia

Wives:
Khadijah bint Khuwaylid (595-619)
Sawda bint Zamʿa (619-632)
Aisha bint Abi Bakr (619-632)
Hafsah bint Umar (624-632)
Zaynab bint Khuzayma (625-627)
Hind bint Abi Umayya (629-632)
Zaynab bint Jahsh (627-632)
Juwayriya bint al-Harith (628-632)
Ramlah bint Abi Sufyan (628-632)
Rayhana bint Zayd (629-631)
Safiyya bint Huyayy (629-632)
Maymuna bint al-Harith (630-632)
Maria al-Qibtiyya (630-632)

Children:
Sons: al-Qasim, 'Abd-Allah, Ibrahim
Daughters: Zainab, Ruqayyah, Umm Kulthum, Fatimah Zahra

Parents:
Father: `Abd Allah ibn `Abd al-Muttalib
Mother: Aminah bint Wahb
Relatives: Ahl al-Bayt:

Timeline of Muhammad in Mecca:
Important dates and locations in the life of Muhammad in Mecca

569	Death of his father, Abdullah
570	Possible date of birth, April 26th: Mecca
576	Death of his mother, Aminah
578	Death of his grandfather
583	Takes trading journeys to Syria
595	Meets and marries Khadijah
610	First reports of Qur'anic revelation
613	Begins spreading message of Islam publicly to all Makkans
614	Begins to gather followers in Mecca
615	Emigration of Muslims to Ethiopia
616	Banu Hashim clan boycott begins
618	Medinan War
619	Banu Hashim clan boycott ends
619	The year of sorrows: Khadijah(his wife and Abu Talib (his uncle) die
620	Isra and Mi'raj (the ascension to heaven to meet God)
622	Emigrates to Medina (was called Yathrib) (Hijra)

Timeline of Muhammad in Medina:

622	Emigrates to Medina (Hijra)
623	Caravan Raids begin
623	Al Kudr Invasion
624	Battle of Badr: Muslims defeat Meccans
624	Battle of Sawiq, Abu Sufyan escapes capture
624	Expulsion of Banu Qaynuqa
624	Invasion of Thi Amr, Muhammed raids Ghatafan tribes
624	Assassination of Khaled b. Sufyan & Abu Rafi
625	Battle of Uhud: Meccans defeat Muslims
625	Tragedy of Bir Maona and Al Raji
625	Invasion of Hamra al-Asad, successfully terrifies enemy to cause retreat
625	Banu Nadir expelled after Invasion

625	Invasion of Nejd, Badr and Dumatul Jandal
627	Battle of the Trench
627	Invasion of Banu Qurayza, successful siege
628	Treaty of Hudaybiyyah, gains access to Kaaba
628	Conquest of the Khaybar oasis
629	First hajj pilgrimage
629	Attack on Byzantine Empire fails: Battle of Mu'tah
630	Bloodless conquest of Mecca
630	Battle of Hunayn
630	Siege of Ta'if
631	Rules most of the Arabian peninsula
632	Attacks the Ghassanids: Tabuk
632	Farewell hajj pilgrimage
632	Wasal (June 8): Medina

***

Muhammad's wives and children: Muhammad's **wives** were the twelve women married to the Islamic prophet Muhammad. Muslims refer to them as Mothers of the Believers (Arabic: Ummahāt ul-Mu'minin). Muslims use the term prominently before or after referring to them as a sign of respect. The term is derived from **Quran 33:6**

Muhammad's life is traditionally delineated as two epochs: pre-Hijra (emigration) in Mecca, a city in northern Arabia, from the year 570 to 622, and post-Hijra in Medina, from 622 until his death in 632. All but two of his marriages were contracted after the Hijra (migration to Medina).

In Arabian culture, marriage was contracted in accordance with the larger needs of the tribe and was based on the need to form alliances within the tribe and with other tribes. Virginity at the time of marriage was emphasized as a tribal honor. All of Muhammad's marriages had the political aspect of strengthening friendly relationships and were based on the Arabian custom. Some of Muhammad's marriages were aimed at providing a livelihood for widows. Muhammad's first marriage lasted 25 years.

1 –Khadijah bint Khuwaylid:

At age 25, Muhammad wed his wealthy employer, the 40-year-old merchant Khadijah. This marriage, his first, would be both happy and monogamous; Muhammad would rely on the wealthy Khadijah in many ways, until her death 25 years later. They had two sons, Qasim and Abd-Allah (nicknamed al-Ṭāhir and al-Tayyib respectively), both died young, and four daughters—Zaynab, Ruqayyah, Umm Kulthum and Fatimah. During their marriage, Khadijah purchased the slave Zayd ibn Harithah, then adopted the young man as her son at Muhammad's request.

2 –Sawda bint Zam'a:

The death of Khadijah left Muhammad lonely, and, before he left for Medina, it was suggested by Khawlah bint Hakim that he marry Sawda bint Zam'a, who had suffered many hardships after she became a Muslim. Prior to that, Sawda was married to a paternal cousin of hers named As-Sakran bin 'Amr, and had five or six sons from her previous marriage. At about the same period, Aisha was betrothed to him. As Sawda got older, and sometime after Muhammad's marriage to Umm Salama, some sources claim that Muhammad wished to divorce Sawda.

3 –Aisha bint Abi Bakr:

Aisha was the daughter of Muhammad's close friend Abu Bakr. She was initially betrothed to Jubayr ibn Mut'im, a Muslim whose father, though pagan, was friendly to the Muslims. When Khawlah bint Hakim suggested that Muhammad marry Aisha after the death of Muhammad's first wife (Khadijah), the previous agreement regarding marriage of Aisha with ibn Mut'im was put aside by common consent. Aisha was six or seven years old when betrothed to Muhammad. Traditional sources state that she stayed in her parents' home until the age of nine when the marriage was consummated with Muhammad, then 53, in Medina, with the single exception of al-Tabari, who records that she was ten. Both Aisha and Sawda, his two wives, were given apartments adjoined to the Al-Masjid al-Nabawi mosque.

4+5 –Hafsa bint Umar and Zaynab bint Khuzayma:

During the Muslim war with Mecca, many men were killed leaving behind widows and orphans. Hafsa bint Umar, daughter of Umar ('Umar bin Al-Khattab), was widowed at battle of Badr when her husband Khunais ibn Hudhaifa was killed in action. Muhammad married her in 3 A.H./625 C.E. Zaynab bint Khuzayma was also widowed at the battle of Badr. She was the wife of 'Ubaydah b. al-Harith, a faithful Muslim and from the tribe of al-Muttalib, for which Muhammad had special responsibility. When her husband died, Muhammad aiming to provide for her, married her 4 A.H. She was nicknamed Umm Al-Masakeen (roughly translates as the mother of the poor), because of her kindness and charity.

6 – Hind bint Abi Umayya (Umm Salama):

The death of Zaynab coincided with that of Abu Salamah, a devout Muslim, as a result of his wounds from the Battle of Uhud. Abu Salamah's widow, Umm Salama Hind bint Abi Umayya also a devoted Muslim, had none but her young children. Her manless plight reportedly saddened the Muslims, and after her Iddah some Muslims proposed marriage to her; but she declined. When Muhammad proposed her marriage, she was reluctant for three reasons: she claimed to suffer from jealousy and pointed out the prospect of an unsuccessful marriage, her old age, and her young family that needed support. But Muhammad replied that he would pray to God to free her from jealousy, that he too was of old age, and that her family was like his family. She married Muhammad

Internal dissension:

After Muhammad's final battle against his Meccan enemies, he diverted his attention to stopping the Banu Mustaliq's raid on Medina. During this skirmish, Medinan dissidents, begrudging Muhammad's influence, attempted to attack him in the more sensitive areas of his life, including his marriage to Zaynab bint Jahsh, and an incident in which Aisha left her camp to search her lost necklace, and returned with a Companion of Muhammad.

7 – Zaynab bint Jahsh:

Zaynab bint Jahsh was Muhammad's cousin, being the daughter of one of his father's sisters. In Medina, Muhammad arranged Zaynab's marriage, a widow, to Zayd ibn Harithah. Zaynab disapproved of the marriage and her brothers rejected it, because according to Ibn Sa'd, she was of aristocratic lineage and Zayd was a former slave and the adopted son of Muhammad. Muhammad, however, was determined to establish the legitimacy and right to equal treatment of the adopted. It is not clear why Zaynab was unwilling to marry Zayd as Zayd was held in a high place in Muhammad's esteem. Watt discusses the following two possibilities: being an ambitious woman, she was already hoping to marry Muhammad; and the other she may have been wanting to marry someone of whom Muhammad disapproved for political reason. In any case, Watt says, it is almost certain that she was working for marriage with Muhammad before the end of 626. According to Maududi, the Qur'anic verse 33:36 was revealed, thus Zaynab acquiesced and married Zayd. Zaynab's marriage was unharmonious, and eventually became unbearable. Zaynab told Zayd about this, and Zayd offered to divorce her, but Muhammad told him to keep her. The story laid much stress on

Islamic Leaders

Zaynab's perceived beauty and Muhammad's supposedly disturbed set of mind.

The marriage seemed incestuous to Muhammad's contemporaries because Muhammad was marrying the former wife of his adopted son, and the adopted sons were counted the same as a biological son. Muhammad's decision to marry Zaynab was an attempt to break the hold of pre-Islamic ideas over men's conduct in society.[citation needed] Initially, however, he was reluctant to marry Zaynab, fearing public opinion. The Qur'an, however, indicated that this marriage was a duty imposed upon him by God. When Zaynab's waiting period was complete, Muhammad married her. However, the marriage was justified by verse 33:37 of the Qur'an, which implied that treating adopted sons as real sons was objectionable, and that there should now be a complete break with the past. The delivery of these verses, thus, did not end the dissent.

8 –Juwayriyya bint al-Harith:

One of the captives from the skirmish with the Banu Mustaliq was Juwayriyya bint al-Harith, who was the daughter of the tribe's chieftain. Her husband, Mustafa bin Safwan, had been killed in the battle. She initially fell among the booty of Muhammad's companion Thabit b. Qays b. Al-Shammas. Upon being enslaved, Juwayriyya went to Muhammad requesting that she – as the daughter of the lord of the Mustaliq – be released, however the Prophet refused. Meanwhile her father approached Muhammad with ransom to secure her release, but Muhammed still refused to release her. Muhammad then offered to marry her, and she accepted. When it became known that tribes persons of Mustaliq were kinsmen of the prophet of Islam through marriage, the Muslims began releasing their captives. Thus, Muhammad's marriage resulted in the freedom of nearly one hundred families whom he had recently enslaved.

9 –Rayhana bint Zayd:

In 626, Rayhana bint Zayd, was among those enslaved after the defeat of the Banu Qurayza tribe. Her relationship with Muhammed is disputed. The sources regarding her status differ as to whether she was a concubine or whether she eventually married him. Most of the sources reveal that she was a slave woman.

10 –Safiyya bint Huyeiy Ibn Akhtab:

In 629, after the Battle of Khaybar, Muhammad freed Safiyya bint Huyayy a noblewoman and the daughter of Huyeiy Ibn Akhtab, of the defeated Jewish tribe Banu Nadir, where her father and husband were killed in battle. Muhammad freed her from her captor Dihya and proposed marriage. Safiyya accepted. Scholars believe that Muhammad married Safiyya as part of reconciliation with the Jewish tribe and as a gesture of goodwill. Safiyyah had been previously married to Kenana ibn al-Rabi, a commander who was executed, and before that to the poet Sallam ibn Mishkam, who had divorced her. He then convinced Safiyya to convert to Islam and marry him. She was then seventeen and known for her extreme beauty. Because she was the daughter of a tribal chief, she was given the offer of marrying the Prophet and remaining free, rather than be enslaved. She accepted this offer. She greatly respected Muhammed as "Allah's Messenger". She was intelligent, learned and gentle. She had many good moral qualities. Upon entering Muhammad's household, Safiyya became friends with Aisha and Hafsa, and also offered gifts to Fatima. But when Muhammad's other wives spoke ill of Safiyya's Jewish descent, Muhammad intervened, pointing out to everyone that Safiyya's "husband is Muhammad, father is Aaron, and uncle is Moses", a reference to revered Islamic prophets.

The Prophet Muhammad apologized to Safiyyah for the killing of her father and her husband by saying, "Your father charged the Arabs against me and committed heinous act," he apologized to the extent that made Safiyyah get rid of her bitterness against the Prophet.

Safiyyah moved to the house of the Prophet. He loved, appreciated and honored her. Safiyyah(R) remained loyal to the Prophet until he died. The marriage to Safiyyah(R) had a political significance as well, as it helped to reduce hostilities and cement alliances. Safiyyah was a humble worshiper and a pious believer.

Safiyyah was a very charitable and generous woman.

When Muhammad was in his final illness, Safiyyah felt deep and sincere sadness for him. She said: *"O Messenger of Allah, I wish it was I who was suffering instead of you."*

11 –Ramla bint Abi Sufyan (Umm Habiba):

In the same year, Muhammad signed a peace treaty with his Meccan enemies, the Quraysh, effectively ending the state of war between the two parties. He soon married the daughter of the Quraysh leader, Abu Sufyan ibn Harb, aimed at further reconciling his opponents. He sent a proposal for marriage to Ramla bint Abi Sufyan who was in Abyssinia at the time, when he learned her husband had died. She had previously converted to Islam (in Mecca) against her father's will. After her migration to Abyssinia her husband had converted to Christianity, and although she remained a steadfast Muslim. Muhammad dispatched 'Amr bin Omaiyah Ad-Damri with a letter to the Negus (king), asking him for Umm Habiba's hand — that was in Muharram, in the seventh year of Al-Hijra.

12 –Maria al-Qibtiyya:

Maria al-Qibtiyya was an Egyptian Coptic Christian slave, sent as a gift to Muhammad from Muqawqis, a Byzantine official. and bore him a son Ibrahim ibn Muhammad, who died in infancy.

13 –Maymuna bint al-Harith:

As part of the treaty of Hudaybiyyah, Muhammad visited Mecca for the lesser pilgrimage. There Maymuna bint al-Harith proposed marriage to him. Muhammad accepted, and thus married Maymuna, the sister-in-law of Abbas, a long time ally of his. By marrying her, Muhammad also established kinship ties with the Banu Makhzum, his previous opponents. As the Meccans did not allow him to stay any longer, Muhammad left the city, taking Maymuna with him. Her original name was "Barra" but the Prophet called her "Maymuna", meaning the blessed, as his marriage to her had also marked the first time in seven years when he could enter his hometown Mecca.

Muhammad's widows:

According to the Qur'an, God forbade anyone to marry the wives of Muhammad, because of their respect and honor, after he died.

> Nor is it right for you that ye should annoy Allah's Messenger, or that ye should marry his widows after him at any time.**(Quran 33:53)**

Although **[Qur'an 2:180]** clearly addresses issues of inheritance, Abu Bakr, the new leader of the Muslim Ummah, refused to divide Muhammad's property among his widows and heirs, saying that he had heard Muhammad say:

> "We (Prophets) do not have any heirs; what we leave behind is (to be given in) charity."

Muhammad's widow Hafsa played a role in the collection of the first Qur'anic manuscript. After Abu Bakr had collected the copy, he gave it to Hafsa, who preserved it until Uthman took it, copied it and distributed it in Muslim lands.

The grave of the wives of Muhammad is located at al-Baqīʿ Cemetery, Medina.

Family life:

Muhammad and his family lived in small apartments adjacent the mosque at Medina. According to an account by Anas bin Malik said, "The Prophet used to visit all his wives in a round, during the day and night and they were eleven in number."

Although Muhammad's wives had a special status as Mothers of the Believers, he did not allow them to use his status as a prophet to obtain special treatment in public.

Umm-al-Momineen:
Wives of Muhammad:

1. Khadijah bint Khuwaylid
2. Sawda bint Zam'a
3. Aisha bint Abi Bakr
4. Hafsa bint Umar
5. Zaynab bint Khuzayma
6. Hind bint Abi Umayya
7. Zaynab bint Jahsh
8. Juwayriyya bint al-Harith
9. Rayhana bint Zayd
10. Safiyya bint Huyayy (*)
11. Ramla bint Abi Sufyan
12. Maria al-Qibtiyya (**)
13. Maymuna bint al-Harith

* = Jewish
** = Egyptian Coptic Slave

***

Muhammad ibn al-Qasim (694-715): Prior to his death in 705, the great Umayyad Caliph Abd al-Malik ibn Marwan nominated his eldest son, al-Walid, as his successor and he went on to rule the vast Islamic dominion for a decade, during which he spearheaded some of Islamic history's most astonishing military conquests. Under Caliph al-Walid's leadership, Muslims launched simultaneous military expeditions in Africa, Europe and Asia, and successfully out-maneuvered their opponents on all three continents. While Qutaybah was making rapid progress in Central Asia, the legendary Tariq ibn Ziyad left North Africa and landed in Gibraltar (the name Gibraltar is derived from the Arabic *Jabal al-Tariq* or the 'Mount of Tariq'), and from there moved into Spain; thus for the first time Islam came into direct contact with mainland Europe. Under the inspirational leadership of young Muhammad ibn al-Qasim, Muslims marched as far as the Indus valley and brought a large part of India under Islamic rule for the first time.

Muhammad ibn al-Qasim ibn Abu Aqil was born during the successful reign of Caliph Abd al-Malik. Young Muhammad ibn al-Qasim grew up at a time when his uncle, Hajjaj ibn Yusuf, served as a prominent member of the Umayyad political administration. When Muhammad ibn al-Qasim reached maturity, he married governor Hajjaj's daughter and settled in Kufah.

After establishing Umayyad suzerainty throughout the Eastern province, Hajjaj hoped to send a military expedition to India. It was at the behest of Umayyad Caliph al-Walid that Hajjaj finally got the chance to send an expedition to India. Renowned for their sailing and navigational skills, the early Muslim traders and merchants travelled regularly to distant lands in pursuit of commerce. Some even settled on remote Indian Ocean islands, like Ceylon, where they established businesses and befriended the locals and their rulers.

An army was sent to Sind to out Raja Dahir from power, but the latter defeated the Muslim army. Hajjaj then sent a second force against the Hindu ruler who again crushed the Muslim army with the assistance of his traditional war elephants. The governor turned to Muhammad ibn al-Qasim (his seventeen year old nephew and son-in-law) to take matters into his hands and bring the arrogant Hindu ruler to heel. He instructed the young and inexperienced Muhammad ibn al-Qasim to take the battle to the Hindu ruler. A young but inspirational Muhammad ibn al-Qasim led the Muslim army to Makran – unaware of the fact that he was about to walk straight into the history books as one of the Muslim world's great military generals.

From Iraq, Muhammad ibn al-Qasim travelled swiftly through the province of Fars to the Makran desert and on the way he was joined by another Muslim battalion, thus reinforcing his contingent. Keen to subdue the town quickly, he immediately brought his catapult into action after receiving information from a disgruntled local Hindu priest. On the third attempt, the catapult hit the target and this caused widespread panic and commotion inside the fortress; it was not long before the Muslims captured the town. After releasing all the Muslims from captivity in Debul – and having also secured a part of the Indian Ocean for the Arab navy – Muhammad ibn al-Wasim vowed to bring the treacherous Raja Dahir to justice. In 712, when he was barely eighteen, he took control of this fortress without shedding a drop of blood.

Muhammad ibn al-Qasim preferred to win the hearts and minds of the locals through justice, kindness and fair play, rather than use the sword; indeed, he only used the sword as a last resort.

In June 712, Muhammad ibn al-Qasim led the Muslim army into one of the most decisive battles of his military career. Led by Jai Singh, the defeated Hindus fled to Brahmanabad but Rawar soon fell into the hands of the Muslims.

Unfortunately, due to a family dispute back in Damascus, Caliph Sulaiman later recalled Muhammad ibn al-Qasim from the subcontinent and reportedly had his tortured to death at the age of twenty-one. His tragic and premature death not only deprived the Muslim world of one of its most celebrated military generals, it also delayed Islamic expansion into the rest of the subcontinent by another three hundred years.

***

Muhammad Ilyas (1885-1944): Muhammad ibn al-Qasim's foray into the province of Sind at the beginning of the eighth century brought political Islam directly in contact with India. Unfortunately, his military excursion into India was brought to a sudden halt by the Umayyad Caliph Sulaiman who recalled Muhammad ibn al-Qasim to Damascus following a family dispute. Led by the Sufi missionaries, Muslims poured into India and began to spread the good news of Islam throughout that country. Thanks to the efforts of these Sufi luminaries, large numbers of Hindus embraced Islam and, as a result, the message of Islam began to spread across India. Not surprisingly, therefore, many of these converts continued to lead a Hindu lifestyle while professing to be Muslims. This state of affairs persisted in many parts of India until Muhammad Ilyas founded the *Tablighi Jama'at* (or Organization for Islamic Propagation) to address their religious needs and requirements.

Muhammad Ilyas, also known as Mawlana Ilyas, was born in the town of Kandhla (located close to Delhi). After his father's death in 1898, young Ilyas and his brother were raised by their mother. Prior to his death in 1905, Mawlana Gangohi, a renowned Islamic scholar and Sufi, personally initiated the twenty year old Ilyas into Sufism and during this period he completed his intermediate education and became proficient in Arabic, *Tafsir* (Qur'anic exegesis), *Hadith* (Prophetic traditions) and aspects of Sufism. Then, in 1908, Ilyas enrolled at the famous *dar al-uloom* (Islamic seminary) in Deoband where he completed advanced training in *Tafsir* and *Hadith* under *Shaykh al-hind* Mawlana Mahmud ul-Hasan, and also received training in Sufism under the guidance of Mawlana Khalil Ahmad Saharanpuri.

After qualifying as an Islamic scholar at the age of twenty-five, Ilyas began to teach at M*azahir ul-Islam* seminary at Saharanpur. In 1914, he took leave from teaching and went to Mecca to perform the sacred *hajj*, and resumed teaching on his return. In the same year his brother and mentor, Mawlana Muhammad Yahya, suddenly died. His death profoundly affected Ilyas.

The success of the *Tablighi Jama'at* enhanced his reputation as an eminent scholar and reformer of Islam. Despite being preoccupied with the supervision and expansion of *Tablighi* activities, Ilyas found time to perform his third *hajj* in 1932. On his return home from Mecca, he began to establish *Tablighi* centers throughout Mewat. His religious methodology proved so successful that over time the *Tablighi Jama'at* became one of India's most popular Islamic movements, even during his own lifetime.

Ilyas performed his fourth and last pilgrimage in 1938. Six years later, he died at the age of fifty-nine and was buried in Nizamuddin. New *Tablighi* centers mushroomed in both East and West Pakistan. Subsequently, under the leadership of Mawlana Inam ul-Hasan, *Tablighi Jama'at* spread across the world including Southeast Asia, Africa, Europe, as well as the Americas.

***

Muhammad Iqbal, Sir (1877-1938): During the late nineteenth and early twentieth century, India produced some of the most influential Muslim leaders, thinkers and writers of the modern period. Not willing to live under British rule, the Indian Muslims spearheaded the Indian liberation movement. Sir Muhammad Iqbal, the hugely influential Muslim thinker and poet-philosopher of the subcontinent, belonged to this generation of outstanding Indian Muslims.

Muhammad Iqbal's date of birth is hotly contested by the historians. Some say he was born in 1873; others say he was born in 1877, while according to others he was born in 1876. His ancestors were Hindu Brahmins who originally hailed from Kashmir and embraced Islam during the seventeenth century. Iqbal was born in Sialkot into a lower-middle class Muslim family. A tailor by profession, his father, Nur Muhammad, was an illiterate Sufi who owned a small business.

When he was sixteen, Iqbal joined the Scotch Mission College (the present-day Murray College) and successfully completed his intermediate studies. At the age of about nineteen, he moved to Lahore and enrolled at the Government College. After graduating with honors in Arabic and English literature, and also obtaining a master's degree in philosophy, he became a lecturer in Arabic at the Oriental College in Lahore; he was only twenty-three at the time.

Following Sir Thomas Arnold's departure from Lahore for London in 1904, Iqbal followed suit and moved to England in 1905. After obtaining a degree in philosophy, he moved to Munich University in Germany where he pursued continental philosophy and wrote a doctoral thesis on the development of metaphysics in Persia. Thereafter, he returned to England where he was called to the Bar at London's Lincoln's Inn and qualified as a barrister. Full of life and vitality, he found the European people friendly, hardworking and studious.

Iqbal had left India in 1905 as a young scholar, poet and nationalist, but his stay in Europe radically transformed his view of Islam and its place and role in history. If Western civilization had made great progress in the fields of science and technology, it did so at the expense of moral and spiritual advancement. This, in his opinion, did not constitute progress or advancement; it was similar to building a castle on shifting sand; a disaster waiting to happen. After leaving London in 1908, he returned home to India at the age of thirty-one and began to explore the problems and predicaments of modern civilization in the light of Islamic values and principles. As a gifted poet and philosopher, Iqbal expounded his ideas and thoughts in his elegant and powerful poetry, which he wrote in both Urdu and Persian.

The period from 1908 to 1936 was the most intellectually productive period of Iqbal's life. He expounded his religious ideas and philosophical thoughts in scores of books of poetry published over more than thirty years. He developed a powerful and dynamic philosophy which called on the Muslims to rise up and boldly face the challenges posed by Western modernity, secularism and nationalism. He urged the Muslims to take their destiny in their own hands by freeing themselves from European colonial rule, and to rediscover the creativity and dynamism that is inherent in the meaning and message of Islam.

Iqbal served as a member of Punjab Legislative Council, was knighted in 1922 and became the president of All-India Muslim League in 1930, thus occupying a prominent position in Indian public life. It was during his tenure as president of the Muslim League that he developed the idea of creating a separate homeland for the Muslims of India. Later, in 1947, Muhammad Ali Jinnah pursued and realized his vision in the form of the Islamic Republic of Pakistan. Iqbal did not live long enough to witness this momentous event; he died of illness at the age of sixty-one and was buried next to the famous Badshahi mosque in Lahore.

***

Islamic Leaders

Muhammad, Khalid Shaikh (1965-   ): Al Qaida leader. Born to Pakistani Baluchi parents settled in Kuwait since 1961, Muhammad grew up in a suburb of Kuwait city. When Yousef was arrested in Pakistan in February 1995 in connection with the bombing of the World Trade Center in New York years earlier, which killed six people and injured 1,200 his chief coconspirator turned out to be Muhammad. But by the time the Qatari government tipped off by the US federal Bureau of Investigation got around to issuing an arrest warrant in 1996 Muhammad had absconded. He formally joined Al Qaida. After the formation of the World Islamic Front for Jihad against Crusaders and Jews in February 1998, he was appointed to the military committee headed by Muhammad Atef. Impressed by his record, Atef reportedly made him his deputy. He was arrested in the Pakistani city of Rawalpindi in February 2003 and handed over to US authorities.

***

Muhammad, Khwarazmshah (1200-1220): Ruler of a dynasty in Khwarazm, who tried to establish a strong monarchy in Iran but incurred the wrath of the Mongols and brought about the first Mongol invasions.

***

Muhammad Musadeq (-   ): Iranian politician, Iran's prime minister An eccentric Iranian politician acting as prime minister under a constitutional monarchy, nationalized British oil holdings (1951) against the wishes of Shah Muhammad Riza Pahlavi. He was overthrown with the help of the CIA, and the Shah was restored to power.

***

Muhammad Reza Pahlavi (1944-1979): Shah: the second Pahlavi shah of Iran, whose aggressively modernizing and secularizing policies led to the Islamic revolution. (1919-1980) Shah of Iran (1941-79). The son of Reza Shah Phalavi he succeeded on the abdication of his father. After the fall of Mussadegh in 1953 he gained supreme power and with the aid of greatly increased oil revenues, embarked upon a policy of rapid social reform and economic development, while maintaining a regime of harsh repression towards his opponents. In 1962 he introduced a land reform program to break landlord power. In 1979 he was deposed by a revolution led by the Islamic clergy, notably Ayatollah Khomeini, whose supporters were bitterly opposed to the pro-western regime of the

Shah. He died in exile in Egypt. Shah of Iran at the time of the revolution led by Ayatollah Khomeini in 1979

***

Muhammad Riza Shah (-): Shah as of 1941. Son and successor to Riza Shah; continued anti-Islamic policies of his father, resulting in his overthrow and the establishment of an Islamic State by the Islamic Revolution of 1979 (let by Ayatollah Khomeini).

***

Muhammad V or Mehmet V (1844-1918): Ottoman sultan (1909-18). He succeeded to the throne of the Ottoman Empire (Turkey) when the liberal Young Turk revolution of 1909 deposed his brother, Abd al-Hamid II. He exercised no actual power under the new constitution, and the administration was dominated by Enver Pasha. During Muhammads reign Turkey lost much of its remaining European possessions in the Balkan Wars (1912-1913) and lost Tripoli to Italy in 1911-1912. Germany gained increasing influence over Turkish affairs, resuming the construction of the Baghdad Railway in 1911. Muhammad sided with the Central Powers in World War I. He died shortly before the Turkish surrender and was succeeded by his brother, Muhammad VI.

***

Muhammad Yunus (1940-): When the early Muslim traders and merchants first arrived in the coastal regions of India in the seventh century, they were welcomed with open arms by the locals. Though these pioneering Muslims came primarily to conduct business, over time they married and settled in some of the most remote coastal towns and villages of India, Ceylon, Sumatra and Maldives. When Ibn Battutah, the celebrated fourteenth century Muslim globetrotter, visited those areas he was surprised to find thriving indigenous Muslim communities in all the major coastal regions of India, Ceylon and Sumatra. Muhammad Yunus, one of the most radical economists of contemporary times and arguably the single most influential banker of the twentieth century, hailed from this age-old center of commerce and spirituality.

Born and brought up in a lower-middle class Muslim family, young Yunus attended his local schools where he studied Bengali language, literature, mathematics and aspects of science. The Second World War had started in 1939 and the British – who still maintained their grip on India – had joined the fight against the Nazis in Europe. As an integral part of British India, East Bengal also faced an imminent military invasion from the Japanese who were, at the time, making rapid progress in the East. As it transpired, the British had no choice but to quit India in 1947 after agreeing to Muhammad Ali Jinnah's demand for a separate homeland for the Muslims of India; Yunus was only seven at the time.

After graduating from Dhaka University in 1961, he lectured on economics at Chittagong College until 1965 when he won a Fulbright scholarship to read economics in the United States. He left his native East Pakistan and moved to the United States to pursue research in economics at Vanderbilt University in Tennessee. In 1972 he returned to a new country – now named Bangladesh – with a doctorate in economics. As a Bengali nationalist, Yunus was happy to see Bangladesh appear on the world map. On a personal level, his relationship with his Russian wife, who bore him a daughter, also deteriorated until she finally left him and returned to the United States.

From 1972 to 1976, Yunus explored different ways in which he could improve the economic condition of the local villagers. He came up with the idea of lending small amounts of money to the very poor in order to encourage them to set up small businesses. The borrower was required to repay the sum, plus a nominal amount of interest, over a period of time out of the profits generated from the business. Pioneered by Yunus in 1976, this method of lending small sums of money to some of the world's poorest people became known as the 'system of microcredit'.

In his attempts to obtain bank loans for the poor, Yunus discovered that conventional banks operated on a principle which automatically excluded the very poor from receiving any form of credit. This prompted him to set up the Grameen ('village') Bank experiment in 1977 in order to provide credit to the poor, especially to the women, in rural areas of Bangladesh. "Indeed, more than 98 percent of our loans are repaid, because the poor know this is the only opportunity they have to break out of poverty." From then on, the Grameen Bank gradually expanded across rural Bangladesh so that today it provides help to millions of poor and needy people across Bangladesh through its microcredit self-help schemes. The Grameen Bank has turned the basic banking principle on its head, because it does not operate on the premise of collateral.

The system of micro-credit pioneered by Yunus back in the 1970s has not only proved to be a great success in rural Bangladesh; the concept has since been successfully replicated in more than sixty countries around the world including the United States, United

Kingdom, Canada, France, Australia, Malaysia, China, Norway and Finland.

In his acceptance speech for the World Food Prize, awarded to him in 1994, Yunus stated, "Brilliant theories of economics do not take into account issues of poverty and hunger. They tend to imply that these problems will be solved when the march of economic prosperity will sweep through the nations…I feel very strongly that if the world recognizes poverty alleviation as an important and serious agenda, we can create a world that we can be proud of, rather than feel ashamed of, as we do now."

In July 2005, total loans disbursed by the Grameen Bank topped $5 billion. The bank crossed the first billion dollar mark in March 1995, about eighteen years after it was formally inaugurated in 1976 by lending $27 to forty-two people. It has also established thousands of branches across rural Bangladesh, serving around 5 million borrowers on their doorsteps, in more than forty thousand villages.

According to Yunus, poverty is an example of a cancer which humans have created and foisted upon their fellow humans. It is so widespread because political oppression, economic inequality and social injustice are rife in many parts of the world. Poverty – both relative and absolute – can only be eradicated when the world's most powerful leaders and financial institutions make poverty eradication their first priority. According to Yunus, poverty will not be completely eradicated until the restrictive practices which sustain the structures of global economic inequality and injustice are first dismantled.

In recognition of his outstanding achievements, Yunus has been awarded scores of prestigious international prizes and awards, including the Nobel Peace Prize in 2006. Muhammad Yunus lives in Dhaka, Bangladesh with his wife and daughter.

***

Muhyi al Din, Khalid (1922-   ): Egyptian political. Born into a landowning family in the Nile delta, Muhyi graduated from the Royal Military Academy in Cairo and became a cavalry officer, reaching the rank of major. Active with the Free Officers organization, which staged a coup in July 1952, Muhyi was one of the two leftist members of the ruling eighteen member Revolutionary Command Council (RCC). After Egypt's debacle in the June 1967 Arab Israeli War. Nasser began to cold shoulder leftists and rejected Muhyi's proposal that the armed services be controlled by the ASU with its cadre penetrating their institution, thus ending their isolation from society. Muhyi received the Lenin Peace Prize from the Soviet Union in 1970. After Nasser's death that year, Muhyo's ties with the new government became tenuous. He opposed the Egyptian Israeli Peace Treaty. He was one of the 240 secular dissidents arrested in September 1981 a month before Sadat's assassination. Reviver of Islam.

***

Muhyiddin ibn Arabi (1165-1240): born in Umarcia, Spain. One of the greatest Islamic philosophers. Died in Damascus. the pursuit of esoteric truth became his life purpose "Bezels of Wisdom" dealt with the principle of the unity of all beings. Spanish Muslim thinker.

***

Mu'in al-Din Chishti (1142-1236): All popular Sufi (or Islamic mystical) Orders, like the *Qadiriyyah*, *Naqshbandiyyah*, S*uhrawardiyyah* and S*hadhiliyyah*, trace their spiritual lineage back to the Prophet through his close companions. But after the influx of materialistic values and practices into the Islamic world, Sufism became a label without the reality. During this challenging period in Islamic history, a number of influential Sufis, like Abd al-Qadir al-Jilani, Shihab al-Din Umar al-Suhrawardi, Najm al-Din Kubra and Khwajah Yusuf Hamdani, emerged to champion Islamic morals, ethics and spirituality. A contemporary of these luminaries was Mu'in al-Din Chishti, who became the founder of the C*hishtiyyah* Sufi Order in India.

Mu'in al-Din Muhammad ibn Hasan, also known as Aftab-i Mulk-i Hind (the 'Sun of the Kingdom of India'), was born in Sistan into a noble Muslim family. He was barely fifteen when his father suddenly died and this forced his family to endure considerable financial hardship. To make matters worse, his beloved mother then passed away, which again forced him to experience more personal and financial hardships.

He then travelled extensively in pursuit of knowledge and wisdom. In addition to Bukhara and Samarqand, he visited many other renowned centers of Islamic learning and education, and studied under the guidance of scores of prominent scholars and Sufis. On his arrival in Harwan (a prominent center of Islamic learning and scholarship located on the outskirts of Nishapur), he encountered Khwajah Uthman Harwani, who was a distinguished Islamic scholar and prominent *Chishtiyyah* Sufi. Here he became a member of Khwajah Harwani's Sufi circle and spent the next two decades in his company. After staying in Harwan for almost two decades, he left Khwajah Harwani's company and travelled to Baghdad, the capital of the Abbasid Caliphate. He also met the renowned Central Asian Sufi sage Najm al-Din Kubra, the founder of the *Kubrawiyyah* Sufi Order. Mu'in al-Din soon established his reputation as a master of Sufism and one of its most eloquent exponents.

From Baghdad, he proceeded to Isfahan where he met another distinguished Sufi sage, Shaykh Mahmud al-Isfahani. Mu'in al-Din was in his mid-forties when he moved from Isfahan to Ghazna (in present-day Afghanistan). On his arrival in Ghazna, he was surprised to encounter Khwajah Uthman Harwani, his former mentor and guide. It was Khwajah Harwani who urged him to proceed to India and disseminate the message of Islam in that country.

Either way, he left Ghazna and reached Lahore in 1190. From Lahore he moved to Multan and stayed there for about five years. His asceticism and spirituality captured the imagination of people of all faiths. After reaching Delhi with his band of followers, he settled in Ajmer (located in the Indian State of Rajasthan), which became an integral part of the Delhi sultanate in 1196. Mu'in al-Din was a humble and gracious scholar and Sufi, who was motivated by no desire other than to attain personal purity and disseminate the message of Islam in India.

Though Mu'in al-Din was the founder of the *Chishtiyyah* Sufi Order in India, he was not the originator of the *Chishtiyyah Tariqah* as such. That credit must go to Khwajah Ishaq Ghani Chishti, who was an outstanding exponent of Sufism.

Mu'in al-Din opposed the Hindu caste system and instead argued that all human beings are equal in the sight of God. "We are all children of Adam and Eve," he argued, "and both Adam and Eve were made from clay." His message of love, peace, compassion, equality, freedom and brotherhood struck a chord with Muslims and Hindus alike.

After his death, Mu'in al-Din became a household name in India, Pakistan and Bangladesh.

***

Mujibar Rahman, Sheikh (1920-1975): Bangladeshi statesman. Popularly known as Sheikh Mujib, he came into political prominence as co-founder and general secretary of the Awami League and as a champion of the Bengalis of East Pakistan, who he feared were being dominated by West Pakistan. He was imprisoned in 1954 under the rule of Ayub Khan, and again in 1966, but as leader of the Awami League after the death of Suhrawardy, he became the leading politician of East Pakistan. He was released after the fall of Ayub and led his party to victory in the

1970 elections. In 1975 he and his family were murdered in an army coup.

***

Mullah Sadra (1571-1641): The encounter between Islam and ancient Greek, Syriac and Persian thought and culture first took place during the mid-seventh century, after the Muslim conquest of Egypt, Syria and Iraq. As a result, *falsafah* (Islamic philosophy) emerged as a distinct intellectual tradition in the Muslim world. In this battle of ideas, the traditionalists emerged victorious, which marked the beginning of the end of philosophical thought in much of the Islamic East. But it was in the works of Mullah Sadra that Islamic philosophy found a new, fresh impetus and a degree of intellectual rigor and sophistication.

Sadr al-Din Muhammad ibn Ibrahim al-Qawami al-Shirazi, better known as Mullah Sadra, was born into the Iranian city of Shiraz into a notable Persian family. Impressed by his intellectual abilities, his family enrolled him at his local school for a thorough education in Persian, Arabic, Islamic sciences, literature and philosophy.

As a highly respected authority on Islamic sciences, Baha al-Din became the *Shaykh al-Islam* (supreme religious authority) of Safavid Persia, in addition to being a noted mathematician, alchemist and Sufi (Islamic mystic). Mullah Sadra studied Islamic theological, philosophical and mystical thought. After completing his advance education while he was still in his mid-twenties, Mullah Sadra became very enthusiastic about mysticism, which infuriated the conservative *ulama* (religious scholars) in Isfahan who accused him of espousing un-Islamic ideas and thoughts. When the hostility of the religious scholars became unbearable, he was forced to leave Isfahan and return to Shiraz.

The Shi'a scholars' reaction against his 'unorthodox' interpretation of mysticism eventually convinced Mullah Sadra to leave Shiraz and settle in Kahak, a remote village located on the outskirts of Qom, one of Iran's most famous centers of Shi'a religious learning and scholarship.

After almost a decade in Kahak, Mullah Sadra returned to Shiraz, where he began to lecture on religious sciences and write books and treatises on metaphysics, philosophy, mysticism and Shi'a theology. The Safavids came to power in Persia at the beginning of the sixteenth century and being *Ithna 'Ashari* (Twelver) Shi'as, they made this the official religion of Persia. The Safavid ruler Shah Abbas II reportedly ordered the governor of Fars to build a religious seminary in Shiraz where Mullah Sadra could teach and train a new generation of Shi'a religious scholars and thinkers. Despite his busy teaching schedule, he found time to author many books and treatises. Mullah Sadra wrote about fifty books and treatises in total.

Just as revelatory and mystical approaches to Reality can provide a sound expression of the Truth, in the same way, Mullah Sadra argued, a philosophical approach to Reality can also shed fresh light on the Truth. He claimed Greek philosophers had received inspiration from Abraham who, in turn, received the Truth directly from Adam. This paved the way for him to create a synthesis between Greek philosophy, the Gnostic wisdom of the Sufis and the Peripatetic thought of the *falsafah*, with Shi'a theology. It is this synthesis which became known as H*ikmat al-Muta'aliyyah* (the 'transcendental wisdom').

Mullah Sadra also adopted Ibn al-Arabi's concept of N*ur Muhammadiya* (the 'Muhammadan Light') but vehemently opposed Ibn Sina's notion of the eternity of the world. He stated that the true meaning of the revelation would not become clear until after the advent of the M*ahdi*, the final Shi'a Imam. He attempted to harmonize philosophy, Gnosticism and theology in order to answer some of the most fundamental questions concerning God, His Nature and Attributes, the meaning of life, the purpose of creation and the nature of resurrection – all surveyed through the lenses of revelation, reason, intuition and experience.

Mullah Sadra performed the sacred *hajj* (pilgrimage to Mecca) seven times and died in Basrah at the age of seventy while he was on his way home from completing his seventh pilgrimage.

***

Murad I (1326-1389): Ottoman sultan (1326?-1389), son and successor of Orkhan to the throne of the Ottoman Empire (Turkey). Murad widened the Ottoman hold on European territory, conquering Macedonia and making Adrianople his residence. He granted Muslims sections of conquered lands as fiefs (see feudalism). In 1373 he forced Byzantine Emperor John V to pay tribute. Murad began the policy of compelling Christian youths to join the army corps known as the Janissaries. As a result of his victory at Kosovo Field (see under Kosovo), Serbia came under Ottoman rule. However, Murad was assassinated in his tent by a Serbian warrior; his son Beyazid I succeeded him. The name also appears as Amurath.

***

Islamic Leaders

Murad II (1403-1451): Ottoman sultan (1421-51), son and successor of Muhammad I to the throne of the Ottoman Empire (Turkey). He was opposed at his accession by a pretender, Mustafa, who rapidly gained control over most of the Ottoman possessions in Europe. After defeating his rival, Murad unsuccessfully laid siege (1422) to Constantinople. In a war with Venice he seized (1430) Salonica, thus proving Ottoman naval power, and invaded Greece. In the north Murad fought the resistance led by John Hunyadi. Murad sought to retire from public life on several occasions, but each time was recalled by the pressure of events. In 1444 he won the great victory of Varna against the crusading forces led by King Ladislaus III of Poland and Hungary. Murad was a patron of poetry and learning, and his court was a cultural center. His son Muhammad II succeeded him.

***

Murtadd (-): Female apostate is Murtadah, apostate. The technical Islamic term for an apostate, that is one who has renounced Islam. According to the holy law as traditionally understood, this is a capital offense and the offender must be put to death whatever the circumstances. Even if he later repents and reverses his apostasy he must still be executed. God may forgive him but no human authority is empowered to so. This penalty applies even in the case of a new convert to Islam, of however brief duration, who reverts to his previous faith. The death penalty normally included not only the convert but also anyone responsible for converting him. According to the proponents of Taqiya the apostate may be forgiven if his apostasy is forced and false. In addition to a formal renunciation of the faith, some actions, such as certain forms of blasphemy are considered tantamount to apostasy ad incur the same penalties.

Despite the impossibility of even attempting to convert Muslims, Christian missions of various churches were extremely active under some Muslim governments, notably under the Ottoman Empire. Their purpose was to convert Jews to Christianity and more especially to convert Christians from one church to another. During the long and bitter struggle between Protestants and Catholics in Europe both sides became aware that there was a large untapped reservoir of Christians in the Islamic lands, not committed to either of the contending Western churches. Most of the Middle Eastern Christians belonged to one or other of the Eastern churches-Orthodox, Armenian, Coptic, Syrian. For awhile Catholic missions achieved some success in supporting or creating Uniate churches, that is, autonomous churches with their own rules and rites but in communion with Rome. The best known of these is the Maronite church of Lebanon.

The Protestant missions also succeeded in winning converts from among the Eastern churches. Under the rule of the Western Empires, the missionaries had free reign. Since the ending of Western imperial rule, their activities had been more circumscribed and in some countries in accordance with the old laws, totally forbidden. In general by conversion to Islam and migration the ancient Christian communities of the Middle East have been dwindling steadily.

Musa ibn Nusayr (639-716): Though Muslims first made inroads into North Africa during the reign of Caliph Umar, the Byzantines re-conquered their lost territories during the conflict which ensued between Caliph Ali and Muawiyah; thus the Muslims were not able to consolidate their presence in North Africa at the time. After Muawiyah ascended the Umayyad throne in 661, he not only reunited the Muslim world under his leadership but also launched expeditions to North Africa and thereby brought a large part of that region back under Umayyad authority. Under the able leadership of Uqba ibn Nafi, the Umayyad forces drove out the Byzantines and in 670 the Muslims founded the historic city of Qayrawan (in present-day Tunisia), thus consolidating Islamic power in that region for the first time.

Yazid then ascended the Umayyad throne in 680 and, having taken his eyes off events in North Africa, he engaged in a war of attrition with fellow Muslims at home. This enabled the Byzantines to recover and inflict a crushing defeat on the North African Muslims. Soon afterwards, Uqba and his forces were soundly defeated by the North African Berber tribes and, again, the Umayyad grip on that region became precarious until the heroic Muslim general Musa ibn Nusayr emerged to permanently establish an Islamic presence in that part of the world.

Musa ibn Nusayr was born during the reign of Caliph Umar. His family hailed from the noble Arab tribe of Lakhm, whose members once occupied prominent positions in the Lakhmid dynasty of Hira (in present-day Iraq). Raised in a relatively wealthy family, young Musa aspired to follow in the footsteps of his father and join the Umayyad military service. Known for his bravery, courage and tactical ability, he made his mark as a soldier on the battlefield, and played an active part in the Umayyad conquest of Cyprus during the reign of Caliph Muawiyah.

When Abd al-Malik ibn Marwan ascended the Umayyad throne in 685, he appointed his brother, Abd al-Aziz, to the post of governor of Egypt. Musa served the Caliph and his brother in various capacities until 692, when he was sent to Basrah to take over the vacant post of chief revenue collector. Musa then went to Egypt with the governor and helped Abd al-Aziz restructure his civil service with great skill and determination.

Musa helped the governor consolidate his political authority across Egypt, until in 699 Abd al-Aziz appointed him commander of a large military expedition. The purpose of this expedition was to sweep through North Africa and crush the growing unrest, whipped up by the Berbers, against Umayyad rule. Musa's success pleased Abd al-Aziz who handsomely rewarded him for his efforts. Subsequently, Abd al-Aziz recalled Hassan ibn al-Nu'man, the incumbent governor of North Africa, and replaced him with Musa.

Musa was about sixty when he moved to North Africa with his extended family and took up his new post. Upon his arrival in Qayrawan, he launched military expeditions against rebellious Berber tribes who were bent on wreaking havoc in the Umayyad territories. Most astonishingly, within a few months of his arrival, Musa managed to restore peace and security across North Africa. However, after Abd al-Aziz's sudden death in 704, the Caliph appointed his brother, Abdullah, governor of Egypt. Although he supported Musa in his efforts to strengthen Umayyad rule in North Africa, a year later Caliph Abd al-Malik also died. Hereafter, Musa was required to report directly to Caliph al-Walid in Damascus.

Despite the Berber's stiff resistance, Musa triumphantly marched into Tangier where Ilyan (or Julian), the Christian ruler, submitted to Umayyad authority without a fight – as he had done previously to Uqba ibn Nafi. A few years later, Ilyan played a pivotal role in the Islamic conquest of both Gibraltar and Spain under the leadership of the legendary Muslim general Tariq ibn Ziyad.

After annexing the entire Maghreb, Musa appointed Tariq as his deputy governor of Morocco. His efforts bore fruit as the Berbers began to enter the fold of Islam in their droves. Indeed, the credit for establishing a permanent Islamic presence in North Africa and the Maghreb must go mainly to Musa. After securing Tangier, he returned to Qayrawan as North Africa's most effective and powerful governor. It was also Musa who nominated Tariq ibn Ziyad to spearhead the campaign to conquer Gibraltar and Spain. When Tariq's expedition proved a success, Musa joined forces with him and brought a significant part of Spain under Umayyad control. Spain remained a Muslim country for more than another seven hundred years.

Unfortunately Caliph Sulaiman, al-Walid's successor, completely ignored the great Muslim conqueror. Musa died in poverty at the age of around seventy-seven and was buried in Wadi al-Qura, located in Syria. Commander of the invading Berber army who conquered all of Spain for the Muslims in 313.

***

Musavi, Mir Hussein (1942-): Iranian politician: Prime minister 1981-89. Born in Khamane near Tabriz, Musavi obtained a degree in architecture at a university in Tehran in 1969. An activist in Islamic circles, h was jailed briefly in 1973 for antigovernment activities. An economic radical, he favored nationalization of foreign and domestic trading. When after his reelection as president in 1985 Ali Hussein Khamanei considered dropping Musavi as premier, Ayatollah Ruhollah Khomeini, intent on maintaining a balance between radicals and moderates, publicly praised Musavi. Later, leader Ayatollah Ali Khamanei nominated him to the Expediency Consultation Council System.

***

Muslim ibn al-Hajjaj (817-875): Scholars like Malik ibn Anas, al-Zuhri, al-Awza'i, Abdullah ibn Mubarak, Yahya ibn Ma'in and Ahmad ibn Hanbal have left their indelible marks in the annals of *Hadith* literature. However, the names of two remarkable scholars, al-Bukhari and Muslim, have today become household names across the Muslim world on account of their selfless devotion, assiduous scholarship and seminal contributions to the collection and dissemination of the Prophetic traditions. The popularity of Muslim ibn al-Hajjaj must not be underestimated, the collections of both al-Bukhari and Muslim are today regarded as two of the most authentic and authoritative anthologies of Prophetic traditions ever produced.

Abul Hussain Asakir al-Din Muslim ibn al-Hajjaj ibn Muslim ibn Ward was born in Nishapur (located in the Persian province of Khurasan) into a respected Arab family of the tribe of Qushair. Following the rapid expansion of Islam during the reign of Caliphs Umar and Uthman, Muslims began to move from Arabia and settle in the newly-conquered territories in Syria, Egypt and Persia to pursue commerce and also engage in missionary activities. Indeed, it was his father's profound reverence and admiration for the Prophetic traditions which inspired Muslim to specialize in *Hadith* literature.

Muslim went to Makkah to perform the sacred pilgrimage (*hajj*), and thereafter studied *Hadith* under al-Bukhari's tutelage for a period and polished his knowledge and understanding of *Hadith* and *Usul al-Hadith*. Students like Bukharis and Muslim had no choice but to travel extensively in search of knowledge and in process they met with, and studied *Hadith* under the guidance of, hundreds of eminent scholars and traditionalists of their time.

When Muslim was convinced that he had acquired an unrivalled mastery of Prophetic traditions, he returned home to Nishapur where his fame began to spread far and wide. Prominent scholars like al-Tirmidhi,

Ibn Khuzaimah, Ibrahim ibn Muhammad ibn Sufyan and Ibn Abu Hatim al-Razi attended his lectures.

Although Muslim composed more than twenty books on different aspects of *Hadith*, only six of his books have survived, including *al-Jani al-Sahih* (better known as *Sahih Muslim*). This anthology of *Hadith* is not only his most famous work, but, along with *Sahih al-Bukhari*, it is today considered to be one of the most authentic books of Islamic teachings after the Qur'an itself. Muslim incorporated around seven thousand *ahadith* in his anthology. For a *Hadith* to be considered beyond reproach, it had to have a sound M*atn* (text) as well as a sound I*snad* (chain of narration), among other things. After completing this voluminous work, Muslim presented copies to some of his great contemporaries, including Abu Zur'ah of Rayy. *Sahih Muslim* is one of the most authoritative anthologies of *Hadith* ever produced.

Muslim ibn al-Hajjaj died at the age of about fifty-nine and was buried in his native Nishapur.

***

Mussadiq, Muhammad (1881-1967): Iranian politician, prime minister 1951-53. Son of a wealthy public official in Ahmadabad, Mussdiq pursued his university education in Paris and then obtained his doctorate in law at Lausanne University, Switzerland. When he opposed the coronation of Reza Khan as Shah of Iran in 1925, he was forced to retired from public life. With the disposition of Reza Shah in 1941 Mussadiq's fortunes rose. He was elected to parliament in 1944. Three years later he challenged Muhammad Reza Shah Pahlavi's nominee for premier, Ibrahim Hakimi and lost by a single vote. In 1949 he co founded the National Front.

In late April 1951 the Majlis decided by a large majority to go ahead with the nationalization and to appoint Mussadiq as premier. This happened on 1 May 1951. This alienated Mussadiq from clerical circles. In mid January 1953 he won a yearlong extension of his emergency powers from parliament. Mussadiq declared on 12 August 1953 that he would order fresh parliamentary elections. When the Shah's attempt to dismiss Mussadiq failed, the shah fled. Actively aided by US Central Intelligence Agency, mounted a successful coup against Mussadiq. By 19 August the shah was back in power.

***

Mustafa IV (1778-1808): Ottoman sultan (1807-8), son of Abd al-Hamid I. He was raised to the throne by the reactionary Janissaries who had deposed Mustafa's cousin, Selim III, because they opposed his attempted reforms. When a Turkish army marched on the capital to restore Selim, Mustafa had him murdered, but the rebels killed Mustafa and placed his brother, Mahmud II, on the throne.

***

Mustafa Kemal Ataturk (1881-1938): Mustafa Kemal Ataturk (19 May 1881 by a posteriori–10 November 1938) was an Ottoman and Turkish army officer, revolutionary statesman, writer, and the first President of Turkey. He is credited with being the founder of the Republic of Turkey.

Ataturk was a military officer during World War I. Following the defeat of the Ottoman Empire in World War I, he led the Turkish national movement in the Turkish War of Independence. Having established a provisional government in Ankara, he defeated the forces sent by the Allies. His military campaigns gained Turkey independence. Ataturk then embarked upon a program of political, economic, and cultural reforms, seeking to transform the former Ottoman Empire into a modern, westernized and secular nation-state. The principles of Ataturk's reforms, upon which modern Turkey was established, are referred to as Kemalism.

Early life:

Mustafa was born either in the Ahmed Subaş neighborhood or in Islahhane Street (present-day Apostolu Pavlu Street) in the Koca Kasım Pasha neighborhood (this house is preserved as a museum) in Salonica (present-day Thessaloniki), Ottoman Empire, to his mother Zübeyde Hanım (a housewife) and father Ali Rıza Efendi (a militia officer, title-deed clerk and lumber trader). Only one of Ataturk's siblings, a sister named Makbule (Atadan) survived childhood; she died in 1956. He was born into a family which was Muslim, Turkish-speaking and precariously middle-class. *Time* magazine states that Mustafa Kemal's father was of Albanian and his mother was of Macedonian origin.

Born Mustafa, his second name Kemal (meaning Perfection or Maturity) was given to him by his mathematics teacher. In his early years, his mother encouraged Mustafa to attend a religious school, something he did reluctantly and only briefly. His parents wanted him to learn a trade, but without consulting them, Ataturk took the entrance exam for the Salonica Military School in 1893. In 1896, he enrolled into the Monastir Military High School. On 14 March 1899, he enrolled at the Ottoman Military Academy in the neighborhood of Pangaltı within the Şişli district of the Ottoman capital city Constantinople and graduated in 1902. He later graduated from the Ottoman Military College in Constantinople on 11 January 1905.

Military career (*Committee of Union and Progress, and Young Turk Revolution*):

Following graduation, he was assigned to the Fifth Army based in Damascus as a Staff Captain in the company of Ali Fuat (Cebesoy) and Lütfi Müfit (Özdeş). He joined a small secret revolutionary society of reformist officers led by a merchant Mustafa Elvan (Cantekin) called Vatan ve Hürriyet ("Motherland and Liberty"). On 20 June 1907, he was promoted to the rank of Senior Captain (*Kolağası*) and on 13 October 1907, assigned to the headquarters of the Third Army in Manastır. On 22 June 1908, he was appointed the Inspector of the Ottoman Railways in Eastern Rumelia. In July 1908, he played a role in the Young Turk Revolution which seized power from Sultan Abdulhamid II and restored the constitutional monarchy.

In 1910 he was called to the Ottoman provinces in Albania. At that time Isa Boletini was leading Albanian uprisings in Kosovo and there were revolts in Albania. In 1910 he met with Eqerem Vlora. In early 1911, he worked at the Ministry of War (*Harbiye Nezareti*) headquarters in Istanbul for a short time.

Italo-Turkish War (1911-1912) (*Battle of Tobruk (1911)*):

Later in 1911, he was assigned to the Ottoman Tripolitania Vilayet (present-day Libya) to fight in the Italo-Turkish War, mainly in the areas near Benghazi, Derna and Tobruk. A massive Italian amphibious assault force of 150,000 troops had to be countered by 20,000 Bedouins and 8,000 Turks (a short time before Italy declared war, a large portion of the Ottoman troops in Libya were sent to the Ottoman province of Yemen in order to put down the rebellion there, so the Ottoman government was caught with inadequate resources to counter the Italians in Libya; and the British government, which militarily controlled the *de jure* Ottoman provinces of Egypt and Sudan since the Urabi Revolt in 1882, didn't allow the Ottoman government to send additional Ottoman troops to Libya through Egypt; causing the Ottoman soldiers like Mustafa Kemal to go to Libya either dressed as Arabs (risking imprisonment if noticed by the British authorities in Egypt), or through very few available ferries (the Italians, who had superior naval forces, effectively controlled the sea routes to Tripoli).)

However, despite all the hardships, Mustafa Kemal's forces in Libya managed to successfully repel the Italians in a number of occasions, such as the Battle of Tobruk on 22 December 1911. On 6 March 1912 Mustafa Kemal became the Commander of the Ottoman forces in Derna. He managed to defend and retain the city and its surrounding region until the end of the Italo-Turkish War on 18 October 1912. The Treaty of Ouchy (First Treaty of Lausanne) signed ten days later, on 18 October.

Balkan Wars (1912-1913) (*First Balkan War and Second Balkan War*):

On 1 December 1912, Mustafa Kemal arrived at his new headquarters on the Gallipoli peninsula and during the First Balkan War, he took part in the amphibious landing at Bulair on the coast of Thrace that was commanded by Binbaşı Fethi Bey, but this offensive was repulsed during the Battle of Bulair by Georgi Todorov's 7th Rila Infantry Division under the command of Stiliyan Kovachev's Bulgarian Fourth Army.

In June 1913, during the Second Balkan War, he took part in the Ottoman Army forces commanded by Kaymakam Enver Bey that recovered Dimetoka and Edirne (Adrianople, the capital city of the Ottoman Empire between 1365 and 1453, thus of utmost historic importance for the Turks) together with most of eastern Thrace from the Bulgarians. In 1913, he was appointed the Ottoman military attaché to all Balkan states (his office was in Sofia, Bulgaria) and promoted to the rank of Kaymakam (Lieutenant Colonel / Colonel) on 1 March 1914.

First World War (1914-1918) (*Battle of Gallipoli and Middle Eastern theatre of World War I*):

In 1914, the Ottoman Empire entered the European and Middle Eastern theatres of World War I allied with the Central Powers. Mustafa Kemal was given the task of organizing and commanding the 19th Division attached to the Fifth Army during the Battle of Gallipoli. Mustafa Kemal became the front-line commander after correctly anticipating where the Allies would attack and holding his position until they retreated. Following the Battle of Gallipoli, Mustafa Kemal served in Edirne until 14 January 1916. He was then assigned to the command of the XVI Corps of the Second Army and sent to the Caucasus Campaign after the massive Russian offensive had reached the Anatolian key cities. On 7 August, Mustafa Kemal rallied his troops and mounted a counteroffensive. Two of his divisions captured Bitlis and Muş, upsetting the calculations of the Russian Command.

Following this victory, the CUP government in Constantinople proposed to establish a new army in Hejaz (*Hicaz Kuvve-i Seferiyesi*) and appoint Mustafa Kemal to its command, but he refused the proposal and this army was never established. Instead, on 7 March 1917, Mustafa Kemal was promoted from the command of the XVI Corps to the overall command of the Second Army, although the Czar's armies were soon withdrawn when the Russian Revolution erupted.

In July 1917 he was appointed to the command of the Seventh Army, replacing Fevzi Pasha on 7 August 1917, who was under the command of the German general Erich von Falkenhayn's Yildirim Army Group (after the British forces of General Edmund Allenby captured Jerusalem in December 1917. Mustafa Kemal resigned from the Seventh Army and returned to Constantinople. There, he was assigned with the task of accompanying the crown prince (and future sultan) Mehmed Vahideddin during his train trip to Austria-Hungary and Germany.

When Mehmed VI became the new Sultan of the Ottoman Empire in July 1918, he called Mustafa Kemal to Constantinople, and in August 1918 assigned him to the command of the Seventh Army in Palestine. Mustafa Kemal arrived in Aleppo on 26 August 1918, then continued south to his headquarters in Nablus. The Seventh Army was holding the central sector of the front lines. On 19 September, at the beginning of the Battle of Megiddo, the Eighth Army was holding the coastal flank, but fell apart and Liman Pasha ordered the Seventh Army to withdraw to the north in order to prevent the British from conducting a short envelopment to the Jordan River. The Seventh Army retired towards the Jordan River but was destroyed by British aerial bombardment during its retreat from Nablus on 21 September 1918. The Armistice of Mudros was signed on 30 October 1918 and all German and Austro-Hungarian troops in the Ottoman Empire were granted ample time to withdraw. On 31 October, he was appointed to the command of the Yıldırım Army Group, replacing Liman von Sanders. He organized the distribution of weapons to the civilians in Antep in case of a defensive conflict against the invading Allies.

Kemal's last active service in the Ottoman Army was organizing the return of the troops left behind to the south of this line. In early November 1918 the Yıldırım Army Group was officially dissolved and Mustafa Kemal returned to an occupied Constantinople, the Ottoman capital, on 13 November 1918. Along the established lines of the partitioning of the Ottoman Empire, the Allies (British, Italian, French and Greek forces) occupied Anatolia. The occupation of Constantinople, which was followed by the occupation of Smyrna (the two largest Ottoman cities in that period) sparked the establishment of the Turkish national movement and the Turkish War of Independence.

Turkish War of Independence (1919-1922):
On 19 May 1919, he reached Samsun. His first goal was the establishment of an organized national resistance movement against the

occupying forces. In June 1919, he issued the Amasya Circular, declaring the independence of the country was in danger. He resigned from the Ottoman Army on 8 July and the Ottoman government issued a warrant for his arrest. Later, he was condemned to death.

The last election to the Ottoman parliament held in December 1919 gave a sweeping majority to candidates of the "Association for Defense of Rights for Anatolia and Roumelia", headed by Mustafa Kemal, who himself remained in Ankara. Mustafa Kemal called for a national election to establish a new Turkish Parliament seated in Ankara – the "Grand National Assembly" (GNA). On 23 April 1920, the GNA opened with Mustafa Kemal as the speaker; this act effectively created the situation of diarchy in the country.

On 10 August 1920, the Ottoman Grand Vizier Damat Ferid Pasha signed the Treaty of Sèvres, finalizing plans for the partitioning of the Ottoman Empire, including the regions that Turkish nationals viewed as their heartland. Mustafa Kemal insisted on the country's complete independence and the safeguarding of interests of the Turkish majority on "Turkish soil". He persuaded the GNA to gather a National Army. The GNA Army faced the Caliphate army propped up by the Allied occupation forces and had the immediate task of fighting the Armenians forces in the Eastern Front and the Greek forces, that advanced eastward from Smyrna (modern day Izmir) that they had occupied in May 1919, on the Western Front.

The GNA military successes against the Democratic Republic of Armenia in the autumn of 1920 and later against the Greeks were made possible by a steady supply of gold and armaments to the Kemalists from the Russian Bolshevik government from the autumn 1920 onwards.

After a series of battles during the Greco-Turkish war, the Greek army advanced as far as the Sakarya River, just eighty kilometers west of the GNA. On 5 August 1921, Mustafa Kemal was promoted to Commander in chief of the forces by the GNA. The ensuing Battle of Sakarya was fought from 23 August to 13 September 1921 and ended with the defeat of the Greeks. After this victory, on 19 September 1921, Mustafa Kemal Pasha was given by the Grand National Assembly the rank of "Marshal" and the title of "Ghazi". The Allies, ignoring the extent of Kemal's successes, hoped to impose a modified version of the Treaty of Sèvres as a peace settlement on Ankara, but the proposal was rejected. In August 1922, Kemal launched an all-out attack on the Greek lines at Afyonkarahisar in the Battle of Dumlupınar and Turkish forces regained control of Smyrna on 9 September 1922. On 10 September 1922, Mustafa Kemal sent a telegram to the League of Nations saying that the Turkish population was so worked up that the Ankara Government would not be responsible for massacres.

Establishment of the Republic of Turkey:
The Conference of Lausanne began on 21 November 1922. Turkey, represented by İsmet İnönü of the GNA, refused any proposal that would compromise Turkish sovereignty, such as the control of Turkish finances, the Capitulations, the Straits and other issues. On 24 July 1923, the Treaty of Lausanne was signed by the Powers with the GNA, thus recognizing the latter as the government of Turkey. On 29 October 1923, the Republic of Turkey was proclaimed.

Presidency:
With the establishment of the Republic of Turkey, efforts to modernize the country started. The new government analyzed the institutions and constitutions of Western states such as France, Sweden, Italy, and Switzerland and adapted them to the needs and characteristics of the Turkish nation. Mustafa Kemal capitalized on his reputation as an efficient military leader and spent the following years, up until his death in 1938, instituting political, economic, and social reforms. In doing so, he transformed Turkish society from perceiving itself as a Muslim part of a vast Empire into a modern, democratic, and secular nation-state.

Domestic policies:
Kemal's basic tenet was the complete independence of the country. He led wide-ranging reforms in social, cultural, and economical aspects, establishing the new Republic's backbone of legislative, judicial, and economic structures.

This defining ideology of the Republic of Turkey is referred to as the "Six Arrows", or Kemalist ideology. Kemalist ideology is based on Mustafa Kemal's conception of realism and pragmatism. The fundamentals of nationalism, populism and etatism were all defined under the Six Arrows.

Emergence of the state, 1923-1924:
In forging the new republic, the Turkish revolutionaries turned their back on the perceived corruption and decadence of cosmopolitan Constantinople and its Ottoman heritage. For instance, they made Ankara the country's new capital.

The revolutionaries faced challenges from the supporters of the old Ottoman regime, and also from the supporters of newer ideologies such as communism and fascism. Mustafa Kemal saw the consequences of fascist and communist doctrines in the 1920s and 1930s and rejected both. It was necessary to protect the young Turkish state from succumbing to the instability of new ideologies and competing factions.

The heart of the new republic was the GNA, established during the Turkish War of Independence by Mustafa Kemal. The elections were free and used an egalitarian electoral system that was based on a general ballot. Initially, it also acted as a legislative power, controlling the executive branch and, if necessary, acted as an organ of scrutiny under the Turkish Constitution of 1921. The Turkish Constitution of 1924 set a loose separation of powers between the legislative and the executive organs of the state, whereas the separation of these two within the judiciary system was a strict one. Mustafa Kemal, then the President, occupied a powerful position in this political system.

The single-party regime was established *de facto* in 1925 after the adoption of the 1924 constitution. The only political party of the GNA was the "People's Party", founded by Mustafa Kemal in the initial years of the independence war. On 9 September 1923 it was renamed the Republican People's Party.

Civic independence and the Caliphate, 1924-1925:

Abolition of the Caliphate was an important dimension in Mustafa Kemal's drive to reform the political system and to promote the national sovereignty. By the consensus of the Muslim majority in early centuries, the caliphate was the core political concept of Sunni Islam. Caliph Abdülmecid II was elected after the abolishment of the sultanate (1922).

The caliph had his own personal treasury and also had a personal service that included military personnel; Mustafa Kemal said that there was no "religious" or "political" justification for this. He wanted to integrate the powers of the caliphate into the powers of the GNA. His initial activities began on 1 January 1924, when İnönü, Çakmak and Özalp consented to the abolition of the caliphate. On 1 March 1924, at the Assembly, Mustafa Kemal said

> "The religion of Islam will be elevated if it will cease to be a political instrument, as had been the case in the past."

On 3 March 1924, the caliphate was officially abolished and its powers within Turkey were transferred to the GNA. A "Caliphate Conference" was held in Cairo in May 1926 and a resolution was passed declaring the caliphate "a necessity in Islam", but failed to implement this decision. Two other Islamic conferences were held in Mecca (1926) and Jerusalem (1931), but failed to reach a consensus.

The removal of the caliphate was followed by an extensive effort to establish the separation of governmental and religious affairs. Education was the cornerstone in this effort. Mustafa Kemal changed the classical Islamic education for a vigorously promoted reconstruction of educational institutions. Kemal linked educational reform to the liberation of the nation from dogma, which he believed was more important than the Turkish war of independence.

In the summer of 1924, Mustafa Kemal invited American educational reformer John Dewey to Ankara to advise him on how to reform Turkish education. He wanted to institute compulsory primary education for both girls and boys; since then this effort has been an ongoing task for the republic. The state schools established a common curriculum which became known as the "unification of education."

Unification of education was put into force on 3 March 1924 by the Law on Unification of Education (No. 430). With the new law, education became inclusive, organized on a model of the civil community. Concurrently, the republic abolished the two ministries and made clergy subordinate to the department of religious affairs, one of the foundations of secularism in Turkey.

Beginning in the fall of 1925, Mustafa Kemal encouraged the Turks to wear modern European attire. He was determined to force the abandonment of the sartorial traditions of the Middle East and finalize a series of dress reforms, which were originally started by Mahmud II. The fez was established by Sultan Mahmud II in 1826 as part of the Ottoman Empire's modernization effort. The Hat Law of 1925 introduced the use of Western-style hats instead of the fez. Mustafa Kemal first made the hat compulsory to civil servants. The last part of reform on dress emphasized the need to wear modern Western suits with neckties as well as Fedora and Derby-style hats instead of antiquated religion-based clothing such as the veil and turban in the Law Relating to Prohibited Garments of 1934.

> "The religious covering of women will not cause difficulty ... This simple style [of head covering] is not in conflict with the morals and manners of our society."

> "...The Turkish republic cannot be a country of sheiks, dervishes, and disciples. The best, the truest order is the order of civilization..."

On 2 September the government issued a decree closing down all Sufi orders and the tekkes. Mustafa Kemal ordered their dervish lodges to be converted to museums, such as Mevlana Museum in

Konya. The institutional expression of Sufism became illegal in Turkey; a politically neutral form of Sufism, functioning as social associations, was permitted to exist. The abolition of the caliphate and other cultural reforms were met with fierce opposition.

Opposition to Kemal in 1924-1927:
In 1924, while the "Issue of Mosul" was on the table, Sheikh Said began to organize the Sheikh Said Rebellion. Sheikh Said was a wealthy Kurdish Tribal chief of a local Naqshabandi order. Members of the government saw the Sheikh Said Rebellion as an attempt at a counter-revolution. They urged immediate military action to prevent its spread. The "Law for the Maintenance of Public Order" was passed to deal with the rebellion on 4 March 1925. It gave the government exceptional powers and included the authority to shut down subversive groups, but was repealed on 4 March 1929. Mustafa Kemal said, "the Turkish nation is firmly determined to advance fearlessly on the path of the republic, civilization and progress".

On 17 November 1924, the breakaway group established the Progressive Republican Party (PRP) with 29 deputies and the first multi-party system began. The PRP's economic program suggested liberalism.

During 1926, a plot to assassinate Mustafa Kemal was uncovered in Izmir. It originated with a former deputy who had opposed the abolition of the Caliphate. The investigations found a link between the members of the PRP and the Sheikh Said Rebellion. The PRP was dissolved following the outcomes of the trial. Mustafa Kemal's saying, "My mortal body will turn into dust, but the Republic of Turkey will last forever," was regarded as a will after the assassination attempt.

Modernization efforts, 1926-1930:
In the years following 1926, Mustafa Kemal introduced a radical departure from previous reformations established by the Ottoman Empire. For the first time in history, Islamic law was separated from secular law, and restricted to matters of religion.

On 1 March 1926, the Turkish penal code was passed. It was modeled after the Italian Penal Code. On 4 October 1926, Islamic courts were closed. He and his staff discussed issues like abolishing the veiling of women and the integration of women into the outside world.

Mustafa Kemal needed a new civil code to establish his second major step of giving freedom to women. The first part was the education of girls and was established with the unification of education. On 4 October 1926, the new Turkish civil code passed. It was modeled after the Swiss Civil Code. Under the new code, women gained equality with men in such matters as inheritance and divorce.

Kemal believed that "culture is the foundation of the Turkish Republic." and described modern Turkey's ideological thrust as "a creation of patriotism blended with a lofty humanist ideal." The pre-Islamic culture of the Turks became the subject of extensive research, and particular emphasis was laid upon Turkish culture widespread before the Seljuk and Ottoman civilizations. He instigated study of Anatolian civilizations--Phrygians and Lydians, Sumerians and Hittites. He also stressed the folk arts of the countryside as a wellspring of Turkish creativity.

In the spring of 1928, Mustafa Kemal met in Ankara with several linguists and professors from all over Turkey where he unveiled to them a plan of his to implement a new alphabet for the written Turkish language based on a modified Latin alphabet. The new Turkish alphabet would serve as a replacement for the old Arabic script and as a solution to the literacy problem in Turkey.

Over the next several months, Mustafa Kemal pressed for the introduction of the new Turkish alphabet as well as made public announcements to the upcoming overhaul of the new alphabet. On 1 November 1928, Mustafa Kemal introduced the new Turkish alphabet and abolished the use of Arabic script. At the time, literate citizens of the country comprised as little as 10% of the population. The first Turkish newspaper using the new alphabet was published on 15 December 1928. Kemal himself travelled the countryside in order to teach citizens the new alphabet. The country's adaptation to the new alphabet was very quick, and literacy in Turkey jumped from 10% to over 70% within two years. Beginning in 1932, the People's Houses (Turkish: Halk Evleri) opened throughout the country in order to meet the requirement that people between the ages of four and 40 were required to learn the new alphabet as mandated.

Turkish women were taught not only child care, dress-making and household management, but also skills needed to join the economy outside the home. Turkish education became an integrative system, aimed to alleviate poverty and used female education to establish gender equality.

Opposition to Kemal in 1930-1931:

On 11 August 1930, Mustafa Kemal decided to try a multiparty movement once again and asked Ali Fethi Okyar to establish a new party. He insisted on the protection of secular reforms. The brand-new Liberal Republican Party succeeded all around the country. Without the establishment of a real political spectrum, once again, the party became the center to opposition of Ataturk's reforms, particularly in regard to the role of religion in public life.

On 23 December 1930, a chain of violent incidents occurred, starting with the rebellion of Islamic fundamentalists in Menemen, a small town in the Aegean region.

In November 1930, Ali Fethi Okyar dissolved his own party. A more lasting multi-party period of the Republic of Turkey began in 1945. In 1950, the RPP released the majority position to the Democratic Party. In one of his many speeches about the importance of democracy, Mustafa Kemal said in 1933:

> "Republic means the democratic administration of the state. We founded the Republic, reaching its tenth year. It should enforce all the requirements of democracy as the time comes.

Modernization efforts, 1931-1938:

In 1931, Mustafa Kemal established the Turkish Language Association for conducting research works in the Turkish language (Turkish: *Turk Dil Kurumu*). The Turkish Historical Society (Turkish: *Turk Tarih Kurumu*) was established in 1931, and began maintaining archives in 1932 for conducting research works on the history of Turkey. On 1 January 1928, he established the Turkish Education Association.

Mustafa Kemal dealt with the translation of scientific terminology into Turkish. He wanted the Turkish language reform to be methodologically based. He personally oversaw the development of the Sun Language Theory (Turkish: *Güneş Dil Teorisi*), which was a linguistic theory which proposed that all human languages were descendants of one Central Asian primal language. He introduced the Sun Language Theory into Turkish political and educational circles in 1935, although he did later correct the more extremist practices. Ataturk supported and encouraged the visual and the plastic arts, which had been suppressed by the Ottoman leaders, who regarded depiction of the human form as idolatry.

In 1932, a Qur'an in the Turkish language was read before a live audience and broadcast over the radio. All Qur'ans at the time were printed in Old Arabic. These Turkish Qur'ans were fiercely opposed by religious people. With the support of Mustafa Kemal, the Parliament approved the project and the Directorate of Religious Affairs enlisted, Mehmet Akif (Ersoy), to compose a Qur'an translation and a Islamic scholar Elmalılı Hamdi Yazır to author a Turkish language Qur'anic commentary (Tafsir) titled "Hak Dini Kur'an Dili." It was only in 1935 that the version read in public found its way to print. In 1934, Mustafa Kemal commissioned the first Turkish operatic work, *Özsoy*.

On 5 December 1934, Turkey moved to grant full political rights to women, before several other European nations. Mustafa Kemal said that

> "There is no logical explanation for the political disenfranchisement of women. ...Women must have the right to vote and to be elected..."

Change came slowly; in the 1935 elections there were only 18 female MPs out of a total of 395 representatives.

Foreign policies:

Ataturk's foreign policy followed his motto, "peace at home and peace in the world." The Turkish War of Independence was the last time Ataturk used his military might in dealing with other countries. Foreign issues were resolved by peaceful methods during his presidency.

Issue of Mosul:

The "Issue of Mosul", a dispute with the United Kingdom over control of Mosul Province, was one of the first foreign affairs-related controversies of the new Republic. During the Mesopotamian campaign, General Marshall followed the British War Office's instruction that "every effort was to be made to score as heavily as possible on the Tigris before the whistle blew", capturing Mosul three days after the signature of the Armistice of Mudros (30 October 1918). In 1920, the *Misak-ı Milli*, which consolidated the "Turkish lands", declared that Mosul Province was a part of the historic Turkish heartland. The Iraqi revolt against the British was put down by the RAF Iraq Command during the summer of 1920.

In 1923, Mustafa Kemal tried to persuade the GNA that accepting the arbitration of the League of Nations at the Treaty of Lausanne over Mosul did not mean relinquishing Mosul, but rather waiting for a time when Turkey might be stronger. The artificially drawn border had an unsettling effect on both sides of the population. Later, it was claimed that Turkey began where the oil ends as the border was drawn by the British geophysicists based on the oil reserves. Ataturk did not want this separation. The British Foreign Secretary attempted to disclaim any existence of oil in the Mosul area. On 23 January 1923, Lord Curzon argued that the existence of oil was no more than hypothetical. "England wanted oil. Mosul and Kurds were the key."

In 1925, the League of Nations formed a three-member committee to study the case while the Sheikh Said Rebellion was on the rise. By the end of March 1925, the necessary troop movements were completed, and the whole area of the Sheikh Said rebellion was encircled. As a result of these maneuvers, the revolt was put down. Britain, Iraq and Kemal made a treaty on 5 June 1926, which mostly followed the decisions of the League Council. A large section of the Kurdish population and the Iraqi Turkmen were left on the other side of the border. In 1925, the population was largely illiterate and disparate. Turkey was in ruins, reconstruction was difficult, poverty was everywhere and people were in pain, which fed separatist violence.

Relations with the RSFSR/Soviet Union:
In 1920 alone, the Lenin government supplied the Kemalists with 6,000 rifles, over 5 million rifle cartridges, 17,600 projectiles as well as 200.6 kg of gold bullion; in the subsequent 2 years the amount of aid increased.

In March 1921, the GNA representatives in Moscow signed the "Friendship and Brotherhood" Treaty with Soviet Russia, which was a major diplomatic breakthrough for the Kemalists.

The two country's relations were friendly but were based on the fact that they were fighting against a common enemy: Britain and the West. Nevertheless, the entire Turkish communist leadership was assassinated on 28 January 1921 at Kemal's behest.

After the Turks, on 16 December 1925, withdrew their delegation from Geneva, thus leaving the League of Nations Council to grant a mandate for the Mosul region to Britain without their consent, Kemal countered by concluding a non-aggression pact with the USSR on 17 December the same year. In 1935, the pact was prolonged for another 10 years. During the second half of the 1930s, Mustafa Kemal tried to establish a closer relationship with Britain and other major western powers, which caused displeasure on the part of the Soviets.

Turkish-Greek alliance:
The post-war leader of Greece, Eleftherios Venizelos, was also determined to establish normal relations between the two states. The war devastated Western Anatolia, and the financial burden of Ottoman Muslim refugees from Greece blocked rapprochement. Venizelos moved forward with the agreement despite accusations of conceding too much on the issues of the naval armaments, and the properties of the Ottoman Greeks from Turkey according to the Treaty of Lausanne.

Ultimately, many Greeks consider the reconciliation with Turkey among the greatest foreign policy achievements of Venizelos' final term as Prime Minister. Greece renounced all its claims over Turkish territory and the two sides concluded an agreement on 30 April 1930. On 25 October, Venizelos visited Turkey, and signed a treaty of friendship. Indeed, Venizelos' successor Panagis Tsaldaris came to visit Ataturk in September 1933 and signed a more comprehensive agreement, called the Entente Cordiale, a stepping stone for the Balkan Pact.

Neighbors to the east:
From 1919, Afghanistan was in the midst of a reformation period under Amanullah Khan. Afghan Foreign Minister Mahmud Tarzi was a follower of Mustafa Kemal's domestic policy. During the late 1920s, Anglo-Afghan relations soured over British fears of an Afghan-Soviet friendship. On 20 May 1928, Anglo-Afghan politics gained a positive perspective, when Amanullah Khan and the Queen were received by Mustafa Kemal in Constantinople. This meeting was followed by a Turkey-Afghanistan Friendship and Cooperation pact on 22 May 1928. In 1934, Afghanistan's relations with the international community gained a huge boost when it joined the League of Nations. In 1937, King Zahir Shah became a signatory of the Treaty of Saadabad. Mahmud Tarzi received Mustafa Kemal's personal support until he died on 22 November 1933 in Istanbul.

Mustafa Kemal and Reza Shah had a common approach regarding British imperialism and its influence in their region, creating a slow but continuous rapprochement between Ankara and Tehran. The relations were strained after the abolishment of the Caliphate. Iran's Shi'a clergy did not accept Kemal's position. Iranian religious power centers perceived the real motive behind Ataturk's reforms was to undermine the power of the clergy. An admirer of Mustafa Kemal and close student of his reforms, Reza Shah followed the same type of modernization efforts. By the mid-1930s, Reza Shah's efforts had upset the clergy throughout Iran, thus widening the gap between religion and government. Mustafa Kemal feared the occupation and dismemberment of Iran as a multi-ethnic/multi-tribal society by Russia or Great Britain. Like Mustafa Kemal, Reza Shah wanted to secure Iran's borders. Reza Shah visited him in 1934. In 1935, the draft of what would become the Treaty of Saadabad was paragraphed in Geneva, but the signing of it was delayed because of the border dispute between Iran and Iraq. Iran challenged the validity of both the Treaty of Erzerum and the Constantinople Protocol in 1934.

On 8 July 1937, Turkey, Iraq, Iran and Afghanistan signed the Saadabad Pact at Tehran. The signatories undertook to preserve their common frontiers, to consult together in all matters of common interest and to commit no aggression against one another's territory. The treaty united the Afghan king's call for greater Oriental-Middle Eastern cooperation, Reza Shah's goal in securing relations with Turkey that would help Iran free herself from Soviet and British influence, and Mustafa Kemal's foreign policy of securing stability in the region. The immediate outcome was to deter Mussolini from adventures in the region.

Turkish Straits:

On 24 July 1923, the Treaty of Lausanne included the Lausanne Straits Agreement. The Lausanne Straits Agreement stated that the Dardanelles should remain open to all commercial vessels: Turkey could not limit any military passage during wartime. The Lausanne Straits Agreement stated that the waterway was to be demilitarized, and its management left to the Straits Commission. The defense of Constantinople was impossible without having the sovereignty over the water that passed through it.

In March 1936, Hitler's reoccupation of the Rhineland gave Mustafa Kemal the opportunity to resume full control over the Straits. Mustafa Kemal demanded that the members of the Turkish Foreign Office devise a solution that would transfer full control over the waterway to Turkey.

On 20 July 1936, the Montreux Convention was signed, with the participation of Bulgaria, Great Britain, Australia, France, Japan, Romania, the Soviet Union, Turkey, Yugoslavia and Greece. It became the primary instrument governing the passage of commercial and war vessels through the Dardanelles Strait. It was ratified by the GNAT on 31 July 1936. It went into effect on 9 November 1936, and is still valid today.

Balkan Pact:

By the end of 1925, Turkey had signed fifteen joint agreements with Western states. In the early 1930s, changes and developments in world politics required Turkey to make multilateral agreements to improve its security. Mustafa Kemal strongly believed that a close cooperation between the Balkan states based on the principle of equality would have an important effect on European politics. These states had been ruled by the Ottoman Empire for centuries, and had formed a powerful force.

The Balkan Pact was negotiated by Mustafa Kemal with Greece, Romania, and Yugoslavia. This mutual-defense agreement intended to guarantee the signatories' territorial integrity and political independence against attack by another Balkan state such as Bulgaria or Albania. He thought of the Balkan Pact as a medium of balance in the relations with the European countries.

The Balkan Pact provided for regular military and diplomatic consultations.

> "The borders of the allies in the Balkan Pact are a single border. Those who covet this border will encounter the burning beams of the sun. I recommend avoiding this. The forces that defend our borders are a single and inseparable force."

It was signed by GNA on 28 February The Greek and Yugoslav Parliaments ratified the agreement a few days after. The unanimously ratified Balkan pact became a reality on 18 May 1935 and lasted until 1940. The goal of Ataturk, to protect southeast Europe, failed with the dissolution of the pact. The only state which arose intact after the war was Ataturk's Republic of Turkey.

Issue of Hatay:
In 1936, Ataturk raised the "Issue of Hatay" at the League of Nations. Hatay was based on the old administrative unit of the Ottoman Empire called the Sanjak of Alexandretta. On behalf of the League of Nations, the representatives of France, the United Kingdom, the Netherlands, Belgium and Turkey prepared a constitution for Hatay, which established it as an autonomous Sanjak within Syria. Despite some inter-ethnic violence, in the midst of 1938 an election was conducted by the local legislative assembly. The cities of Antakya (Antioch) and İskenderun (Alexandretta) joined Turkey in 1939.

Economic policies:
Mustafa Kemal's vision regarding early Turkish economic policy was apparent during the Izmir Economic Congress of 1923 which was established before the signing of the Lausanne Treaty. The initial choices of Mustafa Kemal's economic policies reflected the realities of his period. After World War I, due to the lack of any real potential investors to open private sector factories and develop industrial production, Kemal established many state-owned factories for agriculture, machinery, and textile industries.

State intervention, 1923-1929:
For Mustafa Kemal, as for his supporters, tobacco remained wedded to his policy in the pursuit of economic independence. Turkish tobacco was an important industrial crop, while its cultivation and

manufacture were French monopolies under capitulations of the Ottoman Empire. The control of tobacco was the biggest achievement of the Kemalist political machinery's "nationalization" of the economy for a country that did not produce oil. They accompanied this achievement with the development of the cotton industry, which peaked during the early 1930s. Cotton was the second biggest industrial crop in Turkey.

In 1927, Turkish State Railways was established. Because Mustafa Kemal considered the development of a national rail network as another important step in industrialization, it was given high priority. However, in 1937, the 22,000 km of roads in Turkey augmented the railways.

Great Depression, 1929-1931:
The young republic, like the rest of the world, found itself in a deep economic crisis during the Great Depression. However, Turkey could not finance essential imports; its currency was shunned and zealous revenue officials seized the meager possessions of peasants who could not pay their taxes.

In 1929, Mustafa Kemal signed a treaty that resulted in the restructuring of the nation's debt with the Ottoman Public Debt Administration. He did not fault the Ottoman debt.

In 1931, Mustafa Kemal's intention to establish the Central Bank of the Republic of Turkey was realized. The bank's primary purpose was to have control over the exchange rate, and Ottoman Bank's role during its initial years as a central bank was phased out. Later specialized banks such as the Sümerbank (1932) and the Etibank (1935) were founded.

From the political economy perspective, Mustafa Kemal had to face the same problems which all countries faced: political upheaval.

Liberalization and planned growth, 1931-1939:
The first (1929–1933) and second five year economic plans were performed under the supervision of Mustafa Kemal. The first five year economic plan promoted consumer substitution industries. However, these economic plans changed drastically with the death of Kemal and the rise of World War II.

In 1931, Mustafa Kemal watched the first national aircraft, MMV-1, develop. He realized the important role of aviation. In his words, "the future lies in the skies". Turkish Aeronautical Association was founded in 16 February 1925 by his directive. Operational American Curtiss Hawk fighters were being produced soon after his death and before the onset of World War II.

In 1936 Nuri Demirağ established the first Turkish aircraft factory in the Beşiktaş district of Istanbul. The first Turkish airplanes, Nu D.36 and Nu D.38, were produced in this factory. During 1935, Turkey was becoming an industrial society on the Western European model set out by Ataturk. However, the gap between Mustafa Kemal's goals and the achievements of the socio-political structure of the country was not closed.

Personal life:
On 29 January 1923, Mustafa Kemal married Latife Uşaklıgil; they were divorced on 5 August 1925. He never remarried. During his lifetime, Ataturk adopted twelve daughters and a son.

During 1937, indications that Ataturk's health was worsening started to appear. In early 1938, while he was on a trip to Yalova, he suffered from a serious illness. He went to Istanbul for treatment, where he was diagnosed with cirrhosis of the liver due to heavy alcohol consumption. He died on 10 November 1938, at the age of 57, in the Dolmabahçe Palace, where he spent his last days. The clock in the bedroom where he died is still set to the time of his death, 9:05 in the morning. Mustafa Kemal's remains were originally laid to rest in the Ethnography Museum of Ankara, and transferred on 10 November 1953, 15 years after his death in a 42-ton sarcophagus, to a mausoleum that overlooks Ankara.

Legacy:
At the exact time of his death, on every 10 November, at 09:05 am, most vehicles and people in the country's streets pause for one minute in remembrance.

Outlawing insults to his reminiscence:
In 1951, the Turkish Parliament issued a law (5816) outlawing insults to his reminiscence (Turkish: *Hatırası*) or destruction of objects representing him.

In 2010 the French-based NGO Reporters Without Borders declared that the Turkish laws to protect the memory of Kemal Ataturk are in contradiction with the current European Union standards of freedom of speech in news media.

Mustafa Kemal Ataturk:
1st President of the Republic of Turkey:
In office:
29 October 1923 - 10 November 1938 (15 years, 12 days)

Military service: Allegiance:
Ottoman Empire (1893 - 8 July 1919)
Republic of Turkey (9 July 1919 - 30 June 1927)

Service/branch: Army
Rank:
Ottoman Empire: General (Pasha)
Republic of Turkey: Mareşal (Marshal)

***

Nabulsi, Suleiman (1908-1976): Jordanian political, prime minister, 1956-57. Born into a notable family in Salt, Jordan, Nabulsi graduated in la and social studies from the American University in Beirut. He was Jordan's ambassador to Britain from 1953-54. It merged the Arab legion with the (Palestinian dominated) National Guard to create a 35,000 strong army. When parliament abrogated the 1948 Anglo Jordanian Treaty, the monarch did not overrule it. In April 1957 the king resisted a challenge from the Free Officers, led by Ali Abu Nawar who had succeeded Sir John Bagot Glubb as chief of staff.

***

Nadir Shah (1688-1747): Ruler of Persia (1736-1747) and scourge of Central Asia and India. Of Turkish origin until 1726 a bandit chieftain, he rose to prominence under the Safavid shahs of Persia, acting as king-maker during an era of disputed succession. In 1736 when the infant shah died he seized the throne and immediately embarked on expeditions against neighboring states. In 1739 he attacked Delhi, capital of Mogul India, but retreated after slaughtering the citizens. Campaigns against Russia and Turkey followed but military adventures were by then at the price of Persia's economic stability. His own subjects suffered as much as his enemies from his ruthless methods, and he was assassinated by his own troops. Nadir Shah or Nader Shah, 1688-1747, shah of Iran (1736-47), sometimes considered the last of the great Asian conquerors.

He was a member of the Afshar tribe. Although taken prisoner by the Uzbeks while he was still a child, he escaped and entered the service of the governor of Khorasan. There he earned a reputation for bravery. He then entered the service of Tahmasp, the son of Shah Sultan Husayn, who was asserting his claims against the Afghans under Mahmud, who had usurped the Persian throne. Nadir took the name Tahmasp Kuli Khan [Tahmasp's slave] and proceeded to win a series of battles against the Afghans. Decisively beaten, they retired to Kandahar, and Tahmasp was restored to the rule over Iran. Nadir, however, was the powerful figure of the realm.

    He fought against the Turks successfully, and when the shah turned victory to disaster by a conciliatory peace, Nadir in 1732 deposed him. Tahmasp's infant son Abbas III was placed on the throne with Nadir as regent. The conquests continued, and the western boundary was restored to what it had been before the Afghan invasions. In 1736 Nadir deposed Abbas and himself became shah, thus ending the rule of the Safavid dynasty. He attempted to weld Iran and the Ottoman Empire by unifying the Shiites and Sunnis. This led to much dissatisfaction in Shiite Iran, and the plan was discarded. In 1738-39 Nadir invaded Mughal India.

    He was brilliantly successful, taking and sacking Delhi and Lahore and carrying off vast treasure, including the Koh-i-noor diamond and the Peacock Throne. He also continued his conquests in other directions. Bukhara was subdued, and the limits of Iran were extended to the greatest that they had been since the days of the Sassanids. War with the Turks occupied his attention from 1743 to 1746. Nadir's later years were darkened by a turn toward tyranny, suspicion, and greed. So much did he fear opposition that he had his own son blinded. In 1747, during a campaign against rebellious Kurds, Nadir Shah was assassinated by officers of his own guard. Although the dynasty he founded, the Afshar dynasty (1736-49), was short-lived, Nadir is generally regarded as one of the greatest of all rulers of Persia.

***

Nahas (Pasha), Mustafa (1879-1965): Egyptian politician, prime minister 1928, 1930,1935-1937, 1942-1944, 1950-1952 Born into a wealthy Cairene family, Nahas obtained a law degree from the University of Cairo. Nahas served in the Wafd government under Zaghlul. When Zaghlul died in 1927, Nahas succeeded him as leader of the party. In 1928 and 1930 he served as prime minister, but was forced by the monarch to resign. Nahas was dismissed from office in December 1937 by King Faruq. In February 1942 when German troops were advancing on Egypt from Libya, the British intervened militarily by surrounding the royal palace with tanks and gave Faruq the choice of abdicating or appointing the pro British Nahas as prime minister. When his talks on the future of the 1936 Treaty and the British military presence in the Suez Canal zone failed, Nahas unilaterally abrogated the Treaty in 1951.

Following the July 1952 coup all political parties including Wafd were outlawed. Nahas Pasha (Mustafa Nahas Pasha), 1876-1965, Egyptian statesmen, leader (1927-52) of the Wafd party. He was premier five times between 1928 and 1952. During World War II the British forced (1942) King Farouk to appoint Nahas as head of a government favorable to the Allies. When he became premier for the last time (1951), he denounced the Anglo-Egyptian treaty of alliance, which he had signed as premier in 1936. Agitation against the British led to rioting in Cairo in Jan., 1952, and Nahas was dismissed by the king. After the king's abdication later in the year, Nahas supported the new Egyptian government, but he was subsequently forced to disband the Wafd. He and his wife were imprisoned in 1953. After their release in 1954 he retired into private life.

***

Nasir al-Din al-Tusi (1201-1274): The thirteenth century was one of the most destructive periods in Islamic history. The Abbasid Caliph's apparent weakness made the Islamic East vulnerable to foreign attack; in fact, the fragility of the Caliph's position became all too clear when the Mongol hordes emerged from Asia and threatened to overwhelm the heartlands of Islam. Once a great seat of Islamic political, military and intellectual dominance, Baghdad now was a shadow of its former self. Thanks to the *bait al-Hikmah* (House of Wisdom) of the early Abbasid era and the Nizamiyyah College of the Seljuk period, the Muslim world once led the world in intellectual and literary pursuits. During this sad and tumultuous period in Islamic history, Nasir al-Din al-Tusi emerged to reinvigorate the Islamic intellectual world by founding one of Islamic history's most prominent institutions of higher education.

Abu Ja'far Muhammad ibn Muhammad ibn Hasan Nasir al-Din al-Tusi was born in Tus, in the Persian province of Khurasan. Al-Tusi developed his thirst for knowledge and wisdom from an early age. After completing his elementary education at home, he went to Nishapur to pursue advanced education in Islamic, philosophical and other sciences of the day.

Al-Tusi was a Shi'a scholar of the *Ithna 'Ashari* (Twelver) tradition. He was only in his early twenties when Khurasan was invaded by the Mongols and this forced him to seek sanctuary with the followers of the neo-Ismaili Assassin (*Nizari*) sect. Founded by Hasan-i-Sabbah, this extremist religious sect became notorious for assassinating their opponents.

Following the Mongol capture of Alamut in 1255, al-Tusi experienced considerable personal hardship and suffering. But, impressed by his vast learning and erudition, the Mongol ruler Hulagu appointed him his personal advisor. Al-Tusi was with the Mongol warlord when he launched his devastating attack on Baghdad, the seat of the Abbasid Caliphate, in 1258. According to some Shi'a sources, it was al-Tusi who urged the Mongols to attack Baghdad because he was eager to bring down the Sunni Abbasid Caliphate.

Nonetheless, the Mongol sack of Baghdad was a truly unprecedented event. From being once the home of some of the Muslim world's finest schools, colleges, libraries and hospitals, the Mongols turned Baghdad into rubble. His failure to save the city's libraries probably inspired al-Tusi to construct the Maraghah Observatory which later became one of the Islamic world's finest institutions of higher education and learning. Ironically, this was achieved thanks largely to the generous patronage of Hulagu himself. After the Observatory was completed in 1261, this institution housed more than forty thousand books on all the sciences of the day; some of the books were most probably rescued from the ransacked libraries of Baghdad and Damascus.

Most significantly, in the field of astronomy he proposed a new theory of planetary motion which was different from the Ptolemaic theory, and which later inspired Qutb al-Din Shirazi, Ulugh Beg, Ibn al-Shatir and Copernicus to formulate their own theories of planetary motion.

Al-Tusi's defense of Ibn Sina was instrumental in the revival of Peripatetic philosophy in Persia. As an adherent and exponent of Twelver Shi'ism, al-Tusi wrote prolifically on *Ithna 'Ashari* theology; indeed, he was one of the first to systematically formulate the fundamental tenets of Shi'a belief and practices. Keen to promote religious tolerance and cultural harmony, his ethical discourse sought to unite people of all religious and racial backgrounds on the basis of our common humanity.

Author of more than one hundred books and treatises on almost all the sciences of his day, al-Tusi died at the age of seventy-three during the reign of Abaqa, the son and successor of Hulagu, and was buried in Kazimayn (located on the outskirts of Baghdad).

***

Nasser, Gamal Abdul (1918-1970): Egyptian military leader and political, President 1956-70, prime minister 1954-1956. Born in Bani Mor village, Asyut province, Nasser, son of a postal clerk, was a graduate of the Royal Military Academy in Cairo. He underwent further training at the staff college and participated in the Palestine War (1948-1949) as a major in the Egyptian army. Promoted to colonel in 1950 he was appointed lecturer at the Royal Military Academy. Nasser was a charismatic leader of the clandestine Free Officers organization, which ousted King Faruq on 22 July 1952 and set up the ruling Revolutionary Command Council with Brig, Gen. Muhammad Neguib as its head.

After America had refused to sell him arms, he accepted an arms sales offer from Czechoslovakia. When the United states reacted by withdrawing its offer of aid for the Aswan High Dam project and getting the World Bank to do the same, Nasser nationalized the Suez Canal and accepted aid from Moscow. America, Britain, France and Israel fielded teams to assassinate Him. They failed. The withdrawal of the aggressors from Egypt by March 1957 raised Nasser's prestige at home and in the region. Following the ascendancy in Damascus n early 1966 of radical Ba'athists, who escalated the Palestinian guerilla attacks against Israel, Nasser once again found himself upstaged by Syria. To overcome the problem, in November 1966, he signed a defense pact with Syria, which specified a joint command for the Egyptian and Syrian forces in the event of war.

King Hussein of Jordan who hitherto had been hostile to Nasser, rushed to sign a mutual defense pact with Egypt on 30 May. This was the zenith of Nasser's power and prestige. Once Israel had realized that the international community would not force Nasser to reopen the Straits of Tiran to Israel ships, on 5 June it mounted devastating preemptive attacks on the air forces of Egypt, Syria, and Jordan. The debacle of the June 1967 Arab Israeli War virtually destroyed Nasser and Nasserism. In November 1967 he accepted UN Security Council Resolution 242 which called for the peaceful coexistence of Israel and the Arab states in return for Israel's evacuation of the Occupied Arab Territories. He withdrew Egyptian troops from the North Yemeni Civil War in December 1967. It was the strain of these negotiations that caused Nasser to have a fatal heart attack. A charismatic figure, Nasser was the first Egyptian to rule Egypt for a very long time, since King Fariq's family was originally from Albania.

***

Neguib, Muhammad (1901-1984): Egyptian military leader and politician: prime minister. 1952-53. president, 1953-54. Born to an Egyptian military officer and his wife in Khartoum, Sudan, Neguib graduated from the Royal Military Academy in Cairo. As an army officer, he rose steadily in rank and was a brigadier in 1948 when Egypt participated in the Palestine War. Promoted to brigadier general in 1950, he became commander of the ground forces the following year. Through Abdul Hakim Amer, his operations officer, Neguib was in touch with the Free officers organization. He accepted its offer to head the Revolutionary Command Council RCC after the July 1952 Coup. His differences with Gamal Abdul Nasser, the real leader of the RCC and the republic, came to the fore in February 1954 when the RCC banned the Muslim Brotherhood without consulting him. RCC dismissed him as president and put him under house arrest. He was freed in 1971 after the death of Nasser. He backed Anwar Sadat but did not reenter public life.

***

Nizam al-Mulk (1020-1092): One Muslim statesman and educationalist played a far greater role in the rise and development of a world-class educational system in the Muslim world than probably any other. His love of knowledge and desire to eliminate illiteracy throughout his dominion led to the emergence of a new vibrant culture of learning across the Muslim world. As the founder and patron of the famous Nizamiyyah Colleges, Nizam al-Mulk is today considered to be one of the Islamic history's most celebrated philanthropic statesmen and educators.

Abu Ali Hasan ibn Ali ibn Ishaq, better known as Nizam al-Mulk, was born in Radhkan, a small village located in Tus in the Persian province of Khurasan. After completing his elementary education, he travelled to Nishapur where he received advanced training in Arabic and Persian literature, mathematics and traditional Islamic sciences. In Nishapur, his classmates included Umar Khayyam, the famous poet, scientist and mathematician, and Hasan-i-Sabbah, the infamous founder of the neo-Ismaili Assassin sect.

Named after their ancestral leader Seljuk (Saljuq), the Turkish Oghuz (also known as Ghuzz or Dokuz) clans converted to Islam during the early part of the eleventh century. They became one of the Muslim world's most powerful political dynasties of the time. After restoring the traditional Caliphate in Baghdad, the Seljuks successfully thwarted Fatimid attempts to gain full control of the Muslim world. Grateful to the Seljuks for defending the Abbasid Caliphate from Fatimid encroachment, the reigning Abbasid Caliph Malik al-Rahm officially crowned the first Seljuk ruler, Tughrul Beh, as the 'King of the East and West'.

Following the death of Tughrul Beg in 1063, a protracted power struggle broke out within the Seljuk royal family, but eventually Alp Arsalan emerged victorious and became the Sultan of the Seljuk dynasty. Immediately after ascending the throne, he promoted Nizam al-Mulk to the post of *Wazir* (or Prime Minister) of his vast kingdom. Alp Arsalan broke away from his family tradition and appointed Nizam al-Mulk, who was of Persian origin, to the highest post in the land. They were keen to preserve the Baghdad-based Abbasid Caliphate from the Fatimids of Egypt, who were at the time busy planning its downfall.

By reorganizing and unifying the civil and administrative systems of the Government – whose remit extended from Syria at one end, to Iran at the other – Nizam al-Mulk was able to stamp out corruption and malpractice, and improve accountability and efficiency. Under his stewardship, the Seljuk dynasty became one of the most powerful, prosperous and culturally advanced dynasties of its time.

Nizam al-Mulk despised illiteracy so much that he promoted free education throughout the dominion. Begun in 1066, when he was only forty-six, these educational institutions were established in all the major cities of the Seljuk kingdom including Nishapur, Baghdad and Damascus. These institutions were the Harvard and Oxford of their time.

Nizam al-Mulk closely supervised the collection and distribution of *zakat* (obligatory alms). In addition, he constructed medical clinics and hospitals which offered free health care and medication to the people. Following in the footsteps of the Abbasid Caliph Harun al-Rashid, he built resting places along the main trade routes as well. He became one of the most influential and revered Muslim statesmen of all time – along with Umar ibn Abd al-Aziz, Abd al-Rahman III, Sultan Nur al-Din Zangi, Salah al Din Ayyubi and Sulaiman the Magnificent.

Nizam al-Mulk was fifty-two when Sultan Alp Arsalan was brutally murdered in 1072, but Malik Shah, his son and successor, asked him to stay on as Prime Minister. It is worth pointing out that Nizam al-Mulk wrote on political thought and administration around three hundred years before Machiavelli was born. Attacked by an agent of Hasan-i-Sabbah while he was on his way to Baghdad, he died at the age of seventy-two.

The grand vizier of the Seljuks Sultans Alp Arslan and Malik shah and author of the Siyasetname or Book of Counsel for Kings. Under his administration considerable change is in the Iqta were made, order and peace were maintained within the Seljuk dominions and Nizamiyya madrasahs established throughout the Seljuk Empire.

***

Nizar (-   ): The older son of Isma'il; destabilized the Seljuks through assassinations. They were known by the Crusaders as the "Assassins" (mostly Sunni leaders). The sect was led by Rashid Al-Din Sinan "The Old Man of the Mountain". A violent sect that plagued the Abbasid caliphs; an offshoot of the Shi'a, also known as "The Assassins".

***

Nur Al-Din Zangi (1117-1174): After four hundred years of unrivalled political supremacy and military domination of the Middle East, the Muslims became politically disunited during the eleventh century. Hitherto the Abbasids had ruled the Islamic world without much opposition, but by the middle of the eleventh century, the Abbasid Empire had become fragmented into several fiefdoms. After the Umayyad rule of Islamic Spain came to an abrupt end in 1031, political chaos and anarchy became the order of the day in that part of the world. Although the rise of the Seljuk dynasty did usher in a period of peace and prosperity for a time, after the death of the Seljuk ruler Malik Shah in 1092, this dynasty also began to decline rapidly. As political rivalry and social chaos spread across much of the Muslim world, the Crusaders entered the Muslim sphere of influence in 1096 and established a Crusader Kingdom in Palestine. After capturing Jerusalem, Islam's third holiest city, the Crusaders threatened to overwhelm the entire Islamic East until Sultan Nur al-Din Zangi, the famous Saint-King of the Zangid dynasty, emerged to rally the Muslim world to confront the Crusaders for the first time.

Nur al-Din Mahmud Zangi, known as Nur al-Din Zangi for short, was born in the northern city of Mosul. His father, Imad al-Din Zangi, was a Turkish military commander who at the time was in the service of the Seljuks. Young Nur al-Din was therefore brought up and educated in his father's luxurious and secluded mansion in Mosul. In 1127, when Nur al-Din was only ten, the Seljuk ruler Sultan Mahmud II appointed Imad al-Din governor of Mosul. Soon after becoming governor, Imad al-Din declared his independence from the Seljuks and established a separate political entity consisting of the cities of Sinjar, Nasibin, Jazirat ibn Umar and Harran, with his political headquarters based in Mosul.

A year later, Imad al-Din took advantage of the chaos which prevailed in Aleppo at the time and added that city to his expanding empire. He then annexed the territories of Hamah and Hims but, to his huge disappointment, he failed to capture the historic city of Damascus.

Not willing to fight on two fronts simultaneously, he turned his attention toward Edessa, the capital of the oldest Crusader State in the Muslim world. The capture of this city by the Muslims under the leadership of Imad al-Din in 1144 sent a shudder through the ranks of the Crusaders, and reinvigorated the Muslims' determination to drive out the Crusaders from the Islamic East. Two years after the capture of Edessa, Imad al-Din was murdered by his bodyguard in 1146. As the news of his death spread across the Zangid kingdom, chaos and confusion ensued until Nur al-Din, his second son, emerged to restore peace and order across the region.

Nur al-Din succeeded his father as the Sultan of the Zangid kingdom in 1146 at the age of twenty-nine. As a ruler and statesman, the Sultan was determined to reunite the Muslim world under the banner of Islam and drive out the Crusaders from the Islamic East. After appointing his brother, Sayf al-Din, governor of Mosul and its surrounding territories, he moved to Aleppo to take care of that strategically important principality. On his arrival in Syria, he received news that Edessa had again fallen into the hands of the enemy. Nur al-Din organized an expeditionary force and marched to Edessa at a lightning speed. He arrived there even before the Crusaders could organize their defenses properly. The recapture of Edessa without a fight not only won him widespread acclaim, but also helped to consolidate his position as supreme ruler of the Zangid dynasty.

However, the Crusaders' siege of Damascus backfired in spectacular fashion when Mu'in al-Din's forces inflicted a crushing defeat on the powerful Frankish army. A year after the Franks' humiliating defeat at the Battle of Damascus, Mu'in al-Din died, leaving the door wide open for Sultan Nur al-Din to move in and further expand his empire. As expected, in 1149, the Sultan captured Antioch and five years later added Damascus to his expanding empire. Inspired by his desire and determination to reclaim Jerusalem from the Crusaders, Nur al-din now became a powerful adversary of the Crusader kingdom. With Jerusalem now very much within his reach, his dream of liberating Islam's third holiest site from the grip of the Crusaders seemed a real possibility. But his plans were thwarted by a powerful earthquake which struck Syria in 1167 and completely devastated the country. In the same year, he fell seriously ill.

Again, as the Sultan contemplated the possibility of taking the fight to the Crusaders in Jerusalem, he received news of Byzantine military activity to the north of Syria. When he made contact with the Byzantine Emperor Manuel, the latter assured him that he had no intention of attacking Zangid territories. Even so, the presence of Byzantine forces close to his borders prevented the Sultan from launching an expedition against the Franks. Most unexpectedly, during this period, Egypt rather than Palestine became the main theater of warfare. After Egypt became a Fatimid stronghold during the tenth century, it was ruled by a succession of Caliphs who saw themselves as rivals of the Abbasid Caliphs in Baghdad. But, by the middle of the twelfth century, the Fatimid grip on Egypt had become very precarious. So much so that from 1163 to 1169 the Fatimids clashed with the Franks and the Zangids on more than one occasion over the rich prize that was Egypt.

At the insistence of his gifted general Asad al-Din Shirkuh, the uncle of the famous Salah al-Din (Saladin), Sultan Nur al-Din eventually authorized a large-scale military expedition against Egypt in order to add this country to his empire. Amalric, a Frankish ruler who was eager to annex this strategically important Muslim country, and the third was Shirkuh, the Kurdish general in the service of Sultan Nur al-Din. These three men fought each other for nearly a decade to gain control of Egypt until Shirkuh, assisted by his young nephew Salah al-Din, finally triumphed in 1169. His victory enabled Nur al-Din to add Egypt to his expanding empire. However, after Shirkuh's unexpected death, young Salah al-Din exercised power in Egypt on behalf of Sultan Nur al-Din. And although Salah al-Din remained loyal to the Sultan, in reality he came to be seen as an independent ruler in his own right.

As time passed, Sultan Nur al-Din's dream of reclaiming Jerusalem from the grip of the Crusaders began to slowly fade away. Confined to his bed as a result of an angina attack, his health was now deteriorating rapidly. The credit for unifying the Islamic East must go to Sultan Nur al-Din. More importantly, he paved the way for Salah al-Din to take the fight to the Crusaders and re-establish Islamic political authority across the region. Not surprisingly, renowned historians like Ibn al-Athir, Ibn Khallikan and Ibn al-Jawzi have lavished much praise on Nur al-Din, often referring to him as the 'Saint-King' of Islam. He encouraged his officials to serve the public with honesty, dedication and care. He led such an exemplary lifestyle that even a bold and stubborn Salah al-Din never dared to cross his path.

Sultan Nur al-Din Mahmud Zangi, the famous 'Saint-King' of Islam, passed away at the age of sixty-one and was buried in Damascus.

***

Oqba ibn Nafi (-) nephew of Amr and an almost legendary figure of conquest and exploration from the annals of the first Muslim conquests. He participated in the conquest of Egypt, commanded the raids that would penetrate the Libyan Sahara, and was repelled from the Sudan before founding the city of Kairouan as an advance base for the conquest of North Africa.

***

Orkhan (1288-1362): Ottoman sultan (1326-1362?), son and successor of Osman I as leader of the Ottoman Turks. He defeated Byzantine Emperor Andronicus III and conquered large parts of Asia Minor, including Nicaea and Izmit. In 1345 the Ottomans first crossed into Europe to aid Byzantine Emperor John VI (John Cantacuzene). Orkhan married John's daughter Theodora. Orkhan crossed the Dardanelles two more times, assisting John against Stephen Dusan of Serbia and gaining for the Ottomans a foothold in Europe. He left a well-organized state to his son and successor, Murad I. Orkhan was the first Ottoman ruler to assume the title of sultan.

***

Osman I (1258-1326): Founder (1300) of the Ottoman Empire. He was the leader of the famed 'four hundred tents', who turned his band of Turkish nomads from raiding to permanent conquest. In 1290 he declared his independence from the Seljuk Turks and expanded his territory by capturing minor Christian kingdoms in north-western Turkey. Osman I or Othman I, 1259-1326, leader of the Ottoman Turks and founder of the dynasty that established and ruled the Ottoman Empire. The Osmanli or Ottoman Turks derive their name from Osman. He proclaimed (1290) his independence from his overlord, the Seljuk Turks, upon the collapse of their empire. Aided by an influx of Muslim warriors, he expanded his state in NW Asia Minor at the expense of the petty Christian lords who were his neighbors. He nevertheless inaugurated a policy of religious tolerance. Just before his death in 1326, his son and successor, Orkhan, took the city of Bursa form the Byzantines.

***

Pahlavi, Muhammad Reza Shah (1919-1980): Shah en shah (emperor) of Iran 1941-1979. Born in Tehran, Pahlavi was educated at a private school in Switzerland and the Tehran Military Academy. Pahlavi succeeded his father, Reza Shah Pahlavi in September 1941, who abdicated in his favor when angered at his neutrality in the Second World War, British and Soviet troops began to march toward Tehran. It was only after the Soviet troops had withdrawn in May 1946 and the Iranian forces had quelled autonomous governments in Kurdistan and Azerbaijan in December that Pahlavi was able to exercise authority over all of Iran.

Following a failed assassination attempt on him in February 1949, Pahlavi imposed martial law and banned the Tudeh Party. However in his tussle with the nationalist leader, Premier Muhammad Mussadiq. Pahlavi yielded to parliament's will to nationalize the British owned Anglo Iranian Oil Company in 1951. The ensuing power struggle led to the flight of Pahlavi to Rome on 16 August 1953. But three days later, aided by the US Central Intelligence Agency and royalist military officers Pahlavi staged a comeback. Under pressure from US President John F. Kennedy, Pahlavi began a land reform program in 1961. He dissolved parliament and ruled by decree. This led to increased opposition including from Ayatollah Ruhollah Khomeini. In January 1963 Pahlavi launched a six point White Revolution and repressed the groups that called for a boycott of the referendum on it.

It won 91 percent approval. But when after his release from prison in April 1964, Khomeini resumed his opposition. Pahlavi expelled him from Iran in November. In October 1971 Pahlavi celebrated 2,500 years of unbroken monarchy in Iran at the ancient capital of Persepolis near Shiraz. On the 10th anniversary of the White Revolution in January 1973 Pahlavi announced the nationalization of the Western oil consortium. On 16 January 1979 Pahlavi left Iran, ostensibly for a holiday in Aswan, Egypt. Pahlavi was allowed to enter the United States clandestinely in October for medical treatment. Iran demanded Pahlavi's extradition, which was refused. In March 1980 Egyptian President Anwar Sadat invited him to Cairo. He died there four months later, leaving behind his widow, Farah and their only son, Reza Cyrus.

***

Pahlavi, Reza Shah (1878-1944): Shah en Shah emperor of Iran, 1925-1941. Son of a military officer in a village in northern Mazandaran province, Pahlavi joined the army as a youth. Pahlavi centralized and modernized the state, creating a national civil service and police force. He pressured the Anglo Persian Oil Company in 1932 to increase its oil royalties and reduced its concessionaire area by 80 percent. The building of 14,000 miles of roads and Trans Iranian Railway by August 1938 boosted industrialization. Following the rise of Adolph Hitler in Germany in 1933, Pahlavi tried to use Berlin as a counterpart to the commercial and political dominance of London and Moscow. By the time the Second World War erupted in September 1939, Germany accounted for nearly half of Iran's foreign trade. Pahlavi declared Iran's neutrality in the conflict. In late August Soviet and British troops invaded Iran at five points. Fearing an imminent march of Soviet troops into Tehran. Pahlavi abdicated on 16 September in favor of his eldest son, Muhammad Reza. He left for the British ruled island of Mauritius, and then for South Africa.

***

Qaboos ibn Said (1940-   ): *Sultan of Oman, 1970 --; Prime Minister, 1970—* Born in Salalah, Qaboos was educated privately at the royal palace and then at a private college in Bury St. Edmonds, Britain. Some of them were used by London to plot the deposition of Sultan Said, which occurred on 23 July 1970. Qaboos was along in the Arab world in endorsing Egypt's Camp David Accords with Israel, and did to cut ties with it after the signing of a peace treaty between the two countries. While refusing to provide Oman with a written constitution, he transferred the existing 45 member advisory body into a 60 member consultative council. Having endorsed the Oslo Accord I in September 1993, he hosted a multilateral conference, sponsored as part of the middle East peace process. In Washington's war against the Taliban-administered Afghanistan in October 2001, Qaboos allowed the Pentagon use of its military facilities after it agreed to sell Oman advanced weapons worth $1.2 billion.

***

Qaddafi, Muammar al- (1942- 2011): Libyan statesman. Qaddafi served in the Libyan army and overthrew King Idris I in a military coup in 1969. He became Chairman of the Revolutionary Command Council (RCC) and, in 1970, Prime Minister. He then nationalized the majority of foreign petroleum assets, closed British and US military bases, and seized Italian and Jewish properties. He used his nation's vast oil wealth to support the Palestine Liberation Organization and other revolutionary causes and his government became involved in a number of incidents with neighboring states, most persistently Chad.

In retaliation for alleged acts of terrorism against US nationals, President Reagan authorized the bombing of the Libyan capital in 1986. His ambition for a single North African Arab Federation from Egypt to Morocco remained unrealized but he did help to form the Maghreb Union, an economic alliance, in 1989. In 1991 he maintained a neutral stance over the crisis leading to the Gulf War, but was accused of harboring terrorists responsible for the bombing of a US airplane over Lockerbie, Scotland. This led to the imposition on Libya of UN sanctions in 1992. In 1995 Qaddafi again caused controversy by expelling thousands of Palestinian refugees from Libya.

***

Qasim, Abdul Karim (1914-1963): *Iraqi military leader and politician; prime minister, 1958-63* Born of a Sunni father and a Shi'a mother in a lower-middle-class home in Baghdad, Qasim graduated from the local military academy and became a commissioned officer in 1938. He fought in the 1948-49 Palestine War as a lieutenant-colonel. Along with Col. Abdul Salam Arif, Qasim led the Free officers group from its formation in 1956. It over-threw King Faisal II on 14 July 1958, assassinated the royal family, and declared a republic. He became known as the Sole Leader.

Having made peace with Kurdish nationalists, Qasim invited their leader, Mustafa Barzani, to return home from the Soviet Union. But, when Barzani autonomy, mounted a campaign against the Kurds. Qasim withdrew Iraq from the Baghdad Pact. He hosted a conference of Iran, Iraq, Kuwait, Saudi Arabia, and Venezuela in September 1960 to form the Organization of Petroleum Exporting Countries (OPEC) to serve as a collective bargaining agency. In June 1961, when Kuwait became independent, Qasim claimed that it was part of Iraq. And alliance of Ba'athist civilians and military officers, and Abdul Salam Arif, toppled Qasims regime on 8 February 1963 and executed Qasim and his close aides.

***

Qassam, Izz al Din (1881-1935): *Palestinian leader* Born into a religious family in Jabla, northern Syria, Qassam received an Islamic education in Latakia and joined al Azhar University in Cairo. Qassam fled to the Palestinian city of Haifa and became a preacher there. Calling for a jihad against the British mandate and the Zionist colonizers, he coined the slogan: "God's book in one hand and a rifle in the other." However, this first armed confrontation between Palestinians and the British, coupled with Qassam's martyrdom, boosted Arab morale. It paved the way for the Arab Revolt, which erupted in 1936 and lasted three years, the first Palestinian Intifada. This became apparent when during the Intifada in the Occupied Territories in the late 1980s both Hamas and Islamic Jihad named their respective military wings the Izz al Din Qassam Brigade.

***

Rabi'a al-Adawiyyah (717-801): Although Islamic history is replete with heroic deeds performed by Muslim women, unfortunately the majority of Islamic historians have failed to acknowledge their contribution to the development of Islamic thought, culture and civilization. Indeed, the first person to embrace Islam was Khadijah. Following in her footsteps, other distinguished women like Fatimah bint Muhammad, Umm Atiyya, Asma bint Abu Bakr, Umm Ammara, Asma bint Yazid, Hafsah bint Umar and Aishah bint Abu Bakr became important figures in the early Muslim community. One such remarkable woman was Rabi'a al-Adawiyyah, who is today considered to be one of the most famous and influential female spiritual figures of Islam, along with Khadijah, Aishah and Fatimah.

Rabi'a al-Adawiyyah, also known as Rabi'a al-Basri, was born in the Iraqi city of Basrah. Her parents died while she was still a child. To make matters worse, famine then struck Basrah and this forced her to endure considerable personal hardship and suffering. During the famine young Rabi'a – having been displaced from her family – fell into the hands of an unscrupulous trader who sold her into slavery for six Dirhams. The man who purchased her not only treated her badly, but also forced her to work round the clock without any respite. In desperation, she tried to escape from bondage, but her attempts proved unsuccessful. Eventually, she accepted her condition and became a devout Muslim. Moved by her unflinching faith and piety, her master freed her. Eventually she returned to Basrah and lived in a tiny apartment, and devoted the rest of her life to prayers, fasting and other devotional activities.

Rabi'a became fascinated by Islam from very early in life and thereafter regularly engaged in meditation and other devotional activities. As one of Islam's earliest mystics, she renounced all worldly comforts in favor of asceticism (*Zuhd*). She also made a conscious decision not to marry and remained a confirmed spinster all her life. This also prompted many influential men like Muhammad ibn Sulaiman al-Hashimi, the ruler of Basrah, to send marriage proposals to her. Al-Hashimi even offered her a handsome dowry of a hundred thousand dinars and a generous monthly stipend of ten thousand dinars, but she shunned him saying, 'It does not please me that you should be my slave and that all you possess should be mine or that you should distract me from God for a single moment.'

Rabi'a's sole objective in life was to transcend from the temporal to the highest spiritual plane through single-minded devotion and dedication to God. And in so doing she became immersed in the ocean of Divine love and gnosis. This, according to Rabi'a, was more satisfying and enduring than the transient joys and comforts of this world. In her opinion, to obey God out of fear of Divine retribution – or to serve and worship Him in order to receive a handsome reward – was tantamount to selfishness. For instance, she used to say, 'O God, if I worship You for fear of Hell, burn me in Hell, and if I worship You in hope of Paradise, exclude me from Paradise. But if I worship You for Your Own sake, grudge me not Your everlasting Beauty.' Despite being illiterate, Rabi'a was a very beautiful and eloquent Arabic speaker. This also became the central pillar of her religious thought and mystical philosophy which influenced and inspired generations of Sufis.

Inspired by both Rabi'a and Hasan al-Basri, the message of Sufism attracted hundreds of thousands of followers from across the Muslim world. Rabi'a became a major source of inspiration for Muslims during her own lifetime and even more so after her death. In the West the prominent British poet Richard Monckton Milnes became one of the first to publish a small collection of poems under the title of *The Sayings of Rabi'a* during the nineteenth century. Rabi'a, the great mystical thinker and Sufi saint of Islam, died around the age of eighty-four and was buried in her native Basrah.

***

Rafsanjani, Ali Akbar Hashemi (1934-): *Iranian religious and political leader, president 1989-)* Born into a religious family in Behraman, Kerman province, Rafsanjani went to Qom for his theological studies. During the power struggle between Premier Muhammad Mussadiq and Muhammad Reza Shah Pahlave from 1951-53, he sided with Mussadiq.

Rafsanjani was arrested and tortured in the mid-1970s. One of the co-founders of the Tehran branch of the Association of Combatant Clergy Organization of Militant Clergy (OMC), Rafsanjani was actively involved in the 1977-78 revolutionary movement, particularly the formation of the Revolutionary Komitchs.

During the Iran-Iraq War, when in mid-1982 Iran recovered the area lost earlier to its foe, Rafsanjani advocated advancing into Iraq if the latter did not meet Iran's demands, including a compensation payment of $100 billion for war damages. After Khomeini's death in June 1989, when President Ali Husseini Khamanei was promoted to succeed him, Rafsanjani resigned his speakership and ran for the presidency. He secured 95 percent of the votes on a turn-out of 70 percent. In 1997 Khamanei appointed him president of the Expediency Consultation Council System.

***

Rajagopalachariar, Chakravarti (1878-1972): Indian nationalist politician. He became a close associate of Mohandas Gandhi and was imprisoned on several occasions for non-co-operation with the British. Himself a Hindu, he was tolerant of the right of Indian Muslims to demand special minority safeguards and of the creation of the separate state of Pakistan. He served as governor-general of India (1948-50) and chief minister of the Madras government (1952 – 54). In 1959 he was one of the founders of the conservative Swantantra party.

***

Rajai, Muhammad Ali (1933-1981): *Iranian politician; prime minister, 1980-81, president 1981* Born to a poor shopkeeper in Qasvin, Rajai quit school at sixteen and traveled to Tehran, where he became a bricklayer. Rajai joined the Liberation Movement, and in 1967 he cofounded the Islamic Welfare and Mutual Assistance Foundation, a front organization for political activity. He joined the Mujahedin-e Kalq in 1970, but was unhappy with the leftward drift of the organization and left two years later. After the revolution in February 1979, Rajai was appointed education minister. Following the Iraqi invasion of Iran in September 1980, Rajai argued at the United Nations Security Council that the United States was the chief instigator. An incendiary bomb killed Rajai and Premier Muhammad Javad Bahonar on 30 August during a National Security Council meeting.

***

Rajavi, Massoud (1948-   ): *Iranian politician* Born into a middle-class family in Tabas, Khorasan province, Rajavi studied political science at Tehran University. Since the Mujahedin-e Khlaq had abstained in the referendum on the constitution, Ayatollah Ruhollah Khomeini disqualified Rajavi from contesting the presidential election in January 1980. Rajavi then backed Abol Hassan Bani-Sadr, who was elected president. After Bani-Sadr's dismissal from office, both he and Rajavi went underground. In July they flew to Paris together.

There they jointly established the National Resistance Council, which conducted sabotage and guerrilla attacks on suitable targets in Iran. Toward the end of the Iran-Iraq War, in July 1988 Rajavi's forces, operating as the National Liberation Army, penetrated deep into Iran only to be surrounded by the Iranian troops and decimate. With Washington mounting a global war on terrorism in the wake of attack on it on 11 September 2001, there was no prospect of its rehabilitation there. Following the attacks on the Mujahedin-e Khlaq bases during the Gulf War III in April 2003, Rajavi's whereabouts became a matter of speculation.

***

Ranjit Singh (1780-1839): Ruler of a Sikh kingdom in the Punjab (1799-1839). His state was based on Lahore, which he secured in 1799. In 1801 he took the title 'Maharaja of the Punjab' and in 1802 extended his rule over the Sikh holy city of Amritsar. By agreement with Britain (Amritsar 1809), the eastern boundary of his state remained on the Sutlej River, but with his large army, trained by French offices, he expanded further afield. He extended his rule westwards (1813-21) and also took control of Kashmir. In 1834 he annexed Peshawar. At the end of the Sikh Wars (1849) most of his territory was taken by Britain.

***

Rashid Ali al-Ghailani (1892-1965): Iraqi statesman. Member of a well-known religious family, he served as prime Minister on four occasions. In April 1941 he seized power by a military coup that also deposed Abd al-Ilah, regent for the child-king, Faisal II. Believing he new government to be pro-Axis, Britain intervened to expel Rashid Ali in May 1941 and restored the regent.

***

Reza Shah Pahlavi (1878-1944): Shah of Iran (1925-1941). An officer of the Persian Cossack Brigade, he achieved power through an army coup (1921) and established a military dictatorship. He was successively Minister of War and Prime Minister before becoming Shah. He followed a policy of rapid modernization, constructing a national army, a modernized administrative, new legal and educational systems, and economic development, notably through the Trans-Iranian Railway (1927-38). He crushed tribal and other opposition to his policies. In World War II this refusal to expel German nationals led to the invasion and occupation of Iran by soviet and British forces. He was forced to abdicate in favor of his son, Muhammad Reza Shah Pahlavi, and died in exile in South Africa.

***

Saad ibn Abu Waqqas: early convert to Islam who was among the first seventy believers to migrate to Medina and the first to draw blood in the subsequent ten year war against the Pagans of Mecca. He commanded the vast Arab army that achieved the decisive victory over the Persian Empire at the battle of al Qadisiya and would be among the group of six close Companions chosen by Omar to elect the next Caliph. Muhammad's cousin.

***

Saada, Antun (1902-1949): *Lebanese politician* Born to a Greek Orthodox doctor who migrated with his family to Brazil, Saada grew up there and working on a magazine started by his father. In 1929 he traveled to Damascus, where he became a journalist with *al Ayyam (Arabic: The Days.)* Saada demanded an end to the French mandate and independence for Syria-Lebanon. After he had brought the organization into the open as the Syrian nationalist Party and held its first plenary conference in December 1935, he was jailed by the French. When Saada returned to Lebanon in 1947, the country had regained its independence. But under pressure from Lebanon and the anti-SSNP forces in Syria, Zaim agreed to Saada's extradition to Lebanon. After a secret, summary military trial, he was executed in July.

***

Sabri, Ali (1920-1991): *Egyptian military officer and politician; prime minister 1962-65* Born in Cairo, Sabri graduated from the Cairo Military Academy in 1939 and became a commission officer. A member of the Free Officers group, he liaised between its leadership and the U.S. Embassy before and during the July 1952 coup. In 1966 the SYO carried out a campaign against feudalism. ASU and SYO activists played a crucial role in the demonstrations in Cairo on 9-10 June 1967 to persuade Nasser to reverse his decision to resign in the wake of Egypt's defeat in the Six-Day War. Nasser stayed, but replaced his vice-presidents, including Sabri. Sabri was charged with treason and abuse of power during Nasser's presidency. He was found guilty and condemned to death, but his sentence was commuted to life imprisonment. After his release in May 1981 he stayed away from public life.

***

Sadi or Saadi, Bin shiraz (1184-1291): Persian poet, Used Ghazal. Orphaned at an early age, Sadi studied in Baghdad, where he met Suhrawardi, a major Sufi figure. Having to flee Baghdad because of the Mongol threat, he went on a long journey that took him to central Asia and India, then to Yemen and Ethiopia through Mecca. Sadi was captured by the Franks in Syria and worked at hard labor until ransomed. He proceeded to N Africa and Anatolia, before returning to his native Shiraz in 1256. His *Bustan* [fruit garden], an ethical-didactic text, was composed in *Mathnawi* (rhyming couplets). Even more popular is his *Gulistani* [Garden of Roses], written in rhyming prose. Sadi is also the author of many *qasidas* (long panegyrics) in Persian and Arabic, of mystical *ghazal* (love poems), and of satiric poetry. His tomb in Shiraz is a shrine

***

Sa'id Nursi (1877-1960): The decline of Ottoman political power and authority in the face of a European assault on its territories in both Europe and the Middle East, coupled with the rise of the Young Turks within the Ottoman State, propelled Mustafa Kemal (who was an ambitious Turkish military commander) to rise to the challenge of defending mainland Turkey from European encroachment. After six hundred years of Ottoman rule, Mustafa Kemal sent the last Ottoman Caliph, Abd al-Majid, into exile in Switzerland and inaugurated the Turkish Republic in 1924. When the true color of his socio-cultural reforms became clear for all to see, an influential Turkish Muslim thinker and reformer emerged to challenge Mustafa Kemal's secular crusade. This great Islamic scholar and reformer was none other than Sa'id Nursi.

Bediuzzaman Sa'id Nursi was born in the village of Nurs, in the eastern Turkish province of Bitlis. Of Kurdish origin, his parents were devout Muslims who led a simple and pious lifestyle. He became attracted to Sufism (Islamic mysticism) during his early years and the life and teachings of the famous Abd al-Qadir al-Jilani, the influential founder of the *Qadiriyyah* Sufi Order, fascinated him the most. He committed the entire to Qur'an to memory with ease. However, after obtaining a diploma in Islamic sciences at the age of fourteen, he considered abandoning formal education for good. Shaykh Fetullah Efendi, a notable local scholar, bestowed the title of *Bediuzzaman* (the 'Wonder of the Age') on him.

Once a great Islamic superpower, the Ottoman State now faced imminent political and economic collapse in the face of Russian – and subsequently Anglo-French – assault on its territories. This gave rise to the 'Young Turk' movement which, in turn, led to the removal of the Sultan from the Ottoman throne. The revolution of 1908 may have brought much-needed relief to the masses, but the Young Turks also failed to consolidate their grip on power. Amidst the prevailing chaos, Mustafa Kemal emerged to save his country from European encroachment. The victory of 1922 confirmed his position as the founder and undisputed ruler of the new Turkish republic.

During this period Sa'id became actively involved in the socio-political affairs of the State, and even participated in the war against the Russians on the Caucasian front. Captured by the Russians, he spent two years a prisoner of war in Russia. He managed to escape in 1918 and returned to Istanbul, via Vienna. 'Old Sa'id' became transformed into 'New Sa'id'. Hereafter, the Qur'an became his main source of guidance and spiritual illumination. He became a widely admired religious scholar and in 1923 Mustafa Kemal personally invited him to Ankara, the capital of the new Turkish republic, in order to officially recognize his contribution to the Turkish War of Independence.

Said's short visit to Ankara had confirmed his worst fears; the new Turkish rulers were no better than their predecessors. In fact, he considered Mustafa Kemal's eagerness to de-Islamicize Turkish society by introducing Western-style reforms both alarming and dangerous. By abolishing the Caliphate; banning the traditional Turkish attire; replacing the *Hijri* calendar with the Georgian one, and by overhauling the Turkish traditional educational system in favor of a secular Western model, Mustafa Kemal hoped to thoroughly undermine all major symbols of Turkey's Islamic past, but the *ulama* (Islamic scholars) and the Sufis led a rebellion against his reforms. However, as the Turkish authorities became suspicious of all the prominent religious scholars and Sufis, he was forced to flee to Western Anatolia. Here he spent the next twenty-five years living in exile. During this period he found time to teach and train hundreds of students who later became prominent members of the *Nurculuk* (or the 'Nur Movement') founded by Sa'id in order to preserve Turkey's glorious Islamic history, culture and heritage.

Later, Sa'id was arrested and charged with 'crimes' such as writing seditious books, and aiding and abetting political opposition against the ruling junta, among other things. During this period he authored his *Risale-i-Nur* (The Epistle of Light), a monumental commentary on the Qur'an of more than six thousand pages. Since Sa'id considered Western philosophy to be purely rationalistic, and modern science to be entirely atheistic, he deliberately pursued a logical, rational and scientific approach to the Qur'an in order to protect the Turkish people from the menace of Western atheistic thoughts and ideologies.

As expected, his intellectual assault on the Kemalist secular idol made Sa'id an open target for the ruling junta who felt he was seeking to undo their entire program of Westernization and secularization in Turkey. By the time of his death at the age of eighty-three, he had tens of thousands of followers across the country. Likewise, his *Nurculuk* movement became a powerful force in Turkish society.

***

Sadat, Muhammad Anwar (1918-1981): *Egyptian military officer and politician; president, 1970-81; prime minister 1973-1974, 1980-1981*
Son of a petty civil servant in Mit Abul Kom village in the Nile delta, Sadat grew up in Cairo. Found guilty of spying for the Germans, Sadat, a captain in the signals corps, was jailed in the summer of 1942. He escaped in 1944 and went underground until the detention order was lifted. He rejoined the army in late 1949, regaining his rank of captain. He was posted to Rafah in the Sinai, where he came into contract with Gamal Abdul Nasser. Sadat participated in the 22 July 1952 coup mounted by the Free Officers organization and secured a seat on the ruling eighteen-member Revolutionary Command Council (RCC). Sadat edited *Al Gumburiya* (The Republic), the regimes mouthpiece.

From 1959 to 1969 he served as speaker of the parliament; and from 1964 to 1966 he was one of the four vice presidents. In September 1969, three months later Nasser, performing a rightward shift, appointed Sadat as sole vice president. On Nasser's death in September 1970, Sadat became acting president. Sadat's power struggle with Ali Sabri ended in May 1971 when he arrested Sabri and his close aides. Sadat signed a fifteen-year Egyptian–Soviet Friendship Treaty in late May 1971. Some 15,000 Soviet personnel left, taking with them fighter aircraft, interceptors, and surface-to-air missiles. Sadat became prime minister (stepping down in 1974) and began to plan an invasion of the Israeli-occupied Arab territories. During the October 1973 Arab-Israeli

War the Egyptian troops performed unprecedentedly well, capturing land in the Sinai from the Israelis and retaining it.

After Moscow had refused to reschedule the Egyptian debts of US $10-12 billion, Sadat unilaterally abrogated the Soviet Friendship Treaty. In November, in a dramatic move he addressed the Israeli Knesset in Jerusalem. *In Search of Identity* (1978). Washington began to provide military aid to Egypt. Sadat signed the Camp David Accords with Israeli Premier Menachem Begin at the White House in Washington on 18 September 1978 in the presence of U.S. President Jimmy Carter. General Ghani Gamassy, Mustafa Khalil.

In March 1979 Sadat and Begin signed the bilateral Egyptian-Israeli Peace Treaty at the White House. This resulted in the immediate suspension of Egypt from the Arab league and the Islamic Conference Organization (ICO), and the severing of links by the Arab League members, except Oman. His sweeping crackdown on dissidents in September 1981 resulted in some 2,000 arrests. The next month he was assassinated by four Islamic militants, led by Khalid Ahmad Shawki Islambouli, during a military parade on the anniversary of the October 1973 Arab-Israeli War. In contrast to the mass grief demonstrated at the death of Nasser, most Egyptians were unmoved by Sadat's demise.

***

Saladin, Jalal Ad-Din Ayyubi (1138-1193): Ṣalāḥ ad-Din Yusuf ibn Ayyub (Arabic: Ṣalāḥ ad-Din Yusuf ibn Ayyub, Kurdish: Selah'edînê Eyubî) (ca. 1138 – March 4, 1193), better known in the Western world as Saladin, was an Arabized Kurdish Muslim, who became the first Sultan of Egypt and Syria, and founded the Ayyubid dynasty. He led Muslim and Arab opposition to the Franks and other European Crusaders in the Levant. At the height of his power, his sultanate included Egypt, Syria, Mesopotamia, Hejaz, Yemen, and parts of North Africa.

Under his personal leadership, his forces defeated the Crusaders at the Battle of Hattin, leading the way to his re-capture of Palestine, which had been seized from the Fatimid Egyptians by the Crusaders 88 years earlier. As such, Saladin is a prominent figure in Kurdish, Arab, and Muslim culture. Saladin was a strict adherent of Sunni Islam. His noble and chivalrous behavior was noted by Christian chroniclers. He became a celebrated example of the principles of chivalry.

Early life:

Saladin was born in Tikrit, Iraq. His personal name was *Yusuf*, the Arabic form of Joseph; *Salah ad-Din* is a *laqab*, a descriptive epithet, meaning "Righteousness of the Faith". His family was of

Arabized Kurdish background and ancestry, and had originated from the city of Dvin, in medieval Armenia. His father, Najm ad-Din Ayyub, was banished from Tikrit and in 1139, he and his uncle Asad al-Din Shirkuh, moved to Mosul. He later joined the service of Imad ad-Din Zengi who made him commander of his fortress in Baalbek. After the death of Zengi in 1146, his son, Nur ad-Din, became the regent of Aleppo and the leader of the Zengids.

Saladin was able to answer questions on Euclid, the Almagest, arithmetic, and law, but this was an academic ideal and it was study of the Qur'an and the "sciences of religion" that linked him to his contemporaries. During the First Crusade, Jerusalem was taken in a surprise attack by the Christians. He knew the *Hamasah* of Abu Tammam by heart.

Saladin's military career began under the tutelage of his uncle Asad al-Din Shirkuh, an important military commander under Nur ad-Din. In 1163, the vizier to the Fatimid caliph al-Adid, Shawar, had been driven out of Egypt by rival Dirgham, a member of the powerful Banu Ruzzaik tribe. He asked for military backing from Nur ad-Din, who complied and in 1164, sent Shirkuh to aid Shawar in his expedition against Dirgham. Saladin, at age 26, went along with them. After Shawar was successfully reinstated as vizier, he demanded that Shirkuh withdraw his army from Egypt for a sum of 30,000 dinars, but he refused insisting it was Nur ad-Din's will that he remain.

After the sacking of Bilbais, the Crusader-Egyptian force and Shirkuh's army were to engage in a battle on the desert border of the Nile River, just west of Giza. Saladin played a major role, commanding the right wing of the Zengid army, while a force of Kurds commanded the left, and Shirkuh stationed in the center. After scattered fighting in little valleys to the south of the main position, the Zengid central force returned to the offensive; Saladin joined in from the rear.

The battle ended in a Zengid victory, and Saladin is credited to have helped Shirkuh in one of the "most remarkable victories in recorded history". Saladin and Shirkuh moved towards Alexandria where they were welcomed, given money, arms, and provided a base.

Emir of Egypt:

Shirkuh engaged in a power struggle over Egypt with Shawar and Amalric I of the Kingdom of Jerusalem, in which Shawar requested Amalric's assistance. In 1169, Shawar was reportedly assassinated by Saladin, and Shirkuh died later that year. Nur ad-Din chose a successor for Shirkuh, but al-Adid appointed Saladin to replace Shawar as vizier.

He was eventually accepted by the majority of *emirs*. Al-Adid's advisers were also suspected of attempting to split the Syria-based

Zengid ranks. The bulk of the Syrian rulers supported Saladin due to his role in the Egyptian expedition, in which he gained a record of military qualifications.

Inaugurated as Emir on March 26, Saladin repented "wine-drinking and turned from frivolity to assume the dress of religion."

Later in the year, a group of Egyptian soldiers and emirs attempted to assassinate Saladin, but having already known of their intentions, thanks to his intelligence chief Ali bin Safyan, he had the chief conspirator, Naji, Mu'tamin al-Khilafa—the civilian controller of the Fatimid Palace—arrested, and killed. The day after, 50,000 black African soldiers from the regiments of the Fatimid army opposed to Saladin's rule along with a number of Egyptian emirs and commoners staged a revolt. By August 23, Saladin had decisively quelled the uprising, and never again had to face a military challenge from Cairo.

Towards the end of 1169, Saladin—with reinforcements from Nur ad-Din—defeated a massive Crusader-Byzantine force near Damietta. Afterward, in the spring of 1170, Nur ad-Din sent Saladin's father to Egypt in compliance with Saladin's request, as well as encouragement from the Baghdad-based Abbasid caliph, al-Mustanjid, who aimed to pressure Saladin in deposing his rival caliph, al-Adid. He began granting his family members high-ranking positions in the region and increased Sunni influence in Cairo; he ordered the construction of a college for the Maliki branch of Sunni Islam in the city, as well as one for the Shafi'i denomination to which he belonged in al-Fustat.

After establishing himself in Egypt, Saladin launched a campaign against the Crusaders, besieging Darum in 1170. Amalric withdrew his Templar garrison from Gaza to assist him in defending Darum, but Saladin evaded their force and fell on Gaza instead. He destroyed the town built outside the city's castle and killed most of its inhabitants after they were refused entry into the castle.

Sultan of Egypt:

According to Imad ad-Din, Nur ad-Din wrote to Saladin in June 1171, telling him to reestablish the Abbasid caliphate in Egypt, which Saladin coordinated two months later after additional encouragement by Najm ad-Din al-Khabushani, the Shafi'i *Faqih*, who vehemently opposed Shi'a rule in the country. Several Egyptian *emirs* were thus killed, but al-Adid was told that they were killed for rebelling against him. He then fell ill, or was poisoned according to one account. He died on September 13 and five days later, the Abbasid *khutbah* was pronounced in Cairo and al-Fustat, proclaiming al-Mustadi as caliph.

On September 25, Saladin left Cairo to take part in a joint attack on Kerak and Montreal, the desert castles of the Kingdom of Jerusalem, with Nur ad-Din who would attack from Syria. Also, there was a chance that the Crusader kingdom—which acted as a buffer state between Syria and Egypt—could have collapsed had the two leaders attacked it from the east and the coast. This would have given Nur ad-Din the opportunity to annex Egypt. Saladin claimed he withdrew amid Fatimid plots against him, but Nur ad-Din did not accept "the excuse."

During the summer of 1172, a Nubian army along with a contingent of Armenian refugees were reported on the Egyptian border, preparing for a siege against Aswan. The *emir* of the city had requested Saladin's assistance and was given reinforcements under Turan-Shah—Saladin's brother. Consequently, the Nubians departed, but returned in 1173 and were again driven off. This time Egyptian forces advanced from Aswan and captured the Nubian town of Ibrim. Seventeen months after al-Adid's death, Nur ad-Din had not taken any action regarding Egypt, but expected some return for the 200,000 dinars he had allocated to Shirkuh's army which seized the country. Saladin paid this debt with 60,000 dinars, "wonderful manufactured goods", some jewels, an ass of the finest breed, and an elephant. While transporting these goods to Damascus, Saladin took the opportunity to ravage the Crusader countryside.

On July 31, 1173, Saladin's father Ayyub was wounded in a horse-riding accident, ultimately causing his death on August 9. In 1174, Saladin sent Turan-Shah to conquer Yemen to allocate it and its port Aden to the territories of the Ayyubid Dynasty. Yemen also served as an emergency territory, to which Saladin could flee in the event of an invasion by Nur ad-Din.

Acquisition of Syria: Capture of Damascus:

In the early summer of 1174, Nur ad-Din was mustering an army, sending summons to Mosul, Diyarbakir, and al-Jazira in an apparent preparation of attack against Saladin's Egypt. The Ayyubid dynasty held a council upon the revelation of his preparations to discuss the possible threat and Saladin collected his own troops outside Cairo. On May 15, Nur ad-Din died after being poisoned the previous week and his power was handed to his eleven-year-old son as-Salih Ismail al-Malik. His death left Saladin with political independence and in a letter to as-Salih, he promised to "act as a sword" against his enemies and referred to the death of his father as an "earthquake shock."

In the wake of Nur ad-Din's death, Saladin faced a difficult decision; he could move his army against the Crusaders from Egypt or wait until invited by as-Salih in Syria to come to his aid and launch a war from there. He could also take it upon himself to annex Syria before it could possibly fall into the hands of a rival, but feared that attacking a land that formerly belonged to his master—which is forbidden in the Islamic principles he followed—could portray him as hypocritical and thus, unsuitable for leading the war against the Crusaders. Saladin saw that in order to acquire Syria, he either needed an invitation from as-Salih or warn him that potential anarchy and danger from the Crusaders could rise.

When as-Salih was removed to Aleppo in August, Gumushtigin, the *emir* of the city and a captain of Nur ad-Din's veterans assumed guardianship over him. The *emir* prepared to unseat all of his rivals in Syria and al-Jazira, beginning with Damascus. In this emergency, the *emir* of Damascus appealed to Saif al-Din (a cousin of Gumushtigin) of Mosul for assistance against Aleppo, but he refused, forcing the Syrians to request the aid of Saladin who complied. Saladin rode across the desert with 700 picked horsemen, passing through al-Kerak then reaching Bosra and according to him, was joined by "*emirs*, soldiers, Kurds, and Bedouins—the emotions of their hearts to be seen on their faces." On November 23, he arrived in Damascus amid general acclamations and rested at his father's old home there, until the gates of the Citadel of Damascus were opened to him four days later. He installed himself in the castle and received the homage and salutations of the citizens.

Further conquests:

Leaving his brother Tughtigin as Governor of Damascus, Saladin proceeded to reduce other cities that had belonged to Nur ad-Din, but were now practically independent. His army conquered Hamah with relative ease, but avoided attacking Homs because of the strength of its citadel. Saladin moved north towards Aleppo, besieging it on December 30 after Gumushtigin refused to abdicate his throne. As-Salih, fearing capture by Saladin, came out of his palace and appealed to the inhabitants not to surrender him and the city to the invading force. One of Saladin's chroniclers claimed "the people came under his spell."

Gumushtigin requested from Rashid ad-Din Sinan, grand-master of the Assassins of Syria, who were already at odds with Saladin since he replaced the Fatimids of Egypt, to assassinate Saladin in his camp. A group of thirteen Assassins easily gained admission into Saladin's camp, but were detected immediately before they carried out their attack. One was killed by a general of Saladin and the others were slain while trying to escape.

Meanwhile, Saladin's rivals in Syria and Jazira waged a propaganda war against him, claiming he had "forgotten his own condition [servant of Nur ad-Din]" and showed no gratitude for his old master by besieging his son, rising "in rebellion against his Lord."

Saladin aimed to counter this propaganda by ending the siege, claiming he was defending Islam from the Crusaders; his army returned to Hama to engage a Crusader force there. The Crusaders withdrew beforehand and Saladin proclaimed it "a victory opening the gates of men's hearts." Soon after, Saladin entered Homs and captured its citadel in March 1175, after stubborn resistance from its defenders.

Saladin's successes alarmed Saif al-Din. As head of the Zengids, including Gumushtigin, he regarded Syria and Mesopotamia as his family estate and was angered when Saladin attempted to usurp his dynasty's holdings. Saif al-Din mustered a large army and dispatched it to Aleppo whose defenders anxiously had awaited them. The combined forces of Mosul and Aleppo marched against Saladin in Hama. Seeing that confrontation was unavoidable, Saladin prepared for battle, taking up a superior position on the hills by the gorge of the Orontes River. On April 13, 1175, the Zengid troops marched to attack his forces, but soon found themselves surrounded by Saladin's Ayyubid veterans who crushed them. The battle ended in a decisive victory for Saladin who pursued the Zengid fugitives to the gates of Aleppo, forcing as-Salih's advisers to recognize Saladin's control of the provinces of Damascus, Homs and Hama, as well as a number of towns outside Aleppo such as Ma'arat al-Numan.

After his victory against the Zengids, Saladin proclaimed himself king and suppressed the name of as-Salih in Friday prayers and Islamic coinage. The Abbasid caliph in Baghdad graciously welcomed Saladin's assumption of power and declared him "Sultan of Egypt and Syria."

The Battle of Hama did not end the contest for power between the Ayyubids and the Zengids, with the final confrontation occurring in the spring of 1176. Saladin had gathered massive reinforcements from Egypt while Saif al-Din was levying troops among the minor states of Diyarbakir and al-Jazira. He reached the Sultan's Mound, c. 25 km from Aleppo, where his forces encountered Saif al-Din's army. A hand-to-hand fight ensued and the Zengids managed to plow Saladin's left wing, driving it before him, when Saladin himself charged at the head of the Zengid guard. The Zengid forces panicked and most of Saif al-Din's officers ended up escaped. The Zengid prisoners of war, however, were given gifts and freed. All of the booty from the Ayyubid victory was accorded to the army, Saladin not keeping anything himself.

A'zaz capitulated on June 21, and Saladin then hurried his forces to Aleppo to punish Gumushtigin. His assaults were again resisted, but he managed to secure not only a truce, but a mutual alliance with Aleppo, in which Gumushtigin and as-Salih were allowed to continue their hold on the city and in return, they recognized Saladin as the sovereign over all of the dominions he conquered. The *emirs* of Mardin and Keyfa, the Muslim allies of Aleppo, also recognized Saladin as the King of Syria.

Campaign against Assassins:
Saladin had by now agreed truces with his Zengid rivals and the Kingdom of Jerusalem (latter occurred in the summer of 1175), but faced a threat from the Hashshashin sect or "Assassins" led by Rashid ad-Din Sinan. Based in the al-Nusayri Mountains, they commanded nine fortresses built atop high elevations. As soon as he dismissed the bulk of his troops to Egypt, Saladin led his army into the al-Nusayri range in August 1176. He retreated the same month, after laying waste to the countryside, but failing to conquer any of the forts.

Saladin told his guards to settle an agreement with Sinan. Realizing he was unable to subdue the Assassins, he sought to align himself with them, consequently depriving the Crusaders of aligning themselves against him.

Return to Cairo and forays in Palestine:
After leaving the al-Nusayri Mountains, Saladin returned to Damascus and had his Syrian soldiers return home. He left Turan Shah in command of Syria, and left for Egypt with only his personal followers, reaching Cairo on September 22. The 280 feet (85 m) deep Bir Yusuf ("Joseph's Well") was built on Saladin's orders. The chief public work he commissioned outside of Cairo was the large bridge at Giza, which intended to form an outwork of defense against a potential Moorish invasion.

In November 1177, he set out upon a raid into Palestine; the Crusaders had recently forayed into the territory of Damascus and so Saladin saw the truce was no longer worth preserving. The Christians sent a large portion of their army to besiege the fortress of Harim north of Aleppo and so southern Palestine bore few defenders. Saladin found the situation ripe, and so marched to Ascalon, which he referred to as the "Bride of Syria." William of Tyre recorded that the Ayyubid army consisted of 26,000 soldiers, of which 8,000 were elite forces and 18,000 were black slave soldiers from the Sudan. This army proceeded to raid the countryside, sack Ramla and Lod, and dispersed themselves as far as the Gates of Jerusalem.

Battles and truce with Baldwin:
The Ayyubids did allow King Baldwin to enter Ascalon with his Gaza-based Templars without taking any precautions against a sudden attack. Although the Crusader force consisted only of 375 knights,

Saladin hesitated to ambush them due to the presence of highly skilled generals. Initially, Saladin attempted to organize his men into battle order, but as his bodyguards were being killed, he saw that defeat was inevitable and so with a small remnant of his troops mounted a swift camel, riding all the way to the territories of Egypt.

Not discouraged by his defeat at Tell Jezer, Saladin was prepared to fight the Crusaders once again. In the spring of 1178, he was encamped under the walls of Homs and a few skirmishes occurred between his generals and the Crusader army. His forces in Hama won a victory over their enemy and brought the spoils, together with many prisoners of war to Saladin who ordered the captives to be beheaded for "plundering and laying waste the lands of the Faithful." He spent the rest of the year in Syria without a confrontation with his enemies.

Saladin's intelligence services reported to him that the Crusaders were planning a raid into Syria. As such, he ordered one of his generals, Farrukh-Shah, to guard the Damascus frontier with a thousand of his men to watch for an attack, then to retire avoiding battle and lighting warning beacons on the hills on which Saladin would march out. In April 1179, the Crusaders led by King Baldwin expected no resistance and waited to launch a surprise attack on Muslim herders grazing their herds and flocks east of the Golan Heights. Baldwin advanced too rashly in pursuit of Farrukh-Shah's force which was concentrated southeast of Quneitra and was subsequently defeated by the Ayyubids. With this victory, Saladin decided to call in more troops from Egypt; he requested 1,500 horsemen to be sent by al-Adil.

In the summer of 1179, King Baldwin had set up an outpost on the road to Damascus and aimed to fortify a passage over the Jordan River, known as Jacob's Ford, that commanded the approach to the Banias plain (the plain was divided by the Muslims and the Christians). The engagement ended in a decisive Ayyubid victory and many high-ranking knights were captured. Saladin then moved to besiege the fortress which fell on August 30, 1179.

In the spring of 1180, while Saladin was in the area of Safad, anxious to commence a vigorous campaign against the Kingdom of Jerusalem, King Baldwin sent messengers to him with proposals of peace. Due to droughts and bad harvests hampering his commissariat, Saladin agreed to a truce.

Domestic issues:

Previously, Saladin offered to mediate relations between Nur al-Din and Kilij Arslan II—the Seljuk Sultan of Rum—after the two came into conflict. The latter demanded Nur al-Din return the lands given to him as a dowry for marrying his daughter when he received reports that she was being abused by him and was used to gain to Seljuk territory. Nur al-Din requested assistance from Saladin, but Arslan refused.

After Nur al-Din and Saladin met at Geuk Su, the top Seljuk *emir*, Ikhtiyar al-Din al-Hasan, confirmed Arslan's submission, after which an agreement was drawn up.

Leaving Farrukh-Shah in charge of Syria, Saladin returned to Cairo at the beginning of 1181; According to Abu-Shama, he intended to spend the fast of Ramadan in Egypt and then make the *hajj* pilgrimage to Mecca.

Empire expansions:
Conquest of Mesopotamian hinterland:

Saif al-Din had died earlier in June 1181 and his brother Izz al-Din inherited leadership of Mosul. On December 4, the crown-prince of the Zengids, as-Salih, died in Aleppo. Prior to his death, he had his chief officers swear an oath of loyalty to Izz al-Din, as he was the only Zengid ruler strong enough to oppose Saladin.

On May 11, 1182, Saladin along with half of the Egyptian Ayyubid army and numerous non-combatants left Cairo for Syria; he never saw Egypt again. Knowing that Crusader forces were massed upon the frontier to intercept him, he took the desert route across the Sinai Peninsula to Ailah at the head of the Gulf of Aqaba. He arrived in Damascus in June to learn that Farrukh-Shah had attacked the Galilee, sacking Daburiyya and capturing Habis Jaldek, a fortress of great importance to the Crusaders. In July, Saladin dispatched Farrukh-Shah to attack Kawkab al-Hawa. Later, in August, the Ayyubids launched a naval and ground assault to capture Beirut; Saladin led his army in the Bekaa Valley. The assault was leaning towards failure and Saladin abandoned the operation to focus on issues in Mesopotamia.

Kukbary, the emir of Harran, invited Saladin to occupy the Jazira region, making up northern Mesopotamia. He complied and the truce between him and the Zengids officially ended in September 1182. Before he crossed the Euphrates, Saladin besieged Aleppo for three days, signaling that the truce was over.

From ar-Raqqah, he moved to conquer al-Fudain, al-Husain, Maksim, Durain, 'Araban, and Khabur — all of which swore allegiance to him.

In the midst of these victories, Saladin received word that the Crusaders were raiding the villages of Damascus. Meanwhile, in Aleppo, the *emir* of the city Zangi raided Saladin's cities to the north and east, such as Balis, Manbij, Saruj, Buza'a, al-Karzain. He also destroyed his own citadel at A'zaz to prevent it from being used by the Ayyubids if they were to conquer it.

Possession of Aleppo:

Saladin turned his attention from Mosul to Aleppo, sending his brother Taj al-Mulk Buri to capture Tell Khalid, 130 km northeast of the city. A siege was set, but the governor of Tell Khalid surrendered upon the arrival of Saladin himself on May 17 before a siege could take place.

Zangi did not offer long resistance. He was unpopular with his subjects and wished to return to his Sinjar, the city he governed previously. An exchange was negotiated where Zangi would hand over Aleppo to Saladin in return for the restoration of his control of Sinjar, Nusaybin, and ar-Raqqa. Zangi would hold these territories as Saladin's vassals on terms of military service. On June 12, Aleppo was formally placed in Ayyubid hands. Although he was short of money, Saladin also allowed the departing Zangi to take all the stores of the citadel that he could travel with and to sell the remainder—which Saladin purchased himself. From his standpoint, he could now threaten the entire Crusader coast.

After spending one night in Aleppo's citadel, Saladin marched to Harim, near the Crusader-held Antioch. The city was held by Surhak, a "minor *Mamluk*." Saladin offered him the city of Busra and property in Damascus in exchange for Harim, but when Surhak asked for more, his own garrison in Harim forced him out. He was then arrested by Saladin's deputy Taqi al-Din on allegations that he was planning to cede Harim to Bohemond III of Antioch. When Saladin received its surrender, he proceeded to arrange the defense of Harim from the Crusaders. He reported to the caliph and his own subordinates in Yemen and Baalbek that was going to attack the Armenians. Before he could move, however, there were a number of administrative details to be settled. Saladin agreed to a truce with Bohemond in return for Muslim prisoners being held by him and then he gave A'zaz to Alam ad-Din Suleiman and Aleppo to Saif al-Din al-Yazkuj—the former was an *emir* of Aleppo who joined Saladin and the latter was a former *Mamluk* of Shirkuh who helped rescue him from the assassination attempt at A'zaz.

Fight for Mosul:

As Saladin approached Mosul, he faced the issue of taking over a large city and justifying the action. Saladin immediately laid siege to the heavily fortified city.

After several minor skirmishes and a stalemate in the siege that was initiated by the caliph, Saladin intended to find a way to withdraw from the siege without damage to his reputation while still keeping up some military pressure. He decided to attack Sinjar which was now held by Izz al-Din's brother Sharaf al-Din. It fell after a 15-day siege on December 30. Saladin's commanders and soldiers broke their discipline, plundering the city; Saladin only managed to protect the governor and his officers by sending them to Mosul.

On March 2, al-Adil from Egypt wrote to Saladin that the Crusaders had struck the "heart of Islam." Raynald de Châtillon had sent ships to the Gulf of Aqaba to raid towns and villages off the coast of the Red Sea.

Ibn Jubair was told that sixteen Muslim ships were burnt by the Crusaders who then captured a pilgrim ship and caravan at Aidab. He also reported they intended to attack Medina and remove Muhammad's body. Al-Maqrizi added to the rumor by claiming Muhammad's tomb was going to be relocated to Crusader territory so Muslims would make pilgrimages there. Fortunately for Saladin, al-Adil had his warships moved from Fustat and Alexandria to the Red Sea under the command of an Armenian mercenary Lu'lu. They broke the Crusader blockade, destroyed most of their ships, and pursued and captured those who anchored and fled into the desert. The surviving Crusaders, numbered at 170, were ordered to be killed by Saladin in various Muslim cities.

Nur al-Din swore allegiance to Saladin, promising to follow him in every expedition in the war against the Crusaders and repairing damage done to the city. Saladin aimed to persuade the caliph claiming that while he conquered Egypt and Yemen under the flag of the Abbasids, the Zengids of Mosul openly supported the Seljuks (rivals of the caliphate) and only came to the caliph when in need. He also promised that if Mosul was given to him, it would lead to the capture of Jerusalem, Constantinople, Georgia, and the lands of the Almohads in the Maghreb, "until the word of God is supreme and the Abbasid caliphate has wiped the world clean, turning the churches into mosques." Instead of asking for financial or military support from the caliph, he would capture and give the caliph the territories of Tikrit, Daquq, Khuzestan, Kish Island, and Oman.

Wars against Crusaders:

On September 29, 1182 Saladin crossed the Jordan River to attack Beisan which was found to be empty. The next day his forces sacked and burned the town and moved westwards. They intercepted Crusader reinforcements from Karak and Shaubak along the Nablus road and took a number of prisoners. After a few Ayyubid raids—including attacks on Zir'in, Forbelet, and Mount Tabor—the Crusaders still were not tempted to attack their main force, and Saladin led his men back across the river once provisions and supplies ran low.

However, Crusader attacks provoked further responses by Saladin. Raynald of Châtillon, in particular, harassed Muslim trading and pilgrimage routes with a fleet on the Red Sea, a water route that

Saladin needed to keep open. In response, Saladin built a fleet of 30 galleys to attack Beirut in 1182. Raynald threatened to attack the holy cities of Mecca and Medina. Raynald responded by looting a caravan of pilgrims on the Hajj in 1185. Raynald captured Saladin's sister in a raid on a caravan, although this claim is not attested in contemporary sources.

The defenders of Mosul, when they became aware that help was on the way, increased their efforts, and Saladin subsequently fell ill, so in March 1186 a peace treaty was signed.

In July 1187 Saladin captured most of the Kingdom of Jerusalem. On July 4, 1187, at the Battle of Hattin, he faced the combined forces of Guy of Lusignan, King Consort of Jerusalem and Raymond III of Tripoli. In this battle alone the Crusader army was largely annihilated by the motivated army of Saladin. It was a major disaster for the Crusaders and a turning point in the history of the Crusades. Saladin captured Raynald de Châtillon and was personally responsible for his execution in retaliation for his attacking Muslim caravans.

Guy of Lusignan was also captured. Seeing the execution of Raynald, he feared he would be next. But his life was spared by Saladin with the words, talking about Raynald:

> It is not the wont of kings, to kill kings; but that man had transgressed all bounds, and therefore did I treat him thus.

Capture of Jerusalem:

Saladin had captured almost every Crusader city. Jerusalem capitulated to his forces on October 2, 1187, after a siege. When the siege had started, Saladin was unwilling to promise terms of quarter to the Frankish inhabitants of Jerusalem until Balian of Ibelin threatened to kill every Muslim hostage, estimated at 5000, and to destroy Islam's holy shrines of the Dome of the Rock and the al-Aqsa Mosque if quarter was not given. Saladin consulted his council and these terms were accepted. Patriarch Heraclius of Jerusalem organized, and contributed to a collection which paid the ransoms for about 18,000 of the poorer citizens, leaving another 15,000 to be enslaved, Saladins brother al-Adil, "asked Saladin for a thousand of them for his own use and then released them on the spot." Most of the foot soldiers were sold into slavery. Upon the capture of Jerusalem, Saladin summoned the Jews and permitted them to resettle in the city. In particular, the residents of Ashkelon, a large Jewish settlement, responded to his request.

Tyre, on the coast of modern-day Lebanon, was the last major Crusader city that was not captured by Muslim forces (strategically, it would have made more sense for Saladin to capture Tyre before Jerusalem—however, Saladin chose to pursue Jerusalem first because of the importance of the city to Islam). The city was now commanded by Conrad of Montferrat, who strengthened Tyre's defenses and withstood two sieges by Saladin.

Third Crusade:

Hattin and the fall of Jerusalem prompted the Third Crusade, financed in England by a special "Saladin tithe". Richard I of England (Richard the Lionheart) led Guy's siege of Acre, conquered the city and executed 3,000 Muslim prisoners, including women and children. Saladin retaliated by killing all Franks captured from August 28 – September 10.

The armies of Saladin engaged in combat with the army of King Richard at the Battle of Arsuf on September 7, 1191, at which Saladin's forces were defeated. After the battle of Arsuf, Richard moved his forces towards Ascalon. Anticipating Richard's next move, Saladin emptied the city and camped a few miles away from the city. When Richard arrived at the city, he was stunned to see the city abandoned and the towers demolished. The next day when Richard was preparing to retreat to Jaffa, Saladin attacked his Army. After a furious battle, Richard managed to save some of his troops and retreated to Ascalon. This was the last major battle between the two forces. All military attempts and battles made by Richard the Lionheart to re-take Jerusalem were defeated and failed.

Richard only had 2,000 fit soldiers and 50 fit knights to use in battle. With such a small force, Richard could not hope to take Jerusalem even though he got near enough to see the Holy City. However, Saladin's relationship with Richard was one of chivalrous mutual respect as well as military rivalry. At Arsuf, when Richard lost his horse, Saladin sent him two replacements. Richard proposed that his sister, Joan of England, Queen of Sicily, should marry Saladin's brother and that Jerusalem could be their wedding gift. However, the two men never met face to face and communication was either written or by messenger.

As leaders of their respective factions, the two men came to an agreement in the Treaty of Ramla in 1192, whereby Jerusalem would remain in Muslim hands but would be open to Christian pilgrimages. The treaty reduced the Latin Kingdom to a strip along the coast from Tyre to Jaffa.

Death:

Saladin died of a fever on March 4, 1193, at Damascus, not long after Richard's departure. In Saladin's possession at the time of his death were 1 piece of gold and 47 pieces of silver. He had given away his great wealth to his poor subjects and there was none left to pay for his funeral. He was buried in a mausoleum in the garden outside the Umayyad Mosque in Damascus, Syria.

Seven centuries later, Emperor Wilhelm II of Germany donated a new marble sarcophagus to the mausoleum. Saladin was, however, not placed in it. Instead the mausoleum, which is open to visitors, now has two sarcophagi: the empty one made of marble and the original wooden one, which holds Saladin.

Family:

According to Imad al-Din, Saladin had fathered five sons before he left Egypt in 1174.

Recognition and legacy:
Muslim world:

In 1898 German Emperor Wilhelm II visited Saladin's tomb to pay his respects. The visit, coupled with anti-colonial sentiments, led nationalist Arabs to reinvent the image of Saladin and portray him as a hero of the struggle against the West.

The legacy of Saladin within the Arab World continues to this day. With the rise of Arab nationalism in the Twentieth Century, particularly with regard to the Arab-Israeli conflict, Saladin's heroism and leadership gained a new significance. Saladin's recapture of Palestine from the European Crusaders is considered inspiration for the modern-day Arabs' opposition to Zionism.

For this reason, the Eagle of Saladin became the symbol of revolutionary Egypt, and was subsequently adopted by several other Arab states (United Arab Emirates, Iraq, the Palestinian Territory, and Yemen).

Western world:

Though Saladin faded into history after the Middle Ages, he appears in a sympathetic light in Sir Walter Scott's novel The Talisman (1825). Despite the Crusaders' slaughter when they originally conquered Jerusalem in 1099, Saladin granted amnesty and free passage to all common Catholics and even to the defeated Christian army, as long as they were able to pay the aforementioned ransom. An interesting view of Saladin and the world in which he lived is provided by Tariq Ali's novel *The Book of Saladin*.

In April 1191, a Frankish woman's three month old baby had been stolen from her camp and had been sold on the market. The Franks urged her to approach Saladin herself with her grievance. According to Bahā' al-Din, Saladin used his own money to buy the child back.

According to some sources, British Commander General Edmund Allenby during World War I, proudly declared "today the wards of the Crusaders are completed" by rising up his sword towards statue of Saladin after capture of Damascus from Turkish troops.

Ṣalāḥ ad-Din Yusuf ibn Ayyub, Sultan of Egypt and Syria:

Buried: Umayyad Mosque, Damascus, Syria

***

Salam, Saeb (1905-2000): *Lebanese politician; prime minister, 1952, 1953, 1960-61, 1970-73* Born into a notable Sunni family in Beirut, Salem graduated from the American University of Beirut and finished his postgraduate studies at the London School of Economics and Political Science. When Suleiman Franjieh became president in 1970, he called on Salem to form the next government. Salem purged the army and civil service of the reformists inspired by ex-president Faud Chehab. After the assassination of Bashir Gemayel in September, Salem played a crucial role in the election of Amin Gemayel as president. As the civil conflict continued well into the 1980s, Salem's influence declined sharply.

***

Salih, Ali Abdullah (1942-   ): *Yemeni military officer and politician, president of North Yemen, 1978-90; president of Yemen, 1990-* A member of the Sanhan tribe of the Hashid tribal confederation, Salih was born in the northern region. Following Ghashmi's assassination in June 1978, Salih became chief of staff and a member of the Presidential Council. A month later, seventy-six of the ninety-six People's Constituent Assembly members elected his president. In October 1980 Salih replaced premier Abdul Aziz Abdul Ghani with Abdul Karim Iryani. In the Kuwait crisis of 1990-91 Salih refused to side with the Saudi-US alliance against Iraq.

Yemen, the only Arab member of the United Nations Security Council, voted against the US stance and abstained on crucial resolutions on the Kuwait crisis and the Second Gulf War. In 1995 Salih was elevated to chairman of the GPC, a new post. Two years later the GPC improved its parliamentary strength from 123 to 187. In October

2000 a suicide bomb attack on USS Cole while refueling in Aden killed seventeen sailors. The Islamic Army of Aden-Abyan claimed responsibility. After the terrorist attacks on the United States in September 2001, Salih's government cooperated with Washington to capture Al Qaida activists based in Yemen.

***

Sallal, Abdullah (1917-2001): *Yemeni military officer and politician; president, 1962-67; prime minister, 1962-63, 1966-67* Born in a Zaidi blacksmith family in the north, Sallal was sent to Baghdad Military Academy, where he graduated in 1938. Sallal became a protégé of Crown Prince Muhammad al Badr, who made him commander of his guard in 1956, and of the newly established military academy three years later. When al Badr acceded the throne on 18 September 1962, he made Sallal, then a brigadier general, commander of the royal guard. With the failure of Nasser's peacemaking efforts, Sallal was allowed to return to Sanaa in September 1966. Because of the June 1967 Arab-Israeli War, which diverted Egypt's resources. Cairo decided to withdraw its forces from North Yemen, and this weakened the position of Sallal, who was seen as an Egyptian protégé. He was overthrown in November 1967 during his visit to Moscow. He went into exile in Baghdad, in October 1981.

***

Salman II ibn Hamad (1895-1961): ruler of Bahrain, 1942-1961. Born in Manama, al Khalifa began to acquire administrative experience in his early twenties. Al Khalifa's close ties with Britain became a point of contention during the 1956 Suez War when the Anglo French Israeli alliance invaded Egypt, and his subjects mounted massive pro Egyptian demonstrations.

***

Sarkis, Elias (1924-1985): *Lebanese politician; president, 1976-82* Born into a middle-class Maronite family in Beirut, Sarkis obtained a law degree from Saint Joseph University. He came to represent moderate Maronite opinion, which was rare after the start of the Lebanese Civil War in April 1975. Sarkis became a favorite of Syrian President Hafiz Assad following the latter's intervention in the war on the Maronite side in June 1976. In June 1982, within a week of invading Lebanon, the Israeli forces expelled Sarkis from his presidential palace in Baabda.

***

Saud: The ruling family of Saudi Arabia. Originally established at Dariyya in Wadi Hanifa. Nejd, in the 15th century, its fortunes grew after 1745 when Muhammad ibn Saud allied himself with the Islamic revivalist Abd al-Wahhab (Wahhabism), who later became the spiritual guide of the family. The first wave of Saudi expansion ended with defeat by Egypt in 1818, but Saudi fortunes revived under Abd al-Aziz ibn Saud (1889-1953), who captured Riyadh (1902), al-Hasa (1913), Asir (1920-26), Hail (1921), and the Hejaz (1924-25), thus assembling the territories that formed the kingdom of Saudi Arabia in 1932. He imposed a settled way of life onto many of the nomadic tribes, but reduced tribal conflicts and crime, especially crimes against pilgrims traveling to Mecca. He granted drilling rights to US oil companies to exploit Saudi oil, much of the revenue from which was spent by the royal family Abd al-Aziz was succeeded by his sons Saud 1953-64), whose lack of administrative control and extravagant lifestyle almost bankrupted the country Faisal Ibn Abd Al-Aziz (1964-75, Khalid (1975-82), and Fahd (1982-), Fahd briefly handed power over to Crown Prince Abdullah in late 1995, after suffering a stroke, but resumed control of the country in February 1996.

***

Sawdah (-): second wife of the Prophet who came into his household after the death of Khadijah as a thirty year old widow and a stepmother to his daughters. She had been one of the first Muslims to escape persecution by pagan Mecca and emigrate to Ethiopia. Cousin and sister-in-law of Suhayl, Chief of Amir. Married Muhammad.

***

Sayyab, Badr Shakir (1926-1964): *Iraqi poet* Born into a Shi'a family near Basra, Sayyab secured a diploma from the Teachers' College, Baghdad, where he specialized in Arabic and English literature. He applauded the revolution of July 1958 in Iraq, which saw the end of the pro-British monarchy He celebrated the victory of the Algerian Front for National Liberation against French imperialism in 1962 by using the symbol of Sisyphus discarding his rock. During his terminal illness he produced poetry of despair, often portraying himself as Job, an Old Testament prophet who suffered affliction with fortitude and faith.

***

Sayyid Qutb (1906-1966): As viceroys of the Ottomans, the Muhammad Ali Pasha dynasty ruled Egypt for more than half a century before the British occupied Egypt in 1882. During this period, a large part of the Muslim world was colonized by the leading European nations. The influx of European culture and values into the Muslim world led to considerable socio-cultural tension and confusion. In Egypt, the spread of nationalist fervor during the early part of the twentieth century forced the British to grant formal independence to Egypt. Both the secular and socialist models had been tried, tested and found wanted. Only an Islamic approach to nation-building was, in their opinion, most appropriate for a great Muslim nation like Egypt. One of the most influential Egyptian Islamic thinkers and ideologues of the time was Sayyid Qutb, whose ideas and thoughts have exerted a profound influence on twentieth century Islam.

Sayyid Qutb Ibrahim Hussain Shadhili was born in the village of Musha, near Asyut in Upper Egypt. Although his family originally hailed from the Arabian Peninsula, it was his immediate ancestors who moved to Egypt. Keen to provide a good education for his son, Hajj Qutb ensured his son committed the entire Qur'an to memory before he was ten. After completing his elementary and intermediate studies, Qutb left his native Musha and, in 1921, settled in Cairo (*al-Qahira*), the capital of Egypt and a bustling center of intellectual, cultural and literary activities.

In Cairo, Qutb lived with his uncle and enrolled at a preparatory college in order to secure a place at *dar al-uloom* (the present-day Cairo University). Keen to pursue a career in teaching, Qutb completed his preparatory courses and secured a place at *dar al-uloom* to study for a degree in education. From 1927 to 1930, he immersed himself in his studies and became actively engaged in cultural and literary activities. He was not a supporter of the Western modernism and secularism which was being imported in Egypt from Europe and promoted throughout the country by the Egyptian elite. By now, Qutb was considered to be a talented writer and literary critic in his own right.

After graduating from *dar al-uloom* in 1933, he taught at local schools before joining the Ministry of Education. The Egyptian Government was only too eager to please the British elites and, as expected, this made Qutb very angry. Increasingly considered to be a loose cannon by his colleagues, his superiors at the Ministry of Education were relieved when he finally agreed to go to America. Qutb joined Wilson Teacher's College in Washington DC to learn English. He then moved to Colorado and also visited California, Chicago and San Francisco before returning home to Egypt in 1951.

Qutb's stay in America transformed his outlook on life forever. As an educated, cultured and sensitive man, Qutb felt American society had very little to offer him. He considered American values and way of life to be riddled with both moral and ethical contradictions. Convinced that American morals and values were not the answer for Muslim society, Qutb experienced an intellectual, as well as a cultural, transformation. In his *America Allati Raiyto* (America as I saw it), Qutb not only demolished the argument that American culture and values were worth emulating by the Egyptians; he also exposed the fallacies inherent in Western materialistic values and philosophies.

In 1949, while Qutb was confined to his bed in George Washington University Hospital suffering from recurring respiratory problems, he received news of Hasan al-Banna's assassination. After the murder of the Egyptian Prime Minister, Nuqrashi Pasha, allegedly by a member of *Ikhwan al-Muslimun* (The Muslim Brotherhood), al-Banna was gunned down on the streets of Cairo by the Egyptian secret service. Founded by al-Banna in 1929, the Muslim Brotherhood was a mass Islamic movement which resisted the Egyptian elite's attempts to promote Western morals and values in Egypt. This movement became so popular that by the early 1940s, it became too powerful and influential for the liking of the Egyptian authorities. On his return to Egypt in 1951, Qutb closely studied the ideas, thoughts and methodology of the Brotherhood, and a year later he formally joined the organization. Instantly he became one of its most prominent figures, along with Hasan Ismail al-Hudaybi. Qutb formulated his conceptual and ideological approach to Islam in a number of books he authored at the time. This propelled him into political activism under the banner of the Muslim Brotherhood.

Having no family commitments and responsibilities – Qutb did not marry; he remained a confirmed bachelor all his life – he advocated the need for *jihad* (or the individual and collective struggle) to change the status quo in favor of an Islamic socio-political order. He also assimilated Mawdudi political ideas and thoughts to develop his own ideological interpretation of Islam. But Jamal Abd al-Nasir (who assumed power following the overthrow of King Farouk by the Free Officers) was determined to steer the country toward a secular path. However, when the Brotherhood began to oppose Nasir's secularist overtures, they were censured by the authorities. Two years later, in 1954, the Brotherhood was outlawed by Nasir's regime after an alleged attempt on his life by a member of the Brotherhood. As a result, all the prominent leaders of the Brotherhood were arrested, including Qutb.

After a botched trial, he was sentenced to fifteen years' incarceration, during which he authored his monumental *Fi Zilal al-*

Qur'an (In the Shade of the Qur'an), a voluminous commentary on the Qur'an. Although released from prison in 1964 due to poor health, a year later he was rearrested for actively supporting and co-operating with the Brotherhood. Accused of advocating the violent overthrow of the Government, a military tribunal established by the authorities tried and sentenced him to death at the age of sixty. He walked to his death without any fear or remorse.

Qutb was not steeped in traditional Islamic thought and scholarship; in that sense he was indeed a radical Islamic thinker and activist.

***

Seku Ahmadu Lobbo (1775-1845): West African religious leader. A student of Uthman Dan Fodio, Ahmadu participated in Uthman's *jihad* (or holy war) before settling in the province of Macine (in Mali), where he founded an independent Muslim community. Expelled from Macina by the pagan king of Segu, he established a new capital at Hamdullahi and in 1818 proclaimed a *jihad*, capturing Macina, and extending his authority around it. He established a strictly theocratic Muslim Fulani state which survived until 11859, when it was absorbed in the Tukulor empire of Umar Ibn Said Tal.

***

Selim I (1470–1520): Ottoman sultan , known in English as 'the Grim', thought 'Relentless' better conveys the meaning of his name in Turkish. Recalled from Crimean exile after an aborted attempt to ensure his own succession, he defeated and killed his brother Ahmed in 1513. In 1514, responding to Safavid-inspired subversion in Asia Minor, he crushed a Persian army at Chaldiran. Turning against the Mamluks, he next conquered Syria and Egypt and took the titles of Caliph and protector of the holy cities of Mecca and Medina.

***

Selim III (1761-1808): Ottoman sultan (1789-1807), nephew and successor of Abd al-Hamid I to the throne of the Ottoman Empire (Turkey). He suffered severe defeats in the second of the Russo-Turkish Wars with Catherine II, but suffered no major territorial losses when peace was made at Jassy in 1792. An ardent reformer, Selim set out to rebuild the Turkish navy on European lines, to reform the army, and to curb the Janissaries. In 1798 Selim joined the second coalition against France in the French Revolutionary Wars. Turkish forces lost Jaffa to Napoleon

Bonaparte, who had invaded (1799) Syria after taking Egypt, but they held out at Acre and forced Napoleon to retreat.

In 1801 the French left Egypt, which was restored to the sultan. In 1804 the Serbs under Karageorge revolted. In 1806 war with Russia broke out again. A revolt of the Janissaries and conservatives who opposed his reforms led to Selim's deposition and imprisonment in 1807. Mustafa IV was placed on the throne. A loyal army marched on Constantinople to restore Selim. It entered the city in 1808, just after Selim had been strangled on Mustafa's orders. Mustafa was executed and another of Selim's cousins, Mahmud II, was put on the throne. During Selim's reign Egypt became virtually independent under Muhammad Ali, as did Albania under Ali Pasha. Selim's well-intentioned and efficient reforms came too late to arrest the decay of the Ottoman empire.

***

Shah Jahan (1592-1666): Founded by Zahir al-Din Babar (Babur) in 1526, the Mughal dynasty ruled the Indian subcontinent for more than three centuries with great splendor and munificence. Expanded and consolidated by Akbar the Great during his long reign of forty-nine years, the Mughal dynasty subsequently became one of the Muslim world's foremost political and military powers, along with the Ottomans and the Safavids. After the death of Akbar in 1605, his son Salim (also known as Emperor Jahangir) ascended the throne and attempted to further consolidate Mughal power and authority. After securing Mughal rule in Bengal, he built some of the most beautiful fountains and gardens ever constructed by a Mughal ruler. And unlike his father, Jahangir was highly educated and wrote his autobiography. Peace and prosperity reigned supreme during his rule. Jahangir was eventually succeeded by his son, Shah Jahan, who went on to become one of the Muslim world's most famous and romantic rulers.

Abu Muzaffar Shihab al-Din Muhammad Sahib-i-Qiran II, better known as Shah Jahan ('King of the World'), was born during the long and successful reign of his grandfather, Akbar the Great. Overjoyed at the birth of his third grandson, Akbar named him Khurram, meaning 'joy and happiness'. Brought up by his father, young Shah Jahan received a thorough education in the languages, arts and religious sciences.

In 1611, when Shah Jahan was only nineteen, his father married Mihr al-Nisa, popularly known as Nur Jahan ('Light of the World'), who was the daughter of a Persian immigrant. She then married her daughter by her first husband to Jahangir's youngest son, Prince Shahryar, thus further strengthening her position in the Mughal hierarchy. Not surprisingly, during this period Shah Jahan served his father with much loyalty and distinction including leading several military expeditions against their rivals. Indeed, when he captured the kingdom of Ahmadnagar in 1616, Jahangir was so delighted with his son's achievement that he conferred on him the royal title of 'Shah Jahan'.

Exasperated by Nur Jahan's political intrigues and by his father's apparent inability to restrain her, Shah Jahan eventually revolted against the emperor. After suffering defeat on the battlefield, Shah Jahan went on the run, only to be reconciled with his ailing father in 1625. By then, however, considerable loss and damage had already been inflicted on Mughal power and authority.

After Jahangir's death, Shah Jahan swiftly moved to Agra, the capital of the Mughal dynasty, and found a powerful supporter and ally in the person of Asaf Khan, his father-in-law and the incumbent Prime Minister. In the ensuing battle, Shah Jahan's forces, led by Asaf Khan, routed Shahryar's army, thereby paving the way for Shah Jahan to formally ascend the Mughal throne at the age of thirty-six. Unlike his father, Shah Jahan was a bold and decisive ruler.

During the next two years Shah Jahan remained busy dealing with the appalling impact of famine in both Deccan and Gujarat. According to Abd al-Hamid Lahori, the noted Mughal historian, this famine was so devastating that the people were forced to devour human remains. During this period he also had to come to terms with the death of his beloved wife and consort, Mumtaz Mahal (meaning 'Chosen One of the Palace'), the daughter of Prime Minister Asaf Khan. Mumtaz was the real love and passion of his life, and her premature death in 1631 was a major blow to Shah Jahan. She not only bore him fourteen children, her death completely changed his outlook on life.

As a prolific builder, during his thirty year reign Shah Jahan constructed some of the subcontinent's most dazzling works of architecture. Undoubtedly the most dazzling work of architecture ever produced by a Muslim is the world-famous Taj Mahal (Crown Palace), which is the mausoleum constructed in memory of Shah Jahan's beloved wife, Mumtaz Mahal. He personally chose the site, located on the banks of the river Yamuna in Agra, and authorized the construction of this immortal building in 1632. After many years of careful planning and hard work, the Taj Mahal was eventually completed in 1648. Made entirely from white marble, it is today considered to be one of the seven architectural wonders of the world.

Shah Jahan restored the faith and confidence of the *ulama* (traditional Islamic scholars) and the Muslim masses in the Mughal authorities. He offered full protection and support to all his Hindu subjects. Indeed, he allowed the Hindus to observe their religious rites and cultural practices without any hindrance whatsoever.

Unlike his grandfather, Akbar, Shah Jahan was not a military conqueror. Perhaps the only unprovoked military campaign he undertook was the attempt to annex Samarqand, the land of his legendary ancestor, Amir Timur. The campaign to conquer the 'Blue Pearl of the Orient' thus proved to be disastrous for the Mughals both financially and militarily. Their only consolation was that they recaptured Qandahar from the Persians.

Shah Jahan's reign is today considered to be the 'Golden Age' of Muslim rule in India. In 1657, he fell seriously ill, which sparked off a civil war between his four sons as they each simultaneously laid claim to the Mughal throne. Shah Jahan died at the age of seventy-four and was buried next to his beloved wife, Mumtaz Mahal, inside the immortal Taj Mahal in Agra.

Mogul Emperor of India (1628-58) whose outwardly splendid reign ended in imprisonment by his son and successor. He extended Mogul power, notably in the Deccan, and rebuilt the capital at Delhi. His buildings there and in Agra, notably the Taj Mahal, mark the high peak of Indo-Muslim architecture. His severe illness in 1657 caused a succession war between his four sons in which Aurangzer, the third son, killed his rivals, imprisoned his father in the Agra palace, and seized the throne. One his death Shah Jahan was buried with his favorite wife in the Taj Mahal.

***

Shah Waliullah (1703-1762): As the signs of Islamic political, economic and intellectual decline became all too clear for everyone to see during the early years of the eighteenth century, the once-great dynastic powers like the Ottomans, Safavids and the Mughals faced challenges at home and external threats from foreign powers. The Muslim rulers of the time struggled to maintain their grip on power. Amidst the prevailing chaos and confusion, however, there emerged a number of remarkable Muslim scholars and reformers. One such remarkable intellectual and reformer was Shah Waliullah, who emerged to champion Islamic thought, culture and practices at a time when Muslim India was passing through one of the most difficult periods in its history.

Qutb al-Din Ahmad ibn Abd al-Rahim, better known as Shah Waliullah Dihlawi, was born in the Indian district of Muzaffarnagar into a prominent Muslim family of religious scholars and Sufi luminaries. Shah Abd al-Rahim's father, Shah Wajih al-Din Ghazi, had served as a commander in the Mughal army and was awarded the title of *ghazi* (or warrior) by Emperor Awrangzeb on account of his exceptional bravery and loyalty.

Shah Waliullah spent his early years in Muzaffarnagar and then moved to Delhi with his father, where the latter had established *madrasah-i-Rahimiyyah*, a religious seminary, in which he taught Islamic sciences. Shah Waliullah therefore grew up in Delhi under the care of his father and committed the entire Qur'an to memory by the age of seven. After completing his undergraduate studies at fifteen, he married by unfortunately his wife died a few years later. In 1719, when Shah Waliullah was only sixteen, his father died and suddenly the full operational responsibilities of *madrasah-i-Rahimiyyah* fell on his shoulders.

During this period Shah Waliullah read widely and expanded his intellectual horizons so he could think in a multi-disciplinary way. He then received initiation into the *Shadhiliyyah* Sufi Order, which was widely followed in Egypt and other Arab countries at the time. On his return to India he witnessed the same socio-political commotion as he had seen in Arabia. Indeed, after the death of Awrangzeb (the last of the great Mughal rulers) in 1707, the Mughal dynasty began to decline rapidly as a result of incessant political rivalry and infighting within the royal family. As one Mughal ruler after another tried but failed to reassert their authority across the empire, their grip on India became increasingly precarious.

Shah Waliullah inspired the Muslims to renew their faith and strengthen their commitment to Islam by leading and Islamic lifestyle. As an intellectual rather than a politician, he devoted the next three decades of his life to writing and researching on all aspects of Islam, and in so doing he developed a powerful and compelling Islamic intellectual response to the challenges of his time.

After centuries of Mughal rule, the Indian Muslims now felt threatened by the Hindus within India, and the European colonial powers from outside. As a multi-disciplinary thinker, Shah Waliullah tackled these complex and overlapping social. political, economic, cultural, philosophical and religious issues in more than forty books which he authored in both Arabic and Persian. Indeed, he argued that there existed a common thread across all branches of knowledge which unified the core structures of human thought. To him, Indian Muslims had lost touch with the original, pristine sources of Islam. That is why he translated the Qur'an into Persian, despite the opposition of the conservative *ulama* (religious scholars), so as to make the Qur'an more accessible to the masses. He later inspired his talented son, Shah Abd al-Aziz, to produce an Urdu translation for the first time in the history of India.

Shah Waliullah died at the age of fifty-nine and was buried in Meruli, a suburb of Delhi, in India.

***

Shamil (1798-1871): Leader of Muslim resistance to the Russian occupation of the Caucasus from 1834 to 1859. He became Imam of a branch of the Sufi Naqshabandi order known as Muridism which recommended strict adherence to Islamic law and preached *jihad* (holy war) against Russian. After the Crimean War Russia employed some 200,000 troops in the Caucasus to encircle and subdue Shamil and his followers. He was captured (1859) and imprisoned, but allowed to go on a pilgrimage to Mecca (1870), where he died.

***

Shamyl of Daghestan (1796-1871): The demise of the Soviet Union during the early 1990s heralded a new era in the history of Muslim Central Asia. Historically speaking, the people of this region began to embrace Islam during the Caliphate of Uthman in the middle of the seventh century and, as a result, this region became a flourishing center of Islamic learning, culture and civilization. Tough, talented and unusually brave, the people of this region not only survived the horrors of Mongol invasion in the thirteenth century, they also resisted the formidable Russian and Soviet military machines for more than a century. But, following the disintegration of Soviet Union in the 1990s, the Central Asian Muslim countries finally gained their independence. The man who inspired the Caucasian Muslims to rise up and liberate their homeland from Russian domination, and revive their Islamic culture and heritage was none other than the legendary Muslim warrior and freedom fighter, Shamyl of Daghestan.

Born in the village of Gimiri in North-eastern Daghestan into a noble Muslim family, Shamyl's real name was Ali, but he later became known as Imam Shamyl. He became highly skilled in one-to-one combat and warfare. It was the custom of the Caucasian people to provide basic Islamic education to their young ones before they received training in archery, horse-riding and the use of a dagger.

Gripped by all sorts of superstitious beliefs and practices, the people of Daghestan hardly ventured outside their homes after dark, but Shamyl's unflinching faith in the power and majesty of God left no room for fear of men or evil spirits. As the *Naqshbandiyyah* Sufi *Tariqah* was one of Central Asia's most widely followed Sufi Orders, Shamyl became an adherent and exponent of this *Tariqah*. He knew it was the petty religious-cum-political differences within his society which represented the main obstacle to unity and solidarity. But it was Shamyl who was destined to bring about wide-ranging social and religious reform in and around Daghestan, and in so doing unite his people under his leadership to fight against Russian encroachment.

Despite being a strict adherent of the *Naqshbandiyyah* Sufism (which was well known for its ascetic ways and practices), Shamyl married more than once and had an extended family of his own. According to him, both the law (*Shari'ah*) and the principle (Sufism) were indispensable for leading a balanced Islamic life.

As early as 1801, the Russians had conquered Georgia and made their way toward the mountainous region of Daghestan and Chechnya in order to add these territories to their expanding empire. The Russians knew that the Caucasian people were great warriors who came to the battlefield, wearing their Sufi robes, to die rather than live under foreign occupation. Shamyl and his people united to fight their enemy and defend their motherland. In the ensuing battle, the Tsar's vastly superior forces bulldozed village after village, until there was hardly anything left standing in Chechnya.

After Ghazi Mullah died fighting in 1832, Hamzah Beg succeeded him as *imam* of Chechnya and Daghestan. Two years later he was assassinated, and Shamyl succeeded him as the political and spiritual leader of the Caucasus. As a brave and accomplished warrior (*Mujahid*), Shamyl personally spearheaded the battle against the Russian army. For the next quarter of a century (that is, from 1834 to 1859), the brave people of Chechnya and Daghestan fought against the mighty Russian war machine under Shamyl's inspirational leadership.

To save his beleaguered people from total annihilation, Shamyl reluctantly agreed to sign a peace treaty with the Tsar, which temporarily brought Chechen resistance to an end. Shamyl eventually died in exile at the age of seventy-five and was buried in Madinah (in present-day Saudi Arabia).

***

Shapur I (or Sapor I 241-272): king of Persia, son and successor of Ardashir I, of the Sassanid or Sassanian dynasty. He was an able warrior king. Although he was defeated by the Roman emperor, Gordian III, in 242, Gordian's successor, Philip (Philip the Arabian), concluded a peace with him guaranteeing Shapur's power in Armenia and Mesopotamia. In 260 he achieved his greatest triumph by defeating the Roman emperor Valerian at Edessa-a landmark in the decline of Rome. The rise of Odenathus of Palmyra cut into Shapur's territories and even threatened

Ctesiphon. Yet Shapur not only maintained Persian power in the west but also rebuilt Persian economy. He promoted a program of public works, and in later years he commissioned the translation of numerous Greek and Indian writings. He placed Mani, the found of Manichaeism, under his protection

***

Shariati, Ali (1933-1977): *Iranian Islamic thinker* Born into the family of an Islamic intellectual in Mazinan village near Mashhad [*qv*], Shariati grew up partly in Mazinan and partly in Mashhad. During the oil nationalization crisis of 1951-53, he backed Muhammad Mussadiq [*qv*] and was detained briefly. After receiving his doctorate in sociology and theology in 1964, Shariati traveled home overland with his family and was arrested at the Turkish-Iranian frontier as a suspected subversive. Bitterly opposed to the regime of Muhammad Reza Shah Pahlavi [*qv*], Shariati advocated participation in politics by the masses.

***

Shariatmadari, Muhammad Kazem (1903-1986): *Iranian Islamic leader* Born into a religious, Azeri-speaking [*qv*] family in Tabriz [*qv*] in 1924, Shariatmadari went to Qom [*qv*] to undertake Islamic studies. In January 1978, after the security forces had broken into his theological college in Qom and killed two of his students, he voiced opposition and demanded the return to the 1906-07 constitution. After the revolution in February, Khomeini's leadership was balanced by Ayatollah Mahmud Taleqani [*qv*] on the left, and Shariatmadari on the right.

***

Shaykh Ahmad Sirhindi (1564-1624): The reign of the Mughal Emperor Akbar the Great is generally considered to be the Golden Age of Muslim rule in India. After ascending the Mughal throne during the middle of the sixteenth century, he ruled India for five decades and completely transformed the fortunes of the Mughal dynasty. As a military commander and strategist Akbar was supremely successful, but as a politician and reformer he proved to be controversial, to say the least. As a religious freethinker, he advocated a form of religious pluralism which antagonized both the Muslims and Hindus. During this critical period in the history of Muslim India, Shaykh Ahmad Sirhindi, a pioneering Sufi thinker and influential Islamic reformer, emerged to defend the cause of traditional Islam and reformulate one of the most powerful doctrines of Islamic mystical philosophy.

Also known as M*ujaddid-i alf-i Thani* (Renewer of the Second Millennium of Islam), Shaykh Ahmad Sirhindi was born in the town of Sirhind (located in the Indian State of Punjab) into a respected family of religious scholars and Sufi saints. Brought up in a deeply religious family, young Ahmad was encouraged by his father to commit the entire Qur'an to memory before he was ten. After completing his early education under the guidance of his learned father, he moved to Lahore and Sialkot (in present-day Pakistan). At the age of seventeen, he returned home after success-fully completing his studies and began to teach at his local Islamic seminary.

But subsequently he left his native town and moved to Agra, the capital of the Mughal dynasty, where he joined Emperor Akbar's circle of courtiers. After his father's death in 1598, Ahmad left Sirhind to perform the sacred pilgrimage to Mecca but, on his way, he encountered the acclaimed Naqshabandi Sufi Khwajah Abd al-Baqi, better known as Khwajah Baqi Billah, who helped him to progress through all the stages of mystical experience. After Khwajah Baqi Billah's death in 1603, he again returned to Sirhind where he devoted the rest of his life to the pursuit of Islamic knowledge, wisdom and spirituality, and also became a powerful champion of traditional Islam in Muslim India.

In his opinion, the majority of Sufis failed to clearly distinguish the Eternal and Infinite Creator from His mortal and finite creatures. Ibn al-Arabi's doctrine of *wahdat al-Wujud* stipulated there was only One Being and that everything existed therein. Such a concept, argued Ahmad, had no basis whatsoever in the traditional Islamic worldview. *Tawhid Wujudi*, therefore, contradicted one of the most fundamental concepts of traditional Islam and as such it must be rejected, he argued. God is absolutely transcendent, while man is a mere mortal and a servant of God (*Abd Allah*). The realization that man is God's creature and servant is, according to Ahmad, the highest stage of mystical experience. He referred to this stage as U*budiyah* (or servanthood). After Ahmad's stinging critique of *Tawhid Wujudi*, the majority of India's *Naqshbandiyyah* Sufis rejected this doctrine in favor of *Tawhid Shuhudi*.

At the time, the Mughal Emperor Akbar the Great and his courtiers attempted to dilute the fundamental principles and practices of Islam in order to appease the Hindus.

Ahmad's disciples even took his message beyond the borders of India and established *Naqshbandiyyah* Sufi centers in Afghanistan, Iran and parts of Central Asia. As a prolific writer, he composed more than five hundred epistles on different aspects of Islam and Sufism. He died at the age of sixty and was buried in his native Sirhind. After his death, his religious mission was continued by his four sons, Muhammad Sadiq, Muhammad Sa'id, Muhammad Ma'sum and Muhammad Yahya.

***

Shaykh Sa'di of Shiraz (1174-1290): The words 'ethics' and 'morality' are often used interchangeably even though they do not mean the same thing. Derived from the Greek *ethikos*, ethics means 'ethos and character'. The words 'custom' and 'usage' also fall within the wider definition of ethics. By contrast, the word 'morality' comes from its Greek root M*oralis*, which refers to the nature of a human action rather than the character of the actor.

Influential Muslim philosophers like al-Kindi and al-Farabi formulated new ethical theories in the light of the Islamic worldview. The works of these early Muslim thinkers laid the foundations for a new science which became known as *Ilm al-Akhlaq* (or the 'science of ethics'). However, it was Shaykh Sa'di of Shiraz who became one of the most influential exponents of practical ethics; indeed, he not only clearly defined the 'common good', he also played a pivotal role in popularizing Islamic morality and ethics.

Abu Abdullah Sharaf al-Din ibn Muslih al-Din Sa'di, known as Shaykh Sa'di for short, was born in the Persian city of Shiraz into a middle-class Muslim family. The poverty and destitution experienced by Sa'di during his childhood remained fixed in his mind and was later recalled most vividly in his writings. His devotion to his studies impressed his teachers and this also prompted a local wealthy patron to volunteer to pay for his education. Some of the leading centers of Islamic learning and education at the time were in Baghdad, Damascus, Basrah, Nishapur, Hira and Isfahan. Accordingly, Sa'di proceeded to Baghdad for his higher education and there he composed scores of essays and poems on both religious and moral themes; he was around twenty-one at the time.

As the capital of the Abbasid Caliphate, Baghdad at the time was home to some of the Muslim world's leading scholars and thinkers, who willingly imparted knowledge and wisdom to those who were eager to learn. During his stay in Baghdad, Sa'di also encountered the celebrated Sufi sage Shihab al-Din Umar al-Suhrawardi, the founder of the *suhrawardiyyah* Sufi Order, who initiated him into his *Tariqah*.

Sa'di eventually returned home to Shiraz. Here, he discovered to his dismay, how the socio-political situation had become very volatile and unpredictable. To make matters worse, the Mongols were threatening to wreak havoc throughout that region. This prompted Sa'di to leave Shiraz and travel in pursuit of knowledge. For the next three decades (that is, from 1226 to 1256), he travelled extensively across the Muslim world and explored the lifestyle, culture, tradition and habits of Muslims and non-Muslims alike. From North Africa, he travelled to Turkistan, Afghanistan and India where he met the Hindus for the first time. Rooted in the timeless axis of Divine wisdom, his global ethic was all about the 'common good'; the common good of all humanity rather than that of a specific group or nation. After returning to his native Shiraz in 1256 at the age of eighty-one, he authored most of his books, treatises and poetry.

The Mongol hordes emerged from Asia and marched into Baghdad. The Mongol attack on Baghdad was so devastating that it shocked and horrified Muslims and non-Muslims. Sa'di must have been devastated by the brutal nature of Mongol assault on the seat of the Abbasid Caliphate. When the Mongol advance was eventually halted in 1260 by the Mamluks of Egypt, the entire Muslim world breathed a sigh of relief.

Comprising more than four thousand couplets, Sa'di's *Bustan* is today considered to be one of the most widely-read works of Persian poetry. His understanding of Islam was primarily a moral and ethical one – underpinned by the universal Qur'anic principles and Prophetic wisdom. In his *Bustan*, Sa'di spoke a universal language – which transcended formal speech – by addressing the human heart, which he considered to be the mirror of universal truth. That is to say, his moral philosophy sought to connect mankind to Divinity at a practical level. At the same time, he refused to condemn those who fell short of his high moral and ethical standards. He was wise and entertaining, and never dull or boring. A reader of the *Gulistan* cannot help but smile, reflect and ponder, and do so without having to stretch themselves either physically or intellectually.

As a writer and a poet, Sa'di is considered to be one of the most polished and gifted Muslim poets of all time. Originally written in Persian, Sa'di's *Gulistan* and *Bustan* have also been translated into all the prominent languages of the world including English, Arabic, Hindi, Urdu, French, German, Bengali, Russian, Turkish and even Latin. Sa'di was laid to rest in his native Shiraz. The following couplet is from his *Gulistan* (which has also been inscribed on the Hall of the United Nations): 'The humanity are the limbs of one frame, as in Creation their origin is the same. If fate causes one of the limbs to sting, others too will cry in suffering.' (The Book of Adab-i-Shabat or 'Manners of Companionship').

***

Shihab al-Din Suhrawardi (1154-1191): As the father of Islamic philosophy, the careers of Abu Yusuf Yaqub ibn Ishaq al-Kindi (Al-kindus) flourished in the ninth century during the reign of Abbasid Caliphs al-Ma'mun, Mu'tasim and Wathiq. Following al-Ghazali's stinging critique of Peripatetism, philosophy rapidly declined in the Islamic East. At a time when the Islamic East turned its back on Peripatetic philosophy – and the Islamic West openly embraced what the East had rejected – Shihab al-Din Suhrawardi emerged to develop a powerful synthesis between Peripatetic philosophy and mysticism.

Shihab al-Din Yahya ibn Habash Suhrawardi, also known as *Shaykh al-Ishraq* (Master of Illumination), was born in Suhraward in North-western Persia. Eager to pursue higher education in Islamic philosophical sciences, he left his native Suhraward and moved to Maraghah to study under the guidance of Majd al-Din al-Jili, a notable Persian scholar and thinker. He then left Maraghah and proceeded to the historic Persian city of Isfahan where he conducted research in logic and philosophical sciences. He travelled extensively during this period and visited Anatolia and other prominent Islamic cities and provinces, before finally settling in Aleppo. Suhrawardi lived during one of the most politically turbulent periods in Islamic history, when the Crusaders emerged from Europe and threatened to overwhelm the Islamic East. Thankfully, their advance was first checked by the Zangids, before the heroic figure of Salah al-Din Ayyubi, better known in the West as Saladin, defeated the Franks and recaptured Jerusalem (*al-Quds*), the third sacred city of Islam, from the Crusaders.

Born in 1138 in northern Iraq, Salah al-Din became a prominent Zangid military commander during the reign of Sultan Nur al-Din Mahmud. After the Sultan's death in 1174, Salah al-Din consolidated his powerbase in Egypt and then went on to annex Syria, Iraq, Western Arabia and parts of North Africa, including Tunisia. As a result, he carved out a vast empire which extended from Yemen in the south, to Tunisia in the west; thus he successfully united the Islamic East under his able leadership, with a view to confronting the Frankish Crusaders once and for all.

It was the governor of Aleppo, Malik al-Zahir Ghazi, Sultan Salah al-Din's young son, who summoned Suhrawardi to his court and offered him a lucrative Government post. Young Malik al-Zahir Ghazi was so impressed with Suhrawardi's learning that he began to study aspects of philosophy and Islamic mysticism under his guidance.

Suhrawardi authored most of his influential books and treatises in Arabic, and did so after his arrival in Aleppo in 1183. However, it was his four philosophical works which subsequently exerted immense influence on Muslim philosophers and mystics, especially in Persia. In fact, he was an original thinker who mastered Islamic sciences, Peripatetic philosophy, Sufi thought and ancient Zoroastrian wisdom, in addition to concepts and information from many other sources. The synthesis created by Suhrawardi became known as the 'philosophy of illumination; (or *Hikmat al-Ishraq*). Suhrawardi created a new philosophic-cum-mystical synthesis which he delineated in his major philosophical works, especially his *Hikmat al-Ishraq* (The Philosophy of Illumination).

Suhrawardi argued that Truth cannot be discovered through rational effort alone. By the same token, he felt the mystical approach was not in itself sufficient for attaining the Truth – and the whole Truth. Instead, he proposed a new methodology which combined elements of rationality, experiential wisdom and intellectual intuition which, he argued, was more likely to lead to a deeper and comprehensive understanding of the Truth as such.

Heavily influenced by the philosophical thought of Ibn Sina, Suhrawardi became an ardent Neo-Platonist during his early years. After many years of intensive study and research, he finally discovered the 'philosophy of illumination' which he considered to be a far superior system of thought than Peripatetic philosophy. Since Sultan Salah al-Din Ayyubi and his family members were strict Sunni Muslims, the charge of promoting a heterodoxical creed (consisting of elements of Zoroastrianism, Neoplatonic thought and Shi'a theology and mysticism) was bound to offend the senior courtiers at Aleppo. A petition – formulated by the eminent judge and jurist al-Fadil – stated that Suhrawardi espoused heretical theological and philosophical views which were similar to those of the Ismailis, and urged Sultan Salah al-Din to order his son to execute Suhrawardi. Sultan Salah al-Din agreed with the petition and ordered his son to put Suhrawardi to death.

At the time the Sultan was facing an imminent attack from the Crusaders and therefore decided not to upset the senior courtiers in Aleppo by refusing to comply with their demand. The master of the 'philosophy of illumination' (*Shaykh al-Ishraq*) was sentenced to death at the age of thirty-seven.

***

Shishkali, Adib (1901–1964): *Syrian military leader and politicians; president, 1953–54* Born into a middle-class Sunni family in Hama, Shishkali pursued a military career by joining the Special Forces of the French mandate. A nationalist officer, he backed Rashid Ali Gailani in his fight with the British in 1941. In June 1953 Shishkali became prime minister and was elected president with wide powers in a referendum.

Shishkali subsequently lived in Lebanon, Saudi Arabia, and France. Charged with plotting a coup against the Syrian regime in 1957, Shishkali was tried in absentia and convicted. In 1960 he migrated to Brazil, where he was assassinated by a Druze in revenge for the bombing of the Druze Mountains, which had been ordered by him.

***

Shuqairi, Ahmad (1908–1980): *Palestinian politician* Born into an eminent religious-political family in Acre, Shuqairi trained as a lawyer at the Jerusalem Law School and the American University in Beirut. In 1963 Syria and Iraq proposed at the Arab League that a Palestine National Council be elected and that its chief delegate should occupy the Palestinian seat at the Arab League. Under Shuqairi the PLO had the full backing of Egyptian President Gamal Abdul Nasser, who allowed Shuqairi to run a radio station from Cairo. Following the Arab debacle in the war, Shuqairi was forced to resign his chairmanship of the PLO in December 1967. This ended his public life.

***

Solh, Riyad (1894-1951): *Lebanese politician; prime minister, 1943-45, 1946-51* Also spelled Sulh. Born into a notable Sunni family in Beirut, Solh joined the Arab nationalist movement as a youth. During the Second World War Solh was one of the two main architects of the 1943 National Pact, the other being Bishara Khouri, a Maronite leader. He became prime minister (1943-45) and played a leading role in getting Lebanon chosen as a cofounder of the Arab League

***

Suharto (1921-2008): Indonesian statesman and general. Having played a prominent role in the Indonesian Revolution, he became chief-of-staff of the army in 1965. He crushed a communist coup attempt by the PKI in 1965 and in 1966 President Sukarno, who had been implicated in the coup, was forced to give him wide powers. Having united student and military opponents of the Sukarno regime, he became acting President in 1967, assuming full powers the following year. He ended the Konfrontasi with Malaysia and revitalized the Indonesian economy, as well as restoring the country to the Western capitalist fold. Increasingly dictatorial in the 1980s and 1990s, he has faced considerable domestic opposition, most notably from the Islamic Fundamentalist movement. The sudden collapse of Indonesia's economy in January 1998 prompted widespread civil disorder, which was met with repressive measures by the government.

***

Sukarno, Achmad (1901–1970): Indonesian statesman and founder of Indonesia's independence. A radical nationalist, he emerged as leader of the PNI (Indonesian Nationalist Party) in 1926 and spent much of the 1930s either in prison or exile. During the Japanese occupation, he consolidated his position as the leading nationalist figure and claimed the title of President of Indonesia in 1945. He then led his country through the Indonesian Revolution (1945-49), remaining President after the legal transfer of power from the Netherlands in 1949.

A leading spokesman for the non-aligned movement, he hosted the Bandung Conference in 1955, but found that his dictatorial tendencies aroused increasing resistance at home. Economic difficulties, and the Konfrontasi with Malaysia, further undermined his position in the mid-1960s. Seeking increasing support from the communists, he was implicated in the abortive left-wing officer coup of 1965. Thereafter he effectively lost power to the army. Officially stripped of his power in 1967, he was succeeded as President by General Suharto.

***

Sulaiman the Magnificent (1494-1566): Historians often classify Islamic history into what is known as the 'classical' and 'modern' periods. Two of the greatest empires of the classical period were the Umayyad and the Abbasid dynasties which collectively ruled the Muslim world for around six centuries without serious opposition. Three of the most influential political powers of this period were the Ottomans, the Safavids and the Mughals. At the height of its power, the Ottoman Empire extended across three continents, namely Europe, Africa and Asia. Founded in 1300 by Uthman Bey, a Turkish chieftain, the Ottoman Empire became a formidable political and military superpower during the sixteenth century under the wise and able stewardship of Sulaiman the Magnificent, the tenth ruler of the Ottoman Empire.

Born in the Asiatic province of Trabzon, Sulaiman's great-grandfather was Sultan Muhammad II, the conqueror of Constantinople; his father, Sultan Salim I, ascended the throne relatively late in life in 1512, and ruled for eight years with some success. His mother, Aishah, was a noble lady who became his first tutor and guide.

In 1520, Sultan Salim died at the age of fifty-four, having successfully spearheaded a series of military expeditions and thereby consolidated Ottoman rule across much of Europe, Asia and Africa. As expected, Sulaiman succeeded his father without facing any political or military opposition. Only twenty-six at the time of his accession, he instantly became one of the most powerful rulers of his time. Sulaiman outshone all his contemporaries by the force of his sublime character and personality. With Islam being the official religion of the State, he made Turkish the main language of his empire and promoted it throughout his dominion.

Sulaiman also freed all the slave laborers his father had brought from Egypt. His wise and decisive actions instantly won over the people to his side. He made it clear that he would not tolerate injustice and oppression, no matter who happened to be the perpetrator. Since the main purpose of his reforms was to eradicate injustice and corruption from all levels of his administration, he established an imperial council (*divan*).

After setting up the imperial council, Sulaiman reformed the archaic Ottoman legal system. The legal system implemented by Sulaiman enabled both Muslims and non-Muslims to seek redress for their grievances through the Ottoman courts; these courts applied a combination of *Shari'ah* (Islamic law) and imperial Ottoman law (*Qanun*). It was not long before Sulaiman succeeded in restoring peace, security and prosperity across the Ottoman Empire. Impressed by his political, social, economic and legal reforms, his subjects conferred on him the coveted title of the 'law-giver' or Q*anuni*.

Faced with open rebellion in Syria, Sulaiman mustered a large army and sent an expedition to Syria to bring its treacherous governor to heel. In the ensuing battle, the governor and his supporters were routed by Sulaiman's forces. Sulaiman was also forced to take action against the King of Hungary for humiliating his emissary, who had gone there to collect the annual levy from the King. So it was that in 1521, at the age of twenty-seven, Sulaiman organized a large expedition and marched toward the city of Belgrade, which he captured after seven days of heavy fighting. After establishing a garrison in Belgrade, he began to devise his next military plan.

A year later, Sulaiman moved toward the strategically important Mediterranean island of Rhodes, which at the time was firmly in the grip of the fanatical Knights of St John. Accompanied by a one hundred thousand strong force and three hundred formidable vessels, Sulaiman spearheaded a massive military assault on the island. The Knights fought back with great determination and resisted the Ottoman army for nearly nine months before they were forced to surrender.

Then, in 1526, Sulaiman authorized one of the most important campaigns of his reign, namely the Ottoman invasion of Hungary.

Equipped with superior weaponry, the Ottoman forces left their military base in Belgrade and marched toward Budapest, the capital of Hungary. In the ensuing battle Louis II, the King of Hungary, and his senior officials died fighting as the Ottoman forces, led by Sulaiman, crushed the Hungarians. But a few years later, in 1529, Sulaiman was again forced to return to Budapest to put an end to a civil war which had broken out there between his governor and a rival militia. Following a fierce battle, he entered Budapest and restored peace and security throughout the city. He then proceeded to Vienna and laid siege to that historic city. The Ottoman failure to take Vienna represented a major turning-point in both Islamic and European history, because this brought an end to the Ottoman advance into the rest of Europe. This day became known throughout Europe as 'the Day of Deliverance'.

History shows that Sulaiman was a veteran military commander who personally led no fewer than thirteen major military expeditions during his rule, ten of which were in Europe, and the other three in Asia. The Ottoman navy had complete supremacy of the seas and the Ottoman Empire became one of the world's great military superpowers.

Sulaiman's most famous architectural works include the magnificent Sulaimaniyyah Complex built in Istanbul by Mimar Sinan between 1550 and 1557; Sinan was his personal builder and one of the world's greatest architects.

Sulaiman also became recognized as the undisputed ruler and champion of the Muslim world at the time. That is why he became known throughout Europe as *el magnifico* (or 'the Magnificent').

In his spare time, Sulaiman used to commit the Qur'an to paper, and copies of the Qur'an written by his own hand are still extant to this day. Sulaiman died at the age of seventy-two and was buried in his beloved Istanbul. After his death, the Ottoman Empire began to decline irreversibly.

***

Sultan Husayn (1694-1729): Safavid shah of Persia. A weak and superstitious man, Shah Sultan Husayn was surrounded by astrologers and fanatics and was able to offer little opposition to the uprising of the Afghans. He gave up his throne, and the bloody rule of Mahmud followed. Persian administration was restored only later by Nadir Shah.

***

Sultan Muhammad II (1429-1481): The Ottoman Empire (known in Arabic as *al-Khilafah al-Uthmaniyyah*) was one of the most powerful and enduring dynasties to have emerged in Islamic history. It was founded in 1300 by the Turkish chieftain Uthman Bey (who was also known as Osman or Ottoman). In all, thirty-six Sultans ruled the Ottoman Empire from 1300 to 1922. At its zenith, the Ottoman dynasty stretched from Yemen in the Middle East, as far as Greece, Bulgaria, Romania, Hungary, Albania and the former Yugoslav States of Serbia, Croatia, Bosnia, Macedonia and Kosovo in the West. More than five centuries of Ottoman achievements and legacy are today admired by Muslims and Europeans alike. The reign of one of its greatest sons, Sultan Muhammad II, represents the complete opposite, namely the Ottoman's greatest triumph over its European adversaries.

When Sultan Murad II, the father of Muhammad II, ascended the Ottoman throne in 1421, he inherited a strong a united empire which he further consolidated during his reign of three decades, and in so doing established Ottoman dominance across a significant part of Europe, Asia and the Middle East. Born eight years after his father's accession to power, Muhammad II was considered far too weak and feeble to follow in his father's footsteps and take on the enormous responsibility of ruling a vast empire. He had very limited contact with the outside world during his early days.

While he was still in his teens, Muhammad was appointed governor of the province of Amasya by his father to prepare him to ascend the Ottoman throne after his death. In 1451, Sultan Murad II died of apoplexy and, as expected, he was succeeded by his son, who became known as Sultan Muhammad II. For the next thirty years, the Sultan not only sat securely on the Ottoman throne, he also carved out a unique place for himself in the annals of history by becoming one of the Muslim world's most successful military commanders, strategists and statesmen. He also championed the cause of toleration, coexistence and mutual understanding between all his subjects. If anyone dared to cross his path, he taught them a lesson they never forgot. As for his avowed opponents, he relentlessly pursued them without any mercy or forgiveness.

The Sultan signed peace treaties with all the rival powers of his time. Caliph Muawiyah ibn Abi Sufyan, the founder of the Umayyad dynasty, was one of the first Muslim rulers to send an expedition to capture Constantinople. Many other attempts were later made by other Muslim rulers to annex Constantinople, but they also failed to capture this historic capital. As destiny would have it, the onus of taking this last bastion of the Holy Roman Empire fell on the shoulders of Sultan Muhammad II. The Sultan was determined to liberate Constantinople.

Known to antiquity as Byzantium, Constantinople was named after the Roman Emperor Constantine, who moved the capital of his empire from Rome to this ancient and strategically situated city on the Bosphorus, bridging the continents of Asia and Europe.

The Sultan began by recruiting military experts and engineers from Hungary and paid them handsomely to design a large quantity of cannonballs and several delivery systems. As the weapons were being prepared, the Sultan gathered his one hundred and fifty thousand strong army, which included his twelve thousand elite infantrymen known as the Janissaries (derived from the Turkish *yen Cheri*, meaning 'new troops'). In 1453, the Sultan marched toward Constantinople with his contingent and camped close to the city's walls. This prompted the Sultan to law siege to the city in April 1453.

For the next month, the Ottoman army pounded the walls of Constantinople both from the land and sea. The defense put up by the Byzantines proved highly effective both on land and on sea. It was at this point, with the siege of Constantinople reaching its climax, that the Sultan showed his true colors as a military genius. He ordered his fleet of vessels to be transferred from the Bosphorus into the Golden Horn by land. He ordered his army to construct a road, made from wooden planks, from one end of the Bosphorus and leading to the Golden Horn. The Ottoman army took the enemy by complete surprise. They smashed the walls of Constantinople to rubble. The Ottoman army, led by the Sultan, then marched into the historic city of Constantinople. As for the Byzantine Emperor and his troops, they died fighting bravely.

By conquering the historic city of Constantinople, the Sultan became known to posterity as *al-Fatih*, meaning 'the Conqueror', on 29th May 1453. As expected, the Sultan went straight to the splendid surroundings of the Hagia Sophia (Aya Sofia) and offered his prayers there. He treated the inhabitants of the city with respect and courtesy, allowing the Christians and Jews to continue to live there with their wealth and properties, if they so wished. He also ordered two minarets to be added to the exquisite Hagia Sophia, which came to symbolize Islam's great victory over its Byzantine rival. He then transferred the capital of the Ottoman Empire from Adrianople (Edirne) to Constantinople (Istanbul). Most astonishingly, the Sultan was only twenty-two years old when he achieved the unprecedented feat of conquering Constantinople.

During the next twenty-eight years of his reign, he helped to rebuild and repopulate the entire city, and in so doing transformed Istanbul into one of the world's most beautiful and attractive cities, thus reflecting its former glory again. The Ottoman Empire became one of the great superpowers of its time. And his fleet of vessels, which roamed the seas without any opposition, was also considered to be the world's most advanced naval power of the time. After annexing Greece and venturing as far as Italy, the Sultan effectively became the Muslim world's (and also Europe's) most powerful political and military leader. The venerable Sultan died at the age of forty-nine and he was the first Muslim ruler to be buried in Istanbul.

***

Tahman, Tungku (Prince) Abdul (1903–1990): Malaysian statesman. He entered the Kedah state civil service in 1931 and in 1952 succeeded Dato Onn bin Ja'far as leader of the United Malays national Organization (UMNO). He played a central role in organizing UMNO's alliance with the moderate Malayan Chinese Association (founded in 1949 by Tan Cheng Lock) which provided the political base for the achievement of independence. After becoming the leader of the Federal Legislative Council in 1955, he became Malaya's first Prime Minister (1957-63) and in 1963 he successfully presided over the formation of the Federation of Malaysia, which he led as Prime Minister (1963-70). He remained in office until the political crisis caused by the riots of 1969 between the Malays and the Chinese forced him to stand down.

***

Taimur ibn Faisal (1885-1956): *Sultan of Oman, 1913-1932* Born in Muscat, Taimur succeeded his father, Faisal, in 1913. The subsequent uneasy peace allowed the British Political Agent in Muscat to initiate peace talks in 1918. The efforts of British civil servants to salvage the situation failed, and in 1932 Britain forced Taimur to abdicate in favor of his son, Said.

***

Talabani, Jalal (1933-   ): *Iraqi Kurdish leader* Born into a landowning family in Koy Sanjak, Irbil province, Talabani obtained a law degree at Baghdad University and practiced as a lawyer. He then moved to Damascus to become the KDP's envoy there. Disagreeing with Barzani's decision to flee to Iran in the wake of the March 1975 Algiers Accord, Talabani left the KDP to cofound the Kurdish Workers League. In 1984, pressured by the demands of its war with Iran, the Iraqi government began to negotiate with Talabani, but nothing came of it. This paved the way for Talabani's ties with Iran. Following Iraq's invasion of Kuwait in August 1990, Talabani was elected to a six-member coordination committee of the Iraqi opposition.

After the Second Gulf War, Talabani helped trigger a Kurdish uprising against Baghdad in early March 1991. Emboldened by Iran's arms supplies, Talabani mounted an offensive against the KDP in August 1996. When, after defeating the Taliban regime in Afghanistan in late 2001, the U.S. administration of President George W. Bush turned its attention to overthrowing Saddam's government by force, the importance of Talabani as well as Barzani rose. On the eve of the Gulf War III in 2003, Talabani agreed to coordinate his party's military plans with those of the KDP.

***

Talal ibn Abdullah al Hashem (1909-1972): *King of Jordan, 1951-52* Born in Mecca to Abdullah ibn Hussein al Hashem, Talal ascended the throne of Jordan in July 1951 following the assassination of his father. He was forced to abdicate in favor of his son Hussein, a minor, in August 1952 and was committed to a mental clinic in Istanbul, where he died twenty years later.

***

Taleqani, Mahmud (1910-1979): *Iranian Islamic leader* Born into a religious Shi'a family in Taleqan village, Mazandaran province, Taleqani went to Qom for his Islamic studies. After graduating in 1938, he taught at a theological school in Tehran. He was sentenced to ten years of imprisonment in January 1964 for participating in the protest movement of June 1963. In terms of popular support, which spanned a wide political spectrum, Taleqani was second only to Khomeini, upon whom he was a moderating influence.

***

Tariq ibn Zaid (700-712): A freedman of Musa ibn Nusayr, Umayyad governor of North Africa. In 711 he was sent to conquer Spain with 7,000 men, landing near the famous rock that has immortalized his name, Jabal al-Tariq (Mount of Tariq), that is, Gibraltar. On 19 July 711 he defeated the Visigoth king Roderick and went on to conquer half of Spain. In 712 Musa crossed to Spain and, out of jealousy at Tariq's success, put him in chains. His subsequent fate is unknown.

***

Tariq ibn Ziyad (650-728): Within a few decades following the death of the Prophet, Muslims burst out of Arabia and overwhelmed the Persian and Byzantine Empires, two great superpowers of the time. After assuming full control of the region known today as the Middle East, Muslim forces marched into Africa. Although it was during the reign of Caliph Umar that Muslims first made in-roads into North Africa, it was Muawiyah ibn Abi Sufyan, the first Umayyad ruler, who commissioned large-scale campaigns into that part of the world. Thanks to Caliph Abd al-Malik's efforts, Islamic rule became firmly established in North Africa.

In 708, the Umayyad ruler al-Walid appointed the great Muslim general Musa ibn Nusayr as governor of the North Africa. Within a very short period, Musa became the undisputed master of all North Africa. It was also during Musa's reign as governor of North Africa that Muslims first sailed across the sea and marched into Spain under the command of the legendary Muslim general Tariq ibn Ziyad.

Tariq hailed from the North African Berber tribe of Nafzawah and was born into a poor Muslim family. Trained in military strategy and warfare by the illustrious Musa ibn Nusayr, Tariq soon began to shine and out-smart his peers. Soon afterward, Musa appointed him governor of Tangier (in present-day Morocco).

In contract, the situation across the sea in the Iberian Peninsula could not have been more desperate. King Roderick (or Rodrigo), the reigning Visigoth ruler of Spain, presided over a people who still lived in the Dark Ages. The King mercilessly pursued and punished the Jewish population of Iberia with the support and approval of the Catholic Church. As the masses intensified their campaign for freedom and liberation from the despotic rule of King Roderick, Musa ibn Nusayr felt the situation was ripe for external intervention.

Musa summoned his favorite general, Tariq ibn Ziyad, and instructed him to lead a sortie into Iberia. Ilyan promised the supply the Muslim army with boats so that they could cross the sea which separated Iberia from North Africa. Tariq told them: they must either conquer *al-Andalus* or die fighting for Islam. Hereafter this place became known as Gibraltar, derived from the Arabic *Jabal at-Tariq* (the Mount of Tariq), and thus the name of Tariq ibn Ziyad became immortalized.

The two armies met at Guadalete. Standing before his men, Tariq delivered one of the most inspirational speeches ever composed by a Muslim military commander.

Tariq had no doubt that the Muslims would win the Battle of Rio Barbate. And so it proved. Under his inspirational leadership, the Muslim forces completely routed Roderick and his much larger, superior army. Victory over Roderick opened the door to the rest of Iberia: Tariq moved swiftly to other parts of the peninsula and conquered a large part of the country before proceeding to Toledo. When Musa received the news of Tariq's success, he also crossed into Iberia, in 712, with a large army and successfully conquered such prominent Iberian cities as Sidonia, Carmona and Seville before joining Tariq in Toledo. Both Tariq and Musa remained in Muslim Spain for three years.

Those who chose to remain Christian were tolerated and allowed to live in peace, along with a significant number of Jews who continued to live and thrive in Islamic Spain. Under Muslim patronage, Judaism flourished throughout Spain and this period became known as the Golden Age of Judaism in Europe, where great Jewish scholars and thinkers like Musa bin Maimon (better known as Maimonides), Ibn Gabirol and Ibn Daud later lived and produces some of their most influential works. Tariq deserves to be recognized as one of the most influential and pioneering military geniuses of all time.

Caliph al-Walid in Damascus ordered both Tariq and Musa to report to him immediately. Caliph al-Walid's unexpected intervention not only saved France, it also saved the rest of Europe from Muslim domination.

Tari was not only the first Muslim to set foot on mainland Europe, he was also responsible – along with Abd al-Rahman I – for initiating more than seven centuries of Islamic rule in Spain.

***

Tewfik Pasha (Muhammad Tewfik 1852-1892): Khedive of Egypt (1879-92). He acceded to office when his father, Ismail Pasha, was deposed. In 1880, Tewfik accepted joint French-British control over the nation's finances. This act provoked a nationalist uprising that forced Tewfik to appoint a cabinet hostile to the European powers. The British and the French, however, quickly compelled the cabinet to resign. Later, in 1882, Great Britain, alarmed by renewed agitation, bombarded Alexandria and landed troops. France had refused to support this action and ended participation in Egyptian affairs, thus leaving Great Britain in sole control. Tewfik, who was generally Western in his outlook, devoted much attention to educational and legal reforms. He was succeeded as khedive by his son Abbas II.

***

Timur the Conqueror (1336-1405): There is no doubt that Alexander the Great, Genghis Khan, Hannibal and Napoleon were great conquerors. Alexander burst out of Macedonia in 334BC and overwhelmed the mighty Persian Empire, although unfavorable circumstances forced him to return home without conquering India. After instigating a series of remarkable conquests within a short period, he died at the age of thirty-two. The Mongols. led by Genghis Khan, suddenly emerged from North-east Asia in the twelfth century and rapidly conquered China, India, Persia and southern Russia. The Mongols' reputation for carrying out wholesale massacres and brutality made their opponents shake in their boots.

Genghis Khan died in 1227 after falling off his horse. Hannibal, on the other hand, was appointed commander of the Carthaginian army when he was only twenty-six. With a contingent of forty thousand men, thirty-eight elephants and some horses, he fought a vicious battles against the Romans and successfully conquered northern Italy. Fearing betrayal, he poisoned himself in 183BC. By contrast, Napoleon Bonaparte received training at the military academy in Paris and fought numerous battles before becoming the Emperor of continental Europe. Following crushing defeats at Leipzig (1814) and Waterloo (1815), he died in 1821. Timur was undoubtedly history's most successful conqueror.

Amir Timur, known as Tamerlane in the West, was born into a noble Muslim family in the village of Khoja Ilgar close to Shakhrisabz, the Green City, in modern-day Uzbekistan. The name Timur, meaning lion, says much about the character, attitude and aspirations of the Turkicized descendants of Genghis Khan who became known as the Tartars. The Tartars were tough, resilient and ruthless warrior-like people, who became famous for their bravery, sense of purpose and military prowess.

After receiving training in combat, archery and horse-riding, Timur became a skilled hunter. During this period he suffered a serious injury which earned him the nickname 'Timur the Lame' (derived from the Persian T*imur-i Lang*). For this reason, he later became widely-known in the West as Tamerlane. Despite his crippling injury, he became an accomplished polo and chess player. Timur became fascinated by combat and warfare. As expected, he followed in the traditions of his people and become a skilled archer, huntsman, soldier and military tactician.

Timur was born during a chaotic period in the history of Central Asia. After the death of Genghis Khan in 1227, the Mongol Empire began to disintegrate rapidly as his descendants engaged in a protracted succession battle. Young Timur witnessed the bitter political rivalry which prevailed at the time between Amir Qazaghan of Mawarahnahr and Moghul Khan of Moghulistan. The two men fought tooth and nail for power, until Amir Qazaghan was assassinated in 1358. Timur returned to Barlas with a group of young fighters and decided to defend his homeland against the encroaching Moghul Khan. Instead he offered his services to Moghul Khan, who rewarded him handsomely and made him the leader of the Barlas clan; he was only twenty-five at the time.

Given his meager resources, Timur could not dare to challenge Moghul Khan. So he decided to forge an alliance with Amir Hussain, the grandson of Qazaghan, who at the time was the ruler of Balkh (located in northern Afghanistan). Timur strengthened his relationship with Amir Hussain by marrying his sister, Aljai Turkhan-Agha, and also agreed to collaborate with him in order to oust Moghul Khan. Timur's guerrilla activities eventually culminated in the subjugation of the small Sarbadar Kingdom of Samarqand. After the overthrow of the Sarbadars, he installed himself as the new ruler of that kingdom.

As a strong, fearless and intelligent warrior, Timur trained and rewarded his fighters better than any of his rivals. Being a ruthless and ambitious warrior, he was not interested in ruling a small kingdom; he was determined to conquer and rule the whole world.

Timur then launched several other military campaigns against the Moghuls before finally defeating them in 1383. He then returned to Samarqand in 1372, only to discover his son, Jahangir, had died of flu.

The Persian city of Sultaniyya was a strategically important center and it succumbed soon afterward. This was followed by the annexation of Tabriz, the capital of Azerbaijan. Almost unstoppable, he was now on a rampage. Thus, in 1387 he reached Tbilisi, the capital of Georgia, and ransacked the entire city. After subduing Azerbaijan, Georgia and Armenia, his forces marched toward Asia Minor at a lightning speed and captured the historic cities of Isfahan and Shiraz. By 1385, Timur had carved out a huge empire. He then turned his eyes toward the Islamic East and soon captured Baghdad. Although the brave people of Baghdad put up a determined resistance, Timur's forces entered the city and created much havoc there. From Baghdad, his forces then proceeded toward the Caucasus.

Later, in 1398, Timur marched into India and subjugated Delhi, leaving behind only a pile of dust and rubble. He then captured Aleppo and Damascus in 1400 and 1401, respectively, but his greatest victory was yet to come. In 1402, he took on the might of the Ottoman Empire and inflicted a humiliating defeat on the forces of Sultan Bayazid at the Battle of Ankara. Ironically, it took one emerging Muslim power to inflict defeat on another great Islamic superpower. Timur set out for his final military campaign, in 1405, against the Ming Emperor of China, but on his arrival in Otrar (in modern Kazakhstan) he died of fever at the age of sixty-nine. Nonetheless, he had already carved out one of the largest empires in history, and in so doing he became one of the most powerful men who ever lived.

As a military genius, Timur carefully identified his military targets and pursued them ruthlessly; he had no time for love, emotion or tears, except only for those who were very close and dear to him. Toward the end of his life, he liked to sit in the company of the religious scholars and Sufis. He lies buried in the Gur Amir mausoleum in Samarqand (also known as Samarkand).

Timur or Tamerlane, c. 1336-1405, Mongol conqueror, b. Kesh, near Samarkand. He is also called Timur Leng [Timur the lame]. He was the son of a tribal leader, and he claimed (apparently for the first time in 1370) to be a descendant of Genghis Khan. With an army composed of Turks and Turkie-speaking Mongols, remnants of the empire of the Mongols, Timur spent his early military career in subduing his rivals in what is now Turkistan; by 1369 he firmly controlled the entire area from his capital at Samarkand. Campaigns he waged against Persia occupied him until 1387. By that time he had in his possession the lands stretching E from the Euphrates River.

He advanced (1392) across the Euphrates, conquered the territory between the Caspian and Black seas, and invaded several of the Russian states. By weakening the Crimean Tatars he helped clear the way for the conquests of the grand duchy of Moscow. Timur abandoned some of his Russian conquests to return to Samarkand and invade (1398) India along the route of the Indus River. He took Delhi and brought the Delhi Sultanate to an end, but he withdrew with little addition to his domain. In 1400, Timur ravaged Georgia and proceeded to the Levant, where he took Aleppo and Baghdad. His next war was fought in Asia Minor against the Ottoman Turks, and in 1402, at Angora, he captured their sultan, Beyazid I, who, contrary to popular belief, was well treated. Timur died while planning an invasion of China. His tomb at Samarkand was long known to archaeologists, but it is only recently that his skeleton, buried in a deep crypt, was found.

Timur's reputation is that of a cruel conqueror. After capturing certain cities he slaughtered thousands of the defenders (perhaps 80,000 at Delhi) and built pyramids of their skulls. Although a Muslim, he was scarcely more merciful to those of his own faith than to those he considered infidels. His positive achievements were the encouragement of art, literature, and science and the construction of vast public works. He had little hope that his vast conquests would remain intact, and before his death he arranged for them to be divided among his sons. The Timurids are the line of rulers descended from him.

***

Tipu Sultan (1753-1799): Sultan of Mysore (1782-99). He inherited the kingdom recently created by his father, Hyder Ali and was a formidable enemy to both the British and neighboring Indian states. Failures to secure active French support left him without allies in resisting the British. He was finally besieged in his own capital, Seringapatam, when unfounded rumors that he had secured an alliance with Revolutionary France gave the British the necessary pretext for a final assault. He was killed in the attack.

***

Touma, Emile (1918-1985): *Palestinian writer and politician* Born into a Greek Orthodox middle-class family in Haifa, Touma moved to Jerusalem for his university education. When Maki split in 1965, Touma joined Rakah, which was recognized by the international department of the Communist Party of the Soviet Union two years later.

***

Toure (Ahmed) Sekou (1922-1984): African statesman. President of Guinea (1958-84). In 1946, together with other African leaders, including Houphouet-Boigny, he was a founder of the Tassmblement Democratique Africain. He became Secretary-General of the CGT (Confederation Generale de Travail) for Africa in 1948. In 1955 he was ejected Mayor of Conakry and took his seat in the French National Assembly in 1956. In 1957 he became Vice-President in the Guinea cabinet. He was elected president when Guinea became independent in 1958 and broke all links with the French community. A convinced Marxist, he received aid or Guinea from the Soviet bloc. Following his death in 1984 the armed forces stage a coup.

***

Ubaydallah ibn Jahsh: Muhammad's cousin; became a Muslim and then converted to Christianity. Muhammad's cousin and brother-in-law had died in Abyssinia. His wife later married Muhammad (Ramlah, known as Umm Habiba) daughter of Abu Jakyan.

***

Umar, al-Hajj (1797-1864): West African mystic and warrior, who founded the Tukolor Empire of the Senegambia region. Born in the Futa Toro (in present-day Senegai), the son of a Tukolor Muslim scholar, he was given a good education, joined the Tijaniyya brotherhood, and married a daughter of Muhammad Bello, sultan of Sokoto (1781?-1837). In the 1820s he made a pilgrimage to Mecca, and the returned inspired to further the spread of Islam. Getting a horde of adherents and arming them with guns, he launched a jihad, or holy war, in 1852, winning control of several pagan Bambara and Mandinka states in the Senegal-Niger basins. From there he turned eastward to Segou, which he defeated in 1861, and the kingdom of Macina, a fellow Muslim state, which he overran the following year. In 1863 he captured Tuaregs and revolting Fulani from Macina destroyed his army in 1864, and Umar himself was killed. His empire, under his son Ahmadu (1833?-98), was finally subdued by the French in 1893.

***

Umar Al-Khayyam (1048–1131): Was a Persian polymath, philosopher, mathematician, astronomer and one of the most famous Muslim poets in the Western world. It is rare for a person to excel in science, as well as in poetry. He also wrote treatises on mechanics, geography, mineralogy, music, climatology and Islamic theology. He poked fun at people who wore the cloak of religiosity outwardly, but failed to live by the moral, ethical and spiritual demands of their faith. He was steeped in Islamic morality and T*asawwuf* (or Islamic mysticism and spirituality).

The period from the eighth to the sixteenth century is generally considered to be that age of Islamic supremacy. During this period Muslims dominated a significant part of Asia, Africa and Europe. Under the patronage of prominent Muslim rulers and statesmen like Harun Alashi, Abdullah al-Ma'mun, Nizam al-Mulk, Sultan Mahmud of Ghazna, Akbar the Great and Suleiman the Magnificent, the Muslim world led the rest of the world in educational, artistic and cultural pursuits. The tenth and eleventh centuries were, arguable, the most intellectually and culturally progressive period in the annals of Islam. Omar Khayyam, who was a renowned astronomer and mathematician and one of the most famous Muslim poets in the Western world, also lived during this unusually creative period in the intellectual history of Islam.

His significance as a philosopher and teacher and his few remaining philosophical works, have not received the same attention as his scientific and poetic writings. Al-Zamakhshari referred to him as "the philosopher of the world". Many sources have testified that he taught for decades the philosophy of Avicenna in Nishapur where Khayyam was born and buried and where his mausoleum today remains a masterpiece of Iranian architecture visited by many people every year.

Thomas Hyde (1636–1703) was the first non-Persian to study him. The most influential of all was Edward Fitzgerald (1809–83), who made Khayyam the most famous poet of the East in the West through his celebrated translation and adaptations of Khayyám's rather small number of quatrains in the *Rubáiyát of Omar Khayyam*, which became an instant hit in the English-speaking world soon after its publication. It was Fitzgerald's fault that the saying of the Alexandrian Philistine in Theocritius, "Homer is enough for all," became "Omar is enough for all."

Omar Khayyam died in 1131 and is buried in the Khayyam Garden at the mausoleum of Imamzadeh Mahruq in Nishapur. In 1963 the mausoleum of Omar Khayyam was constructed on the site by Hooshang Seyhoun.

Early life:

Khayyám's full name was Ghiyāth ad-Din Abu'l-Fath 'Umar ibn Ibrahim an-Nīshāpūrī al-Khayyāmī. He was born in Nishapur, modern-day Iran, but then a Seljuq capital in Khorasan, which rivaled Cairo or Baghdad in cultural prominence in that era. He is thought to have been born into a family of tent-makers (*khayyami* "tent-maker").

He spent part of his childhood in the town of Balkh (present northern Afghanistan), studying under the well-known scholar Sheikh Muhammad Mansuri. He later studied under Imam Mowaffaq Nishapuri, who was considered one of the greatest teachers of the Khorasan region. Throughout his life Omar Khayyam was dedicated to his efforts and abilities, in the day he would teach Algebra and geometry in the evening he would attend the Seljuq court as an adviser of Malik-Shah I and at night he would study Astronomy and complete the important aspects of the Jalali calendar.

Mathematician:

Khayyam Sikander was famous during his times as a mathematician. He wrote the influential *Treatise on Demonstration of Problems of Algebra* (1070), which laid down the principles of algebra, part of the body of Persian Mathematics that was eventually transmitted to Europe. In particular, he derived general methods for solving cubic equations and even some higher orders.

In the *Treatise* he wrote on the triangular array of binomial coefficients known as Pascal's triangle. In 1077, Khayyam wrote *Sharh ma ashkala min Musadarat kitab Uqlidis* (Explanations of the

Difficulties in the Postulates of Euclid) published in English as "On the Difficulties of Euclid's Definitions". An important part of the book is concerned with Euclid's famous parallel postulate, which attracted the interest of Thabit ibn Qurra.

Omar Khayyam had notable works in geometry, specifically on the theory of proportions. His notable contemporary mathematicians included Al-Khazini and Abu Hatim al-Muzaffar ibn Ismail al-Isfizari

Theory of parallels:

Khayyam wrote a book entitled *Explanations of the difficulties in the postulates in Euclid's Elements*. The book consists of several sections on the parallel postulate (Book I), on the Euclidean definition of ratios and the Anthyphairetic ratio (modern continued fractions) (Book II), and on the multiplication of ratios (Book III).

The treatise of Khayyam can be considered as the first treatment of parallels axiom which is not based on petitio principii, but on more intuitive postulate. Khayyam refutes the previous attempts by other Greek and Persian mathematicians to *prove* the proposition. And he, as Aristotle, refuses the use of motion in geometry and therefore dismisses the different attempt by Ibn Haytha, too. In a sense he made the first attempt at formulating a non-Euclidean postulate as an alternative to the parallel postulate,

Geometric Algebra:

This philosophical view of mathematics has had a significant impact on Khayyám's celebrated approach and method in geometric algebra and in particular in solving cubic equations. In that his solution is not a direct path to a numerical solution and in fact his solutions are not numbers but rather line segments. In this regard Khayyám's work can be considered the first systematic study and the first exact method of solving cubic equations.

In an untitled writing on cubic equations by Khayyam discovered in the 20th century, where the above quote appears, Khayyam works on problems of geometric algebra. Regarding more general equations he states that the solution of cubic equations requires the use of conic sections and that it cannot be solved by ruler and compass methods. A proof of this impossibility was plausible only 750 years after Khayyam died.

Binomial theorem and extraction of roots:

This particular remark of Khayyam and certain propositions found in his Algebra book has made some historians of mathematics believe that Khayyam had indeed a binomial theorem up to any power.

Khayyam was the mathematician who noticed the importance of a general binomial theorem. The argument supporting the claim that Khayyam had a general binomial theorem is based on his ability to extract roots.

Khayyam-Saccheri quadrilateral:
The Saccheri quadrilateral was first considered by Khayyam in the late 11th century in Book I of *Explanations of the Difficulties in the Postulates of Euclid*.

It wasn't until 600 years later that Giordano Vitale made an advance on Khayyam in his book *Euclide restituo* (1680, 1686).

Astronomer:
Like most Persian mathematicians of the period, Khayyam was famous as an astronomer. In 1073, the Seljuq Sultan Jalal al-Din Malik-Shah Saljuqi (Malik-Shah I, 1072–92), invited Khayyam to build an observatory, along with various other distinguished scientists. According to some accounts, the version of the medieval Iranian calendar in which 2,820 solar years together contain 1,029,983 days (or 683 leap years, for an average year length of 365.24219858156 days) was based on the measurements of Khayyam and his colleagues. Another proposal is that Khayyám's calendar simply contained eight leap years every thirty-three years (for a year length of 365.2424 days). In either case, his calendar was more accurate to the mean tropical year than the Gregorian calendar of 500 years later. The modern Iranian calendar is based on his calculations.

Heliocentric Theory:
It is sometimes claimed that Khayyam demonstrated that the earth rotates on its axis by presenting a model of the stars to his contemporary al-Ghazali in a planetarium.

Calendar Reform:
Khayyam is claimed to be a member of a panel that introduced several reforms to the Iranian calendar. On March 15, 1079, Sultan Malik Shah accepted this corrected calendar as the official Persian calendar.

As a gifted scientist and mathematician, Khayyam thrived under Seljuk patronage as did his many colleagues. One of the fruits of their research was the calendar known as the Jalali calendar named after their Seljuk patron, Jalal al-Din Malik Shah the Sultan and was in force across Greater Iran from the 11th to the 20th centuries. It is the basis of the Iranian calendar which is followed today in Iran and Afghanistan.

While the Jalali calendar is more accurate than the Gregorian calendar produced in Rome in 1582 by Pope Gregory, it is based on actual solar transit, similar to Hindu calendars, and requires an ephemeris for calculating dates. The lengths of the months can vary between 29 and 31 days depending on the moment when the sun crosses into a new zodiacal area (an attribute common to most Hindu calendars). This meant that seasonal errors were lower than in the Gregorian calendar.

The modern-day Iranian calendar standardizes the month lengths based on a reform from 1925, thus minimizing the effect of solar transits. Seasonal errors are somewhat higher than in the Jalali version, but leap years are calculated as before.

Poet:

He is believed to have written about a thousand four-line verses or Rubáiyát (quatrains). In the English-speaking world, he was introduced through the *Rubáiyát of Omar Khayyam* which is rather free-wheeling English translations by Edward FitzGerald (1809–1883).

Poetry:

Omar Khayyám's poems have been translated many times in many languages and many translators have claimed that their translations of the Rubáiyát of Omar Khayyam literal, poetic and less controversial than that of Edward Fitzgerald.

> A Book of Verses underneath the Bough,
> A Jug of Wine, a Loaf of Bread--and Thou,
> Beside me singing in the Wilderness,
> And oh, Wilderness is Paradise now.

> Myself when young did eagerly frequent
> Doctor and Saint, and heard great Argument
> About it and about: but evermore
> Came out of the same Door as in I went.

> With them the Seed of Wisdom did I sow,
> And with my own hand labored it to grow:
> And this was all the Harvest that I reap'd –
> "I came like Water, and like Wind I go."

> Into this Universe, and why not knowing,
> Nor whence, like Water willy-nilly flowing:
> And out of it, as Wind along the Waste,
> I know not whither, willy-nilly blowing.

And that inverted Bowl we call The Sky,
  Whereunder crawling coop't we live and die,
Lift not thy hands to It for help - for It
  Rolls impotently on as Thou or I.

Views on religion:
There have been widely divergent views on Khayyam. According to Seyyed Hossein Nasr no other Iranian writer/scholar is viewed in such extremely differing ways. At one end of the spectrum there are nightclubs named after Khayyam, and he is seen as an agnostic hedonist. On the other end of the spectrum, he is seen as a mystical Sufi poet influenced by platonic traditions.

It is almost certain that Khayyam objected to the notion that every particular event and phenomenon was the result of divine intervention. Nor did he zealously believe in an afterlife with a Judgment Day or rewards and punishments. Instead, he supported the view that laws of nature explained all phenomena of observed life.

If with wine you are drunk be happy,
If seated with a moon-faced (beautiful), be happy,
Since the end purpose of the universe is nothing-ness;
Hence picture your nothing-ness, then while you are, be happy!
Thou hast said that Thou wilt torment me,
But I shall fear not such a warning.
For where Thou art, there can be no torment,
And where Thou art not, how can such a place exist?

The rotating wheel of heaven within which we wonder,
Is an imaginable lamp of which we have knowledge by similitude?
The sun is the candle and the world the lamp,
We are like forms revolving within it.

A drop of water falls in an ocean wide,
A grain of dust becomes with earth allied;
What doth thy coming, going here denote?
A fly appeared a while, then invisible he became.

Philosopher:
Khayyam himself rejects to be associated with the title *falsafi* "philosopher" in the sense of Aristotelianism and stressed he wishes "to know who I am". In the context of philosophers he was labeled by some of his contemporaries as "detached from divine blessings".

Khayyam the philosopher could be understood from two rather distinct sources. One is through his Rubáiyát and the other through his own works in light of the intellectual and social conditions of his time.

Legacy:
- A lunar crater *Omar Khayyam* was named after him in 1970.
- A minor planet called *3095 Omarkhayyam*, discovered by Soviet astronomer Lyudmila Zhuravlyova in 1980, is named after him.

***

Umar ibn Abd al-Aziz (682-719): The era of the first four Caliphs of Islam is widely considered to be the Golden Age of Islam. Caliphs Abu Bakr, Umar, Uthman and Ali were not only close companions of the Prophet, they were also exceptionally loyal and gifted Muslims. However, after the period of the first four Caliphs, the Muslim world entered a long phase of dynastic rule. Founded by Muawiyah ibn Abi Sufyan, the Umayyads became the first dynasty in Islamic history and went onto rule the Muslim world for nearly a century. During the rule of this dynasty, a hugely inspirational Muslim leader emerged who became known as the 'fifth rightly-guided' Caliph. His name was Umar ibn Abd al-Aziz.

Abu Hafs Umar ibn Abd al-Aziz ibn Marwan ibn Hakam was born in Madinah into an aristocratic family of the Umayyad dynasty. He then received advanced training in Arabic grammar, literature, poetry and *Hadith*. By virtue of his scholarly achievements, he became known throughout Madinah as one of the most learned of the Umayyad princes.

After completing his formal education, Umar moved to Egypt where his father, Abd al-Aziz ibn Marwan, served as governor. Not surprisingly, he came to symbolize the pomp, pride and material extravagance of the ruling Umayyad family. After the death of his father Abd al-Aziz, the reigning Caliph Abd al-Malik offered the hand of his daughter, Fatimah bint Abd al-Malik, to him.

Appointed governor of the province of Khanasarah by Caliph Abd al-Malik, his father-in-law, Umar took charge of this region and became very popular with the locals for his sense of justice, fairness and equality. After the death of Caliph Abd al-Malik, his son al-Walid ascended the Umayyad throne and he promoted Umar to the governorship of Madinah. Soon after becoming governor, Umar invited all the leading scholars and citizens of Madinah to dinner and established a consultative (*Shura*) council. Since his jurisdiction also encompassed Makkah and Ta'if, his willingness to listen to the people and address their concerns quickly won him the support of the locals, who pledged to co-operate with him fully.

Then, to his dismay, Umar noticed how the *Masjid al-Nabi* (the 'Prophet's Mosque') had been neglected by his predecessors. He therefore wrote to Caliph al-Walid for his permission to expand the mosque. When Caliph al-Walid gave the go-ahead, Umar summoned all the prominent scholars of Madinah (including al-Qasim, Salim and Abu Bakr ibn Abd al-Rahman) to seek their advice on the matter. Following the consultation, the old mosque was demolished and a new one was built. This mammoth project took nearly two years to complete, and Caliph al-Walid came to inspect it during the *hajj* (pilgrimage) season in 709.

Umar remained governor of Madinah for six years before he was removed from his post in 711. 'From Allah we come and to Him we will return.' and fainted.

With his accession to the Umayyad throne in 717, Umar became one of the most powerful rulers of his time. Thus, despite being one of the most powerful rulers of his time, he preferred to live like a hermit rather than a King.

Umar then refused to move into the plush Caliphal Palace; instead he erected a tent for himself. 'O people, it is incumbent upon you to obey one who obeys God. It is not incumbent upon you to obey one who disobeys God. As long as I obey God, obey me. As soon as I disobey Him, you cease to owe me any obedience.'

With the full backing of the people, Umar focused his full attention on the affairs of the vast Umayyad Empire. None of the Umayyad rulers were popular with the masses except Umar, who dramatically reversed the policies of his predecessors and returned to the people their stolen goods, properties and lands. He pursued this policy so ruthlessly that every member of the Umayyad family, including his own wife Fatimah, was asked to return to the public all that goods that had been taken from them unlawfully. Soon all the members of the Umayyad family found themselves on the verge of poverty and destitution. 'For fear of punishment on the Day of Judgment prevents me from disobeying God.'

Umar also reminded all his provincial governors that it was incumbent upon them to restore to the people all the lands, properties and goods which had been wrongfully confiscated from them in the past. Some of the meven began to secretly conspire against the Caliph. But unable to topple him, they reportedly poisoned him instead. According to some of his biographers, after twenty day's illness, Caliph Umar ibn Abd al-Aziz passed away at the age of around thirty-seven.

When the news of Umar's death was relayed to the Byzantine Emperor, he also paid him one of the most glowing tributes, saying, 'If there was any man after Jesus who could have brought the dead back to life, it was Umar ibn Abd al-Aziz…'

***

Umar ibn al-Khattab, Al-Farooq (586-644): c. 2 November (Dhu al-Hijjah 26, 23 Hijri), was a leading companion and adviser to the Islamic prophet Muhammad who later became the second Muslim Caliph after Muhammad's death.

After converting to Islam in the 6th year after Muhammad's first revelation, he spent 17 years as a companion of Muhammad. He succeeded Caliph Abu Bakr on 23 August 634 and played a significant role in Islamic history. Under his rule the Islamic empire expanded at an unprecedented rate, conquering the whole territory of the former Sassanid Empire and more than two thirds of the Byzantine Empire. His legislative abilities, his firm political and administrative control over a rapidly expanding empire and his brilliantly coordinated attacks against the Sassanid Persian Empire that resulted in the conquest of the Persian Empire in less than two years, marked his reputation as a great political and military leader. He was assassinated by a Persian captive.

Sunni Muslims view him as the Second Rightly-Guided Caliph and know him as al-Farooq (he who knows truth from falsehood).

Early life:

Umar was born in Mecca to the Banu Adi clan, which was responsible for arbitrations among the tribes. His father was Khattab ibn Nufayl and his mother was Hantammah daughter of Hashaam. He was the cousin of Khalid ibn al-Walid, a general who would play an important role later in his life and during a wrestling match between the two, Umar had his leg broken. Umar said, "My father Al-Khittab was a ruthless man. He used to make me work hard; if I didn't work he used to beat me and he used to work me to exhaustion.

Despite literacy being uncommon in pre-Islamic Arabia, Umar learned to read and write in his youth. Although not a poet himself, he developed a love for poetry and literature. He was blond, white skinned with redness in his face, tall and physically powerful and soon became a renowned wrestler. Umar was also a gifted orator and due to his intelligence and overwhelming personality, he succeeded his father as an arbitrator of conflicts among the tribes.

In addition, Umar followed the traditional profession of the Quraish. He became a merchant and had several journeys to Rome and

Persia, where he is said to have met various scholars and analyzed the Roman and Persian societies closely.

During the era of Muhammad, Umar's hostility to Islam:
In 610 Muhammad started delivering the message of Islam. Umar, alongside others in Makkah, opposed Islam and threatened to kill Muhammad. He resolved to defend the traditional, polytheistic religion of the Arabia. He was most adamant and cruel in opposing Muhammad and very prominent in persecuting the Muslims. Umar was the first man who resolved that Muhammad had to be murdered in order to finish Islam. Umar firmly believed in the unity of the Quraish and saw the new faith of Islam as a cause of division and discord among the Quraish.

Due to the persecution at the hands of the Quraish, Muhammad ordered his followers to migrate to Abyssinia. As a small group of Muslims migrated, Umar felt worried about the future unity of the Quraish and decided to have Muhammad assassinated.

Conversion:
Umar converted to Islam in 616, one year after the Migration to Abyssinia. Umar was 27 when he became Muslim. Following his conversion, Umar went to inform the chief of Quraish, Amr ibn Hishām, about his new faith. At this stage, Umar even challenged anyone who dared to stop the Muslims from praying, although no one dared to interfere with Umar when he was openly praying.

Umar's conversion to Islam gave power to the Muslims and the faith in Mecca. It was after this that Muslims offered prayers openly in *Masjid al-Haram* for the first time. All these things earned Umar the title of Farooq, meaning he who knows/tells truth from falsehood.

Migration to Medina:
In 622 due to the growing popularity of Islam in the city of Yathrib (later renamed Al-Madinah Al-Munawwarah, the enlightened city, or simply Medina) Muhammad ordered his followers to migrate to Medina. Muslims usually migrated at night due to fear of Quraish's resistance to that migration, but Umar is reported to have migrated openly during the day time. Umar migrated to Medina accompanied by his cousin and brother-in-law Saeed ibn Zaid.

Life in Medina:
Medina became the new center of Islam and the religion spread rapidly across Arabia. When Muhammad arrived in Medina, he paired off each immigrant *(Muhajir)* with one of the residents of the city *(Ansari),* joining Muhammad ibn Maslamah with Umar(R.A) making

them brothers in faith. Muslims remained in peace in Medina for approximately a year before the Quraish raised an army to attack them. In 624 Umar participated in the first Battle between Muslims and Quraish of Mecca i.e. Battle of Badr. In 625 he participated in the Battle of Uhud. In the second phase of Battle when Khalid ibn Walid's cavalry attacked Muslims at the rear changing the victory of Muslims to defeat rumors of Muhammad's death were spread.

Many Muslim warriors were routed from the battle field. Umar, too, was initially routed, but hearing that Muhammad was still alive he went to Muhammad at the mountain of Uhud and prepared for the defense of the hill to keep the Quraishi army away. Later in the year Umar was part of a campaign against the Jewish tribe of Banu Nadir. In 625 Umar's(R.A) daughter Hafsah was married to Muhammad. Later in 627 he participated in the Battle of the Trench and also in the Battle of Banu Qurayza campaign. In 628 Umar participated in the Treaty of Hudaybiyyah and was made one of the witnesses over the pact. In 628 he was a part of Muslims' campaign to Khaybar. In 630 when Muslim armies rushed for the Conquest of Mecca he was part of that army. Later in 630 he was part of Battle of Hunayn and Siege of Ta'if. He was part of Muslim's army that went for the campaign of Tabuk under Muhammad's command and he was reported to have given half of his wealth for the preparation of this expedition. He also participated in the farewell Hajj of Muhammad in 631.

Military expeditions led by Umar:

During the time of Muhammad, Umar led 1 military expedition called the Expedition of Umar ibn al-Khattab, which took place in Turbah, around February 628 or the 3rd Month 7 AH of the Islamic calendar.

Umar's troop travelled by night and hid by day. By the time the Muslim army arrived at the habitation, Banu Hawazin already got news of the impending Muslim attack and they fled for their lives, according to the Muslim scholar "Saifur Rahman al Mubarakpuri", author of the Sealed Nectar (a famous award winning biography of Muhammad).

Death of Muhammad:

Muhammad died on 8 June 632. Umar was full of grief upon hearing the news of demise of Muhammad. Umar, the devoted disciple, could not accept the reality that the "Messenger of God" had died. At this point, Abu Bakr is reported to have come out to the Muslim community and gave his famous speech which included:

Whoever worshipped Muhammad, let them know that Muhammad is dead and whoever worshipped God, let them know that God is alive and never dies.

Abu Bakr then recited these verses from the Qur'an:

"Muhammad is but a messenger; messengers (the like of whom) have passed away before him. If, then, he dies or is killed, will you turn back on your heel"?

Hearing this from Abu Bakr, the most senior disciple of Muhammad, Umar then fell down on his knees in great sense of sorrow and acceptance of the reality.

Caliph Abu Bakr's era:
During Abu Bakr's reign as caliph, during which he was active in the Ridda wars, Umar was one of his chief advisers and secretary. Umar along with Khalid ibn Walid, probably was the architect and main strategist behind the collapse of rebellion in Arabia. Khalid ibn Walid by late 632 had successfully united Arabia after consecutive victories against the rebels. Later during his own reign, Umar would mostly adopt the policy of avoiding wars and consolidating his power in the conquered land rather than expanding Islamic empire through continuous warfare. It was Umar who advised Abu Bakr to compile Qur'an in the form of a book, after the death of 300 memorizers of the Qur'an in the Battle of Yamamah. Abu Bakr appointed Umar as his successor prior to his death in 634. He was confirmed in the office thereafter.

Appointment as a Caliph:
When Abu Bakr was close to death, he nominated Umar to succeed him as the next Caliph.
Umar was still well known for his extraordinary will power, intelligence, political astuteness, impartiality, justice and care for poor and underprivileged people. Abu Bakr is reported to have said to the high-ranking advisers:

"If I will be asked by the God to whom I have appointed my successor, I will tell him that I have appointed the best man among your men."

Abu Bakr before his death called Uthman to write his will in which he declared Umar his successor. In his will he instructed Umar to continue the conquests on Iraq and Syrian fronts. Abu Bakr's decision proved to be crucial in the strengthening of the nascent Islamic empire.

Reign as Caliph:

On 22 August Caliph Abu Bakr died. The same day Umar assumed the office of Caliphate. After the assumption of office as the Caliph, Umar addressed the Muslims in his Inaugural address as:

> "O ye faithful! Abu Bakr is no more amongst us. He has the satisfaction that he has successfully piloted the ship of the Muslim state to safety after negotiating the stormy sea. He successfully waged the apostasy wars and thanks to him, Islam is now supreme in Arabia. But now that in national interest, the responsibility for leading the Muslims has come to vest in me, I assure you that I will not run away from my post and will make an earnest effort to discharge the onerous duties of the office to the best of my capacity in accordance with the injunctions of Islam. I will seek guidance from the Holy Book and will follow the examples set by the Holy Prophet and Abu Bakr. In this task I seek your assistance. If I follow the right path, follow me. If I deviate from the right path, correct me so that we are not led astray."

Initial challenges:

The first challenge for Umar was to win out his subjects and members of Majlis al Shura. Umar was a gifted orator and he would use his ability to get a soft corner in the hearts of people.

Umar's addresses greatly moved the people. Next time he addressed the people as:

> "I will be harsh and stern against the aggressor, but I will be a pillar of strength for the weak."

> "I will not calm down until I will put one check of a tyrant on the ground and the other under my feet and for the poor and weak, I will put my check on the ground."

Umar's stress was on the well being of poor and underprivileged people. As this class made a bulk of any community, the people were soundly moved by Umar's speeches and his popularity grew rapidly and continuously over the period of his reign. In the Ridda wars, thousands of prisoners from rebel and apostate tribes were taken away as slaves during the expeditions. Umar ordered the general amnesty for the prisoners and their immediate emancipation. Umar took a bold decision of retrieving Khalid ibn Walid from supreme command on Roman front.

Political and civil administration:

The government of Umar was more or less a unitary government, where the sovereign political authority was the Caliph. The empire of Umar was divided into provinces and some autonomous territories such as Azerbaijan and Armenia which had accepted suzerainty to the Caliphate. The provinces were administered by the provincial governors or *Wali*. The Selection of which was made personally by Umar, who was very fastidious in it. Provinces were further divided into districts and there were about 100 districts in the empire.

In some districts there were separate military officers, though the Governor (Wali) was in most cases the Commander-in-chief of the army quartered in the province. Every appointment was made in writing.

Umar's general instructions to his officers were:

> "Remember, I have not appointed you as commanders and tyrants over the people. I have sent you as leaders instead, so that the people may follow your example. Give the Muslims their rights and do not beat them lest they become abused. Do not praise them unduly, lest they fall into the error of conceit. Do not keep your doors shut in their faces, lest the more powerful of them eat up the weaker ones. And do not behave as if you were superior to them, for that is tyranny over them."

The principal officers were required to come to Mecca on the occasion of the Hajj, during which people were free to present any complaint against them. In order to minimize the chances of corruption, Umar made it a point to pay high salaries to the staff. Provincial governor received as much as five to seven thousand dirham annually besides their shares of the spoils of war *(if they were also the commander in chief of the army of their section)*.

Umar was first to established a special department for the investigation of complaints against the officers of the State. This department acted as Administrative court, where the legal proceedings were personally led by Umar. The Department was under the charge of Muhammad ibn Maslamah, one of Umar's most trusted men.

Reforms:

Umar is regarded as one of the greatest political geniuses in history. While under his leadership, the empire was expanding at a unprecedented rate, he also began to build the political structure that would hold together the vast empire that was being built. He undertook many administrative reforms and closely oversaw public policy. He established an advanced administration for the newly conquered lands, including several new ministries and bureaucracies and ordered a census of all the Muslim territories. In 638, he extended and renovated the Masjid al-Haram (Grand Mosque) in Mecca and the Al-Masjid al-Nabawi (Mosque of the Prophet) in Medina.

Umar also ordered the expulsion of the Christian and Jewish communities of Najran and Khaybar allowing them to reside in Syria or Iraq. Umar also forbade non-Muslims to reside in the Hejaz for longer than three days. He was first to establish the army as a state department. Umar was the founder of Fiqh, the Islamic jurisprudence. He is regarded by Sunni Muslims to be one of the greatest Faqih. Umar as a jurist started the process of codifying Islamic Law. In 641, he established Bayt al-mal, a financial institution and started annual state sponsored allowances for the poor Muslims in Makkah and Al Madinah. In 639, his fourth year as caliph and the seventeenth year since the Hijra, he decreed that the Islamic calendar should be counted from the year of the Hijra of Muhammad from Mecca to Madinah.

Military expansion:
Under Umar, the Islamic empire grew at an unprecedented rate. In 638, after the conquest of Syria, Umar dismissed Khalid, his most successful general due to his ever growing fame and influence. Later, however, Umar regretted this decision. During his reign the Levant, Egypt, Cyrenaica, Tripolitania, Fezzan, eastern Anatolia, almost the whole of the Sassanid Persian Empire including Bactria, Persia, Azerbaijan, Armenia, Caucasus and Makran were annexed to the Islamic Empire. According to one estimate more than 4050 cities were captured during these military conquests. Prior to his death in 644, Umar had ceased all military expeditions apparently to consolidate his rule in Egypt and the newly conquered Sassanid Empire (642-644). At his death in November 644, the domain of his rule extended from present day Libya in west to the Indus River in the east and the Oxus River in the north.

The great famine:
In the year 638, Arabia fell into severe drought followed by a famine. Bedouin people began to die because of hunger and epidemic disease. Umar wrote to the provincial governors of Syria, Palestine and Iraq for aid. A state of emergency was declared in Madinah and Arabia. The timely aid of Umar's governors saved the lives of thousands of

people throughout Arabia. Umar hosted a dinner every night at Madinah, which according to one estimate had attendance of more than hundred thousand people. By early 639 conditions began to improve.

The great plague:
While famine was ending in Arabia, many districts in Syria and Palestine were devastated by plague. Abu Ubaidah died in 639 due to plague, which also cost the life of 25,000 Muslims in Syria. After the plague had weakened in late 639, Umar visited Syria for political and administrative re-organization, as most of the veteran commanders and governors had died of plague.

Family:
Umar married a total of nine women in his lifetime and had fourteen children, ten sons and four daughters.

Taraweeh:
Taraweeh, the night prayers during Ramadan, were institutionalized during Umar's reign as Caliph. A majority of Sunni Muslims have followed the same practice since then. The Shi'a do not give credence to the institutionalization of this prayer during Umar's caliphate.

Assassination:
In 644, at zenith of his power, Umar was assassinated. His assassination was carried out by a Persian, in response to the Muslim conquest of Persia. It is related that when Umar stood at Mount Arafat he heard a voice saying:

"O Caliph, never again will you stand on the Mount of Arafat".

During one of the rituals of Hajj, the Ramy al-Jamarat *(stoning of the Devil)*, someone threw a stone on Umar that wounded his head. A voice was heard that Umar will not attend the Hajj ever again. It was Abu Lulu who was assigned the mission of assassinating Umar.

Abu Lulu brought a conjectural complaint to Umar about the high tax charged from him by his master Mughirah. Umar wrote to Mughirah and inquired about the tax. Mughirah's reply was satisfactory. Umar held that the tax charged from Abu Lulu was reasonable, owning to his daily income. Umar then is reported to have asked Abu Lulu:

I heard that you make windmills; make one for me, as well. In a sullen mood, Firoz said, "Verily I will make such a mill for you, that whole world would remember it".

On 3 November 644, Umar was attacked, while leading the morning prayers, Abu Lulu stabbed him six times in the back and last in the chest, that proved fatal. Umar was left profusely bleeding while Abu Lulu tried to flee, but people from all sides rushed to capture him. He in his efforts to escape, is reported to have wounded twelve other people, six or nine of them later died. At last he was captured, but committed suicide from the same dagger. Umar died of the wounds four days later on Sunday, 7 November 644.

As per Umar's will, he was buried next to Al-Masjid al-Nabawi alongside Muhammad and Caliph Abu Bakr by the permission of Aisha.

Aftermaths:

On his death bed Umar vacillated to appoint his successor. Umar finally appointed a committee of six persons comprising,

1. Ali ibn Abi Taleb
2. Saad ibn Abi Waqqas
3. Talha ibn Ubaidullah
4. Uthman ibn Affan
5. Abd-al-Rahman ibn Awf
6. Zubayr ibn al-Awwam

Their task was to choose a caliph from amongst them. Umar appointed a band of fifty armed soldiers to protect the house where the meeting was proceeding. Until the appointment of the next caliph Umar appointed a notable Sahabi, a Mawali, Suhayb ar-Rumi *(Suhayb the Roman)* as a caretaker Caliph. After the mystery of assassination got uncovered by the two of the most notable governmental figures, it seemed clear that the assassination was planned by the Persians residing in Medina. Infuriated by this, Umar's younger son, Ubaidullah ibn Umar sought to kill all the Persians in Madinah. It is also believed that Umar's daughter, Hafsah bint Umar provoked Ubaidullah to take the punitive action. When Umar was informed about the incident, he ordered that Ubaidullah should be imprisoned and the next Caliph should decide his fate. Umar died on 7 November 644; on 11 November Uthman succeeded him as the Caliph.

Legacy:

Umar is regarded as one of the most influential figures in Islamic history. He was in a true sense the architect of the Islamic Empire. As a leader, 'Umar was known for his simple, austere lifestyle.

Political legacy:

Umar is considered as a political genius, as an architect of the Islamic Empire he is regarded as the 52nd most influential figure in history. During Abu Bakr's era, he actively participated as his secretary and main adviser. After succeeding Abu Bakr as caliph, Umar won over the hearts of the Bedouin tribes by emancipating all their prisoners and slaves taken during the Ridda wars. His excellent oratory skills helped him gain broader support among the poor and the underprivileged. He is best known to build up an efficient administrative structure of the empire that held together his vast realm. His judicial reforms were fairly modern and advanced in nature, when compared to contemporary systems of his era. Their local administration was kept un-touched and several of the former Byzantine and Persian officials were retained in their posts under Umar's governors.

Umar was very painstaking in every matter. He never appointed governors for more than two years, for they might get influence in their county. He dismissed his most successful general, Khalid bin Walid, due to his immense popularity and growing influence, he feared that the Muslims might think it was Khalid who gave them victory not God. Rather than tenacious conquest, he stressed more on consolidating his rule in the conquered land, a fact that saved the Byzantine Empire from complete disappearance.

It is said that Umar's whip was feared more than the sword of another man. He is famous for covert night tours of the city to know the secret life of his domain, a tradition that was later followed by some of the Abbasid Caliphs and even Mughul rulers of Indian Subcontinent.

Social justice and accountability:

It has been recorded in the annals of Muslim chronicles, that at the time of the Zuhr prayers, Sophronius invited Umar to pray in the rebuilt Church of the Holy Sepulcher. Umar declined, fearing that accepting the invitation might endanger the church's status as a Christian temple and that Muslims might break the treaty and turn the temple into a mosque.

Military legacy:

It has been reported that Umar was a champion wrestler of his time and though not distinguished as a swordsman, he would later attain prominence as a master strategist. Along with Khalid, he is said to be one of the key figures in the collapse of the Arabian rebellion, the greatest triumph of Abu Bakr. One of his greatest strategic marvels was his brilliant fission of the Persio-Roman alliance in 636, when Emperor Heraclius and Emperor Yazdegerd III allied against their common enemy Umar. These troops proved decisive in the Battle Qadisiyyah. Both the battles, thus, fought proved decisive and are noted as two of the most decisive battles in history.

Umar's orders to invade the very homeland of the Christian Arab forces besieging Emesa, the Jazirah. A three prong attack against Jazirah was launched from Iraq. This incursion from the Byzantines, however, resulted in Muslim annex, Mesopotamia and parts of Byzantine Armenia.

Nonetheless, the greatest triumph of Umar remained the Conquest of Persian Empire. After years of non-offensive policy according to which Umar wished the Zagros Mountains to be the frontiers between Muslims and Persians, after the Battle of Nahavand, Umar launched a whole scale invasion of the Sassanid Persian Empire. The final expedition was launched against Khurasan, where after the Battle of Oxus River, Persian Empire ceased to exist and Emperor Yazdegerd III fled to Central Asia. He founded the city of Cairo, conquered 36,000 cities or castles and built 1400 mosques.

Religious legacy
Sunni views: *Sunni view of Umar:*

Sunnis Muslims view him as the Second Rashidun and know him as Farooq the great. Umar ibn al-Khattab is the founder of Ijtehad, which later benefited Islam in interpretation of Qur'an and Hadith. Sunni remember Umar as a Strong Muslim of a sound and just disposition in matters of the religion of Allah, a man they title *Farooq*, meaning "leader, jurist and statesman" and the second of the rightly-guided Caliphs, always riding his donkey without the saddle, rarely laughing and never joking with anyone.

Shi'a views:

Umar is viewed negatively in Shi'a literature. He is regarded as an usurper of Ali's rights of succession. According to Shi'a beliefs, his role during Muhammad's lifetime is questioned as he was not assigned to any civil or military authority. The Shi'a believe that Fatima, wife of Ali and daughter of Muhammad, was physically abused by him. These sources report that the event caused her to miscarry her child and eventually led to her death soon after.

Islamic Leaders

Western views:
> The whole history of Omar shows him to have been a man of great powers of mind, inflexible integrity and rigid justice. He was more than anyone else, the founder of the Islam empire; confirming and carrying out the inspirations of the prophet; aiding Abu Bakr with his counsels during his brief caliphate; and establishing wise regulations for the strict administration of the law throughout the rapidly-extending bounds of the Muslim conquests. He forbade that any female captive who had borne a child should be sold as a slave.

***

Umar ibn Said Tal (or al-Hajj Umar or Umar Tal) (1797-1864): Muslim ruler of a state in Mali (1848-64). Born among the Tukolor people, he established the Tukolor Empire. He set out on the pilgrimage to Mecca c. 1920, where he was designated caliph for Black Africa. He established himself in the Senegal River area and in 1854 proclaimed a *jihad* (holy war) against all pagans. He created a vast Tukolor empire, but failed to win many converts. He became a harsh ruler. In 1863 he captured Timbuktu but soon lost it to a combined force of Fulani and Tauregs. He was killed in 1864 but the Tukolor Empire survived until 1897, ruled by his son Ahmadu Seku.

***

Umar II (717-720): An Umayyad Caliph who tried to rule according to the principles of the religious movement. He was the first caliph to encourage positively the conversion of the subject people of the Empire to Islam.

***

Umm Salamah (-): wife of the Prophet. She was the widow of Muhammad's first cousin, Abu Salama, who had died of wounds received at the battle of Uhud. She had been in exile in Ethiopia and brought her young children into the protection of the Prophet's household. It was her sage advice that broke the brief spell of disobedience at Hudaibiyah.

***

Usama bin Zayd (-   ): Muhammad's grandson through his adopted son Zayd. He won Aisha's friendship by supporting her in her hour of need and would be placed in command of the Muslim army by the Prophet Muhammad in the last month of his life. Muhammad's first grandchild.

***

Uthman Dan Fodio (1754-1817): Islam became an integral part of Africa as early as the seventh century. After the Muslim conquest of parts of North Africa during the Caliphates of Umar and Uthman, Islamic rule was reasserted throughout that region during the reign of Muawiyah, thus permanently establishing an Islamic presence in North African and the region which the early Muslim historians referred to as B*ilad al-Sudan* (the land of Sudan) in East Africa. Some of Africa's most powerful and enduring Islamic revivalist movements also emerged in West Africa. It was, however, the nineteenth century *jihad* movement of Shaykh Uthman Dan Fodio in Hausaland which became a great source of inspiration for the West African Muslims.

Uthman ibn Muhammad ibn Ithman ibn Salih, known as Uthman (or Usuman) Dan Fodio for short, was born in the town of Maratta in the Hausa State of Gobir. Brought up in a strongly Islamic environment, Uthman learned Arabic and memorized the whole Qur'an before he was ten. Thanks to his vast learning and spiritual ability, he soon attracted a sizeable following and established his reputation as an up-and-coming religious scholar and leader of his people.

The religious scholars, who were supposed to be the custodians of faith, knowledge and wisdom, had also succumbed to worldly pleasures and luxuries. Indeed, the plight of the ordinary people – who were forced to endure untold personal suffering and hardship – moved Uthman so much that he decided to do something to change the status quo.

While still in his early twenties, Uthman became a prolific writer and speaker. As a gifted scholar, he was not only aware of the burning issues of his time, he was also eager to tackle those issues head-on. When the reform movement initiated by Uthman became very popular with the locals, the official *ulama* (who were in the pay of the ruling elites) tried to undermine his credentials as a religious scholar and leader. However, he felt the *ulama* of his community had abandoned this noble duty by currying favor with the local ruling elites.

During this period Uthman wrote prolifically, authoring more than fifty books and treatises on a wide range of Islamic topics. He encouraged the Hausa women to pursue education and engage in literary activities.

Islamic Leaders

As the Islamic movement continued to expand rapidly, Uthman's followers began to oppose the oppressive policies of the local rulers. When the situation became unbearable, in 1804 Uthman ordered his close disciples to migrate (*Hijrah*) to Gudu, a town located on the northern outskirts of Gobir. An all out military conflict soon ensued in which his forces inflicted a crushing defeat on their enemies and in the process they captured Gobir (the most powerful State in Hausaland) in 1808, thus securing a great victory for Islam. Circumstances forced Uthman to assume both political and religious leadership. After five years of internecine warfare, the entire political, civil and administrative systems of Government in Hausaland lay in ruins, as did the local economy. Uthman then implemented the *Shari'ah* (Islamic law) across the land and gradually the political and economic situation in Hausaland began to improve.

Uthman spent the last years of his life in Sifawa, situated on the outskirts of Sokoto, where he eventually died at the age of sixty-three, without nominating a successor. The Caliphate founded by Uthman endured until the beginning of the twentieth century.

In total, Uthman wrote more than one hundred books and treatises on all aspects of Islam. He considered the adherents of the *Tijaniyah* Sufi Order to be his own followers. In short, Uthman was a great Islamic scholar, thinker and one of the most influential Muslim reformers of the nineteenth century.

(or Usuman Dan Fodio) West African religious and political leader. A Muslim Fulani, he began teaching in about 1775 among the Hausa and established the Emirates of Northern Nigeria (1804-08) after waging a *jihad* (holy war). He conceived the latter as a primary duty, not only against infidels, but against any departure, public or private, from the original and austere ideals of Islam. Under his rule as caliph, and that of his son, Muhammad Bello (d. 1837), Muslim culture flourished in the Fulani Empire.

***

Uthman ibn Affan (579-656): Strict transliteration: Uthman ibn Affan) (579 – 17 July 656) was one of the companions of Islamic prophet, Muhammad. He played a major role in early Islamic history as the third of the Sunni Rashidun or Rightly Guided Caliphs.

Uthman was born into the Umayyad clan of Mecca, a powerful family of the Quraish tribe. He was a companion of Muhammad who assumed the role of leader (caliph) of the Muslim Empire at the age of 65 following Umar ibn al-Khattab. Under his leadership, the empire expanded into Fars in 650 (present-day Iran), some areas of Khorasan (present-day Afghanistan) in 651 and the conquest of Armenia was begun in the 640s. Some of Uthman's notable achievements were the economic reforms he introduced, and the compilation of the Qur'an into the unified, authoritative text that is known today.

Early life:

Uthman was born in Ta'if, which is situated on a hill, and the presumption is that he was born during the summer months, since wealthy Meccans usually spent the hot summers in the cooler climate of Ta'if. He was born into the wealthy Umayyad (Banu Umayya) clan of the Quraysh tribe of Mecca, seven years after Muhammad. Uthman's father, Affan, died young while travelling abroad but left a large inheritance to Uthman. Uthman followed the same profession as his father, and his business flourished, making him one of the richest men among the Qurayshi tribe.

Conversion to Islam:

Uthman was an early convert to Islam and is said to have spent a great amount of his wealth on charity, therefore he gained the epithet "Uthman Ghani", which means "Uthman the giver". On returning from a business trip to Syria in 611, Uthman found out that Muhammad had declared his mission. After a discussion with his friend Abu Bakr Uthman decided to convert to Islam, and Abu Bakr took him to Muhammad to whom he declared his faith. Uthman thus became the fourth male to convert to Islam, after Ali, Zayd and Abu Bakr. His conversion to Islam angered his clan, the Banu Ummayyah, who strongly opposed Muhammad's teachings. Because of his conversion to Islam, Uthman's wives deserted him, and he subsequently divorced them. Muhammad then asked Uthman to marry his daughter Ruqayyah bint Muhammad.

Migration to Abyssinia:

Uthman and his wife Ruqayyah migrated to Abyssinia (modern Ethiopia) in 614–615, along with 11 men and 11 women, all Muslims. As Uthman already had some business contacts in Abyssinia, he continued to practice his profession as a trader. He worked hard and his business soon flourished. After two years the news had spread among the Muslims in Abyssinia that the Quraysh of Mecca had accepted Islam, and that persuaded Uthman, Ruqayyah and some other Muslims to return. However when they reached Mecca it transpired that the news about the Quraysh's acceptance of Islam was false. Some of the Muslims who had come from Abyssinia returned but Uthman and Ruqayyah decided to stay. In Mecca Uthman had to start his business afresh, but the contacts that he had already established in Abyssinia worked in his favor and his business prospered once again.

Migration to Medina:
In 622, Uthman and his wife, Ruqayyah, migrated to Medina. They were amongst the third batch of Muslims who migrated to Medina. On arrival in Medina, Uthman stayed with Abu Talha ibn Thabit of the Banu Najjar. After a short while, Uthman purchased a house of his own and moved there. In Medina, the Muslims were generally farmers and were not very interested in trade, and thus most of the trading that took place in the town was handled by the Jews. Thus, there was considerable space for the Muslims in promoting trade and Uthman took advantage of this position, soon establishing himself as a trader in Medina. He worked hard and honestly, and his business flourished, soon becoming one of the richest men in Medina.

Life in Medina:
In 624 some Muslims from Medina departed to assist in the capture of a Quraysh caravan. At this time Uthman's wife, Ruqayyah, suffered from malaria and then caught smallpox. Uthman stayed at Medina to look after the ailing Ruqayyah and did not join those who left with Muhammad. Ruqayyah died during the time the Battle of Badr was being fought, and the news of the victory of Badr reached Medina as she was being buried. Because of the battle Muhammad could not attend the funeral of his daughter.

After the Battle of Uhud Uthman married Muhammad's second daughter, Umm Kulthum bint Muhammad. The next year Fahida bint ghazwan's son, Abd-Allah ibn Uthman, died. When the Battle of the Trench was fought in 627, Uthman was in charge of a sector of Medina. After the battle a campaign was undertaken against the Jews of Banu Qaynuqa, and when they were taken captive the question of the disposal of the slaves became a problem. Uthman solved the issue by purchasing all the slaves and depositing their price in the Bayt al-mal (Treasury). Any of these slaves who accepted Islam were set free by Uthman in the name of Allah.

Treaty of Hudaibiyah:
In March 628 (6 Hijri), Muhammad set out for Mecca to perform the ritual pilgrimage of Umra. The Quraysh denied the Muslims entry into the city and posted themselves outside Mecca, determined to show resistance, even though the Muslims had no intention or preparation for battle. Muhammad camped outside Mecca, at Hudaybiyyah, and sent Uthman as his envoy to meet with the leaders of Quraysh and negotiate

Muslim entry into the city. The Quraysh made Uthman stay longer in Mecca than he originally planned and refused to inform the Muslims of his whereabouts. This caused the Muslims to believe that Uthman had been killed by the people of Quraysh. On this occasion, Muhammad gathered his nearly 1,400 soldiers and called them to pledge to fight until death and avenge the rumored death of Uthman, which they did by placing a hand on top of Muhammad's. This pledge took place under a tree and was known as the Pledge of the Tree and was successful in demonstrating to the Quraysh the determination of the Muslims. They soon released Uthman and sent down an ambassador of their own, Suhail ibn Amr to negotiate terms of a treaty that later became known as the Treaty of Hudaybiyyah.

Muhammad's last years:

In 629, Uthman fought in the Battle of Khaybar and later that year, he followed Muhammad to perform Umrah in Mecca. While in Mecca he visited his mother and found that his family was not as hostile to Islam as they used to be. In 630, the Quraysh broke the treaty of Hudaibiyah, and the Muslims attacked and conquered Mecca. General amnesty was granted to the people of the city, although an exception was made in the case of half a dozen people. Following the Conquest of Mecca Uthman's family converted to Islam and he rejoined his mother and siblings. Two weeks later, under the command of Muhammad, he participated in the Battle of Hunayn which was followed by the Siege of Ta'if.

Uthman's wife, and the daughter of Muhammad, Umm Kulthum bint Muhammad, died soon after the conquest of Mecca. In 630 Muhammad decided to lead an expedition to Tabuk on the Syrian border. In order to finance the expedition Muhammad invited contributions from his followers. Uthman made the largest contribution: 1,000 dinars in cash, 1,000 camels for transport, and horses for the cavalry, which Muhammad greatly appreciated. In 631, along with other Muslims, Uthman moved to Mecca to perform Hajj under Abu Bakr while Muhammad stayed in Medina. In Mecca Uthman married Umm Saeed Fatima bint Al Walid b Abd Shams, a Qurayshi lady, and returned to Medina with her.

In 632, along with Muhammad, Uthman participated in The Farewell Pilgrimage. In 632 Muhammad died.

Caliph Abu Bakr's era (632–634):

Uthman had a very close relationship with Abu Bakr, as it was due to him that Uthman had converted to Islam. When Abu Bakr was elected as the Caliph, Uthman was the first person after Umar to offer his allegiance. During the Ridda wars (Wars of Apostasy), Uthman remained at Medina, acting as Abu Bakr's adviser. On his death bed, Abu Bakr dictated his will to Uthman, saying that his successor was to be Umar.

Caliph Umar's era (634–644):

Uthman was the first person to offer his allegiance to Umar. During the reign of Umar, Uthman remained at Medina as his adviser, and a member of his advisory council. Umar did not allow the companions, including Uthman, to leave Medina. The reason for this was that Umar didn't wish for the companions, who were famous and respected among the Muslims, to spread and have their own followers, which would, it was felt, have resulted in unnecessary divisions in Islam.

During the reign of Umar, considerable wealth flowed into the public treasury. Uthman advised that some amount be reserved in the treasury for future needs, instead of giving all of it as stipends to the Muslims, and this was accepted by Umar. A controversy then arose about the land in conquered areas. The army was of the view that all lands in conquered territories should be distributed among the soldiers of the conquering army, but others thought that the lands should remain as the property of the original owners, and the lands without claimants should be declared as state property. Uthman supported the latter view and this view was ultimately accepted.

At the time of the conquest of Jerusalem the Christians asked that Umar come to Jerusalem to accept the surrender of the city. Uthman was of the view that it was not necessary for the Caliph of the Muslims to go to Jerusalem and that the enemy, when defeated, would surrender the city unconditionally. There was much force in Uthman's argument, but in order to win the good will of the Christians, Umar decided to go to Jerusalem to accept the surrender of the city. In the time of Umar, a severe famine broke out in the country and a large caravan belonging to Uthman that was carrying a large supply of food grains served the poor well.

Election of Uthman:

Umar, on his death bed, formed a committee of six people to choose the next Caliph from amongst themselves.

This committee was:

- Ali
- Uthman ibn Affan

- Abdur Rahman bin Awf
- Sa'd ibn Abi Waqqas
- Al-Zubayr
- Talhah

Umar asked that, after his death, the committee reach a final decision within three days and the next Caliph should take the oath of office on the fourth day. On the fourth day after the death of Umar, 11 November 644, 5 Muharram 24 Hijri, Uthman was elected as the third Caliph, with the *title* "Amir al-Mu'minin"

Reign as a Caliph (644-656):

On assuming office, Uthman issued a number of directives to the officials all over the dominions, ordering them to hold fast the laws made by his predecessor Umar. Uthman's realm extended in the west to Morocco, in the east to South east Pakistan and in the north to Armenia and Azerbaijan. During his caliphate, the first Islamic naval force was established, administrative divisions of the state were revised and many public projects were expanded and completed.

In total, Uthman ruled for twelve years. The first six years were marked by internal peace and tranquility and he remained the most popular Caliph among the Rashidun; but during the second half of his caliphate a rebellion arose.

Uthman had the distinction of working for the expansion of Islam and he sent the first official Muslim envoy to China in 650. The envoy, headed by Sa'd ibn Abi Waqqas, arrived in the Tang capital, Chang'an, in 651 via the overseas route. The Hui people generally consider this date to be the official founding of Islam in China. Although the envoy failed to convince the Emperor to embrace Islam, the emperor allowed him to proselytize in China and ordered the establishment of the first Chinese mosque in the capital to show his respect for the religion. Uthman also sent official Muslim envoys to Sri Lanka.

Reforms of Uthman's era:

Uthman was a shrewd businessman and a successful trader from his youth, which contributed greatly to the Rashidun Empire. Umar had fixed the allowance of the people and on assuming office, Uthman increased it by about 25%. Umar had placed a ban on the sale of lands and the purchase of agricultural lands in conquered territories. Uthman withdrew these restrictions, in view of the fact that the trade could not flourish. The lands in conquered territories were not to be distributed among the combatants, but were to remain the property of the previous owners. The army once again raised the demand for the distribution of the lands in conquered territories among the fighting soldiers but Uthman turned down the demand and it favored the Dhimmis (non-Muslims in Islamic state). In 651, the first Islamic coins were struck during the caliphate of Uthman, these were the Persian Dirhams that had an image of the Persian emperor Yazdgerd III with the addition of the Arabic sentence Bismillah (in the name of Allah). However the first original minting of the Islamic dirham was done in 695 during Umayyad period. Uthman did not draw any allowance from the treasury for his personal use, nor did he receive a salary, he was a wealthy man with sufficient resources of his own, but unlike Umar, Uthman accepted gifts and allowed his family members to accept gifts from certain quarters.

Public works:
Under Uthman the people became economically more prosperous and they invested their money in the construction of buildings. Many new and larger buildings were constructed throughout the empire. During the caliphate of Uthman as many as five thousand new mosques were constructed. Uthman enlarged, extended and embellished the Al-Masjid al-Nabawi at Medina and the Kaaba as well.

During the caliphate Uthman, guest houses were provided in main cities to provide comfort to the merchants coming from faraway places. In Iraq, Egypt and Persia numerous canals were dug, which stimulated agricultural development. Water was brought to Kufa and Basra by canals.

Administration:
Under Umar, Egypt was divided into two provinces, Upper and Lower Egypt. Uthman made Egypt one province and created a new province for Efriqya. Under Umar, Syria was divided into two provinces, but Uthman made it one province. During Uthman's reign the empire was divided into twelve provinces. These were:

1. Medina
2. Mecca
3. Yemen
4. Kufa
5. Basra
6. Jazira
7. Faris
8. Azerbaijan
9. Khorasan
10. Syria

11. Egypt
12. Efriqya (lit. "Africa", signifying N. Africa)

The provinces were further divided into districts (more than 100 districts in the empire) and each district or main city had its own Governor, Chief judge and Amil (tax collector). The governors were appointed by Uthman and every appointment was made in writing. Uthman appointed his kinsmen as governors of four provinces: Egypt, Syria, Basra and Kufa. Uthman felt that he could trust his own kin not to revolt against him. However, Shiah did not see this as prudence; they saw it as nepotism and an attempt to rule like a king rather than as the first among equals.

Qur'an:

Uthman is perhaps best known for forming the committee which produced multiple copies of the text of the Qur'an as it exists today. The reason was that various Muslim centers, like Kufa and Damascus, had begun to develop their own traditions for reciting the Qur'an and writing it down with stylistic differences.

During the time of Uthman, by which time Islam had spread far and wide, differences in reading the Quran in different dialects of Arabic language became obvious. A group of companions, headed by Hudhayfah ibn al-Yaman, who was then stationed in Iraq, came to Uthman and urged him to "save the Muslim Ummah before they differ about the Quran". Uthman obtained the complete manuscript of the Qur'an from Hafsah, one of the wives of the Islamic prophet Muhammad who had been entrusted to keep the manuscript ever since the Qur'an was comprehensively compiled by the first Caliph, Abu Bakr . Uthman then again summoned the leading compiling authority, Zayd ibn Thabit, and some other companions to make copies of the manuscript. Zayd was put in charge of the task. The style of Arabic dialect used was that of the Quraysh tribe to which the Prophet Muhammad belonged. Hence this style was emphasized over all others.

Zayd and his assistants produced several copies of the manuscript of the Qur'an. One of each was sent to every Muslim province with the order that all other Qur'anic materials, whether fragmentary or complete copies, be destroyed. As such, when the standard copies were made widely available to the Muslim community everywhere, then all other material was burnt voluntarily by the Muslim community themselves. The annihilation of these extra-Qur'anic documents remained essential in order to eradicate scriptural incongruities, contradictions of consequence or differences in the dialect from the customary text of the Qur'an. The Caliph Uthman kept a copy for himself and returned the original manuscript to Hafsah.

While Shi'a and Sunni accept the same sacred text, the Qur'an, some claim that Shi'a dispute the current version, i.e. they add two additional surahs known as al-Nurayn and al-Wilaya. Nonetheless, Shi'as claim that they are falsely accused of this, as they believe, like Sunnis, that the Qur'an has never been changed and it is with reference from Sunni Hadith books that this inference is drawn not only by uninformed Shi'as, but Sunnis, too.

Military expansion:

Islamic empire expanded at unprecedented rate under Caliph Umar, following the death of Caliph Umar, almost whole of the former Sassanid empire's territory rebelled from time to time until 650, when the last Sassanid emperor was assassinated. Caliph Uthman thus directed several military expeditions to crush rebellion and re-capture the Persia and their vassal states. The main rebellion was in the Persian provinces of Armenia, Azerbaijan, Fars, Sistan, Tabaristan, Khorasan, and Makran. These provinces were across present days Pakistan, Iran, Afghanistan, Azerbaijan, Dagestan, Turkmenistan and Armenia. After the death of Caliph Umar, Byzantine emperor Constantine III launched an attack but was repulsed, due to which Uthman ordered annual raids in Anatolia to cut off the power of Byzantine.

The truce that followed made it possible for Constans II to hold on to the western portions of Armenia. A naval force was built and island of Cyprus was captured in 649 followed by the capture of Crete and Rhodes. After a naval victory against Byzantine fleet a part of Sicily was also captured. In 654–655 Uthman ordered for the preparation of an expedition to capture Constantinople, it was about to be launched when Uthman was murdered. North Africa was invaded in 647 and Byzantine Exarchate of Africa which had declared its independence under its King Gregory the Patrician was annexed. Nubia was invaded in 652 and its capital Dongola was sacked. Though battle remained inconclusive and a peace offer from Nubian King was accepted according to which no party will any aggressive moves against each other. In 652–653 the Iberian Peninsula was invaded and its coastal areas were captured, before further expansion could be made Caliph was murdered and forces were pulled back from Iberia and north Africa during Muslim civil war.

Anti-Uthman sentiment:

According to Muslim sources, unlike his predecessor, Umar, who maintained discipline with a stern hand. Uthman was less rigorous upon his people; he focused more on economic prosperity. Under Uthman, the people became economically more prosperous and on the political plane they came to enjoy a larger degree of freedom. In view of the lenient policies adopted by Uthman, the people took advantage of such liberties, which became a headache for the state and it culminated in the assassination of Uthman.

According to some viewpoints, under such circumstances, leaders like Abdullah Ibn Saba, felt that it was a good opportunity to accomplish their arms of rebellion by starting arguments over religion. However, the figure Abdullah Ibn Saba is believed by many Shi'a Muslims to be an imaginary one created by certain Sunni historians to stir up anti-Shi'a sentiment.

It is believed that the movement had its links with foreign countries. Due to the lack of any particular political department to deal with the growing political agitation in the Islamic state, the political leaders in various towns campaigned against Uthman. Initially, they started with arguments over Uthman's kinsmen, who were governors of Egypt, Bosra and Kufa and they were joined by the companions who supported Ali.

The actual reason for the anti-Uthman movement is disputed among the Shi'a and Sunni Muslims. Many anonymous letters were written to the leading companions of Muhammad complaining about the alleged tyranny of Uthman's appointed governors. The movement, however, exploited differences between the Hashemite (Ali's clan) and Umayyad (Uthman's clan) clans of Quraysh.

Uthman's emissaries to the provinces:
The situation was becoming tense and so the Uthman administration had to investigate the origins and extent of anti-government propaganda and its aims. Sometime around 654, Uthman called all the governors of his 12 provinces to Medina to discuss the problem. The rebels had carried on with their propaganda in favor of the Caliphate of Ali. Ammar ibn Yasir had been affiliated with Ali; he left Uthman and instead joined the opposition in Egypt.

Further measures:
In 655, Uthman directed the people who had any grievance against the administration to assemble at Mecca for the Hajj. He promised them that all their legitimate grievances would be redressed. He directed the governors and the "Amils" throughout the empire to come to Mecca on the occasion of the Hajj. In response to the call of Uthman, the opposition came in large delegations from various cities to present their grievances before the gathering.

Uthman addressed the people and gave a long explanation of the criticism about himself and his administration and then said: "I have had my say. Now I am prepared to listen to you. If any one of you has any legitimate grievance against me or my Government you are free to give expression to such grievance, and I assure you that, I will do my best to redress such grievance."

The rebels realized that the people in Mecca supported the defense offered by Uthman and were not in the mood to listen to them. That was a great psychological victory for Uthman. Muawiyah then suggested that he be allowed to send a strong force from Syria to Medina to guard Uthman against any possible attempt by rebels to harm him. Uthman rejected it too, saying that the Syrian forces in Medina would be an incitement to civil war, and he could not be party to such a move.

Agitation in Medina:

After the Hajj of 655 things remained quiet for some time. With the dawn of the year 656, Medina, the capital city of Uthman, became a hotbed of intrigue and unrest. Muhammad ibn Abu Bakr returned to Medina from Egypt and assisted in leading a campaign against the Caliphate of Uthman.

When the crisis deepened in Medina, Uthman addressed the congregation in the Masjid-e-Nabawi and gave an explanation and rebuttal of all the claims against him. The general public was again satisfied with Uthman.

Armed revolt against Uthman:

The politics of Egypt played the major role in the propaganda war against the caliphate, so Uthman summoned Abdullah ibn Saad, the governor of Egypt, to Medina to consult with him as to the course of action that should be adopted. Abdullah ibn Saad came to Medina, leaving the affairs of Egypt to his deputy, and in his absence, Muhammad bin Abi Hudhaifa staged a coup d'état and took power.

In middle of 656, Uthman's governor of Kufa, Abu-Musa al-Asha'ari, was unable to control the province. In Basra the governor, Abdullah ibn Aamir, left for Hajj, and in his absence the affairs of the province fell into a state of confusion. The three main provinces of Egypt (which was already the center of the dissident movement), Kufa, and Basra became essentially independent from the Caliphate of Uthman, and became the center of revolt.

Rebels in Medina:

From Egypt a contingent of about 1,000 people were sent to Medina, with instructions to assassinate Uthman and overthrow the government. Similar contingents marched from Kufa and Basra to Medina. In proposing alternatives to Uthman as Caliph, the rebels neutralized the bulk of public opinion in Medina and Uthman's faction could no longer offer a united front. Uthman had the active support of the Umayyads, and a few other people in Medina, but the rest of the people of Medina chose to be neutral and help neither side.

Siege of Uthman:

The situation in Medina was a big gain for the rebels. When they felt satisfied that the people of Medina would not offer them any resistance, they entered the city of Medina and laid siege to the house of Uthman, essentially taking it over but not confining the Caliph. The rebels declared that no harm from them would come to any person who chose not to resist them. Uthman strongly instructed his supporters to refrain from violence, but his various servants (about 40 of them) appealed for permission to fight against the rebels, along with a thousand other citizens of Medina. Uthman, who was a wealthy man even from the days before Islam, freed all 40 of his slaves and ordered them to stay away from the civil war between the Muslims.

Tempers flared up on both sides, hot words were exchanged between the parties and that led to the pelting of stones at one another. One of the stones hit Uthman, he fell unconscious and was carried to his house, still unconscious.

When the rebels felt that the people of Medina were not likely to offer active support of Uthman, they changed their strategy and tightened the siege of the house of Uthman, thus confining Uthman to his home. Uthman was denied the freedom to move about and was not allowed to go to the mosque.

As the days passed, the rebels intensified their pressure against Uthman. They forbade the entry of any food or provisions and later water, as well, into his house.

During the siege, Uthman was asked by his supporters, who outnumbered the rebels, to let them fight against the rebels and route them. Uthman prevented them in an effort to avoid the bloodshed of Muslim by Muslim. Unfortunately for Uthman, violence occurred anyhow. The gates of the house of Uthman were shut and guarded by the renowned warrior, Abd-Allah ibn al-Zubayr. The sons of Ali, Hasan ibn Ali and Husayn ibn Ali, were also among the guards. Among the supporters of Uthman, Hasan ibn Ali, Marwan and some other people were wounded.

When Uthman came to know of this action he said: No, I do not want to spill the blood of Muslims, to save my own neck.

Assassination:

Finding the gate of Uthman's house strongly guarded by his supporters, the rebels climbed the back wall and sneaked inside, leaving the guards on the gate unaware of what was going on inside. The rebels entered his room and struck blows at his head. Naila, the wife of Uthman, raising her hand to protect him she had her fingers chopped off and was pushed aside and further blows were struck until he was dead. The supporters of Uthman then counterattacked the assassins and, in turn, killed them.

The rioters wanted to mutilate his body and were keen that he be denied burial. When some of the rioters came forward to mutilate the body of Uthman, his two widows, Nailah and Ramlah bint Sheibah, covered him, and raised loud cries which deterred the rioters. The rebels left the house and the supporters of Uthman at gate hearing it, entered, but it was too late.

Funeral:

The body was lifted at dusk, and because of the blockade, no coffin could be procured. The body was not washed, as Islamic teaching states that martyrs' bodies are not supposed to be washed before burial. Thus Uthman was carried to the graveyard in the clothes that he was wearing at the time of his assassination. His body was buried by Hassan, Hussein, Ali and others however some people reject that Ali attended the funeral. The body was carried to Jannat al-Baqi, the Muslim graveyard.

It appears that some people gathered there, and they resisted the burial of Uthman in the graveyard of the Muslims. The supporters of Uthman insisted that the body should be buried in Jannat al-Baqi. They later buried him in the Jewish graveyard behind Jannat al-Baqi. Some decades later, the Umayyad rulers demolished the wall separating the two cemeteries and merged the Jewish cemetery into the Muslim one to ensure that his tomb was now inside a Muslim cemetery.

Family of Uthman:

Uthman belonged to the Umayyad branch of the Quraish tribe. He was the son of Affan ibn Abi al-'As and Urwa bint Kariz. Urwa bore only two children from Affan: Uthman and his sister Anma. After the death of Affan, Urwa married Uqbah ibn Abu Mu'ayt, to whom she bore three sons and a daughter:

1. Walid ibn Uqba
2. Khalid ibn Uqba
3. Amr ibn Uqba
4. Umm Kulthum bint Uqba

Legacy:

It is said that Uthman was one of the most handsome and charming men of his time. Uthman was well known for his reported generosity. During Muhammad's time, while in Medina, he financed the project for the construction of the al-Masjid al-Nabawi and purchased the well *Beer Rauma,* which he dedicated to the free use of all Muslims. Uthman's generosity continued after he became caliph.

Uthman apparently led a simple life even after becoming the Caliph of the Rashidun Empire, though it would have been easy for a successful businessman such as him to lead a luxurious life. Uthman also developed a custom to free slaves every Friday, look after the widows and orphans and give unlimited charity. He was a devoted Muslim. As a way of taking care of Muhammad's wives, he doubled their allowances. Uthman's sister Amna bint Affan was married to Abdur Rahman bin Awf, one of the closest companions of Muhammad.

Sunni view of Uthman:

According to the Sunni account of Uthman, he was married to two of Muhammad's daughters at separate times, earning him the name *Zun-Nurayn (Dhun Nurayn)* or the "Possessor of Two Lights." In this he was supposed to outrank Ali, who had married only one of Muhammad's daughters.

Sunni Muslims also consider Uthman as one of the ten Sahaba (companions) for whom Muhammad had testified that they were destined for Paradise . He was a wealthy and very noble man. When he became Khalifah, he used the same method Umar did.

Uthman is regarded by Sunnis as a beacon of light who refused to participate in the civil conflict.

Non-Muslims:

Uthman compiled the Qur'an and burnt its other copies. Uthman's governing policies and nepotism led to openly rise of dissatisfaction and resistance throughout most of the empire, especially among noble companions of Muhammad.

Uthman ibn Affan
Banu Umayya

Islamic Leaders

Cadet branch of the Quraysh
Died: July 17 656

Sunni Islam titles
Preceded by **Rashidun Caliph** Succeeded by
Umar 644-656 **Ali**

Regnal titles
Preceded by **Ruler of Persia Merged into**
Yazdgerd III 651-656 **Caliphate**

The Sahaaba:
Among the Companions of Prophet Muhammad (pbuh)Sahaaba is a group of ten Companions who are given glad tidings of Paradise by the Prophet (pbuh), known as Ashrah Mubash-sharah which means the ten Sahaaba about whom Rasullullah (pbuh) gave the glad tidings of Janaat. Rasullullah informed that these ten Sahaaba have already been promised Janaat, hence we have to believe with certainty that the following ten companions are Janaati. The Blessed Ten Companions are:

1-Abu Bakr As-Siddiq
2-'Umar Al-Farooq
3-Uthman bin Affa'an
4-Ali bin Abi Talib
5-Abdur-Rahman bin A'uf
6-Sa'ad bin Abi Waqqas
7-Sa'id ibn Zayd
8-Abu Ubaydah bin Al-Jirrah
9-Talhah bin Ubaydullah
10-Zubair bin Al-Awaam

Uthman ibn Affan:

Reign   11 November 644 – 17 July 656

Wives   Ramla bint Shuibat
Ruqayyah bint Muhammad
Naila
Fatima bint Al-Walid
Fakhtah bint Ghazwan
Umm Kulthum bint Muhammad
Umm Al-Banin bint Unaib
Umm Amr bint Jundub

***

455

Velayati, Ali Akbar (1945-   ): *Iranian politician* Born into a middle-class family, Velayati obtained a medical degree from Tehran University and engaged in postgraduate studies in the United States. During the 1980-88 Iran Iraq War, Velayati repeatedly tried to persuade the members of the Gulf Cooperation Council (GCC) to stay neutral in the conflict by stressing that peaceful coexistence with its neighbors was part of Iran's foreign policy. Under the presidency of Ali Akbar Hashemi Rafsanjani (1989-71), Belayati pursued the policy of reconciliation in the Gulf region not only with the Arab monarchies, but also with Iraq.

***

Waraqah ibn Mawfal (-   ): Khadija's uncle and a Christian priest; he is supposed to have confirmed Muhammad's prophetic status; traditional scribe, publisher, printer, notary and book copier; later converted to Islam. A Hanif; cousin of Khadijah; scholar in Jewish and Christian scriptures. He was the first to recognize the authenticity of Muhammad's revelations.

***

Wazir, Khalil (1935-1988): *Palestinian political-military leader* Born into a middle-class household in Ramla, Palestine, Wazir and his family fled during the 1948-49 Palestine War. He grew up in al-Bureij refugee camp in the Gaza Strip. Before the capture of Gaza by Israel in the 1956 Suez War, Wazir escaped to Cairo, where he became active in Palestinian student politics, dominated by Yasser Arafat. the military wing of Fatah, called Assifa *(Arabic: storm)*, was headed by Wazir. With Fatah becoming the leading constituent of the Palestine Liberation Organization (PLO) in 1968, the importance of Assifa and Wazir rose. Following the outbreak of the intifada in December 1987, Wazir worked closely with the PLO's Occupied Homeland Directorate to give direction to the uprising. Wazir was assassinated by a Mossad hit team in April 1988 at his Tunis home. He was buried in Damascus.

***

Yahya al-Nawawi (1233-1277): After the Qur'an declared the Prophet Muhammad to be the best role model (U*swatun Hasana*) for all people, the need for recording and preserving his sayings and exhortations became a major preoccupation for his companions and the early Islamic scholars. Known as the *Muhaddithun* (traditionists), these scholars dominated Islamic thought and scholarship from the very outset. *Al-*

Muwatta of Malik ibn Anas, *al-Musnad* of Ahmad ibn Hanbal, *Jami al-Sahih* of both Muhammad ibn Ismail al-Bukhari and Muslim ibn al-Hajjaj, and the *Sunan* of Abu Dawud, among others, belonged to this period. These famous traditionists collected and systematically scrutinized hundreds of thousands of *Hadith* before compiling their celebrated anthologies for the benefit of posterity. But the most famous *Muhaddith* of the pre-modern era was Yahya al-Nawawi who played an influential role in popularizing the Prophetic traditions.

Muhyi al-Din Abu Zakariya Yahya ibn Sharaf ibn Muri ibn Hasan ibn Hussain ibn Muhammad ibn Juma ibn Hizam al-Hizami al-Damashqi, known as Imam al-Nawawi for short, was born in the village of Nawa, near Damascus in Syria. As a studious child, he successfully committed the entire Qur'an to memory before the age of twelve. After completing his early education, al-Nawawi's father, impressed with his son's achievements, sent him to Damascus for further education so that he could realize his full potential.

During the Umayyad period, the city not only became the seat of the Caliphate and the dazzling capital of the Islamic world, but also became the pre-eminent center of Islamic learning, culture and civilization. Although by the thirteenth century Damascus had lost much of its former glory, it nevertheless retained its position as one of the Muslim world's leading centers of learning and scholarship. Indeed, Damascus boasted no fewer than three hundred religious seminaries and colleges. In 1251, when al-Nawawi was only eighteen, he moved to Damascus and enrolled at *madrasah al-Rawahiyyah* for his intermediate and advanced education.

After completing his education at *madrasah al-Rawahiyyah*, al-Nawawi accompanied his father to Makkah to perform the sacred pilgrimage. Despite being a prominent authority on Islamic jurisprudence, his fame spread far and wide on account of his unrivalled mastery of *Hadith* literature.

This sorry state of affairs persisted until the Mongol hordes appeared from Asia like a thunderbolt from the heavens and destroyed Baghdad, the political capital of the Muslim world, in 1258 and threatened to overwhelm Syria and Egypt in turn. With the Mongol threat looming on the horizon, the Mamluk rulers of Syria and Egypt were forced to muster their forces and face the Mongols at the Battle of *Ayn Jalut* (or 'the Spring of Goliath') in 1260. By inflicting a crushing defeat on the Mongols, the Mamluks saved Syria and Egypt from the same fate that had visited Baghdad two years earlier. Rukn al-Din Baibars, the Turkish Mamluk commander who led the charge against the Mongol forces, was later crowned the fourth Mamluk Sultan of

Syria and Egypt and, as such, he became a staunch defender of the Islamic East.

Al-Nawawi was not only a brave scholar, but also a man of sound principles and practices. The *Riyadh as-Saliheen* is rated very highly by Islamic scholars and it has also been translated and published in all the prominent languages of the world. However, his most popular and influential work is *Kitab al-Arba'in*. Like his *Riyadh al-Saliheen*, this small collection of forty *Hadith* has been translated into all the main languages of the world, including Persian, Urdu, Hingi, Bengali, French and English.

Al-Nawawi lived in Damascus for more than twenty-five years and he studied, taught and authored all his books during this period. Most interestingly, despite being a strict adherent to the Prophetic *sunnah*, he refused to marry and instead remained a confirmed bachelor all his life. He passed away at the age of forty-four; his father was still alive at the time of his death. He was buried in Nawa.

***

Yamani, Ahmad Zaki (1930-   ): *Saudi oil expert and politician* Born into the family of a religious judge in Mecca, Yamani studied law, first at Cairo University and then at new York and Harvard Universities in the United States. ...in 1962 to minister of petroleum and mineral resources. In the mid-1960s he became chairman of the state-owned General Petroleum and Mineral Organization and a director of the Arabian American Oil Company (Aramco). Yamani served as secretary-general of the Organization of Petroleum Exporting Countries (OPEC) from 1968-69. On 21 December 1975, when OPEC oil ministers, meeting in Vienna, were taken hostage by the commandos led by Ilich Ramirez Sanchez—alias Carlos Martinez—Yamani was one of their chief targets. In early October 1986, after meeting the Iranian oil minister in Riyadh, King Fahd ibn Adul Aziz backed the idea of a fixed price of $18 a barrel. When Yamani refused to endorse this, Fahd dismissed him on 29 October.

***

Yassin, Ahmad (1937-   ): *Palestinian leader* Born into a land-owning household in Jora in Palestine, a village near the northern border of what later became the Gaza Strip, Yassin and his family sought shelter in a refugee camp in the Gaza Strip during the First Arab-Israeli War (1848-49). He joined the clandestine Muslim Brotherhood (Egypt) in the mid-1950s, a few years after suffering crippling injuries in a sporting accident, which left him wheel-chair-bound. After the Gaza Strip was occupied by Israel in 1967, he was released. As a result of another prisoner exchange in the wake of Mossad's failed attempt to assassinate, in Amman, Khalid Mashaal, a leader of Hamas in Jordan, in 1997, Yassin was freed in 1997.

***

Yazid II, bin Abd al-Malik (687-724): Yazid bin Abd al-Malik or Yazid II (687–724) was an Umayyad caliph who ruled from 720 until his death in 724.

According to the medieval Persian historian Muhammad ibn Jarir al-Tabari, Yazid came to power on the death of Umar II on February 10, 720. His forces engaged in battle the Kharijites with whom Umar had been negotiating. After initial setbacks, Yazid's troops prevailed and the Kharijite leader Shawdhab was killed. Yazid ibn al-Muhallab had escaped confinement on the death of Umar. He made his way to Iraq. There he was much supported. He refused to acknowledge Yazid II as caliph and led a very serious uprising. Initially successful, he was defeated and killed by the forces of Maslamah ibn Abd al-Malik.

Numerous civil wars began to break out in different parts of the empire such as in the Al Andalus (the Iberian Peninsula), North Africa and in the east. In A.H. 102 (720-721) in Ifriqiyah, the harsh governor Yazid ibn Muslim was overthrown and Muhammad ibn Yazid, the former governor, restored to power. The caliph accepted this and confirmed Muhammad ibn Yazid as governor of Ifriqiyah.

Al-Djarrah ibn Abdullah, Yazid's governor in Armenia and Azerbaijan, pushed into the Caucasus, taking Balanjar in A.H. 104 (722-723). That same year Yazid's governor in Medina, Abd al-Rahman ibn al-Dahhak, incurred the caliph's displeasure because the governor was exerting undue pressure trying to force a woman to marry him. She appealed to Yazid who replaced Abd al-Rahman with Abd al-Walid ibn Abdallah.

Anti-Umayyad groups began to gain power among the disaffected. Al-Tabari records that Abbasids were promoting their cause in A.H. 102 (720-721). They were already building a power base that they would later use to topple the Umayyads in CE 750.

An anecdote told of Yazid is that his wife Sudah learning he was pining for an expensive slave girl, purchased this slave girl and presented her to Yazid as a gift. This woman's name was Hababah and she predeceased Yazid (at Tabari v. 24, p. 196).

Yazid II died in 724 of tuberculosis. He was succeeded by his brother Hisham.

***

Zaghlul Pasha, Saad (1850-1927): Egyptian nationalist leader, founder of the Wafd party. He suffered both arrest (1882) and exile (1919) for his attempts to end foreign domination in Egypt. Having founded (1919) the Wafd party, he became premier in 1924, but the opposition of Great Britain and the Egyptian court soon forced him to resign. The last year of his life he served as president of the Egyptian parliament.

***

Zahedi, Fazullah (180-1963): *Iranian politician; prime minister, 1953-55* Born into a landlord family in Hamadan, Zahedi graduated from the Military Academy in Tehran in 1916. Under the guise of the Retired Officers Club, Zahedi organized the secret Committee to Save the Fatherland, consisting of the military officers retired by Mussadiq in 1952. Zahedi was dismissed from his office in April 1955, a sign of the Shah's growing confidence.

***

Zaid ibn Sultan, Al Nahyan (1915-2004): President, United Arab Emirates, 1971-; ruler, the Abu Dhabi Emirate 1966-Born in al Ain to the ruling Aal Nahyan family of the Aal Bu Falah tribe, Nahyan learned the Quran as a boy as well as falconry riding and marksmanship. As ruler of the Abu Dhabi emirate he appointed a cabinet led by a premier, responsible to him, in July 1971. When a single federal council of ministers came into being in December 1973, he abolished the Abu Dhabi cabinet and appointed a fifty member consultative council. During the early phase of the 1980-88 Iran Iraq war, Nahyan sided with Baghdad. But as the conflict dragged on and Iran's position grew stronger, Nahyan took an increasingly neutral stance. During Nahyan's rule of the UAE emerged from being a collective of medieval emirates to an efficiently run modern state with one of the highest per capita incomes in the world.

***

Zaim, Hosni (1890-1949: *Syrian military leader and politician; president, 1949* Born into a Kurdish family in Aleppo, Zaim was trained to become an officer in the Ottoman Turkish army. Working in conjunction with the U.S. Embassy in Damascus, intent on securing recognition of Israel by its Arab neighbors, Zaim mounted the country's first military coup on 30 March 1949. On 20 July he signed an armistice agreement with Israel whereby he gave up the small enclave Syria held in Palestine. Pro-American in foreign policy, Zaim backed Washington's proposal for a Middle East military pact. On 14 August a group of military officers, led by Col. Sami Hinnawi, staged a coup against Zaim. Following a summary trial by a military court, he was executed.

***

Zayd ibn Ali (695-740): The brother of the Fifth Imam, Zayd was a political activist and the Fifth Imam may have developed his quietest philosophy in order to counter his claim to the leadership. There after Shiis who engaged in political activism and eschewed the Twelvers withdrawal from politics were sometimes known as Zaydites.

***

Zayd ibn Harithah (-): Captured in a Bedouin raid as a boy and brought to Mecca's annual fair of Ukaz as a slave boy. He was bought at auction and given to Khadijah by one of the wealthy nephews. She in turn gave Zayd to Muhammad and he later rose to become one of the key military commanders of early Islam until his death at the Battle of Mutah. Muhammad's adopted son and the first husband of Zaynab bint Jahsh.

***

Zaynab bint Jaysh (-): Cousin and sixth wife of the Prophet, first married to Muhammad's adopted son Zayd. This marriage was ended and she was given as recorded in a Koranic verse to the Prophet as an additional wife to bring his household in Medina up to five women. Muhammad's daughter in law, whom he subsequently married by what he represented as a command of Allah. Daughter of Khuzaymah, the fifth wife of the Prophet was the daughter of an influential Bedouin chieftain of the Amir tribe. She was widowed after her first husband died at the battle of the wells of Badr. Famously generous to the poor, died eight months after her marriage to the Prophet. Zaynab Jewish sorceress at Khaybar who attempted to avenge her community by trying to poison the Prophet. Daughter of Muhammad, married to one of her mother's favorite nephews, the handsome Abu al As who remained a pagan in Mecca until almost the last. Mother of Umamah.

***

Zayyad (-): Shrewd political operator who, like Mughira, was from the Thawif tribe of the city of Ta'if. As the bastard of a prostitute owned by a foreign merchant, he had no social status or clan allies to help him through life but he would nevertheless rise to become a trusted secretary, then governor, and finally governor of both Basra and Kufa and all Persia for Muawiya. Zayyad was officially adopted into

Muawiya's family and his sons were awarded lesser governorships within the regime, which helped bind his family into total loyalty to the Umayyads. It was one of Zayyad's sons, Ubaydallah ibn Zayyad, governor of Kufa, who masterminded the chain of events that led to the tragedy of Karbala.

***

Zubayr ibn al Awwam (-): Early believer who would be placed in charge of an army of reinforcements sent by Omar to support Amr ibn al As's raid into Egypt. He would win renown among his men by leading an assault on the Byzantine fortress of Babylon. One of the committee of six chosen to select a Caliph after the death of Omar, he joined Aisha in her revolt against Ali.

END***END

Islamic Leaders

About the Author

(ISBN 978-0-9777117-3-4)   (ISBN 978-0-9777117-8-9)

Saul Silas Fathi was born to a prominent Jewish family in Baghdad, Iraq. At age 10, he and his younger brother were smuggled out of Baghdad through Iran and eventually reached the newly formed state of Israel. He began writing a diary at age 11 and had several stories published in Israeli youth magazines.

Saul enrolled at the Israel Airforce Academy of Aeronautics, a 4-year program, where he earned his high-school diploma and became certified in electrical engineering. In 1958, he worked his way to Brazil where he nearly starved. Through perseverance and luck, he started his own electrical business and earned a patent for climate-controlled windows used in the building of Brasilia, Brazil.

In 1960, he came to the U.S. on a student exchange visa, studying sculpture at the Brooklyn Museum of Art and American history and public speaking at the New School of Social Studies. After 8 months, Saul volunteered to serve in the U.S. Army for three years, having been promised a college education and U.S. citizenship at the conclusion of his duties. After Basic Training in Fort Benning, Georgia, he was sent to helicopter school at Fort Bragg, North Carolina, and there enrolled at the University Of Virginia. Within a few months, Saul was shipped to South Korea where he served as Chief Electrical Technician with the 1st Cavalry Division, 15th Aviation Company, the famed helicopter division in the Vietnam War.

Back in the U.S., Saul battled the immigration department while studying at the University of Virginia, finally earning a Bachelor of Science degree in electrical engineering. This launched an impressive career as a high-level executive with several Fortune-500 companies. Later, he founded and managed three high-tech companies.

Saul retired in 2003 and began writing his memoirs, Full Circle: Escape from Baghdad and the Return. Today, he lives in Long Island, New York, with his wife Rachelle. They have three U.S.-born daughters and two grandchildren. He is also a certified linguist, fluent in English, Hebrew, Arabic, and Portuguese.

COMPELLING LECTURES!!!

SUBJECTS (Average 2 Hours):

1. The War in Iraq: A Unique Perspective
2. Prospects for War with Iran: Options
3. History of Islam and the Middle-East
4. Jewish Life in Arab Countries
5. Current (International) Affairs
6. Cosmology: The Big Bang, Black Holes and UFO's
7. Saladin and the Crusades
8. Full Circle: Escape from Baghdad and the return
9. Biblical Stories: From Abraham to Jesus
10. Great Women in World History

27 Broadlawn Drive Central Islip, NY 11722-4616
Tel/Fax: (631) 232-1638 • www.saulsilasfathi.com • fathi@optonline.net

DETAILS ON NEXT PAGE

www.ingramcontent.com/pod-product-compliance
Lightning Source LLC
Chambersburg PA
CBHW001207230426
43666CB00015B/2672